T0230339

Lecture Notes in Computer Science 639
Edited by G. Goos and J. Hartmanis

A. U. Frank I. Campari U. Formentini (Eds.)

Theories and Methods of Spatio-Temporal Reasoning in Geographic Space

International Conference
GIS – From Space to Territory:
Theories and Methods of Spatio-Temporal Reasoning
Pisa, Italy, September 21-23, 1992
Proceedings

Springer-Verlag
Berlin Heidelberg New York
London Paris Tokyo
Hong Kong Barcelona
Budapest

Series Editors

Gerhard Goos
Universität Karlsruhe
Postfach 69 80
Vincenz-Priessnitz-Straße 1
W-7500 Karlsruhe, FRG

Juris Hartmanis
Department of Computer Science
Cornell University
5149 Upson Hall
Ithaca, NY 14853, USA

Volume Editors

Andrew U. Frank
Dept. of Geo-Information E127, Technical University of Vienna
Gusshausstr. 27-29, A-1040 Vienna, Austria

Irene Campari
CNUCE, Consiglio Nazionale delle Ricerche
Via Santa Maria 36, I-56126 Pisa, Italy

Ubaldo Formentini
Dept. of Environmental Sciences, University of Pisa
Via San Giuseppe 22, I-56000 Pisa, Italy

CR Subject Classification (1991): H.2, I.2-3, E.1-2, E.5, I.5-6, I.2

ISBN 3-540-55966-3 Springer-Verlag Berlin Heidelberg New York
ISBN 0-387-55966-3 Springer-Verlag New York Berlin Heidelberg

Printed in Germany

Typesetting: Camera ready by author/editor
Printing and binding: Druckhaus Beltz, Hemsbach/Bergstr.
45/3140-543210 - Printed on acid-free paper

Foreword

This volume collects the papers presented at the conference "GIS: From Space to Territory — Theories and Methods of Spatio-Temporal Reasoning." It is – to the best of our knowledge – the first international conference dedicated to spatial and temporal reasoning in geographic space.

Temporal, but also spatial, reasoning has attracted interest in the artificial intelligence community. Spatial and temporal reasoning is found to be a very common form of reasoning, so prevalent that one often does not identify it as a particular kind of reasoning. Within the National Center for Geographic Information and Analysis (NCGIA) the importance of spatial and temporal reasoning in Geographic Information Systems was recognized several years ago, and is now being pursued as a topic in its own right under Research Initiative 10 "Spatio-Temporal Reasoning in Geographic Information Systems."

Initial research found that spatial reasoning in geographic or large scale space is different from spatial reasoning in small scale space, as usually dealt with in robotics and expert systems, which reason about simple mechanical devices. David Mark and Andrew Frank organized a workshop on "Cognitive and Linguistic Aspects of Geographic Space" in Las Navas (Spain) in 1990 to explore the specific methods and the relevant approaches for spatial reasoning in geographic space. This international conference continues with this topic and integrates it with temporal reasoning in geographic space.

We hoped to bring together experts from different disciplines, most notably computer science, geography, economy, cognitive science but also linguistics. The goal of the Conference is to open an interdisciplinary dialog. An international call for papers, mostly distributed by electronic mail, with a short deadline for submission of full papers resulted in over 70 papers submitted. They were of high quality and covered a very broad field of different disciplines. Each paper was distributed for assessment to three members of the program committee or other experts in the field. The program committee met in Pisa on May 5 and had the difficult task to select the 23 best papers to be presented at the meeting and to be included in the proceedings. Comments from the reviewers were then sent back to the authors to help them to produce the final copy. We are very thankful for the quick responses of the authors and reviewers that allowed us to progress rapidly and have this volume ready for the conference.

The conference also includes a number of distinguished scientists as invited speakers, each opening the topic from the perspective of a particular science. Two of them were able to provided us with manuscripts to be included in this volume, namely Reginald Golledge's paper on "Do People Understand Spatial Concepts: The Case of First-Order Primitives" and Richard Snodgrass' paper on "Temporal Databases".

We are grateful to all the people who have helped shape the topic and organize the conference. The contributions from our colleagues from the NCGIA, in particular from Max Egenhofer (University of Maine), Reginald Golledge (University of California at Santa Barbara) and David Mark (State University of New York at Buffalo) have influenced over the years our conceptualization of space and time. The members of the program committee and the additional reviewers must be thanked for their generous help.

One must also not forget the local organizers and the administrative support from Leonardo Leonardini (ETS, Pisa), which made the conference possible. The support from CNUCE and from NCGIA is gratefully acknowledged. Finally, it is a pleasure to thank Roberto Scopigno (CNR-CNUCE, Pisa), Benedetto Biagi (IEI-CNR, Pisa), Silvano Bonotto (Università di Torino) and Paolo Ghelardoni (Università di Parma) for particular contributions to bring together the conference.

Pisa, July 1992

Andrew Frank
Irene Campari
Ubaldo Formentini

Program Committee

Chairs:

Andrew U. Frank	Technische Universität Wien
Irene Campari	CNUCE-CNR, Pisa
Carlo Da Pozzo	Università di Pisa
Mario Pinna	Università di Pisa
Antonio Albano	Università di Pisa
Giorgio Ausiello	Università di Roma "La Sapienza"
Bruno Bara	Università Statale di Milano
Flavio Bonfatti	Università di Modena
H. Théry	Maison de la Géographie, Université de Montpellier
Stefano Ceri	Politecnico di Milano
Helen Couclelis	NCGIA, University of California, Santa Barbara
Mario Di Massa	CISPEL, Roma
Soumitra Dutta	INSEAD, Fontainbleau
Max Egenhofer	NCGIA, University of Maine, Orono
Franco Farinelli	Università di Bologna
Antonio Fernandez Perez de Talens	IFC-CNR, Pisa
Giacomo Ferrari	Università di Pisa
Herbert Freeman	Rutgers University, Piscataway, New Jersey
Christian Freksa	Universität Hamburg
Aldo Gargani	Università di Pisa
Reginald Golledge	NCGIA, University of California, Santa Barbara
Mike Goodchild	NCGIA, University of California, Santa Barbara
Georg Gottlob	Technische Universität, Vienna
Vincenzo Guarrasi	Università di Palermo
Remo Job	Università di Padova
Milan Konecny	Masaryk University, Brno
Giampiero Maracchi	IATA-CNR, Firenze
David Mark	NCGIA, State University of New York, Buffalo
Armando Montanari	ISEMEM-CNR, Napoli
Piero Pierotti	Università di Pisa
David Rhind	Birkbeck College, London
Mauro Salvemini	Università di Roma "La Sapienza"
Hanan Samet	University of Maryland
Fabio Sforzi	IRPET, Firenze
G. W. Skinner	University of California, Davis
Maurizio Talamo	Università di Roma "La Sapienza"
Costantino Thanos	IEI-CNR, Pisa
Maria Tinacci Mossello	Università di Firenze
Angelo Turco	Università dell'Aquila

Additional Referees

Renato Barrera (USA)
Michael Batty (USA)
Renzo Beltrame (Italy)
Peter Burrough (The Netherlands)
S.-K. Chang (USA)
J.P. Cheylan (France)
Berardo Cori (Italy)
David Cowen (USA)
Giorgio Faconti (Italy)
Oliver Günther (Germany)
Daniel Hernandez (Germany)
John Herring (USA)
Steve Hirtle (USA)
Erland Jungert (Sweden)
Werner Kuhn (Austria)
Diego Latella (Italy)
Gail Langran (USA)
David McKeown (USA)
Matt McGranaghan (USA)
Claudio Montani (Italy)
Tim Nyerges (USA)
Alan Saalfeld (USA)
Hans-Jörg Schek (Switzerland)
Toni Schenk (USA)
Roberto Scopigno (Italy)
Cliff Shaffer (USA)

Sponsorship

The Commission of the European Communities
Consiglio Nazionale delle Ricerche
- Istituto CNUCE
- Istituto di Elaborazione dell'Informazione

U.S. National Center for Geographic Information and Analysis
Università degli Studi di Pisa
Regione Toscana
IRI
ENEL
Amministrazione Provinciale di Pisa
AICA-Associazione Italiana Calcolo Automatico
CISPEL-Confederazione Italiana dei Servizi Pubblici degli Enti Locali
IRPET-Istituto Regionale per la Programmazione Economica della Toscana

Local Organizing Committee

Chair:

Ubaldo Formentini (Università di Pisa)

Irene Campari (CNUCE-CNR, Pisa)
Benedetto Biagi (IEI-CNR, Pisa)
Paolo Ghelardoni (Università di Parma)
Silvano Bonotto (Università di Torino)
Giuseppe Pozzana (IRPET, Firenze)
Leonardo Leonardini (ETS, Pisa)
Alina Potrykowska (Polska Akademia Nauk Warszawa)
Nicola Silvestri (Università di Pisa)

Contents

Invited Papers

Technical Papers

Section I

Section II

Section III

Do People Understand Spatial Concepts: The Case of First-Order Primitives

Reginald G. Golledge

Department of Geography
and
Research Unit on Spatial Cognition and Choice
University of California Santa Barbara
Santa Barbara, CA 93106-4060 USA

Abstract. The purpose of this paper is to examine whether people in general understand elementary spatial concepts, and to examine whether or not naive spatial knowledge includes the ability to understand important spatial primitives that are built into geographic theory, spatial databases and geographic information systems (GIS). The extent of such understanding is a partial measure of spatial ability. Accurate indicators or measures of spatial ability can be used to explain different types of spatial behavior. In this paper I first examine the relation between spatial ability and spatial behavior, then present experimental evidence of the ability of people to understand spatial concepts such as nearest neighbors (proximity), and spatial distributions. A final commentary is made about the possible difference between "common sense" and "expert" spatial knowledge, and the implications of such results for the comprehension of space at all scales.

1. Purpose

It is sometimes argued that instead of developing a cognitive map people develop a cognitive atlas. This atlas would contain representations of many different environments at many different scales. Depending on the purpose behind a specific problem solving task, specific components of the cognitive atlas would be accessed. The question immediately arises as to whether such a cognitive representation is simply an internalized geographic information system. A major purpose of this project is to begin examining this question by determining the degree to which selected processes involved in compiling and using cognitive maps are similar to those involved in compiling and using GIS. In particular, the project will focus on a selection of key concepts found in both cognitive mapping and GIS regardless of geographic scale. An attempt is made to determine how well the latent spatial information embedded in distributions displayed on a map can be understood and interpreted by lay people.

The larger project from which this research is abstracted continues research on the components of spatial knowledge. In particular, research is being conducted on the extent to which people understand geographic terms and concepts needed in cognitive mapping and GIS development and use. Since all such terms and concepts can be found in the domain of configurational knowledge, this will provide a focus for the research. The parent project includes the design of specific tasks: (a) to identify similarities between the processes of cognitive mapping and the processes of building a GIS (i.e. to see if correspondence occurs between the two processes or to see if cognitive maps are internalized GISs); (b) to determine the order of difficulty for completing a variety of spatial inference tasks that require the same level of understanding as is assumed in GIS functions (such as overlay, compression, pattern recognition, hierarchical ordering, recognition of spatial distribution membership, adjacency and connectivity, orientation and direction, spatial sequencing and ordering, locational designation and cue recognition); (c) to logically extend current work to include "higher order" processing such as developing an ability to overlay several discrete patterns without losing the initial information while concurrently creating new knowledge; (d) to examine the concepts of neighborhood, regions and regionalization and how they enter into spatial knowledge structures; (e) to examine the concept of spatial hierarchy, to identify how such hierarchies are formed and used by people to store and recall spatial information; and, (f) to evaluate individual abilities to recognize spatially associated geographic patterns presented in visual format. It is anticipated that much of this research will be cumulative, with the solutions to some problems depending on the prior solution of others; the research is projected over a multi-year period. This paper reports only on experiments relating to recognition of characteristics of spatial distributions.

2. Background

This project from which this paper is drawn examines the nature and components of configurational (survey) knowledge. Such knowledge is presumed by developmental and life span theories to be the final stage of the spatial knowledge acquisition process. Hence it incorporates all components of spatial knowledge. From the geographer's view, configurational knowledge should include the ability to identify distributions, patterns, shapes, associations and relations of phenomena in both proximal and macro environments. For the geographer it is a level of knowledge that facilitates comprehension of pattern in the distribution of natural and human phenomena over the earth's surface. Despite the ready acceptance of its necessary existence, we know little about configurational knowledge and how well people can develop it. The characteristics of this stage of knowledge as outlined theoretically by Piaget & Inhelder (1967) have been shown to occur at many stages of the life span (Liben, Patterson & Newcombe, 1981). Recently Anderson (1982) hypothesized that spatial knowledge requires only a declarative base and a set of procedural rules to allow understanding of complex spatial environments. Other research (Gale, et al. 1990; Golledge, et al. 1991) have thrown some doubts on whether this is so. The parent project aims in part to evaluate whether the integration of a declarative knowledge base with sets of procedural rules *can* produce the configurational or survey level understanding of spatial phenomena that it is assumed normal adults develop. Multiple tasks will assess the degree of integration of spatial knowledge at a variety of micro and macro scales to see if more than one level of configurational understanding exists. Based on the outcome of recent NSF funded research (Golledge, 1991, 1992) it is hypothesized that most individuals develop only a "common sense" configurational understanding of spatial phenomena, which accounts for incomplete and fuzzy cognitive representations of environments, and partly accounts for many spatially irrational behaviors. It is also suggested that people are not necessarily aware of all they "know," in the sense of not developing the necessary inference rules and logical procedures needed to obtain a full comprehension of the spatial information contained in their knowledge set. For example, one may *know* that A>B and B>C but not be aware of the logical outcome

A>C. A lack of rules or poverty of spatial inference capability may account for many spatial misperceptions, misunderstandings, and inabilities to recognize fundamental spatial concepts such as distance decay, nearest neighbor, distribution membership, region membership, or hierarchical dominance This project is exploring the latter hypothesis by designing and carrying out spatial tasks whose successful completion provides evidence of the existence of and ability to use rules or procedures involving spatial inference.

3. Relevant Literature

The literature on both cognitive mapping and spatial knowledge acquisition has strong ties to psychological developmental theory (Piaget & Inhelder, 1967). As interpreted by Hart & Moore (1973) and Siegel & White (1975), individuals pass through stages from egocentric to allocentric knowledge, from topological to fully metric comprehension of space, and from knowledge structures dominated by landmarks to those where landmarks and connections between them are proceduralized into routes, to full configurational understanding of the layout of a specific environment. Over the last decade in particular, traditional developmental theory has been questioned by life-span theorists and others interested in spatial knowledge acquisition (Liben, Patterson, & Newcombe, 1981; Evans, Marrero, & Butler, 1981), who suggest that progression through developmental stages may only partially account for progressive changes in spatial abilities. Increasing quantities of evidence indicates that the spatial abilities formerly hypothesized to come into existence only at particular ages have been found at earlier ages (Acredolo, 1976, 1978, 1981, 1987; Evans, 1980; Liben, 1982). It is also suggested that when one learns about an unfamiliar environment one does not automatically obtain understanding at a level equivalent to one's developmental stage. Rather, one goes through all stages from egocentric to allocentric and topological to metric as part of the learning process (Golledge, 1977a&b; Evans, et al., 1981). Kuipers (1977) provides a reason for this. He suggests that knowledge is acquired by a piecemeal "bottom-up" process dependent on experiencing an environment. Bits and pieces of declarative knowledge are absorbed experientially. This information is collected from a human-level perspective rather than a birds-eye perspective and must be integrated by a set of procedural rules to produce the latter ("survey") type of comprehension. Such rules develop a "common sense" understanding of an environment, allowing one to use the sensed bits of information in an integrated way to solve problems of spatial movement. This theory has been most useful for the building of computational process models (CPMs) of environmental knowledge acquisition (e.g., CRITTER, Kuipers, 1985; TURTLE, Zimring & Gross, 1991; TOUR, Kuipers, 1977; and NAVIGATOR, Gopal, Klatzky, & Smith, 1989). The importance of proceduralizing piecemeal knowledge to facilitate spatial problem solving was conceptualized by Anderson (1976, 1982), who provided the general framework for knowledge acquisition processes that has proven useful for investigating how different types of learning occur. Since this model was not specifically designed for spatial learning, however, there are questions as to whether or not it can account for all stages or types of spatial understanding. One problem researched in this project is to investigate how higher order concepts involving associations and relations of phenomena can be achieved via proceduralizing bits of information learned in different contexts. This question has only recently been raised (Carey & Diamond, 1977; Golledge, et al.,

1988; Freundschuh, 1989; Gale, et al., 1990). It is, however, of great importance to understanding the nature of spatial reasoning, and the types of inferences that can produce the type of spatial understanding that geographers generally assume people have, or are capable of developing after instruction and exposure to learning aids such as maps.

4. Configurational Knowledge

Although much of the research on cognitive mapping implies that configurational or survey level understanding exists in adult humans, few researchers have probed the nature of this type of knowledge structure and little is known about how it is differentiated from proceduralized declarative knowledge. Since configurational understanding is a knowledge state in which much geographical information is presented, particularly in map format, it has been the focus of attention of geographers since the earliest discussion of mental maps (Gould, 1966, 1969, 1972; Downs & Stea, 1973a; Gould & White, 1974). The nature of configurational knowledge as represented in a cognitive map compiled using multidimensional scaling techniques has been discussed extensively by Golledge and his co-workers (Golledge, 1974; Zannaras, 1973a&b; Golledge & Zannaras, 1973; Rivizzigno, 1976; Spector, 1978; Golledge & Spector, 1978; Golledge, Rayner, & Rivizzigno, 1982; Golledge 1987; Golledge & Timmermans, 1990). These researchers tried to recover the latent spatial information contained in an individual's long term memory using multidimensional scaling and hierarchical clustering techniques. Their efforts differed markedly from the space preference surfaces typical of earlier work on mental maps and explored the coincidence or fit between map-like representations of cognized spatial information and real-world objective configurations of the same data. Similar efforts at comparing cognitive and objective maps have been undertaken by Moar & Bower (1983), Baird (1979), Curtis, et al. (1981), Tversky (1981), and Siegel (1981, 1982). More recent examinations of survey-type knowledge have been completed by Aitken & Prosser (1990), who examine the configurational understanding of residents of different San Diego neighborhoods. Notions of configurational understanding as a function of neurobiological development have been suggested by Budd, et al. (1985), while several papers by Evans, et al. (1981, 1984) have examined configurational structure, configurational accuracy, and the significance of features such as context and frame-of-reference, as factors contributing to spatial knowledge acquisition and understanding.

Much of the literature on configurational understanding focuses on the layout of the everyday physical environment (e.g., Gärling, et al., 1981, 1986). Research on spatial layout incorporates not only landmark or place knowledge in its pure form but also the system of associations and relations between each individual bit of information in a specified environment. Golledge (1977b) has offered a variety of multidimensional measurement procedures for recovering spatial layout information and comparing it with objective reality. More recently, Golledge (1990) has speculated on the composition of configurational knowledge systems and has stressed the need for further research into this important but fuzzy topic, particularly since it represents the expert knowledge system that is at the heart of the discipline of geography. Factors such as hierarchical structuring (Hirtle & Jonides, 1985) and regionalization (Stevens and Coupe, 1978; Tversky, 1981) have been identified as important components of configurational knowledge systems, and appear natural areas of expansion for geographic research efforts. The question of scale arises in a configurational context (Kirasic, et al., 1984) with particular emphasis being placed on the difference between the immediate observable perceptual domain (small-scale) and the larger-scale environment that generally exists beyond the immediate visual field. The relative significance of active (field) versus passive (laboratory/model) experiences in obtaining configurational understanding has been discussed by Gale, et al. (1990) and Lloyd (1989a,b,c). In a series of papers, Siegel and his co-workers (Siegel & Schadler, 1977; Siegel, Kirasic & Kail, 1978; Siegel, Herman, Allen & Kirasic, 1979; Siegel & Cousins, 1983) have illustrated how conventional cartographic and surveying techniques such as triangulation, intersection, and projective convergence can be used to recover external representations of spatial layout or configurational knowledge. It is in this area that the methods and concepts of geography appear to have considerable potential in representing and understanding the nature of configurational or survey knowledge.

The major shortcoming of research activity to date is that while specific components of spatial knowledge have been identified and more light has been thrown on types of spatial knowledge, it has not yet clearly identified whether or not people in general are able to use the logic and inference needed to extend their naive spatial understanding into the "expert" domain. As geographers, we assume everyone *has* the ability to do this, and we develop methods for assisting such a transition. But often we are *not* aware of the nature of the reasoning and inferential processes that are required in as "simple" a matter as reading a map.

During the past year, NSF has funded research by co-workers James Pellegrino and myself on the following tasks:

a. *Identification of spatial distributions* of selected land-use features;
b. *Evaluation of nearest neighbor* concepts;
c. Comparison of knowledge acquired after *learning routes from maps or visual simulations of routes*; and
d. Examination of ability to *integrate information* acquired from routes into configurational understanding.

Each of these tasks is directed towards understanding the degree to which basic reasoning and inference processes can be used to solve the spatial problems we somehow handle in our daily activities. In the next section I review a selection of these tasks. As part of this review, let us now turn to a discussion of spatial abilities, spatial behavior, and spatial competence in the specific context of knowing properties of spatial distributions.

5. Spatial Abilities

Elsewhere, co-workers and I have discussed the nature of spatial ability (Self, Gopal, Golledge & Fenstermaker, 1992). This discussion is summarized below.

Spatial abilities include: the ability to think geometrically; the ability to image complex spatial relations at various scales, from national urban systems to interior room designs or tabletop layouts; the ability to recognize spatial patterns in distributions of functions, places and interactions at a variety of different scales; the ability to interpret macrospatial relations such as star patterns; the ability to give and comprehend directional and distance estimates as required by navigation, or the path integration and short-cutting procedures used in wayfinding; the ability to understand network structures used in planning, design and engineering; and the ability to identify key characteristics of location and association of phenomena in space. This definition extends beyond that usually found in discussion of spatial aptitude tests, but includes traditional things such as orientation and re-orientation after rotation, translation (or other transformation), perspective viewing, knowing locations, and integrating partial (linearized) information into configurational wholes.

Spatial ability is often measured in terms of achieving scores on tests such as the Differential Aptitude Test (DAT), the Thurstone test of Primary Mental Abilities (PMA), and many others (see Eliot & McFarlane-Smith, 1983). Such tests measure performance based on different tasks relating to the two main hypothesized dimensions, spatial visualization and spatial orientation. Test scores are interpreted as revealing the degree of "spatial competence" of tested subjects, and are the basis for making generalizations about differences in performance (i.e., bèhavior). All these measures involve laboratory testing of the presence or absence of skills. None evaluate performance outside of the laboratory test arena. None determine an individual's spatial competence in problem-solving situations in the field. It is accepted that the skills exhibited on the abstract manipulative tasks encoded in paper and pencil tests can be transferred immediately to larger-scale environmental settings and to active decision-making situations. There is some doubt that this is so, a point made previously by geographers Gilmartin and Patton (1984). My first hypothesis, therefore, is that traditional definitions of spatial ability are task dependent, are at best partial, and fall short of measuring the "spatial competence" they claim to measure.

6. Spatial Activities and Spatial Behavior

The restricted definition of spatial ability as incorporated into many aptitude tests contrasts with the richness of the general literature on spatial activities and spatial behavior. The term "spatial activities" includes both covert and overt activity, although it is usually interpreted in a traditional geographic way, being limited to overt activities that have observable spatial ranges (i.e., "revealed" behavior). For our purposes, however, spatial activities may include sedentary actions such as playing a musical instrument, playing chess, doing needlepoint, and so on. Activities requiring significant use of geographic space (i.e., personal relocation and movement between places) on the other hand, might involve sports, recreation, and a variety of social or want satisfying behaviors, such as shopping. The spatial skills required in many of these behaviors differ substantially. Some require visualization skills; some require visualization plus motor coordination (as in hitting a tennis ball or kicking a football). Some involve cognitive processes and physiological functioning (such as when a pedestrian explores an unfamiliar neighborhood). Other behaviors involve spatial sequencing, as might be the case in wayfinding. Consumers able to effectively use a range of shopping opportunities in a city require some understanding of hierarchical order and spatial dominance. Reading a map requires skills in symbol identification and orientation. Direction-giving requires the ability to image and verbalize information stored in memory. Drawing a sketch map may require the ability to integrate information about landmarks, routes, and neighborhoods into an organized whole contained within some bounding scheme or frame of reference (Self, et al., 1992). What is not at all obvious is how the scores on the spatial components of different aptitude tests, relate to and/or are able to predict the spatial skills necessary in many of these problem solving situations. My hypothesis is, therefore, that spatial competence is a concept that requires integration of both psychological measures of performance on spatial ability tests together with measures of performance on a range of spatial activities and/or behaviors. Few examples of this larger integrated psychological/geographical interpretation of spatial ability can be found.

The tie between spatial ability and (revealed) spatial behavior may not be immediately obvious. Co-workers Self, Gopal, Fenstermaker, and I have explored this tie elsewhere in the context of gender differences in spatial ability. I shall briefly review these ties again here. "Spatial behavior" is mostly defined as the overt act of moving from place to place. For decades geographers have discussed and built into their theories and models simple criteria for understanding such behaviors - e.g., least effort, shortest path, spatial rationality. More often than not, these assumptions do not match actual behaviors. Much literature has been written on how activities such as multiple purpose and multiple place shopping distort these simple assumptions. Much behavioral research has indicated that it is not the physical proximity of places in objective reality that is important, but rather their perceived proximity - with such a perception being measured in time or cost or distance units. In many cases choice of an opportunity is said to depend on how familiar the traveler is with possible destinations. Destinations close to anchoring nodes of home or work are often chosen over other more spatially rational opportunities because they may be more frequently experienced as part of the habitual journey to work, because the temporal scheduling of household activities prevents any other choice, or because encoding information near anchors is easier and more reliable. All these reasons rely on the ability of a person to acquire and process spatial information (e.g., locational and linkage information) from an environment, to integrate that information into a memorized spatial layout, and to undertake behavior on the basis of such acquired spatial knowledge or "cognitive map" (Self, et al., 1992)

The degree that information included in one's cognitive map reflects real world structures depends on the spatial ability of individuals to comprehend characteristics such as location, connectivity, dominance, hierarchy, proximity, region, and pattern, among others. The less one understands these concepts, the more inaccurate is the encoding of spatial information. The more errors built into the information coded and stored in long-term memory, the less accurately one can perform tasks that rely on recall, and the more error prone any consequent behaviors that rely on that recall. The question arises therefore, when attempting to understand people's use of space, as to just what features and characteristics of the spatial properties of any given environment can we expect people to be aware?

7. Components of Spatial Knowledge

Elsewhere (Golledge, 1991) I have examined in detail the elementary spatial components that exist in any environment at any scale, and have discussed the cognitive equivalents of such features. Briefly the components are:

a. Location of occurrences, with each occurrence having a minimal descriptor set including identity, magnitude, location and time. An additional cognitive component might be familiarity. Occurrences are often called environmental cues, nodes, landmarks, or reference points;

b. Spatial distributions of phenomena: each distribution has a pattern or shape, a density, and an internal measure of spatial variance, heterogeneity or dispersion; occurrences in distributions also have characteristics such as proximity, similarity, order, and dominance;

c. Regions or bounded areas of space in which either single or multiple features occur with specified frequency (uniform regions) or over which a single feature dominates (nodal region). In geographic space examples might be a residential neighborhood (uniform region) or a store's market area (nodal region);

d. Hierarchies or multiple levels or nested levels of phenomena, including features such as public school districts combining high, middle, and elementary schools (nested hierarchy) or the commercial structure of a city (simple hierarchy of Central Business District, Regional Center, Community Center, and Neighborhood Center);

e. Networks or linked features having characteristics, connectivity, centrality, diameter, density, including physical links such as transportation systems, or non-visual links such as telephone call frequency or migration frequency;

f. Spatial associations including spatial autocorrelation, distance decay, and contiguities; examples include interaction frequencies, or geographic and areal associations such as the coincidence of features within specific places (e.g., corn and pigs);

g. Surfaces or generalizations of discrete phenomena, including densities of occurrence, flows over space and through time (as in the spatial diffusion of information or phenomena).

Of these components, most attention in spatial cognition research has focused on the first and simplest of these features - location of occurrences represented as environmental cues, landmarks, nodes or reference points, while aptitude testing includes some shape and pattern recognition both before and after transformation. Other components of geographic space have received less attention. In the remainder of this paper I propose to partially remedy this by examining features of the second component listed above - that of spatial distributions.

8. Spatial Distributions and Nearest Neighbors

In this experiment we simply wished to find out if people became aware of functional distributions (e.g., shops, schools) and their spatial properties when asked to learn about an environment. No explicit instructions were given about *what* was to be learned. We wanted to find out what information common sense examination produced. Initiating a learning process probably could produce more specific understanding, but such a procedure is more representative of a different type of inference and assumes a different set of operating procedures - (ones that I plan to investigate in a later paper).

8.1 Procedures

Subjects: Subjects were 32 adults, sixteen males and sixteen females. Each male and female group were divided equally between geographers and non-geographers. Ages ranged from 20 to 35 years.

Fig. 1. The Base Map

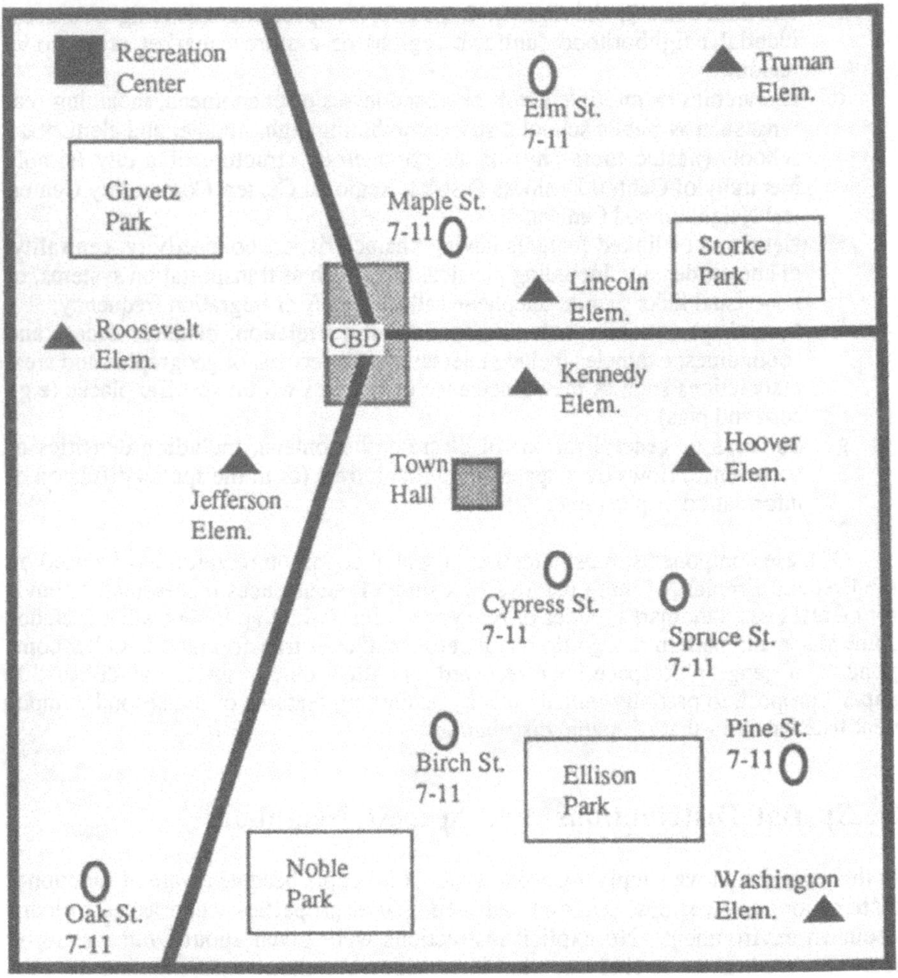

Tasks: All groups were required to study the first map given for five minutes (Fig. 1). After viewing the composite map, two initial conditions were established, one in which we focused on the distribution of stores (Condition 1); the other in which we focused on the distribution of schools (Condition 2). The 2 x 2 x 2 (condition by sex by discipline background) design was examined via ANOVA procedures.

The first task following the initial study period was investigation of the nearest neighbor concept. Each occurrence of a feature of one type (e.g., stores) was examined in turn. Subjects were given a list of the names of features in the group: Group A represented the 7-11 convenience stores and Group B were the elementary schools. These two features were chosen because they have similar population thresholds and ranges, and would therefore occur with similar frequency in an environment. Such a relationship precludes one feature from being (a priori) considered to be a more dominant occurrence. Subjects were required to choose from the list that feature that was closest (in distance terms) to the target feature. This procedure was done on a computer screen in the following manner. The name of one of the 7-11s (schools) taken from the map previously studied appeared in the center of the screen. A list of the other 7-11s (schools) was placed on the right of this feature name. The subject was then asked to remember which feature was closest to the target feature presented in the center of the screen. Response involved typing the first letter of the name of the choice made from the list of remaining features.

This task was followed by a mapping task. Again, depending on the condition they were first exposed to, subjects were asked to locate all the stores (schools) at their correct locations on a paper outline map by penciling an X on the map and labeling it with the name of the appropriate feature. The map sheet consisted of the same sized bounded area as the original map. Prior to beginning the task, subjects were placed in one of three groups - the first group was given a sheet with the boundaries and North line and no other information ("the Blank Sheet"); the second group had boundaries and North line as well as the location of two centrally located distractor cues (the Central group); a third group were given two peripheral distractor cues in addition to the boundaries and North line (the Peripheral group). Our interest here was in examining whether or not providing an additional piece of information other than a blank sheet would have an impact on the ability to perform the given task.

In the next task, subjects were tested on the distribution of the second feature - that is if at first tested on the distribution of stores, the second test focussed on the distribution of schools (or vice versa). This time the subjects were told that a feature name would appear in the center of the screen, followed by a list of the remaining feature names to the right of the target. Subjects were then asked to rank order the members of the feature list in terms of increasing distance from the target. Responses involved typing in turn the first letter of all the stores (schools) from the appropriate lists. Subjects were specifically requested to first type the letter of the feature that was closest to the target school (where closest was measured as the shortest distance away). This was the same as was done with the previous computer task. Subjects were then asked to consecutively type the letter of the school (store) that is next closest to the one shown (i.e., identifying the second shortest distance away), and the third closest, and so on. They were asked to continue until all six features had been ranked in order of distance from the target. As reinforcement they were specifically told that the last letter entered must be for the school (store) that is farthest from the target. Subjects were provided with paper and pencil check lists as scratch paper to make sure that they used features only once for each ranking task. However, in this task each feature in turn was taken as the target and all remaining features were ranked with respect to increasing distance from that target.

Following this task another map task was undertaken in which again the features for the condition were mapped in their appropriate perceived locations. The same "blank," "central," and "peripheral" conditions were used. After these maps had been collected they were then asked to perform an evaluation task in which they assessed the degree of similarity between the two distributions they had been tested on in each condition. Degree of similarity was recorded on a seven point scale anchored by the terms "not all similar" and "identical."

As a follow-up task, subjects were again shown the original map. After this map was removed they were then given a single target feature, and were asked to rank the other features in order of increasing distance away from the one presented. The procedure used was the same as before, (i.e., typing the letter of the closest school followed by letters of the next closest until the furthest was chosen). Again they were allowed to cross off names on a check list so that each feature could only occur once in the ranking. This task was designed to provide a final check on consistency of choice of both closest alternative and rank ordering.

8.2 Results

Task 1: Closest location (first nearest neighbor). The data collected for this task consisted of the number of times the subject correctly chose the closest feature. There were seven observations for each person. A 2 x 2 x 2 ANOVA (condition x sex x geography background) showed a marginally significant main effect of group, and a significant interaction between sex and group ($F_{1,24} = 3.90$; $p > .05$). The mean number of times the first nearest neighbor was correctly identified in Condition 1 was 2.375 while for Condition 2 the mean was 3.4375. In general, Condition 2 males performed best with a mean number of correctly identified nearest neighbors of 4.25, followed by Condition 1 females having a mean of 3.0 correct times, Condition 2 females with a mean of 2.625 correct, and Condition 1 males with 1.75 correct followed. For some reason, females did better when starting with the stores while males did better when starting with the schools. Geographical background had no significant effect in this task.

Task 2: Ranking: For the ranking experiment, the data consisted of seven observations per person in which six locations other than the target were ranked each time. Again, from the 2 x 2 x 2 ANOVA there was a main effect of condition in which those working with Condition 2 (schools) averaged 2.15 features ranked correctly while the members of the other condition (stores first) had only 1.83 correct. There was a significant interaction between sex and geography background and condition ($F_{6,19} = 3.96$; $p > 0.009$) In this task, female non-geographers generally scored highest (mean correct = 2.25) followed by male geographers (mean = 2.21). Male non-geographers (mean = 1.83) and female geographers (mean = 1.66) performed worst of all. The non-geography group that did the schools first averaged 2.46 correct, while the geography group starting with stores averaged 2.04 correct; the geography schools group averaged 1.84 correct, and the non-geographers starting with stores averaged 1.63 correct.

As a follow-up to this analysis, we computed a random guessing distribution which is obtained by analyzing the number of possible configurations and combinations given a task of ranking with respect to a single target location and considering all possible targets. When comparing the random distribution with an observed distribution, observed and random distributions were compared using a chi-squared statistic. The results showed rejection of the null hypothesis (i.e., no similarity) (χ^2 = 1196.97; df = 5, α =0.90 = 9.236) (Fig. 2).

Fig. 2. Theoretical and observed cumulative probabilities of ranking k cues correctly

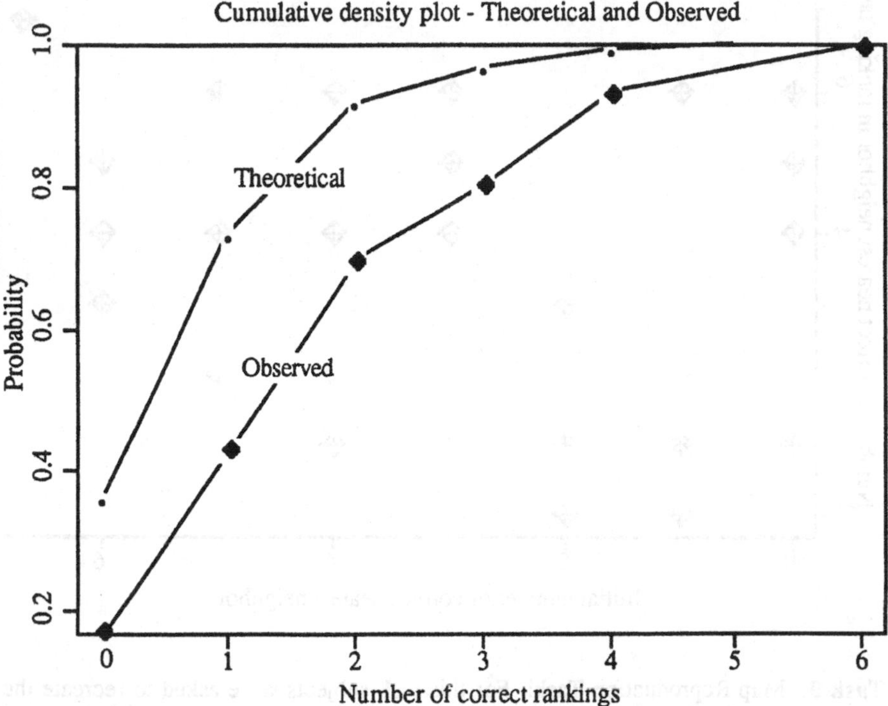

Another analysis focused on the success subjects achieved picking only the closest or first nearest neighbor in the six location ranking task. Here we compared performance on the single task of choosing the closest location to how they performed when ranking all locations by closeness. If subjects were consistent across tasks, the feature chosen as the closest should be the same in both cases. Results showed that there was no consistency in their ranking (Fig. 3).

Fig. 3. Relation between R^2 values for stores versus schools

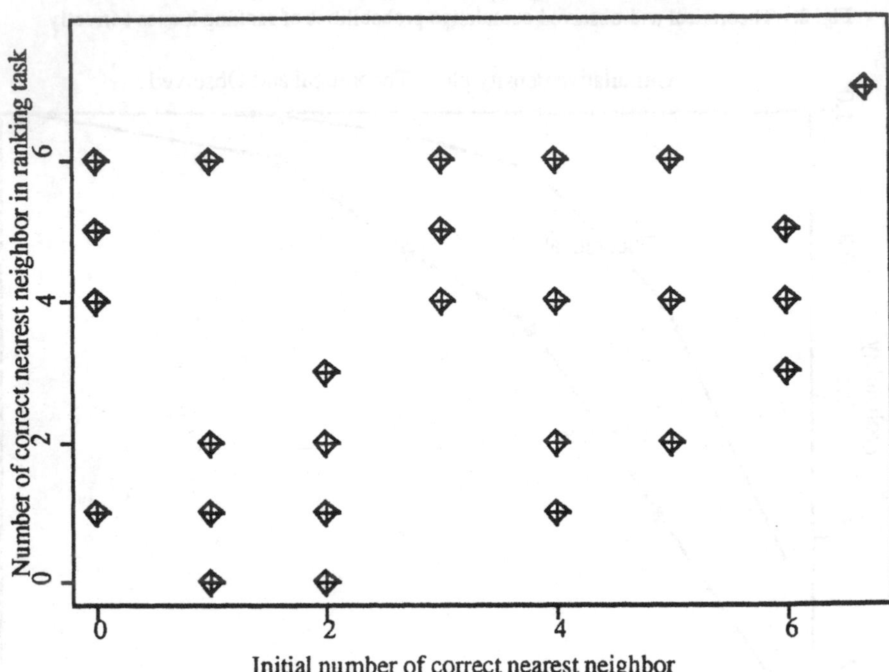

Task 3: Map Reproduction Task: For this task subjects were asked to recreate the map pattern of either the stores or the schools following their ranking tasks. The resulting configurations were compared via bi-dimensional correlation (Tobler, 1978) to the actual mapped patterns. Bi-dimensional correlation provides a statistic somewhat similar to an r-square and has been used extensively to compare maps of point distributions (Golledge & Rayner, 1982; Gale, 1982, 1985; Richardson, 1980, 1982). The r-squares for the 32 subjects are given in Table 1.

For the store maps, 12 of the 32 subjects had r-squares greater than .60; for the schools, 10 of the 32 had correlations greater than .60. Only 6 of the 32 subjects performed consistently well on both tasks (#16, 18, 19, 21, 26, and 28). Eight others performed consistently poorly, while the other 18 had varied success from one situation to the next. In general, there was no clear pattern of consistent performance on both tasks ($r^2 = .1818$).

Table 1. Individual subject correlations between objective and subjective cue locations

	Bidimensional Regression results	
Observation	Store ranking analysis R-Square	School ranking analysis R-Square
1	0.2771	0.0729
2	0.6656	0.0153
3	0.6368	0.1409
4	0.7805	0.1739 **
5	0.8491	0.0261
6	0.7093	0.2180
7	0.0470 **	0.0000
8	0.0982	0.1284
9	0.4829	0.7058
10	0.4582	0.5953
11	0.0962	0.9520
12	0.0017	0.1293
13	0.0834	0.2838
14	0.3372	0.0389
15	0.2822	0.8290
16	0.8760	0.7781
17	0.0129	0.0325
18	0.8760	0.8999
19	0.9469	0.9603
20	0.0550	0.3003
21	0.8571	0.7526
22	0.3566	0.3159
23	0.2823	0.9406
24	0.4146	0.4700
25	0.0240	0.0292
26	0.9375	0.6177
27	0.6697	0.2406
28	0.9313	0.8998
29	0.0420	0.0254
30	0.4439	0.0779
31	0.5607	0.2178
32	0.0117	0.0038

** Observation has missing coordinates.

9. Discussion

The overall results from these experiments were not particularly encouraging. First it appeared that even simple first order geographic primitives such as the idea of pair proximity or nearest neighbor, is not necessarily well understood in the complex map situation tested here, whether or not the distribution which is examined is embedded in a map including other information. Since both configurations of stores and schools had exactly the same internal spatial relations, with one merely being locationally displaced and rotated ninety degrees in the plane, the evidence shows first that the two distributions were not regarded as being similar, and that even performing common tasks on each distribution produced significantly different results. Our attempts to examine whether or not there was a gender basis in terms of this particular spatial ability showed no significant differences overall. Similarly our attempts to evaluate whether those trained in geography or non-geographers could perform better on these tasks also showed no significant differences.

Other information that can be gathered from this study includes examination of whether locations are imaged as being in the correct region (e.g., as defined by the road system on the map), and whether or not the point patterns of the cues have any common interpretation. One reason for a lack of good performance on the cue location reproduction task for example might be that people regionalized the initial map and that this interfered with their ability to comprehend the functional distribution as a single entity. Since the schools and stores can be regionalized differently, this would again account for the lack of observed similarity between distributions.

Another reason for the lack of ability to recognize distribution features and similarities may lie in the choice of labels for each location. For example when debriefing subjects, some claimed it was "easier" to remember details of the stores because they were all associated with tree names and remembering which trees were located near one another was easier than remembering which schools (named after Presidents) were near each other, particularly since many people learn presidents' names in temporal order and the spatial arrangement followed no clear temporal sequence. But, even these explanations fail to explain the significant differences between better performance using schools first for men and stores first for women.

Another intriguing feature was the lack of difference between geographers and non-geographers. We presumed that geographic training would produce a greater ability to recognize spatial distributions and their characteristics. We could not support this hypothesis.

The question remains then, how effective are people at recognizing spatial distributions of like phenomena? The answer appears to be "not very effective." But, is this true only for naive subject? Can we, through repeated trials, dramatically improve people's ability to recognize and interpret this fundamental component of geographical space? How can this skill/ability be taught? Must it be part of all training for spatially aware professionals, including those designing and using GIS? And, to what extent is this skill/ability needed when undertaking spatial analysis at any scale? Can we be sure that interpreters of spatial data will get all relevant information *without* such training? And, is the ability to recognize a distribution and its documentation an integral part of spatial knowledge that should occur in any aptitude or ability test? These and many other questions arise automatically from studies such as the above, and point the way to an important area of future research for all interested in space and territory at geographic and other scales.

10. Summary

Practical needs have lead to the investigation of a variety of methods and techniques for describing spatial relations. They have also raised important questions as to what sets of spatial relations are the most fundamental, and the most important to include in an environmental knowledge base. In today's GIS, for example, many queries are based on some form or another of spatial concepts (Dangermond, 1983; Peuquet 1984). It is essential both to understand what those concepts may be and how people are able to interpret or understand them. For example, we need to be aware of and be able to describe spatial objects standing alone, in sequence (chain) or list form, or regionalized. The lack of a comprehensive theory of spatial relations has been identified by the NCGIA as a major shortcoming and impediment to further GIS development (NCGIA, 1990). The problem inherent here is one of determining which spatial relations should be identified, how to define them, and to understand their various semantic interpretations.

What are the consequences of this research?

1. Even simple spatial concepts may not be well comprehended by many people (e.g. nearest neighbor; shortest path; location, orientation, and direction).
2. The spatial terms we freely use to "help understand" the distribution of phenomena and the interactions between them are not widely used or understood (e.g. nearest neighbor; "distance decay," distribution of a function; region).
3. Without specific prompting (or teaching), people may be unaware of spatial characteristics of an environment (e.g. may not appreciate that like functions form a spatial distribution and that properties of distributions may be similar or different).
4. That the "naive" or "common sense" understanding and use of spatial information and spatial relations is error ridden, naive, and very incomplete, resulting in misconceptions and misunderstandings (e.g. which are closer? which way is shorter?).
5. That many of the criteria that geographers use in models to comprehend and explain spatial relations and spatial properties are *not* the ones typically used in common sense spatial problem solving.
6. To handle spatial problems appropriately, there is a need for an expert language base, expert concept and model building, and an expert training/teaching program capable of using appropriate language, interpretative and manipulative skills. There is, in fact, a need for a distinct spatial discipline designed to handle these functions: Geography is such a discipline, but it has developed on a set of assumptions about people's abilities to understand spatial relations that may be woefully incorrect. We need to know more about the skills and abilities required in spatial thinking and problem solving, and this knowledge must be examined at all spatial scales and under both active and passive experimental conditions.

Acknowledgments: Much of the research reported in this paper was funded by National Science Foundation (NSF) Grant #SES-9023047. Acknowledgments are due to Amy Ruggles, Erika Ferguson, Joanna Schulman and Alan Murray for their valuable assistance and comments.

References

1. L.P. Acredolo: Frames of referenced used by children for orientation in unfamiliar spaces. In: G.T. Moore, R.G. Golledge (eds.): Environmental knowing. Stroudsburg, PA: Dowden, Hutchinson and Ross 1976, pp. 165—172
2. L.P. Acredolo: Development of spatial orientation in infancy. Developmental Psychology 14, 224—234 (1978)
3. L.P. Acredolo: Small- and large-scale spatial concepts in infancy and childhood. In: L. Liben, A. Patterson, N. Newcombe (eds.): Spatial representation and behavior across the life span: Theory and application. New York: Academic Press 1981
4. L.P. Acredolo: Early development of spatial orientation in humans. In: P. Ellen, C. Thinus-Blanc (eds.): Cognitive processes and spatial orientation in animal and man. Volume II: Neurophysiology and developmental aspects. NATO ASI Series, Series D: Behavioural and Social Sciences - No. 37. Dordrecht: Martinus Nijhoff 1987, pp. 185—201
5. S.C. Aitken, R. Prosser: Residents' spatial knowledge of neighborhood continuity and form. Geographical Analysis 22, 301—325 (1990)
6. J.R. Anderson: Language, memory and thought. Hillsdale, NJ: Erlbaum 1976
7. J.R. Anderson: Acquisition of cognitive skill. Psychological Review 89, 369—406 (1982)
8. J.C. Baird: Studies of the cognitive representation of spatial relations: I. Overview. Journal of Experimental Psychology, General 108, 90—91 (1979)
9. B.E. Budd, P.R. Clance, D.E. Simerly: Spatial configurations: Erikson reexamined. Sex Roles 12, 571—577 (1985)
10. S. Carey, R. Diamond: From piecemeal to configurational representation of faces. Science 195, 312—314 (1977)
11. L. Curtis, A. Siegel, N. Furlong: Developmental differences in cognitive mapping: Configurational knowledge of familiar large-scale environments. Journal of Experimental Child Psychology 31, 456—469 (1981)
12. J. Dangermond: A classification of software components commonly used in GIS. In: D.J. Peuquet, J. O'Callaghan (eds.): Design and implementation of computer-based Geographic Information Systems. Amherst, NY: IGU Commission on Geographical Data Sensing and Processing 1983, pp. 70-91
13. R.M. Downs, D. Stea: Image and environment: Cognitive mapping and spatial behavior. Chicago: Aldine 1973a
14. J. Eliot, I.M. McFarlane-Smith: An international directory of spatial tests. Oxford: NFER-Nelson Publishing Company 1983
15. G.W. Evans: Environmental cognition. Psychological Bulletin 88, 259—287 (1980)
16. G.W. Evans, D.G. Marrero, P.A. Butler: Environmental learning and cognitive mapping. Environment and Behavior 13, 83—104 (1981)
17. G.W. Evans, M.A. Skorpanich, K.J. Bryant, B. Bresolin: The effects of pathway configuration, landmarks, and stress on environmental cognition. Journal of Environmental Psychology 4, 323—335 (1984)
18. S.M. Freundschuh: Can survey (map view) knowledge be acquired from procedural knowledge? Presented at the Annual Meeting, Association of American Geographers, Baltimore, MD 1989

19. N.D. Gale: Some applications of computer cartography to the study of cognitive configurations. Professional Geographer 34, 313—321 (1982)
20. N.D. Gale: Route learning by children in real and simulated environments. Ph.D. Dissertation, University of California, Santa Barbara 1985
21. N.D. Gale, R.G. Golledge, J.W. Pellegrino, S. Doherty: The acquisition and integration of neighborhood route knowledge in an unfamiliar neighborhood. Journal of Environmental Psychology 10, 3—26 (1990)
22. T. Gärling, A. Böök, E. Lindberg, T. Nilsson: Memory for the spatial layout of the everyday physical environment: Factors affecting the rate of acquisition. Journal of Environmental Psychology 1, 263—277 (1981)
23. T. Gärling, J. Säisä, A. Böök, E. Lindberg: The spatio-temporal sequencing of everyday activities in the large-scale environment. Journal of Environmental Psychology 6, 261—280 (1986)
24. P.P. Gilmartin, J. Patton: Comparing the sexes on spatial abilities: Map-use skills. Annals of the Association of American Geographers 74, 605—619 (1984)
25. R.G. Golledge (ed.): On determining cognitive configurations of a city: Volume I - Problem statement, experimental design and preliminary findings. NSF Grant #GS-37969 (1974)
26. R.G. Golledge: Environmental cues, cognitive mapping, spatial behavior. In: D. Burke, et al., (eds.) Behavior-environment research methods. Institute for Environmental Studies, University of Wisconsin 1977a, pp. 35—46
27. R.G. Golledge: Learning about an urban environment. In N. Thrift, D. Parkes, T. Carlstein (eds.): Timing space and spacing time. London: Aldine 1977b
28. R.G. Golledge: Environmental cognition. In: D. Stokols, I. Altman (eds.): Handbook of environmental psychology. New York: John Wiley & Sons 1987, pp. 131—174
29. R.G. Golledge: The conceptual and empirical basis of a general theory of spatial knowledge. In: M.M. Fischer, P. Nijkamp, Y.Y. Papageorgiou (eds.): Spatial choices and processes. North-Holland: Elsevier Science Publishers B.V. 1990, pp. 147—168
30. R.G. Golledge: Cognition of physical and built environments. In: T. Gärling, G. Evans (eds.): Environment, cognition, and action: An integrated approach. New York: Oxford University Press 1991, pp. 35—62
31. R.G. Golledge: The acquisition and integration of components of spatial knowledge by children and adults. NSF Grant #SES-8407160. Department of Geography, University of California at Santa Barbara 1991
32. R.G. Golledge: Spatial properties of configurational knowledge. NSF Grant #SES-9023047. Department of Geography, University of California at Santa Barbara 1992
33. R.G. Golledge, J. Loomis, R.L. Klatzky, J.W. Pellegrino, S. Doherty, J. Cicinelli: Environmental cognition and assessment: Spatial cognition of the blind and visually impaired. Paper delivered at Environmental Cognition and Assessment Conference, Umeå, Sweden 1988
34. R.G. Golledge, J.W. Pellegrino, N.D. Gale, S. Doherty: Acquisition and integration of route knowledge. The National Geographical Journal of India 37, 130—146 (1991)

35. R.G. Golledge, J.N. Rayner: Proximity and preference: Problems in the multidimensional analysis of large data sets. Minneapolis, MN: University of Minnesota Press 1982
36. R.G. Golledge, J.N. Rayner, V.L. Rivizzigno: Comparing objective and cognitive representations of environmental cues. In: R.G. Golledge, J.N. Rayner (eds.): Proximity and preference: Problems in the multidimensional and analysis of large data sets. Minneapolis, MN: University of Minnesota Press 1982, pp. 233—266
37. R.G. Golledge, A. Spector: Comprehending the urban environment: Theory and practice. Geographical Analysis 10, 403—426 (1978)
38. R.G. Golledge, H. Timmermans: Applications of behavioural research on problems, I: Cognition. Progress in Human Geography 14, 57—99 (1990)
39. Golledge, G. Zannaras: Cognitive approaches to the analysis of human spatial behavior. In: W. Ittelson (ed.): Environmental cognition. New York: Seminar Press 1973, pp. 59—94
40. S. Gopal, R.L. Klatzky, T.R. Smith: Navigator: A psychologically based model of environmental learning through navigation. Journal of Environmental Psychology 9, 309—332 (1989)
41. P. Gould: On mental maps. Discussion paper No. 9, Community of Mathematical Geographers, Michigan University, Ann Arbor, Michigan 1966
42. P. Gould: Problems of space preference measures and relationships. Geographical Analysis 1, 31—44 (1969)
43. P. Gould: Location in information space. Paper presented at the Symposium on Conceptual Issues in Environmental Cognition, Environmental Design Research Association meeting, Los Angeles, CA, January 1972
44. P. Gould, R. White: Mental maps. Harmondsworth, England: Penguin 1974
45. R.A. Hart, G.T. Moore: The development of spatial cognition: A review. In: R. Downs, D. Stea (eds.): Image and environment: Cognitive mapping and spatial behavior. Chicago: Aldine 1973, pp. 246—288
46. S.C. Hirtle, J. Jonides: Evidence of hierarchies in cognitive maps. Memory and Cognition 13, 108—217 (1985)
47. K.C. Kirasic, G.L. Allen, A.W. Siegel: Expression of configurational knowledge of large-scale environments. Environment and Behavior 16, 687—712 (1984)
48. B.J. Kuipers: Representing knowledge of large scale space. AI-TR-418, AI Laboratory, MIT 1977
49. B.J. Kuipers: The map-learning critter. AI-TR-85-17, University of Texas at Austin, Austin, Texas 1985
50. L.S. Liben: Children's large-scale spatial cognition: Is the measure the message? In: R. Cohen (ed.): New directions for child development: Children's conceptions of spatial relationships. San Francisco: Jossey-Bass 1982
51. L.S. Liben, A. Patterson, N. Newcombe (eds.): Spatial representation and behavior across the life span. New York: Academic Press 1981
52. R.E. Lloyd: Encoding information into and obtaining information from cognitive maps. Unpublished Manuscript, Department of Geography, University of South Carolina 1989a
53. R.E. Lloyd: Cognitive maps: Encoding and decoding information. Annals of the American Association of Geographers 79, 101—124 (1989b)

54. R.E. Lloyd: The estimation of distance and direction from cognitive maps. The American Cartographer 16, 109—122 (1989c)
55. I. Moar, G. Bower: Inconsistency in spatial knowledge. Memory and Cognition 11, 107—113 (1983)
56. National Center for Geographic Information and Analysis: NSF Proposal for Continuation of Cooperative Agreement No. SES88-010917 for period 12/1/90 through 11/30/91 (1990)
57. D.J. Peuquet: A conceptual framework and comparison of spatial data models. Cartographica 21, 66—113 (1984)
58. J. Piaget, B. Inhelder: The child's conception of space. New York: Norton 1967
59. G.D. Richardson: Comparing two cognitive mapping methodologies. In: R.G. Golledge, J. Parnicky, J. Rayner (eds.): The spatial competence of selected populations. The Ohio State University Research Foundation Project 761142/711173 - Final Report, November. NSF Grant #SOC77-26977-A02, 1980, pp. 165-184
60. G.D. Richardson: Spatial cognition. Ph.D. Dissertation, University of California at Santa Barbara 1982
61. V.L. Rivizzigno: Uncovering individual differences in the cognitive structuring of an urban area using multidimensional scaling. In: R.G. Golledge, J. Rayner (eds.): Cognitive configurations of a city: Volume II. NSF Grant #GS-37969 (1976), pp. 75—114
62. C. Self, S. Gopal, R.G. Golledge, S. Fenstermaker: Gender-related differences in spatial abilities. Progress in Human Geography (In Print) 1992
63. A.W. Siegel: The externalization of cognitive maps by children and adults: In search of better ways to ask better questions. In: L. Liben, A. Patterson, N. Newcombe (eds.): Spatial representation and behavior across the life span: Theory and application. New York: Academic Press 1981, pp. 167—194
64. A.W. Siegel: Toward a social ecology of cognitive mapping. In: R. Cohen (ed.): New directions for child development: Children's conceptions of spatial relationships, No. 15. San Francisco, Jossey-Bass 1982
65. A.W. Siegel, J. Cousins: The symbolizing and symbolized child in the enterprise of cognitive mapping. In: R. Cohen (ed.): The development of spatial cognition. Hillsdale, NJ: Lawrence Erlbaum Associates 1983
66. A.W. Siegel, J. Herman, G.L. Allen, K.C. Kirasic: The development of cognitive maps of large- and small-scale space. Child development 50, 582—585 (1979)
67. A.W. Siegel, K.C. Kirasic, R.V. Kail: Stalking the elusive cognitive map: The development of children's representations of geographic space. In: J.F. Wohlwill, I. Altman (eds.): Human behavior and environment: Children and the environment, Volume 3. New York: Plenum Press 1978
68. A.W. Siegel, M. Schadler: Young children's cognitive maps of their classroom. Child Development 48, 388—394 (1977)
69. A.W. Siegel, S.H. White: The development of spatial representation of large scale environments. In: H. Reese (ed.): Advances in child development and behavior. New York: Academic Press 1975, pp. 9—55
70. A.N. Spector: An analysis of urban spatial imagery. Unpublished Ph.D. dissertation. Columbus, OH: Ohio State University 1978

71. A. Stevens, P. Coupe: Distortions in judged spatial relations. Cognitive Psychology 10, 422—437 (1978)
72. W.R. Tobler: Comparison of plane forms. Geographical Analysis 10, 154—162 (1978)
73. B. Tversky: Distortions in memory for maps. Cognitive Psychology 13, 407—433 (1981)
74. G. Zannaras: An analysis of cognitive and objective characteristics of the city: Their influence of movements to the city center. Unpublished Ph.D. dissertation, Department of Geography, Ohio State University 1973a
75. G. Zannaras: The cognitive structure of urban areas. EDRA IV, April 1973b
76. C. Zimring, M. Gross: The environment in environmental cognition research. In: T. Gärling, G. Evans (eds.): Environment, cognition, and action. New York: Oxford University Press 1991

Temporal Databases

Richard T. Snodgrass

Department of Computer Science, University of Arizona, Tucson, AZ 85721
rts@cs.arizona.edu

Abstract. This paper summarizes the major concepts, approaches, and implementation strategies that have been generated over the last fifteen years of research into data base management system support for time-varying information. We first examine the time domain, its structure, dimensionality, indeterminacy, and representation. We then discuss how facts may be associated with time, and consider data modeling and representational issues. We survey the many temporal query languages that have been proposed. Finally, we examine the impact to each of the components of a DBMS of adding temporal support, focusing on query optimization and evaluation.

1 Introduction

Time is an important aspect of all real-world phenomena. Events occur at specific points in time; objects and the relationships among objects exist over time. The ability to model this temporal dimension of the real wold is essential to many computer applications, such as econometrics, banking, inventory control, accounting, law, medical records, land and geographical information systems, and airline reservations.

Conventional databases represent the state of an enterprise at a single moment of time. Although the contents of the database continue to change as new information is added, these changes are viewed as modifications to the state, with the old, out-of-date data being deleted from the database. The current contents of the database may be viewed as a shapshot of the enterprise. In such systems the attributes involving time are manipulated solely by the application programs; the database management system (DBMS) interprets dates as values in the base data types. No conventional system interprets temporal domains when deriving new relations.

Application-independent DBMS support for time-varying information has been an active area of research for about 15 years, with approximately 400 papers generated thus far [13, 92, 130, 132]. This paper attempts to capture and summarize the major concepts, approaches, and implementation strategies that have been generated by that research.

We first examine the time domain: its structure, dimensionality (interestingly, there are several time dimensions) and temporal indeterminacy, followed by issues in representing values in this domain. We demonstrate that time is actually more complex than the spatial domain, as the former's dimensions are non-homogeneous.

Section 3 follows a similar organization in examining how facts may be associated with time. Data modeling issues are first examined, then representational alternatives are explored, with frequent comparisons with space. We briefly consider how facts may be simultaneously associated with both space and time, a common phenomena in land and geographic information systems.

We next consider languages for expressing temporal queries. We illustrate the various types of queries through examples in the temporal query language TQuel, and briefly appraise various standards efforts.

Temporal DBMS implementation is the topic of Sec. 5. We examine the impact to each of the components of a DBMS of adding temporal support, discussing query optimization and evaluation in some detail.

We conclude with a summary of the major accomplishments and disappointments of research into temporal databases.

We omit one major aspect, that of database design, due to lack of space.

2 The Time Domain

In this section we focus on time itself: how it is modeled and how it is represented. The next section will then combine time with facts, to model time-varying information.

2.1 Structure

We initially assume that there is one dimension of time. The distinctions we address here will apply to each of the several dimensions we consider in the next section.

Early work on *temporal logic* centered around two structural models of time, *linear* and *branching* [145]. In the linear model, time advances from the past to the future in a totally ordered fashion. In the branching model, also termed the *possible futures* model, time is linear from the past to now, where it then divides into several time lines, each representing a potential sequence of events [149]. Along any future path, additional branches may exist. The structure of branching time is a tree rooted at now. The most general model of time in a temporal logic represents time as an arbitrary set with a partial order imposed on it. Additional axioms introduce other, more refined models of time. For example, linear time can be specified by adding an axiom imposing a total order on this set. Recurrent processes may be associated with a *cyclic* model of time [15, 87, 88].

In spatial models, there is much less diversity, and a linear model is generally adequate.

Axioms may also be added to temporal logics to characterize the *density* of the time line [145]. Combined with the linear model, *discrete* models of time are isomorphic to the natural numbers, implying that each point in time has a single successor [18]. *Dense* models of time are isomorphic to either the rationals or the reals: between any two moments of time another moment exists. *Continuous* models of time are isomorphic to the reals, i.e., they are both dense and unlike the rationals, contain no "gaps."

In the continuous model, each real number corresponds to a "point" in time; in the discrete model, each natural number corresponds to a nondecomposable unit of time with an arbitrary duration. Such a nondecomposable unit of time is refered to as a *chronon* [7, 19] (other, perhaps less desirable, terms include "time quantum" [6], "moment" [5], "instant" [41] and "time unit" [100, 138]). A chronon is the smallest duration of time that can be represented in this model. It is not a point, but a line segment on the time line.

Although time itself is generally perceived to be continuous, most proposals for adding a temporal dimension to the relational data model are based on the discrete time model. Several practical arguments are given in the literature for this preference for the discrete model over the continuous model. First, measures of time are inherently imprecise [6, 18]. Clocking instruments invariably report the occurrence of events in terms of chronons, not time "points." Hence, events, even so-called "instantaneous" events, can at best be measured as having occurred during a chronon. Secondly, most natural language references to time are compatible with the discrete time model. For example, when we say that an event occurred at 4:30 p.m., we usually don't mean that the event occurred at the "point" in time associated with 4:30 p.m., but at some time in the chronon (perhaps minute) associated with 4:30 p.m. [6, 19, 34]. Thirdly, the concepts of chronon and interval allow us to naturally model events that are not instantaneous, but have duration [6]. Finally, any implementation of a data model with a temporal dimension will of necessity have to have some discrete encoding for time (Sec. 2.4).

Space may similarly be regarded as discrete, dense, or continuous. Note that, in all three of these alternatives, two separate space-filling objects cannot be located in the same point in space and time: they can be located in the same place at different times, or at the same time in different places.

Axioms can also be placed on the *boundedness* of time. Time can be bounded orthogonally in the past and in the future. The same applies to models of space.

Models of time may include the concept of *distance* (most temporal logics do not do so, however). Both time and space are *metrics*, in that they have a distance function satisfying four properties: (1) the distance is nonnegative, (2) the distance between any two non-identical elements is non-zero, (3) the distance from time α to time β is identical to the distance from β to α, and (4) the distance from α to γ is equal to or greater than the distance from α to β plus the distance from β to γ (the triangle inequality).

With distance and boundedness, restrictions on range can be applied. The scientific cosmology of the "Big Bang" posits that time begins with the Big Bang, 14 ± 4 billion years ago. There is much debate on when it will end, depending on whether the universe is *open* or *closed* (Hawking provides a readable introduction to this controversy [54]). If the universe is closed then time will have an end when the universe collapses back onto itself in what is called the "Big Crunch." If it is open then time will go on forever.

Similar considerations apply to space. In particular, an open universe implies unbounded space. However, many applications assume a bound as well as a range; geographical information systems don't need to contend with values greater than approximately 70 million meters.

Finally, one can differentiate *relative* time from *absolute* time (more precise terms are *unachored* and *anchored*). For example, "9A.M., January 1, 1992" is an absolute time, whereas "9 hours" is a relative time. This distinction, though, is not as crisp as one would hope, because absolute time is with respect to another time (in this example, midnight, January 1, A.D. 1). We will show in Sec. 2.4 how to exploit this interaction. Relative time differs from distance in that the former has a direction, e.g., one could envision a relative time of -9 hours, whereas a distance is unsigned.

One can also differentiate between relative and absolute space, with the same provisos.

2.2 Dimensionality

Time is multi-dimensional [123]. *Valid time* concerns the time a fact was true in reality. The valid time of an event is the wall clock time at which the event occurred in the real world, independent of the recording of that event in some database. Valid times can also be in the future, if it is known that some fact will be true at a specified time in the future. *Transaction time* concerns the time the fact was present in the database as stored data. The transaction time (an interval) of an event identifies the transactions that inserted the information about the event into the database and removed this information from the database. As with space, these two dimensions are orthogonal. A data model supporting neither is termed *snapshot*, as it captures only a single snapshot in time of both the database and the enterprise that the database models. A date model supporting only valid time is termed *historical*; one that supports only transaction time is termed *rollback*; and one that supports both valid and transaction time is termed *bitemporal* (*temporal* is a generic term implying some kind of time support).

Figure 1 illustrates a *single* bitemporal relation (i.e., table) composed of a sequence of historical states indexed by transaction time. It is the result of four transactions starting from an empty relation: (1) three tuples (i.e., rows) were added, (2) one tuple was added, (3) one tuple was added and an existing one terminated (logically deleted), and (4) the starting time of a previous tuple [the middle one added in transaction (1)] was changed to a somewhat later time (presumably the original starting time was incorrect) and a recently added tuple (the bottom one) was deleted (presumably it should not have been there in the first place.) Each update operation involves copying the historical state, then applying the update to the newly created state. Of course, less redundant representations than the one shown are possible. While we'll consider only linear time, branching transaction time provides a useful model for *versioning* in computer-aided design tasks [33] such as CAD [36, 69] and CASE [9, 56].

A different depiction that has proven useful is to time-stamp each fact with

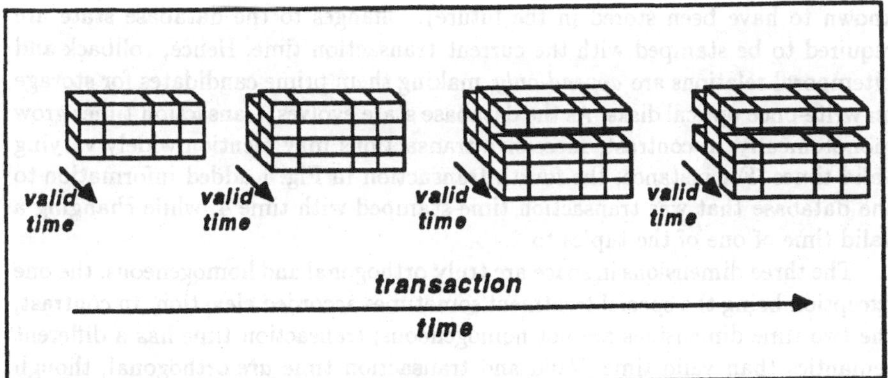

Fig. 1. A bitemporal relation

a *bitemporal element*[1], which is a set of *bitemporal chronons*. Each bitemporal chronon represents a tiny rectangle in valid-time/transaction-time space. Figure 2 shows the bitemporal element associated with the middle tuple of Fig. 1. Historical and rollback databases effectively record *historical chronons* and *rollback chronons*, respectively.

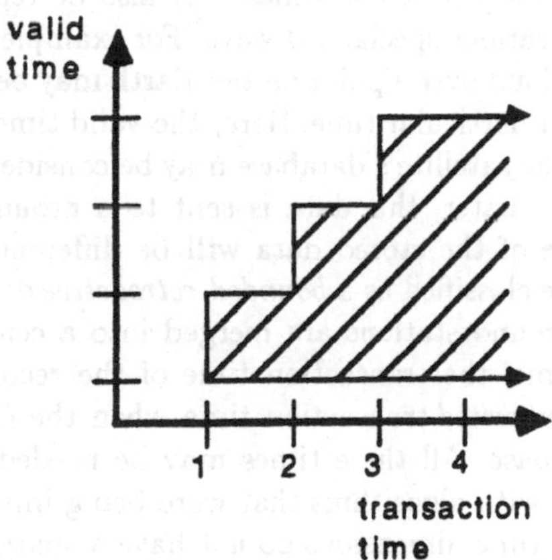

Fig. 2. A bitemporal element

While valid time may be bounded or unbounded (as we saw, cosmologists feel that it is at least bounded in the past), transaction time is bounded on both ends. Specifically, transaction time starts when the database is created (before which time, nothing was stored), and doesn't extend past now (no facts are

[1] This term is a generalization of *temporal element*, previously used to denotes a set of single dimensional chronons [43]. An alternative, equally desirable term is *bitemporal lifespan* [20].

known to have been stored in the future). Changes to the database state are required to be stamped with the current transaction time. Hence, rollback and bitemporal relations are *append-only*, making them prime candidates for storage on write-once optical disks. As the database state evolves, transaction times grow monotonically. In contrast, successive transactions may mention widely varying valid times. For instance, the fourth transaction in Fig. 1 added information to the database that was transaction time-stamped with time 4, while changing a valid time of one of the tuples to 2.

The three dimensions in space are truly orthogonal and homogeneous, the one exception being the special treatment sometimes accorded elevation. In contrast, the two time dimensions are not homogeneous; transaction time has a different semantics than valid time. Valid and transaction time *are* orthogonal, though there are generally some application dependent correlations between the two times. As a simple example, consider the situation where a fact is recorded as soon as it becomes valid in reality. In such a *specialized* bitemporal database, termed *degenerate* [61], valid and transaction time are identical. As another example, if a cloud cover measurement is recorded at most two days after it was valid in reality, and if it takes at least six hours from the measurement time to record the measurement, then such a relation is *delayed strongly retroactively bounded with bounds six hours and two days.*

Multiple transaction times may also be stored in the same relation, termed *temporal generalization* [61]. These times may also be related to each other, or to the valid time, in various specialized ways. For example, a particular value for the reflectivity of a cloud over a point on the Earth may be recorded by an Earth Sensing Satellite at a particular time. Here, the valid time and transaction time are correlated, and the satellite's database may be considered to be a degenerate bitemporal database. Later, this data is sent to a ground station and stored; the transaction time of the stored data will be different from the valid time; this database may be classified as a *bounded retroactive* database. Later still, the data from several ground stations are merged into a central database, storing the original valid time, the transaction time of the recording into the central database, and the *inherited* transaction time when the data was stored in the ground station database. All three times may be needed, for instance, if data massaging was done with algorithms that were being improved over time. Such multiple transaction time dimensions do not have a spatial analogue.

2.3 Indeterminacy

Information that is *historically indeterminate* can be characterized as "don't know exactly when" information. This kind of information is prevalent; it arises in various situations, including the following.

- *Finer system granularity* — In perhaps most cases, the granularity of the database does not match the precision to which an event time is known. For example, an event time known to within one day and recorded on a system with time-stamps in the granularity of a millisecond happened sometime *during* that day, but during which millisecond is unknown.

- *Imperfect dating techniques* — Many dating techniques are inherently imprecise, such as radioactive and Carbon-14 dating. All clocks have an inherent imprecision [34].
- *Uncertainty in planning* – Projected completion dates are often inexactly specified, e.g., the project will complete three to six months from now.
- *Unknown or imprecise event times* — In general, event times could be unknown or imprecise. For example, if we do now know when an individual was born, the individual's date of birth could be recorded in the database as either unknown (she was born between now and the beginning of time) or imprecise (she was born between now and 100 years ago).

There have been several proposals for adding historical indeterminacy to the time model [44, 67], as well as more specific work on accommodating multiple time granularities [75, 148]. The *possible chronons* model unifies treatment of both aspects [34]. In this model, an event is *determinate* if it is know when (i.e., during which chronon) it occurred. A determinate event cannot overlap two chronons. If it is unknown when an event occurred, but known that it did occur, then the event is historically indeterminate. The indeterminacy refers to the *time* when the event occurred, not *whether* the event did or did not occur.

Two pieces of information completely describe an indeterminate event: a *set of possible chronons* and an *event probability distribution.* A single chronon from the set of possible chronons denotes when the indeterminate event actually occurred. However, it is unknown *which* possible chronon is the actual one. The event probability distribution gives the probability that the event occurred during each chronon in the set of possible chronons.

The implementation of the possible chronons model supports a fixed, minimal chronon size. Multiple granularities are handled by representing the indeterminacy explicitly. For example, if the underlying chronon is a microsecond and an event is known to within a day, then this indeterminate event would be associated with a set of 86,400,000 possible chronons, and perhaps a uniform event probability distribution.

As a practical matter, events that occurred in the prehistoric past cannot be dated as precisely as events that occur in the present. There is an implicit "telescoping view" of time. Dating of recent events can often be done to the millisecond while events that occurred 400 million years ago can be dated to, perhaps at best the nearest 100,000 years. Dating future events is also problematic. It is impossible to say how many seconds will be between Midnight January 1, 1992 and Midnight January 1, 2300 because we don't know how many leap second will be added to correct for changes in the rotational clock. We can guess at the number of seconds, but "leap shifts" to the current clock are likely to invalidate our guess.

Historical indeterminacy occurs only in valid time. The granularity of a transaction time time-stamp is the smallest inter-transaction time. Transaction times are always determinate since the chronon during which a transaction takes place is always known.

Most of the above may be applied to space. Information that is *spatially indeterminate* can be characterized as "don't know exactly where" information. It is also prevalent, due to granularity concerns, measurement techniques, and unknown or imprecise location specifiers. One could envision an analogous "possible space quanta" model that could capture the variety of spatial indeterminacy. The telescoping view phenomenon also occurs in space, as distant locations are less precisely known.

As with time, a spatial *data granularity* coarser than the *database management system (DBMS) granularity* is often adopted. One of the more common models, Type 0 (Sec. 2.2), covers the two-dimensional space with a grid, with point locations and associated attributes reported to the nearest cell center. In this model, the data is a multiple of the underlying DBMS granularity. For example, the DBMS granularity might be a meter, with all location specifiers being expressed in this unit, while the grid cells may be 2 kilometers on a side.

2.4 Representation

Since time and space are metrics, a system of units is required to represent particular events or locations. A time-stamp or location specifier has a *physical realization* and an *interpretation*. The physical realization is a pattern of bits while the interpretation is the meaning of each bit pattern, that is, the time or location each pattern represents.

Interpretation. For time, the central unit is the *second*. However, there are at least seven different definitions of this fundamental unit [34].

Apparent solar — 1/86400 of the interval from noon to noon; varies from day to day.

Mean solar (UT0) — 1/86400 of a *mean solar day*, averaged over a year; varies from year to year.

Mean sidereal — 1/86400 of a *mean sidereal day*, measuring the rotation of the Earth with respect to a distant star; varies from year to year.

UT1 — UT0 corrected for polar wander.

UT2 — UT1 corrected for seasonal variations.

Ephemeris — mean solar second for the year 1900; does not vary. This was the standard definition from 1960 to 1967.

International System of Units (SI) — the duration of 9,192,631,770 periods of the radiation corresponding to the transition between the two hyperfine levels of cesium-133 atoms [104].

When a range of less than 10,000 years is supported, the differences between these definitions are generally inconsequential, except for the apparent solar second, which varies by 1% over the course of a year. When ranges of several billion years are supported, however, all of these definitions differ significantly.

Different regions of the time line are used by different communities. For example, apparent solar time is important to historians, who care about whether something happened in the daylight or in darkness, as well as to users of cadastral (real estate) databases, which utilize civil calendars [58]. Ephemeris time is used by astronomers, while the SI second is the basis for radioactive dating used by geochronologists. Because of these different needs, as well as the telescoping view of time, we have proposed a specific temporal interpretation termed the *base-line clock* that constructs a time-line by using different well-defined clocks in different periods. This clock, shown in Fig. 3 (not to scale), partitions the time line into a set of contiguous *periods*. Each period runs on a different clock. A *synchronization point*, where two clocks are correlated, delimits a period boundary. The synchronization points occur at Midnight on the specified date.

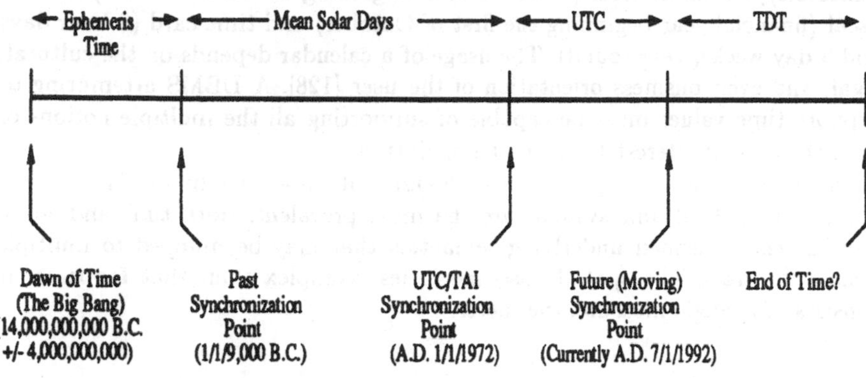

Fig. 3. The base-line clock

From the Big Bang until Midnight January 1, 9000 B.C. the base-line clock runs on ephemeris time. This clock is preferable to the solar clock since ephemeris time is independent of the formation of the Earth and the Solar System. Also, we prefer using the ephemeris clock to the solar clock because an ephemeris year is a fixed duration, unlike the tropical year. For historic events, 9000 B.C. to January 1, 1972, the base-line clock follows the mean solar day clock. Historic events are usually dated with calendars. Calendar dates invariably count days and use an intercalation rule to relate the number of days to longer-term celestial clocks, e.g., the Gregorian calendar relates days to months and tropical years. At Midnight January 1, 1972 the base-line clock switches to Universal Coordinated Time (UTC). Midnight January 1, 1972 is when UTC was synchronized with the SI definition of second and the current system of leap seconds was adopted. The base-line clock runs on UTC until one second before Midnight, July 1, 1992. This is the next time at which a leap second may be added (a leap second will be added on this date according to the latest International Earth Rotation Service bulletin [102]). After Midnight July 1, 1992, until the "Big Crunch" or the end of our base-line clock, the base-line clock follows Terrestrial Dynamic Time (TDT), an "idealized atomic time" [46] based on the SI second, since both

UTC and mean solar time are unknown and unpredictable.

The situation is much simpler for space. Here, the (SI) *meter* is the commonly accepted unit, with a single accepted definition, the length of the path traveled by light in vacuum during a time interval of 1/299,792,458 of a second [104]. Distance is defined in terms of time, rather than the other way around, because time can be measured more accurately (1 part in 10^{10} over long intervals and 1 part in 10^{15} for between a minute and a day [105, 106]).

The base-line clock and its representation are independent of any calendar. We used Gregorian calendar dates in the above discussion only to provide an informal indication of when the synchronization points occurred. Many calendar systems are in use today; example calendars include academic (years consists of semesters), common fiscal (financial year beginning at the New Year), federal fiscal (financial year beginning the first of October) and time card (8 hour days and 5 day weeks, year-round). The usage of a calendar depends on the cultural, legal, and even business orientation of the user [128]. A DBMS attempting to support time values must be capable of supporting all the multiple notions of time that are of interest to the user population.

Space also has multiple notions, though with less variability. The metric, U.S., and nautical unit systems are the most prevalent. Both time and space have precisely defined underlying semantics that may be mapped to multiple display formats. The spatial base-line is less complex than that for time; it consists of a single measure, the meter.

Physical Realization. The base-line clock defines the meaning of each time-stamp bit pattern in the physical realization of a time-stamp. The chronons of the base-line clock are the chronons in its constituent clocks. We assume that each chronon is one second in the underlying constituent clock. A chronon may be denoted by an integer, corresponding to a *single (DBMS) granularity*, or it may be denoted by a sequence of integers, corresponding to a *nested granularity*. For example, if we assume a granularity of a second relative to Midnight, January 1, 1980, then in a single granularity the integer 164,281,022 denotes 9:37:02AM March 15, 1985. If we assume a nested granularity of ⟨year, month, day, hour, minute, second⟩, then the sequence ⟨6,3,15,9,37,2⟩ denotes that same time.

Various time-stamps are in use in commercial database management systems and operating systems; a summary is provided in Table 1. This table compares formats from operating systems (specifically Unix, MSDOS, and the MacIntosh operating systems), the database systems DB2 [27], SQL2 [25, 97], and several proposed formats to be discussed shortly. The SQL2 `datetime` time-stamp appears twice in the comparison, once with its optional fractional second precision field set to microseconds, and once without the optional field. The last three representations have recently been proposed, and will be discussed shortly.

Size is the number of bytes devoted to the representation, while *range* refers to the difference between the youngest and oldest time values that can be represented. The *granularity* of a time-stamp is the precision to which a time value can be represented. If a representation has more than one *component*, it is of a

SYSTEM	*Size (bytes)*	*Range*	*Granularity*
OS (several)	4	≈ 136 years	second
DB2 —`date`	4	10,000 years	day
DB2 —`time`	3	24 hours	second
DB2 —`timestamp`	10	10,000 years	microsecond
SQL2 —`datetime`	20	10,000 years	second
SQL2 —fractional `datetime`	27	10,000 years	microsecond
Low Resolution	8	≈ 36 billion years	second
High Resolution	8	≈ 17400 years	microsecond
Extended Resolution	12	≈ 36 billion years	nanosecond

SYSTEM	*Number of Components*	*Bytes Needed*	*Space Efficiency*
OS (several)	1	4	100%
DB2 —`date`	3	2.9	71%
DB2 —`time`	3	2.2	72%
DB2 —`timestamp`	7	7.3	73%
SQL2 —`datetime`	5	4.8	24%
SQL2 —fractional `datetime`	6	7.3	27%
Low Resolution	1	7.6	95%
High Resolution	3	7.5	93%
Extended Resolution	4	11.3	94%

Table 1. A comparison of some physical layouts

nested granularity. The extreme is the DB2 `timestamp` representation, in which the year, month, day, hour, minute, second, and number of microseconds are individually represented. *Space efficiency* is a measure of how much of the representation is actually needed. It is computed as a percentage of the number of bits needed to represent every chronon in the temporal interpretation (DB2 and SQL2 both use the Gregorian calendar temporal interpretation) versus the number of bits devoted to the physical realization. The minimum number of *bytes needed* to store the number of chronons dictated by a time-stamp's granularity and range is shown as a separate column. For instance, SQL2's `datetime` time-stamp uses 20 bytes, but only 4.8 bytes of space are needed to store a range of 10,000 years to the granularity of a second.

The evaluated time-stamps fall into two camps: OS-style time-stamps and database-style time-stamps. OS-style time-stamps have a limited range and granularity; these limitations are dictated by the size of the time-stamp. OS-style time-stamps are maximally space efficient, having a single granularity. The time-stamp itself is merely a count of the number of chronons that have elapsed since the origin in the temporal interpretation. But optimal space efficiency is attained at the expense of some *time efficiency*.

In contrast, database-style time-stamps, as exemplified by the DB2 `timestamp` format, are generally larger than OS-style time-stamps; they have a wider range and finer granularity. But, as a group, they also have poorer space utilization, having a nested granularity. The advantage of representing values separately is that they can be quickly accessed. Extracting the number of years from an OS-style time-stamp is more involved than performing a similar task on an DB2 **`timestamp`**.

These existing time-stamp representations suffer from inadequate range, too coarse a granularity, excessive space requirements, or a combination of these drawbacks. Finally, none of the time-stamps are able to represent *historical indeterminacy*. Consequently, we recently proposed new time-stamp formats, incorporating features from both the OS-style and database-style time-stamps. These formats combine high space efficiency with high time efficiency for frequent time-stamp operations [34].

There is a natural tradeoff between range and granularity in time-stamp development. Using the same number of bits, a time-stamp designer can make the granularity coarser to extend the range, or she can limit the range to support finer granularities. These observations imply that a format based on a single 32 bit word is inadequate for our purposes; there are simply not enough bits. Since we wanted to keep the time-stamp formats on 32 bit word boundaries, we allocated the next word increment, 64 bits, to our basic format. Using 64 bits, it is possible to represent all of time (that is, a range of 34 billion years) to the granularity of a second, and a range of historical time to granularities much finer than a second.

There are three basic types of time-stamps: events, spans, and intervals [128]. We developed three new event time-stamp formats, with different *resolutions*, high, low, and extended. Resolution is a rough measure of a time-stamp precision. The low resolution format can represent times to the precision of a second. High resolution narrows the precision to a microsecond while extended resolution is even more precise; it can represent times to the precision of a nanosecond. High resolution has limited range but extended precision while low resolution has extended range but limited precision. Extended resolution handles those uncommon cases where the user wants both an extended range and an extended precision, at the cost of an extra word of storage.

Interval time-stamp formats are simply two event time-stamps, one for the starting event of the interval and one for the terminating event of the interval. We use this representation because all operations on intervals are actually operations on their delimiting events [129]. There are sixteen interval time-stamp formats in toto. The type fields in the delimiting event time-stamps distinguish each format.

Spans are relative times. There are two kinds of spans, fixed and variable [128]. A *fixed span* is a count of chronons. It represents a fixed duration (in terms of chronons) on the base-line clock between two time values. The fixed span formats use exactly the same layouts as the standard event formats, with a different interpretation. The chronon count in the span representation is independent of the origin, instead of being interpreted as a count from the origin. The sign bit indicates whether the span is positive or negative rather than indicating the direction from the origin.

A *variable span*'s duration is dependent on an associated event. A common variable span is a *month*. The duration represented by a month depends on whether that month is associated with an event in June (30 days) or in July (31 days), or even in February (28 or 29 days). Variable spans use a specialized format requiring 64 bits.

To represent indeterminate events, we added nine formats, three of each resolution. There are three analogous formats for low resolution, and three for extended resolution. The most common, for high resolution with a uniform distribution, requires only 64 bits.

As we have seen in other areas, the considerations for space are similar, yet considerably simpler. A spatial representation of 32 bits (per dimension) for a range required to map the Earth results in a granularity of one decimeter, and of one centimeter for the third dimension (the atmosphere, the oceans, and the Earth's interior) or for restricted areas such as the United States or Europe. Moving up to 64 bits makes spatial indeterminacy representations feasible, and reduces the granularity to a nanometer, which should be adequate for quite a while.

3 Associating Facts with Time

The previous section explored models and representations for the time domain. We now turn to associating time with facts.

3.1 Underlying Data Model

Time has been added to many data models: the entity-relationship model [31, 71], semantic data models [53, 144], knowledge-based data models [29], deductive databases [14, 15, 16, 66], and object-oriented models [30, 90, 99, 107, 116, 117, 150]. However, by far the majority of work in temporal databases is based on the relational model. For this reason, we will assume this data model in subsequent discussion.

3.2 Attribute Variability

There are several basic ways in which an attribute associated with an object can interact with time and space. A *time-invariant* attribute [101] does not change over time. Some temporal data models require that the key of a relation be time-invariant; some others identify the object(s) participating in the relation with a time-invariant surrogate, a system-generated, unique identifier of an item that can be referenced and compared for equality, but not displayed to the user [52]. Secondly, the *value* of an attribute may be drawn from a temporal domain. An example is *date stamping*, where cadastral parcel records in a land information system contain fields that note the dates of registration of deeds, transfers of titles, and other pertinent historical information [146]. Such temporal domains are termed *user-defined time* [123]; other than being able to be read in, displayed, and perhaps compared, no special semantics is associated with such domains. Interestingly, most such attributes are time-invariant. For example, the transfer date for a particular title transfer is valid over all time.

An analogous sitation exists for space. There are space-invariant attributes as well as attributes that are drawn from spatial domains, an example being an attribute recording the square feet of a residence, which is a relative spatial measure in two dimensions.

Time- and *space-varying* attributes are more interesting. There are five basic cases to consider.

- The value of an attribute associated with a *space-invariant* object may vary over time, termed *attribute temporality* [146]. An example is percentage of cloud cover over the Earth, which has a single value at each point in time, but varies over time. The value is uniquely specified by the temporal coordinate(s) (either valid time, or a combination of valid and transaction time).
- The value of an attribute associated with a region in space may be time invariant. An example is elevation: the value varies spatially but not temporally (assuming historical time; certainly the elevation varies over geologic time!). The value is unique given spatial coordinates.
- The value of an attribute associated with a region in space may vary over time. An example is the percentage of cloud cover over each 10-kilometer square grid element. Here, the object is identified spatially, and each object is associated with a time-varying sequence of values. Both the temporal and the spatial coordinates are required to uniquely identify a value.
- The boundary lines identifying a cadastral object, e.g., a particular land packet, may vary over time, termed *temporal topology* [146]. The orientation and interaction of spatial objects change over time; such objects could nevertheless have time-invariant attributes, such as initial purchase price. The temporal and spatial coordinates are required to uniquely identify a value, but this identification is indirect, via the topology.
- The final case is the most complex: the value of an attribute, which varies over time, is associated with a cartographic feature that also varies over time [76]. An example is the appraised value of a land packet. The appraised value may change yearly, and the boundary of the land packet changes as it is reapportioned and parts sold to others. As with the previous two cases, both temporal and spatial coordinates are required to identify a value, but the temporal coordinate(s) are utilized twice, first to identify a cartographic feature and then to select a particular attribute value associated with that feature.

A further categorization is possible concerning which temporal domains are involved (only valid time, only transaction time, or both) and which spatial domains are involved (two dimensions, $2\frac{1}{2}$ dimensions, or a full three dimensions).

The first case is the traditional domain of temporal DBMS's. The second case is the domain of conventional LIS's and GIS's. While there has been some conceptual work on merging temporal and spatial support, as discussed throughout this paper, current implemented systems are fairly weak in this regard.

3.3 Representational Alternatives

Over two dozen extensions to the relational model to incorporate time have been proposed over the last 15 years. These models may be compared by asking four basic questions: how is valid time represented, how is transaction time represented, how are attribute values represented, and is the model *homogeneous*, i.e., are all attributes restricted to be defined over the same valid time(s) [43].

Data Models. Table 2 lists most of the temporal data models that have been proposed to date. If the model is not given a name, we appropriate the name given the associated query language, where available. Many models are described in several papers; the one referenced is the initial journal paper in which the model was defined. Some models are defined only over valid time or transaction time; others are defined over both. Whether the model is homogeneous is indicated in the next column. Tuple-timestamped data models, to be identified in the next section, and data models that use single chronons as time-stamps are of necessity homogeneous. The issue of homogeneity is not relevant for those data models supporting only transaction time. The last column indicates a short identifier which denotes the model; the table is sorted on this column.

We omit a few intermediate data models, specifically Gadia's multihomogeneous model [41], which was a precursor to his heterogeneous model (Gadia-2), and Gadia's two-dimensional temporal relational database model [10], which is a precursor to Gadia-3. We also do not include the data model used as the basis for defining temporal relational completeness [142], because it is a generic data model that does not force decisions on most of the aspects to be discussed here.

More detail on these data models, including a comprehensive comparison, may be found elsewhere [96, 124].

Valid Time. Two fairly orthogonal aspects are involved in representing valid time. First, is valid time represented with single chronon identifiers (i.e., event time-stamps, Sec. 2.4), with intervals (i.e., as interval time-stamps, Sec. 2.4), or as historical elements (i.e., as a set of chronon identifiers, or equivalently as a finite set of intervals)? Second, is valid time associated with entire tuples or with individual attribute values? A third alternative, associating valid time with sets of tuples, i.e., relations, has not been incorporated into any of the proposed data models, primarily because it lends itself to high data redundancy. The data models are elevated on these two aspects in Table 3. Interestingly, only one quadrant, time-stamping tuples with an historical element, has not been considered (but see Sec. 3.3)

Data Model	*Citation*	*Temporal Dimension(s)*	*Homogeneous*	*Identifier*
—	[123]	both	yes	Ahn
Temporally Oriented Data Model	[7]	both	yes	Ariav
Time Relational Model	[8]	both	yes	Ben-Zvi
Historical Data Model	[17]	valid	yes	Clifford-1
Historical Relational Data Model	[20]	valid	no	Clifford-2
Homogeneous Relational Model	[43]	valid	yes	Gadia-1
Heterogeneous Relational Model	[42]	valid	no	Gadia-2
TempSQL	[45]	both	yes	Gadia-3
DM/T	[59]	transaction	N/A	Jensen
LEGOL 2.0	[65]	valid	yes	Jones
DATA	[70]	transaction	N/A	Kimball
—	[82]	transaction	N/A	Lomet
Temporal Relational Model	[87]	valid	no	Lorentzos
—	[89]	transaction	yes	Lum
—	[95]	both	no	McKenzie
Temporal Relational Model	[101]	valid	yes	Navathe
HQL	[110]	valid	yes	Sadeghi
HSQL	[113]	valid	yes	Sarda
Temporal Data Model	[118]	valid	yes	Shoshani
TQuel	[124]	both	yes	Snodgrass
Postgres	[134]	transaction	no	Stonebraker
HQuel	[137]	valid	no	Tansel
Accounting Data Model	[140]	both	yes	Thompson
Time Oriented Databank Model	[147]	valid	yes	Wiederhold

Table 2. Temporal Data Models

	Single chronon	Interval (pair of chronons)	Historical element (set of chronons)
Time-stamped attribute values	Lorentzos Thompson	Gadia-2 McKenzie Tansel	Clifford-2 Gadia-1 Gadia-3
Time-stamped tuples	Ariav Clifford-1 Lum Sadeghi Shoshani Wiederhold	Ahn Ben-Zvi Jones Navathe Sarda Snodgrass	

Table 3. Representation of Valid Time

Transaction Time. The same general issues are involved in transaction time, but there are about twice as many alternatives. Transaction time may be associated with

- a single chronon, which implies that tuples inserted on each transaction signify the termination (logical deletion) of previously current tuples with identical keys, with the time-stamps of these previously recorded tuples not requiring change.
- an interval. A newly inserted tuple would be associated with the interval starting at now and ending at the special value U.C., *until-changed.*
- three chronons. Ben-Zvi's model records (1) the transaction time when the valid start time was recorded, (2) the transaction time when the valid stop time was recorded, and (3) the transaction time when the tuple was logically deleted.
- a transaction-time element, which is a set of not-necessarily-contigous chronons.

Another issue concerns whether transaction time is associated with individual attribute values, with tuples, or with sets of tuples.

The choices made in the various data models are characterized in Table 4. Gadia-3 is the only data model to time-stamp attribute values; it is difficult to efficiently implement this alternative directly. Gadia-3 also is the only data model that uses transaction-time elements (but see Sec. 3.3). Ben-Zvi is the only one to use three transaction-time chronons. All of the rows and columns are represented by at least one data model.

	Single chronon	Interval (pair of chronons)	Three Chronons	Transaction-time element (set of chronons)
Time-stamped attribute values				Gadia-3
Time-stamped tuples	Ariav Jensen Kimball Lomet	Snodgrass Stonebraker	Ben-Zvi	
Time-stamped sets of tuples	Ahn Thompson	McKenzie		

Table 4. Representation of Transaction Time

Attribute Value Structure. The final major decision to be made in designing a temporal data model is how to represent attribute values. There are six basic alternatives. In some models, the time-stamp appears as an explicit attribute; we do not consider such attributes in this analysis.

- *Atomic valued*—values do not have any internal structure. Ariav, Ben-Zvi, Clifford-1, Jensen, Jones, Kimball, Lomet, Lorentzos, Lum, Navathe, Sadeghi, Sarda, Shoshani, Snodgrass, Stonebraker and Thompson all adopt this approach. Tansel allows atomic values, as well as others, listed below.
- *Set valued*—values are sets of atomic values. Tansel supports this representation.
- *Functional, atomic valued*—values are functions from the (generally valid) time domain to the attribute domain. Clifford-2, Gadia-1, Gadia-2, and Gadia-3 adopt this approach.
- *Ordered pairs*—values are an ordered pair of a value and a (historical element) time-stamp. McKenzie adopts this approach.
- *Triplet valued*—values are a triple of attribute value, valid from time, and value to time. This is similar to the ordered pairs representation, except that only one interval may be represented. Tansel supports this representation.
- *Set-triplet valued*—values are a set of triplets. This is more general than ordered pairs, in that more than one value can be represented, and more general than functional valued, since more than one attribute value can exist at a single valid time [137]. Tansel supports this representation.

In the conventional relational model, if attributes are atomic-valued, they are considered to be in *first normal form* [22]. Hence, only the data models placed in the first category may be considered to be strictly in first normal form. However, in several of the other models, the non-atomicity of attribute values comes about because time is added. It turns out that the property of "all snapshots are in first normal form" is closely associated with homogeneity (Sec. 3.3).

Separating Semantics from Representation. It is our contention that focusing on data *presentation* (how temporal data is displayed to the user), on data *storage*, with its requisite demands of regular structure, and on efficient *query evaluation* has complicated the central task of capturing the time-varying semantics of data. The result has been, as we have seen, a plethora of incompatible data models, with many query languages (Sec. 4.1), and a corresponding surfeit of database design and implementation strategies that may be employed across these models.

We advocate instead a very simple *conceptual temporal data model* that captures the essential semantics of time-varying relations, but has no illusions of being suitable for presentation, storage, or query evaluation. Existing data model(s) may be used for these latter tasks. This conceptual model time-stamps tuples with bitemporal elements, sets of *bitemporal chronons*, which are rectangles in the two-dimensional space spanned by valid time and transaction time (see Fig. 2). Because no two tuples with mutually identical explicit attribute values (termed *value-equivalent* tuples) are allowed in a bitemporal relation instance, the full time history of a fact is contained in a single tuple.

In Table 3, the conceptual temporal data model occupies the unfilled entry corresponding to time-stamping tuples with historical elements, and occupies the entry in Table 4 corresponding to time-stamping tuples with transaction-time elements. An important property of the conceptual model, shared with the conventional relational model but not held by the representational models, is that relation instances are semantically unique; distinct instances model different realities and thus have distinct semantics.

It is possible to demonstrate equivalence mappings between the conceptual model and several *representational* models [62]. Mappings have already been demonstrated for three data models: Gadia-3 (attribute time-stamping), Jensen (tuple time-stamping with a single transaction chronon), and Snodgrass (tuple time-stamping, with interval valid and transaction times). This equivalence is based on *snapshot equivalence*, which says that two relation instances are equivalent if all their snapshots, taken at all times (valid and transaction), are identical. Snapshot equivalence provides a natural means of comparing rather disparate representations. An extension to the conventional relational algebraic operators may be defined in the conceptual data model, and can be mapped to analogous operators in the representational models. Finally, we feel that the conceptual data model is the appropriate location for database design and query optimization.

In essence, we advocate moving the distinction between the various existing temporal data models from a semantic basis to a physical, performance-relevant basis, utilizing the proposed conceptual data model to capture the time-varying semantics. Data presentation, storage representation, and time-varying semantics should be considered in isolation, utilizing different data models. Semantics, specifically as determined by logical database design, should be expressed in the conceptual model. Multiple presentation formats should be available, as different applications require different ways of viewing the data. The storage and processing of bitemporal relations should be done in a data model that emphasizes efficiency.

4 Querying

A data model consists of a set of objects with some structure, a set of constraints on those objects, and a set of operations on those objects [141]. In the two previous sectins we have investigated in detail the structure of and constraints on the objects of temporal relational databases, the temporal relation. In this section, we complete the picture by discussing the operations, specifically temporal query languages.

Many temporal query languages have been proposed. In fact, it seems obligatory for each researcher to define their own data model and query language (we return to this issue at the end of this section). We first summarize the twenty-odd query languages that have been proposed thus far. We then briefly discuss the various activities that should be supported by a temporal query language, using a specific language in the examples. Finally, we touch on work being done in the standards arena that is attempting to bring highly needed order to this confusing collection of languages.

We do not consider the related topic of *temporal reasoning* (also termed *inferencing* or *rule-based search*) [16, 67, 68, 77, 120, 131] that uses artificial intelligence techniques to perform more sophisticated analyses of temporal relationships, generally with much lower query processing efficiency.

4.1 Language Proposals

Table 5 lists the major temporal query language proposals to date. While many of these languages each have several associated papers, we have indicated the most comprehensive or most readily available reference. The underlying data model is a reference to Table 2. The next column lists the conventional query language the temporal proposal is based on, from the following.

SQL Structured Query Language [26], a tuple calculus-based language; the lingua franca of conventional relational databases.

Quel The tuple calculus based query language [55] originally defined for the Ingres relational DBMS [133].

QBE Query-by-Example [151], a domain calculus based query language.

IL_s An intensional logic formulated in the context of computational linguistics [98].

relational algebra A procedural language with relations as objects [21].

DEAL An extension of the relational algebra incorporating functions, recursion, and deduction [32].

Most of the query languages have a formal definition. Some of the calculus-based query languages have an associated algebra that provides a means of evaluating queries.

More comprehensive comparisons may be found elsewhere [96, 124].

4.2 Types of Temporal Queries

We now examine the types of temporal queries that each of the above-listed query languages support to varying degrees. We'll use TQuel [126] in the examples, as it is the most completely defined temporal language [124].

Schema Definition. We will use one relation in these examples.

Example. *Define the* `Cities` *relation.*

```
create persistent interval Cities(Name is char, State is char,
        Population is I4, IncorporationDate is event,
        Size is area)
```

`Cities` has five explicit attributes: two strings (denoted by `char`), a 4-byte integer (denoted by `I4`), a user-defined event, and a user-defined area. The ***persistent*** and ***interval*** keywords specify a bitemporal relation, with four implicit time-stamp attributes: a valid start time, a valid end time, a transaction start time, and a transaction end time. The valid time-stamps define the interval when the attribute values were true in reality, and the transaction time-stamps specify the interval when the information was current in the database. □

Name	*Citation*	*Underlying Data Model*	*Based On*	*Formal Semantics*	*Equivalent Algebra*
HQL	[111]	Sadeghi	DEAL	partial	[110]
HQuel	[137]	Tansel	Quel	yes	[137]
HSQL	[113]	Sarda	SQL	no	[112]
HTQuel	[43]	Gadia-1	Quel	yes	[43]
Legol 2.0	[65]	Jones	relational algebra	no	N/A
Postquel	[135]	Stonebraker	Quel	no	none
TDM	[118]	Shoshani	SQL	no	none
Temporal Relational Algebra	[87]	Lorentzos	relational algebra	yes	N/A
TempSQL	[45]	Gadia-3	SQL	partial	none
Time-By-Example	[139]	Tansel	QBE	yes	[137]
TOSQL	[7]	Ariav	SQL	no	none
TQuel	[124]	Snodgrass	Quel	yes	[95]
TSQL	[101]	Navathe	SQL	no	none
—	[8]	Ben-Zvi	SQL	yes	[8]
—	[17]	Clifford-1	IL_s	yes	N/A
—	[20]	Clifford-2	relational algebra	yes	N/A
—	[41]	Gadia-2	Quel	no	none
—	[60]	Jensen	relational algebra	yes	N/A
—	[95]	McKenzie	relational algebra	yes	N/A
—	[140]	Thompson	relational algebra	yes	N/A
—	[142]	*several*	relational algebra	yes	N/A

Table 5. Temporal query languages

Quel Retrieval Statements. Since TQuel is a strict superset of Quel, all Quel queries are also TQuel queries [124]. Here we give one such query, as a review of Quel.

The query uses a **range** statement to specify the *tuple variable* `C`, which will remain active for use in subsequent queries.

Example. *What is the current population of the cities in Arizona?*

```
range of C is Cities

retrieve (C.Name, C.Population)
where C.State = "Arizona"
```

The *target list* specifies which attributes of the qualifying tuples are to be retained in the result, and the where clause specifies which underlying tuples from the underlying relation(s) qualify to participate in the query. Because the defaults have been defined appropriately, each TQuel query yields the same result as its Quel counterpart. □

Rollback (Transaction-time Slice). The ***as of*** clause rolls back a transaction-time relation (consisting of a sequence of snapshot relation states) or a bitemporal relation (consisting of a sequence of valid-time relation states) to the state that was current at the specified transaction time. It can be considered to be a transaction time analogue of the where clause, restricting the underlying tuples that participate in the query.

Example. *What was the population of Arizona's cities as best known in 1980?*

```
retrieve (C.Name, C.Population)
where C.State = "Arizona"
as of begin of |January 1, 1980|
```

This query uses an event temporal constant, delimited with vertical bars, "|···|". TQuel supports multiple calendars and calendric systems [127, 128, 129]. In this case, the default is the Gregorian calendar with English month names. □

Valid-time Selection. The ***when*** clause is the valid-time analogue of the where clause: it specifies a predicate on the event or interval time-stamps of the underlying tuples that must be satisfied for those tuples to participate in the remainder of the processing of the query.

Example. *What was the population of the cities in Arizona in 1980 (as best known right now)?*

```
retrieve (C.Name, C.Population)
where C.State = "Arizona"
when C overlap |January 1, 1980|
as of present
```

A careful examination of the prose statement of this and the previous query illustrates the fundamental difference between valid time and transaction time. The ***as of*** clause selects a particular transaction time, and thus *rolls back* the relation to its state stored at the specified time. Corrections stored after that time will not be incorporated into the retrieved result. The particular ***when*** statement given here selects the facts *valid in reality* at the specified time. All corrections stored up to the time the query was issued are incorporated into the result. In this case, all corrections made after 1980 to the census of 1980 will be included in the resulting relation. □

Example. *What was the population of the cities in Arizona in 1980, as best known at that time?*

```
retrieve (C.Name, C.Population)
```

```
where C.State = "Arizona"
when C overlap |January 1, 1980|
as of |January 1, 1980|
```

The result of this query, executed any time after January 1, 1980, will be identical to the result of the first query specified, "*What is the current population of the cities in Arizona?*", executed exactly on midnight of that date. □

Valid Time Projection. The ***valid*** clause serves the same purpose as the target list; it specifies some aspect of the derived tuples, in this case, the valid time of the derived tuple.

Example. *For what date is the most recent information on Arizona's cities valid?*

```
retrieve (C.All)
valid at begin of C
where C.State = "Arizona"
```

This query extracts relevant events from an interval relation. □

Aggregates. As TQuel is a superset of Quel, all Quel aggregates are still available [125].

Example. *What is the current population of Arizona?*

```
retrieve (sum(C.Population where C.State = "Arizona"))
```

Note that this query only counts city residents. □

This query applied to a bitemporal relation yields the same result as its conventional analogues, that is, a single value. With just a little more work, we can extract its time-varying behavior.

Example. *How has the population of Arizona flucuated over time?*

```
retrieve (sum(C.Population where C.State = "Arizona"))
when true
```

□

New, temporally-oriented aggregates are also available in TQuel. One of the most useful computes the interval when the argument was rising in value. This aggregate may be used wherever an interval expression is expected.

Example. *For each growing city, when did it start growing?*

```
retrieve (C.Name)
valid at begin of rising(C.Population by C.Name
                         where C.State = "Arizona")
```

□

Historical Indeterminacy. Indeterminacy aspects can hold for individual tuples, or for all the tuples in a relation.

Example. *The information in the* `Cities` *relation is known only to within thirty days.*

```
modify cities to indeterminate span = %30 days%
```

`%30 days%` is a *span*, an unanchored length of time [127]. Spans can be created by taking the difference of two events; spans can also be added to an event to obtain a new event. □

Example. *What cities in Arizona definitely had a population over 500,000 at the beginning of 1980?*

```
retrieve (C.Name)
where C.State = "Arizona" and C.Population > 500000
when C overlap |January 1, 1980|
```

The default is to only retrieve tuples that fully satisfy the predicate. This is consistent with the Quel semantics. □

Historical indeterminacy enters queries at two places, specifying the *credibility* of the underlying information to be utilized in the query, and specifying the *plausibility* of temporal relationships expressed in the when and valid clauses. We'll only illustrate plausibility here.

Example. *What cities in Arizona had a population over 500,000 probably at the beginning of 1980?*

```
retrieve (C.Name)
where C.State = "Arizona" and C.Population > 500000
when C overlap |January 1, 1980| probably
```

Here, "probably" is syntactic sugar for "`with plausibility 70`". □

Schema Evolution. Often the database schema needs to be modified to accommodate a changing set of applications. The `modify` statement has several variants, allowing any previous decision to be later changed or undone. Schema evolution involves transaction time, as it concerns how the data is stored in the database [94]. As an example, changing the type of a relation from a bitemporal relation to an historical relation will cause future intermediate states to not be recorded; states stored when the relation was a temporal relation will still be available.

Example. *The* `Cities` *relation should no longer record all errors.*

```
modify Stocks to not persistent
```

□

4.3 Standards

Support for time in conventional data base systems (e.g., [103, 136]) is entirely at the level of user-defined time (i.e., attribute values drawn from a temporal domain). These implementations are limited in scope and are, in general, unsystematic in their design [27, 28]. The standards bodies (e.g., ANSI) are somewhat behind the curve, in that SQL includes no time support. Date and time support very similar to that in DB2 is currently being proposed for SQL2 [97]. SQL2 corrects some of the inconsistencies in the time support provided by DB2 but inherits its basic design limitations [127].

An effort is currently underway within the research community to consolidate approaches to temporal data models and calculus-based query languages, to achieve a consensus extension to SQL and an associated data model upon which future research can be based. This extension is termed the *Temporal Structured Query Language*, or TSQL (not to be confused with an existing language proposal of the same name).

5 System Architecture

The three previous sections in concert sketched the boundaries of a temporal data model, by examining the temporal domain, how facts may be associated with time, and how temporal information may be queried. We now turn to the implementation of the temporal data model, as encapsulated in a temporal DBMS.

Adding temporal support to a DBMS impacts virtually all of its components. Figure 4 provides a simplified architecture for a conventional DBMS. The *database administrator (DBA)* and her staff design the database, producing a physical schema specified in a *data definition language (DDL)*, which is processed by the *DDL Compiler* and stored, generally as system relations, in the *System Catalog*. Users prepare queries, either ad hoc or embedded in procedural code, which is submitted to the *Query Processor*. The query is first lexically and syntactically analyzed, using information from the system catalog, then optimized for efficient execution. A query evaluation plan is sent to the *Query Evaluator*. For ad hoc queries, this occurs immediately after processing; for embedded queries, this occurs when the cursor associated with a particular query is opened. The query evaluator is usually an interpreter for a form of the relational algebra annotated with access methods and operator strategies. While evaluating the query, this component accesses the database via a *Stored Data Manager*, which implements concurrency control, transaction management, recovery, buffering, and the available data access methods.

In the following, we visit each of these components in turn, reviewing what changes need to be made to add temporal support.

5.1 DDL Statements

Relational query languages such as Quel and SQL actually do much more than simply specify queries; they also serve as data definition languages (e.g., through

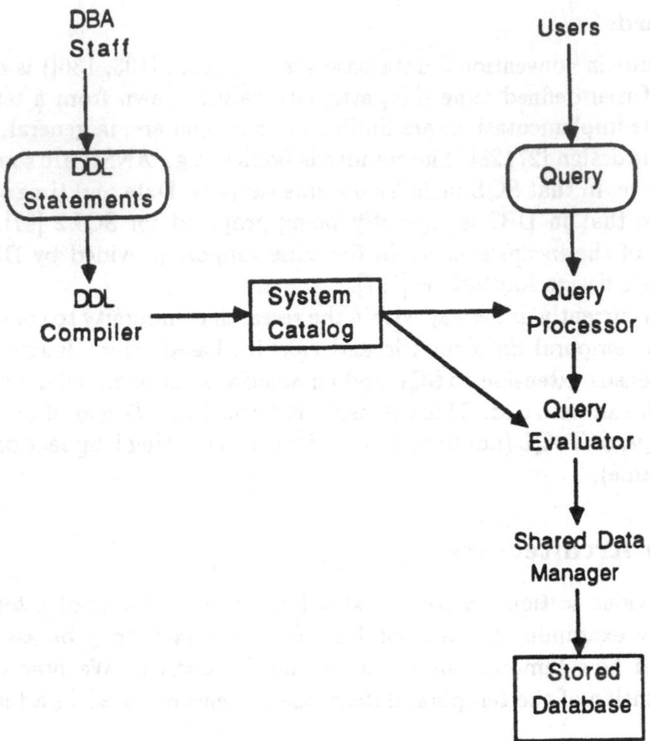

Fig. 4. Components of a data base management system

Quel's ***create*** statement, c.f., Sec. 4.2) and as data manipulation languages (e.g., through SQL's `INSERT`, `DELETE` and `UPDATE` statements). The changes to support time involve adding temporal domains, such as event, interval, and span [127] and adding constructs to specify support for transaction and valid time, such as the TQuel keywords ***persistent*** and ***interval***.

5.2 System Catalog

The big change here is that the system catalog must consist of transaction-time relations. Schema evolution concerns only the recording of the data, and hence does not involve valid time. The attributes and their domains, the indexes, even the names of the relations all vary over transaction time.

5.3 Query Processing

There are two aspects here, one easily extended (language analysis) and one for which adding temporal support is much more complex (query optimization).

Language analysis needs to consider multiple calendars, which extend the language with calendar-specific functions. An example is `monthof`, which only makes sense in calendars for which there are months. The changes to language processing, primarily involving modifications to semantic analysis (name resolution and type checking), have been worked out in some detail [129].

Optimization of temporal queries is substantially more involved than that for conventional queries, for several reasons. First, optimization of temporal queries is more critical, and thus easier to justify expending effort on, than conventional optimization. The relations that temporal queries are defined over are larger, and are growing monotonically, with the result that unoptimized queries take longer and longer to execute. This justifies trying harder to optimize the queries, and spending more execution time to perform the optimization.

Second, the predicates used in temporal queries are harder to optimize [78, 79]. In traditional database applications, predicates are usually equality predicates (hence the prevalence of equi-joins and natural joins); if a less-than join is involved, it is rarely in combination with other less-than predicates. On the other hand, in temporal queries, less-than joins appear more frequently, as a conjunction of several inequality predicates. As an example, the TQuel **overlap** operator is translated into two less-than predicates on the underlying time-stamps. Optimization techniques in conventional databases focus on equality predicates, and often implement inequality joins as cartesian products, with their associated inefficiency.

And third, there is greater opportunity for query optimization when time is present [79]. Time advances in one direction: the time domain is continuous expanding, and the most recent time point is the largest value in the domain. This implies that a natural clustering or sort order will manifest itself, which can be exploited during query optimization and evaluation. The integrity constraint $beginof(t) < endof(t)$ holds for every time-interval tuple t. Also, for many relations it is the case that the intervals associated with a key are contiguous in time, with one interval starting exactly when the previous interval ended. An example is salary data, where the intervals associated with the salaries for each employee are contiguous. *Semantic query optimization* can exploit these integrity constraints, as well as additional ones that can be inferred [121].

In this section, we first examine local query optimization, of a single query, then consider global query optimization, of several queries simultaneously. Both involve the generation of a *query evaluation plan*, which consists of an algebraic expression annotated with access methods.

Local Query Optimization. A single query can be optimizing by replacing the algebraic expression with an equivalent one that is more efficient, by changing an access method associated with a particular operator, or by adopting a particular implementation of an operator. The first alternative requires a definition of equivalence, in the form of a set of tautologies. Tautologies have been identified for the conventional relational algebra [40, 122, 143], as well as for many of the algebras listed in Table 5. Some of these temporal algebras support the standard tautologies, enabling existing query optimizers to be used.

To determine which access method is best for each algebraic operator, *meta-*

data, that is, statistics on the stored temporal data, and *cost models*, that is, predictors of the execution cost for each operator implementation/access method combination, are needed. Temporal data requires additional meta-data, such as *lifespan* of a relation (the time interval over which the relation is defined), the lifespans of the tuples, the surrogate and tuple arrival distributions, the distributions of the time-varying attributes, regularity and granularity of temporal data, and the frequency of null values, which are sometimes introduced when attributes within a tuple aren't synchronized [47]. Such statistical data may be updated by random sampling or by a scan through the entire relation.

There has been some work in developing cost models for temporal operators. An extensive analytical model has been developed and validated for TQuel queries [3, 4], and *selectivity estimates* on the size of the results of various temporal joins have been derived [47, 48].

Global Query Optimization. In global query optimization, a collection of queries is simultaneously optimized, the goal being to produce a single query evaluation plan that is more efficient than the collection of individual plans [114, 119]. A state transition network appears to be the best way to organize this complex task [63]. *Materialized views* [11, 12, 108, 109] are expected to play an important role in achieving high performance in the face of temporal databases of monotonically increasing size. For an algebra to utilize this approach, incremental forms of the operators are required (c.f., [59, 93]).

5.4 Query Evaluation

Achieving adequate efficiency in query evaluation is very important. We first examine operations on time-stamps, some of which are critical to high performance. We then review a study that showed that a straightforward implementation would not result in reasonable performance. Since joins are the most expensive, yet very common, operations, they have been the focus of a significant amount of research. Finally, we will examine the many temporal indexes that have been proposed.

Domain Operations. In Sec. 2 we outlined the domain of time-stamps. Query evaluation performs input, comparison, arithmetic, and output operations on values of this domain. Ordered by contribution to execution efficiency, they are comparison (which is often in the "inner loop" of join processing), arithmetic (which is most often performed during creation of the resulting tuple), output (which is only done when transferring results to the screen or to paper, a much slower process than execution or even disk I/O), and finally input (which is done exactly once per value). However, the SQL2 format, with its five components (see Table 1) is optimized for the relatively infrequent operations of (Gregorian) input and output, and is rather slow at comparison and addition. The proposed formats instead optimize comparison at the expense of input and output. For a sequence of operations that inputs two relations and computes and outputs the overlap (favoring input and output more than expected), the high resolution format is more efficient, with only 50 tuples, than the SQL2 format, even though the high resolution format has much greater range and smaller granularity [35].

Performing these operations efficiently in the presence of historical indeterminacy is more challenging. For the default range credibility and ordering plausibility, and for comparing events whose sets of possible chronons do not overlap, there is little overhead even when historical indeterminacy is supported [34]. The average *worse case* for comparison, over all plausibilities, when the sets of possible chronons overlap signficantly, is less than 100 microseconds on a Sun-4, or about the time to transfer a 100-byte tuple from disk.

A Straightforward Implementation. The importance of efficient query optimization and evaluation for temporal databases was underscored by an initial study that analyzed the performance of a brute-force approach to adding time support to a conventional DBMS. In this study, the university Ingres DBMS was extended in a minimal fashion to support TQuel querying [1]. The results were very discouraging for those who might have been considering such an approach. Sequential scans, as well as access methods such as hashing and ISAM, suffered from rapid performance degradation due to ever-growing overflow chains. Because adding time creates multiple tuple versions with the same key, reorganization does not help to shorten overflow chains. The objective of work in temporal query evaluation then is to avoid looking at all of the data, because the alternative implies that queries will continue to slow down as the database accumulates facts.

There were four basic responses to this challenge. The first was a proposal to separate the *historical* data, which grew monotonically, from the *current* data, whose size was fairly stable and whose accesses were more frequent [89]. This separation, termed *temporal partitioning*, was shown to significantly improve performance of some queries [3], and was later generalized to allow multiple cached states, which further improves performance [63]. Second, new query optimization strategies were proposed (Sec. 5.3). Third, new join algorithms, to be discussed next, were proposed. And finally, new temporal indexes, also to be discussed, were proposed.

Joins. Three kinds of temporal joins have been studied: binary joins, multiway joins, and joins executed on multiprocessors.

A wide variety of binary joins have been considered, including *time-join*, *time-equijoin* (TE-join) [20], *event-join*, *TE-outerjoin* [49], *contain-join*, *contain-semijoin*, *intersect-join* [79], and *contain-semijoin* [81]. The various algorithms proposed for these joins have generally been extensions to nested loop or merge joins that exploit sort orders or local workspace.

Leung argues that a checkpoint index (Sec. 5.4) is useful when stream processing is employed to evaluate both two-way and multi-way joins [81].

Finally, Leung has explored in depth partitioning strategies and temporal query processing on multiprocessors [80].

Temporal Indexes. Conventional indexes have long been proposed to reduce the need to scan an entire relation to access a subset of its tuples. Indices are even more important in temporal relations that grow monotonically in size. In table 6 we summarize the temporal index structures that have been proposed to date. Most of the indexes are based on B$^+$-Trees [23], which index on values of a single key; the remainder are based on R-Trees [51], which index on ranges (intervals) of multiple keys. There has been considerable discussion concerning the applicability of point-based schemes for indexing interval data. Some argue that structures that explicitly accommodate intervals, such as R-Trees and their variants, are preferable; others argue that mapping intervals to their endpoints is efficient for spatial search [86].

If the structure requires that exactly one record with each key value exist at any time, or if the data records themselves are stored in the index, then it is designated a *primary* storage structure; otherwise, it can be used either as a primary storage structure or as a secondary index. The checkpoint index is associated with a particular indexing condition, making it suitable for use during the processing of queries consistent with that condition.

A majority of the indexes are tailored to transaction time, exploiting the append-only nature of such information. Most utilize as a key the valid-time or transaction-time interval (or possibly both, in the case of the Mixed Media R-Tree). Lum's index doesn't include time at all; rather it is a means of accessing the history, represented as a linked list of tuples, of a key value. The Append-only Tree indexes the transaction-start time of the data, and the Lop-Sized B$^+$-Tree is most suited for indexing events such as bank transactions. About half the indexes utilize only the time-stamp as a key; some include a single non-temporal attribute; and the two based on R-Trees can exploit its multi-dimensionality to support an arbitrary number of non-temporal attributes. Of the indexes supporting non-temporal keys, most treat such keys as a true separate dimension, the exceptions being the indexes discussed by Ahn, which support a single composite key with the interval as a component.

While preliminary performance studies have been carried out for each of these indexes in isolation, there has been little effort to compare them concerning their space and time efficiency. Such a comparison would have to consider the differing abilities of each (those supporting no non-temporal keys would be useful for doing temporal cartesian products, but perhaps less useful for doing temporal joins that involved equality predicates on non-temporal attributes) as well as various underlying distributions of time and non-temporal keys (the indexes presume various non-uniform distributions to achieve their performance gains over conventional indexes, which generally assume a uniform key distribution).

5.5 Stored Data Manager

We examine three topics, storage structures (including page layout), concurrency control, and recovery. Page layout for temporal relations is more complicated than conventional relations if non-first normal form (i.e., non-atomic attribute values) are adopted, as is proposed in many of the temporal data models listed in

Name	Citation	Based On	Primary/ Secondary	Temporal Dimension(s)	Temporal Key(s)	Non-Temporal Key(s)
Append-only Tree	[50]	B^+-Tree	primary	transaction	event	0
Checkpoint Index	[81]	B^+-Tree	secondary	transaction	event	0
Lop-Sided B^+-Tree	[74]	B^+-Tree	both	transaction	event	0
Monotonic B^+-Tree	[39]	Time Index	both	transaction	interval	0
—	[89]	B^+-Tree or Hashing	primary	transaction	none	1
Time-Split B-Tree	[83]	B^+-Tree	primary	transaction	interval	1
Mixed Media R-Tree	[72]	R-Tree	both	transaction, trans+valid	interval, pairs of intervals	k ranges, $k \geq 1$
Time Index	[37]	B^+-Tree	both	both	interval	0
Two-level Combined Attribute/Time Index	[38]	B^+-Tree +Time Index	both	both	interval	1
—	[3]	B^+-Tree, Hashing	*various*	*various*	interval	1
SR-Tree	[73]	Segment Index + R-Tree	both	both	interval, pairs of intervals	k ranges, $k \geq 1$

Table 6. Temporal Indexes

Sec. 3.3. Often such attributes are stored as linked lists, for example representing a valid-time element (set of valid-time chronons) as a linked list of intervals. Hsu has developed an analytical model to determine the optimal block size for such linked lists [57].

Many structures have been proposed, including *reverse chaining* (all history versions for a key are linked in reverse order) [8, 24, 89], *accession lists* (a block of time values and associated tuple id's between the current store and the history store), *clustering* (storing history versions together on a set of blocks), *stacking* (storing a fixed number of history versions), and *cellular chaining* (linking blocks of clustered history versions), with analytical performance modeling [2] being used to compare their space and time efficiency [3].

Several researchers have investigated adapting existing concurrency control and transaction management techniques to support transaction time. The subtle issues involved in choosing whether to time-stamp at the beginning of a transaction (which restricts the concurrency control method that can be used) or at the end of the transaction (which may require data earlier written by the transaction to be read again to record the transaction) have been resolved in favor of the latter through some implementation tricks [24, 84, 134]. The Postgres system is an impressive prototype DBMS that supports transaction time [135]. Time-stamping in a distributed setting has also been considered [84]. Integrating temporal indexes with concurrency control to increase the available concurrency has been studied [85].

Finally, since a transaction-time database contains all past versions of the database, it can be used to recover from media failures that cause a portion or all of the current version to be lost [86].

6 Conclusion

We conclude with a list of accomplishments, a list of disappointments, and a pointer to future work.

There have been many significant accomplishments over the past fifteen years of temporal database research.

- The semantics of the time domain, including its structure, dimensionality, and indeterminacy, is well-understood.
- Representational issues of time-stamps have recently been resolved.
- Operations on time-stamps are now well-understood, and efficient implementations exist.
- A great amount of research has been expended on temporal data models, addressing this extraordinarily complex and subtle design problem.
- Many temporal query languages have been proposed. The numerous types of temporal queries are fairly well-understood. Half of the proposed temporal query languages have a strong formal basis.
- Temporal joins are well-understood, and a multitude of implementations exist.
- Approximately a dozen temporal index structures have been proposed.
- The interaction between transaction time support and concurrency control and transaction management has been studied to some depth.
- Several prototype temporal DBMS implementations have been developed.

There have also been some disappointments.

- The user-defined time support in the SQL2 standard is poorly designed. The representation specified in that standard suffers from inadequate range, excessive space requirements, and inefficient operations.
- There has been almost no work done in comparing the two dozen temporal data models, to identify common features and define a consensus data model upon which future research and commercialization may be based. It is our feeling that expecting a data model to simultaneously express time-varying semantics while optimizing data presentation, data storage, and query evaluation is unrealistic. We advocate a two-tiered data model, with a conceptual data model expressing the semantics, and with several representational data models serving these other objectives.

- There is also a need to consolidate approaches to temporal query languages, identify the best features of each of the proposed languages, and incorporate these features into a consensus query language that could serve as the basis for future research into query optimization and evaluation. Also, more work is needed on adding time to so-called fourth generation languages that are revolutionizing user interfaces for commercially available DBMS's.
- It has been demonstrated that a straightforward implementation of a temporal DBMS will exhibit poor performance.
- More empirical studies are needed to compare join algorithms, and to possibly suggest even more efficient variants.
- While there are a host of individual approaches to isolated portions of a DBMS, no coherent architecture has arisen. While the analysis given in Sec. 5 may be viewed as a starting point, much more work is needed to integrate these approaches into a cohesive structure.
- There has been little effort to compare the relative performance of temporal indexes, making selection in specific situations difficult or impossible.
- Temporal database design is still in its infancy, hindered by the plethora of temporal data models.
- There are as yet no prominent commercial temporal DBMS's, despite the obvious need in the marketplace.

Obviously these disappointments should be addressed. In addition, future work is also needed on adding time to the newer data models that are gaining recognition, including object-oriented data models and deductive data models. Finally, there is a great need for integration of spatial and temporal data models, query languages, and implementation techniques.

7 Acknowledgements

This work was supported in part by NSF grant ISI-8902707. James Clifford was helpful in understanding structural aspects of models of time. Curtis Dyreson, Christian S. Jensen, Nick Kline and Michael Soo provided useful comments on a previous draft.

8 Bibliography

1. Ahn, I., Snodgrass, R. Performance Evaluation of a Temporal Database Management System, in **Proceedings of ACM SIGMOD International Conference on Management of Data**. Zaniolo, C. (Ed.), Association for Computing Machinery, Washington, DC, (May 1986), 96–107.

2. Ahn, I. **Performance Modeling and Access Methods for Temporal Database Management Systems**. Ph.D. Dissertation, Computer Science Department, University of North Carolina at Chapel Hill, (July 1986).

3. Ahn, I., Snodgrass, R. Partitioned Storage for Temporal Databases. *Information Systems* 13, 4 (1988), 369–391.

4. Ahn, I., Snodgrass, R. Performance Analysis of Temporal Queries. *Information Sciences* 49 (1989), 103–146.

5. Allen, J.F., Hayes, P.J. A Common-Sense Theory of Time, in **Proceedings of the International Joint Conference on Artificial Intelligence**. Los Angeles, CA, (August 1985), 528–531.

6. Anderson, T.L. Modeling Time at the Conceptual Level, in **Proceedings of the International Conference on Databases: Improving Usability and Responsiveness**. Scheuermann, P. (Ed.), Academic Press, Jerusalem, Israel, (June 1982), 273–297.

7. Ariav, G. A Temporally Oriented Data Model. *ACM Transactions on Database Systems* 11, 4 (December 1986), 499–527.

8. Ben-Zvi, J. **The Time Relational Model**. Ph.D. Dissertation, Computer Science Department, UCLA, (1982).

9. Bernstein, P. A. Database System Support for Software Engineering- An Extended Abstract, in **Ninth International Conference on Software Engineering**. IEEE, ACM, Computer Society Press, Monterey, CA, (March 1987), 166–178.

10. Bhargava, G., Gadia, S.K. **A 2-dimensional temporal relational database model for querying errors and updates, and for achieving zero information-loss**. Technical Report TR#89-24, Department of Computer Science, Iowa State University, (December 1989).

11. Blakeley, J.A., Larson, P.-A., Tompa, F.W. Efficiently Updating Materialized Views, in **Proceedings of ACM SIGMOD International Conference on Management of Data**. Zaniolo, C. (Ed.), Association for Computing Machinery, Washington, DC, (May 1986), 61–71.

12. Blakeley, Jose A., Martin, Nancy L. Join Index, Materialized View, and Hybrid-Hash Join: A Performance Analysis, in **Proceedings of the Sixth International Conference on Data Engineering**. (February 1990), 256–263.

13. Bolour, A., Anderson, T.L., Dekeyser, L.J., Wong, H.K.T. The Role of Time in Information Processing: A Survey. *SigArt Newsletter* 80 (April 1982), 28–48.

14. Chomicki, J., Imelinski, T. Temporal Deductive Databases and Infinite Objects, in **Proceedings of the Seventh ACM SIGAct-SIGMod-SIGArt Symposium on Principles of Database Systems**. Association for Computing Machinery, Austin, Texas, (March 1988), 61–73.

15. Chomicki, J., Imelinski, T. Relational Specifications of Infinite Query Answers, in **Proceedings of ACM SIGMOD International Conference on Management of Data**. (May 1989), 174–183.

16. Chomicki, J. Polynomial Time Query Processing in Temporal Deductive Databases, in **9th Annual ACM SIGACT-SIGMOD-SIGART Symposium on Principles of Database Systems**. Nashville, TN, (April 1990).

17. Clifford, J., Warren, D.S. Formal Semantics for Time in Databases. *ACM Transactions on Database Systems* 8, 2 (June 1983), 214–254.

18. Clifford, J., Tansel, A.U. On an Algebra for Historical Relational Databases: Two Views, in **Proceedings of ACM SIGMOD International Conference on Management of Data**. Navathe, S. (Ed.), Association for Computing Machinery, Austin, TX, (May 1985), 247–265.

19. Clifford, J., Rao, A. A Simple, General Structure for Temporal Domains, in **Proceedings of the Conference on Temporal Aspects in Information Systems**. AFCET, France, (May 1987), 23–30.

20. Clifford, J., Croker, A. The Historical Relational Data Model (HRDM) and Algebra Based on Lifespans, in **Proceedings of the International Conference on Data Engineering**. IEEE Computer Society, IEEE Computer Society Press, Los Angeles, CA, (February 1987), 528–537.

21. Codd, E.F. *Relational Completeness of Data Base Sublanguages*, Data Base Systems, vol. 6. Prentice Hall, Englewood Cliffs, N.J., (1972), 65–98.

22. Codd, E.F. *Further Normalization of the Data Base Relational Model*, Data Base Systems, vol. 6. Prentice hall, Englewood Cliffs, N.J., (1972).

23. Comer, D. The Ubiquitous B-tree. *Computing Surveys* 11, 2 (1979), 121–138.

24. Dadam, P., Lum, V., Werner, H.-D. Integration of Time Versions into a Relational Database System, in **Proceedings of the Conference on Very Large Databases**. Dayal, U., Schlageter, G., Seng, L.H. (Ed.), Singapore, (August 1984), 509–522.

25. Date, C. J. An Overview of SQL2. *Info. Database* 4, 1 (Spring 1989), 8–12.

26. Date, C. J. *A Guide to the SQL Standard (Second Edition)*. Addison-Wesley, (August 1989).

27. Date, C. J., White, C. J. *A Guide to DB2*, vol. 1, 3rd edition. Addison-Wesley, Reading, MA, (September 1990).

28. Date, C.J. A Proposal for Adding Date and Time Support to SQL. *SIGMOD Record* 17, 2 (June 1988), 53–76.

29. Dayal, U., Smith, J.M. *PROBE: A Knowledge-Oriented Database Management System*, On Knowledge Base Management Systems: Integrating Artificial Intelligence and Database Technologies. Springer-Verlag, (1986).

30. Dayal, U., Wuu, G. **A Uniform Approach to Processing Temporal Queries**. Technical Report, Bellcore, (1992).

31. DeAntonellis, V., Degli, A., Mauri, G., Zonta, B. Extending the Entity-Relationship Approach to Take Into Account Historical Aspects of Systems, in **Proceedings of the International Conference on the E-R Approach to Systems Analysis and Design**. Chen, P. (Ed.), North Holland, (1979).

32. Deen, S.M. DEAL: A Relational Language with Deductions, Functions and Recursions. *Data and Knowledge Engineering* 1 (1985).

33. Dittrich, Klaus R., Lorie, Raymond A. Version Support for Engineering Database Systems. *IEEE Transactions on Software Engineering* 14, 4 (April 1988), 429–437.

34. Dyreson, C. E., Snodgrass, R. T. **Historical Indeterminacy**. Technical Report TR 92-16a, Computer Science Department, University of Arizona, (July 1992).

35. Dyreson, C. E., Snodgrass, R. T. **Time-stamp Semantics and Representation**. TempIS Technical Report 33, Computer Science Department, University of Arizona, (Revised May 1992).

36. Ecklund, D. J., Ecklund, E. F., Eifrig, R. O., Tonge, F. M. DVSS: A Distributed Version Storage Server for CAD Applications, in **Proceedings of the Conference on Very Large Databases**. Brighton, England, (1987), 443–454.

37. Elmasri, R., Wuu, G., Kim, Y. The Time Index - An Access Structure for Temporal Data, in **Proceedings of the Conference on Very Large Databases**. Brisbane, Australia, (August 1990).

38. Elmasri, R., Kim, Yeong-Joon, Wuu, G. T. J. Efficient Implementation Techniques for the Time Index, in **Proceedings of the Seventh International Conference on Data Engineering**. (1991).

39. Elmasri, R., Jaseemuddin, M., Kouramajian, V. Partitioning of Time Index for Optical Disks, in **Proceedings of the International Conference on Data Engineering**. Golshani, F. (Ed.), IEEE, Phoenix, AZ, (February 1992), 574–583.

40. Enderton, H.B. *Elements of Set Theory*. Academic Press, Inc., New York, N.Y., (1977).

41. Gadia, S.K. Toward a Multihomogeneous Model for a Temporal Database, in **Proceedings of the International Conference on Data Engineering**. IEEE Computer Society, IEEE Computer Society Press, Los Angeles, CA, (February 1986), 390–397.

42. Gadia, S.K., Yeung, C.S. A Generalized Model for a Relational Temporal Database, in **Proceedings of ACM SIGMOD International Conference on Management of Data**. Association for Computing Machinery, Chicago, IL, (June 1988), 251–259.

43. Gadia, S.K. A Homogeneous Relational Model and Query Languages for Temporal Databases. *ACM Transactions on Database Systems* 13, 4 (December 1988), 418–448.

44. Gadia, S.K., Nair, S., Poon, Y.-C. Incomplete Information in Relational Temporal Databases, in **Proceedings of the Conference on Very Large Databases**. Vancouver, Canada, (August 1992).

45. Gadia, Shashi K. **A Seamless generic extension of SQL for querying temporal data**. Technical Report TR-92-02, Computer Science Department, Iowa State University, (May 1992).

46. Guinot, B., Seidelmann, P.K. Time scales: their history, definition and interpretation. *Astronmy & Astrophysics* 194 (1988), 304–308.

47. Gunadhi, H., Segev, A., Shantikumar, G. **Selectivity Estimation in Temporal Databases**. Technical Report LBL-27435, Lawrence Berkeley Laboratories, (1989).

48. Gunadhi, H., Segev, A. A Framework For Query Optimization In Temporal Databases, in **Fifth International Conference on Statistical and Scientific Database Management Systems**. (1989).

49. Gunadhi, H., Segev, A. Query Processing Algorithms for Temporal Intersection Joins, in **Proceedings of the 7th International Conference on Data Engineering**. Kobe, Japan, (1991).

50. Gunadhi, H., Segev, A. Efficient Indexing Methods for Temporal Relations. *IEEE Transactions on Knowledge and Data Engineering (forthcoming)* (1991).

51. Guttman, A. R-Trees: A Dynamic Index Structure For Spatial Searching, in **Proceedings of ACM SIGMOD International Conference on Management of Data.** Yormack, B. (Ed.), Association for Computing Machinery, Boston, MA, (June 1984), 47–57.

52. Hall, P., Owlett, J., Todd, S. J. P. Relations and Entities, in **Modelling in Data Base Management Systems.** Nijssen, G. M. (Ed.), North-Holland, (1976), 201–220.

53. Hammer, M., McLeod, D. Database Description with SDM: A Semantic Database Model. *ACM Transactions on Database Systems* 6, 3 (September 1981), 351–386.

54. Hawking, S. *A Brief History of Time.* Bantam Books, New York, (1988).

55. Held, G.D., Stonebraker, M., Wong, E. INGRES–A Relational Data Base Management System, in **Proceedings of the AFIPS National Computer Conference.** AFIPS Press, Anaheim, CA, (May 1975), 409–416.

56. Hsieh, D. Generic Computer Aided Software Engineering (CASE) Databases Requirements, in **Proceedings of the Fifth International Conference on Data Engineering.** Los Angeles, CA, (February 1989), 422–423.

57. Hsu, S.H., Snodgrass, R.T. **Optimal Block Size for Repeating Attributes.** TempIS Technical Report No. 28, Department of Computer Science, University of Arizona, (December 1991).

58. Hunter, G., Williamson, I. The Development of a Historical Digital Catastral Database. *International Journal for Geographical Information Systems* 4, 2 (1990), 169–179.

59. Jensen, C. S., Mark, L., Roussopoulos, N. Incremental Implementation Model for Relational Databases with Transaction Time. *IEEE Transactions on Knowledge and Data Engineering* 3, 4 (December 1991), 461–473.

60. Jensen, C. S., Mark, L. Queries on Change in an Extended Relational Model. *IEEE Transactions on Knowledge and Data Engineering,* to appear (1992).

61. Jensen, C. S., Snodgrass, R. Temporal Specialization and Generalization. *IEEE Transactions on Knowledge and Data Engineering,* to appear (1992).

62. Jensen, C. S., Soo, M. D., Snodgrass, R. T. **Unification of Temporal Relations.** Technical Report 92-15, Computer Science Department, University of Arizona, (July 1992).

63. Jensen, C.S., Mark, L., Roussopoulos, N., Sellis, T. Using Caching, Cache Indexing, and Differential Techniques to Efficiently Support Transaction Time. *VLDB Journal,* to appear (1992).

64. Jones, C.B. Data structures for three-dimensional spatial information systems in geology. *International Journal of Geographical Information Systems* 3, 1 (1989), 15–31.

65. Jones, S., Mason, P., Stamper, R. LEGOL 2.0: A Relational Specification Language for Complex Rules. *Information Systems* 4, 4 (November 1979), 293–305.

66. Kabanza, F., Stevenne, J-M, Wolper, P. Handling Infinite Temporal Data, in **9th Annual ACM SIGACT-SIGMOD-SIGART Symposium on Principles**

of Database Systems. Nashville, TN, (April 1990).

67. Kahn, K., Gorry, G. A. Mechanizing Temporal Knowledge. *Artificial Intelligence* (1977), 87–108.

68. Karlsson, T. **Representation and Reasoning about Temporal Knowledge**. SYSLAB Working Paper Nr 105, The Systems Development and Artificial Intelligence Laboratory, University of Stockholm, (1986).

69. Katz, R.H., Chang, E., Bhateja, R. Version Modeling Concepts for Computer-Aided Design Databases, in **Proceedings of ACM SIGMOD International Conference on Management of Data**. Zaniolo, C. (Ed.), Association for Computing Machinery, Washington, DC, (May 1986), 379–386.

70. Kimball, K.A. **The DATA System**. Master's Thesis, University of Pennsylvania, (1978).

71. Klopprogge, M.R. TERM: An Approach to Include the Time Dimension in the Entity-Relationship Model, in **Proceedings of the Second International Conference on the Entity Relationship Approach**. Washington, DC, (October 1981), 477–512.

72. Kolovson, C., Stonebraker, M. Indexing Techniques for Historical Databases, in **Proceedings of the Fifth International Conference on Data Engineering**. Los Angeles, CA, (February 1989), 127–137.

73. Kolovson, C., Stonebraker, M. **S-Trees: Database Indexing Techniques for Multi-Dimensional Interval Data**. Technical Report UCB/ERL M90/35, University of California, (April 1990).

74. Kolovson, C.P. **Indexing Techniques for Multi-Dimensional Spatial Data and Historical Data in Database Management Systems**. Ph.D. Dissertation, University of California, Berkeley, (November 1990).

75. Ladkin, P. **The Logic of Time Representation**. Ph.D. Dissertation, University of California, Berkeley, (November 1987).

76. Langran, G., Chrisman, N. A Framework for Temporal Geographic Information. *Cartographica* 25, 3 (1988), 1–14.

77. Lee, R.M., Coelho, H., Cotta, J.C. Temporal Inferencing on Administrative Databases. *Information Systems* 10, 2 (1985), 197–206.

78. Leung, T.Y., Muntz, R. Query Processing for Temporal Databases, in **Proceedings of the 6th International Conference on Data Engineering**. Los Angeles, California, (February 1990).

79. Leung, T.Y., Muntz, R. **Stream Processing: Temporal Query Processing and Optimization**. Technical Report, University of California, Los Angeles, (December 1991).

80. Leung, T.Y., Muntz, R. **Temporal Query Processing and Optimization in Multiprocessor Database Machines**. Technical Report CSD-910077, Computer Science Department, UCLA, (November 1991).

81. Leung, T.Y., Muntz, R. Generalized Data Stream Indexing and Temporal Query Processing, in **Second International Workshop on Research Issues in Data**

Engineering: Transaction and Query Processing. (February 1992).

82. Lomet, D., Salzberg, B. Access Methods for Multiversion Data, in **Proceedings of ACM SIGMOD International Conference on Management of Data.** (June 1989), 315–324.

83. Lomet, D., Salzberg, B. The Performance of a Multiversion Access Method, in **Proceedings of ACM SIGMOD International Conference on Management of Data.** Atlantic City, (May 1990), 353–363.

84. Lomet, D. **Consistent Timestamping for Transactions in Distributed Systems.** Technical Report CRL90/3, Digital Equipment Corporation, (September 1990).

85. Lomet, D., Salzberg, B. **Concurrency and Recovery for Index Trees.** Technical Report CRL 91/8, Digital Equipment Corporation, (August 1991).

86. Lomet, D. Grow and Post Index Trees: Role, Techniques and Future Potential, in **Proc. of the Second Symposium on Large Spatial Databases.** (1991).

87. Lorentzos, N., Johnson, R. Extending Relational Algebra to Manipulate Temporal Data. *Information Systems* 13, 3 (1988), 289–296.

88. Lorentzos, N.A. **A formal extension of the relational model for the representation and manipulation of generic intervals.** Ph.D. Dissertation, Birkbeck College, University of London, (1988).

89. Lum, V., Dadam, P., Erbe, R., Guenauer, J., Pistor, P., Walch, G., Werner, H., Woodfill, J. Designing DBMS Support for the Temporal Dimension, in **Proceedings of ACM SIGMOD International Conference on Management of Data.** Yormark, B (Ed.), Association for Computing Machinery, Boston, MA, (June 1984), 115–130.

90. Manola, F., Dayal, U. PDM: An Object-Oriented Data Model, in **Proceedings of the International Workshop on Object-Oriented Database Systems.** (1986).

91. Mark, D.M., Lauzon, J.P., Cebrian, J.A. A review of quadtree-based strategies for interfacing coverage data with digital elevation models in grid form. *International Journal of Geographical Information Systems* 3, 1 (1989), 3–14.

92. McKenzie, E. Bibliography: Temporal Databases. *ACM SIGMOD Record* 15, 4 (December 1986), 40–52.

93. McKenzie, E. **An Algebraic Language for Query and Update of Temporal Databases.** Ph.D. Dissertation, Computer Science Department, University of North Carolina at Chapel Hill, (September 1988).

94. McKenzie, E., Snodgrass, R. Schema Evolution and the Relational Algebra. *Information Systems* 15, 2 (June 1990), 207–232.

95. McKenzie, E., Snodgrass, R. **Supporting Valid Time in an Historical Relational Algebra: Proofs and Extensions.** Technical Report TR-91-15, Department of Computer Science, University of Arizona, (August 1991).

96. McKenzie, E., Snodgrass, R. An Evaluation of Relational Algebras Incorporating the Time Dimension in Databases. *ACM Computing Surveys* 23, 4 (December 1991), 501–543.

97. Melton, J. (ed.) Solicitation of Comments: Database Language SQL2. American National Standards Institute, Washington, DC, (July 1990).

98. Montague, R. *The proper treatment of quantification in ordinary English*, Approaches to Natural Language. D. Reidel Publishing Co., Dordrecht, Holland, (1973).

99. Narasimhalu, A. **A Data Model for Object-Oriented Databases with Temporal Attributes and Relationships.** Technical Report, National University of Singapore, (1988).

100. Navathe, S. B., Ahmed, R. TSQL-A Language Interface for History Databases, in **Proceedings of the Conference on Temporal Aspects in Information Systems.** AFCET, France, (May 1987), 113–128.

101. Navathe, S. B., Ahmed, R. A Temporal Relational Model and a Query Language. *Information Sciences* 49 (1989), 147–175.

102. U.S. Naval Observatory **Time Service Announcement.** Series 14, Washington, D.C., (February 1992).

103. Oracle Computer, Inc. ORACLE Terminal User's Guide. Oracle Corporation, (1987).

104. Petley, B.W. Time and Frequency in Fundamental Metrology. *Proceedings of the IEEE* 79, 9 (July 1991), 1070–1077.

105. Quinn, T.J. The BIPM and the Accurate Measurement of Time. *Proceedings of the IEEE* 79, 9 (July 1991), 894–906.

106. Ramsey, N.F. The Past, Present, and Future of Atomic Time and Frequency. *Proceedings of the IEEE* 79, 9 (July 1991), 936–943.

107. Rose, E., Segev, A. TOODM - A Temporal Object-Oriented Data Model with Temporal Constraints, in **Proceedings of the 10th International Conference on the Entity Relationship Approach.** (October 1991).

108. Roussopoulos, N. View Indexing in Relational Databases. *ACM Transactions on Database Systems* 7, 2 (June 1982), 258–290.

109. Roussopoulos, N. An Incremental Access Method for ViewCache: Concept, Algorithms, and Cost Analysis. *ACM Transactions on Database Systems* 16, 3 (september 1991), 535-563.

110. Sadeghi, R. **A Database Query Language for Operations on Historical Data.** Ph.D. Dissertation, Dundee College of Technology, (December 1987).

111. Sadeghi, R., Samson, W.B., Deen, S.M. **HQL — A Historical Query Language.** Technical Report, Dundee College of Technology, (September 1987).

112. Sarda, N. Algebra and Query Language for a Historical Data Model. *The Computer Journal* 33, 1 (February 1990), 11–18.

113. Sarda, N. Extensions to SQL for Historical Databases. *IEEE Transactions on Knowledge and Data Engineering* 2, 2 (June 1990), 220–230.

114. Satoh, K., Tsuchida, M., Nakamura, F., Oomachi, K. Local and Global Query Optimization Mechanisms for Relational Databases, in **Proceedings of the Conference on Very Large Databases.** Pirotte, A., Vassiliou, Y. (Ed.), Stockholm, Sweden, (August 1985), 405–417.

115. Committee on Earth Sciences **Our Changing Planet: A U.S. strategy for global change research.** (January 1989). (unpublished).

116. Sciore, E. Using Annotations to Support Multiple Kinds of Versioning in an Object-Oriented Database System. *ACM Transactions on Database Systems* 16, 3 (September 1991), 417-438.

117. Sciore, E. **Versioning and Configuration management in an Object-Oriented Data Model.** Technical Report, Boston College, (1991).

118. Segev, A., Shoshani, A. Logical Modeling of Temporal Data, in **Proceedings of the ACM SIGMOD Annual Conference on Management of Data**. Dayal, U., Traiger, I. (Ed.), Association for Computing Machinery, ACM Press, San Francisco, CA, (May 1987), 454–466.

119. Sellis, T.K. Global Query Optimization, in **Proceedings of ACM SIGMOD International Conference on Management of Data**. Zaniolo, C. (Ed.), Association for Computing Machinery, Washington, DC, (May 1986), 191–205.

120. Sheng, R. L. **A Linguistic Approach to Temporal Information Analysis.** Ph.D. Dissertation, University of California, Berkeley, (May 1984).

121. Shenoy, S., Özsoyoğlu, Z. Design and Implementation of a Semantic Query Optimizer. *IEEE Transactions on Data and Knowledge Engineering* 1, 3 (September 1989), 344-361.

122. Smith, J.M., Chang, P.Y-T. Optimizing the Performance of a Relational Algebra Database Interface. *Communications of the Association of Computing Machinery* 18, 10 (October 1975), 568–579.

123. Snodgrass, R., Ahn, I. Temporal Databases. *IEEE Computer* 19, 9 (September 1986), 35–42.

124. Snodgrass, R. The Temporal Query Language TQuel. *ACM Transactions on Database Systems* 12, 2 (June 1987), 247–298.

125. Snodgrass, R., Gomez, S., McKenzie, E. Aggregates in the Temporal Query Language TQuel. *IEEE Transactions on Knowledge and Data Engineering*, to appear (1993).

126. Snodgrass, R.T. *An Overview of TQuel*, Temporal Databases: Theory, Design, and Implementation. Benjamin/Cummings Pub. Co., (1993), chapt. 6.

127. Soo, M., Snodgrass, R. **Mixed Calendar Query Language Support for Temporal Constants.** TempIS Technical Report 29, Computer Science Department, University of Arizona, (Revised May 1992).

128. Soo, M., Snodgrass, R. **Multiple Calendar Support for Conventional Database Management Systems.** Technical Report 92-7, Computer Science Department, University of Arizona, (February 1992).

129. Soo, M., Snodgrass, R., Dyreson, C., Jensen, C. S.,, Kline, N. **Architectural Extensions to Support Multiple Calendars.** TempIS Technical Report 32, Computer Science Department, University of Arizona, (Revised May 1992).

130. Soo, M. D. Bibliography on Temporal Databases. *ACM SIGMOD Record* 20, 1 (March 1991), 14–23.

131. Sripada, S. A Logical Framework for Temporal Deductive Databases, in **Proceedings of the Conference on Very Large Databases.** Los Angeles, CA, (1988),

171–182.

132. Stam, R., Snodgrass, R. A Bibliography on Temporal Databases. *Database Engineering* 7, 4 (December 1988), 231–239.

133. Stonebraker, M., Wong, E., Kreps, P., Held, G. The Design and Implementation of INGRES. *ACM Transactions on Database Systems* 1, 3 (September 1976), 189–222.

134. Stonebraker, M. The Design of the POSTGRES Storage System, in **Proceedings of the Conference on Very Large Databases**. Hammersley, P. (Ed.), Brighton, England, (September 1987), 289–300.

135. Stonebraker, M., Rowe, L., Hirohama, M. The Implementation of POSTGRES. *IEEE Transactions on Knowledge and Data Engineering* 2, 1 (March 1990), 125–142.

136. Tandem Computers, Inc. ENFORM Reference Manual. Cupertino, CA, (1983).

137. Tansel, A.U. Adding Time Dimension to Relational Model and Extending Relational Algebra. *Information Systems* 11, 4 (1986), 343–355.

138. Tansel, A.U., Arkun, M.E. HQuel, A Query Language for Historical Relational Databases, in **Proceedings of the Third International Workshop on Statistical and Scientific Databases**. (July 1986).

139. Tansel, A.U., Arkun, M.E., Özsoyoğlu, G. Time-By-Example Query Language for Historical Databases. *IEEE Transactions on Software Engineering* 15, 4 (April 1989), 464–478.

140. Thompson, P.M. **A Temporal Data Model Based on Accounting Principles**. Ph.D. Dissertation, Department of Computer Science, University of Calgary, (March 1991).

141. Tsichritzis, D.C., Lochovsky, F.H. *Data Models* (Software Series). Prentice-Hall, (1982).

142. Tuzhilin, A., Clifford, J. A Temporal Relational Algebra as a Basis for Temporal Relational Completeness, in **Proceedings of the Conference on Very Large Databases**. Brisbane, Australia, (August 1990).

143. Ullman, Jeffrey David *Database and Knowledge - Base Systems — II: The New Technologies*, vol. II. Computer Science Press, 1803 Research Boulevard, Rockville, MD 20850, (1988).

144. Urban, S.D., Delcambre, L.M.L. An Analysis of the Structural, Dynamic, and Temporal Aspects of Semantic Data Models, in **Proceedings of the International Conference on Data Engineering**. IEEE Computer Society, IEEE Computer Society Press, Los Angeles, CA, (February 1986), 382–389.

145. Van Benthem, J.F.K.A. *The Logic of Time*. Reidel, (1982).

146. Vrana, R. Historical Data as an Explicit Component of Land Information Systems. *International Journal for Geographical Information Systems* 3, 1 (1989), 33–49.

147. Wiederhold, G., Fries, J.F., Weyl, S. Structured Organization of Clinical Data Bases, in **Proceedings of the AFIPS National Computer Conference**. AFIPS, (1975), 479–485.

148. Wiederhold, G., Jajodia, S., Litwin, W. Dealing with Granularity of Time in Temporal Databases, in **Proc. 3rd Nordic Conf. on Advanced Information Systems**

Engineering. Trondheim, Norway, (May 1991).

149. Worboys, M.F. **Reasoning About GIS Using Temporal and Dynamic Logics**. (October 1990). (unpublished).

150. Wuu, G., Dayal, U. A Uniform Model for Temporal Object-Oriented Databases, in **Proceedings of the International Conference on Data Engineering**. Tempe, Arizona, (February 1992), 584–593.

151. Zloof, M. Query By Example, in **Proceedings of the National Computer Conference**. AFIPS, (1975).

This article was processed using the LaTeX macro package with LLNCS style

People Manipulate Objects (but Cultivate Fields): Beyond the Raster-Vector Debate in GIS

Helen Couclelis

Department of Geography, University of California
Santa Barbara, CA 93106, USA

Abstract. The ongoing debate in GIS regarding the relative merits of vector versus raster representations of spatial information is usually couched in technical terms. Yet the *technical* question of the most appropriate data structure begs the *philosophical* question of the most appropriate conceptualization of geographic space. The paper confronts this latter question in the context of the opposition between the "object" and "field" views of space. I suggest that GIS can turn a rather dry debate into a source of insights regarding the nature of its subject matter by learning from how people actually experience and deal with the geographic world. Human cognition indeed appears to make use of both the object and field views, but at different geographic scales, and for different purposes. These observations suggest a list of *desiderata* for the next round of thinking about spatial representation in GIS.

1 Introduction

Is the geographic world a jig-saw puzzle of polygons, or a club-sandwich of data layers? Probably neither, notwithstanding what the ongoing vector-raster debate in GIS might suggest (Gahegan and Roberts, 1988; Goodchild, 1989; Peuquet, 1984). It is fair to say that most participants in that debate would sooner stay clear of the shoals of ontology: GIS is, after all, a technical field. Still, the technical question of the most appropriate data structure for the representation of geographic phenomena begs the philosophical question of the most appropriate conceptualization of the geographic world. It is this latter issue that the present paper sets out to confront, initially in the context of the vector-vs.-raster controversy, more appropriately rephrased, for our purposes, as the opposition between the "object" and "field" views of geographic space. This, it turns out, is closely analogous to the opposition between the atomic and plenum ontologies in the philosophy of physics, which remains equally open.

I suggest that, unlike physics, GIS has the means to turn a rather sterile debate into a positive source of insights regarding the nature of its subject matter. The key is to be sought in human cognition, in learning from how people actually experience and deal with the geographic world. Seen from that perspective, both the object and field views, as they currently stand, appear very limited, but some directions for further development and synthesis can be discerned. The paper ends with a list of *desiderata*, not quite yet for the next generation GIS, but for the next round of thinking about spatial representation.

2 Objects and Vectors

The intellectual pedigrees of vector and raster GIS reveal a lot about both their contrasting underlying ontologies of geographic space, and their status in the field relative to each other. Vector GIS is firmly rooted in the view of geography as spatial science, formulated in the 1950's and 60's, which resulted in the geometrization of the geographic world and its reduction to a body of theories about relations between points, lines, polygons, and areas. In more recent years, the computational geometry developed for CAD/CAM systems designed to model actual geometric objects, provided a critical part of the technical toolkit necessary for the computational representation of geographic space in the spatial science tradition. Points, lines, polygons and areas representing geographic entities thus became geometric "objects", inheriting the sensible qualities of the prototypical objects that surround us: their discrete and independent existence, their relative permanence of identity, attribute, and shape, and their manipulability. Objects in a vector GIS may be counted, moved about, stacked, rotated, colored, labeled, cut, split, sliced, stuck together, viewed from different angles, shaded, inflated, shrunk, stored, and retrieved, and in general, handled like a variety of everyday solid objects that bear no particular relationship to geography.

There are problems with this view of the geographic world, of course. For one, Euclidean points, lines, and polygons do not exist in the natural, full-scale geographic world, any more than trend lines exist in a scatter plot of data. It is only at some phenomenon-specific but generally ill- defined scale that points, lines and polygons become reasonable approximations, if at all. (The only notable exceptions are visually induced structures and configurations such as the horizon, ridge lines, or constellations). This is true not only of straight lines and regular polygons (a la Christaller), but even of features such as stream networks, shore lines, fault lines and capes ("points"), notwithstanding their geometric- sounding names: witness the relatively recent excitement over the fractal representation of coastlines, or the continuing perplexity generated by the resistance to mapping of phenomena such as soil quality or natural vegetation. The lesson to be learned from the success of fractal geometry in modeling the appearance of many natural features, is not just that surfaces are coarse and lines wiggly. Rather, it is the interpenetration and blending of matter, form and phenomenon at practically every geographic scale -- the problem of deciding where the valley ends and the hill begins, the doubt about the actual course of the water channel, the challenge of trying to geo-code the soil of type A versus that of type B, the futility of even thinking to vectorize the hurricane, the avalanche, or the rain cloud -- briefly, the difficulty of carving up the continuous landscape into discrete objects, the resistance of natural geographic phenomena to being treated like plane geometric figures or table-top things.

The points, lines and polygons that do exist in the geographic world are practically all human artifacts, falling into two broad categories: (a) *engineering* works such as roads, bridges, dykes, runways, railway lines, and surveying landmarks, and (b) administrative and property *boundaries*. (It is instructive to remember, in this context, the origin of geometry in the need to safeguard property boundaries in the ever-flooded Nile valley. As for the association of lines in the landscape with man-made projects, remember how earlier in this century, some recently observed linear features on Mars were interpreted as canals and seen as proof of the existence of Martians!).

Throughout the history of Western culture, these two categories of Euclidean features have been essential to the regulation, domination and control of the geographic world: the natural world, in the case of engineering works; the social world, in the case of boundaries. The profound cultural significance of boundaries in particular has been extensively analyzed by scholars in the traditions of political and critical geography. In an early essay on this subject, Soja (1971) discusses the Western bias of rigidly compartmentalized space, and the concomitant hierarchy of nested bounded areas, from the modern nation-state all the way dowm to the individual parcel. Western culture is apparently unique in its treatment of land as *property*, as commodity capable of being bought, subdivided, exchanged, and sold at the market place. It is at this lowest level of *real* estate (from the Latin *res*, meaning thing), that we find the cultural grounding of the notion of space as object. Further up the hierarchy, at the level of counties, states, or nations, precise boundaries are needed again to determine what belongs to whom, who controls whom and what, and for what purpose. As Soja (1971) put it,

> It is almost as if the world were considered a cadastral map, with clear boundaries separating the "property" of the French and Germans, the Americans and Mexicans, just as the conventional cadastral map outlines the property of the Joneses and the Smiths, the factory and the business corporation. (p. 9)

One way or the other, boundaries carve out distinct objects in space, characterized by the prototypical object qualities of discrete identity, relative permanence of structure and attribute, and potential to be manipulated.

The view of the geographic world as composed of Euclidean objects also puts the focus on the kinds of spatial *relations* that may hold among such objects: namely, metric, projective, and topological relations. But, as Sack (1986) notes, this misses out a good part of relevant relations in human geography, namely the relations characterizing territorial behavior. In his words,

> Territoriality, as the basic geographic expression of influence and power, provides an essential link betwen society, space, and time. Territoriality is the backcloth of geographical context - it is the device through which people construct and maintain spatial organizations... Its geographical alternative is non-territorial spatial behavior. Focussing on the latter has led geography and social science to emphasize the effects on human behavior of such metrical properies of space as distance. Unfortunately, this focus has been too constraining to permit development of a complex spatial logic. (p 216)

Indeed, the problem with natural human territories, the reason why they elude spatial analysis, is that they lack some of the basic properties of objects. First, they require constant effort to establish and maintain. Second, they are defined by a nexus of social relations rather than by intrinsic object properties. Third, their internal structure changes not through the movement of anything physical, but through changes in social rules and ideas. Fourth, they do not partition space, although they may share it. Fifth, their intensity at any time varies from place to place. Sixth, they are context- and place-specific: one cannot move a territory like one moves a factory to another more suitable location. The same is not true of boundaries, as the sad case of Poland in our century attests. Possibly the majority of tensions and armed conflicts between neighboring nations in history have been at least in part the result of the discrepancy between established ethnic territories (which need not partition space, and are thus non-exclusive) on the one hand, and arbitrarily drawn political boundaries (which do partition space, and are thus exclusive), on the other. Territorial views, behaviors, and relations also underlie more localized spatio-social phenomena such as the NIMBY (Not In My Back Yard) syndrome, which has been called the problem of the decade in American planning. It is no wonder that neither GIS-based approaches, nor any of the conventional "rational" planning methodologies have been able to make a dent at that problem.

3 Fields and Rasters

If vector-based GIS over-determines the geographic world by forcing it into a uniform mold of geometric objects, the raster-based alternative is guilty of feigning maximal ignorance as to the nature of things in that world. All of us have experienced frustration at some time or other looking at a remote-sensed image in which the phenomenon of interest is blithely bisected by the image frame, and resented the mindless mechanical eye for which everything in the world is just another array of pixels. But just as vector-based GIS derives its credibility from the spatial analysis tradition, raster-based GIS is strongly supported by the increasing importance of satellite imagery not only in geography, but in wide areas of applied natural science. Raster GIS shares with these developments in the earth sciences not only a convenient direct compatibility in data structures, but also an implicit view of the geographic world as a vector field of measurable values, discretized into a pixel array. Groupings of pixels in particular configurations, or sharing particular attributes, can be identified with specific "features" on the Earth's surface, but it is understood that a different range of measurements (say, made within a different band of the electromagnetic spectrum, or represented by a different data layer in the GIS), may not reveal these same features, or any features at all. Features may be purely accidental clusters or patterns of values, they may be unstable at the relevant time-scales, they may or may not be bounded in Euclidean space, they may be part of an object, or themselves contain several objects. This fleeting nature of "features" is in stark contrast with the strong individuality of "objects" in vector-based GIS, which are identified and defined as discrete, localized individuals prior to any attributes they may possess.

The object-vs.-field debate in GIS closely parallels a much more fundamental controversy in the philosophy of science, that between the atomic and the plenum ontologies. Both these views exist in parallel in modern physics, and allow two conflicting hypotheses about the world to be formulated:

a. there exist things in time and space which have (known and unknown) attributes;

b. the spatio-temporal clusters of known attributes are the things.

The first, more conventional view, which grants things an existence somehow independent from their properties, entails that object identity must persist throughout any abstraction or simplification or generalization process by which non- essential attributes are eliminated. This is because, according to this view,

> all laws (in particular the laws of change) are reducible to fundamental laws concerning spatio-temporal relations among fundamental individuals [the "things"], and their fundamental properties. (Hooker, 1973, p. 211)

In contrast to this, the "plenum" view implies that each different cluster of properties is simply a different (abstract) object, and it cannot be expected to behave like another, sufficiently different cluster of properties (another object), even if both are abstractions from the same real thing. Thus

> the laws of nature will concern fundamentally the relations among properties and property-complexes, and again, prior to any roles which they might play in actual scientific theories, all such relations are on an equal footing. (Hooker, 1973, p. 211)

This view is especially popular in cosmology and quantum physics, both of which deal with objects outside any direct human experience, objects that many suspect to be no more than theoretical artifacts. Accordingly, it is the relations among different kinds of measurements that give rise to the laws of physics, rather than any relations among fundamental individuals which happen to be carriers of the properties measured. Put in a spatial context, the atomic-plenum debate is also one between the Newtonian view of space as inert container populated with objects, and the more contemporary, dynamic view whereby space is a "plenum" characterized by a ubiquitous field. As Einstein (1960) wrote in *Relativity*,

> There is no such thing as empty space, i.e. space without field. Space-time does not claim existence on its own, but only as a structural quality of the field. (p. 155)

Outside physics, the atomic-plenum debate has a bearing on all theoretical model-building, because of the opposing answers these two views give to the question of theoretical abstraction. Will the same object, described by two sufficiently different subsets of its attributes, continue behaving roughly "like itself" in any valid model that involves that object (the atomic view), or will it become two different theoretical objects (the plenum view)? Formal model theory has dealt with this issue, and Zeigler (1976) clearly sides with the plenum ontology when he defines the Real World as "the universe of potentially acquirable data".

I explored the theoretical and practical implications of the plenum ontology for geographical modeling in my PhD dissertation (see Couclelis, 1982), where I demonstrated that different definitions of geographic space and human populations, involving different subsets of attributes for each, must necessarily lead to very different and often mutually incompatible model structures.

4 Cognitive Geography

Applied geography has a major advantage (or disadvantage) over theoretical physics, in that it describes not a system of abstract equations, but a visible, tangible, empirical world. Human cognition had sorted out the basic properties of that world long before digital spatial databases came about, and (unlike what is the case with the next law in quantum electrodynamics), it probably has little to learn from the next spatial data model that is built. Thus, in applied geography - the geography that GIS is supposed to serve - the question of whether an object or field view is more correct, is neither a philosophical nor a theoretical issue, but largely an empirical one: how is the geographic world understood, categorized, and acted in by humans?

It appears that cognitive geography will not side with either the object nor the field side of the controversy, but supports a little of each, and much beyond. It is interesting to note in this connection that traditional pen- and-paper cartography, which GIS and its cousin, computer cartography, are about to render obsolete, used to accommodate both the object and the field views of geographic space. Lakes may be polygons, and coastlines may be lines, but the contour lines of topography only work in concert, as in a field: they are not independent objects, slices to be sorted, stacked and manipulated, and checked for illegal overlaps. Similarly, the seasonal stream may be shown by a blue line, but that line gets thinner and gradually disintegrates as we follow it up the canyon. And where is the bounding polygon around that marsh, indicated by dainty blue plant symbols strewn across the lowlands? Map symbolism evolved over the centuries through extensive trial and error, guided by the need to minimize the distance between the cognitive and the graphical representations of the geographic world. There may be a baby in the bathwater we are about to throw out.

Spatial cognition is flexible, dynamic, eclectic, and opportunistic: it does not abide by the Boolean *either-or*'s of theory, methodology, or technique. How the geographical world is understood is a function of at least two kinds of separate considerations: one has to do with geographic scale, the other with human intentionality, or *purpose*.

A growing body of work in cognitive psychology, anthropology and linguistics, some of it explored in Initiative 2 of the NCGIA (see, for example, Frank and Mark, 1991), supports the "experiential" hypothesis that human understanding of space develops against a background of largely preconceptual bodily and cultural experience (Lakoff and Johnson, 1980; Lakoff, 1987). Herskovits (1986) has explored in more detail the subconscious spatial idealizations that seem to underlie the use of prepositions and other locative expressions in natural language. Along similar lines, Couclelis (forthcoming) has proposed a theoretical framework for cognitive geography, according to which spatial cognition is established at several levels simultaneously (physical, biological, kinesthetic, perceptual, syntactic, cultural), of which only one, the syntactic level, supports the kinds of symbolic manipulations of abstract spatial objects represented in formal geometries. Consistent with the experiential hypothesis is also Zubin's (1989) cognitive typology of spatially distributed percepts as a function of geographic scale. This agrees well with the framework outlined in Couclelis (forthcoming): indeed, the cognitive means by which the physical world is known vary greatly with scale, and this is likely to result in a range of qualitatively different spatial experiences. Zubin's typology distinguishes a sequence of four categories of space of increasing geographic scale, designated as A, B, C, and D, and briefly outlined in the following:

A-spaces are those of everyday objects smaller than the human body, which are contained in a static visual field, and can be manipulated. Thus, knowledge of space A is strongly grounded at the physical and kinesthetic levels of spatial cognition, and it is consistent with the Newtonian notion of container space and with Euclidean properties. This is the scale of prototypical "objects": chairs, books, cups, keys. Since this is also the first space to be explored by the developing infant, it appears to have a psychological primacy that may explain the intuitive appeal of the Kantian notion of Euclidean space as a synthetic *a priori.*

B-space, the space of larger every-day objects, is very similar to space A, despite the fact that the visual appearance of these objects must be pieced together from many non-simulataneous views, and their knowledge is not aided by manipulation. But while an elephant cannot be picked up like a cat, and a real house cannot be put back in its box like a doll house, such objects are sufficiently similar to scaled-up versions of space-A objects to inherit the basic cognitive properties of the latter.

C-spaces contain the vast landscapes seen from some vantage point - apprehended through a sweeping glance, but otherwise not directly accessible to sensorimotor experience. Here, perspective, depth, atmospheric distortions, and the curvature of the Earth, cancel many properties of Newtonian spaces and objects, including the fundamental ones of a rectangular Cartesian reference frame, and of Euclidean transformations.

D-spaces, finally, are those of regions and realms beyond the range of direct experience, spaces pieced together by means of a very diverse range of spatial and other knowledge, information, and belief. Decades of work on mental maps and environmental cognition by geographers and psychologists has provided insights into both the contents and the partial structure of such spaces (for a review, see Garling and Golledge, 1988). It is evident that higher cognitive functions of inference and calculation, as well as world knowledge and cultural conditioning, are involved in their construction. Still, the Columbus of D-space is likely not yet born.

The point of this classification is that the experience of geographic space is not homogeneous, but varies with scale. More significantly for our discussion, it appears that the perception of a Newtonian space of Euclidean objects is confined to spaces A and B, which are below the range of geographical scales proper. The experience of landscapes and territories, by contrast, is most active at the levels of cognition (perceptual, syntactic, cultural) which are not directly grounded in the world of classic Newtonian bodies, and their physical and kinesthetic properties. Spatial experience of a natural landscape seen from above (C-space), for example, is more field-like than object-like. There are things in it - valleys, hills, marshes, forests and fog banks - but these are not "objects" to pick up and move about: they are salient *features*, breaks in a plenum that is otherwise *continuous*, not by the mathematical criterion of infinite subdivisibility, but because of the indefinite number of different ways one could draw boundaries around these features. It is even harder to say what D-type spaces might be "like" as formal approximations, especially given the pervasive influence of geographic imagery (maps, charts, GIS layers, subway plans, satellite pictures, space shuttle photographs...) on modern human consciousness: is the whole Earth now cognized as a vast landscape, much vaster, but not dissimilar to the one seen from the local hilltop - or are there still Terrae In-cogn-itae beyond the visible, imparting to the cognitive map a wholly different topological order?

But human cognition is also *intentional*, not content with a single passive set of representations. Next to geographic scale, *purpose* also determines how the geographic world is conceptualized. I commented earlier, in my discussion of engineering works and boundaries, on how the purpose of surveillance, control and manipulation of both the natural and the social worlds requires things to be objectified that are not, strictly speaking, objects.

I would further suggest that a scientific description of the geographic world is best compatible with the field perspective. As the supporters of the plenum ontology in physics have pointed out, quantitative descriptions can only deal with relations between properties, not between things, and it is properties, not things, that mathematical fields are about. Also, a field-based framework is much better suited to modeling change, and therefore time, because it is much easier both for our minds and for our formal tools to deal with volatile variables than with volatile objects. The Cheshire Cat would have not made literary history if it had just sat there and gradually lost its grin.

If the purpose however is neither scientific description nor control, but simply to carry out the spatial tasks of everyday practical existence, things can be considerably more complex. When we *manipulate* spatial concepts mentally, these too need to be made into *objects*. In their study of language and metaphor, Lakoff and Johnson (1980) have pointed out that we categorize and bound in discourse even what is continuous and unbounded: we pedal our bicycle *around* the hill and meet *at* street corners. But that objectification is intentional, contextual, reflexive, and fleeting. It is as if *ad hoc* objects were pulled out of a continuum of largely uninterpreted features, temporarily invested with whatever required properties, highlighted and used, then let to sink back in a background of tacit world knowledge. That background may itself be as interesting to study as the objects themselves, and the notion of *territory*, briefly discussed above, may be part of what is to be found there. Territories too become objects when they need to be defended or fenced, but it is in their field- like, background form that they appear to have their most pervasive effects on human behavior.

The flexibility of cognitive objectification extends to the treatment of spatial relations themselves. Indeed, unlike what is the case in any known geometry, the meaning of spatial relations appears to change with the nature of the entities being related, and their role in discourse. Examples of these phenomena abound in the work of cognitive linguists such as Lakoff and Johnson (1980), Lakoff (1987), Herskovits (1986), and Talmy (1983), and have by now become common intellectual property among those of us involved in NCGIA Initiative 2. Remember the case of "the boat on the lake" (object A supported by surface B), versus "the house on the lake" (object A just outside the boundary of polygon B), versus "the fish in the lake" (object A inside volume B): what should then be the "objective" representation of the "lake" object, and what does *on* really mean?.

The intentional, contextual, and reflexive quality of cognitive objectification is manifest in areas well outside the study of language. In environmental psychology, for example, a *landmark* is something that stands out relative to its surroundings, that is used for the purpose of place recognition, orientation, or behavioral adjustment in navigation, that is subjectively chosen, that is a function of geographic scale, and that is not a landmark unless someone sees it as such. Similarly, the quintessential question of spatial cognition, the "where am I" question, cannot be usefully answered either in latitude-longitude coordinates, nor in bee-line distances from Paris, San Diego, and the Hard Rock Cafe. (As the anthropologist Paul Bohannan notes, "We are the only people in the world who use seafaring instruments to determine our position on the ground": reported in Soja, 1971; and giving someone's home address in UTM coordinates is a practical joke among some geographers). Indeed, the meaningful answer to the personal locational question is rather something like "in the classroom", "thirty miles offshore", "five minutes from home", or "a few inches from the precipice", depending on the purpose and context of the question. It is as if landmarks, places, and other geographic entities were defined in neither an absolute nor a relative, but in a *relational* space, where object identity itself is at least in part a function of the nexus of contextual relations with other objects.

To go back to our original theme, not too much should be made of the object versus field debate, as both miss much that is fundamental to spatial representation. After all, as every GIS expert knows, vector and raster operations are inter-convertible. Topologically, object and field spaces are duals of each other [manuscript in preparation], and both, in their current formulations, support the classical view of categories that cognitive science has shown to be too restricted. For many of the purposes that GIS serves, one or the other of the two views will usually be fully sufficient. In other respects, however, it looks like we may still have a long way to go.

A basic underlying assumption throughout this last part of the paper has been that the human mind still remains the most accomplished system for the representation, explanation, and prediction of geographic phenomena. This much was ensured by natural selection, since the world of applied geography (as opposed to, say, the rarified worlds of physics, chemistry, or geometry), is the actual world in which humans evolved. The scientific representations of the Earth and social sciences can extend what the cognitive representational system can do into scales of space and time and levels of detail that are beyond the direct reach of the latter. In doing so, they inevitably modify the contents of cognition itself (though not its basic properties). Still, it is useful to think of "cognitive geography" as both the starting point and the guiding thread for the construction of meaningful, applicable formal geographies. Scientific representations of geographic space, and GIS in particular, cannot and should not try to mimic spatial cognition. On the other hand, in its search for better spatial languages and representations, the brash newcomer still has a great deal to learn from the old master. This paper argued that the field-object debate is just one such area where insights from spatial cognition can bring valuable illumination. I believe there will be many, many more.

These thoughts, tentative and speculative though they may be, lead to the formulation of some provisional

5 Desiderata for the Next but One Generation of GIS (Users)

1 Choose your system to fit your main purpose. All applications with the word "management" in their title require an object perspective, more consistently implemented in vector-based GIS. The same is true of social-science work based on statistical analysis of census-type data, which presuppose the rigidly partitioned spaces of official surveillance and control. But stick to the field perspective (and raster GIS) if you do research in a mathematical earth science. Don't be misled to think that features and objects are the same.

2 If in doubt, choose raster, as it is better compatible with phenomena at geographic scales (i.e., the scales of Zubin's spaces C and D, where objects fade into features, and Euclidean absolute space gives way to the relative space of fields and properties).

3 Better still, demand a system that supports both raster and vector equally, and that allows the purposive creation of temporary objects out of features.

4 Consider the possibility of spatial data structures that are neither raster- nor vector-oriented. Fields may not always have to be represented as data layers; objects (e.g., objects as defined in object-oriented programming) need not always be Euclidean points, lines, areas, and polygons.

5 Be open to the notion of spatial representations that may not be mappable, and to GIS that do not work primarily through map-like displays.

6 Ask whether we can represent *relational* as well as absolute and relative space, i.e., a space in which spatial units carry information about their relations to other relevant spatial units in the vicinity. One way to

their relations to other relevant spatial units in the vicinity. One way to approach this notion would be as a generalization of the potential field concept. Getis (unpublished) is working on operationalizing this notion of relational (or "proximal") space, which is discussed in connection with modeling in Couclelis (1991).

7 Be humble. The most significant geographic spaces may never make it into a computer. Even so, the quest for their representation may prove the most exciting kind of geography we've ever done.

References

Couclelis, H. (1982). Philosophy in the Construction of Geographic Reality. In P. Gould and G. Olsson (eds.): *A Search for Common Ground.* London: Pion, pp. 105-140.

Couclelis, H. (1991). Requirements for Planning-Relevant GIS: a Spatial Perspective. *Papers in Regional Science* 70, 1, 9-19.

Couclelis, H. (forthcoming). A Linguistic Theory of Spatial Cognition. *Annals of the Association of American Geographers.*

Einstein, A. (1960). *Relativity: the Special and the General Theory.* London: Methuen.

Frank A., Mark D. M. (1991). Language Issues for GIS. In D. J. Maguire, M. F. Goodchild, D. W. Rhind (eds.): *Geographical Information Systems: Principles and Applications*, Vol 1. Essex: Longman.

Frank A., M. Egenhofer, W. Kuhn (forthcoming). Computational Topology: Data Structures and Algorithms. *Cartography and GIS.*

Gahegan, M. N., Roberts, S. A. (1988). An Intelligent Object-Oriented Geographical Information System. *International Journal of Geographical Information Systems* 2, 101-110.

Getis, A. (unpublished). Some Thoughts on Developing Proximal Data Bases.

Garling, T., Golledge, R. (1988). Environmental Perception and Cognition. In E. Zube, G. Moore (eds): *Advances in Environmental Behaviour and Design*, Vol 2, New York: Plenum Press, pp. 203-238.

Goodchild, M. F. (1989). Modeling Error in Vectors and Fields. In M. F. Goodchild, S. Gopal (eds.) *Accuracy of Spatial Databases.* , New York: Taylor and Francis, pp. 107-13.

Herskovits, A. (1986). *Language and Spatial Cognition.* Cambridge:

Cambridge University Press

Hooker, C. A. (1973). Metaphysics and Modern Physics: a Prolegomenon to the Understanding of Quantum Theory. In C.A. Hooker (ed.): *Contemporary Research in the Foundations and Philosophy of Quantum Theory.* Dordrecht: Routledge & Kegan Paul.

Lakoff, G. (1987). *Women, Fire, and Dangerous Things.* Chicago: University of Chicago Press.

Lakoff, G., Johnson, M. (1980). *Metaphors We Live By.* Chicago: University of Chicago Press.

Peuquet, D. J. (1984). A Conceptual Framework and Comparison of Spatial Data Models. *Cartographica* 21 (14), 66-113.

Sack, R. (1986). *Human Territoriality: its Theory and History.* Cambridge: Cambridge University Press.

Soja, E. (1971). The Political Organization of Space. *Resource Paper # 8.* Washington, DC: Association of American Geographers.

Talmy, L. (1983). How Language Structures Space. In H. Pick, L. Acredolo (eds.): *Spatial Orientation: Theory, Research, and Applications.* New York: Plenum Press.

Zeigler, B. (1976). *Theory of Modelling and Simulation.* New York: Wiley.

Zubin, D. (1989). Oral presentation, NCGIA Initiative 2 Specialist Meeting, Santa Barbara. Reported in D. Mark (ed.): Languages of Spatial Relations: Researchable Questions & NCGIA Research Agenda, *NCGIA Report 89-2A*, NCGIA.

TIME AND SPACE: AN ECONOMIC MODEL

By

Robbin R. Hough Ph.D.

School of Business Administration, Oakland University
Rochester, MI 48307-4401

Abstract. Technology enables us to assemble ever and ever larger quantities of data and ever deepening data structures. These developments are not sufficient. Humans must have stories, images, habits and rules-of-thumb to live by and with in complex environments and they are just not available as they relate to the globe which is shared by all. Simply browsing through a world atlas or looking at a globe is an exercise in looking at more information than it is possible to handle at once. The remote sensing and geographic information system communities have the opportunity to engage in the construction of tools which, in their maturity, will enable new ways of comprehending our global state of affairs. The purpose of the paper which follows is to contribute to a framework for such an undertaking.

1 A Problem of The Policy Sciences

This paper is about the role of policy, resources and the environment in economic and social development. Though it draws substantially upon the methodologies of modern economics, the world view which it attempts to sketch for the reader will be alien to many who perceive economics as a policy science increasingly concerned with abstract "macro" entities. To be of use to humankind, policies for humans must be on a human scale. Moreover, it is of central importance that peoples be moved to perceive the objectives of the policies as important to them.

To be of use, policies must also anticipate the consequences of action or inaction. Specifically, the policy actors must be prepared to forecast the behaviors of the actors impacted by their policies. The problem here is not with the models but with the social and policy sciences themselves. Though widely used, the term "behavior" is so ambiguous as to lack meaning. There must, in truth, be an entity which behaves and specific acts which can be discussed as instances of behavior. Attempts at metaphor which speak of nation-states as though they were persons can be colorful and illuminating, but frequently fail under close scrutiny. Consider then an alternative foundation of objects for study.

2 The City-State

This section will set forth a broad conceptual framework with which to think about the idea of a city-state as an alternative construction for viewing human activities. The remainder of the paper will then explore the explanatory power of that framework in the context of a global database constructed to test the framework. Consider first, the matter of land tenure.

2.1 Land Tenure in the City-State

It is possible to describe a very simple framework within which to pursue the economics of the city-state. Assume, to begin, a flat plain of abundant and equal fertility everywhere. Assume that the plain is occupied by a population for which the total production of the plain is always adequate for the population. In large measure the state of the American Indian before the arrival of the white man depicts a similar situation. So long as the plain continues to produce sufficient food to sustain the population there will be no reason to expect accumulations of population anywhere on the plain. In essence the population will be distributed randomly about its uniform surface.

Assume now that weather conditions alter and total production is adequate to supply the population, but that the adequacy of production in a given place may fall short from time to time. In the absence of a system of land ownership, the population may move about following the weather patterns. If, however, there is a system of land ownership, the shortages which result from the weather may be handled in one of two ways. Either a futures market may arise in which those with shortfalls pledge future crops to obtain present consumption or the land itself may be chatteled to obtain needed sustenance.

There are further consequences of the assumed change in weather conditions. If either type of bargain is to be struck, the best place at which to strike the bargain will be at the center of the plain where buyers may most efficiently be brought together with sellers. Moreover, since the distance of a given property from the center of the space will determine the costs of transportation, the value of the land will decline with its distance from the center of the space. The existence of these transport costs lead to a most interesting conclusion.

From our understanding of perfect competition, all farms would come to equilibrium at a zero economic profit. Since such an equilibrium rewards all factors at the value of their marginal product, it follows that the operation of the markets will produce a condition in which all farms are equal in value but their size will vary as their distance from the center of the space. Obviously a perfect matching of this state is dependent upon the assumption of uniform fertility. It is further dependent upon the assumption that there are no internal economies of scale in agricultural production.

2.2 The Center of the City-State

From the point of view of its economics, a "city-state" is an economic entity with a marketplace at its center. The existence of the center facilitates trade in ways which have long been well understood. It is far more efficient for buyers and sellers to converge on the center for the purposes of trade than to wander at random about the space in search of one-another. But the center is not simply a financial center and a place where goods are traded. It is also a place where tools are fashioned, where goods are processed, where services are rendered, where processed goods and imports to the city-state are distributed and where potential exports from the city-state are gathered and shipped.

Here again, a very simple model is an aid to understanding. Assume that the rainfall over the plain of the previous section is uniform and that the plain is, for all practical purposes, flat. Under such circumstances, the desirability of the plain as a habitat for humans will be influenced by the porosity of the surface, the rate at which the sun evaporates the rain, the rate at which plants transpire the moisture from the soil and the degree to which variation in the surface of the plain allows water to collect in lakes. That is, the rain will partially be absorbed into the groundwaters, evaporate or transpire, or collect in lakes. Acidity and alkalinity problems aside, it is possible to imagine a climate which will just provide ample rain for growing plants and lakes for human use. Water, of course, has many uses. It is needed for health, sanitation, a variety of manufacturing processes, and may provide an excellent means of transportation for humans and goods. It would be expected that the non-agricultural activities would take place around the lakes.

Assume, in contrast, that the plain is very steep. Its steepness may, at the limit, approach that of a mountainside. The surface would be a difficult one from the point of view of agriculture, and the water will simply run straight off the "plain."

The habitable surfaces of the earth occupy a place on a spectrum between the two postulated extremes. Where they lie on the spectrum is extremely important to the placement of regional centers. In essence, the falling rain will etch a pattern of rivers on the surface. Human settlements will grow up along those rivers. If it is assumed that a given technology requires a fixed quantity of water per human, the scale of the settlements will be limited by the flow of water. Of key interest then, are the factors which determine the rate of flow of rivers.

Studies in hydrology tell us that two factors govern the rate of flow of a river. These factors are the slope of the basin and the order of the basin where an order 1 river has no tributaries, an order 2 river has order 1 rivers as tributaries, an order 3 river has order 2 rivers as its tributaries and so on.

The Missouri-Mississippi river basin is one of the largest continuously habitable surfaces on the face of the earth. The two left hand columns of Table 1. were constructed assuming that thirty percent of the rainfall over the Missouri-Mississippi basin would reach the mouth of the river and that each tributary in turn split into two tributaries. Column three displays the support capacity of the river assuming that each cubic foot per second of water flow would support ten human beings. The third and fourth columns of the table display the actual size distribution of the cities in the basin.

Given the prevailing technology of water use, City-states, as described, are limited spatially by the available fresh water.

Given the technology of transportation, they are also limited spatially to a scale which is consistent with the prevailing means of transportation. That is, city-states are places where people live and work. Since people will not generally spend more than one hour commuting to work, the prevailing technology tends to limit the radius of a city-state to the distance that can be travelled in one hour.

Finally, they are limited spatially by the presence of physical or political barriers which limit the effectiveness of the prevailing means of transport.

Table 1. Actual and Predicted City Size Distributions for the Missouri-Mississippi Basin (1970).

Predicted Tributary Flow Rate	Number of City Sites	Actual Number of Cities	Population Size Class of Cities
610,000	1	1	6,100,000
305,000	2	2	3,050,000
152,500	4	6	1,525,000
76,250	8	10	762,500
38,125	16	15	381,250
18,063	32	19	180,063
9,531	64	59	95,310
4,765	128	154	47,650
2,383	256	390	23,830
1,191	512	623	11,915
596	1024	1,133	5,960

The distribution of city-state sizes shows that there are relatively few sites which will provide sufficient water for very large populations. There are additional important reasons to believe that some cities will come to dominate an area much larger than the prevailing commuter distance. In general, it can be said that there are substantial economies of scale in the production of a wide variety of the services required by a producing society. Bulk transport, bulk storage, energy production, and financial services are important examples. The provision of these services will tend, therefore, to concentrate in regional centers. In some measure, these centers will follow the water limited placement pattern of other city-states. To some degree, however, the nature of their function will allow their scale to increase well beyond the measured flow available to support them directly.

It is just at this point that the potential importance of human behavior in altering the shape of regions must be considered.

2.3 Human Behavior

In some cases, the city-state may be viewed as a single isolated entity. One hundred or more small island city-states are examples. In most cases however, a number of city-states occupy a larger *region* with other city-states. In such a regional space, the single community with the most advantageous location will come to occupy a central place in the region. It will enjoy a locational advantage in relation to the other city-states of the region.

Each such structure, regardless of the number of city-states involved, is shaped by linkages which have been elsewhere identified as *support, survival, and culture* (Hough and Hollebone, 1992). Each of the linkages can be viewed on a bipolar continuum. The support linkages are based roughly on the sophistication of the technologies of transport/communications and the level of energy consumption. The city-states, on this dimension, are *centralized* or *dispersed*. For example, the radical changes in transportation technology during the period from 1850 to 1950 very importantly shifted the regions of the midwest from relatively dispersed to a relatively centralized. The survival linkages refer to the city-states relationships to the region which are described as *regarding* or *imposing*. Agricultural communities tend toward the regarding end of the survival continuum while mining communities often inhabit the imposing end. The cultural linkages among city-states define them as *independent* or *interdependent*. Common languages, religions, and technologies may bind communities together while their absence may keep them apart.

In essence, the region may be viewed as an *energy well* dimensioned on the three continuums (Hollebone and Hough, 1991). The region's constituent communities are bound together in that energy well. Given a clear understanding of the scale, limits and dimensions of the energy well, the general structure outlined earlier may serve to describe given city-states or "communities" under a wide range of conditions *so long as the conditions do not threaten the existence of the well itself.* In this fundamental sense, regions should be regarded as disequilibrium systems. Their structures are dependent upon the continuums identified, making the problem of identifying truly independent policy variables a difficult problem indeed.

With the foregoing caveat, plausible models can be constructed to argue on behalf of one or another of the identified policy variables. Thus, taxes, immigration laws, tarrifs, technology transfers, development aid, land use, energy use and the like become the central issues on which policy discussions focus. These conventional economic models focus on the control of one or more resources. The four resources seen as critical, are human, water, land and energy/mineral.

A city-state based on the control of these resources may "develop" in a variety of ways. The development track for a city-state most familiar to western readers is founded upon private or public "development" for the common good. In fact, the ownership of the resource is tangential to a development process in which the few produce a specialized product for the many. A market must develop at the center of the city-state, and its extent will be proportional to the extent of the four critical resources used in production. The controllers of water, land and energy will develop a technology for the combining of those resources in production.

The temporal aspects of the development process are thus fairly simple to conceptualize. Assume a given technology and a given water-energy-land-labor resource base. So long as the population of a region and its constituent city-states do not face an absolute technological limit, conventional economics supplies descriptions of the ways in which regions will solve their problems.

Economic analysis has concentrated a great deal on the human behaviors of *exchange* and *migration*. The arguments can be developed as follows (Hansen,1970). If the resources are free to move from region to region, the prices of the resources will be everywhere equal. Obviously land and natural resources are not mobile. To what extent do these immobilities upset the structure of relative prices and hence the equilibrium of the markets? Heckshere and Ohlin suggested that trade among the regions in the final products would result in equal factor prices. Somewhat later along, Samuelson and Learner suggested the precise conditions under which such market equilibria would occur. They were that: (1) the number of commodities be equal to or greater than the number of resources; (2) the commodities move freely among the regions; (3) the production function is everywhere the same; and (4) the factor proportions differ between the products.

The conceptual structures devised cope easily with other equally explicit human behaviors including *mitosis* (subsidies), *parisitism* (confiscation and taxes). If it is assumed that the information underlying the technology migrates freely from region to region, the market models handle *commensalism* (technology transfer) as well. If the equilibrium conditions are expressed as inequalities, even the cases where certain of the factors will not be utilized because their costs exceed the value of their marginal product are covered *(the subsistence economies)*.

Consider now, the application of the concepts toward the development of a global model. Specifically, we shall attempt to construct a profile of the regions of the globe.

3 Toward a Global Model: Agriculture

Since the United States is the steward of nearly 1/3 of the globe's arable land, and a significant share of its other resources it is appropriate to expect that a model which fails to deal with the detailed texture of the U.S. economy will fail miserably elsewhere. The next step toward a global model will therefore begin with a detailed look at the United States both from the point of view of agriculture and of manufacturing. The remainder of the present section will consider the outlines of agriculture in the U.S. and the following section will develop a parallel view of other industries. Specifically, this chapter will examine the influences of weather and other factors on agricultural production in the United States.

3.1 Climate and Agriculture

It has been said that to "do science" is to follow injunctions like "look down that microscope". The present construction should be taken in that spirit. Utilizing the 494 Rand McNally "basic trading areas" of 1970, the City-County Data Book was utilized to construct a 1980 profile of each of the 494 United States regions defined. The use of this particular set of regions will be considered in the following section.

There is significant commercial agriculture in 488 of the 494 trading areas. In 1979, the total production of the areas was nearly 85 billion dollars with the smallest marketing a mere $31000 in crops and livestock, while the largest sold over $2 billion.

Table 2. below contains an estimate of the overall U.S. agricultural production function based on the 474 regions for which complete data were available. The results seem to support the following observations.

Ignoring for the moment the three other significant factors, there would appear to be important economies of scale operating at the regional level. That is, the sum of the labor and capital coefficients is significantly greater than one. It might be speculated that there are a number of plausible sources for these economies: The sharing by individual farms of large scale farm equipment, storage facilities, feedlots, transportation equipment and irrigation works seem among the more obvious. More detailed work would be necessary to identify specific sources.

Whatever the economies at the regional level, they would not appear to extend to the individual farms. This observation obviously grows from the significance of the negative coefficient of farm size. Again further study would be warranted in order to separate the influences of area economies from those of the individual farm operation.

Finally, it seems quite clear that weather and elevation play an important role even within the limited latitude and elevation ranges of the continental United States. This, I believe, is the most important observation because of its portent for findings in the more extreme ranges found across the globe.

Table 2.
A Production Function Estimate for U. S. Agriculture

n = 474
F = 498.436
r^2 = .842

Crops + Livestock = 1.24328 (.59012)

	t	Beta
Persons on farms^.30228	(4.674)	.241
Value land and bldgs^.880648	(13.696)	.735
Growing degree days^-.43136	(-4.033)	-.105
Elevation in meters^-.101136	(-4.819)	-.083
Ave farm size acres^-.07941	(-1.765)	-.051

It may be noted here that the production function holds without knowledge of the mix of livestock and crops in production. Under the conditions that livestock sales as a percentage of total sales is known, several changes in the coefficients may be conjectured. It should be expected that the coefficient of technology would increase susbstantially insofar as feeding cattle is a less efficient approach to producing the same nutritional output. The importance of land and buildings would decline insofar as the livestock feeding sheds, barns and other facilities are associated with the livestock. Since cattle forage well and are raised at higher elevations some detraction from the coefficient of elevation may occur. In addition, animals may obviously be protected from the weather with much greater ease than crops. Lastly, since the ranches on the steppes are both distant from area centers and on less desirable soil, there may be a positive impact on the average farm size coefficient.

As can be seen from a comparison of Table 3. with Table 2., the overall regression is improved and the changes in the coefficients are in the expected directions. A smaller number of regions was included since some regions did not have livestock production which exceeded 1% of the total agricultural products sold. A review of the individual residuals suggests that an important fraction of the remaining variation is due to misclassification of the sources of production in the computation of reporting error corrections. For example, the volume of sales reported for Amarillo, Texas and Dodge City,

Table 3.
An Alternative Production Function Estimate

n = 446
F = 559.199
r^2 = .884

Crops + Livestock = 3.53512 (.451899)

	t	Beta
Persons living on farms ^ .299925	(5.476)	.252
Value of land and bldgs ^ .800404	(14.357)	.722
Growing degree days ^ –.601619	(–6.710)	–.123
Elevation in meters ^ –.100381	(–5.819)	–.114
Ave. farm size in acres ^ .02804669	(.724)	.019
Livestock as % of crop ^ –.1003365	(–3.182)	–.060

Kansas are multiples of the expected values. However, the removal of the two observations does not significantly effect the values of the coefficients.

Now, if the agricultural model outlined is correct, the value of all farms will be identical except for the external influences on farm value identified in our estimate of the production function. More specifically, in an ideal world the product of the value per acre of the farm with the acreage of the farm would be a constant. It has just been demonstrated that the plains are not flat, the weather is uneven, cows graze in the timber and farms are not all equal in size. It is however, implied that a function with an elasticity of one is being shifted about by the factors identified in the estimate of the production function. In addition it is possible to distinguish between those centers with major financial, transportation, and service capabilities and all others (i. e. the Ranally Major Trading Areas). It may be expected that a specific city–state's distance from those urban population centers imposes a further transportation and communications burden on the region.

The results displayed in Table 4. appear to bear out the hypothesis. While the sum of the coefficients is somewhat larger than one, each of the coefficients is highly significant. Moreover, we know that the price of agricultural land is frequently driven up by the competing demands of other uses. It is possible to obtain some sense of the magnitude of the several

Table 4.
Factors Bearing on Farm Values

n = 445

F = 166.652

r^2 = .654

Value per acre = 13.5444 (.394032)

	t	Beta
* average farm size ^– .444754	(–17.997)	–.591
* percentage of livestock ^– .241934	(–9.594)	–.288
* distance from major center^– .121791	(–5.137)	–.159
* elevation^– .0642942	(–4.458)	–.147
* growing degree days^– .314098	(–4.126)	–.129

demands from the following regression. Three additional variables were included in the analysis. The extent of industrial, commercial and residential demands is represented by population density. The robustness of agricultural demands is represented by a caloric production index the value of which is one if the region produces just enough food to meet the needs of its population. The third variable is a simple count of the number of major extractive industry facilities in the region. Unfortunately (or fortunately) only 97 of the 494 regions have major extractive facilities so that only those regions were included.

Table 5.
Some Factors Competing for Farm Land

n = 97
F = 75.25
r^2 = .872

Value per acre = 10.3342 (.29814)

	t	Beta
* average farm size ^- .374217	(-6.987)	-.501
* percentage of livestock ^- .182972	(-3.27)	-.145
* distance from major center^- .00566036	(-.142)	-.007
* elevation ^- .0513742	(-2.231)	-.108
* growing degree days ^- .23672	(-2.001)	-.087
* per capita food production ^.24581	(6.984)	.425
* population density ^.312145	(7.957)	.636
* major extractive facilities^.135874	(2.168)	.105

As can be seen from a comparison of the two regressions, the changes in the agricultural coefficients are small but for the distance factor which is presumably washed out by the entry of the population density. The signs of the added variables are correct and their coefficients significant. A review of residuals reveals that the key missing influences on land prices relate to the peculiar features of seaports and financial centers as will be discussed in the following section.

3.2 An Overview of Agriculture

What has been sketched shows that mankind cannot escape the influences of weather and geography even in the richest agricultural nation on earth. What is more, if the output required of commercial agriculture is known, the results obtained allow an estimate to be made of the number of farms (hence the commercial farmers and investment) required to produce that output under the particular circumstances of the climate of the region. That is: a farm is a farm is a farm.... but for the influences of climate and geography. The very significant and very simple regression following illustrates the point beyond words.

Table 6.
An Output Function for Agriculture

n = 474
F = 354.366
r^2 = .698

Total Output = 5.93778 (.819)

	t	Beta
* number of farms^1.19979	(32.182)	855
* elevation^.0830663	(−3.124)	−.086
* growing degree days^− .467309	(−3.262)	−.09

We turn now to the development of an industrial profile.

4 Toward a Global Model: Industry

Earlier, the role of water in the support of city–states was highlighted. Given the technology of the 1960's, it can be said that the U. S. was well into the final stages of the development of its water resources as can be inferred from the close fit of the size distribution of cities to the theoretical limits of the basin under the reigning technology. Since that time, the sensitivity to those limits has improved and further improvements may be expected. In addition, the costs of water may be expected to press for changes which are water–saving in their nature.

With some justification because of the land areas of Canada which drain into the Columbia and St. Lawrence basins, we may extend the hypothetical analysis of Chapter II to the continental U. S. Assume that the average worker is willing to commute no further than 30 miles, and that one cubic foot per second of water flow will support 10 persons. Table 7. displays the limit river flow of the United States of a 30 inch rainfall over the continental land area. We thus conclude that there are a maximum of about 500 regions which will support more than 39000 persons.

Table 7.
Predicted and Actual U.S. River Flows

Basin Order	River Flow	Predicted Regions	Actual Regions
1	1989040	1	1
2	994521	2	2
3	497261	4	7
4	248630	8	18
5	124315	16	41
6	62157.6	32	71
7	31078.8	64	122
8	15539.4	128	154
9	7769.7	256	68
10	3884.85	512	10

In column 4 are displayed the actual number of Basic Trading Areas identified by Rand Mc Nally in the construction of their 1970 Trading Area Manual. Two important forces would appear to account for the distortions in the actual when compared to the predicted. On the one hand, nature has provided a number of lakes including the Great Lakes which allow the development of regions beyond those predicted by the simple river model. On the other hand, the artful use of technology has created major man-made lakes, aqueducts, pumps which will pull from underground aquifers and rivers, and water filtration plants. Each of these artifacts is capable of providing water where it might not otherwise be available.

The Ranally Basic Trading Areas may thus provide a tolerable first approximation to the city-state as the concept has been used to the present point in our analysis. Consider then, the industrial structure of the city-states.

The next concept to be explored is Alexander's idea of a "basic" and "non-basic" industry dichotomy. Alexander proposed that certain industries enhanced the income base of the local economy through their exports while others simply re-circulated local dollars. Cast in employment form, each employee in a basic industry can be said to generate employment for others. If Alexander is correct, manufacturing employment, Federal employment, and military employment should explain the size of the total labor force in a "simple" city-state at any point in time. Moreover, since commercial agriculture is necessary to provide food for those working in the center, non-export commercial agriculture should be proportional to the sum of employment in the basic industries.

Given a structure of support, survival and culture, it is conectured in this section that the economies of scale in the provision of a range of goods and services imposes a regional structure over the otherwise independent structure of city-states. The matter of regional structure will be examined in some detail in the next section, but it is important to note here that central banking facilities, deep water ports, communications centers, intermediate-haul transportation and governmental services are among the goods included. The most obvious and direct effects of the provision of these factors will be their employment impact on the communities in which they are centralized.

The results seem to bear out the hypothesis in the 494 U. S. cases. The average city-state employs a total of 214747 persons. The average basic employment is distributed as follows:

Federal employees = 5947
Manufacturing employees = 44362
Military personnel = 3309

The apparent importance of manufacturing activity to total city-state market economy employment shown in the equation of Tabl;e 8. makes it imperative that its importance be confirmed by an alternative and independent procedure. According to the Oxford Economic Atlas of the World, the 494 city-states have 1361 sites of major economic activity. The 378 city-states with manufacturing sites have a total employment in manufacturing of 20529027. The 116 city-states without manufacturing sites have a total manufacturing employment of 1385727. This observation would tend to indicate that an appropriate definition of "major" was utilized in the identification of the manufacturing sites.

Table 8.
Some Determinants of Employment

n = 494
F = 6256.51
r^2 = .99

Total Labor Force = −2185.12 (51221)

	t	Beta
+ 3.46725 * Federal employees	(23.513)	.14
+ 3.4431 * Manufacturing employees	(97.368)	.734
+ 2.45411 * Military personnel	(8.705)	.046
+ .095442 * Value crop and livestock prod	(9.461)	.044
+ 1638770 * Eastern Financial Center	(25.456)	.142
+ 304837 * Major port	(14.08)	.079
+ 11715.7 * Energy production center	(4.863)	.027
+ 5.0751 * State Government Revenue	(6.437)	.029

A simple linear regression of sites against manufacturing employment suggests that there are 12804.5 employees per site. The standard error of the estimate is 5 times the (negative) intercept term while the t statistic for the coefficient is 22.725 and the F statistic is 516.442. In this case the scale of the coefficient (one fourth of the total regional manufacturing employment) again points to an appropriate definition of "major". It is, however, possible to probe a great deal deeper.

As can be seen from the regression of Table 9. below, the industrial sites labelled account for nearly 85% of the manufacturing employment in the regions identified as having major industrial sites. Since a number of generally small–shop industries are not included, the results seem plausible.

Table 9.
The Sources of Manufacturing Employment

n = 378
F = 205.21
R^2 = .848
Mfg Empl = -8945.54 (49166.2)

	t	Beta
+ 15473.3 * Univ	12.389	.43
+ 82107.6 * Auto	11.272	.28
+12695.2 * Textiles	5.854	.124
+ 10695.3 * Energy	4.566	.115
+ 27020.7 * Plane	4.738	.121
+16678.4 * Computers	3.431	.089
+ 10088.6 * Ships	.775	.017
+ 19033.7 * Rail	1.946	.042
+ 20049.4 * Steel	3.045	.072
+ 7220.7 * Paper	1.939	.045

It has often been observed that universities are information factories. To my knowledge, it has not been demonstrated that they are very substantial generators of manufacturing employment as such. The university variable was not entered until the final stage of the analysis. The other terms, including the ship-building term were significant and explained over 80% of the variance before the University variable was entered. It should be noted that the numbers of colleges and community colleges bear no important relationship to employment. Simply reclassifying certain of the sites produces the following distribution of manufacturing sites which emphasizes those industries with major wage differences from the average manufacturing wage and relatively low levels of unemployment.

236 Textile plants
48 Auto plants
409 Chemical plants
148 Rubber plants
845 Other manufacturing plants

Several important conclusions can be reached which are evidenced in the Table 10. which is a regression of average annual earnings of employees in manufacturing by region against the distribution of the manufacturing sites in those regions.

First, because the precise earnings will depend upon the mix of manufacturing industries, location and the other noted influences, it is impossible to make direct comparison of the wage estimates above on a cardinal basis. Nevertheless, the per employee Census figures for the four industries named clearly sort into the correct rank order.

Secondly, the clear wage differentials and their explanation in terms of the distribution of employment by industry at once support the integrity of the regional definition and give further support to the site classification scheme.

Third, the magnitude and direction of the wage slope from south to north confirms popular belief and suggests compensation related to the costs of providing heat.

Table 10.
Some Influences on Manufacturing Earnings

n = 378

F = 17.022

r^2 = .24

Mfg Earn = 11296.1 (4140.21)

			t	Beta
+	154.61	* Other manufacturing	(1.741)	.096
-	910.09	* Textile plants	(-5.09)	-.211
+	731.40	* Rbr, plstc & synth	(244.322)	
+	226.99	* Latitude north	(6.124)	
-	5.66	* Farm/mfg empl	(-4.437)	
+	2119.44	* Auto plants	(3.547)	
-	224.71	* % unemployment	(-2.775)	
-	9587.93	* Finance center	(-2.797)	
+	271.71	* Chemical Plants	(1.831)	

Table 11.
Selected Wage Estimates

Industry	Payroll/Employee
Auto	$21933
Chemical	$20082
Rubber	$14420
Textile	$11320

Finally, the factor proportions vary greatly between the industries.

5 Regions of The U.S.

The U.S. evidence supporting the existence of city-states has been reviewed and found to coincide with the simple model set forth in the second section. The final step in providing a basis for examining agricultural and industrial activity on a global scale is that of reviewing the evidence which may be brought in support of the regional concept advanced in the second section.

Several approaches to the problem of defining regions are possible. The so-called "Major Trading Areas" of the Ranally Atlas were defined by including each Basic Trading Area within the scope of a Major Trading Area which provided it with banking, wholesaling, advertising and other services.

It is important to now note again that the construction of the city size distribution was importantly influenced by the plausible commuting radius of individual workers. If the technology, income or energy supplies were insufficient to support the postulated radius, the city-states would be bounded at a smaller radius. New forms of personal or public transportation technology might be utilized to expand the radius or increases in the costs might be expected to shrink the radius. It seems most appropriate to think of the forces acting upon regional structures along similar lines. That is, the natural forces discussed in previous chapters lead to a roughly triangular distribution of city sizes. Economies of scale in warehousing, finance, distribution, and communications give certain of the larger city-states further cost advantages over their smaller neighbors in spatial terms. Moreover, the costs of intermediate-haul transportation enhance the cost advantages of city-states nearer the center of the regions.

The logic of the region must differ somewhat from the logic of its subsystems. The scale of the region and transport costs may place the city-states or space in city-states beyond a given distance from the center at such a disadvantage that they simply do not participate in the market economy. Such spaces will tend to be dry, mountainous and large. These areas will be the locus of subsistence agriculture, so long as the organization of production and the productivity of the land will support the subsistence population. At such time as the capabilities of these marginal areas will not support their population, it may be expected that conditions will drive the surplus population from the land into the kind of urban subsistence economy visible in the barrios of Central and South America.

Secondly, the regions themselves suffer advantage or disadvantage in relation to the centers of foreign trade and commerce. Thus, as New York and San

Francisco play special roles in foreign trade, regions will incur cost disadvantages in proportion to their distance from those two regions.

The regression of Table 12. and Table 13. which describes the regional centers may be interpreted as follows in relation to the regions of the United States. The industrial northeast has plentiful lakes including the Great Lakes as well as the St. Lawrence, Hudson, Connecticut and numerous other rivers. It has relatively high levels of rainfall as well as a temperate climate which reduces evaporation and transpiration. The resulting city-states have smaller land areas and higher populations than might otherwise be expected. Indeed, they are so small that many of them are close enough to New York City to come to depend upon it for the several services which they cannot themselves provide.

Table 12.
The Determinants of Regional Land Area

n = 50
F = 17.94
$R^2 = .661$

Land Area = 3.43739 (.566284)

		t	Beta
* number of city-states^.974279		(6.075)	.701
* precipitation^-.599441		(-5.276)	-.487
* percent of poverty^1.113414		(4.008)	.433
* distance from NY or SF^.257733	(2.826)	.284	
* degrees north lat^1.64016	(2.537)		.308

At the other end of the spectrum, the large, arid and mountainous spaces of San Antonio and El Paso coupled with the adjacent areas of northern Mexico represent regions with plenty of space for subsistence agriculture and display the high percentages of poverty associated with living beyond the market economy. So framed, of course, Los Angeles appears as a region whose population has grown to create (albeit less visibly) the urban barrios associated with her neighbors south of the border.

It is thus concluded that climatic and hydrological conditions provide the orderly basic conditions under which city-states come to exist and to be associated in energy wells called regions. Moreover, following the conditions outlined in Chapter II have been met: (1) the number of commodities is equal to or greater than the number of resources; (2) the commodities move freely among the regions; (3) the production function is everywhere the same; and (4) the factor proportions differ between the products as evidenced by the clear wage differentials between the industries. So long as the equilibrium conditions are stated as inequalities, the existence of unused resources in a subsistence economy at the fringes of the regions will not disturb the equilibrium.

Table 13.
Table of Regional Centers

REGION	CITY-STATES		AREA	PRECPVERTY		DISTANCE	LAT
				(cm)		(pct.)	NY/SF
New York	25		64759	557	2	10	43
Minneapolis	23		231692	481	2	1000	44
Charlotte	23		74446	552	4	700	34
Chicago	23		57559	566	2	700	40
Dallas	21		194071	446	3	1400	32
Detroi	20		47395	414	2	500	42
Philadelphia	17		23073	559	2	100	39
Pittsburgh	17		24581	509	2	300	40
Milwaukee	16		45927	486	2	700	43
San Francisco	15		144489	49	3	10	37
Spokane	14		227333	143	3	800	46
Denver	13		261792	268	3	800	38
Des Moines	12		67886	553	2	800	41
Boston	12		48865	506	2	200	42
St Louis	11		63569	621	3	800	37
Atlanta	11		59692	590	4	800	32
Richmond	11		33788	602	3	300	37
Seattle	11		34920	238	2	700	51
Birmingham	10		39536	679	4	600	33
Memphis	10		54915	656	5	900	33
Indianapolis	10		17704	555	2	600	39
Los Angeles	9		98603	50	3	300	34
Omaha	9		84362	565	2	1100	40
Kansas City	9		61607	618	2	1100	38
Cleveland	9		9924	503	2	400	40
Portland	8		89639	231	3	500	43
Salt Lake City	8		177645	121	3	600	40
Oklahoma City	8		43855	537	3	1100	35
Jacksonville	8		30833	877	4	800	29
Washington	8		17249	563	2	200	38
Columbus	8		12981	551	3	500	39
New Orleans	7		29447	834	4	1100	30
Louisville	7		37556	573	4	600	36
Cincinnati	7		13809	551	2	500	38
Phoenix	6		89012	76	4	300	33
Little Rock	6		40635	587	5	1100	34
Houston	6		38028	530	3	1300	29
Buffalo	5	1	3839	487	2	300	42
San Antonio	4		48087	451	6	1200	27

REGION	CITY-STATES	AREA	PRECP	VERTY	DISTANCE	LAT
			(cm)		(pct.)	NY/SF
Wichita	4	34770	511	2	700	37
Knoxville	4	17567	662	5	300	35
Tulsa	4	15150	628	3	1300	35
Miami	4	14009	1011	4	1200	25
El Paso	3	55594	133	5	1100	32
Shreveport	3	21509	567	5	1300	31
Tampa/Lakeland	3	9183	805	4	1200	27
Mobile	2	15649	939	5	1100	30
Nashville	2	16198	601	4	500	35
Honolulu	2	6425	49	2	1500	19

6 Toward a Global Model

The results can be used to profile the regions of the globe. Simple questions can be posed. Can the results obtained from the investigation of the United States be generalized to the globe? More specifically, are estimates of a global production function consistent with the idea that a car is a car is a car...? Similarly, is a farm a farm no matter where it is found? Though the concepts coped well with the varying conditions encountered in the United States, will the concepts of region and city-state generalize to a global realm?

A global database of regions was constructed which include as their centers, 740 cities chosen for their scale, their size in relation to their neighbors or their role as largest city in a nation bounded by water or other regions. Based on the Hammond Atlas size given for the cities used as regional centers:

Average size of the largest city	959173
Number of cities per country	3.67052

A profile of manufacturing employment was computed for each region based on the U.S. estimates. That is, each of approximately 13,000 plant sites was assumed to provide the same level of employment provided by its counterpart in the United States. When the resulting estimates are aggregated by country the following result is obtained for 50 countries on which World Bank data is available:

Table 14.
National Income Estimates, Selected Countries

n = 50
F = 158.915
R^2 = .912

National income = .45

* Mfgempl^.54	(5.609)
* Fuel Imports^.23875	(2.12)
* Machine imports^.1767438	(1.393)

The close fit and plausible magnitude of the coefficients are taken as preliminary evidence that the U.S. based estimates will serve as reasonable substitutes for the actual levels of manufacturing employment in the regions.

7 Conclusions and Recommendations

The paper has *described* the spatial organization of human activity in a way which focuses attention on the scarcity of land, water and energy resources. Human populations are shown to be clustered in and around key industrial facilities whose activities are central to their economic well being. These regional spaces can potentially provide the building blocks for diverse but conceptually comparable structures.

The tentative list of key industrial facilities identified, their proximity to and reliance upon flows of fresh water, their uses of energy and air, their relations to nearby agriculture, the employment they generate and the tertiary activities which they support all suggest that there is considerable potential in a global research program which focuses on those facilities. Such a program might include studies which focus on the following kinds of topics:

o The definition of key facilities
o Measures of facility performance
o Estimating ancillary activity
o Multi-source data integration/analysis
o Inter-regional comparisons

Bibliography

Folland, Sherman T. and Hough, Robbin R., The Value of Agricultural Land **Land Economics**, 1991 pp. 30-36.

Hollebone, Bryan C and Hough, Robbin R., Freedom and Limits: The Fundamental Theorem of System Structure, **Systems Research**, Vol. 8., No. 3., 1991, pp.13-20.

Hough, Robbin R., The Impact of Socialization and Specialization on Society: A Preface, **Systems Research**, Vol. 8., No. 3, 1991 pp. 6-11.

_________., Natural Language and Geographic Information Systems, **Advances in Spatial Information Extraction and Analysis for Remote Sensing**, Ed. Manfred Ehlers, Bethesda: American Society for Photogrammetry and Remote Sensing, 1990

_________., Support, Survival and Culture: System Integration, **Problems of Support, Survival and Culture**, Ed. Gerard de Zeeuw, Amsterdam: Center for Innovation and Cooperative Technology, 1991

_________., The Design of Remote Sensing and Geographic Information Systems: A Demographic Image, **The Integration of Remote Sensing and Geographic**

Information Systems, Ed. Jeffrey L. Star Bethesda: American Society for Photogrammetry and Remote Sensing, 1991.

Hough, Robbin R. and Hollebone, Bryan C., Organizational Structure: Defining Process Management, **Cybernetics and Systems Research '92**, Ed. Robert Trappl, Singapore: World Scientific, 1992.

Hough, Robbin R. and Ehlers, Manfred, A Proposal to Extend OUr Understanding of the Global Economy, **Multisource Data Integration in Remote Sensing**, Ed. James C. Tilton, Greenbelt: National Aeronautics and Space Administration, 1991.

Hough, Tor H. and Hough, Robbin R., Database Tools for the Manipulation of Hierarchic Relations, **Advances in Support Systems Research**, Ed. George Lasker and Robbin Hough. Windsor: International Institute for Advanced Studies in Cybernetics and Systems Research, 1990.

The Changing Language of and Persisting Patterns in the Urban Design of Edo/Tokyo

Keiichi TAKEUCHI

Department of Social Geography
Hitotsubashi University
Kunitachi, Tokyo 186

Abstract: The city is an environment formed by the interaction and integration of different practices. The practices of the city involved a great number of individuals and social groups whose cosmologies are different and whose interests are in conflict.
In this paper, the author attempts to analyse the changing signification and persisting vernacular elements of the urban design of Tokyo (called Edo up till 1868) since its beginnings in the seventeenth century.
Topography was the most important factor in the urban design of this period: alluvial plains and reclaimed land were designated for the commercial and residential use of the commoners (these districts being referred to as the *shitamachi*) and the diluvial, hilly parts (referred to as the *yamanote*) were assigned to the feudal lords and their samurai subjects as residential quarters.
Destruction caused by the Kanto earthquake in 1923 and ensuing reconstruction plans were epochal inducements towards the transforming of Tokyo from a canal city into a land-traffic city. Nonetheless, most of the popular commercial centres continued to be found at the junctions of canal traffic systems and at sacred places, where moats and panoramas dominated by distantly seen symbolic mountains (Fuji and Tsukuba) were important elements.

1 Introductory Remarks

Urban design is a language or a means to express an urban utopia, or the cosmology or geographical thought, in the broader sense, of a society. At the same time, the city is an environment formed by the interaction and the integration of different practices in the society of that city [3,10]. These practices involve many individuals and social groups, whose interests are not primarily planning-oriented. The cosmologies and the interests of these individuals and social groups differ from one another and are often in conflict. It is necessary, on the one hand, to distinguish between popular and official approaches to the management of urban space carried on throughout various historical phases. On the other, it is also necessary to provide a proper grammar applicable to the reading of the urban design of Tokyo (called Edo up to 1868), independently of the differences in social classes or in access to political and economic power [1,6,18].

Regarding the historical background, certain specific features of Edo/Tokyo should first be pointed out. In comparison with many cities in western Japan, Edo is of comparatively recent origin; while the origins of the Edo settlement date from the twelfth century, Edo city per se was founded by a local lord in the fifteenth century as a small castle town on the banks of what is now called Tokyo Bay. As a castle town, Edo had certain peculiar characteristics. When at the beginning of the seventeenth century, the shogunate government was first established by the Tokugawa family here, the castle site was originally selected because it could be easily defended; it faced the bay and was surrounded by a moat [14]. But from the seventeenth century, the bay area in front of the castle continuously underwent reclamation in order that a district might be created in which merchants could ply their trades; and the moats and canal systems were reorganised for traffic and communications purposes rather than the purpose of defense [11]. The Tokugawa regime was highly centralised and maintained its rule by means of a huge bureaucratic apparatus. Every local lord (*daimyo*) was required to reside every other year in Edo and was compelled to leave his family behind in Edo, each time he returned to the administration of his own estate in the provinces. The castle of Edo itself was transformed into an administrative centre after the establishment of the shogunate government. Under this arrangement, Edo became a huge centre of consumption with commercial and handicraft manufacturing activities being concentrated there. For the shogunate, the primary concern in the planning of Edo was to settle therein a great number of feudal lords of various ranks and their samurai subjects, and also to settle and regulate a great number of merchants and craftsmen. Hence, in the latter half of the Tokugawa period, with the development of a monetary economy and capital accumulation, the economic forces consisting of merchants and craftsmen became stronger and stronger [5,6,7,17,18].

Thus, the urban design of Edo was completely different from that of ancient capitals such as Nara and Kyoto, which had been constructed largely under the influence of the Chinese concept of a capital city. Most *jokamachi*, or towns developed around a castle, had a certain number of features in common, within the urban design. Strategic considerations governed the composition of the road network and the layout of walls and moats surrounding the predominant castle with its donjon (*tenshukaku*). Edo Castle, however, was, as mentioned above, primarily a place of administrative affairs; the donjon was burnt down in the middle of the seventeenth century and was never reconstructed.

2 The Urban Design of Edo

In the eighteenth century, Edo had a population of one million, which made it the biggest city in the world at that period. In spite of this, the shogunate government never attempted to adopt an integrated town plan covering all the urban areas of Edo. The ground plan of Edo was extremely simple. As in other *jokamachi*, the first principle of settlement policy was the separation of samurai and merchant classes, and also the segregation of merchants according to trade and craftsmen according to craft. This segregation was reflected in place names still in use today such as Ginza, which means "district of silversmiths". The merchants and handicraftsmen were settled on the alluvial plain (called *shitamachi*, literally "downtown area") having an efficient fluvial and canal system and streets laid out in a regular grid pattern; while the residential quarters assigned to the samurai class were located on the diluvial uplands (called *yamanote*, literally "hilly area"), along the principal roads to the provinces. With regard to the concept of "residing", there was a difference between the *shitamachi* and the *yamanote*. For merchants and craftsmen, the primary concern was to have their shops and workshops facing the street or wharf, with a small living area behind the work area. In the *yamanote*, samurai constructed their residences within assigned compounds [5]; in the case of powerful feudal lords,residential compounds also included storehouses and row houses for low-ranking samurai of the *yamanote* area. In this way, because the diluvial uplands were dissected by alluvial valleys, from the beginning Edo was predisposed to urban sprawl along the main roads. The line of demarcation between the *yamanote* and *shitamachi* areas wasvery complicated with the latter area sometimes penetrating deeply into the former. Edo Castle was the site of business for the samurai class only; in the *shitamachi*, there was no one business centre or central forum or square, and this is the origin of the multinuclear character of Tokyo today [1].

Not only because topographical conditions strongly influenced the urban design, but also because natural elements played an important role in the formation of landmarks, nature was very important in the urban design of Edo. There are many place names such as Fujimizaka (Slope with a View of Mt. Fuji), Shiomizaka (Slope with a View of The Sea), which indicate that, very often, in Edo the direction of the streets was not determined by the four cardinal points as in Kyoto, for example, where streets run north to south and east to west, but by the position of certain mountains, notably Fuji and Tsukuba, and the sea, in relation to the city. (When planning to build a house, however, geomantic considerations or the determining of the auspicious cardinal point the house was to face were extremely important.) Many pictorial documents depicted somewhat stereotyped scenes of Edo consisting of a body of water, that is, the sea or sometimes a canal, in the foreground and distant mountains in the background. This peculiarity of the pictorial records indicates that water in and mountains visible from the city were considered to be urban landmarks; very often, shrines were located at places with a panoramic view of Mt. Fuji or the sea, and Buddhist temples were to be found on boundaries between land and water. The locations of shrines and temples were not determined by shogunate decree but depended on popular traditions, which held that mountains and water were sacred elements. Fetes at these shrines and temples constituted important events for the inhabitants of the *shitamachi*. As previously pointed out, the concept of a plaza or square did not exist in Japanese cities, but in Edo, wharves and the foot of bridges, which in the capacity of traffic junctions were animated sites of shopping and amusements, had a function similar to that of squares or plazas in Western cities.

In the *shitamachi* and also in the residential districts of lower class samurai, the neighbourhood community was defined not in terms of the main streets but of the alleys and labyrinthian paths leading off the main streets. Place names were and are still given to the blocks formed by these alleys and paths, and not to the main streets.

In the second half of the period of the shogunate, fireproof warehouses with mortar-faced walls were built along the canals and main streets. Fires were constantly breaking out in Edo, and where merchants and craftsmen were concerned, a mortar-walled warehouse was considered a status symbol.

In 1868, with the Meiji Restoration, which put an end to shogunate rule and opened the way to modernisation, the capital was transferred from Kyoto to Edo, which changed its name to Tokyo. Both politically and economically, the Meiji Restoration was an important time of transformation for this city. The samurai class had lost its privileged position and Tokyo became the site of a modern central government. It is necessary to note, however, that in spite of this large-scale transformation, urban design in Edo did not undergo extensive modification. Many governmental facilities, together with the central managerial functions of big enterprises and foreign embassies were located in the compounds of former residences of *daimyo* and high-ranking samurai. The newly-forming middle class occupied the residential areas of middle- and lower-ranking samurai. This is the case in most parts of present-day Chiyoda and Minato wards. In order to demonstrate the dignity of the emerging state, the central government initiated plans for the construction of Western-style avenues and buildings. One was the development project in Hibiya and Kasumigaseki for governmental offices, and the other involved a proposed street of brick buildings in Ginza. The former with its aim

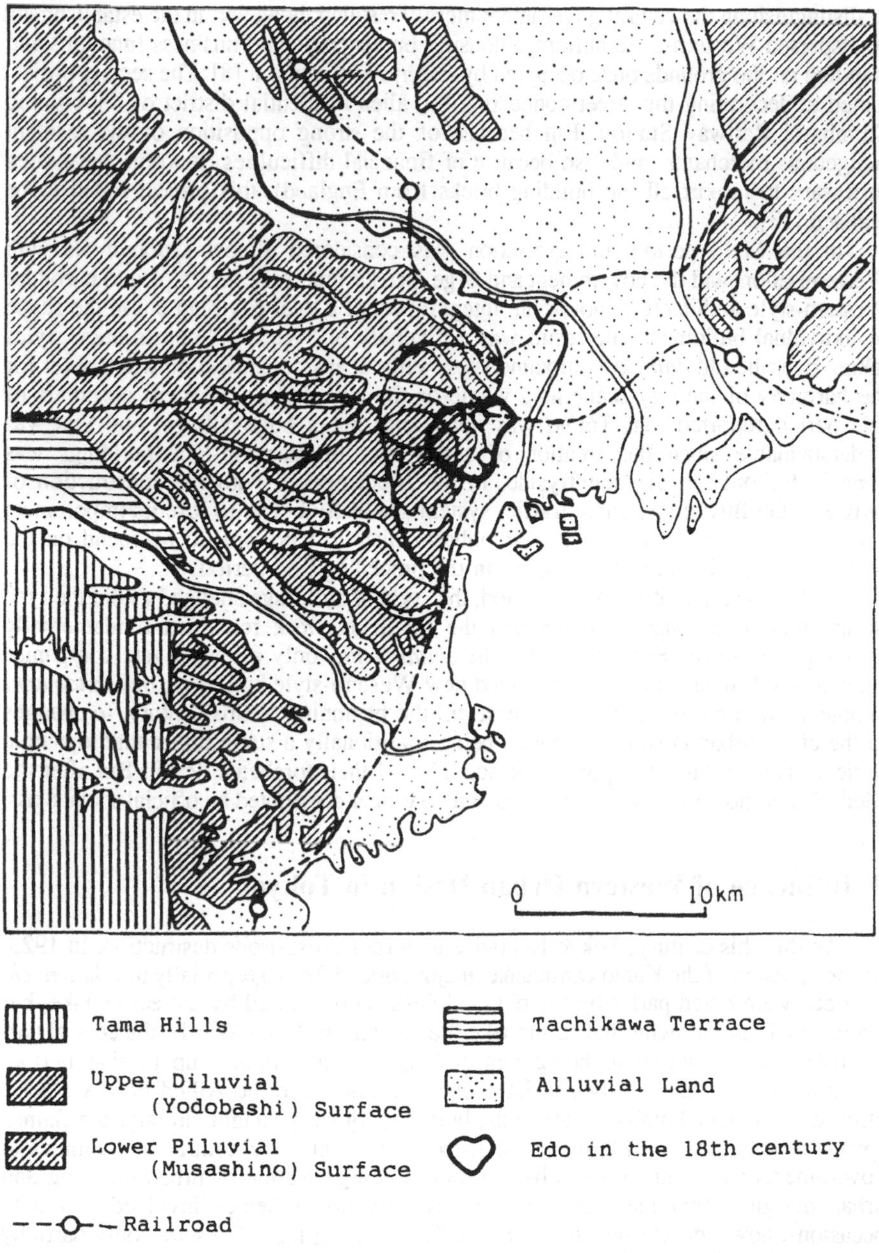

0 10km

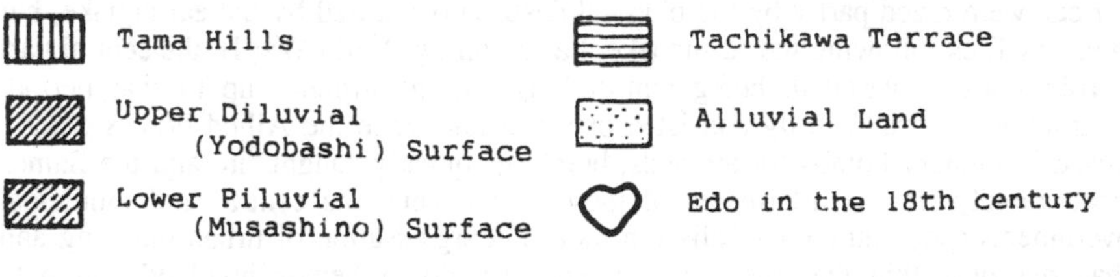

Fig.1 Landform of the Tokyo Area (ca.1960)
(M.Suzuki 1988)

of distinguishing the central government merely resulted, however, in the establishment of dispersed Western-style buildings housing bureaucratic and business functions and standing on the grounds once occupied by *daimyo* and samurai [8]. The second project aimed at decorating the street connecting the alien residential district of Tsukiji and Shimbashi Railway Station. But because of the strong opposition of the resident indigenous merchants, and also because of financial difficulties (it would have been necessary to import all the building bricks from England), this project failed to be realised [13].

In the Meiji period, modernisation was considered almost synonymous with Westernisation, and the government and large private enterprises attempted to introduce Western-style architecture, not as an integral part of a total city plan but in the shape of individual buildings. The result was a diversity of "Western" construction styles taking over the old *daimyo* compound sites, without any consideration whatsoever for the harmony of the city scene as a whole or the city skyline. Western observers of this period reported that Tokyo was not a city but a huge village; and this was understandable since the creation of a diversity of mansion-type buildings was conceivable only in the countryside. In the Meiji period, with the construction of railways, the fluvial and canal traffic system gradually began to lose its importance; but business centres, such as the Nihonbashi district, were still to be found on the wharves and at the foot of bridges as in the preceding Edo period.

In the *yamanote* of the Meiji period, the style of buildings changed as did the type of inhabitants, but land division and the traffic network remained fundamentally unchanged from the Edo period. In the *shitamachi*, only a few private companies such as the Mitsui concern, constructed new Western-style buildings; but *shitamachi* people showed more resistance, at least till the beginning of this century, to changes in the city's urban design; moreover, being traditionally a static rather than dynamic society, they continued to pursue the activities of their forebears [2,16]. But after the Meiji Restoration, merchants and craftsmen no longer constituted an official social class.

3 Influence of Western Urban Design in Tokyo

Within this century, Tokyo has twice undergone disastrous destruction. In 1923, on the occasion of the Kanto earthquake, major parts of Tokyo,especially the *shitamachi* districts, were razed partly by the physical destruction caused by the earthquake, but mainly by fires following the earthquake. Later, during World War II, the central part of Tokyo was devastated, being almost burnt to the ground; up to that period, construction material mostly consisted of wood and since the Allied Forces chiefly utilised incendiary bombs for air raids, buildings quickly caught fire and the flames spread rapidly. In the aftermaths of these two events, the central and municipal governments each time envisualised a radical reorganisation of urban planning and urban design within the frame of the reconstruction schemes involved. On both occasions, however, the transformation of Tokyo along these lines was only partially realised. Moreover the respective circumstances and results of the partial and limited achievements regarding these two events differed somewhat, as follows:

The beginning of this century saw the start of the development of modern manufacturing in the *shitamachi* areas. With the population increase, urban areas in the *yamanote* commenced to expand beyond the municipal boundaries of Tokyo. The Minister of Internal affairs, Shimpei Goto, had been mayor of Tokyo for three years until five months before the occurrence of the Kanto earthquake of 1923. After the

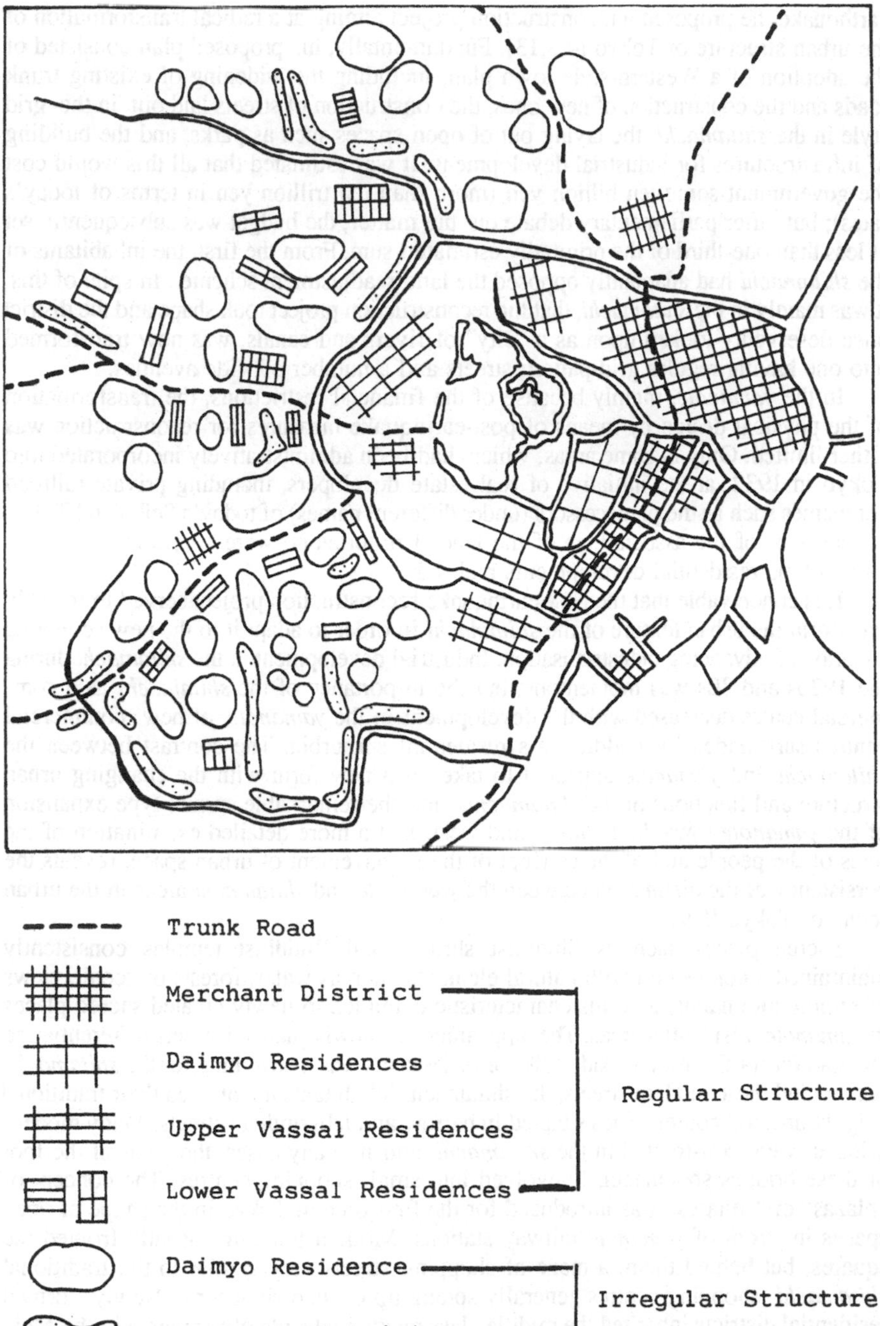

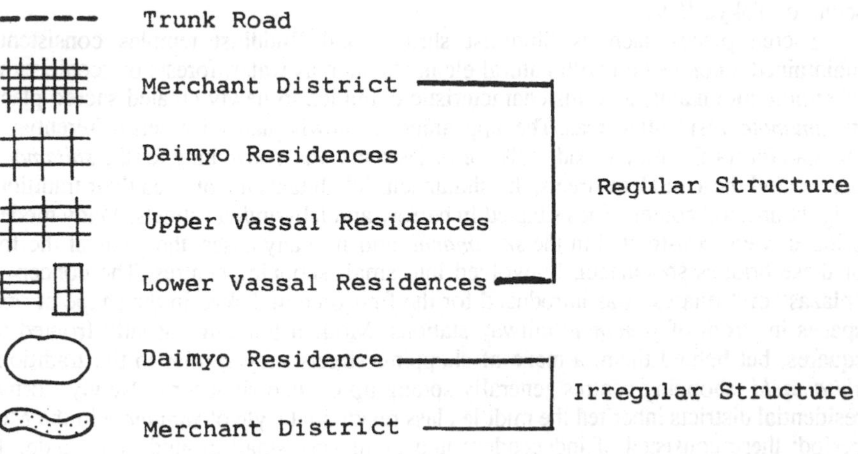

Fig.2 Schematic land use map of Edo (H.Jinnai 1985)

earthquake, he proposed a reconstruction project aiming at a radical transformation of the urban structure of Tokyo [4,8,13]. Fundamentally, his proposed plan consisted of the adoption of a Western-style town plan, including the widening of existing trunk roads and the construction of new ones, the construction of streets laid out in the grid style in the *shitamachi*, the laying out of open spaces such as parks, and the building of infrastructures for industrial development. It was estimated that all this would cost the government some ten billion yen (more than ten trillion yen in terms of today's rates); but after parliamentary debate on the matter, the budget was subsequently set at less than one-third of the originally estimated sum. From the first, the inhabitants of the *shitamachi* had adamantly opposed the land readjustment scheme. In spite of this, it was mainly in the *shitamachi*, that the reconstruction project took shape and the district once deservedly looked upon as a "city" of rivers and canals, was now transformed into one having regular grid-pattern streets and a number of wide avenues.

In the *yamanote*, mainly because of the financial restrictions, the transformation of the physical design by means of post-earthquake measures for reconstruction was rather limited. Only in some areas, which had been administratively incorporated into Tokyo in 1932, at the initiative of real estate developers, including private railroad companies such as the predecessors (under different names) of today's Seibu and Tokyu concerns or of the associations of the landed proprietors, were a certain number of garden-type residential developments realised.

It is conceivable that the post-earthquake reconstruction project served to forcibly transform the urban texture of the *shitamachi* in order to adapt it to the new economic situation of advancing industrialisation. Industrial development in the *shitamachi* during the 1920s and 30s was momentous, but the importance of the *shitamachi* as a commercial centre decreased with the development in the *yamanote* of new commercial centres surrounded by middle-class residential surburbia. The contrast between the *shitamachi* and *yamanote* appeared to take on a new form with the changing urban structure and functions of the *shitamachi*, and the remarkable sprawl-type expansion of the *yamanote* towards the north and west. But a more detailed examination of the lives of the people and of the concept of the management of urban space, reveals the persistency of the distinction between the *yamanote* and *shitamachi* areas in the urban scene of Tokyo [5,9].

Sacred places such as Shintoist shrines and Buddhist temples consistently maintained a connection with natural elements such as water, forests or scenic views of remote mountains, and this characteristic extended to newly created sacred places in *yamanote* residential areas. The appearance of newly planned streets differentiating the road for traffic from the sidewalk for pedestrians was a new thing for the *shitamachi*; but behind these modern streets, the shitamachi inhabitants maintained their traditional neighbour-hood communities situated in narrow and labyrinthian streets. Many modern bridges were constructed in the *shitamachi*, and in many cases, the areas at the foot of these bridges spontaneously evolved into small shopping centres. The concept of "plazas" or "squares" was introduced for the first time in Tokyo in the shape of open spaces in front of *yamanote* railway stations. Modern buildings usually fronted the squares, but behind them, a maze of shopping streets very similar to the traditional *shitamachi* shopping centres generally sprang up of its own accord. Newly formed residential districts inherited the middle class residential style of *yamanote* in the Meiji period: these consisted of independent houses in very small grounds surrounded by small gardens and hedges. The doors of houses and buildings never opened directly onto the street; there was always a garden, however small, or a strip of ground dividing the building from the street.

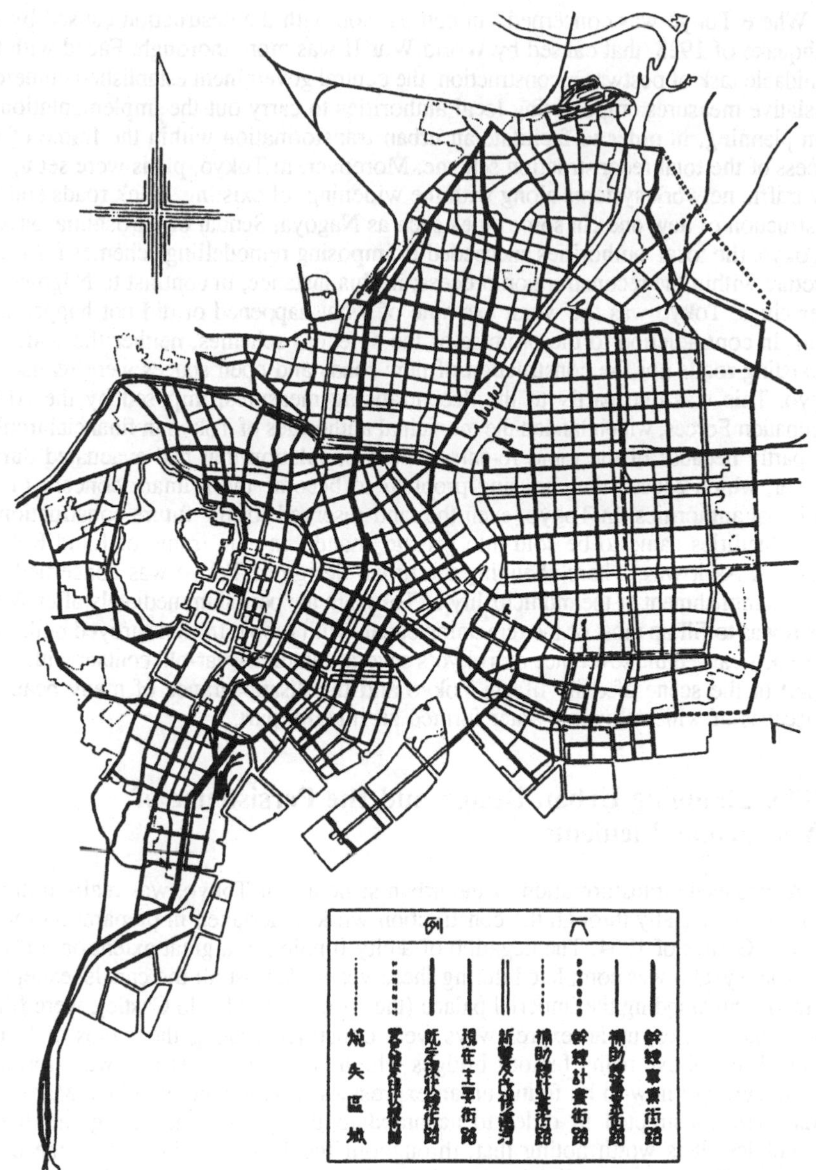

Fig.3 Achieved Reconstruction Project after the 1923 Earthquake (Map made by Ministry of Home Affairs in 1930. Property of Akira Koshizawa and published in his work [8])

Where Tokyo was concerned, in comparison with the destruction caused by the earthquake of 1923, that caused by World War II was more thorough. Faced with the formidable task of postwar reconstruction, the central government established numerous legislative measures empowering local authorities to carry out the implementation of town planning, in order to facilitate an urban transformation within the frame of the process of the total reconstruction scheme. Moreover, in Tokyo, plans were set up for new traffic network systems along with the widening of existing trunk roads and the construction of new ones.In some cities such as Nagoya, Sendai or Hiroshima, as well as Tokyo, the local authorities succeeded in imposing remodelling schemes for urban structure within the reconstruction process; in this instance, in contrast to Nagoya and other cities, Tokyo was the worst example of what happened or did not happen as a result. In contradiction to the promise of the splendid schemes, neither the widening of existing roads nor the construction of new roads and open spaces were realised in Tokyo. This was due partly to the decentralising measures, imposed by the Allied Occupation Forces, which landed the municipal authorities of Tokyo in financial trouble, and partly because of the rapid re-entry of the population that had evacuated during the war, which caused the housing problem to become the primary concern of the municipal authorities. In Tokyo, even the land reserved for the future construction of public facilities came to be sold into private hands, in the frame of Land Reform measures. As it was, where changing the urban design of Tokyo was concerned, the sole accomplishment of the municipality of Tokyo in the period immediately after World War II was to fill up most of the remaining canals with rubble from destroyed buildings. These acts caused the severance of Tokyo's several-hundred-year-old contact with water as part of the scene of daily life in Tokyo and the disappearance of many beautiful landscapes of which flowing water formed an integral part.

4 The Changing Urban Design and the Persistence of Vernacular Elements

A wholesale transformation of the urban structure of Tokyo, was realised during the 1960s, especially through the construction work undertaken in preparation for the Olympic Games of 1964. The negation of a city running to a great extent on a fluvial and canal system was completed during these years. Almost all the canals, except for the moats surrounding the imperial palace (the former site of Edo Castle), were filled, and in many cases, urban expressways were constructed along the routes of former canals. Thus, above many famous bridges which still span roads that were formerly canals, there are now to be found urban expressways with concrete piles. Many new roads were constructed in order to accomodate the rapidly increasing number of automobiles. It is worth noting that, throughout the 1960s, during which the urban structure of Tokyo was radically altered and the heritage of the urban design of Edo/ Tokyo ceased to exist, there was no expression of public opinion or movement to oppose these trends. This was in contrast with other cities such as Kyoto, where already in the 1960s, a civil movement had arisen in protest against constructions such as the Kyoto Tower Building which destroyed the harmony of the traditional urban landscape [6].

In Tokyo, it was only in the 1970s, in the midst of a catastrophic situation involving atmospheric pollution and the worsening of amenities among the inhabitants, that people began to reflect on the consequences of a blind pursuit of economic efficiency. It is very suggestive that, in this process of reflection, a reappraisal of traditional elements in the urban design of Tokyo was carried out. There is now a strong movement towards the restoration of contact with water in the urban life of Tokyo. For instance, after World War II, a number of dikes had been constructed to prevent the flooding of certain *shitamachi* areas which had subsided below sea level in consequence of the excessive pumping up of ground water for industrial use. But these dikes hindered the view of river and sea. Hence, after the middle of the 70s, a decade which to varying degrees reflected a growing concern for the ecology in opposition to the belief that economic supremacy (*keizai shugi*) took priority over other issues, a growing concern for the conservation of the city's cultural heritage and so on, at the strong request of supporters of civil movements, the dikes were finally removed. This action formed part of the so-called waterfront development scheme, and the new dikes substituted for the old restored the view of and access to the water. Utilising the small part of the old canal and fluvial system which fortunately still remained intact, a water-bus service was re-installed and is currently in operation.

After World War II, and especially after the middle of the 1950s, a remarkable increase in the population of Tokyo took place. The Tokyo Metropolitan area, which comprises not only the metropolitan prefecture of Tokyo but also major parts of Kanagawa, Chiba and Saitama Prefectures, now contains about twenty million inhabitants. In line with this population increase, there also occurred a sprawl-type expansion of the urban space, which was essentially a continuation of the urbanisation process following upon the earthquake of 1923. Quantitatively, however, the built-up districts of the Tokyo Metropolitan area have tripled since World War II. Some *yamanote*-type residential areas have been created in the eastern part of the Tokyo Metropolitan area, that is, in Chiba Prefecture, and *shitamachi*-type commercial districts have constantly been created at junctions of the public transportation system, such as areas surrounding suburban railway stations. Where the process of this kind of urban expansion is concerned, private railway companies and real estate agencies have played leading roles.

After the middle of the 1970s, manufacturing industries completely moved out of the central part of the Tokyo Metropolitan area, where due to the concentration of tertiary activities, especially managerial functions, the price of land has enormously increased. Consequently, the residential population in the sectors urbanised before 1923 has drastically decreased. The drastic decrease of the residential population, or the expansion of the CBD in this central part of the Metropolitan area, has resulted in urban renewal or the realisation of a redevelopment scheme; and with the construction of numerous new skyscrapers, the skyline of this central part has undergone a complete change.

In spite of this apparently extensive transformation, it is still possible to discern the continuing existence or persistence of many elements obviously carried over from the past and applied to the present-day management of urban space in Tokyo. Today the CBD covers an area almost equal to the total area of Tokyo in the nineteenth century. But we can still discover a visible contrast between the northern and western parts of Tokyo and the eastern parts of the Tokyo Metropolitan area, which are expansions of the *yamanote* and *shitamachi*, respectively. Gentrified or upper class residential districts are generally found only in the northern and western parts of the Tokyo Metropolitan area, while the eastern sector is generally considered a low-income residential district. Not only does this economic segregation still persist, but a difference in construction patterns and the character of the neighbourhood communities is also evident. In the western and northern parts independent houses owned by the inhabitants and standing in their own small grounds or gardens predominate; while in the eastern parts, a profusion of closely-packed houses and condominiums are generally to be found. The participation of the inhabitants in neighbourhood community events, such as local fetes, is much more active in the eastern parts.

Tokyo's CBD is currently the center of a world-wide financial and informational network. Nonetheless, the landscape still conforms to the Tokyo of the days prior to the development of the CBD. Every skyscraper has been constructed independently of other buildings, with its own design and functions and standing in its own plot designated by the landowner or developer. At no time has there even been an attempt at creating an integrated landscape design incorporating the street or the district as a whole; hence the cityscape is a mixture of various architectural styles, the skyline is jagged and there are gaps between the buildings—all buildings including skyscrapers are required to observe a certain ratio between the built-up space and the open space. This mode of erecting a skyscraper is the same as that applied to constructions in the Meiji period when independent Western-style edifices were built on the comparatively large plots formerly designated as sites of *daimyo* residences.

Tokyo Bay was constantly being reclaimed even in modern times, right up to the middle of the 1960s. Newly reclaimed land used to be invariably designated for industrial and port facilities. Reclamation work after the middle of the 60s took place with even greater rapidity in consequence of the increase in availability of fill-up material resulting from urban development in hilly areas and redevelopment work in the central part of the Tokyo Metropolitan area. After the middle of the 1970s, the development of new residential and business areas, newly reclaimed land and evacuated former industrial land came to the fore. The fact that, in these newly developed areas, the contact with water as a scenic element in recreational spaces has been revived is an important one, since it is the restoration of an element missing since the time of the post-earthquake and, particularly, the post-World War II era. Many trunk roads have been widened in the last thirty years in the course of adapting to the age of the automobile. But surprisingly enough, the pattern of the road network is fundamentally still unchanged from that of the Edo period. The only exceptions, perhaps, are the sectors where the land readjustment scheme was actualised at the time of the post-earthquake reconstruction.

5 Concluding Remarks

The persistence to this day of the original ground plan of the traffic network dating back to the Edo period could be interpreted as the expression of failure on the part of the authorities in the imposition of a comprehensive town planning on modern Tokyo. But it is also possible to consider that the adaptation to topographic conditions, including the happy association with water and the division between *yamanote* and *shitamachi* constitute the fundamental urban culture of Tokyo, and no urban planning has been able to disregard this culture. The division of *shitamachi* and *yamanote* has never been considered by the people as a policy imposed on society for the purpose of social segregation in modern Tokyo; rather, it is an expression of differences in the concepts pertaining to "residing", to the constructing of buildings and the establishing of work places. In connection with these distinctions, sprawl-type urban expansion is proper to the *yamanote* and water-ward expansion is proper to the *shitamachi*. At present, *yamanote*-type districts and *shitamachi*-type districts can no longer be found at their original sites, since all of the original built-up areas of Tokyo have been taken over by the modern CBD. But in both *shitamachi* and *yamanote* areas. Natural elements including the view of remote mountains play important roles in the formation of urban landmarks in the Tokyo Metropolitan area, which has, for instance, more than a hundred streets with Fujimidori (Street with a View of Mount Fuji) as a place name.

To understand the signification of the urban design of a city or to read the city as a text, it is necessary to know the grammar of urban design as language. The grammar of Edo/Tokyo as a Japanese city has many features in common with the grammar of other Japanese cities: traditionally, for example, natural materials are utilised in construction, or the acceptance of Western influence has been selective and so on. The transformation of the urban landscape of Tokyo since its origin, and especially after it became the capital of modern Japan in 1868, has been extraordinary. perhaps more so than in any of the cities of Japan. In spite of this apparent drastic transformation, however, the striking persistence of fundamental elements in the urban design of Tokyo may yet be observed; the planning authorities are compelled to take these elements into consideration even today, for the reason that they are considered proper to Tokyo, regardless or because of their origin. This indicates the fact that historical and cultural elements may very well be largely responsible for the building up of steady mental models of an urban environment, which survive the physical renewal and functional modernisation of the city.

References

1. A. Berque: Paroles sur la ville et expression urbaine, Tokyo années quatre-vingt. In: A. Berque (ed.): La qualité de la ville. Urbanité française, urbanité nippone. Tokyo: Maison Franco-japonaise 1987, pp. 8-15

2. T. Fujimori: Meiji no Tokyo keikaku (Urban planning of Tokyo in the Meiji period) Tokyo: Iwanami 1991

3. M. Gottdiener: Culture, ideology, and the sign of the city. In: M. Gottdiener and A. Ph. Lagopoulos (eds.): The city and the sign. An introduction to urban semiotics. New York: Columbia University Press 1986, pp. 202-218

4. H. Ishizuka: Nihon kindai toshiron: Tokyo 1868-1923 (The city in modern Japan: Tokyo 1868-1923). Tokyo: Tokyo Daigaku Shuppankai 1991

5. H. Jinnai: Tokyo no kukan jinruigaku (Spatial anthropology of Tokyo) Tokyo: Chikuma 1985

6. H. Jinnai: Changement morphologique et continuité de la ville. In: A. Berque (ed.): La qualité de la ville. Urbanité française,urbanité nippone. Tokyo: Maison Franco-japonaise 1987, pp. 73-80

7. H. Jinnai: Yawarakai toshi kozo (Soft urban structure). In: S. Ogi (ed.): Edo Tokyo wo yomu (Reading Edo/Tokyo). Tokyo: Chikuma 1991, pp. 11-24

8. A. Koshizawa: Tokyo toshikeikaku monogatari (Story of the city planning of Tokyo). Tokyo: Nihon Keizaihyoron 1991

9. F. Maki: Miegakure suru toshi (The city now in and now out of sight). Tokyo: Kajima Shuppankai 1980

Toward a Behavioral Theory of Regionalization

Albert Z. Guttenberg

Department of Urban and Regional Planning
University of Illinois at Urbana-Champaign

Abstract. This paper addresses the problem of regionalization from a social science perspective. The author presents a theory of regionalization based on an elementary model of human action. Regions are classified according to the various phases of adaptive human behavior which they represent. The dynamism of regions is shown to derive from the interaction of these phases. Examples are given of how regions generate regions. The paper calls attention to the often unanticipated political consequences of scientific regionalization.

1 Introduction

The purpose of my paper is to present to this gathering my work on a behavioral theory of regionalization, a subject intimately related to the theme of the present Congress. The theme of the Congress, "From Space to Territory" is implicitly a call for theories of regionalization.

How does space become regionalized? How does it become human territory?[1] These are questions with a history. Almost 60 years ago the National Resources Committee, a New Deal agency, produced a landmark report on the origins and programs of "chorography", the ancient name for the practice of describing regions upon the earth's surface. It also, perhaps for the first time, used the modern term "regional science." The Committee reviewed and gave examples of a great number of regions of various types and identified the motives that produce them. In this respect its report anticipated the point of view of the present paper (National Resources Committee, 137-233).

2 What is a Region ?

Every science has some phenomenon as its object. Social science has society, economic science the economy, political science the polity. Presumably, the object of the science of regions is "regionality," the observable division of space (and time) into regions. But what is a region? Generations of social scientists, natural scientists and public administrators have argued over the matter without reaching any generally satisfactory conclusions. Sometimes their frustration has declined into a weary cynicism as exemplified by the following observations:

10. A. Ph. Lagopoulos: Semiotic urban models and modes of production: A socio-semiotic approach. In: M. Gottdiener and A. Ph. Lagopoulos (eds.): The city and the sign. An introduction to urban semiotics. New York: Columbia University Press 1986, pp. 176-201

11. A. Naito: Edo to Edojo (Edo and Edo Castle). Tokyo: Kajima Shuppankai 1966

12. T. Okamoto: Toshi senta to shite no Marunouchi no hensen (Changes in Marunouchi as an urban center). In: S. Ogi (ed.): Edo Tokyo wo yomu (Reading Edo/Tokyo). Tokyo: Chikuma 1991, pp. 125-146

13. T. Shibata: Gendai toshiron (The contemporary city). Tokyo: Tokyo Daigaku Shuppankai 1967

14. M. Suzuki: Edo no Toshikeikaku (Town planning of Edo). Tokyo: Sanseido 1988

15. T. Tamai: Edo: Ushinawareta toshi kukan wo yomu (Edo: Reading the lost urban space). Tokyo: Heibonsha 1986

16. T. Tamai: Yomigaeru Meiji no Tokyo: Tokyo 15 ku shashin-shu (Meiji Tokyo restored: A collection of photographs of 15 Tokyo wards). Tokyo: Kadokawa Spazio 1992

17. A. Tamura: Edo Tokyo machizukuri monogatari (Story of the formation of Edo/Tokyo) Tokyo: Jijitsushin 1992

18. P. Waley: Tokyo: City of Stories. New York-Tokyo: Weatherhill 1991

"A region means an area which a researcher gets a grant to study," (Edward Hoover quoted in Gore, 1984).

"..defining regions precisely is such a nightmare that most regional economists prefer to shy away from the task and are relieved when they are forced to work with administrative regions on the grounds that policy considerations require it, or that data are not available for any other spatial units," (Harry Richardson quoted in Gore).

If defining "region" is frustrating it is in part because of the notion that the word refers to something entirely objective out there which can be identified and whose measure can be taken as though it were solely a natural-world object. In fact, this belief is a delusion, as I shall argue here.

Kenneth Boulding has defined the term "region" as any amount of space or time treated as a unit (Boulding 1985: 19-32). This definition is admirable in its conciseness and comprehensiveness. By including time as a regionable dimension it implies that the study of regions ought also to encompass regions of time, that is, *eras* as well as *areas* -- a fascinating proposition but one that we cannot stop to examine here. Boulding's definition, moreover, doesn't take us very far. It is too general. It leaves us adrift in a sea of possibilities without any idea of what regions are other than that they are units of space, spatial entities, "things".

More useful is Derwent Whittlesey's contribution, upon which my own work is based. A region, Whittlesey wrote, "...is...an entity for purposes of thought, created by the selection of certain factors that are relevant to an areal interest and by the disregard of all features that are considered irrelevant" (Whittlesey 1954, 30). The operative terms here are the words "selection" and "interest". They indicate that regions are a behavioral, not a natural, phenomenon. It is men and women who make regions and they do so in order to understand and manage themselves and the world in which they live. Humankind creates regions as spiders spin webs -- it is a characteristic of the species. Conceivably, it has its most profound roots in animal territoriality.

Given this interpretation of regionalization as a form of adaptive human behavior, the next logical step is to ask: What are the various modes or phases of this behavior? This is a crucial question for it can yield the major kinds of regionalization of which humankind is capable, as well as a taxonomy of regions. In previous writings I have gone into considerable detail in presenting a typology of regions from a behavioral standpoint (Guttenberg, 1977, 1988). In this paper I can only summarize them.

3 Types of Region

Human behavior is motivated by and gives expression to two kinds of knowledge: (1) knowledge for its own sake and (2), knowledge for the sake of human betterment. The latter is divisible into three sub-types: (2a) knowledge about the state of human welfare and the conditions affecting it; (2b) technical knowledge which is concerned with actions that are supposed to bring about an improved state of affairs; and (2c) that knowledge which is a kind of practical dreaming and whose purpose is to keep humankind's gaze focussed on its ideals. When projected spatially, each of these types or sub-types of adaptive knowledge results in a particular kind of region. For purposes of clear reference in the following discussion I have numbered these knowledge Types 1-4.

Where the purpose is knowledge for its own sake (Type 1), regionalization takes the form of reference to (description and analysis of) natural and cultural variations in space. The products are natural and cultural spatial entities: Here is a desert. There is an ocean. Here is an area where the French language predominates. There, most people are English speakers, etc. I call such regions *referential regions.*

Another type of regionalization (Type 4) goes beyond the objective features of the natural or man-made environment. It gives expression to social visions, or the aspirations of certain visionaries. The products might be called *optative regions*, that is, regions expressing a deep wish or desire. Optative regionalization would fashion the world closer to the heart's desire. An example is Pearcy's "38-State United States" which would "perfect" the political the map of the United States in line with certain natural, economic and cultural ideals.

Between these two polar types representing, respectively, the real and the ideal functions of knowledge, there are two kinds of intermediate regions -- *appraisive regions* and *prescriptive regions.* Both types are spatial entities for purposes of social betterment, but each one represents a different phase in the betterment process.[2]

Type 2a, appraisive regions, are spatial entities for the purpose of characterizing the quality of human (or non-human) life. Consequently, they color the map with value terms. Some examples are those areas designated in many countries as "poor or lagging" because they are places of low-income, high unemployment, deficient education and a variety of other social and economic ills. Other areas are characterized as "hazardous" because there is in danger from natural causes (e.g. hurricanes, earthquakes, tornadoes or floods) or from man-made hazards, such as areas subject to air pollution, flooding, etc.

Prescriptive regions, (Type 2b) are spatial entities for the purpose of taking action in the face of perceived social and environmental ills. Land use zoning is a good example of prescriptive regionalization, as are the creation of historic preservation districts, wilderness areas, mosquito abatement districts, national parks, enterprise zones, etc. The latter are one-function prescriptive regions. Type 2b also includes multi-function prescriptive regions, such as cities, states or provinces, and nations. What all these quite diverse spatial entities have in common is that they exist for the purpose of regulating and controlling the activity within them.

4 Dynamics -- How Regions Generate Regions

If the science of regionalization is not to remain a science of static spatial entities it must be concerned with the dynamics of regions. What kinds of change occur in the landscape of regions? What forces cause these changes? A comparison of the way regional change is generally conceived and the way it is conceived here is useful for understanding regionalization as a behavioral process.

In many regional studies the regions appear as static entities (e.g. New England, the Great Plains, etc.). What changes in them is the quantity or quality of their economic, social, political or demographic content, a content for which they serve as convenient, boxlike containers. The population or the wealth or a particular kind of economic activity may wax or wane in one of these boxes, or it may flow from one of them to another, but the boxes themselves never change. The dynamics of this type of region are the dynamics of the content, whereas what is needed for an adequate theory of regions is the dynamics of the box itself.

There are, of course, many other regional studies in which the containers do change. These are studies in which an economic region may be shown to shrink or expand, or shift its geographic center, or migrate from one part of the country to another, or even to another country. An example of several decades ago was the migration of the American textile industry from New England to the South. A current example is the breakup and dispersal of the American automobile-producing region centered in Detroit. But in these cases, the term region refers to a spatially extended but moveable socio-economic system rather than to a fixed and invariant geographic entity, such as the city of Detroit.[3]

The special concern of the present paper is with regional dynamics of quite another sort -- not with the movement of a socio-economic system in physical space, but with movement understood as the generation of one kind of region by another, those that I have named the referential, appraisive, prescriptive and optative regions. If these various regional types may be regarded as having their sources in different phases of human action -- referring, valuing, acting, imagining, etc. -- then regions appear not as mere spatial things but rather as moments in a train of intelligent, willed acts, a manifestation of purposeful human thought. Regionalization is man thinking and behaving in spatial categories. The various phases of this behavior will then appear as a set of regions, logically revealing themselves in space and sequentially in time.

The best way to convey the meaning of inter-regional dynamics in the sense in which I am using it here is by means of a very simple example.

Consider Figure 1, which is an illustration from an article by Frank and Deborah Popper (1986). Frank is an urbanist and his wife, Deborah, a geographer. The shaded area in Figure 1 is an outline of the Great Plains, comprising parts of the states of North Dakota, South Dakota, Nebraska, Kansas, Oklahoma, Montana, Wyoming, Colorado and Texas. From a climatological standpoint, the Great Plains is one of America's natural regions characterized by subhumid conditions; average rainfall is less than 20 inches per year. As a natural spatial entity, it falls in the category of a referential region. In the early years of the present century, the Great Plains was the scene of considerable immigration of peasants from Europe as well as of migrants from the teeming cities of the eastern seaboard. In years when there was greater than average rainfall, the efforts of these farmers flourished, but frequently they, and the soil which they cultivated, were devastated by frequent droughts. There were farm foreclosures, loss of topsoil and many other ills of a failed agriculture. The Great Plains became the scene of considerable economic and social distress and it was

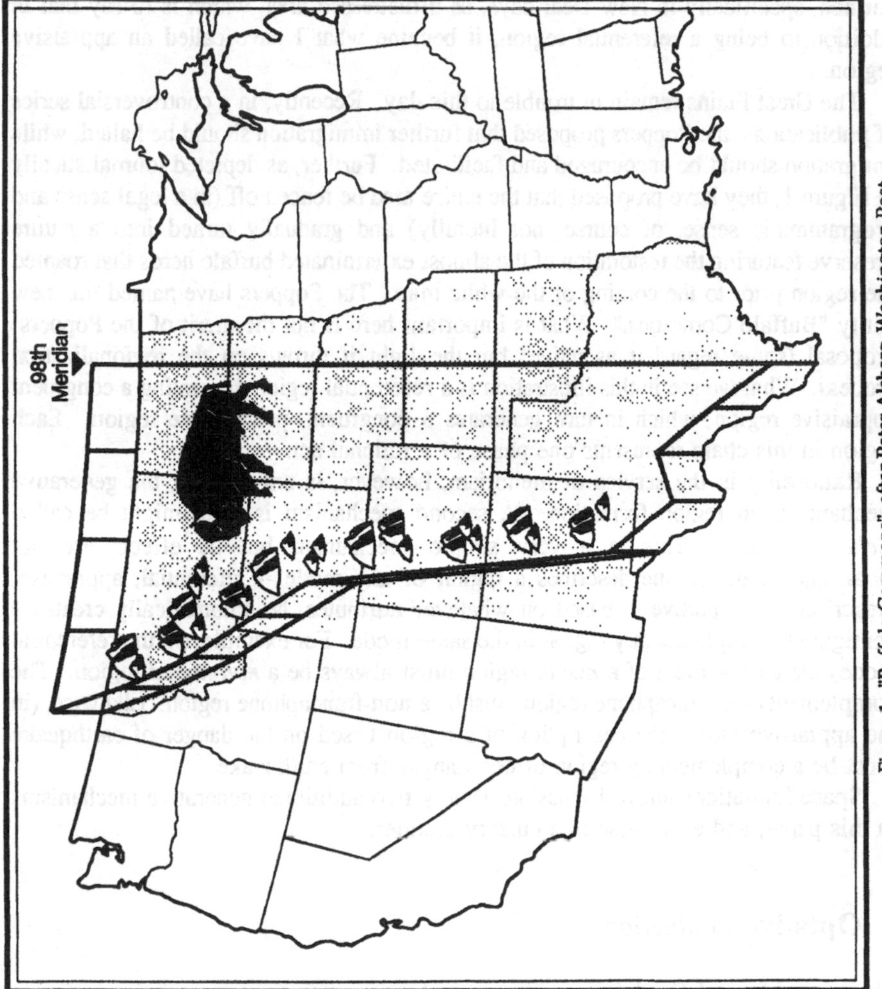

Figure 1. "Buffalo Commons", after Peter Alsberg, Washington Post.

defined, specifically in New Deal days, as a distressed area, which is to say that in addition to being a referential region, it became what I have called an appraisive region.

The Great Plains remain in trouble to this day. Recently, in a controversial series of publications, the Poppers proposed that further immigration should be halted, while emigration should be encouraged and facilitated. Further, as depicted journalistically in Figure 1, they have proposed that the entire area be fenced off (in a legal sense and programmatic sense, of course, not literally) and gradually turned into a nature preserve featuring the restoration of the almost exterminated buffalo herds that roamed the region prior to the coming of the white man. The Poppers have named this new entity "Buffalo Commons." What is important here is not the merit of the Poppers' proposal (some regard it as naive) but the light it throws on the regionalization process. What we see in this illustration is a referential region generating a congruent appraisive region, which in turn generates a congruent, prescriptive region. Each region in this chain represents one phase of a rational act.

Rationality in the service of meliorism, however, is only one of the generative mechanisms in region formation. A second mechanism is what might be called *dichotomization.* This is a very simple mechanism but its effects are not inconsequential. If one describes a region of any mode -- referential, appraisive, prescriptive or optative -- based on whatever attributes, he automatically creates a contiguous, complementary region in the same mode. For example, (in the referential mode) the complement of a *humid* region must always be a *non-humid* region. The complement of a francaphone region must be a non-francaphone region. Likewise, (in the appraisive mode) the description of a region based on the danger of earthquake must be a complementary region of non-danger from earthquake.

Space limitations allow discussion of only two additional generative mechanisms in this paper, and even these in a cursory manner.

5 Optative Projection

Elsewhere I have defined this mechanism as the propensity of a prescriptive region to give rise to two types of optative region, one type smaller than itself (a micro-optative region) which it wholly contains, and the other larger than itself (a macro-optative region) by which it is wholly contained (Figure 2), (Guttenberg 1988, 377-78).

Optative projection is a response to the strains imposed on a society by its prescriptive regions.

As noted above, prescriptive regions are spatial entities for the purpose of control and governance. They include not only entities for the control of single functions, such as land use zones and mosquito abatement districts, but also entities for the control of more than one function. The greater the number of functions a region controls, the closer it is to being a governmental or political region, such as a city, state, province or nation. In short, cities, states and nations are simply the most complex prescriptive regions, controlling the full constitutional range of the activities of their inhabitants. Prescriptive regions are in many instances the products of

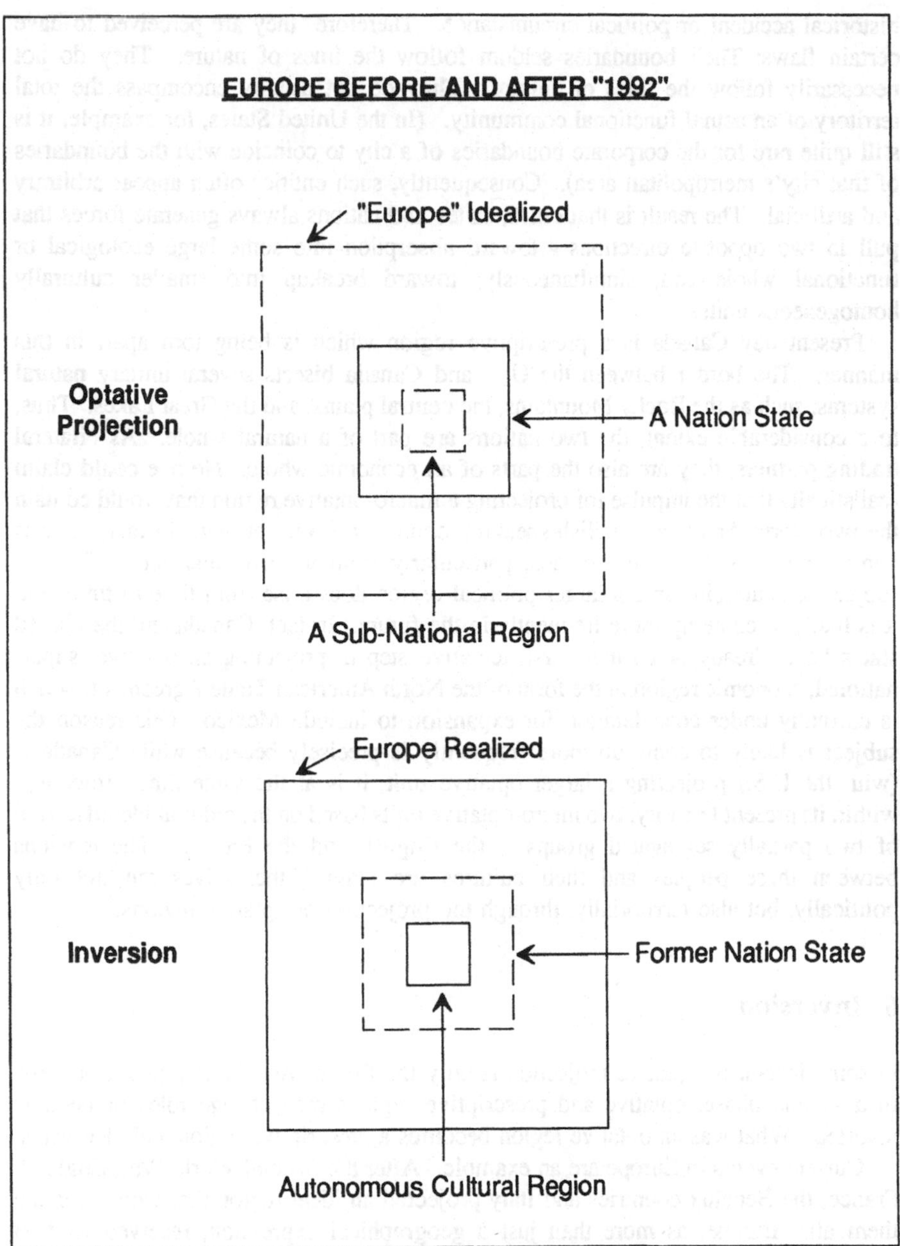

Figure 2. The Projection-Inversion Sequence

historical accident or political circumstance. Therefore they are perceived to have certain flaws: Their boundaries seldom follow the lines of nature. They do not necessarily follow the lines of culture. They do not usually encompass the total territory of an actual functional community. (In the United States, for example, it is still quite rare for the corporate boundaries of a city to coincide with the boundaries of that city's metropolitan area). Consequently, such entities often appear arbitrary and artificial. The result is that cities, states and nations always generate forces that pull in two opposite directions - toward absorption into some large ecological or functional whole and, simultaneously, toward breakup into smaller culturally homogeneous units.

Present day Canada is a prescriptive region which is being torn apart in this manner. The border between the U.S. and Canada bisects several unitary natural systems, such as the Rocky Mountains, the central plains, and the Great Lakes. Thus, to a considerable extent, the two nations are part of a natural whole. As bilateral trading partners, they are also the parts of an economic whole. No one could claim realistically that the impulse for projecting a macro-optative region that would contain the two North American English-speaking countries is very strong. In fact, there is considerable resistance to the idea, particularly from the Canadian side. But the subject of coalescing into a larger political region does arise from time to time, and it is likely to come up more frequently in the future. In fact, Canada and the United states have already taken their first, tentative step in projecting an optative, super-national, economic region in the form of the North American Trade Agreement, which is currently under consideration for expansion to include Mexico. One reason the subject is likely to come up more frequently is precisely because while Canada is (with the U.S.) projecting a larger optative unit, it is at the same time projecting, within its present territory, two micro-optative units based on the cultural identification of two partially segregated groups -- the English and the French. The tensions between these peoples and their cultures are playing themselves out not only politically, but also territorially, through the projection of optative regions.[4]

6 Inversion

In some instances, optative projection is only the first phase of a two-phase process. In a second phase, optative and prescriptive regions may change roles or become inverted. What was an optative region becomes a prescriptive region and vice versa.

Current events in Europe are an example. After the Second World War, England, France, the Benelux countries and Italy projected an ideal region that would contain them all. Europe, as more than just a geographical expression, received its first definite recognition in the Treaty of Rome in 1957. At the same time each of these countries also dreamed of sending power back to its ancient cultural regions. In fact, most have experimented with some degree of denationalization. These two opposed forces -- the ideal of a European super-community and the ideal of a Europe of sub-national (in some cases pre-national) cultural regions represent the optative projection phase of post-World War II regionalization. The inversion phase has been in progress for some time and is scheduled to culminate in 1992 with the transfer of important components of sovereignty from the nations to the new European Community. There is no certainty that "1992" will ever arrive, but if it does what will be the outcome? What use will Brussels and the regional capitals make of each other? Will they be stout allies against any threat of resurgent nationalism? Or will the regions regret their independent-mindedness and seek to reinstate the nation as a buffer against the power of Europe? In England as well as in some other countries a nationalist reaction against unification already flourishes. Whatever the outcome, the image of future European regionalization that this analysis leaves us with is not that of a relentless linear progression toward a continental nation, but of a Europe always pulsing between its "real" (prescriptive) regions and its "ideal" optative units. One hesitates to allude to the experience of the Soviet Union and Yugoslavia because of the violence with which these originally optative regions were converted into prescriptive regions and the violence with which they are now being torn apart, but they do afford additional examples of the interplay between prescriptive and optative regionalization.

What is occurring at a continental scale in Europe is also taking place in the United States locally. The tendency has been to project simultaneously both large-scale metropolitan regions and small scale neighborhoods as alternatives to the established corporate city. In a few cases (Indianapolis, for example), this process has even proceeded to the inversion stage wherein the metropolitan area has actually succeeded the city as the duly constituted political unit, while the original city or a part of it becomes an object of nostalgia, a kind of romantic, ideal region -- "olde towne" (Guttenberg 1988, 381).

7 Conclusion

There are other, more complex, region-generating mechanisms than the ones briefly examined here. Unfortunately, space limitations will not allow us to discuss them in this paper. However, it has not been the purpose of the paper to be exhaustive, but rather to highlight certain facts about regions and regionalization: Regions are not natural objects. They are, as Whittlesey said, "mental constructs." Regions are not inert objects. They are dynamic spatial entities whose appearance and disappearance mirror adaptive human behavior. They are not sterile objects. Once drawn, they give rise to other regions. As our examples have shown, appraisive regions lead to prescriptive regions, prescriptive regions lead to optative regions which in turn lead to prescriptive regions, and so on. The interplay between regions in different modes is never-ending.

My final point is cautionary. Whether we like it or not, going from space to territory also means getting involved in politics. This applies even in the case of the most disinterested acts of regionalization. When an ecologist draws a line around a particular area and labels it "wetland," there is a good chance that the resulting natural (referential) region will soon be supplemented by a prescriptive region for the purposes of preserving or conserving that wetland. This may be a good thing or a bad thing, depending on the interests affected, but its goodness or badness is not the point here. The point is that to describe a region for whatever purpose, may bring in its wake consequences and controversies that the chorographer never imagined or dreamed of. To "chorographize", therefore, is not an act to be entered into lightly or without forethought. Herein lies a lesson not only for chorographers, but for society as whole.

Notes

1. This suggests another question which we cannot deal with here, notwithstanding its importance: How does space become non-human territory, that is, the territory of non-human species? The two forms of territory, of course, are intimately related.

2. The terms "appraisive" and "prescriptive" are borrowed from Charles Morris, who used them to represent two of the functions of language (Morris, 1946).

3. That such a distinction can exist testifies to the ambiguity that inheres in the term "region": Does it denote the space occupying system -- economic, cultural, political, etc. -- or does it rather denote the absolute space occupied?

4. The United States as yet has not projected any micro-optative region (with the possible exception of Puerto Rico) but the current wave of "multiculturalism" may presage such a development.

References

1. Boulding, Kenneth E. "Regions of Time." *Papers of the Regional Science Association*, 57 (1985).

2. Gore, Charles A. *Regions in Question*. London and New York: Methuen (1984).

3. Guttenberg, Albert Z. "Classifying Regions: a Conceptual Approach." *International Regional Science Review*. 2, Fall (1977).

4. Guttenberg, Albert Z. "Regionalization as a Symbolic Process." *Canadian Journal of Regional Science* XL,3 (1988).

5. Guttenberg, Albert Z. "City Encounter and "Desert" Encounter: Two Sources of American Regional Planning Thought." *Journal of the American Institute of Planners*. (1978).

6. Morris, Charles. *Signs, Language and Behavior*. New York: Prentice-Hall (1946).

7. National Resources Committee. *Regional Factors in National Planning and Development*. Washington, D.C.: Government Printing Office (1935).

8. Pearcy, G. Etzel. *A 38-State U.S.A.* Fullerton, CA: Plycon Press (1973).

9. Popper, Frank and Deborah. "Saving the Plains: The Bison Gambit." *The Washington Post*. B-3, August 6 (1986).

10. Whittlesey, Derwent. "The Regional Concept and the Regional Method." In: P.E. James and C. F. Jones (eds.), *American Geography: Inventory and Prospect*. Syracuse, New York: University of Syracuse Press (1954).

Descriptive Modeling and Prescriptive Modeling in Spatial Data Handling

Bianca Falcidieno - Caterina Pienovi - Michela Spagnuolo

Istituto per la Matematica Applicata del C.N.R.
Via L.B. Alberti, 4
16132 Genova (ITALY)

Abstract. Descriptive and prescriptive modeling are here proposed to devise general and comprehensive Spatial Information Systems, which broaden the role of spatial data modeling from relatively passive inquiry to much more active intent. Descriptive modeling corresponds to a bottom up approach to spatial data organization, and provides tools to extract prominent features from the low level geometric model. Prescriptive modeling involves two aspects: exploration and generation. Exploration of a high level description of spatial data is performed to allocate stated geographical configurations, while the generation of low level descriptive models supports the simulation of geographical phenomena. An implementation of the proposed system architecture is presented with examples of both descriptive and prescriptive modeling in the context of digital terrain modeling.

1 Introduction

In spatial data handling, a great deal of effort has gone into research concerning the improvement of computation techniques and the solution of several problems (e.g. interpolation model, data acquisition, ...), whereas not enough attention has been payed to the modeling aspects and to architectural considerations for the development of more general and comprehensive Spatial Information Systems (SIS). Due to this lack of communication between modeling experts and users, many of the commercial systems seem to be mere data bases customized for the particular context, and spatial data are often considered as attributes of application-specific information.

In contrast to this, the peculiar nature of spatial data suggests a more careful choice of the system architecture, based on the opposite approach, where the model of the spatial data takes the leading role and outlines the framework for the organization of the application knowledge. Obviously, the spatial data model should not be considered as a static structure which simply codes the measures of the natural phenomena, but rather as a set of interrelated models each corresponding to a different level of interaction with the data [1].

Traditional spatial data models are important for the development of specific algorithms (visualization, boolean operations,...) but must be further explored to provide higher levels of abstractions that can relate directly to certain properties of the data and can establish an efficient link between geometry and specific information [2].

The aim of this paper is to outline the scheme of a modeling architecture able to handle with complex spatial data and applications in an integrated manner. The basic idea is to highlight the main aspects of modeling, which could be summarized as representation and simulation of the reality.

The representation of the reality is performed by providing suitable structures to store the data and powerful tools to analyze and synthesize the information. In this paper emphasis is put on the need for abstraction mechanisms which should generate high level data descriptions based on prominent features. For example, the analytical extraction of landforms from a digital terrain model is a complex task which has the aim to generate a rich symbolic description which is one step closer to representing the morphological structure of the surface than the sampling data and requires less storage. This approach is here considered as a *descriptive modeling*, which corresponds to a bottom up approach to the information coding.

In dealing with the nature of spatial data and spatial problems we need some sort of conceptual modeling as developed in computer sciences disciplines that provide valuable intellectual aids for solving out different spatial problems.

In devising a general SIS, however, not only tools for analyzing the data should be provided, but a *prescriptive modeling* should be supported too in order to provide means to simulate the reality by interacting with high level concepts. Let us give an example: suppose we need to simulate a terrain with certain morphological characteristics in order to study the effect of some natural phenomena. A concise description of a landscape could be easily given in terms of high level concepts, for example, two chains of mountains, a narrow valley between them, a river at the bottom of the valley and a broad meadow at the end of the valley. A SIS supporting this kind of prescriptive definition of the scene should be able to generate a surface model by decomposing the described terrain into geometric primitives and by building automatically the corresponding geometric model, thus allowing the user to forget low level operations.

In this view, we propose an integrated architecture for Spatial Information Systems, which is based both on geometric models and on conceptual models. In this architecture, descriptive and prescriptive modeling give the possibility to interact with high level abstractions which can be linked to application concepts and can provide a support to prevision tasks, a very important aspect of future GIS.

The remainder of the paper is organized as follows. In the second section, the descriptive approach to spatial data modeling is explained, while the prescriptive approach is sketched in the third section. In the fourth section, the proposed system architecture is described, where prescriptive and descriptive approaches are combined. In the fifth section, some results are presented concerning an application in the context of digital terrain modeling.

2 Descriptive Modeling

Descriptive modeling can be seen as the bottom-up approach to spatial data, which has the main aim to upgrade the knowledge of the observed natural phenomena by extracting information which are implicitly contained in the initial set of data. A typical flow of operations involved in a descriptive interaction with data is depicted in figure 1.

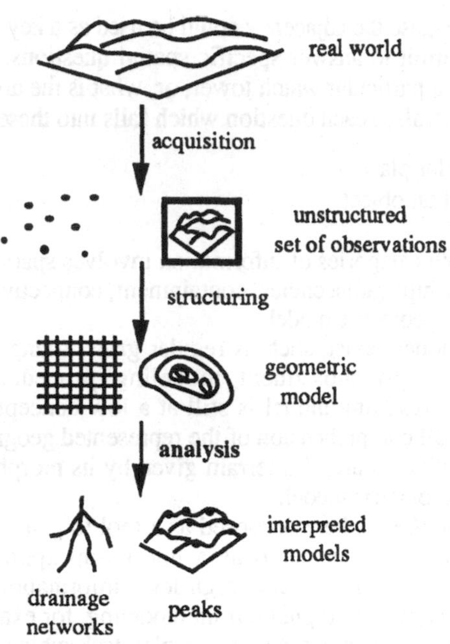

Fig. 1. An example of descriptive interaction with spatial data

In the first phase, which is common and necessary within any SIS, sets of data are acquired from the real world. For example, in the context of digital terrain modeling, data correspond to measures of terrain elevation, while for air pollution studies sets of statistic data will be collected. More precisely, this first level of information consists of original observations of the natural phenomenon, which are generally characterized by *geometric attributes* related to the position (typically triplets of coordinates) and form (dimension, shape...) and by *non geometric attributes* which affect only the geographical meaning (geological data, historical notations, land use, ...). These basic data reflect the best level of knowledge available: if only elevations are collected, then the SIS can handle only this limited information. However, this initial model is not yet a structure suitable for surface modeling and it should be structured and upgraded with the introduction of further information.

Geometric models correspond to a second level of spatial data model and are derived by the basic model through the generation of relationships between individual observations (point, line, polygon topology). The geometric model reflects and highlights the particular nature of spatial data, which can be synthesized by two of its properties: continuity and coherence. In the real geographical world a topographic surface can be visited at any location and thus the geometric model should reflect an underlying view of space as continuous and the need to answer the user who wishes to determine elevation at some arbitrary and precise position. In mathematical terms, the discretized surface should be represented by a continuous approximation of the surface. The spatial coherence is here meant as the tendency for nearby locations to influence each other and to possess similar attributes. Consequently, the geometric model should make the adjacency relationships between its primitive entities (e.g. points, vertices, polygons,...) explicit, because the adjacency could be used as a key to access data.

Geometric models permit to answer specific spatial questions, such as: how much terrain can be seen from a particular watch tower, or, what is the area covered by a type of vegetation, and in general, to each question which falls into these two categories [1]:

- what is in a particular place
- find the position of an object

The determination of both categories of information involves spatial measurements and checking spatial relationships (adjacencies, containment, connectivity,...) which can be directly deduced from the geometric model.

Several geometric models exist, such as regular grids, triangulations or contours, which act as interfaces to subsequent modeling procedures (interpretation, visualization,...) but the resulting model is still at a low conceptual level because it does not support an overall comprehension of the represented geographical phenomena. For example, the qualitative nature of a terrain given by its morphological features, is somehow hidden in the geometric model.

Thus, *descriptive modeling* is here proposed as a tool to generate a further level of spatial data model, and it is considered as a bottom-up approach to spatial data modeling, which allows the user to extract high level information from the low level geometric model. In the context of digital terrain modeling, for example, the automated extraction of topographic features is a rather complex task which has been studied by several authors [3,4,5,6,7]. Methods have been developed mainly for regular grids and with particular attention to the extraction of point and line features.

Descriptive modeling uses powerful interpretation algorithms which perform the analytical extraction of several features in order to generate a richer and more synthetic description, based on prominent features, which codes information in an efficient and effective way. Symbolic descriptions can be regarded as frameworks through which it is possible to point out some properties of interest the surface may have for a specific analysis. The same approach has been adopted in the picture processing context in relation to the similar problem of segmentation. There, the goal is to subdivide an image into maximal disjoint regions each satisfying some uniformity predicate. Image segmentation is usually followed by scene analysis when more global information is used to merge regions and to assign region interpretation.

Symbolic descriptions can be very useful within a SIS not only for the modeling aspects but also because they behave as a directory associated with a computer representation of a natural phenomenon that can be used to facilitate selective access and retrieval of information from the representation. Suppose one wishes to analyze a terrain about the highest peak. Instead of searching the entire digital model to locate this feature, the same information could be easily obtained by interrogating a high level terrain description based on its morphological features. Indeed, when the number of observed points is very large, it becomes essential to determine a procedure to access and retrieve efficiently only those data relevant to the problem at hand in order to avoid the high cost of processing all of the available data points.

3 Prescriptive Modeling

Descriptive modeling is a basic issue in spatial data systems, but alone it is not sufficient to devise comprehensive and efficient systems. Indeed, in each phase of a descriptive interaction, the user has a quite limited role, meaning that he can handle only those data measured from the reality and no tools are given to simulate or predict any natural phenomenon. For this reason, we would like to introduce a new approach to spatial data models that is called *prescriptive modeling*. The aim is to represent facts, to simulate processes, to express judgements or to provide for effective descriptions of geographic phenomena, through sets of properties or constraints. The computer has to generate the potential answers to these descriptions and to present them to the users.

To move from description to prescription, however, implies the development of tools allowing users to describe, generate, explore, visualize and understand classes of geographical phenomena. These techniques broaden the role of modeling from relatively passive inquiry to much more active intent. Descriptive models answer questions, prescriptive models solve problems [8].

The problems addressed by prescriptive models generally involve two different uses of them: exploration and generation (see figure 2).

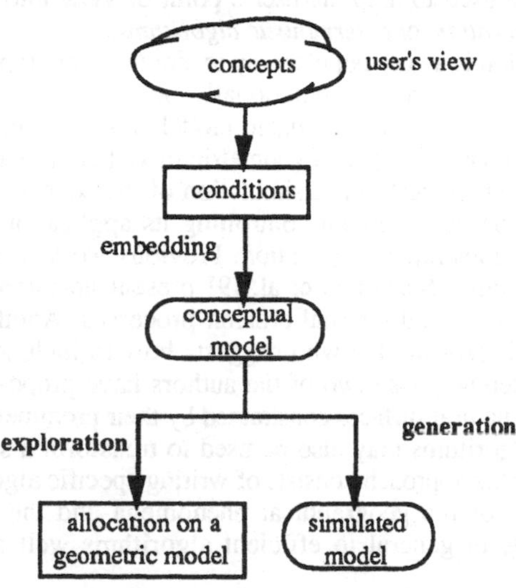

Fig.2. An example of prescriptive interaction with spatial data.

The first use requires a selective exploration of the spatial data model using geometric, topological, geographical properties in order to satisfy stated objectives. This process, also called cartographic *allocation* [8], may range from the siting of a proposed land use to the positioning of fire towers.

The initial statement of an allocation problem is a descriptive task which consists of an explicit specification of some geographic conditions necessary to achieve the stated objective. Different problems occur when stating the set of conditions, properties, or constraints, which should be satisfied by the area of interest:

- defining local or global properties: the first ones are associated to atomic parts of geographic space, while the second ones permit to establish links between groups of locations as integrated wholes;
- providing mechanisms to check the consistency of a set of constraints or the

derivation of new properties when controlling given ones.
The set of conditions expressed by the user defines the *conceptual model* of the spatial phenomena, in a suitable formalism. While it is possible to give a well defined characterization of the geometric model, the definition of conceptual model is harder to give precisely because a detailed definition of the conceptual model depends on the user's requirements. However, it is possible to state some desirable properties of the conceptual model. First of all, it should adhere to the underlying geometric model, so that the interchanges between conceptual and geometric model are possible without troublesome mappings. Then, the conceptual model should be combinatorially less complex than the geometric representation because the conceptual model should be a simplification with respect to the low level description. Following these guide-lines, the conceptual model should be considered as a relational structure which groups sets of low level geometric entities and associates a meaning with these entities.

Another use of prescriptive modeling involves simulation of geographical phenomena, for example to foresee potential site modifications. Two different approaches may be used to map the user's point of view into a simulated geometric model: *random generation* or *deterministic algorithms*.

Random generation is a very popular way to simulate geographical phenomena, since it is very simple to use and computationally not expensive. First, the user has to specify some properties that the simulated model should have, for example by giving its global fractal dimension. Then, a geometric model is automatically generated by a random procedure which performs a simulation of the conceptual model. The random production cannot be used without controlling its application but more properly by applying a sort of constrained generation. Previous work in this category has been published. For example Musgrave et al. [9] present an interesting approach to the simulation of hydraulic and thermal erosion processes. Another approach has been proposed by Mandelbrot in [10] who suggests how to include drainage networks in fractal terrain modeling. Also two of the authors have proposed in [11] a stochastic method to generate natural surfaces constrained by their prominent features.

Deterministic algorithms may also be used to transform a set of constraints into a geometric model. This approach consists of writing specific algorithms which take into account the nature of the geographical phenomena and the relationships with the properties. It leads in general to efficient algorithms well adapted to the desired objectives.

An example of this is an algorithm building a constrained Delaunay Triangulation on a set of points and edges corresponding to surface specific features [12]. Another example of specific algorithm has been proposed by Morris and Flavin [13] to build a hydrologically appropriate digital terrain model. Other papers propose a combination of these two approaches to generate possible solutions which satisfy the prescriptive set of initial conditions.

4 The proposed system architecture

From what we have seen so far, we might hypothesize an "ideal" architecture like that depicted in figure 3, in which both prescriptive and descriptive modeling are integrated.

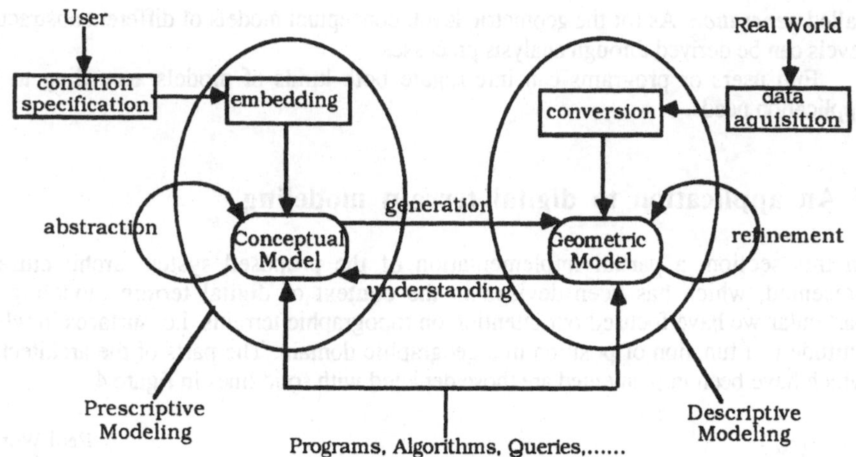

Fig. 3. The proposed system architecture

The system architecture is mainly based on the distinction of the two levels of representation: a *geometric model*, in terms of low level primitive entities, and a *conceptual model*, which is a symbolic representation based on the prominent features of the represented spatial phenomena. It is assumed that the system handles with data somehow acquired from the real world and consisting of quantitative information (coordinates of sample points) and, possibly, qualitative information (attributes, geographical data, ...). Several geometric data models exist, such as regular grids, triangulations or contours, and all of them represent a structured version of the acquired data with their own advantages and disadvantages. At this level the geometric model is not forced to be of any particular kind as different geometric models could be used, according to the user's needs and to the nature of the phenomenon to be represented. However, geometric models play a leading role in the proposed architecture as they represent the background knowledge used by the different applications which should all refer to a geometric representation. The meaning and the structure of a conceptual model has been roughly described in the previous section, where it has been explained that the conceptual model is considered as a tool to link sets of geometric primitives to an application specific interpretation.

The user can handle with these two levels of representation using either a descriptive or a prescriptive interaction.

A typical descriptive activity starts with the acquisition of data from the real world and the conversion of these data into any suitable geometric model. The geometric model can be converted into a conceptual model through *understanding* processes which interpret the low level information and extract high level descriptions of the phenomenon represented by the geometric model. Also, geometric models of different levels of accuracy or fairness can be derived through *refinement* processes.

The prescriptive approach corresponds to a different interaction with data. The first step is the definition a set of conditions (constraints, needs, ...) which will be embedded into a conceptual model, described by using a consistent formalism (entity-relationship, object based, rule based, ...).

Then, the system automatically builds the underlying geometric model by a process called *generation*. As for the geometric level, conceptual models of different abstraction levels can be derived through analysis processes.

End users or programs can interrogate both kinds of models according to the application needs.

5 An application to digital terrain modeling

In this section, a partial implementation of the proposed system architecture is presented, which has been devised in the context of digital terrain modeling. In particular we have focused our attention on topographic terrains, i.e. surfaces in which altitude is a function of position in a geographic domain. The parts of the architecture which have been implemented are those depicted with solid lines in figure 4.

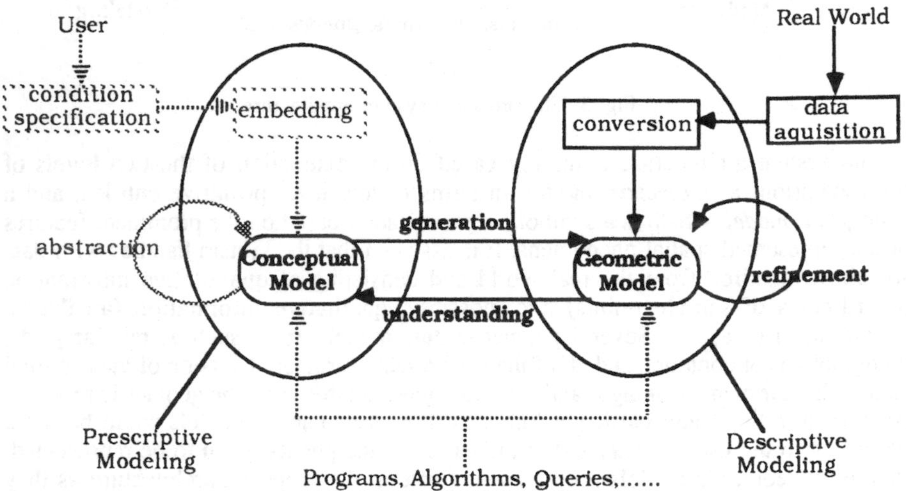

Fig.4. The implemented system architecture

Descriptive modeling deals with sets of elevation data which are acquired from the real world, typically by map digitalization. No assumption is made on the point spatial distribution, which may be regular or irregular. In the conversion step, a triangulation of the sample point is constructed, which is the basis of the adopted geometric model. Indeed, an interpolation based on surface patches preserving the values at the data points is widely considered satisfactory for surfaces of well-distributed data points. Between regular grids and irregular networks, the latter structure has been chosen, since a triangulation can represent a surface at a variable resolution, thus adapting to the local changes and to the roughness of a terrain. For this reason, it is considered the most appropriate data structure for spatial data representation and it has been adopted as the basis of the geometric model used in the implementation of the proposed system architecture. Moreover, in surface approximation problems, an acceptable triangulation is one in which most of the triangles are as equiangular as possible in order to avoid long thin triangles. This criterion is satisfied by *Delaunay triangulation*, considered a standard for surface description [12,14]. The triangulated surface is then represented by a model which makes the adjacency relationships between triangular facets explicit and is defined as a relational graph in which nodes correspond to triangles while arcs correspond to edges shared by two adjacent triangles.

The core of the descriptive approach is the *understanding* operator which has been devised in the context of shape decomposition methods to define a surface characterization based on 2-dimensional shape feature. The understanding operator performs a qualitative curvature analysis of the terrain model and produces a symbolic description of the surface shape, based on its concave, convex, plane and saddle regions. The defined method may be classified as a geometric analysis of the elevation data, and it is mainly based on the idea that combining classical topological techniques with well-known differential geometry can provide simple methods, suitable for computer implementation for evaluating several shape descriptors. First, a geometric classification of the triangulation primitives is performed to enhance the geometric description of the surface. Geometric attributes are assigned to edges, corresponding to the type (concave, convex or plane) of the dihedral angle subtended by the two faces meeting along the edge. Then, the curvature "along" edges and "around" triangles is checked, to extract the surface *characteristic regions*, i.e. regions whose shape can be classified as *concave, convex, plane* or *saddle*. Those regions are defined as particular connected components of the graph surface model and are extracted using a region-growing algorithm which produces a unique surface decomposition, as described in [15]. In figure 5, an example of surface characterization is shown where the convex regions are coloured in white, the concave ones in dark green, the plane regions in light green and finally the saddle regions in red.

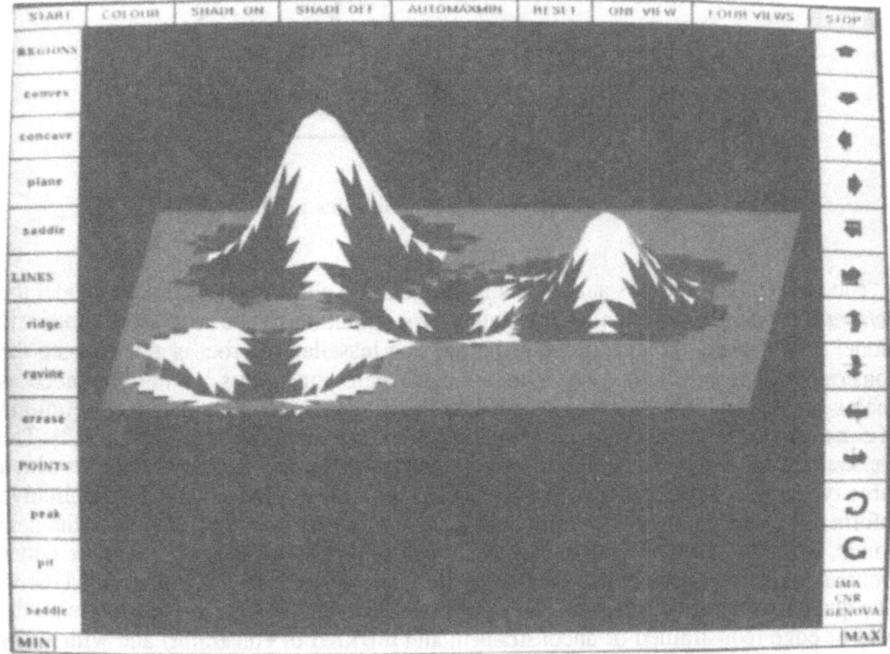

Fig. 5. Understanding operator: the convex regions are coloured in white, the concave ones in dark green, the plane regions in light green and the saddle regions in red.

Two regions never overlap, that is, they can come in contact only through edges belonging to the bounding contours and those edges shared by two region borders define the *characteristic lines* of the surface, which are classified as ridge, ravine or generic crease lines. Similarly, characteristic lines may intersect only at their endpoints and the intersections define the *characteristic points* of the surface, classified as peaks, pits or passes [7]. The resulting conceptual model is the relational structure which encodes the decomposition of the surface by explicitly coding the adjacency relationships between characteristic regions. The structure, called the *Characteristic Region Configuration Graph*, is formally defined as an attributed hypergraph in which characteristic regions correspond to graph nodes, while arcs and hyperarcs represent the relationships between regions defined by the surface characteristic lines and points respectively.

The prescriptive approach is implemented by the *generation* mechanism which operates in two steps. First, the user can specify either a set of conditions describing a certain morphological configuration or a set of parameters defining a global aspect of the surface to be generated. Then, the system automatically produces a triangulation which represents a simulated terrain satisfying the stated conditions.

Let us give an example. Suppose the user wants to simulate a landscape characterized by two mountains meeting at a steep valley. The conceptual model which synthesizes the scene is depicted in figure 6, where each node represents a mountain defined by a closed sequence of edges and by an interior maximum. The arc joining the two nodes represents the valley along which the two mountains should meet.

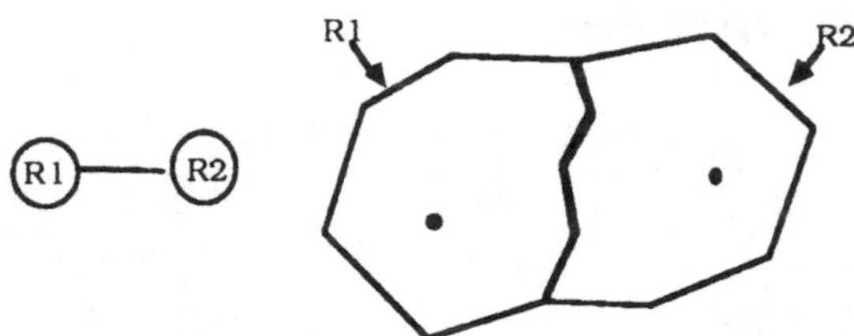

Fig. 6. Conceptual description of two mountains meeting along a valley.

The conceptual model is automatically merged into a low level geometric model the *generation* operator. Assuming a Delaunay triangulation as the low level geometric model of a surface, the generation technique is a tessellation process able to keep the constraints imposed by the conceptual model, where constraints are here intended as chains of edges which must be preserved by the triangulation. To this aim, a definition of *constrained Delaunay triangulation* is required, which has been defined in [12]. The constrained Delaunay triangulation may be represented as a boundary model in which three types of information are stored, namely topological, geometrical and qualitative information. The geometrical information is given by triplets of coordinates of the data points, while the topology of the surface is represented by a graph in which the nodes are triangular faces of the triangulation, the arcs are edges and the hyperarcs are vertices. The qualitative information is coded by attributes associated with every arc to assign the type of edge (constrained or unconstrained, and the kind of constraint) and with every node to assign the type of region to which the triangle belongs (convex, concave, planar, saddle region). In figure 7, the geometric model is depicted corresponding to the conceptual model specified in figure 6, where the constrained primitives are marked by thicker lines.

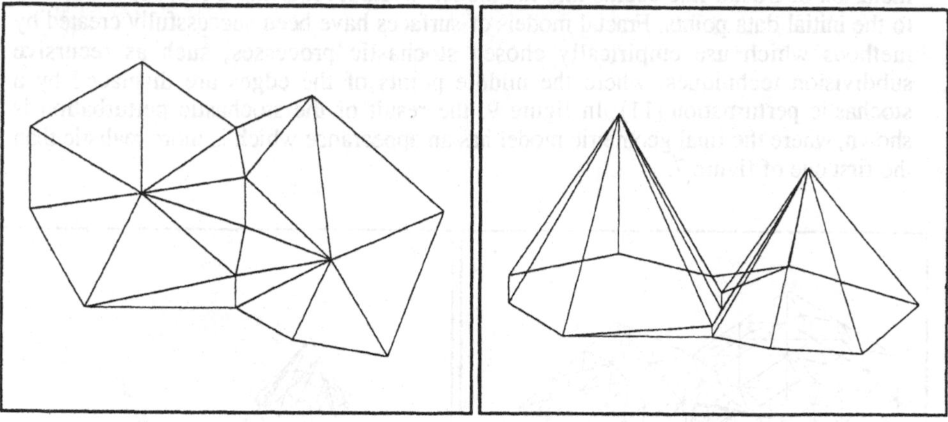

Fig.7. The generated geometric model

Beside the understanding and the generation operator, a *refinement* operator has been defined which can be used to produce refined geometric models of the original conceptual models. Refinement of the basic model may be performed when an approximation closer to a sampled surface is needed because only a subset of the data points have been included as vertices of the model. In figure 8, an example is shown where the basic model has been refined with the introduction of those points giving rise to an approximation error greater than a given tolerance.

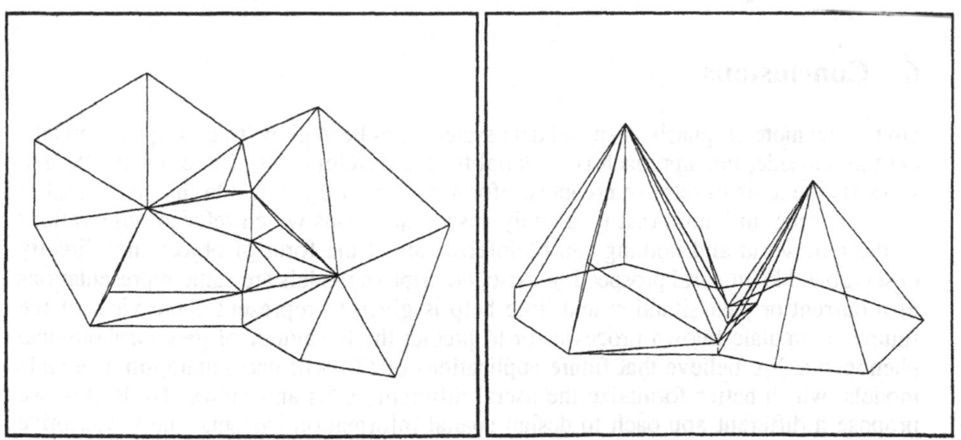

Fig.8. Refinement of the geometric model by introducing further points.

An alternative refinement may be obtained by applying a stochastic perturbation to the geometric model when a realistic visualization is required. This approach permits the inclusion of fractal-like details into the model, without requiring a real approximation to the initial data points. Fractal models of surfaces have been successfully created by methods which use empirically chosen stochastic processes, such as recursive subdivision techniques, where the middle points of the edges are displaced by a stochastic perturbation [11]. In figure 9, the result of the stochastic perturbation is shown, where the final geometric model has an appearance which is more realistic than the first one of figure 7.

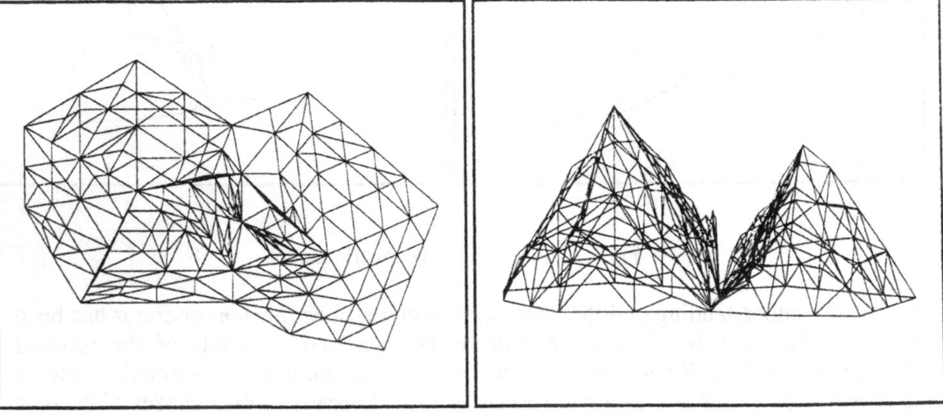

Fig. 9. The geometric model refined with stochastic perturbation.

6 Conclusions

Up to now more emphasis in spatial data systems has been given to descriptive models. On the one side, this approach is essential for the development of intelligent SIS as it supports the tools to retrieve complex information from the data. On the other hand, it has the strong limitation that it can only answer questions which refer to observations of the real world and nothing can be inferred about the form of objects not directly observable, like mineral prospecting. Also, descriptive models are static representations of a current or past situation and little help is given to represent some view of the future to simulate known processes or to predict the behaviour of geomorphological phenomena. We believe that future applications of SIS will necessitate more flexible models, which better formalize the users' different needs and views. To do this, we propose a different approach to design spatial information systems: the prescriptive modeling.

Developing such systems requires to provide description, generation, and understanding tools, together with abstraction and refinement mechanisms. The major point of this approach is that the user has only to specify the set of conditions the overall model has to obey through a list of properties and/or constraints.

The understanding of this formal description and the translation into a classical geometric model are left to the computer.

To be more effective and efficient, prescriptive modeling is integrated with the descriptive way, here considered as a bottom up approach to spatial data modeling which permits to generate symbolic descriptions from low level geometric models.

References

1. R.Laurini, D.Thompson: *Fundamentals of Spatial Information Systems*, Academic Press

2. R.Weiber, M.Heller: A framework for digital terrain modeling. In: K.Brassel,K. Kishimoto (eds.) Proceedings of Spatial Data Handling, (Department of Geography, University of Zürich), 1989, pp. 219-229

3. T.K.Peucker, D.H.Douglas: Detection of surface specific points by local parallel processing of discrete terrain elevation data. Computer Graphics and Image Processing, 4, pp.375-387

4. G.W.Wolf: Metric surface networks. In: K.Brassel, K.Kishimoto (eds.) Proceedings of Spatial Data Handling, (Department of Geography, University of Zürich), 1989, pp. 884-856

5. T.J.Laffey, R.M.Haralick, L.T.Watson: Topographic classification of image intensity surfaces. In Proceedings of the Workshop in Computer Vision: Representation and Control, New York, Computer Society Press, pp.171-177

6. A.Tribe: Automated recognition of valley heads from Digital Terrain Models. *Earth, Surface Processes and Landform*, Vol.15, No 8, 1990

7. B.Falcidieno,M.Spagnuolo: A new method for the characterization of topographic surfaces. International Journal of Geographical Information Systems, vol. 5, No. 4, December 1991

8. C.D.Tomlin: *Geographic Information Systems and Cartographic Modeling*, Prentice Hall, Englewood Cliffs, 1990

9. F.K.Musgrave, C.E.Kolb, R.S.Mace: The synthesis and rendering of eroded fractal terrains. Computer Graphics, Vol. 23, No. 3, July 1989, pp.41-50

10. B.B.Mandelbrot: Fractal landscapes without creases and with rivers. In: H.O. Peitgen, D. Saupe (eds.): The science of fractal images, Springer Verlag, 1988

11. B.Falcidieno,C.Pienovi: Natural surface approximation by constrained stochastic interpolation. Computer-Aided Design, 22, 3, 1990

12. L.De Floriani, B.Falcidieno, C.Pienovi: Delaunay-based representation of surfaces defined over arbitrarily shaped domains. Computer Vision, Graphics and Image Processing, 32, 1985

13. D.G.Morris, R.W.Flavin: A digital terrain model for hydrology. In: K.Brassel, K. Kishimoto (eds.): Proceedings of Spatial Data Handling, (Department of Geography, University of Zürich), 1989, pp. 250-262

14. F.P.Preparata, M.I.Shamos: *Computational Geometry*. New York: Springer Verlag, 1985

15. B.Falcidieno,C.Pienovi, M.Spagnuolo: Discrete surface models: constraint-based generation and understanding: In: Computer Graphics and Mathematics. EG Seminar Series : (to appear)

The Geometry of Environmental Knowledge

Daniel R. Montello

Department of Geography, University of California
Santa Barbara, CA 93106-4060
USA

Abstract. Theoretical and empirical work on the geometry of environmental knowledge is discussed. Certain patterns of distance and directional estimates collected from humans have been interpreted as being due to non-metric or non-Euclidean spatial knowledge. I argue that attempts to determine this geometry are inconsistent with existing theoretical models of human knowledge storage and use. Spatial estimation data are more parsimoniously explained as resulting from: (a) measurement error and ambiguity, (b) multiple and uncoordinated long-term memory representations, and (c) processes taking place when spatial knowledge is activated and used.

1 Introduction

The philosopher Kant maintained that phenomenal space such as that experienced during visual perception or imagery is described by Euclidean geometry [37, 42]. Since space is readily perceived and imagined in this way, Kant reasoned, physical space must be Euclidean. In Kant's terms, the 3-dimensional Euclidean structure of space is *synthetic* (nontrivial, meaningful description of the world) and *a priori* (self-evident and not subject to empirical test). This view is intuitively appealing, as for instance when a 3-dimensional Euclidean sphere is provided for the "visualization" of 2-dimensional Riemannian space. But Kant's arguments for the self-evident geometry of physical space have been criticized frequently, and it is now believed that Euclidean geometry does not best describe the space of the physical universe (e.g., Einstein's general theory of relativity).

But what about the space of the mind -- "space" as it is perceived, imagined, and stored in memory? The intuitive appeal of Euclidean geometry may imply something about *psychological* space that it does not imply about physical space. The fact that space at scales of size relevant to certain topics in physics and astronomy may best be described as non-Euclidean (or hyperdimensional, etc.) does not force us to adopt such models for space at scales relevant to psychology:

> "The description of reality with the help of the four- dimensional schema [one of time] is a result of the construction of physical space from psychological spaces (visual and tactile spaces, etc.). These latter are, however, by no means relative...In these regions, the application of Euclidean geometry is more than an arbitrary convention. Nevertheless, the question as to which geometries shall be constructed for greater or smaller magnitudes, that is, for atomic or astronomical dimensions, is no longer psychologically, but purely physically, determined". [38, p. 296]

In the following essay, I discuss some recent theoretical and empirical work on the geometry of environmental knowledge. Properties of metric spaces in general and Euclidean metric spaces in particular are briefly reviewed. I present a representative sample of research on the estimation of spatial properties of the environment (distance and directional relationships) that has implications for the geometry of environmental knowledge. The importance of several measurement issues is described. Finally, I question assertions about the geometry of environmental knowledge, primarily with respect to implicit assumptions about memory structure and the processes required to externalize this structure as thought and behavior.

My discussion below focuses on knowledge of large-scale or *environmental* spaces, spaces that surround us and generally require movement over time for their apprehension. Because these spaces apparently necessitate considerable information integration in memory over time, their mental representations have been termed *cognitive maps* or *cognitive spaces* [6, 8, 10, 18]. In contrast, *perceptual spaces* are those apprehended relatively simultaneously during perception, usually visual. Evidence in fact suggests that the perspective geometry of perceptual, or visual, space may not best be described as Euclidean. The *Luneberg-Blank* theory states that visual space follows a homogeneous, hyperbolic metric [4, 11, 17, 26]; straight lines behave as though they were on the surface of a hyperbolic plane. Not all features of this theory are universally accepted (Foley [11], for instance, questions the homogeneity of visual space), but the evidence is clearly at odds with a Euclidean metric.

Acknowledging the non-Euclidean nature of perceptual space, however, does not force us to adopt such a geometry for internal spatial representations derived from perceptual events. Encoding processes operating on perceptual input could transform hyperbolic space into Euclidean space, or for that matter, into some other non-Euclidean or non-metric space. For instance, Baird, Wagner, and Noma [3] propose that such processes transform the locally Euclidean metric of the environment into non-Euclidean cognitive space.

2 Alternative Geometries in the Study of Environmental Knowledge

Euclidean space is one member of a general class of *metric spaces*, spaces for which quantitative distances between locations can be defined in a consistent way that does not depend on the direction of measurement between two locations. Metric spaces are characterized by the following axioms (*d* is distance; *m*, *n*, and *o* are locations in space):

a) $d(m,n) \geq 0$ — *nonnegativity*
b) $d(m,n) = 0$, if and only if m and n coincide — *nondegeneracy*
c) $d(m,n) = d(n,m)$ — *symmetry*
d) $d(m,n) + d(n,o) \geq d(m,o)$ — *triangle inequality*

Metric spaces include, but are not limited to, Euclidean spaces. Two-dimensional Euclidean spaces are the flat, infinite, continuous, and isotropic spaces familiar from high school geometry and formally characterized by the five postulates of Euclid's geometry [14, 37].

Euclid's fifth postulate has been the most controversial philosophically. In one of its forms, it states:

Given a straight line and a point not on that line, there is one and only one straight line through the point and parallel to the original line.

Various non-Euclidean metric geometries, such as hyperbolic and spherical geometries, take issue with the fifth postulate, curving planar space so that no parallels or many parallels exist. Alternatively, non-Euclidean metric spaces may be flat but locally nonisotropic. Straight-line distance in these metric but non-Euclidean spaces depends in part on the angular orientation of the points in the space [13, 40]. The *city-block* metric, for instance, is a flat metric that requires distance measurement along orthogonal lines that connect the endpoints, much as road distances in cities follow city blocks.

In the psychological literature on cognitive distance, the term *Euclidean* distance has often been equated with *straight-line* or *as-the-crow-flies* distance, in contrast to *route* or *functional* distance [e.g., 35, 44]. This usage is inexact, however, given that the shortest route between locations on a 2-dimensional surface (the "straight-line" route) would not be a Euclidean straight line if the space was non-Euclidean. An example is the straight-line route of an airplane flying from New York to Moscow -- it follows a great circle, or circumference line, around the globe. Conversely, route distance may or may not be based on a representation with the properties of a Euclidean space, though it would equal straight-line distance only along routes without turns.

The most important historical example of explicit theorizing about the geometry of psychological, as opposed to physical, space comes from the extensive work of Piaget [cf. 33]. He and his colleagues proposed that spatial knowledge develops ontogenetically from topological to projective and fully Euclidean geometry in the mature thinker. However, he did not explicitly attempt to empirically evaluate the geometry of the adult's spatial knowledge in a rigorous fashion.

More recently, psychologists, geographers, and others have attempted to empirically evaluate the metric of environmental knowledge. There are several strategies for doing this. One is to examine estimates of distances in the environment: Are they consistent with the metric axioms? In fact, several researchers have reported violations of the symmetry and triangle inequality axioms [3, 7, 29, 31, 36, 43]. Sadalla et al. [36], for example, found that distance from a campus building high in reference-point saliency to a campus building low in reference-point saliency was estimated as being greater than the same distance in the opposite direction. They attributed this to the role of reference points in the organization of environmental memory representations.

A strategy for determining which metric best describes the geometry of spatial knowledge follows from a theorem derived from Euclid's fifth postulate about parallels: The sum of the angles of the vertices of a triangle will equal 180° if the space is Euclidean, within the limits of measurement error. In the 19th century, Gauss actually attempted to establish the geometry of physical space by summing the angles formed by light rays traveling between three distant mountain peaks ([42] -- Gauss concluded that within limits of measurement accuracy, physical space was Euclidean). By a similar logic, the sum of the vertex angles of a triangle formed by the estimation from memory of the directions between three locations should equal 180° if the knowledge space is Euclidean. For example, Moar and Bower [29] found that the sum of estimated directions between three nonvisible street intersections significantly exceeded 180° in several cases. Although they did not interpret it as such, this finding is consistent with a spherical geometry of strong curvature.

Perhaps a more sophisticated approach to this question has been the use of multidimensional scaling (MDS) algorithms to fit a geometry to a matrix of proximity estimates made between locations. Solutions obtained using spaces of different metrics are compared with respect to their *stress values*, their abilities to reproduce the original values of the proximity estimates [e.g., 13, 45]. The relative stress of Euclidean and non-Euclidean solutions can be compared. Golledge and Hubert [13], for instance, report data from an earlier study of distance estimation within the city of Columbus. The distance estimates of 18% of residents were better fit by a non-Euclidean metric than they were by a Euclidean metric. However, these authors go on to discuss research by Spector and by Richardson in which matrices of distance estimates at intraurban scales were not fit as well by a Euclidean as by a non-Euclidean metric (particularly the city-block metric).

Shepard [40] discusses the MDS approach and some difficulties associated with it, particularly when comparing a Euclidean metric to alternative flat but nonisotropic metrics such as the city-block. Because of differences in the degree of degeneracy of the solutions obtained with these different metrics, expected stress values under random conditions are not equal for the different metrics. Certain extreme metrics will artifactually produce low-stress solutions. Furthermore, if nonmetric paired-comparison data are used as input in the MDS program, the various metrics differ very little in their rank ordering of pairwise distances (the Euclidean and city-block, for instance, would generally differ by no more than one pair reversal). Shepard concludes that "the generally accepted practice of taking, as the correct metric, the one which yields the lowest residual departure from monotonicity is unfounded and probably leads to erroneous conclusions" (p. 401).

Although Shepard's [40] comments are relevant, a couple of caveats about them should be made. The first is that the difficulties of stress comparisons with different metrics may not be as serious when one starts with the objective spatial configuration (i.e., the actual layout of the urban area being estimated) as a starting point for the iterative fitting done by the MDS algorithm. In addition, different metrics do not reproduce rank orders of pairwise estimates as equivalently when one uses incomplete pairwise designs (as has typically been the case) instead of all possible pairwise estimates. Both issues call for further research[1].

3 Measurement and Methodology

As long as any arbitrary pattern or amount of error can be attributed to the measurement process, any geometry for environmental knowledge can be maintained in the face of any empirical evidence [see 3, 5, 12]. The mathematician Poincaré pointed out some time ago that the appropriateness of a Euclidean metric can only be empirically tested if one makes certain *coordinating definitions* [14, 37]. He maintained that decisions about the geometry of a space are conventional, not empirical, because any pattern of data could be explained either by characteristics of the space or by characteristics of the behavior of the measuring device as it is moved about the space [42]. Thus, the requirement that one's measuring rod must remain a constant length across measurements is an important historical example of a coordinating definition.

In a recent article [30], I discuss several issues that are relevant to a coordinating definition about the psychophysical measurement of cognitive distance. One is that subjects generally may have different internal representations of standard distances (the mental "yardsticks"), differences which are generally opaque to the researcher. Another is that magnitudes of estimates made with traditional psychophysical methods such as ratio- and magnitude-estimation apparently depend in systematic ways on the relative sizes of the standard distances used in the estimation procedure. To the degree that such factors influence the magnitudes of estimated distances, even estimates derived from Euclidean representations might be interpreted as indicating non-Euclidean or non-metric geometries.

Failures of the metric axioms in the context of cognitive distance measurement were cited above. In general, however, failures of the metric axioms are ubiquitous whenever pairwise estimates of similarity or proximity are collected [46]. Given stimuli that vary along qualitatively different dimensions (an apple has size, color, aroma, etc.), shifts of context and attention will result in violations of the metric axioms [39]. Users of MDS usually transform or otherwise modify their data so it can be fit with a Euclidean or some other metric representation, preventing the description of the resulting spaces as being non-metric.

Furthermore, people apparently do not always estimate distances along Euclidean straight lines even when their representations would allow them to do so. For example, a city-block metric most accurately describes spaces in which shortest distances between places are along routes containing orthogonal turns instead of along straight routes. But just because one knows that the shortest routes that can actually be traveled are not straight lines does not mean that one's mental representation of the space containing the routes is necessarily non-Euclidean. Maps generated from people's distance estimates may be best fit by a city-block metric [13];

this may just reveal that unless carefully specified, people will tend to estimate distances along accessible routes.

Data collected by Rieser et al. [35] provide some support for this contention. When given no explicit instructions either to estimate route or straight-line distances, their subjects tended to estimate distances as if they had received route instructions. However, when given straight-line instructions, they estimated distances differently -- more like the actual relative straight-line distances. Thus, subjects were not necessarily bound to a city-block metric. They did tend to interpret the estimation task and use their representations differently under different instructions.

Finally, some additional methods that have been used to measure cognitive distance do not allow tests of the geometry of environmental knowledge. Methods that involve the construction of a spatial representation by simultaneous estimation of locations typically force a Euclidean metric onto the representation (or whatever space we take as a description of flat pieces of paper). Examples are map-drawing and model-building tasks.

4 Environmental Knowledge: Structures and Processes

Given that environmental knowledge must be finite (as are all brains and information storage devices), the question becomes whether it can best be described as *locally* Euclidean. Behavioral data, including sketch maps, distance estimates, proximity rankings, and directional judgments, indicate that knowledge of the environment is incomplete, distorted, asymmetric, discontinuous, and imperfectly coordinated [e.g., 7, 15, 25, 27, 29]. A uniform or homogeneous metric would not typically describe it well. People store very different amounts of information about different places, often excluding unfamiliar areas altogether. Discrete, fragmented pieces of represented environments are stored at multiple hierarchical levels [28].

Several theorists [9, 22] have criticized the concept of cognitive maps as falsely implying that environmental knowledge exists in a unitary spatial format, as in a cartographic map. They instead propose modeling environmental knowledge as a conglomeration of multiple representations of space in LTM that are not necessarily coordinated nor mutually consistent, at least not directly. Some of it is not even locally metric, but encodes topological information in non-spatial formats such as verbal and abstract propositional networks (cf. a model by Kuipers and Levitt [23] for navigation by autonomous vehicles). From this perspective, environmental *long-term memory* (LTM) is clearly not a unitary metric representation that is uniform and continuous. Instead, these models suggest that there isn't a single psychological space stored in LTM but rather several spaces -- spaces whose LTM characteristics may not even be spatial.

Given this, using sets of distance or directional estimates to conclude that the space of environmental knowledge is non-Euclidean or even non-metric [e.g., 13, 45] might be considered inappropriate. There is no reason that environmental spatial knowledge should fit any single metric unless it comes from a unitary representation. For example, one might estimate the distance from A to B using a different representation than that used when estimating the distance from B to A, resulting in asymmetric estimates [cf. 36]. As long as the asymmetric estimates are not simultaneously experienced by the estimator, it is possible for the two mutually inconsistent but internally metric representations to coexist in LTM without conflict. (Moar and Bower [29] provide a similar interpretation of apparently non-Euclidean directional estimates). Such an example illustrates the way that statements about the geometry of environmental knowledge are like constructing a patchwork made up of pieces cut from several maps of different styles and sizes, and then remarking on the distorted, non-metric quality of the resulting patchwork.

But there is another serious difficulty with using data from spatial estimation tasks to model the geometry of environmental knowledge. It involves the processes required to activate LTM spatial knowledge and construct spaces in *working memory* (WM) during the estimation task. Such processes are also required during many everyday uses of environmental knowledge, such as non-automatized wayfinding and direction-giving.

Holyoak and Mah [16] discuss transformations in spatial knowledge induced by the retrieval of LTM knowledge during distance estimation tasks. Their *implicit scaling model* states that information from LTM is retrieved when estimating distances and used to construct a "scaled" representation of the space in WM. These representations are categorically structured internal scales of distance from which distance estimates can be made. The reference point used to construct the distance scales will affect the way distance is partitioned on the scale (spatial estimates are relative in so far as they require implicitly generated or explicitly provided points of reference). The discrimination categories make up an interval scale in which categories nearest the reference point will contain the least distance. Greater discriminability of distance is thus found near the reference point. As examples, Holyoak and Mah showed that cities in the Western US were estimated as being further apart relative to the Pacific Ocean than to the Atlantic Ocean. They also used their implicit scaling model to explain patterns of asymmetric distance estimates associated with reference points [36], favoring such an explanation in this case over a model that posits multiple LTM representations for estimates in opposite directions (as I discussed above).

Presumably such a scaling process has evolved as the most efficient way to access spatial information, given limitations on how much information can be maintained in WM (it is useful to be able to make finer discriminations near points of reference). Alternatively, the greater density of knowledge near personal reference points (such as one's home) will lead to a greater representation of information near the reference point on the WM scale. Either way, implicit scaling results in the "stretching" of subjective distance in the vicinity of reference points. For purposes of the present discussion, the distortion from geographic reality resulting from such scaling processes in a single represented space is not so important (it might still result in a Euclidean space). More importantly, such processes operating differently over the course of data collection would typically produce mutually non-metric estimates. Thus, a particular knowledge structure in LTM will be activated and used in WM differently depending on the nature of the task at hand. "Psychological spaces don't exist sui generis; they are constructed on the spot, and their nature and field of view will be task specific" [19, pp. 23-24].

5 Conclusions

Both the pluralistic nature of LTM spatial knowledge and knowledge activation theories such as the implicit scaling model [16] provide reasons that spatial estimation data would not be fit well by a Euclidean metric (or perhaps any metric). These ideas in fact suggest that such an enterprise is mistaken, in so far as it involves the implicit or explicit assumption that environmental knowledge can be meaningfully modeled as a coordinated, unitary representation. Such attempts typically fail to take account of the distinction between WM and LTM knowledge. "Considerable confusion has been engendered by a failure to distinguish between spatial thought [WM] and spatial storage [LTM]" [24, p. 13]. Because behavioral data (maps, distance or proximity estimates, directional judgments) are usually derived from multiple representations that are not simultaneously activated into an internally consistent WM representation, it should come as no surprise that the resulting data violate metric axioms. This does not imply that cognitive space is non-metric or non-Euclidean, only that there is no such omnibus "space" in memory.

What is important for the geometry of mental representations is that it facilitates adaptive spatial behavior in the environment. The structure of LTM is not directly constrained by this need, though both its contents and any mapping procedures used to make this content explicit [9] are thus constrained. The environment may be expected to constrain the structure of WM representations. For instance, Shepard [41] discusses environmental constraints on the form of internal representations that operate via evolutionary processes. He suggests that the geometric properties of the world of "perceiving, imagining, thinking, and dreaming" (*WM representations*) reflect the internalized constraints of a 3-dimensional and locally Euclidean world (except for a nonisotropy due to gravity). O'Keefe and Nadel [32] take a similarly Kantian-like position that the brain innately organizes experience in 3-dimensional, Euclidean terms because of environmental constraints.

To the degree that an attempt to establish the geometry of environmental knowledge is a cogent enterprise, it might be reformulated to refer to WM space rather than to LTM space or to some generic "mental" space. This is similar to one view of the recent analogue-propositional debate concerning the form of mental imagery ([20]; see [34] for a very different view of imagery): WM representations may very well function as if in an analogue, spatial medium even though the LTM representations from which they are generated may take any of several forms, including a propositional form. If one could establish that spatial estimation data reflected the simultaneous content of some WM space, one would be in a position to evaluate the geometric properties of the space.[2]

As did Kosslyn, Ball, and Reiser [21], this endeavor asks what the metric of the spatial information preserved by visual images is. The time required to scan an image from location A to location C, for example, should never be greater than the time required to scan from A to B plus the time to scan from B to C (assuming equal scanning rates, etc.). Or one could examine angular estimates made from an image in order to determine if a Euclidean metric is a good description for it. Using such methods, one might even show that all WM spaces do not share a single geometry (e.g., even within the class of "large-scale" environments, variations in scale of size could be important).

An important and difficult question is whether one can actually determine which WM spaces are stored as internally consistent units in LTM and which are composed from a combination of two or more spatial units in LTM. In essence, what elements of the world (body zones, rooms, buildings, cities, etc.) are treated as single environmental units in various contexts? This is a difficult question to answer given that data reflecting the contents of LTM are expressed via WM (see [1] for a similar point about the analogue-propositional imagery debate). One could hold that metric consistency, equivalent scale and completeness within a set of spatial estimates is evidence of a unitary representation in LTM. But this would beg the question of mental geometry. It would never allow us to claim evidence against the metric nature of environmental knowledge (a *conventionalist* argument).

But the problem may not be intractable. Careful response-time studies might show that patterns of response-times in spatial estimation tasks vary as a function of whether: (a) a single environmental unit is being accessed across time, (b) more than one unit is being accessed sequentially across time, or (c) more than one unit is being accessed and simultaneously integrated because the particular estimation task requires coordinated access to multiple representations. It might also be informative to discuss metric inconsistencies with subjects (e.g., nonsymmetric distance estimates) after collecting a series of spatial estimates. Their responses to such queries might provide some insight into the cause of metric inconsistencies.

Footnotes

1 I am indebted to an anonymous reviewer for alerting me to these important caveats.

2 The relationship mediating WM representations and behavior is also important; if significant transformations of the geometry of WM representations mediate this relationship, behavioral data will not directly inform us of WM geometry.

References

1. J.R.Anderson: Arguments concerning representations for mental imagery. Psychological Review 85, 249-277 (1978)

2. J.C.Baird: Psychophysical analysis of visual space. New York: Pergamon (1970)

3. J.C.Baird, M.Wagner, E.Noma: Impossible cognitive spaces. Geographical Analysis 14, 204-216 (1982)

4. A.A.Blank: Curvature of binocular visual space. Journal of the Optical Society of America 51, 335-339 (1961)

5. B.P.Buttenfield: Comparing distortion on sketch maps and MDS configurations. Professional Geographer 38, 238-246 (1986)

6. M.T.Cadwallader: Cognitive distance in intraurban space. In: G.T.Moore, R.G.Golledge (eds.):

Environmental knowing. Stroudsburg, PA: Dowden, Hutchinson & Ross 1976, pp. 316-324

7. M.T.Cadwallader: Problems in cognitive distance: Implications for cognitive mapping. Environment and Behavior 11, 559-576 (1979)

8. D.Canter, S.Tagg: Distance estimation in cities. Environment and Behavior 7, 59-80 (1975)

9. R.M.Downs: Maps and mappings as metaphors for spatial representation. In: L.S.Liben, A.H.Patterson, N.Newcombe (eds.): Spatial representation and behavior across the life span. New York: Academic 1981, pp. 143-166

10. R.M.Downs, D.Stea: Cognitive maps and spatial behavior: Process and products. In: R.M.Downs, D.Stea (eds.): Image and environment. Chicago: Aldine 1973, pp. 8-26

11. J.M.Foley: The size-distance relation and the intrinsic geometry of visual space. Vision Research 12, 323-332 (1972)

12. T.Gärling, A.Böök, E.Lindberg, C.Arce: Evidence of a response-bias explanation of non-Euclidean cognitive maps. Professional Geographer 43, 143-149 (1991)

13. R.G.Golledge, L.J.Hubert: Some comments on non-Euclidean mental maps. Environment and Planning A 14, 107- 118 (1982)

14. A.Grünbaum: Philosophical problems of space and time, 2nd ed. Dordrecht, The Netherlands: D.Reidel (1973)

15. D.A.Hardwick, C.W.McIntyre, H.L.Pick: The content and manipulation of cognitive maps in children and adults. Monographs for the Society for Research in Child Development 41, 166 (1976)

16. K.J.Holyoak, W.A.Mah: Cognitive reference points in judgments of symbolic magnitude. Cognitive Psychology 14, 328-352 (1982)

17. T.Indow: On geometry of frameless binocular perceptual space. Psychologia 17, 50-63 (1974)

18. W.H.Ittelson: Environment perception and contemporary perceptual theory. In: W.H.Ittelson (ed.): Environment and cognition. New York: Seminar 1973, pp. 1-19

19. P.R.Killeen: Geometric models of proximity data. Unpublished manuscript, Arizona State University, Tempe (1979)

20. S.M.Kosslyn: The medium and the message in mental imagery: A theory. Psychological Review 88, 46-66 (1981)

21. S.M.Kosslyn, T.M.Ball, B.J.Reiser: Visual images preserve metric spatial information: Evidence from studies of image scanning. Journal of Experimental Psychology: Human Perception and Performance 4, 47-60 (1978)

22. B.Kuipers: The 'map in the head' metaphor. Environment and Behavior 14, 202-220 (1982)

23. B.Kuipers, T.S.Levitt: Navigation and mapping in large-scale space. Artificial Intelligence Magazine 73, 25-43 (1988)

24. L.S.Liben: Spatial representation and behavior: Multiple perspectives. In: L.S.Liben, A.H.Patterson, N.Newcombe (eds.): Spatial representation and behavior across the life span. New York: Academic 1981, pp. 3-36

25. R.Lloyd: Cognitive maps: Encoding and decoding information. Annals of the Association of American Geographers 79, 101-124 (1989)

26. R.K.Luneberg: The metric of binocular visual space. Journal of the Optical Society of America 40, 637-642 (1950)

27. K.Lynch: The image of the city. Cambridge, MA:

M.I.T. Press (1960)

28. T.P.McNamara, J.K.Hardy, S.C.Hirtle: Subjective hierarchies in spatial memory. Journal of Experimental Psychology: Learning, Memory, and Cognition 15, 211-227 (1989)

29. I.Moar, G.H.Bower: Inconsistency in spatial knowledge. Memory and Cognition 11, 107-113 (1983)

30. D.R.Montello: The measurement of cognitive distance: Methods and construct validity. Journal of Environmental Psychology 11, 101-122 (1991)

31. J.Muller: Non-Euclidean geographic spaces: Mapping functional distances. Geographical Analysis 14, 189-203 (1982)

32. J.O'Keefe, L.Nadel: The hippocampus as a cognitive map. New York: Oxford University Press (1978)

33. J.Piaget, B.Inhelder: The child's conception of space. London: Routledge & Kegan Paul Ltd. (1956) (Original work published 1948)

34. Z.W.Pylyshyn: The imagery debate: Analogue media versus tacit knowledge. Psychological Review 88, 16-45 (1981)

35. J.J.Rieser, J.L.Lockman, H.L.Pick: The role of visual experience in knowledge of spatial layout. Perception and Psychophysics 28, 185-190 (1980)

36. E.K.Sadalla, W.J.Burroughs, L.J.Staplin: Reference points in spatial cognition. Journal of Experimental Psychology: Human Learning and Memory 6, 516-528 (1980)

37. W.C.Salmon: Space, time, and motion: A philosophical introduction. Dickenson (1975)

38. M.Schlick: The four-dimensional world. In: J.J.C.Smart (ed.): Problems of space and time. New York: The Macmillan Company 1964, pp. 292-296 (Reprinted from chap. 7 of The philosophy of nature,

translated by A.von Zeppelin, Philosophical Library, New York, 1949)

39. R.N.Shepard: Attention and the metric structure of the stimulus space. Journal of Mathematical Psychology 1, 54-87 (1964)

40. R.N.Shepard: Representation of structure in similarity data -- problems and prospects. Psychometrika 39, 373-422 (1974)

41. R.N.Shepard: Ecological constraints on internal representation: Resonant kinematics of perceiving, imagining, thinking, and dreaming. Psychological Review 91, 417-447 (1984)

42. L.Sklar: Space, time, and spacetime. Berkeley: University of California (1974)

43. D.Stea: The measurement of mental maps: An experimental model for studying conceptual spaces. In: K.R.Cox, R.G.Golledge (eds.): Behavioral problems in geography: A symposium. Evanston, IL: Northwestern University 1969, pp. 228-253

44. P.W.Thorndyke, B.Hayes-Roth: Differences in spatial knowledge acquired from maps and navigation. Cognitive Psychology 14, 560-581 (1982)

45. W.Tobler: The geometry of mental maps. In: R.G.Golledge, G.Rushton (eds.): Spatial choice and spatial behavior. Columbus: Ohio State University 1976, pp. 69-81

46. A.Tversky: Features of similarity. Psychological Review 84, 327-352 (1977)

Spatial Reasoning Using Symbolic Arrays

Dimitris Papadias and Timos Sellis[1,2]
Computer Science Division
Department of Electrical and Computer Engineering
National Technical University of Athens
157 73 Zographou, Athens, GREECE
{dp,timos}@theseas.ntua.gr

Abstract. Research in Artificial Intelligence and Cognitive Science has suggested the distinction between visual knowledge (such as shape, volume and colour of objects) and spatial knowledge (that is, spatial relationships among the different objects of a visual scene). We find this distinction applicable to Information Systems concerned with spatial reasoning and especially to Geographic Information Systems. In particular, this paper deals with the representation of spatial information in GIS. The paper presents a representational formalism which captures the knowledge embedded in spatial relationships and provides the ability to represent, retrieve and reason about spatial information not explicitly stored in memory.

1. Introduction

There is extensive research in the areas of Databases, Artificial Intelligence (AI) and Cognitive Science concerning the storage and access of spatial and visual information. Although there are some common research objectives, such as computational and storage efficiency, expressive power and inferential adequacy, the goals depend on the particular viewpoint. Work in AI and Cognitive Science, for instance, is focused more on reasoning and expressive power of knowledge representations, whereas in Databases, work is focused on the efficient management of large amounts of data. The goal of this paper is to combine ideas of the above areas and to propose a computational representation for the manipulation of information regarding spatial concepts. *Spatial concepts* comprise of simpler entities related with spatial relationships. These simpler entities can themselves be spatial concepts which may be further decomposed.

The thesis of the paper is that different representational formalisms should be used for different computational tasks in Database Systems. This idea though, is not new to AI or Cognitive Science. In perceptual systems, for example, multiple image representations have been proposed to derive cognitively useful representations from a visual scene [12]. In the representation scheme for computational imagery [14] three kinds of representations have been described:

---

1 Research partially supported by the National Science Foundation under Grant IRI-9057573 (PYI Award), by DEC and Bellcore, and by UMIACS.

2 On-leave from the Dept. of Computer Science, University of Maryland, College Park, U.S.A.

(1) A spatial concept is stored in long-term memory as a possibly hierarchically organised, descriptive, *deep representation* that contains all the relevant information about the concept.

(2) The *visual representation* contains visual information such as shape, volume and colour, otherwise called the *"what"* information.

(3) Finally, the *spatial representation* of a spatial concept denotes the various components of the concept symbolically and preserves relevant spatial properties, otherwise called the "where" information.

Notice that the term spatial and visual representations do not have the usual meaning as when they are used in Database and Geographic Information Systems terminology. We follow the prevalent notions in Cognitive Science (e.g., [1]), according to which spatial representations preserve information about spatial relationships of objects in a visual scene, without containing information about the objects' appearance which is stored in visual representations. In other words spatial representations can be considered as indexes that spatially connect visual representations to create a scene. Furthermore, it has been suggested by numerous studies (e.g., [2]) that different parts of the brain are responsible for the manipulation of spatial knowledge (that is, the "where" information) and visual knowledge (that is, the "what" information).

We find the idea of distinct visual and spatial representations applicable to Information Systems concerned with spatial reasoning and especially to Geographic Information Systems. Geographic Information Systems (GIS) involve tools and techniques for spatial reasoning and data retrieval, where spatial and visual data (images, etc.) are recalled from long-term memory and then manipulated, transformed, associated with similar forms (constructing spatial analogies), pattern matched, increased or reduced in size, etc. A single representational system is not always suitable for all the different computational tasks involved in GIS and multiple representations might be required to facilitate efficiency. Consider, for example, that we want to retrieve the countries north of Austria which the river Danube crosses. We could take advantage of the knowledge about the spatial relationships among European countries by using spatial representations to retrieve the countries north of Austria and then access the database for these countries in order to locate the particular river coordinates. The paper concentrates on spatial representations and describes a computational formalism which facilitates the retrieval of spatial information that *is not explicitly stored* in the database.

Information in the spatial representation is not stored using a deep representation scheme (database), but it is rather generated out of it, in the same sense that views can be generated out of tables in relational databases. However, one very important difference between views and what we propose later in this paper, lies in the type of operators available for the various types of representation. In relational database systems, views are also accessed through relational algebra, or in general, relational languages, used for base (or real) tables as well. In our proposal, the various levels of representation have their own set of operators which better fit the kind of searches a user performs at that level. It is clear that such functionality can also be offered in Object-Oriented Database Systems, and in systems where the burden of defining and implementing operations on the information is put on the developer/user of the system. However, we believe that in GIS there are simple models that can offer such functionality, one of which is the focus of our research. Section 2 briefly reviews the research that has been carried out in the representation of spatial and visual information and discusses the nature of spatial relationships. Section 3 describes the use of spatial representations in GIS and Section 4 concludes the paper with a discussion about future work.

2. Knowledge Representation for Visual and Spatial Information

Extensive research on visual and spatial knowledge representation has resulted in the development of knowledge representation schemes concerned with the representation of information such as distance, shape, volume and spatial relationships. In *discrimination trees*, objects are sorted by discriminating on their coordinates, as well as, other quantitative and qualitative discriminators [13]. *Quadtrees* represent the two-dimensional space, as trees whose nodes have at most four children. The top node corresponds to the entire picture and each node at the next level corresponds to a square of the picture of the previous level [16]. Similar trees for three dimensional pictures are called *octrees*. Other data structures that have been used in GIS for the storage of geographic information are *fieldtrees* [6] and *R-trees* [17]. Contrary to the above representations that concentrate on the efficient manipulation of large amounts of geographic data, research on spatial knowledge representation in AI and Cognitive Science concentrates more on expressive power and inferential adequacy of representations. In *volumetric descriptions*, objects are described as combinations of volumes. According to [3] each object can be represented as a spatial organisation of simple primitive volumes, called *geons*. Other researchers have proposed alternative primitive volumes, like generalised cones, spheres etc. A major contribution in representational formalisms for visuo-spatial information is the progression of *primal sketch*, *2-1/2D sketch* and *3D sketch* [12]. The primal sketch represents intensity changes in a 2D image. The 2-1/2 sketch represents viewer dependent orientation and depth of surface. Finally, the 3D sketch represents object-centred spatial organisation.

It has been argued from the computational, as well as from the cognitive, point of view that one representational formalism is not suitable for all the types of information processing (see [9] for an extensive discussion on the subject). This paper is concerned with the efficient representation and manipulation of spatial information. As mentioned in Section 1, the term spatial information in the context of this paper does not mean visual information such as shape or volume, but it refers to spatial relationships among spatial concepts. Intuitively, we can distinguish between spatial and non-spatial information by considering the type of information we wish to retrieve. Suppose, for example, we wish to answer the following questions: *What city is further north, Pisa or Rome? Which European countries are to the south of Chile?* These questions involve only spatial relationships (that is, "where" information) and they can be typically answered without constructing the explicit representation of the objects; that is, you can possibly recall the relative position of Chile and Europe on the globe without the need to go into further details about the size or the shape of the countries. The answer to each of these questions relies on retrieving the relative locations of objects within a spatial concept and this information can be encoded in spatial representations. Now consider questions such as: *What is the shape of Germany? What is the closest big city (i.e. population more than a million) to Pisa?* Clearly, to answer these questions one needs to access visual information, which is essential to compute the size, shape, and relative distance of objects, as well as, additional information (e.g., population). In this case the spatial representation does not contain enough information and access of the database files (otherwise called the deep representation) is needed.

Spatial representations are used to encode spatial relationships among physical objects. Physical world spatial relationships have important regularities, which we often use in our everyday reasoning. For instance, if we know that *object a is in front of object b*, and that *object b is in front of object c*, then we can conclude that *object a is in front of object c*. If we know that *country x is north of country y*, we also know that country *y is not north of x*. On the other hand, if we are told that *object a is beside object b* we can conclude that *object b is beside object a*, by performing a trivial deduction. All this world knowledge is embedded in the nature of the spatial relationships. Relationships such as *north-of, south-of, left-of, right-of, up, down, front-of, behind-of* etc., are (according to their usual everyday semantics) asymmetric and transitive. For instance:

A left-of B ⇒ not (B left-of A)

A left-of B and B left-of C ⇒ A left-of C .

On the other hand relationships such as *adjacency, closeness, attachment* etc. are symmetric. For instance, no matter how we define closeness in a specific context: if *A is-close-to B* then *B is-close-to A*. Additional properties of spatial relationships facilitate human spatial reasoning. For instance the fact that *Sweden is north of Greece* leads to the conclusion that *Greece is south of Sweden*. This is due to the fact that *south-of* is used as the inverse of the *north-of* relationship. If we know that *Germany is in Europe* and that *Europe is north of Africa* then we can conclude that *Germany is north of Africa*. This happens because all the countries *in* Europe (*in* is another spatial relationship in this context) inherit the status of Europe with respect to some spatial relationships such as *north-of*. On the other hand if we know that *Europe is adjacent to Asia* we cannot conclude that *Germany is adjacent to Asia*. The above examples involve one-step deductions. We could also have multiple-step deductions. For instance from the fact that *Greece is in Europe* and *Chile is in South America* we can conclude that *Greece is north of Chile*, because *Europe is north of South America*. Furthermore we can use knowledge about spatial relationships to perform induction. If we know that *the book is near the phone* and *the phone is near the printer* then we can infer that *with a high probability the book is near the printer*. An efficient representational formalism should capture the knowledge embedded in spatial relationships and provide the inference tools to extract information not explicitly stored.

Our choice for the representation of spatial relationships is the *symbolic array* structure. Symbolic arrays can be regarded as multidimensional sparse indexes which provide nesting capability. They have been introduced for representing human spatial knowledge [7] and have been used in applications involving cognitive spatial reasoning [14]. However, our interest in symbolic arrays is not from the cognitive but from the computational point of view. This paper treats symbolic arrays as a computational formalism which provides the ability to represent, retrieve and reason about spatial information not explicitly stored in memory. In the next section we examine the advantages of using symbolic arrays as a data structure which indexes information spatially.

3. Symbolic Arrays

A symbolic array is used to capture the spatial structure of a spatial concept, where elements of the array denote the meaningful components of the concept. Symbolic arrays preserve the spatial relationships of the various components, but not the relative sizes or distances, that is, they contain symbolic and not geometric information. The arrays can be interpreted in different ways depending upon the application. For instance, in the Molecular Scene Analysis through Imagery application described in [8] the interpretations involve *symmetry* and *adjacency*, whereas in the domain of geographic maps the interpretations would include predicates such as *north*, *east*, *southeast* etc. Figure 1 illustrates a symbolic array corresponding to a map of the world.

index	
africa	1
america	2
asia	3
europe	4
oceania	5

symbolic array						
2		4	4	3	3	3
2		1			3	
2						5

Figure 1: A Symbolic Array for the five continents

The *index* table associates continents with their cells in the *symbolic array*. As it can be seen in Figure 1 each continent occupies some positions in the symbolic array denoted by a distinct number (instead of having numbers corresponding to index entries we could have pointers from index entries to array elements). Notice that in some cases a component may occupy more than one element in an array (e.g., Europe). This is necessary because one element is not always enough to represent all the spatial relationships of a component in relation to others (e.g., the fact that some parts of Europe are north and some northeast of Africa). Notice also that the array positions for the continents are not related to the actual shape of each continent and they do not contain any information about the size of the continents; the fact that Europe is represented by two elements and Africa by one does not imply that Europe has twice the size of Africa.

Symbolic arrays are nested structures, that is, their elements can themselves be symbolic arrays which can be decomposed in simpler arrays. The hierarchical structure of symbolic arrays can be used to represent complex spatial concepts in various levels of abstraction. For example, in Figure 2 the two elements of Europe have been replaced by the symbolic array corresponding to the map of this continent (not all countries are shown). This *zooming* can be achieved with the FOCUS function described in [9]. The (sub)elements belonging to the sub-array of Europe inherit the properties of the higher level array to which they belong with respect to some spatial relationships; for instance, Figure 2 denotes that all the countries of Europe are north of Africa. The *zooming* procedure can proceed until we reach the level at which we obtain simple concepts that can not be decomposed into simpler ones. For example, we can replace the element denoting Italy, with the symbolic array containing the states of Italy, in the array of Figure 2. We have to point out that there is a large number of symbolic arrays which can represent the same information. Furthermore, there is a trade-off between the size of the symbolic array and the precision of the represented information. For instance, there are some parts of Greece that are north of some parts of Yugoslavia. This information can not be retrieved from the symbolic array of Figure 2 which denotes that all parts of Yugoslavia are north of all parts of Greece. We could increase the resolution of the array to include as much detail as it is needed for a particular application, with a negative effect on storage and speed. On the other hand to retrieve this information in a conventional database system we should retrieve and compare all the coordinate pairs for the two countries, which is computationally expensive.

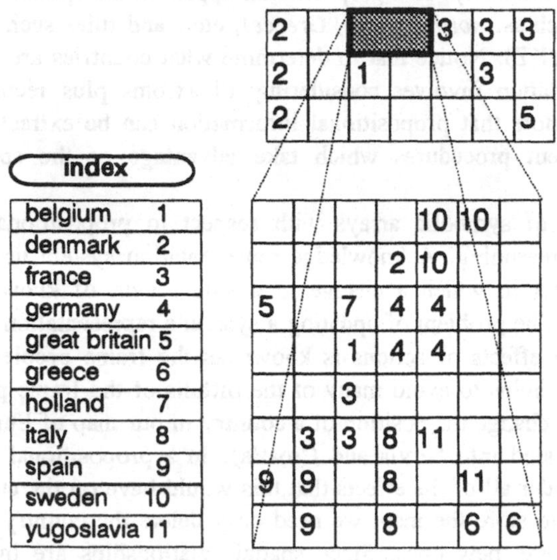

Figure 2: A Symbolic Array for Europe

Approaches to knowledge representation are distinguished by the operations performed on the representations. Thus, the effectiveness of our scheme can be partially measured by how well it facilitates the retrieval of information that it was not explicitly stored. Several functions that operate on symbolic arrays have been developed for Computational Imagery [9]. These functions, as well as new ones, can be used in database queries involving symbolic arrays. As an example consider the query *Is Belgium north of Egypt*? In order to answer this query we use the country index to retrieve the symbolic array that contains Belgium (that is, the array of Europe) and the symbolic array that contains Egypt (that is, the array of Africa) and then we use the UNFOCUS function to retrieve the symbolic array to which both the arrays belong, that is, the array with the continents (Figure 1). Using this array we can determine that Europe is north of Africa and thus Belgium is north of Egypt since the elements inherit the properties of the arrays to which they belong with respect to the *north of* relationship.

Information embodied in a symbolic array can be represented in different ways, for instance, using binary relations or sets of propositions. Although information in the symbolic representation can be expressed as a set of propositions, the representations are not computationally equivalent; that is, the efficiency of the inference mechanisms is not the same [10]. The spatial structure of symbolic arrays possesses properties which help avoid the combinatorial explosion of correct but trivial inferences that must be explicitly represented in a propositional system. Lindsay argues that spatial representations (symbolic arrays in our case) support non-deductive inference by a constraint satisfaction mechanism built into the processes that construct and access them [11]. Consider for example the spatial representation of the map of Europe. To retrieve the information on which European countries are north of Germany, we need only to search a portion of the symbolic array. Alternatively, in a propositional approach the spatial relations would be stored as axioms such as: *north(Britain, Greece)*, etc., and rules such as: *north(X,Z)* ← *north(X,Y) & north(Y,Z)*. Notice that to determine what countries are north of Germany using this representation involves considering all axioms plus recursive calls to the general rule. Also note that propositional information can be extracted from symbolic arrays using efficient procedures which take advantage of the spatial structure of symbolic arrays.

Another advantage of symbolic arrays with respect to propositional representations, concerns temporal reasoning. A knowledge representation system usually deals with a dynamic environment in which a change in a single item of knowledge might have widespread effects. The problem of updating a system's representation of the state of the world to reflect the effects of actions is known as the frame problem [15]. Symbolic array representation helps to avoid many of the pitfalls of the frame problem. Consider for example that we change the position of a country in our map of Europe (for instance, Yugoslavia is separated into Servia and Croatia). In a propositional representation we would have to consider all of the effects that this would have on the current state. Using the symbolic array to store the map, we need only delete the country from its previous position and insert the new ones. Since spatial relationships are interpreted and not logically inferred from symbolic arrays we eliminate some of the problems associated with non monotonicity in domains involving spatial/temporal reasoning. There still remains, though the problem of dealing with truth maintenance if we desire to preserve relations as changes are made. Also notice that the current implementation of symbolic arrays does not provide the expressive power of first-order logic since it cannot express negation, disjunction etc. For example in a symbolic array we cannot express the fact that Greece is north of Egypt or east of Egypt.

4. Conclusions

In this paper we have proposed the use of multi-level knowledge representation techniques for Geographic Information Systems. We believe that adopting different levels of representations can significantly improve the functionality and efficiency of a system. Although we have presented symbolic arrays as a medium for organising spatial knowledge, this is by no means the only way for structuring hierarchical knowledge. Some of the questions we are currently working on include:

1] *Problems of implementation*. This involves the separation of the abstract notion of the symbolic array from the actual implementation. We are currently working on formal methods for representing spatial relationships among physical spatial concepts in symbolic arrays (similar work can be found in [5]) and we are developing algorithms for the creation and update of symbolic arrays in order to have an optimal size without the loss of useful information.

2] *Query Optimisation.* This area involves the study of the relations and the combinations of relations that can be encoded in a symbolic array in order to facilitate query optimisation for some classes of queries.
3] *Learning.* One interesting subject is learning knowledge rules from relational databases. Learning techniques (such as the ones described in [4]) incorporate knowledge encoded in concept hierarchies in order to extract rules from large amounts of data. We believe that symbolic arrays not only provide a means for representing concept hierarchies, but also a means for representing extracted rules.
4] *Deduction and Induction.* Symbolic arrays provide the capability for inference (deduction and induction). Logic interfaces can be used not only to extract propositional information from symbolic arrays, but also to modify symbolic arrays with respect to propositional information.

References

1. Baddeley,A.D., & Lieberman,K. (1980) *Spatial Working Memory.* In R. Nickerson (Ed.) Attention and Performance VIII. Erblaum.

2. Bauer,R.M., & Rubens,A.B. (1985) *Agnosia.* In Heilman & Valenstein (Eds.), Clinical Neuropsychology. Oxford University Press.

3. Biederman, I. (1987) *Recognition by Components: A Theory of Human Image Understanding.* Psychological Review, 94.

4. Cai, Y., Cercone, N., Han, J. (1990) *Learning Characteristic Rules from Relational Databases.* Computational Intelligence, 11.

5. Chang,S., Erland, J., Li, Y. (1989) *The Design of Pictorial Database upon the Theory of Symbolic Projections.* In the proceedings of the First Symposium on the Design and Implementation of Large Spatial Databases (SSD 89).

6. Frank,A.U., Barrera,R. (1989) *The Fieldtree: A Data Structure for Geographic Information Systems.* In the proceedings of the First Symposium on the Design and Implementation of Large Spatial Databases (SSD 89).

7. Glasgow,J.I. (1990) *Artificial Intelligence and Imagery.* Proceedings of the second IEEE conference on Tools for AI.

8. Glasgow,J.I., Fortier,S & Allen,F.H. (1991) *Crystal and Molecular Structure Determination through Imagery,* In Hunter (Ed.), Artificial Intelligence and Molecular Biology, AAAI Press. Also appears in the Proceedings of the Seventh IEEE Conference on Artificial Intelligence Applications.

9. Glasgow,J.I & Papadias,D. (?) *Computational Imagery.* To appear in the Cognitive Science Journal.

10. Larkin,J. & Simon,H.A. (1987) *Why a Diagram is (sometimes) Worth Ten Thousand Words*. Cognitive Science, 10.

11. Lindsay,R.K. (1988) *Images and Inference*. Cognition, 29.

12. Marr,D. (1982) *Vision: A Computational Investigation in the Human Representation of Visual Information*, San Francisco, Freeman.

13. McDermott,D.V.& Davis,E. (1984) *Planning Routes through Uncertain Territory*. Artificial Intelligence, 22.

14. Papadias,D. & Glasgow,J.I. (1991) *A Knowledge Representation Scheme for Computational Imagery*. Proceedings of the 13th Annual Conference of the Cognitive Science Society, Lawrence Erblaum Associates.

15. Raphael,B. (1971) *The Frame Problem in Problem Solving Systems*. In Findler and Meltzer (Eds.), Artificial Intelligence and Heuristic Programming, Edinburgh University Press.

16. Samet,H. (1989) *The Design and Analysis of Spatial Data Structures*. Addison Wesley.

17. Sellis,T., Roussopoulos,N., Faloutsos,C. (1987) *The R^+-tree: A Dynamic Index for Multi-Dimensional Objects*. In P. Stocker and W. Kent (eds.) 13th VLDB conference, Brighton, England.

Using Orientation Information for Qualitative Spatial Reasoning

Christian Freksa

Fachbereich Informatik Universität Hamburg
Bodenstedtstr. 16, 2000 Hamburg 50, Germany
freksa@informatik.uni-hamburg.de

Abstract. A new approach to representing qualitative spatial knowledge and to spatial reasoning is presented. This approach is motivated by cognitive considerations and is based on relative orientation information about spatial environments. The approach aims at exploiting properties of physical space which surface when the spatial knowledge is structured according to *conceptual neighborhood* of spatial relations. The paper introduces the notion of conceptual neighborhood and its relevance for qualitative temporal reasoning. The extension of the benefits to spatial reasoning is suggested. Several approaches to qualitative spatial reasoning are briefly reviewed. Differences between the temporal and the spatial domain are outlined. A way of transferring a qualitative temporal reasoning method to the spatial domain is proposed. The resulting neighborhood-oriented representation and reasoning approach is presented and illustrated. An example for an application of the approach is discussed.

1 Introduction

Spatial orientation information, specifically: directional information about the environment, is directly available to animals and human beings through perception and is crucial for establishing their spatial location and for wayfinding. Such information typically is imprecise, partial, and subjective. In order to deal with this kind of spatial information we need methods for adequately representing and processing the knowledge involved. This paper presents an approach to representing and processing qualitative orientation information which is motivated by cognitive considerations about the knowledge acquisition process.

1.1 Background

In a study investigating cognitive aspects of temporal reasoning, a new approach to qualitative temporal reasoning was developed [Freksa 1992]. The main feature of this approach was the exploitation of *conceptual neighborhood* between related qualitative relations. The use of this neighborhood information results in several advantages compared with previous approaches, for example: (1) processing incomplete knowledge simplifies (rather than complicates) the computational procedure; (2) uncertainty is easily controlled in the case of fuzzy base knowledge; (3) for an important class of operations, a computationally intractable process becomes tractable.

The obvious question was raised whether the approach originally developed for the one-dimensional directed domain *time* could be advantageously transferred to a more-dimensional and/or undirected domain like 2-D or 3-D *space*. Within the spatial domain, the application of the approach both to subject-centered knowledge, i.e. knowledge available from within the domain, and to external knowledge appeared desirable due to cognitive considerations. The current state of our considerations will be presented in this paper for the 2-dimensional case.

1.2 Qualitative Reasoning

After an initial enthusiasm regarding the potential of high-precision quantitative computation, qualitative reasoning has become increasingly popular in artificial intelligence and its application areas. This is due to a variety of reasons. First of all, it has been recognized that computational quantitative approaches do not always have the nice properties of their analytical counterparts; second, the goal of a reasoning process usually is a qualitative rather than a quantitative result: a decision; third, the input for a reasoning process frequently is qualitative: the result of a comparison rather than a description in quantitative terms; fourth, qualitative knowledge is 'cheaper' than quantitative knowledge since it is less informative, in a certain sense; fifth, qualitative representations tend to be more transparent than their quantitative counterparts; and sixth, humans seem to do qualitative reasoning more easily (and sometimes better) than quantitative reasoning. Thus, we must develop methods for dealing with judgements which are non-quantitative in nature and a quantitative representation of these judgements may not be the best solution.

What do we precisely mean by *qualitative* knowledge? In the context of the present discussion, it may suffice to say that qualitative knowledge is obtained by *comparing* features within the object domain rather than by *measuring* them in terms of some artificial external scale. Thus, qualitative knowledge is relative knowledge where the reference entity is a single value rather than a whole set of categories. For example, if we compare two objects along a one-dimensional criterion, say length, we can come up with three possible qualitative judgements: the first object can be *shorter (<)*, *equal (=)*, or *longer (>)* in comparison with the second object.

From a representation-theoretical point of view, a major difference between the two approaches is that measuring requires an intermediate domain in which the scale is defined while comparisons may be performed directly in the object domain. Dealing with an intermediate domain requires mapping functions between the object domain and the scale domain which may be critical for the reasoning process. Thus, qualitative representations aim at avoiding distortions of knowledge due to intermediate mappings. In addition, reasoning based on qualitative information aims at restricting knowledge processing to that part of the information which is likely to be relevant in the decision process: the information which already makes a difference in the object domain.

1.3 Spatial Reasoning

Physical space and its properties play essential roles in all sorts of actions and decisions. Consequently, the ability to reason in and about space is crucial for systems involved in these actions and decisions. In fact, we can raise the question if formal logic or physical space is more fundamental for reasoning processes: should we view spatial reasoning as a special case of 'general' logic-based reasoning or should we rather view logic-based reasoning as an abstraction (and generalization) of spatial reasoning? From a formal position, these two viewpoints may appear equivalent; however, from a cognitive and computational position, they are not: the logic-based view assumes that spatial reasoning involves special assumptions regarding the properties of space which must be taken into account while the space-based view assumes that abstract (non-spatial) reasoning involves abstraction from spatial constraints which must be treated explicitly.

From a biological point of view, the issue raised above corresponds to the question which ability is more 'primitive' and has evolved first, abstract reasoning or spatial reasoning. If we replace the term 'reasoning' by the less presumptuous term 'dealing', it appears evident that nature has chosen to equip plants and animals first with abilities of dealing with space before abilities of dealing with abstract worlds were developed. Some interesting questions arise in this context: does the ability of dealing with abstract worlds require the ability of dealing with the concrete world or are they two completely independent abilities? Do we have representational, computational, or other advantages when using either abstract or concrete approaches to spatial reasoning – independent of the way nature may have chosen? If there are advantages for the space-based approach, how can the approach materialize?

1.4 Existing Approaches to Qualitative Spatial Reasoning

A variety of approaches to qualitative spatial reasoning has been proposed. Güsgen [1989] adapted Allen's [1983] qualitative temporal reasoning approach to the spatial domain by aggregating multiple dimensions into a Cartesian framework. Güsgen's approach is straightforward but it fails to adequately capture the spatial interrelationships between the individual coordinates. The approach has a severe limitation: only rectangular objects aligned with their Cartesian reference frame can be represented in this scheme.

Chang & Jungert [1986] present a knowledge structure for representing relations between arbitrarily shaped 2-dimensional objects on the basis of string representations. Lee & Hsu [1991] also use string representations and develop a 'picture algebra' for rectangles (or projections of convex shapes] in a 2-dimensional Cartesian framework.

Randell [1991] attacks the problem of representing qualitative relationships of concave objects. He introduces a 'cling film' function for generating convex hulls of concave objects; he then lists all qualitatively different relations between an object containing at most one concavity and a convex object. Egenhofer & Franzosa [1991] develop a formal approach to describing spatial relations between point sets in terms of the intersections of their boundaries and interiors.

Schlieder [1990] develops an approach which is not based on the relation between extended objects or connected point sets. Schlieder investigates the properties of projections from 2-D to 1-D and specifies the requirements for qualitatively reconstructing the 2-dimensional scene from a set of projections yielding partial arrangement information.

Hernández [1990] considers 2-dimensional projections of 3-dimensional spatial scenes. He attempts to overcome some deficiencies of Güsgen's approach by introducing 'projection' and 'orientation' relations. Freksa [1991] suggests a perception-based approach to qualitative spatial reasoning; a major goal of this approach is to find a natural and efficient way for dealing with incomplete and fuzzy knowledge.

Frank [1991] discusses the use of orientation grids ('cardinal directions') for spatial reasoning. The investigated approaches yield approximate results, but the degree of precision is not easily controlled. Mukerjee & Joe [1990] present a truly qualitative approach to higher-dimensional spatial reasoning about oriented objects. Orientation and extension of the objects are used to define their reference frames.

2 Qualitative Orientation

As we have seen, there is a number of different approaches and reference systems for representing spatial knowledge. In order to select an appropriate reference system for a given purpose, the availability of the required information must be taken into account. For example, if we want to represent spatial knowledge as acquired by a person through perception, it does not make sense to use Cartesian coordinates for representing object location since this information is not made available by the perception process.

On the other hand, information about relative spatial orientation in 2-D is available through perception. This information is also available to an external observer of a 2-dimensional spatial scene. Thus, relative orientation information is a good candidate for processing subject-centered or external qualitative spatial knowledge. Therefore we develop a representation scheme in which this kind of information can be directly represented.

2.1 Dimensionality of Space and Domain-Inherent Constraints

In qualitative reasoning, we can relate entities of different dimensionality within a domain of a certain dimensionality. We obtain a relation space whose size depends on the dimensions involved and on constraints inherent in the modelled domain. Consider for example the one-dimensional domain 'length' which is spanned by two 0-dimensional entities (points). Within this 1-dimensional domain we can relate two 0-dimensional entities. The relation space consists of three disjoint classes: 'less', 'equal', and 'greater'.

In the one-dimensional domain we also can relate a 0-dimensional entity to a 1-dimensional entity, e.g. a point x to an interval [a, b]. If we permit $b<a$ and $b=a$, the relation space consists of nine disjoint classes: $x<a, x<b$; $x=a, x<b$; $x>a, x<b$; $x>a, x=b$; $x>a, x>b$; $x=a, x>b$; $x<a, x>b$; $x<a, x=b$; $x=a=b$. Domain-inherent properties may not permit $b<a$ (if the domain is uni-directional) or $b=a$ (if we only model extended intervals); both restrictions apply to models of temporal events, for example. In this case, the relation space reduces to five relations. Depending on the specific requirements of the modeled domain, we can construct appropriate qualitative relation spaces, in this way.

Directional orientation in 2-dimensional space is a 1-dimensional feature which is determined by an oriented line; an oriented line, in turn, is specified by an ordered set of two points. We will denote an orientation by an (oriented) line *ab* through two points *a* and *b*; *ba* denotes the opposite orientation. Relative orientation in 2-D is given by two oriented lines or two ordered sets of two points. The feature *orientation* is independent of location and vice versa; therefore, the two ordered sets of points can share one point, without loss of generality. Thus, we can describe the orientation of line *bc* relative to the orientation of line *ab*. This corresponds to describing the point location *c* with respect to reference location *b* and reference orientation *ab* (Figure 1a). Note, that if locations *c* and *b* are identical, orientation *bc* is not defined; nevertheless, we can specify the location of *c* wrt. *a* and *b*.

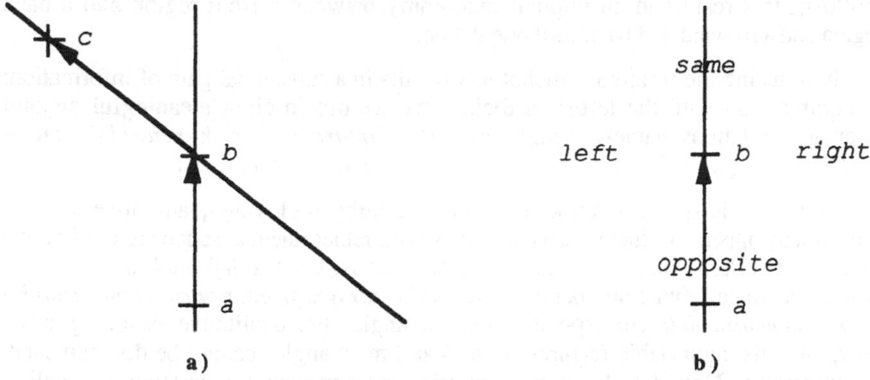

Fig. 1 a) Orientation *bc* relative to orientation *ab*, or: location *c* wrt. location *b* and orientation *ab*; **b)** Orientation relations wrt. location *b* and orientation *ab*.

2.2 Orientation Values and Properties of Qualitative Orientation

The specification of orientation as described in the previous section allows for the distinction of four qualitatively different orientation relations which we have labeled *same, opposite, left, right* (Figure 1b). These relations correspond to point *c* being positioned on line *ab* on the other side of *b* than *a*, on line *ab* on the same side of *b* as *a*, on the left semi-plane of the oriented line *ab*, and on the right semi-plane of the oriented line *ab*, respectively.

Like the qualitative relations *less, equal, greater*, the orientation relation *same* is transitive. The relation *opposite* is periodic in the sense that its repetitive application results in a periodic pattern of resulting orientations, e.g. *opposite* ∞ *left* yields *right*, *opposite* ∞ *opposite* ∞ *left* yields *left*, *opposite* ∞ *opposite* ∞ *opposite* ∞ *left* yields *right*, etc. The qualitative relations *left* and *right* are not periodic, in general; they subsume a wide spectrum of possible quantitative orientations.

Unlike in the case of linear dimensions, incrementing quantitative orientation leads back to previous orientations. In this sense, orientation is a circular dimension. Existing approaches do not deal with periodicity of orientation explicitly. Periodicity is either eliminated by not admitting certain orientations as in [Schätz 1990] or it is ignored by treating different orientations as independent entities as in Frank [1991].

2.3 Augmenting Qualitative Orientation Relations

We can augment the number of orientation relations by introducing additional decision criteria. From a geometrical point of view, the segmentation of 2-dimensional space into two semi-planes perpendicular to the reference orientation *ab* comes to mind immediately. A front/back segmentation already became visible in the *same / opposite* distinction of orientations.

Although people and most animals do not have a perception system for explicit front/back or forward/backward discrimination as they do for left/right discrimination, the segmentation of the plane into a front and a back semi-plane also is meaningful from a cognitive point of view: we conceptualize people, animals, robots, houses, etc. as having an 'intrinsic front side' (compare Pribbenow [1990], Mukerjee & Joe [1990]); this results in an implicit dichotomy between a front region and a back region and a forward and backward orientation.

Introducing the front/back dichotomy results in a substantial gain of information: in combination with the left/right dichotomy we obtain eight meaningful disjoint orientation relations, namely *straight-front (0), right-front (1), right-neutral (2), right-back (3), straight-back (4), left-back (5), left-neutral (6),* and *left-front (7).*

From the viewpoint of a tradition predominantly employing quantitative descriptions it may appear confusing that categories with rather unequal scope are used on the same level of description: the relations *right-front, right-back, left-back,* and *left-front* correspond to an infinite number of angles while *straight-front, neutral-right, straight-back,* and *neutral-left* correspond to a single angle. For qualitative reasoning, however, only distinguishable features count - and most angles cannot be distinguished, in our setting. Note that the orientation relations represent comparative, i.e qualitative values; they do not require a fixed reference system or cardinal directions.

At this point it may be interesting to note the correspondence between orientation and movement. If we view points *a, b,* and *c* as a chain of positions traversed in sequence, then the orientations correspond to the directions of movement while 'undefined orientation' $(c=b)$ corresponds to 'no movement'. The correspondence between orientation and movement is particularly visible in natural language words like *forward* and *backward.*

The arrangement depicted in Figure 1a suggests four ways in which the *front/back* dichotomy can be applied: (1) perpendicular to *ab* in *a,* (2) perpendicular to *ab* in *b,* (3) perpendicular to *bc* in *b,* (4) perpendicular to *bc* in *c.* Eventually we will use all four dichotomies in order to increase the 'qualitative resolution' in spatial reasoning. But we will proceed in stages, in order to make the approach more transparent.

Consider orientation *ab* with a front/back dichotomy introduced in *b* (Figure 2a). We can distinguish eight regions, each corresponding to one qualitative orientation (labeled 0 - 7) and the location *b* corresponding to no orientation. We can do the same for orientation *ba* with a front/back dichotomy introduced in *a.* The result is depicted in Figure 2b.

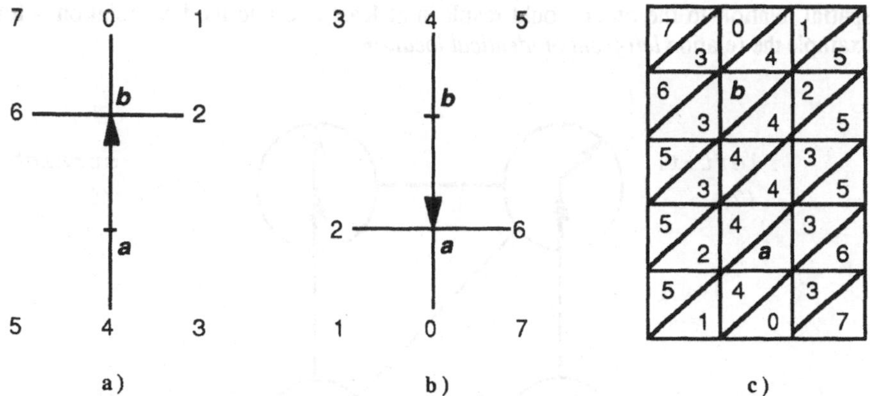

Fig. 2 Combination of left/right and front/back dichotomies into a system of orientations; **a)** front/back dichotomy wrt. *ab* in *b*; **b)** front/back dichotomy wrt. *ba* in *a;* **c)** matrix of combined orientation labels for the 15 qualitative locations.

Figure 2c merges the labels of Figures 2a and 2b into a matrix which distinguishes 15 regions. Each of the regions corresponds to an orientation wrt. *b* (designated in the upper left of the corresponding matrix field) and/or wrt. *a* (designated in the lower right of the corresponding matrix field). The matrix in Figure 2c permits the qualitative description of any location *c* wrt. location *b* and orientation *ab* and wrt. location *a* and orientation *ba*.

The orientation-based qualitative location relation is slightly more general than the qualitative orientation relation since it includes the orientation-less case $c=b$ resp. $c=a$. Therefore we will use it in the following. We will use the same relation labels for denoting qualitative locations as for the corresponding locations; we will denote the orientation-less location by the reference point it corresponds to or by the symbol *i* (identical location).

3 Conceptual Neighborhood and Spatial Knowledge

Freksa [1992] shows for the one-dimensional case of temporal knowledge that there are considerable cognitive and computational advantages to arranging knowledge according to an appropriate *conceptual neighborhood* relation. The conceptual neighborhood principle can be applied to spatial knowledge equally well.

3.1 Conceptual Neighborhood of Spatial Relations

Two relations in a representation are conceptual neighbors, when an operation *in the represented domain* can result in a direct transition from one relation to the other. In physical space, operations can be movements in space or spatial deformations. For example, the relations *left-front (7)* and *left-neutral (6)* and *identical location (i)* are conceptual neighbors by pairs (Figure 3). In contrast, the relations *left-neutral* and *straight-front* are not conceptual neighbors, since any physical operation from one spatial relation to the other would result in at least one intermediate relation – for example the relation *left-front* or *identical location*.

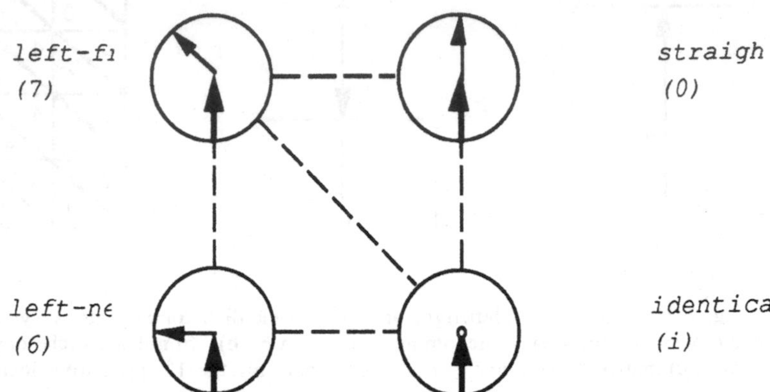

Fig. 3. Relations *7* and *0*, *0* and *i*, *i* and *6*, *6* and *7*, *7* and *i* are conceptual neighbors; relations *6 and 0* are not.

What happens to conceptual neighborhood when we introduce additional differentiations as in Figure 2c? By introducing the second front/back dichotomy through point *a*, we effectively split up the relations *3*, *4*, and *5* into three finer relations each, namely *(3/5, 3/6, 3/7)*, *(4/4, 4/a, 4/0)*, and *(5/3, 5/2, 5/1)*. The coarser original relation becomes a neighborhood of finer relations. Some of the finer relations within a neighborhood are neighbors, some are not. For example, *3/5* and *3/6*, *3/6* and *3/7* are conceptual neighbors, but *3/5* and *3/7* are not.

Note that the finer relations do not resolve the orientation information more finely, although they are defined purely in terms of qualitative orientations. Rather, they distinguish between different qualitative distances. This is shown in Figure 4.

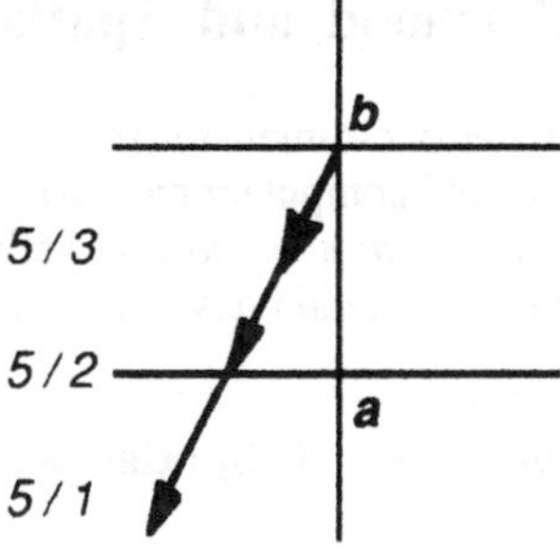

Fig. 4. The combination of orientations wrt. different reference points yields qualitative distance information.

There are also conceptual neighbor relations between fine relations from different neighborhoods, provided that these neighborhoods themselves are neighbors. For example, *3/5* and *4/4* are conceptual neighbors, but *3/5* and *5/3* are not. Figure 5 depicts the conceptual neighbor relations for all 15 location relations. The 15 qualitative relations form 105 (unordered) pairs. 30 of these pairs have the conceptual neighborhood property.

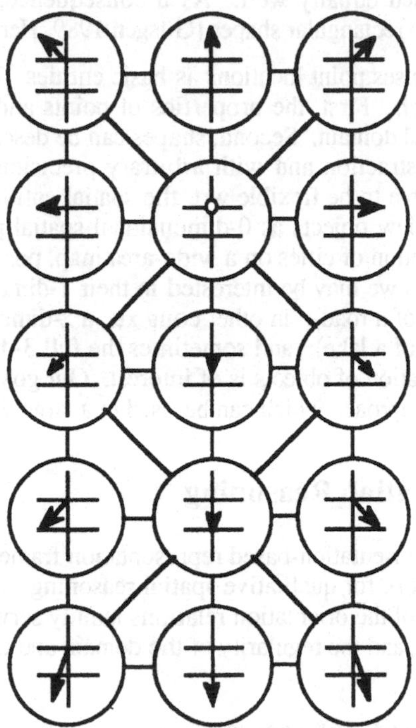

Fig. 5. The 15 qualitative orientation and location relations arranged by conceptual neighborhood. The symbol ‡ depicts iconically line *ab* with the intersections at *a* and at *b*. The arrow depicts the orientation of *bc*.

Conceptual neighborhood structures are important since they intrinsically reflect the structure of the represented world with their operations. Such representations of properties of the represented domain [Furbach et al. 1985] allow us to implement reasoning strategies which are strongly biased towards the operations in the represented domain. They can be viewed as procedural models of this domain. In the case of representing the spatial domain, conceptual neighborhoods contribute to the implementation of imagery processes. From a computational point of view they have the advantage of restricting the problem space in such a way that only operations will be considered which are feasible in the specific domain.

3.2 What are Appropriate Entities to be Spatially Related?

Models of spatial knowledge can either represent abstract point objects or spatially extended objects. Most approaches to representing qualitative spatial knowledge consider the relation between spatially extended objects, or formally speaking between (3-D) volumes, (2-D) areas, or (1-D) intervals. While this approach appears natural, at first glance, considerable drawbacks become apparent upon closer consideration. The main problem is that there is a multitude of possible classes of shapes which cannot be handled equally well. As a consequence, some approaches are restricted to convex or to rectangular shapes [Güsgen 1989, Hernández 1990].

Our representation uses point locations as basic entities. There are several motivations for this approach. First, the properties of points and their spatial relations hold for the entire spatial domain. Second, shapes can be described in terms of points at various levels of abstraction and with arbitrary precision – or can be ignored. Third, it appears desirable to be flexible wrt. the spatial entities and their resolution: in some contexts, we view objects as 0-dimensional spatial points (e.g. position of stars under the sky, position of cities on a wide-area map, position of land marks in a town); in other contexts we may be interested in their 1-dimensional extension (e.g. width of a river, length of a road); in other contexts, a 2-dimensional projection may be of interest (e.g. area of a lake); and sometimes the full 3-dimensional shape of an object or a 3-D constellation of objects is of interest. Our goal has been the development of a fundamental approach which can be used in a large variety of situations.

4 Qualitative Spatial Reasoning

After presenting an orientation-based representation framework we now illustrate how to use this framework for qualitative spatial reasoning. Initially, the conceptual neighborhood structure of the orientation relations mainly serves to help visualize the structure, the operations, and the regularity of the domain and to clarify the approach.

4.1 Orientation-Based Inferences

The representation developed in the foregoing sections enables us to describe one spatial vector with reference to another spatial vector. In analogy to the inference scheme for relating one temporal interval to another temporal interval described by Allen [1983], we develop here an inference scheme for orientation-based spatial inferences.

We will denote the segment between *a* and *b* of the oriented line *ab* as vector ***ab***. Suppose, we know the qualitative spatial relation of vector ***bc*** to vector ***ab*** and the relation of vector ***cd*** to vector ***bc***. We would like to infer the relation of vector ***bd*** to the original reference vector ***ab***.

We will first illustrate the simple case of a single front/back dichotomy, i.e., we consider eight orientation relations for ***bc*** and for ***cd***. The result of the inference is to be expressed in terms of the same eight relations. The front/back dichotomy divides both *ab* and *bc* in point *b*. For reasons of uniformity, we will relate *d* to *cb* instead of *bc;* the front/back dichotomy then is always at the front of the vector (compare Figure 6a). We use the notation (labels *0* through *7*) to denote orientations as introduced in Figure 2.

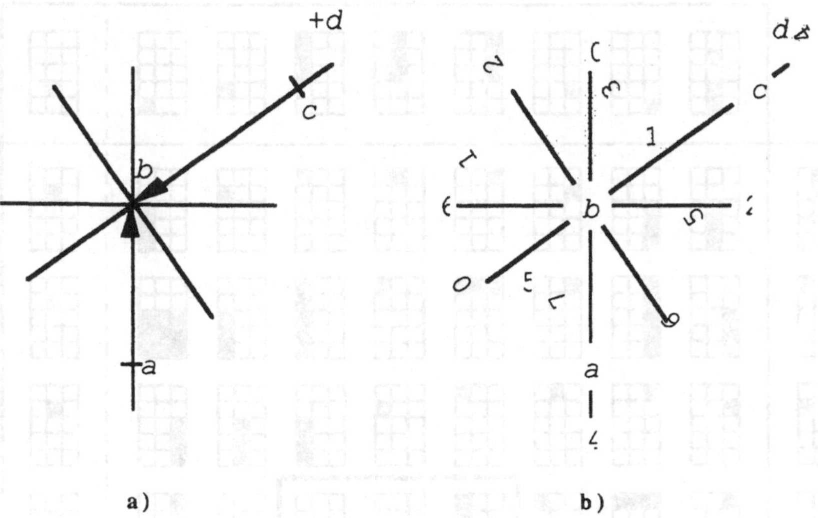

Fig. 6 a) *a, b,* and *c* define two left/right and front/back dichotomies in *b* for describing *d;* **b)** Each pair of dichotomies defines eight orientations; *d* is located in the shaded area.

Take a simple example: Let *c right-front (1)* ***ab*** and *d left-front (7)* ***bc*** (Figure 6a). We do not have a front/back dichotomy of *bc* in point *c;* thus, we cannot represent "*d left-front (7)* ***bc***". We use "*d right-back (3)* ***cb***", instead. This relation describes a more general case, since it also includes part of the region *left-back* ***bc*** (Figure 6b). Informally speaking, we can infer that ***bd*** is ahead of ***ab***; we cannot infer whether *d* is located in the left, straight, or right front region of ***ab***. More formally, we infer: ***bd*** *left-front (7)* ***ab*** or ***bd*** *straight (0)* ***ab*** or ***bd*** *right-front (1)* ***ab***.

Figure 7 depicts the composition table for the 8*8 orientation relations. Each table entry corresponds to an orientation and/or location relation as suggested by Figure 5. The location of *a* and *b* in the icons of the column of initial conditions and in the table is indicated in the top icon of the column of initial conditions; the location of *b* and *c* in the icons of the row of initial conditions is indicated in its leftmost icon. In the column of initial conditions, black squares mark the possible location of *c;* in the row of initial conditions and in the table, black squares mark the possible locations of *d.* The bottom row and the rightmost column display location inferences for the orientation-less cases (*c*=*b* and *d*=*b*, respectively).

The composition table forms the basis for qualitative orientation-based reasoning. The table is arranged in such a way that neighboring rows and columns always correspond to conceptually neighboring initial conditions for the inference. Of course, not all conceptually neighboring relations can be depicted by neighboring rows and columns in a 2-dimensional table. Note that with this arrangement, spatially neighboring table entries (corresponding to the inferences) also are conceptual neighbors.

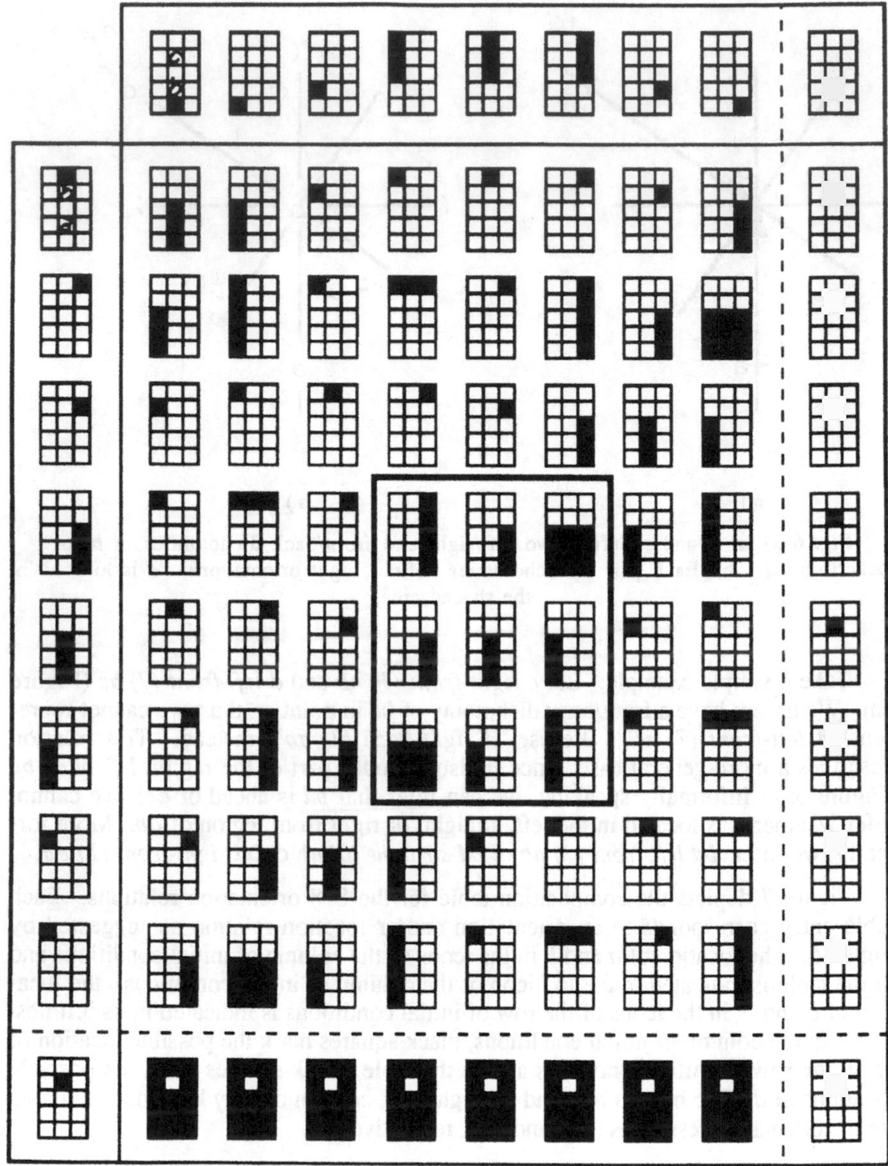

Fig. 7. Iconic composition table for nine location/orientation relations.

The entries in the composition table for the orientations follow a simple formation rule. Let *r* denote the orientation of *c* wrt. ***ab*** and *s* the orientation of *d* wrt. ***bc***. The resulting orientation *t* wrt. ***ab*** then is:

$$t = \left\{ \begin{array}{ll} r+s & \text{for } r \text{ or } s \text{ even} \\ (r+s-1) \ldots (r+s+1) & \text{for } r \text{ and } s \text{ odd} \end{array} \right\} \bmod 8$$

where $(r+s-1) \ldots (r+s+1)$ denotes a range of possible orientations.

Although in one fourth of the cases there is some uncertainty as to which specific qualitative orientation holds – in these cases there is a range of three neighboring possibilities which effectively increase the range of possible angles from 0° or 90° to 180° – we always have certainty about the resulting uncertainty. This is very important, since in certain situations the precision of the result may matter, in others it may not.

Note that the composition table would look more symmetrical if we merged the three lower rows of the icons into one (without loss of information). The expanded graphical notation is used for consistency with the representation for reasoning with higher resolution.

The conclusions obtained through the reasoning procedure can be used for further inferences. Not all conclusion patterns, however, can be found in the composition tables; some conclusions correspond to disjunctions of initial conditions. Accordingly, correct inferences for those patterns are found by forming the logical disjunction of the corresponding compositions. This operation can be visually carried out by superimposing the corresponding icons in our pictorial notation. Alternatively, the composition table could be expanded to explicitly include the complex cases or the conceptual neighborhoods could be exploited for a coarse reasoning approach. These techniques are discussed in detail in Freksa [1992].

4.2 Higher Resolution Reasoning

The reasoning procedure presented in the foregoing section was based on the left/right dichotomy and a single front/back dichotomy for each oriented entity. In this section, we will illustrate how the inferences can be refined by making use of the second front/back dichotomy introduced in section 2.3. This dichotomy corresponds to splitting up rows 4 to 6 of the composition table into three sub-rows each and columns 4 to 6 into three sub-columns each. At the intersection of these rows and columns (marked in Figure 7) we now can make more precise inferences, i.e, we can restrict the range of possible orientations (or locations) of *d* wrt. ***ab***. The result is depicted in Figure 8.

Inferences also can be refined by processing evidence from multiple sources with the same composition table and combining the results. For example, from *c* ***right-front (1) ab*** and *d* ***left-back (5) cb*** follows *d* ***right (1, 2, 3) ab***. From *c'* ***right-front (1) ba*** and *d* ***left-front (7) bc'*** follows *d* ***front (7, 0, 1) ba***. If both descriptions of *d* hold, their conjunction also holds; thus *d* ***left-front ba***. The inference chain is depicted in Figure 9.

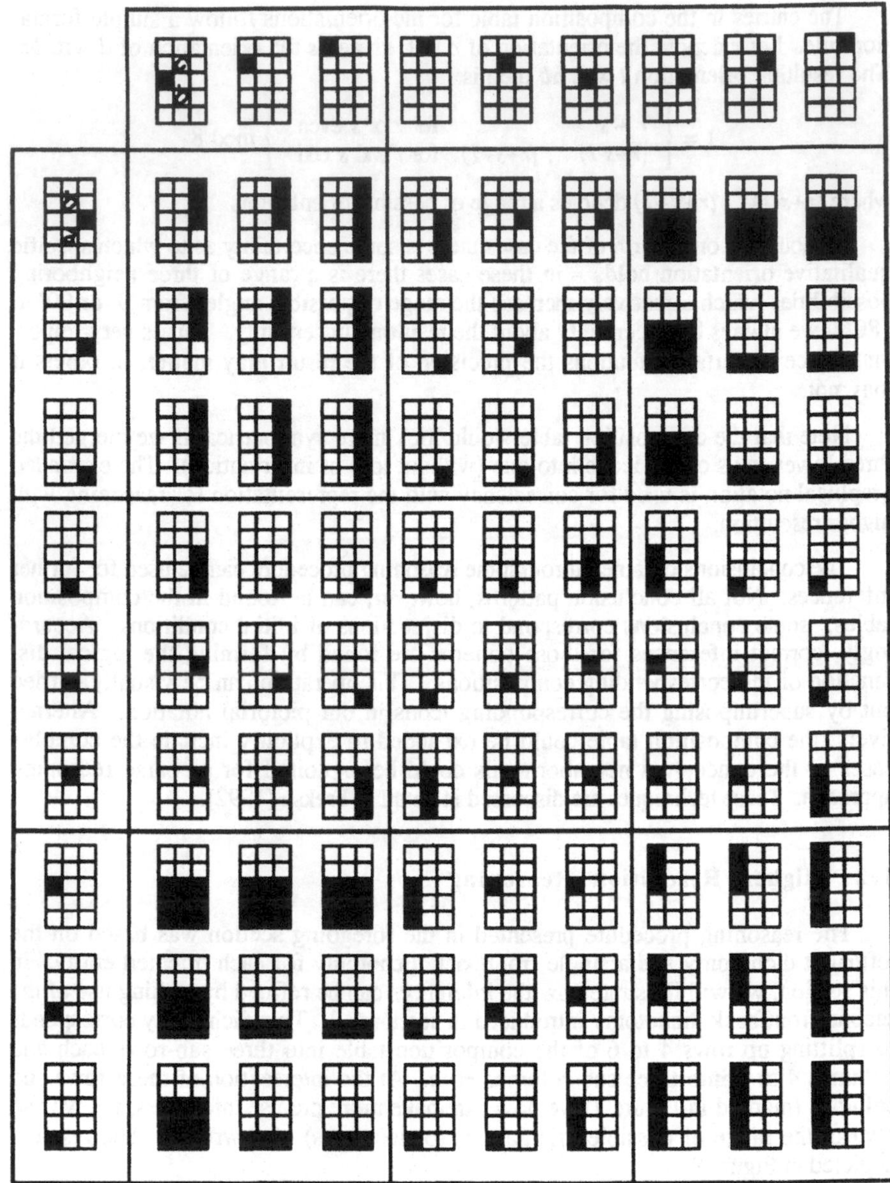

Fig. 8. Fine grain composition table for the marked region in Figure 7.

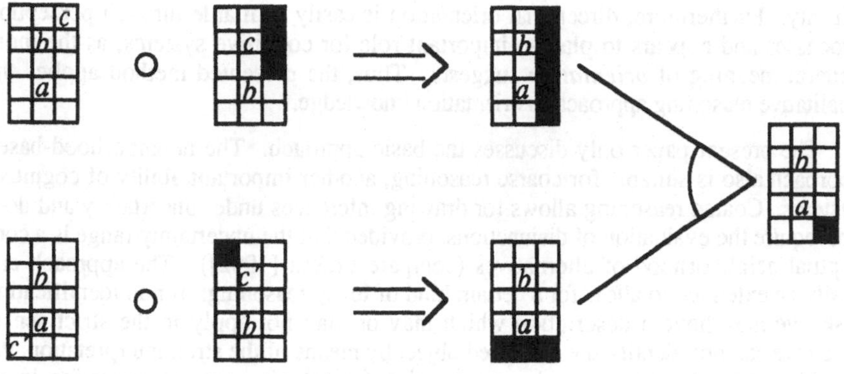

Fig. 9. Refining an inference through multiple evidence.

4.3 Applications

A simple example for an application of orientation-based qualitative spatial reasoning is the process of determining a location in space on the basis of our own location and another location we know. Suppose, we walk from start location *a* to location *c* and we have reached the intermediate location *b*. We can describe orientation and distance of location *c* qualitatively with reference to vector ***ab***, i.e, we compare the road segment ***bc*** to the road segment ***ab*** with respect to their orientation. At position *c*, we can compare the next road segment ***cd*** with the previous stretch, the section ***bc***. The inference step then determines the goal location *d* with respect to the initial road segment ***ab***.

Such an inference can be relevant for a wayfinding process. Suppose, we have a route description from a known location to an as yet unknown place in terms of orientation information (left, straight, right; forward, neutral, backward). We would like to determine the location of the unknown place and the direct route to this place. The described approach can perform this task in qualitative terms, i.e., it can specify a region in which the place can be found.

Suppose, we have two different route descriptions – for example our own description and that of another person. The approach allows us to determine if both routes may lead to the same place; this is the case when the regions described by the inference have a non-empty intersection. Conversely, if we know that both routes in fact lead to the same place, it may be possible to derive a more precise description of the location of this place.

5 Discussion

The approach outlined in this paper is motivated by considerations about spatial knowledge of cognitive systems. More specifically, it is based on the insight that spatial knowledge of natural cognitive systems tends to be qualitative rather than quantitative in nature. The qualitative approach is particularly useful for identification tasks, e.g. for object location tasks, which represent a large fraction of cognitive activity. Furthermore, directional orientation is easily available through perception processes and appears to play an important role for cognitive systems, as the more general meaning of *orientation* suggests. Thus, the presented method applies the qualitative reasoning approach to orientation knowledge.

The present paper only discusses the basic approach. The neighborhood-based approach also is suitable for coarse reasoning, another important ability of cognitive systems. Coarse reasoning allows for drawing inferences under uncertainty and does not require the evaluation of disjunctions, provided that the uncertainty range is a conceptual neighborhood of alternatives (compare Freksa [1992]). The approach can easily be extended to allow for a certain kind of fuzzy reasoning: for an identification task, we may have a description which may or may not apply in the strict sense; when we can not identify the described object by means of the strict interpretation, the neighborhood structure provides information for relaxing the interpretation in an appropriate way. Neighborhood-based reasoning also has computational advantages, specifically for processing perception-based knowledge. For the case of orientation-based reasoning, however, specific analyses have not yet been carried out.

We have discussed in this paper only one of a set of possible spatial inferences one might want to draw: from $c\,R_1\,\boldsymbol{ab}$ and $d\,R_2\,\boldsymbol{bc}$ we inferred $d\,R_3\,\boldsymbol{ab}$. This inference pattern requires a particular sequence of input relations for reasoning through a chain of inference steps. For certain applications, the input knowledge and/or the desired inference may require a different inference pattern. For example, we may want to infer $d\,R_4\,\boldsymbol{ac}$, $b\,R_5\,\boldsymbol{ac}$, $b\,R_6\,\boldsymbol{ad}$, etc. instead. Such inferences require new composition tables which share important properties with the one discussed here. Other variations are conceivable and should be explored.

Acknowledgements

Numerous variations of a previous proposal by the author were worked out in the context of the 'Space Inference Engine' project at the University of Hamburg by Marco Homann, Carsten Wiegand, Antje Wulf, Rolf Sander, and Kai Zimmermann. I also acknowledge critical comments by Daniel Hernández, Ralf Röhrig, Carsten Schröder, and an anonymous referee. The comments and discussions helped improve the approach considerably.

References

Allen, J.F., Maintaining knowledge about temporal intervals, CACM 26 (11) (1983) 832-843.

Chang, S.K., Jungert, E.: A spatial knowledge structure for image information systems using symbolic projections. Proc. of the National Computer Conference, Dallas, Texas, November 2-6, 1986, pp 79-86.

Egenhofer, M., Franzosa, R.: Point-set topological spatial relations. Intern.. Journal of Geographical Information Systems, vol.5, n.2, 161-174, 1991.

Frank, A.U.: Qualitative spatial reasoning with cardinal directions. Proc. Seventh Austrian Conference on Artificial Intelligence, Wien, 157-167, Springer, Berlin 1991.

Freksa, C.: Qualitative spatial reasoning. In: D.M. Mark & A.U. Frank (eds.) Cognitive and Linguistic Aspects of Geographic Space, Kluwer, Dordrecht 1991.

Freksa, C.: Temporal reasoning based on semi-intervals. *Artificial Intelligence* 54 (1992) 199-227.

Furbach, U., Dirlich, G., Freksa, C.: Towards a theory of knowledge representation systems. In: W. Bibel & B. Petkoff (eds.) *Artificial Intelligence Methodology, Systems, Applications* (pp. 77-84). Amsterdam: North-Holland 1985.

Güsgen, H.W.: Spatial reasoning based on Allen's temporal logic. TR-89-049, International Computer Science Institute, Berkeley 1989.

Hernández, D.: Using comparative relations to represent spatial knowledge. In: W. Hoeppner (ed.) Workshop Räumliche Alltagsumgebungen des Menschen, 69-80, Koblenz 1990.

Lee, S.-Y., Hsu, F.-J., Picture algebra for spatial reasoning of iconic images represented in 2D C-string. *Pattern Recognition Letters* 12 (1991) 425-435.

Mukerjee, A., Joe, G.: A qualitative model for space, Proc. AAAI-90, 721-727.

Pribbenow, S.: Interaktion von propositionalen und bildhaften Repräsentationen. In: C. Freksa & C. Habel (eds.) Repräsentation und Verarbeitung räumlichen Wissens, 156-174, Springer, Berlin 1990.

Randell, D.: Analysing the familiar: a logical representation of space and time. 3rd International Workshop Semantics of Time, Space, and Movement, Toulouse 1991.

Schätz, B.: Ein konnektionistischer Ansatz zur verteilten Darstellung von Objektpositionen. In: W. Hoeppner (ed.) Workshop Räumliche Alltagsumgebungen des Menschen, 147-158, Koblenz 1990.

Schlieder, C.: Anordnung. Eine Fallstudie zur Semantik bildhafter Repräsentation. In: C. Freksa & C. Habel (eds.) Repräsentation und Verarbeitung räumlichen Wissens, 129-142, Springer, Berlin 1990.

The Observer's Point of View: An Extension of Symbolic Projections

Erland Jungert
FOA (Swedish Defence Research Establishment)
Box 1165, S-581 11 Linköping, Sweden
telephone + 46 13 11 83 37
fax + 46 13 13 16 65
e-mail jungert@lin.foa.se

Abstract: Spatial reasoning is normally concerned with various methods for reasoning in images that in many cases are symbolic, like for instance, maps. The goal is to identify complex object relations by means of methods operating on a high abstraction level. Several approaches to spatial reasoning have been proposed and one such method is symbolic projections which is closely related to qualitative reasoning. The method that will be discussed here is an extension of symbolic projections that specifically is concerned with the observer's point of view. In other words, the work presented here is concerned with qualitative methods for determination of, among other things, directions, distances and other object relations seen from the observer's perspective, i.e. the projections are in the majority of cases concerned with a singular point.

1 Introduction

Spatial reasoning comprises a group of methods, applied to a large group of problems, that are mainly dealing with the identification of spatial relations between objects in images which in many cases turn out to be symbolic, e.g. maps or drawings. The resemblance among the existing problems is not particularly strong and for that reason it is not likely that a single method can be used for all occurring problems. Most likely, a number of independent methods will be developed in the near future. The approach proposed here is mainly directed towards applications that will occur in geographical information systems. Examples of applications where the approach may be used are in crisis/emergancy management where there is an obvious need for integration of decision support tools. The technique may be used in other types of applications such as in CAD systems although in a somewhat modified way.

Symbolic projections were originally developed by Chang et al. [1] as a method for iconic indexing. Chang and Jungert [2] showed that the method could be used for spatial reasoning as well. Further work by Jungert and Chang [3] has made it possible to develop a symbolic image algebra which comprises a theoretical foundation for improving the technique for spatial reasoning. In [4] Chang and Jungert also showed how symbolic projections can serve as an integrated part in a pictorial information system. The work on symbolic projections is by no means limited to the above, for instance, Lee and Hsu [5] have shown how symbolic projections can be used as a method for similarity retrieval. Furthermore, Holmes and Jungert [6] have given an example of how symbolic projections can be applied to knowledge based route planning in digitized maps. The above list is by no means complete, it just indicates some of the milestones in the development of symbolic projections.

Other approaches to spatial reasoning have been developed as well, for instance, Frank [7] has developed methods for determination of directions and distances in symbolic images in an approach that is founded in techniques for qualitative reasoning. In this respect Frank's approach has similarities with symbolic projections. Actually, Frank's work has partly influenced the work described here.

2 The Basic Problem

Symbolic projection is, basically a method where objects in an image are projected to the x- and y-coordinate axes in the 2D case. The 3D case is a generalization of the 2D case. As a result, two strings can be created, one from each coordinate axis, which show the relative position of the objects. These projection strings can be used for qualitative spatial reasoning. In the original work by Chang et al.[1], these strings described the relative positions along each axes by means of an operator set including just two relational operators, i.e. {<,=}. Later Jungert [8] introduced the edge-to-edge operator. As a consequence, a minimal operator set was defined, i.e. {<,=,|} which can be used for description of any image by means of symbolic projections. However, in the method of symbolic projections some fundamental problems exist among which the most important one is illustrated in figure 1. Shortly, the problem can be stated as follows. Using symbolic projections there is no way to infer on which side of the line object 'l' the two point objects, p1 and p2 lies, if they are situated inside the rectangle spanned up by 'l'.

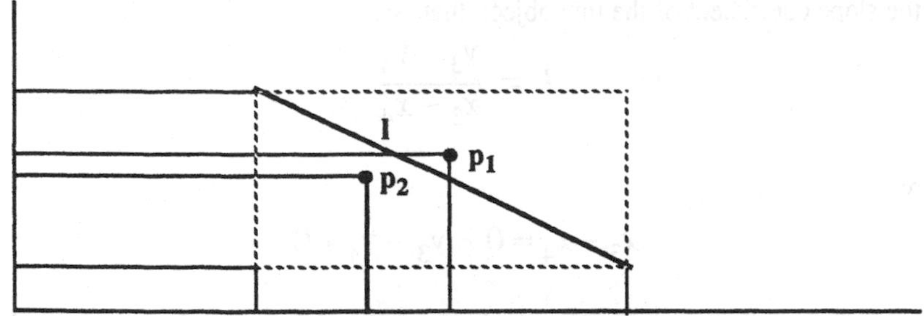

Fig. 1. A fundamental problem in symbolic projections

This problem is due to the fact that lines that are neither horizontal nor vertical cannot be represented such that the knowledge of their slope is preserved in the strings. However, there is quite a simple solution to this problem, illustrated in figure 2.

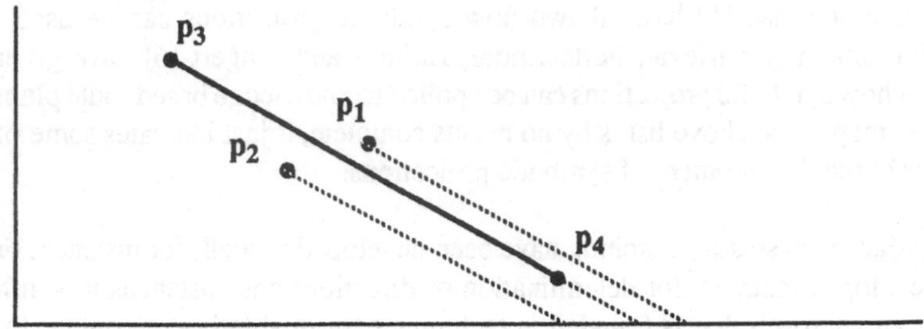

Fig. 2. The solution to the fundamental problem in symbolic projection.

As can be seen, the point objects and the line object are all projected in the direction of the slope of the line object, i.e. they are projected parallel to the line. This projection can either be made down to the x-axis or the y-axis. Both cases are not necessary since either alternative contains all necessary information. The result of this slope-projection, u_l, is:

$$u_l \leftarrow x_{p_1} < x_l < x_{p_2}$$

where

$$x_{p_1} = x_1 - \frac{y_1}{k}$$

$$x_{p_2} = x_2 - \frac{y_2}{k}$$

$$x_l = x_3 - \frac{y_3}{k}$$

k is the slope coefficient of the line object, that is:

$$k = \frac{y_3 - y_4}{x_3 - x_4}$$

where

$$x_3 - x_4 \neq 0 \wedge y_3 - y_4 \neq 0$$

The two extreme cases correspond to the horizontal and the vertical projections, that is the regular projections along the y- and x-axes respectively. In the above, k can take any value beside the extreme cases. The method also works for several lines at different orientations, in which case there must be separate slope projections for each line. However, as will be shown subsequently, it turns out that the most important angles are:

$$\pm\frac{\pi}{4}, \pm\frac{\pi}{8}, \pm\frac{3\pi}{8}$$

The extra cost in operations for this type of projections compared to the regular is thus, 1 division and 1 addition, if the slope is preprocessed. This is a reasonable price for the gained information.

3 Directions

A new way of projecting the symbolic objects was demonstrated in section 2, that contrary to the technique used, so far, is not perpendicular to the coordinate axes. It was demonstrated that the projections could be made in arbitrary directions. This is a solution to a fundamental problem in symbolic projections. However, the approach can be applied to other problems as well, which will be discussed subsequently.

The non-perpendicular approach can be used for determination of directions as well. This is particularly useful in reasoning about geographical directions like north, west and north-east, etc. In such a directional system 8 directions are of particular interest, that is {N, NE, E, SE, S, SW, W, NW}. To illustrate this, only the 3 directions of the first quadrant are considered. However, it is a simple task to generalize the technique into the full space. The first quadrant is thus split into three parts as illustrated in figure 3. The angle between the two dividing lines is $\pi/4$ and the angles between the dividing lines and the coordinate axes are consequently $\pi/8$. The cone between the dividing lines indicates the northeastern direction while the area between a dividing line and a coordinate axis corresponds to half the cone in the northern and eastern directions respectively.

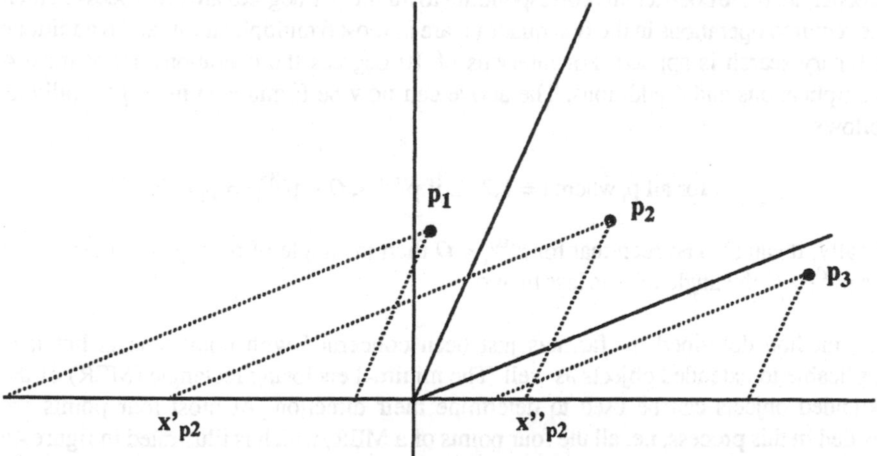

Fig. 3. An illustration of the method for determination of directions in symbolic projections.

The examples in figure 3 show the method for determination of the directions of the points. Here, like in section 2, angular projections are used. The points are projected parallel to the two dividing lines. The result of these projections is, for point p_1, where both projections hit the x-axis to the left of the "origin", subsequently called the observer's position, sine it does not necessarily have to correspond to the origin. p_2 on the other hand lies in the north-eastern cone and the observer's position is in between the projected points. The following rules for deduction of the directions can hence be identified.

$$U_0 \leftarrow x' < x'' < O \Rightarrow north\,(p, O)$$

That is, if the two projections of point p on the x-axis, i.e. x' and x'', are less than the observer's position (*O*) in the U_0-string then the direction of p is north of *O* (as seen in the first quadrant).

Similarly

$$U_0 \leftarrow x' < O < x'' \Rightarrow north - east\,(p, O)$$

Another way of expressing this is by saying that the direction of p in the latter examples is:

$$\frac{\pi}{8} < dir\,(p) < \frac{3\pi}{8}$$

The cost in execution time is two multiplications and two additions which again is acceptable. To use conventional methods would require heavier computation including calculation of the arctan. Observe that the slope coefficient can be preprocessed. In other words, since no extra calculations during the actual run-time is required the method can be refined such that the directions are determined even for much more narrow angle intervals. The extra time required for these calculations are still acceptable. If the coefficients corresponding to all integer degrees are preprocessed then the required operations in the first quadrant are at most 6 multiplications and 6 additions if binary search is applied. For intervals of 10 degrees the operations are at most 4 multiplications and 4 additions. The above can now be formulated more generally as follows

$$\text{for all } p_i \text{ where } i = 1,2, \ldots \text{ if } p^{(\alpha)}{}_i < O < p^{(\beta)}{}_i \Rightarrow p_i \in [\alpha, \beta]$$

Finally, it can also be seen that for $p^{(\alpha)}{}_i < O$ then the angle of p_i is greater than α and for $p^{(\alpha)}{}_i > O$ the angle of p_i is less than α.

The method described, so far, has just been concerned with point objects but it is applicable to extended objects as well. The minimal enclosing rectangle (MER) of the extended objects can be used to determine their direction. At most four points are needed in this process, i.e. all the four points of a MER, which is illustrated in figure 4a through d. Figure 4a illustrates a situation where all four corners of the rectangle fall below the $\pi/8$-line, i.e. the object is east of the observer. In 4b the object is north-east of the observer. Figures 4 c and d are somewhat more complicated. The interpretation of 4c ought to be north-east to east since here we have two points of the rectangle north-east of the observer while the two remaining are to the east. This can be expressed in the following way:

north-east-to-east (A,*O*)

The situation in figure 4d, however, causes some further problems. There are two points to the north, one point to north-east and finally one to the east. The most natural way to interpret this is simply to say that the direction is north-east. If, on the other hand, two points at north had been situated in the second quadrant then it had been more correct to say that the direction is north. Clearly, a more or less exhaustive study of all possible alternatives must be performed. However, this will not change the method as such. As can bee seen, it is quite easy to determine the directions of the four points but in some cases the directions of the objects are subject to personal interpretation. The problem of determination of directional relationships has also been addressed by Peuquet and Ci-Xiang [9].

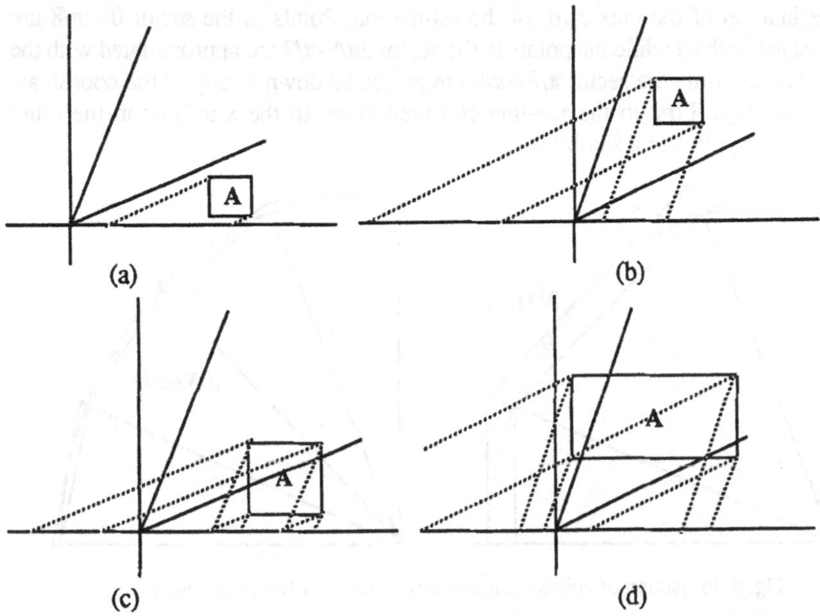

Fig. 4. Four cases illustrating how the direction of extended objects can be determined.

4 Distances

The method can be used for determination of distances as well. However, two different methods can be identified. The first one is concerned with objects that may be fairly apart from each other but are approximately at the same distance from the observer. This method is concerned with approximation of absolute distances. The other method is concerned with qualitative reasoning of distances between observer and objects whose relative distances may vary widely from the observer.

4.1 Approximation of Absolute Distances

Objects at almost the same distances from the observer, but situated in different directions from the observer, are of importance to differentiate from each other. This is especially complicated when the objects are situated in different directions. One way of solving this problem which is based on qualitative reasoning and symbolic projections will be discussed here. The method is accomplished by first determining the direction and than find an approximation of the projection along one of the coordinate axes. Figure 5 a and b illustrate the approach.

In figure 5 a all points on the circle can be projected down to either the x- or the y-axis such that the projected point falls inside the interval of the parallel lines, which is a rough estimation of the max error of the estimation. Points in the sector 0 - $\pi/8$ are approximated with $|x|$ while the points in the sector $3\pi/8$-$\pi/2$ are approximated with the y-value. Points inside the sector $\pi/8$-$3\pi/8$ are projected down to any of the coordinate axes in two steps. First to the $\pi/8$-line and then down to the x-axis or in the other direction to the y-axis in a similar way.

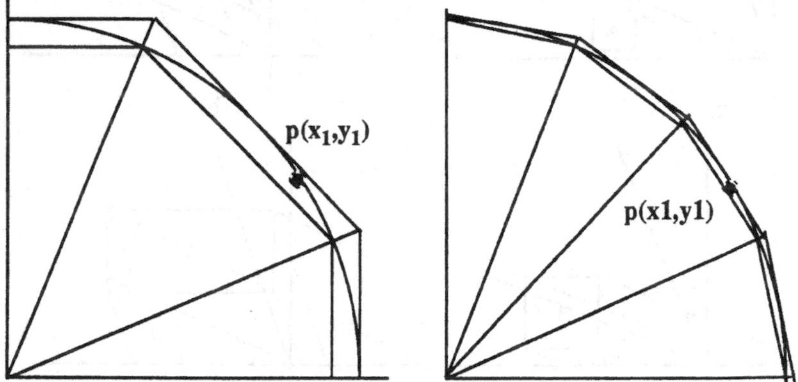

Fig. 5. Projection of points at almost equal distances from the observer.

In the following $k^{(\alpha)}$ means a slope coefficient with an angle 'α'. The point $p(x_1,y_1)$ is on the line $y= -x + m$ where $m = y_1 + x_1$. This line is crossing:

$$y = k^{(\pi/8)} x$$

at

$$x = \frac{x_1 + y_1}{1 + k^{(\pi/8)}}$$

which is the approximation of the distance from the observer to the point object. It can be shown that:

$$1 + k^{(\pi/8)} = 2^{1/2}$$

Consequently, the distance from the observer can be approximated with:

$$(x_1 + y_1)\, 2^{-1/2}$$

The max error is quite large

$$\delta = \sqrt{x_1^2 + y_1^2} - x_1 = \left(1 - \frac{1}{\sqrt{1+k^2}}\right)\sqrt{x_1 + y_1} = 0.076\sqrt{x_1 + y_1}$$

where δ is max for $k = \tan \pi/8$. This is actually too large to be accepted and it turns out that the approximation in 5b is better, i.e.:

$$\delta = \sqrt{x_1 + y_1} - \left(x_1 - \frac{y_1}{k^{(\frac{9\pi}{16})}}\right)$$

$$\delta = 0.0196\sqrt{x_1 + y_1}$$

where $y_1/x_1 = \tan \pi/16$ in the maximum case. In other words, an improvement from about 8% in the 8-sectors case down to almost 2% in the 16-sectors case. In distance transforms Borgefors [10] has showed similar results, i.e. exactly the same result for the 16-sectors case while the 8-sectors case is somewhat larger here. However, the technique described here requires generally a number of operations that is less than for distance transforms although their distances are generated globally in all directions.

The projection technique in both cases is almost the same, except that point objects in the 0-$\pi/8$ sector is projected down to the x-axis with the following approximation:

$$x - \frac{y}{k^{(\frac{\pi}{16})}}$$

In the $\pi/8$- $\pi/4$ sector, the points are first projected to the $\pi/8$-line and then down to the x-axis. The two remaining sectors in the quadrant are analogously projected to the y-axis.

A point (x_1, y_1) in the $\pi/8$-$\pi/4$ sector is first projected down to the intersection between the lines

$$y = k^{(\frac{\pi}{8})} x$$

$$y = k^{(\frac{11\pi}{16})} x + m$$

where

$$m = y_1 - k^{(\frac{11\pi}{16})} x_1$$

This point is

$$x = \frac{y_1 - k^{(\frac{11\pi}{16})} x_1}{k^{(\frac{\pi}{8})} - k^{(\frac{11\pi}{16})}}$$

$$y = k^{(\frac{\pi}{8})} \frac{y_1 - k^{(\frac{11\pi}{16})} x_1}{k^{(\frac{\pi}{8})} - k^{(\frac{11\pi}{16})}}$$

Finally, the point is projected down to the x-axis through the projection

$$d = x + \frac{y}{k^{(\frac{9\pi}{16})}}$$

The final result then becomes

$$d = \left(y_1 - k^{(\frac{11\pi}{16})} x_1\right) C$$

where

$$C = \frac{k^{(\frac{9\pi}{16})} + k^{(\frac{\pi}{8})}}{k^{(\frac{9\pi}{16})}\left(k^{(\frac{\pi}{8})} - k^{(\frac{11\pi}{16})}\right)} \approx 0.48$$

Hence, only two multiplications and one addition are required in the worst case compared to the 8-directions case, which required one multiplication and one addition in the worst case. However, the operations for finding the directions must be included as well, which require two multiplications and two additions at the most. Hence, the total number of operations for getting both distance *and* direction is in the respective cases:

8-sectors 3 multiplications and 3 additions
16-sectors 4 multiplications and 3 additions

The extra multiplication in the 16-sectors case is the price for getting an error that is less than 2% compared to 7.6% in the 8-sectors case. This is affordable when comparing the distances from the observer to two different points. In the 16-sectors case the exact distance lies in the interval [d, d+ δ]. Because of δ, two distances can only be said to be approximately equal when compared. Hence, if two projected distances, d1 and d2, are compared, the following case will occur:

$$d_1 < d_2 \text{ if } d_1 < d_2 - \delta_2$$

$$d_1 > d_2 \text{ if } d_1 - \delta_1 > d_2 \text{ where } \delta_1 \approx 0.02d_1 \text{ and } \delta_2 \approx 0.02d_2$$

For all other cases $d_1 \approx d_2$.

4.2 Qualitative Distances

Using qualitative and relative methods for determination of distances is a technique similar to that introduced by Frank [7]. Frank's technique is based on a method where the space is split into a set of fields {c, m, f} where 'c' corresponds to 'close to' a certain point which can be compared to the observer's position. Similarly 'f' means 'far from' the same point while 'm' is somewhere in the middle. A drawback with Frank's method is that it just works for point objects. In this paper we will see that this limitation can be overcome by means of the extension of symbolic projections. In the following discussion, the method for determination of qualitative distances is entirely based on the same technique as was discussed in section 2 in this paper. For this reason supporting lines, are drawn just for a few selected cases. In figure 6 a set of objects, A through F are shown, illustrating a number of situations corresponding to various distances between the observer's position and the extended objects.

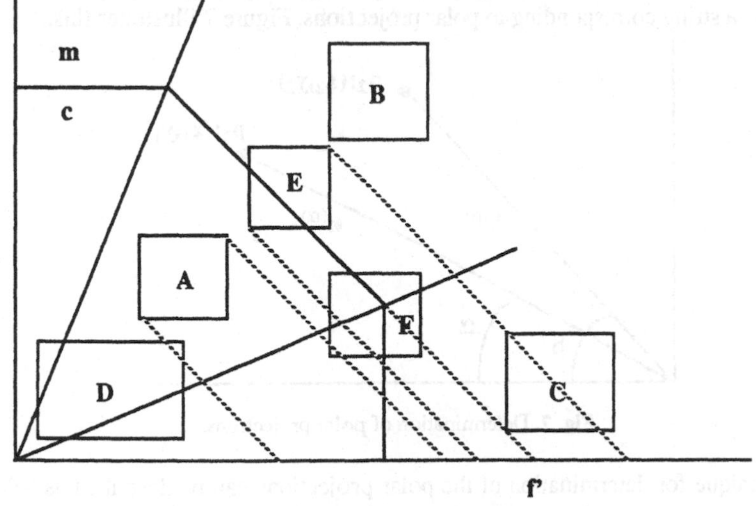

Fig. 6. The distances of extended objects to the observer.

The objects A, B and C have all distances that are unambiguous, since neither of them are crossing any of the lines between the various distance i. e. A is close to O, while B and C are medium far away. E lies on the line between 'm' and 'c'. This is indicated by the judgement that the object is 'fairly close' to O. The same judgement is evidently valid for F. Finally, D, lies close to O. One aspect that is of concern here is that we are considering not just the objects themselves but the minimal enclosing rectangles. Consequently, a rectangle can be 'fairly close' to the observer while the object itself can be 'close' since all the points describing the object lies in the 'close'-area. However here we are performing a qualitative reasoning and for that reason the difference between these two cases can be considered to be of no importance or at least of less importance. Table 1 shows the direction and the distances of the objects in figure 6.

Table 1

Object	direction	distance
A	north-east	close
B	north-east	medium
C	east	medium
D	north-east	close
E	north-east	fairly-close
F	east-north-east	fairly-close

5 Polar Projections

So far, the discussion has been concerned with projections in various directions down to, primarily, the x-axis. Since the direction of a point from the observer's position can be determined relative to a line with a certain angle it will also be possible to determine the relative angle between two points. Consequently, it is possible to project the objects to O, i. e. a string corresponding to polar projections. Figure 7 illustrates this..

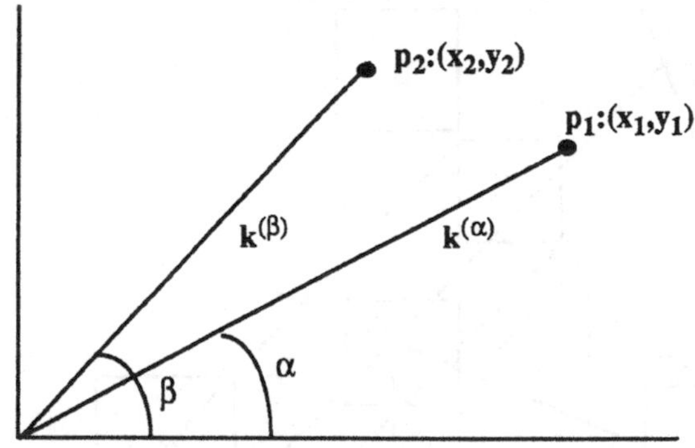

Fig. 7. Determination of polar projections.

The technique for determination of the polar projections can be described as follows. First, the supporting projection lines for each point is projected down to the x-axis to determine the relative angles. From this, a polar projection string P can be generated.

The example in figure 7 thus gives the polar projection string:

$$P \leftarrow p_1 < p_2$$

However the slope coefficients of the supporting lines can be used as a means for distinguishing all points in the space. Those coefficients are simple to calculate

$$k^{(\alpha)} = y_1/x_1 \text{ and } k^{(\beta)} = y_2/x_2 \text{ where } x_1, x_2 \neq 0.$$

The case when $x_i = 0$ is just a simple exception corresponding to the perpendicular case that easily can be handled. For the points p_1 and p_2 in figure 7 the polar projection P follows from:

$$k^{(\alpha)} < k^{(\beta)}.$$

The supporting lines here are used in the same way as in [3], i.e. as cutting lines and for that reason a modified edge-to edge operator for the polar projections can be defined, which here is denoted with '$|_p$' where p stands for polar. Applying the polar projection technique to the extended objects is not too complicated and it can be illustrated with the examples in figures 8a through d. In figure 8a the polar projection string P becomes:

$$P \leftarrow B|_p AB|_p A$$

In this particular case the following relation can, for instance, be inferred:

Partly-behind (B, A, *O*)

which can be interpreted as: 'B is partly behind A seen from *O*'. Moreover, we can also infer;

Right (B, A, *O*),

i.e. 'B is to the right of A seen from *O*'.

In 8b the polar string is:

$$P \leftarrow B < A$$

which can be interpreted as 'B is to the right of A from O'.

Right (B, A, *O*)

Figure 8c corresponds to:

$$P \leftarrow A|_p AB|_p A$$

from which the following can be inferred:

Behind (B, A,*O*).

In figure 8d, finally, the image is somewhat more complicated, i. e:

$$P \leftarrow C|_p CD|_p D|_p BD|_p B|_p AB|_p A$$

In this particular case several different conclusions can be drawn. One is that D is partly visible between C and B. This is determined from the sub-expression CD $|_p$ D $|_p$ BD, where it is easy to see that D is between C and B but also that D can partly be seen fromO since ...$|_p$ D $|_p$... .

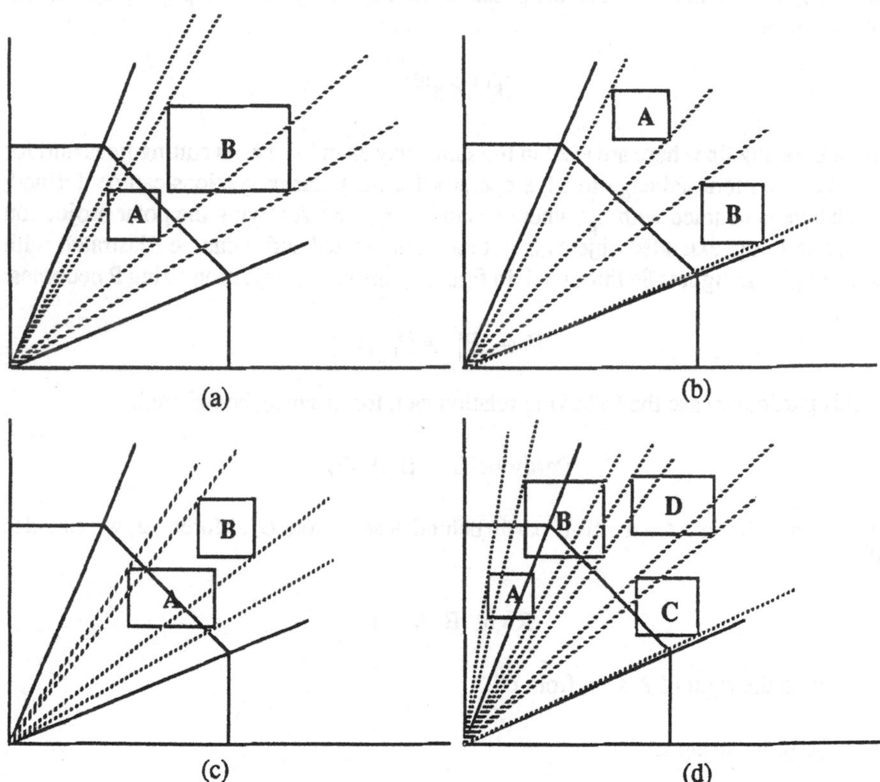

Fig. 8. Four polar projections, (a) partly behind, (b) left of, (c) behind and (d) partly visible.

The method discussed here has some similarities with Hough-transforms, see, e.g. [12]. However, Hough transforms are primarlily concerned with detection of boundaries of various types of objects, for instance, straight lines and other types of curves. Here, on the other hand, we are concerned with methods for qualitative reasoning for identification of various types of relationships between objects.

6 Path Projections.

Path-finding is normally the problem of finding the shortest point -to point description between a start-point and an end-point in a an image that normally is a map. In many applications this is not sufficient. Further information is needed, such as a description of the objects on each side of the path. In [6] Holmes and Jungert showed how a primitive plan describing a path could be created by means of knowledge based rules in an inference system. This technique was a first step in the direction towards a more complete description of a path, but it is not sufficient. A way of solving this problem is to apply the theories described in this paper. This can be done by approximating the path with a sequence of inter-connected straight lines corresponding either to road segments or to any other kind of plan steps. This actually means that the map used here is a map in a lower resolution. Using such a map may sometimes cause problems but this is of less importance since the method does not intend to be exact. A method for generation of a low resolution network which can used here is described in [11]. The objects along the route can be projected down to these lines by using the well-known formula

$$k_o = -\frac{1}{k_r}, k_r \neq 0$$

i.e. the slope coefficient of the objects to be projected down to route-line is the negative inverse of the slope of the route at that point. k_o will subsequently be called the object-to route coefficient and we will talk about object-to-route projections. Figure 9 illustrates the case

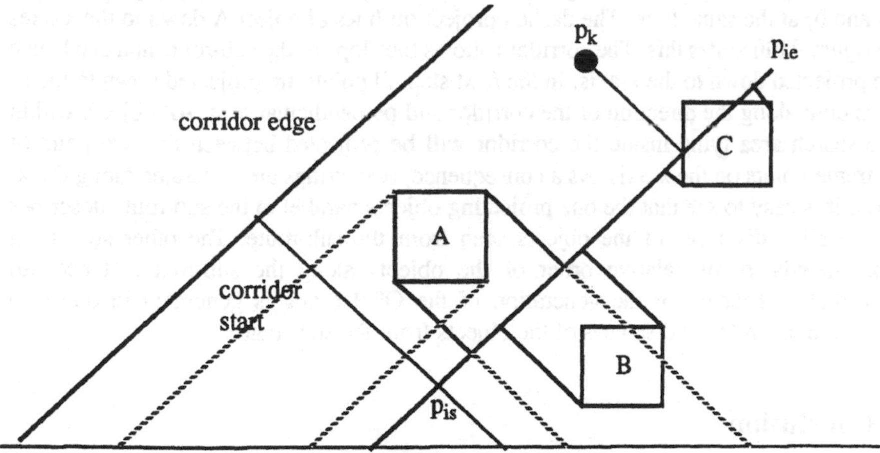

Fig. 9. object-to-route projections.

The projection string from figure 9 down to line segment l_i with start-point p_{is} and end-point p_{ie} is denoted OTR (object to route) which in this particular case becomes:

$$OTR \leftarrow A_L| A_L B_R| B_L < C_R| C_L C_R| p_{kL} C_L C_R| C_L C_R| C_R$$

The subscripts 'L' and 'R' means to the left and to the right of the route segment. As can be seen, the technique works for both extended and for point objects. It must also be noted that the direction of the path must be defined otherwise left and right sides are not defined and may be mixed up. Simple things that can be inferred from the above example are:

- A lies to the left of the route segment (RS),
- B lies to the right of RS,
- A and B lies on opposite sides of the RS and partly face to face,
- The RS is crossing the object C,
- A comes before p_k on the same side.

After line l_i line l_{i+1} follows. Obviously, some of the objects seen from l_i can be seen from l_{i+1} as well. The technique can clearly be used in navigation or just as a means for answering questions like "what object comes next on our route" or "when comes the next object of type X".
A few problems still remain to be solved. The first one concerns the size of the area to be searched for. The question is whether it is just those objects that are neighbours of a sub-route that should be of concern? However, this problem is nearly application dependent and for that reason we just assume that the area has a width of 2d and with the sub-route dividing this area in the middle, i.e. a road passing through a corridor with a width d on each side of the route segment. The second and more serious problem is how to a) find the objects in the corridor among all existing objects and b) generate the OTR-string. There is a fairly elegant solution to this problem which actually solves both a) and b) at the same time. The dashed projection lines of object A down to the x-axes in figure 9 illustrates this. The corridor follows the slope of the sub-route and can hence be projected down to the x-axis. In the next step all points are projected down to the x-axis both along the direction of the corridor and perpendicular to it. All objects within the search area lying inside the corridor will be projected between the two pairs of extreme points on the x-axis. As a consequence, two strings are generated along the x-axis. It is easy to see that the one projecting objects parallel to the sub-route describes the relative distances of the objects seen from the sub-route. The other sub-string corresponds to the relative order of the objects along the sub-route. Hence, all information needed for the generation of the OTR string is generated in one step including the relative distances of the objects from the sub-route.

7 Conclusion

This paper discusses and illustrates an extension of symbolic projection that is the solution to a fundamental problem that was discovered early in the evolution of the theory. It turns out that the solution can be used to solve other problems as well. In those cases the method is basically a method for qualitative reasoning, just like the original approach of symbolic projections and like later extensions to this theory. As a consequence of the new extension, it has been possible to determine such spatial relations as the directions to certain objects seen from an observer's point of view. The theory does not just regard point objects but extended objects as well. It is also possible to determine various kinds of distances in an economical way. Thus also giving rise to polar projections from which it has been possible to identify spatial relations that are seen from the observer's point of view. The technique supports identification of relations corresponding to questions like 'which objects are visible from a certain point'. Furthermore, it has also been demonstrated that the technique of sloping symbolic projection can be used for reasoning about objects situated along a path. Clearly, this extension of symbolic projects constitutes a powerful means for spatial reasoning adding new features to an already rich and powerful methodology.

References

1. Chang, S.-K., Shi, Q.Y and Yan, C. W., "Iconic indexing by 2D strings", IEEE transactions on Pattern Analysis and Machine Intelligence (PAMI), Vol 9, no 3, 1987, pp 413-428.

2. Chang, S.-K. and Jungert, E., "A Spatial Knowledge Structure for Image Information Systems Using Symbolic Projections", Proceedings of the 1986 Fall Joint Computer Conference, Nov 2-6, 1986, Dallas, TX, pp 79-86.

3. Jungert, E. and Chang, S.-K., "An Image Algebra for Pictorial Data Manipulation", To appear in Computer Vision, Graphics and Image Processing (CVGIP): Image Understanding.

4. Chang, S.-K. and Jungert, E."The Design of Pictorial Databases Based upon The Theory of Symbolic Projections", Journal of Visual Languages and Computing, vol 2, no 3, 1991, 195-215.

5. Lee, S. Y. and Hsu, F. J., "Picture Algebra for Spatial Reasoning of Iconic images represented in 2D C-string", Pattern Recognition Letters, no 12, 1991, pp 425-435.

6. Holmes, P. D. and Jungert, E. "Symbolic and Geometric Connectivity Graph Methods for Route Planning in Digitized Maps", IEEE transaction on Pattern Analysis and Machine Intelligence (PAMI), vol 14, no 4, May 1992, pp 549-565.

7. Frank, A. U., "Qualitative Spatial Reasoning about Distances and Directions in Geographic Space", Accepted for the Journal of Visual Languages and Computing.

8. Jungert, E.,"Extended Symbolic Projections Used as a Knowledge Structure for Spatial Reasoning", In Pattern Recognition 1989, Springer Verlag, Heidelberg, 1988, pp 343-351.

9. Peuquet, D. J. and Ci-Xiang, Z., "An Algorithm to Determine the Directional Relationship between Arbitrarily-Shaped Polygons in the Plane", Pattern Recognition, Vol 20, No 1, 1897, pp 65-74.

10. Borgefors, G., "Distance Transforms in Digital Images", Computer Vision, Graphics and Image Processing (CVGIP), Vol 34, 1986, pp 344-371.

11. Persson, J. and Jungert, E., "Generation of Multi-Resolution Maps from Run-Length-Encoded Data", To Appear in the Int. Journal on Geographical Information Systems.

12. Ballard, D. H. and Brown C. M., "Computer Vision", Prentice Hall, Englewood Cliffs, N.J., 1982, pp 123-131.

Reasoning about Gradual Changes of Topological Relationships*

Max J. Egenhofer and Khaled K. Al-Taha

National Center for Geographic Information and Analysis and Department of Surveying Engineering, Boardman Hall, University of Maine, Orono, ME 04469, U.S.A.
{max,kaltaha}@mecan1.maine.edu

Abstract. Geographic objects and phenomena may gradually change their location, orientation, shape, and size over time. A qualitative change occurs if the deformation of an object affects its topological relationship with respect to another object. The observation of such changes is particularly interesting, because qualitative changes frequently require different decisions or trigger new actions. Investigations of a closed set of mutually exclusive binary topological relationships led to a formal model to determine for each topological relationship the relationships closest to it. Applied to the entire set of binary topological relationships between spatial regions, this model describes a partial order over topological relationships and provides a measure to assess how far two relationships are apart from each other. The changes to the binary topological relationship caused by such deformations as translation, rotation, reduction, and expansion of an object are mapped onto this graph. The graphs show characteristic traverses for each kind of deformation. Using these characteristic traverses as knowledge about deformations, one can infer from multiple observations the kind of deformation that caused the change and predict the next topological relationship. Particularly, it provides answers to three kinds of qualitative space-time inferences: (1) Given a process and a state, what is the next most likely state? (2) Given an ordered pair of states, what process may have occurred? (3) Given an ordered pair of states and a process, in what states must the two objects have been in between?

1 Introduction

Spatial relationships between geographic objects are time-dependent and can change due to various phenomena. Water levels of rivers or lakes may rise causing flodding of buildings and roads near the shore line; contamination of soils may spread causing hazards for people living in affected areas; hurricanes may pass over islands or reach the continent; and market areas may expand so that they extend into adjacent political or administrative regions. In all these examples the objects changed their spatial relationships with respect to other spatial objects. A particularly important set of spatial relationships are *topological relationships*, which are preserved under groups of continuous transformations. Models for changes of topological relationships are relevant to spatio-temporal reasoning in geographic space as they derive the most likely configurations and allow

* This work was partially funded by grants from Intergraph Corporation. Additional support from NSF for the NCGIA under grant number SES 88-10917 is gratefully acknowledged.

for predictions about significant changes. Such predictions are important methods of reasoning in large-scale or geographic space, because this kind of reasoning is based primarily on inferences, rather than observations [7].

In the past, formalizations of spatial relationships have concentrated on static situations, i.e., spatial configurations of objects taken as a snapshot at a particular time. These results include various computational models for spatial relationships in raster space [5, 6], cardinal directions [17, 23], topological relationships [11, 12], and reasoning about their combinations [20]. Formalizations of imprecise spatial relationships [9, 10] have been based on fuzzy set theory. Complementary investigations include studies in cadastral systems of temporal changes in spatial relationships [22] and land ownership [2].

Here, we are investigating dynamic aspects of spatial relations, focusing on *changes in topological relations*. Topological changes are of a qualitative nature, rather than quantitative, because they cannot be expressed by conventional measures. For example, a small translation of one object will definitely change the topological relationship between two "equal" objects, while the change may not necessarily modify the topological relationship between two overlapping or disjoint objects. Qualitative changes are often considered particularly interesting information [4, 19], because they influence decisions and trigger actions to be taken. The following example motivates the interest in detecting and predicting changes of topological relations. Over the year, a log close to a lake may go through a variety of topological relationships. During summer, the water level in the lake may be low such that there is some land between the log and the shoreline (Fig. 1a). With increasing rainfall, the water surface will rise and eventually, the log will have an immediate access to the lake, without any land in between them (Fig. 1b). In spring with the melting snow and ice, the log may be first partially under water (Fig. 1c), later completely, but still accessible from the land (Fig. 1d), and finally, the log may become an "island" in the lake (Fig. 1e).

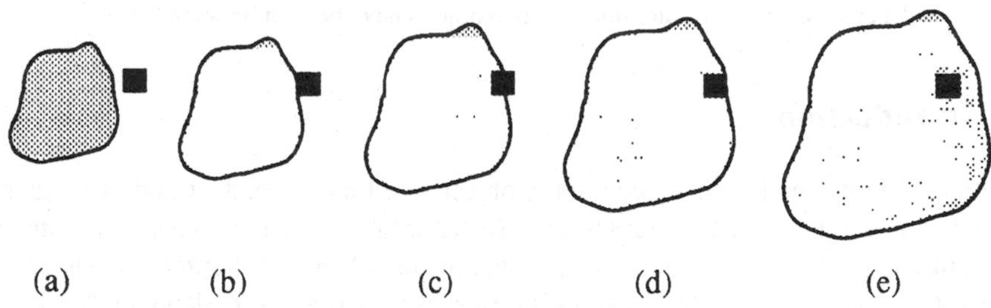

Fig. 1. Changes in the topological relationship between a lake and a log caused by a rise in the water level.

Such qualitative spatial changes have been investigated in Artificial Intelligence, primarily for qualitative kinematics, which deals with solid objects, their motions, and deformations [15]. Their reasoning methods focus on contacts between the objects and rely heavily on the shapes of the objects. The same applies to spatial reasoning about mechanical parts, for which detailed metric information about the parts is necessary [16]. These settings are significantly different from the ones in geographic space, in which incomplete and imprecise information is the standard situation, rather than an exception for human spatial reasoning; therefore, in the absence of more precise geographic information, purely qualitative geographic reasoning may be used as a substitute. While these reasoning processes may provide only approximate, sometimes crude, solutions, they are frequently the only means available to infer new information, though still sufficient to solve a particular geographic reasoning problem.

This paper investigates how an existing model for binary topological relationships [12] can be used as a framework to describe formally how to get from one topological relationship to its "closest" relationship when deforming one of the two objects. The kinds of deformations considered are a scaling (expansion and reduction), translation, and rotation. We are interested in *gradual changes*, i.e., the objects involved are expected not to make discontinuous changes such as jumps, nor may the deformations destroy the topology of a *single* object (e.g., by tearing into pieces). Another assumption made is that only one kind of deformation occurs with the objects involved.

In order not to raise confusion with the notion and concept of *topological transformations*, upon which the definition of binary topological relationships is founded, we reserve the term of *continuous transformations* for topological changes that affect *both* objects so that their binary topological relationship is preserved. On the other hand, the binary topological relationship may be destroyed if a transformation is applied to *only one* of the two objects. The latter transformations will be referred to as *gradual changes* or *deformations*. A gradual change of the location of an object may be interpreted as the movement of the object in either of the dimensions of the embedding space. Changing the size of an object by expanding or reducing it corresponds to a scaling deformation of the object.

The remainder of this paper is structured as follows: the next section summarizes the model used to distinguish between different topological relationships. Section 3 introduces the concept of a topology distance to assess how far apart two topological relationships are, and orders the topological relationships according to their shortest topology distance in the Closest-Topological-Relationship-Graph. Section 4 formalizes the most common deformations (translation, scaling, and rotation) by mapping them onto the Closest-Topological-Relationship-Graph. Section 5 analyzes the characteristic patterns for each kind of deformation and section 6 investigates which kinds of deformations can be inferred from the observation of two different topological relationships for the same two objects. The conclusions in section 7 discuss the significance of the results.

2 9-Intersection

The usual concepts of point-set topology with open and closed sets are assumed [1, 26]. The interior of a set A, denoted by A°, is the union of all open sets in A. The closure of A, denoted by $\overline{A}$, is the intersection of all closed sets of A. The exterior of A with respect to the embedding space $\mathbf{R}^2$, denoted by A^-, is the set of all points of $\mathbf{R}^2$ not contained in A. The boundary of A, denoted by ∂A, is the intersection of the closure of A and the closure of the exterior of A.

The definition of binary topological relationships between two spatial objects, A and B, is based on the nine intersections of A's boundary (∂A), interior (A°), and exterior (A^-) with the boundary (∂B), interior (B°), and exterior (B^-) of B [14]. A 3 x 3-matrix, $\mathcal{M}$, called the *9-intersection*, concisely represents these criteria (Equation 1).

$$\mathcal{M} = \begin{pmatrix} \partial A \cap \partial B & \partial A \cap B^\circ & \partial A \cap B^- \\ A^\circ \cap \partial B & A^\circ \cap B^\circ & A^\circ \cap B^- \\ A^- \cap \partial B & A^- \cap B^\circ & A^- \cap B^- \end{pmatrix} \tag{1}$$

To refer to a particular intersection between two objects, the short form $\mathcal{M}[\_,\_]$ will be used, e.g., $\mathcal{M}[\partial,^-]$ to denote the value of the boundary-complement intersection.

By considering the values empty ($\emptyset$) and non-empty ($\neg\emptyset$) for the 9-intersection, one can distinguish 512 binary topological relationships. The actual relationships that can be realized in a particular space depend on the topological properties of the objects [12, 14] and their codimensions, i.e., the difference between the dimension of the embedding space and the object [12, 21, 24].

The objects of concern in this paper are regions, i.e., 2-dimensional objects homeomorphic to discs. Eight topological relationships can be realized between two regions embedded in $\mathbb{R}^2$ [12, 14]. This set is mutually exclusive and closed for regions, i.e., one and only one of the eight topological relationships holds between any two regions [13]. Fig. 2 shows the 9-intersections of the eight binary topological relationships between two regions and depicts corresponding prototypical geometric interpretations.

Additional topological invariants of non-empty intersections may be used to express more detail about the objects' relationships. Such invariants include the dimension of the intersection and the number of separations in an intersection [13].

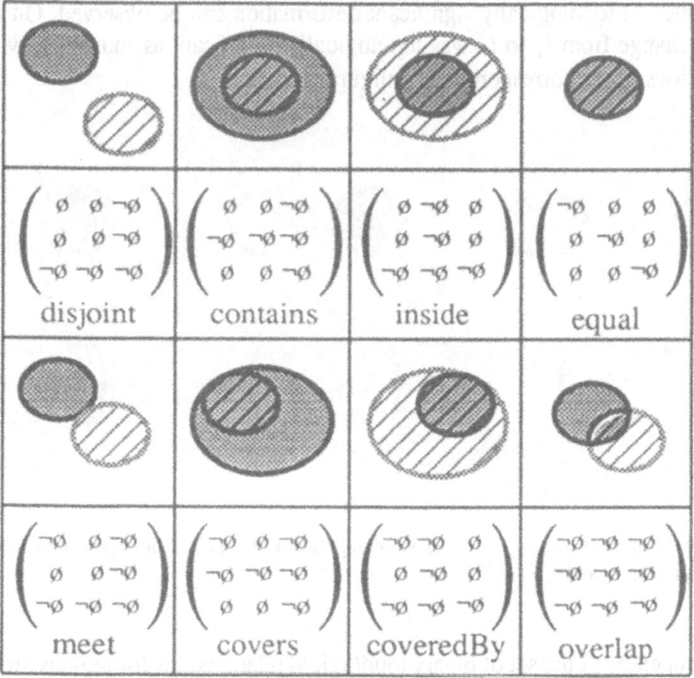

Fig. 2. The specifications and prototypes of the eight topological relationships between two regions in 2-D.

3 Formalizing Topological Changes

The 9-intersection provides a means to determine whether or not two pairs of objects share the same topological relationship. There is an isomorphism between the 9-intersection and the binary topological relationship such that two pairs of objects with the same 9-intersection imply that both pairs have the same binary topological relationship. Reversely, different 9-intersections imply different binary topological relationships. The latter applies immediately to assessing changes in topological relationships. In lieu of comparing two different pairs of objects, one compares the same two objects at two different times, t_0 and t_1. The two objects have undergone a topologically significant change if the 9-intersection at t_0 is different from the 9-intersection at t_1. The reverse statement that a deformation has preserved the topological relationship if the two 9-intersections at t_0 and t_1 are the same cannot be proven, because between t_0 and t_1 two deformations may have occurred that cancel each other. Fig. 3 shows three snapshots at $t_0 \ldots t_2$ and their corresponding 9-intersections. Since the 9-intersections at t_0 and t_1 are the same, no topologically significant deformation can be observed. On the other hand, the change from t_1 to t_2 was topologically significant as indicated by different 9-intersections of the corresponding configurations.

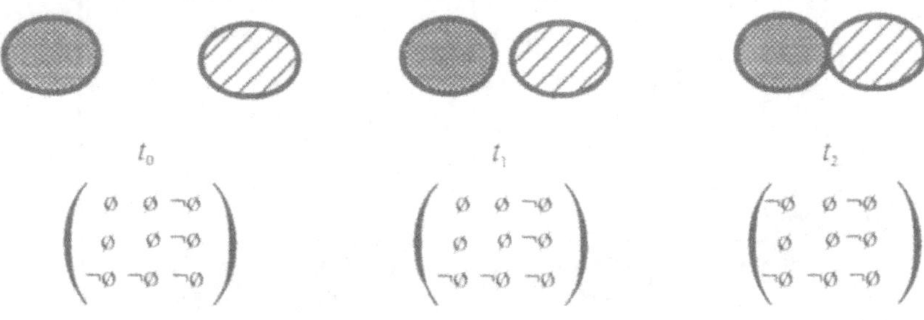

Fig. 3. Three snapshots at t_0, t_1, and t_2 showing that a change in the topological relationship happened between t_1 and t_2.

Two properties of the set of binary topological relationships for regions are relevant for predicting topological deformations: (1) the eight binary topological relationships are a closed set of relationships for regions and (2) the eight relationships are mutually exclusive; therefore, between two regions always one and only one of the eight relationships holds true. This implies that if a deformation changes the topological relationship between the two objects, then the topological relationship must be one of the remaining seven.

The focus is here on identifying which of the transitions can occur when gradually changing the geometry of one object. The most likely topological relationships will be called the *closest topological relationships*. Subsequently, we introduce a model for the closeness of topological relationships, called the topology distance, and use this measure to identify for each of the eight region relationships its closest topological relationships. Recently, a similar model, ordering 1-dimensional interval relations [3], has been called the "conceptual neighborhood" of the relations [18].

3.1 Topology Distance

The topological relationship between two pairs of regions be represented by the 9-intersection. We introduce the difference of empty/non-empty intersections, by mapping the values of empty and non-empty onto the integers 0 and 1, respectively, and applying then common integer subtraction (Equations 2–5).

$$\emptyset - \emptyset = 0 \tag{2}$$

$$\neg\emptyset - \neg\emptyset = 0 \tag{3}$$

$$\emptyset - \neg\emptyset = -1 \tag{4}$$

$$\neg\emptyset - \emptyset = 1 \tag{5}$$

The *topology distance* between two topological relationships, r_A and r_B, determines the number of corresponding elements with different values in their 9-intersections.

Definition 1. The topology distance is the sum of the absolute values of the differences between corresponding enteries of all nine intersections (Equation 6).

$$\mathcal{T}_{r_A,r_B} = \sum_{i=\partial}^{-} \sum_{j=\partial}^{-} |\mathcal{M}_A[i,j] - \mathcal{M}_B[i,j]| \tag{6}$$

or briefly

$$\mathcal{T}_{r_A,r_B} = ||\mathcal{M}_A - \mathcal{M}_B|| \tag{7}$$

where $||x||$ is the absolute norm of $x = \mathcal{M}_A - \mathcal{M}_B$.

For example, the topology distance between *inside* and *contains* is calculated as follows:

$$\mathcal{M}_{inside} = \begin{pmatrix} \emptyset & \neg\emptyset & \emptyset \\ \emptyset & \neg\emptyset & \emptyset \\ \neg\emptyset & \neg\emptyset & \neg\emptyset \end{pmatrix} \quad \mathcal{M}_{contains} = \begin{pmatrix} \emptyset & \emptyset & \neg\emptyset \\ \neg\emptyset & \neg\emptyset & \neg\emptyset \\ \emptyset & \emptyset & \neg\emptyset \end{pmatrix}$$

$$\mathcal{M}_{inside} - \mathcal{M}_{contains} = \begin{bmatrix} 0 & 1 & -1 \\ -1 & 0 & -1 \\ 1 & 1 & 0 \end{bmatrix}$$

$$||\mathcal{M}_{inside} - \mathcal{M}_{contains}|| = 6$$

Theorem 2. For two regions, the values the topology distance may take a value within the range between 0 and 8.

Proof: Each 9-intersection has nine entries. If all entries are the same, then the topology distance is 0. The other extreme case is if the two 9-intersections differ in all nine entries. Table 2 reveals that all eight topological relationships have non-empty exterior-exterior intersections. For the other eight entries, both empty and non-empty values can be found; therefore, two 9-intersections can differ in at most eight entries, which implies that the greatest topology distance possible is 8. □

Subsequently, we will prove that the topology distance fulfills the axioms of a distance function.

Theorem 3. The topology distance between a topological relationship and itself is always zero, i.e.,

$$\mathcal{T}_{r_A,r_A} = 0 \tag{8}$$

Proof: $\mathcal{T}_{r_A,r_B} = \sum_{i=\partial}^{-} \sum_{j=\partial}^{-} |\mathcal{M}_A[i,j] - \mathcal{M}_B[i,j]|$. If the second 9-intersection $\mathcal{M}_B$ is equal to the first, $\mathcal{M}_A$, for each pair of i and j, $|\mathcal{M}_A[i,j] - \mathcal{M}_A[i,j]|$ is zero; therefore, the sum of all differences between corresponding elements in the 9-intersection is 0 as well. □

Theorem 4. The topology distance is symmetric, i.e.,

$$\mathcal{T}_{r_A,r_B} = \mathcal{T}_{r_B,r_A} \tag{9}$$

Proof:

$$\mathcal{T}_{r_A,r_B} = \sum_{i=\partial}^{-} \sum_{j=\partial}^{-} |\mathcal{M}_A[i,j] - \mathcal{M}_B[i,j]| \quad \text{and}$$

$$\mathcal{T}_{r_B,r_A} = \sum_{i=\partial}^{-} \sum_{j=\partial}^{-} |\mathcal{M}_B[i,j] - \mathcal{M}_A[i,j]|$$

For each entry it is true that

$$\begin{aligned} |\mathcal{M}_A[i,j] - \mathcal{M}_B[i,j]| &= |-(\mathcal{M}_A[i,j] - \mathcal{M}_B[i,j])| \\ &= |\mathcal{M}_B[i,j]) - (\mathcal{M}_A[i,j]| \end{aligned}$$

therefore,

$$\sum_{i=\partial}^{-} \sum_{j=\partial}^{-} |\mathcal{M}_A[i,j] - \mathcal{M}_B[i,j]| = \sum_{i=\partial}^{-} \sum_{j=\partial}^{-} |\mathcal{M}_B[i,j] - \mathcal{M}_A[i,j]|$$

which implies

$$\mathcal{T}_{r_A,r_B} = \mathcal{T}_{r_B,r_A}$$

□

Theorem 5. The sum of the topology distances between the topological relationships r_A, r_B and r_B, r_C is greater than or equal to the topology distance of the topological relationship r_A, r_C, i.e.,

$$\mathcal{T}_{r_A,r_B} + \mathcal{T}_{r_B,r_C} \geq \mathcal{T}_{r_A,r_C} \tag{10}$$

Proof: First we prove that for any intersection, the triangle inequality is fulfilled. Then we will show that it also holds true for entire 9-intersections.

The absolute value of the difference between two intersections can be either 0 or 1 (Equation 2–5). If $|\mathcal{M}_A[i,j] - \mathcal{M}_C[i,j]| = 0$, then $\mathcal{M}_B[i,j]$ is either equal to both $\mathcal{M}_A[i,j]$ and $\mathcal{M}_C[i,j]$, or different from both. If it is equal to the two intersections, then

$$|\mathcal{M}_A[i,j] - \mathcal{M}_B[i,j]| + |\mathcal{M}_B[i,j] - \mathcal{M}_C[i,j]| = 0$$

Otherwise, $|\mathcal{M}_A[i,j] - \mathcal{M}_B[i,j]|$ is 1 and $|\mathcal{M}_B[i,j] - \mathcal{M}_C[i,j]|$ is 1, so that

$$|\mathcal{M}_A[i,j] - \mathcal{M}_B[i,j]| + |\mathcal{M}_B[i,j] - \mathcal{M}_C[i,j]| = 2$$

Therefore, the triangle inequality is fulfilled if $|\mathcal{M}_A[i,j] - \mathcal{M}_C[i,j]| = 0$.

If $|\mathcal{M}_A[i,j] - \mathcal{M}_C[i,j]| = 1$, then $\mathcal{M}_B[i,j]$ is either equal to $\mathcal{M}_A[i,j]$ and different from $\mathcal{M}_C[i,j]$, or reverse, such that one of the two differences $|\mathcal{M}_A[i,j] - \mathcal{M}_B[i,j]|$ and $|\mathcal{M}_B[i,j] - \mathcal{M}_C[i,j]|$ is 1 and the other one 0. This implies that their sum is always 1, which is equal to the direct difference between the two intersections.

For each of the nine intersections,

$$|\mathcal{M}_A[i,j] - \mathcal{M}_B[i,j]| + |\mathcal{M}_B[i,j] - \mathcal{M}_C[i,j]| \geq |\mathcal{M}_A[i,j] - \mathcal{M}_C[i,j]|$$

therefore,

$$\sum_{i=\partial}^{-}\sum_{j=\partial}^{-}(|\mathcal{M}_A[i,j] - \mathcal{M}_B[i,j]| + |\mathcal{M}_B[i,j] - \mathcal{M}_C[i,j]|) \geq \sum_{i=\partial}^{-}\sum_{j=\partial}^{-}|\mathcal{M}_A[i,j] - \mathcal{M}_C[i,j]|$$

or, since the summations ($\sum\sum$) distribute over the addition (+),

$$\sum_{i=\partial}^{-}\sum_{j=\partial}^{-}|\mathcal{M}_A[i,j] - \mathcal{M}_B[i,j]| + \sum_{i=\partial}^{-}\sum_{j=\partial}^{-}|\mathcal{M}_B[i,j] - \mathcal{M}_C[i,j]| \geq \sum_{i=\partial}^{-}\sum_{j=\partial}^{-}|\mathcal{M}_A[i,j] - \mathcal{M}_C[i,j]|$$

which implies

$$\mathcal{T}_{r_A,r_B} + \mathcal{T}_{r_B,r_C} \geq \mathcal{T}_{r_A,r_C}$$

□

Table 1 shows the topology distances for the combinations of all binary topological relationships between two spatial regions. It verifies immediately the first two distance axioms for $\mathcal{T}$—all elements along the main diagonal are 0, and the table is symmetric with respect to the main diagonal.

3.2 Closest Topological Relationships

Each of the eight topological relationships has seven candidates for the closest relationship. This may be thought of as a graph in which the nodes represent the topological relationships and the edges, connecting all nodes, stand for the possible changes. With the topology distance we can identify for each node, which of the edges link the topologically closest pairs of relationships. The most likely change of a topological relationship

	disjoint	meet	equal	inside	coveredBy	contains	covers	overlap
disjoint	0	1	6	4	5	4	5	4
meet	1	0	5	5	4	5	4	3
equal	6	5	0	4	3	4	3	6
inside	4	5	4	0	1	6	7	4
coveredBy	5	4	3	1	0	7	6	3
contains	4	5	4	6	7	0	1	4
covers	5	4	3	7	6	1	0	3
overlap	4	3	6	4	3	4	3	0

Table 1. The topology distance, T, between the eight binary topological relationships for two spatial regions.

can be defined as the edge with the smallest distance value for the closest topological relationship(s). The topological relationship A, closest to another topological relationship B, is the one whose topological distance has the least non-zero value (zero distances indicate that a change was not topologically significant).

The table of the topology distances between all pairs of the eight region relationships reveals a number of interesting points:

- The least topological distance is unique for three pairs of relationships (disjoint-meet, inside-coveredBy, and contains-covers).
- The least topological distance is ambiguous for pairs with equal and overlap. For these topological relationships, the least topological distance is 3.
- The least topological distance is not necessarily symmetric. While covers and coveredBy are the relationships closest to equal, equal is not the closest relationships from either covers or coveredBy.

The closest topological relationships form a graph, called the *Closest-Topological-Relationship-Graph*, that corresponds to a partially ordered set (Fig. 4).

4 Interpreting the Closest-Topological-Relationship-Graph

In this section we will demonstrate that the most common deformations (translation, rotation, scalings) correspond to distinct traverses of the Closest-Topological-Relationship-Graph. For each deformation, a number of different scenarios are possible. We will sketch the most general ones only and show that others are subsets thereof.

4.1 Scaling

Scaling may expand or reduce the size of a region. Given two objects, A and B, both deformations may be applied to either object. This gives rise to 4 different scaling operations: (1) an expansion of the reference object A, (2) an expansion of the second region

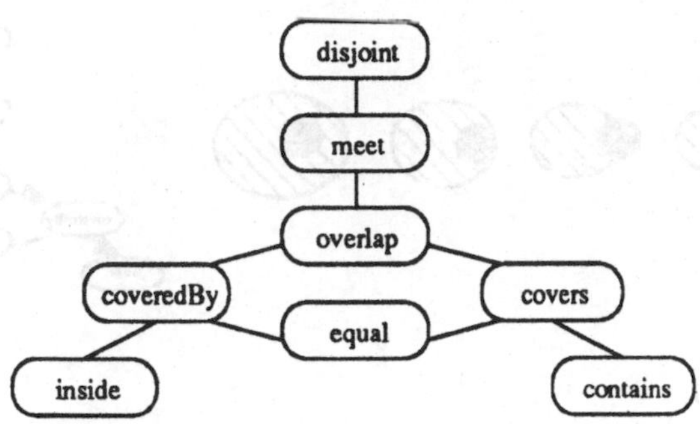

Fig. 4. The Closest-Topological-Relationship-Graph.

B, (3) a reduction of A, and (4) a reduction of B. Depending on the topological relationship between the two regions, the four scalings may have different effects on the relationships.

As the starting conditions, we select the three nodes of degree 1—disjoint, inside, and contains. All other scaling deformations, starting at a node of degree > 1, are covered by these scenarios.

Scenario 1 A and B are disjoint and A is expanded (Fig. 5).

Fig. 5. Expanding A.

The sequence of topological relationships is disjoint, meet, overlap, covers, and contains; therefore, expansion of the reference object corresponds to a top-down traverse of the graph along the right-most branch.

Scenario 2 A and B are disjoint and B is expanded (Fig. 6).

The sequence of topological relationships is disjoint, meet, overlap, coveredBy, and inside; therefore, expansion of the second object corresponds to a top-down traverse of the graph along the left-most branch.

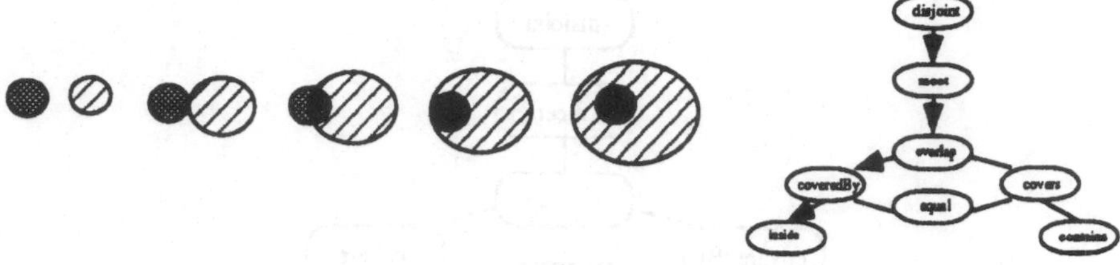

Fig. 6. Expanding B.

The deformation inverse to expansion, the reduction of one object, has no influence on the topological relationship if the objects are disjoint. The graph and the paths for expansion help to verify this: first, expansion corresponds to a top-down traverse, hence, the operation inverse to expansion, reduction, would be a bottom-up traverse; second, disjoint is the top node with degree 1. Hence, there are no other nodes in the graph following the direction opposite to expansion.

Scenario 3 A contains B and A is reduced such that it is ultimately disjoint from B (Fig. 7).

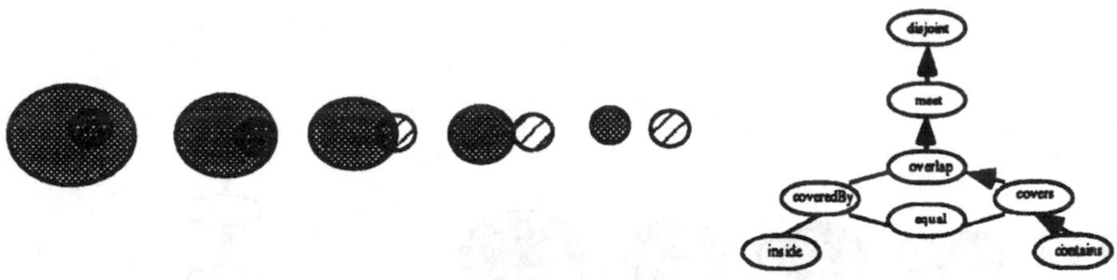

Fig. 7. Reducing A so that it is disjoint from B.

The sequence of topological relationships is contains, covers, overlap, meet, and disjoint; therefore, this deformation is a bottom-up traverse along a left-most branch of the graph.

Scenario 4 A contains B and A is reduced such that it is ultimately inside of B (Fig. 8).

The sequence of topological relationships is contains, covers, overlap, coveredBy, and inside; therefore, this deformation is a right-to-left traverse of the graph passing over the central node "overlap."

Scenario 5 A contains B and B is expanded (Fig. 9).

Fig. 8. Reducing A so that it is inside of B.

Fig. 9. Expanding B.

The sequence of topological relationships is contains, covers, overlap, coveredBy, and inside; therefore, this deformation is a right-to-left traverse of the graph passing over the central node "overlap."

The two graphs in Fig. 8 and 9 show that expanding B has the same effect as reducing A so that it is inside of B. The other two scaling deformations of the relationship A contains B—expanding A and reducing B—have no effect on the topological relationship. This follows from the fact that "contains" is a node of degree 1 in the graph, and the paths for the deformations of reducing A and expanding B point both towards the top. Therefore, their inverse deformations—reducing A and expanding B—point to the opposite direction in which no further nodes exist.

Scenario 6 A is inside of B and A is expanded (Fig. 10).

Their topological relationship changes from inside to coveredBy, overlap, covers, and contains. This scaling deformation corresponds to the shortest horizontal traverse from the left-most to the right-most node passing over the central node "overlap."

Scenario 7 A is inside of B and B is reduced such that ultimately B is disjoint from A (Fig. 11).

This deformation changes their relationships from inside, coveredBy, overlap, meet to disjoint, and corresponds to a bottom-up traverse along the left branch of the graph.

Scenario 8 A is inside of B and B is reduced such that it ultimately contains A (Fig. 12).

Fig. 10. Expanding A.

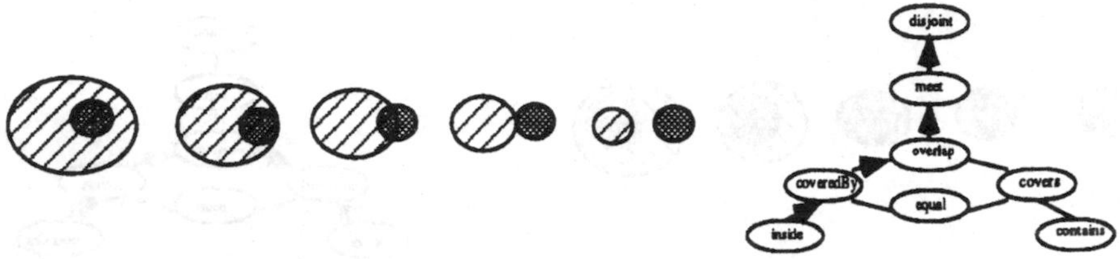

Fig. 11. Reducing B so that it is disjoint from A.

This deformation changes their relationships from inside over coveredBy, overlap, and covers to contains, and corresponds to a left-right traverse in the graph passing over "overlap."

In analogy to the changes of the relationship "contains" we observe that expanding A (Fig. 10) has the same effect as reducing B so that it is disjoint from A (Fig. 12); and the deformations of "inside" by reducing the second region are ambiguous— there are two paths ending at distinct relationships. Likewise, if A is inside of B its topological relationship does not change if A is further reduced or B is expanded.

Scenario 9 A is inside of B and A is expanded such that, at one time, A is equal to B (Fig. 13).

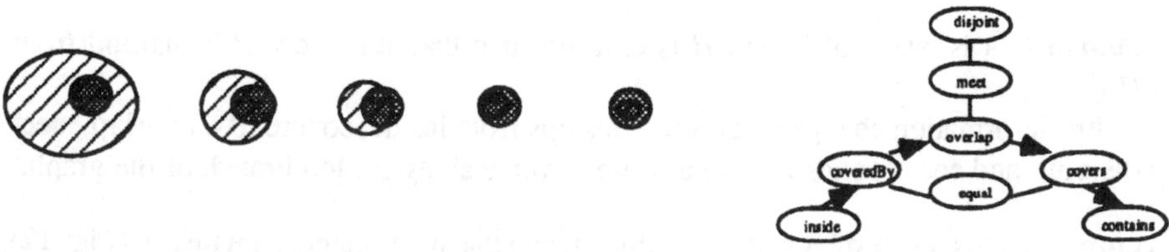

Fig. 12. Reducing B so that it contains A.

Fig. 13. Expanding A so that it is equal to B at one time.

Expanding A will change their topological relationship from inside to equal, and contains. The Closest-Topological-Relationship-Graph does not account for this path.

Scenario 10 A is inside of B and B is reduced such that, at one time, A is equal to B (Fig. 14).

Fig. 14. Reducing B so that it is equal to A at one time.

The sequence of topological relationships is again inside, equal, and contains; therefore, for this particular setting expanding A has the same effect as reducing B.

Scenario 11 A contains B and A is reduced such that, at one time, A is equal to B (Fig. 15).

Fig. 15. Reducing A so that A is equal to B at one time.

This deformation has the reverse effect of expanding A if A is inside of B, i.e., the sequence is contains, equal, and inside.

Scenario 12 A contains B and B is expanded such that, at one time, A is equal to B (Fig. 16).

Fig. 16. Expanding B so that A is equal to B at one time.

The sequence of the topological relationships is contains, equal, and inside; therefore, for this particular setting reducing A has the same effect as enlarging B.

4.2 Translation

Scenario 13 A is smaller than B and A is moved over B (or B over A) (Fig. 17).

The sequence of their topological relationships is disjoint, meet, overlap, coveredBy, inside, coveredBy, overlap, meet, and disjoint and corresponds to a top-down-bottom-up traverse along the left-most branch of the graph.

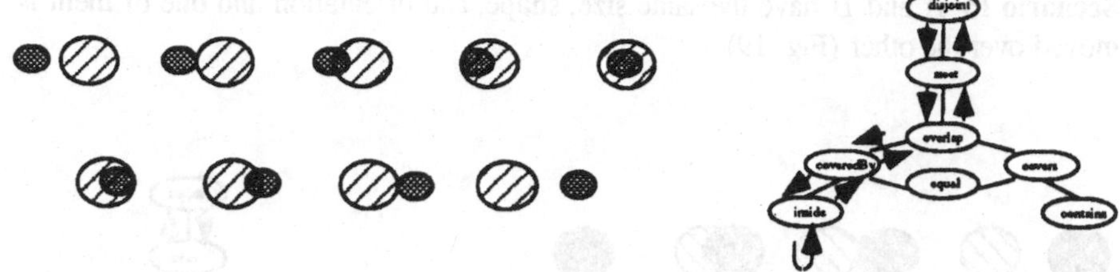

Fig. 17. Moving A over a larger region B.

Scenario 14 A is larger than B and A is moved over B (or B over A) (Fig. 18).

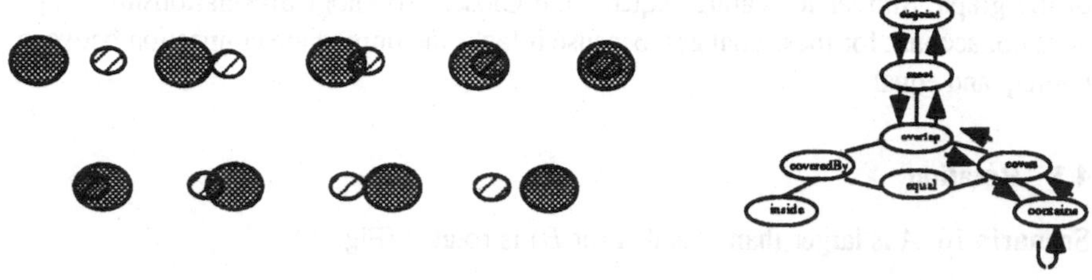

Fig. 18. Moving A over a smaller region B.

The sequence of their topological relationships is disjoint, meet, overlap, covers, contains, covers, overlap, meet, and disjoint. This corresponds to a top-down-bottom-up traverse along the right-most branch of the graph.

Variations of the two scenarios include gradual movements such that the two paths along the outer branches are partially traversed. For example, if A moves across B's boundary without being inside, the sequence of their topological relationships will be disjoint, meet, overlap, meet, disjoint, which is a subset of the sequence of scenarios 17 and 18.

Scenario 15 *A* and *B* have the same size, shape, and orientation and one of them is moved over the other (Fig. 19).

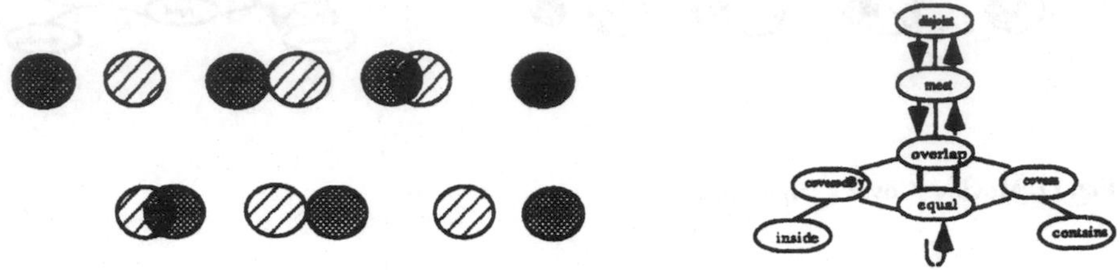

Fig. 19. Moving *A* over a region *B* of equal size, shape, and orientation.

The sequence of their topological relationships is disjoint, meet, overlap, equal, overlap, meet, and disjoint. This corresponds to a top-down-bottom-up traverse in the center of the graph. Similar to scaling "equal," the Closest-Topological-Relationship-Graph does not account for these changes, because it lacks the immediate connection between overlap and equal.

4.3 Rotation

Scenario 16 *A* is larger than *B* and *A* (or *B*) is rotated (Fig. 20).

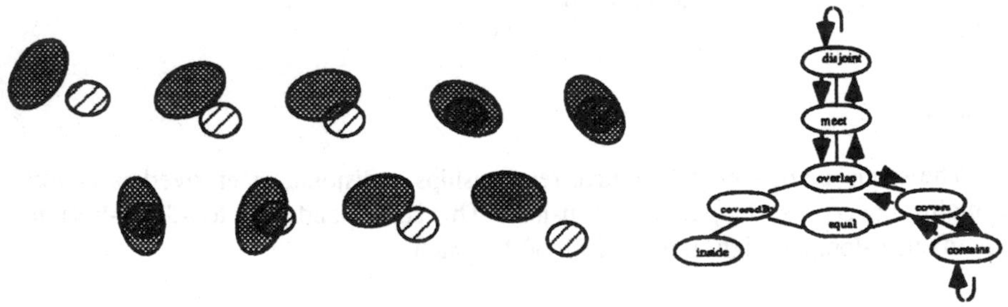

Fig. 20. Rotating a larger *A*.

The sequence of their topological relationships for the first 360° rotation is disjoint, meet, overlap, covers, contains, covers, overlap, meet, and disjoint. This corresponds to a top-down-bottom-up traverse along the right-most branch of the graph. Note that this deformation is cyclic and, therefore, the sequence of relationships may repeat.

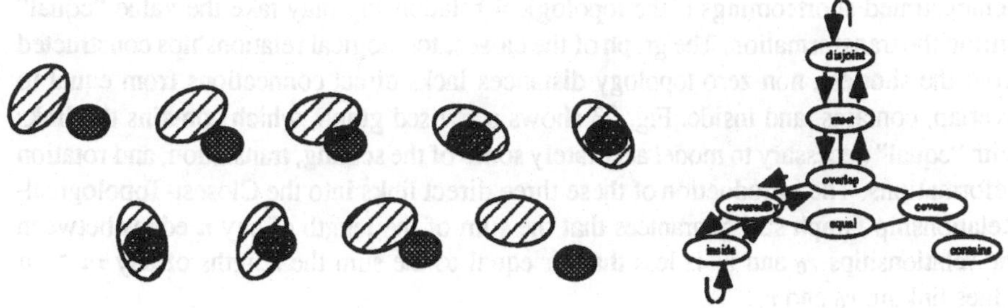

Fig. 21. Rotating a smaller *A*.

Scenario 17 *A* is smaller than *B* and *A* (or *B*) is rotated (Fig. 21).

The sequence of their topological relationships for the first 360° rotation is disjoint, meet, overlap, coveredBy, inside, coveredBy, overlap, meet, and disjoint. This corresponds to a top-down-bottom-up traverse along the left-most branch of the graph.

Scenario 18 *A* is equal to *B* and *A* (or *B*) is rotated (Fig. 22).

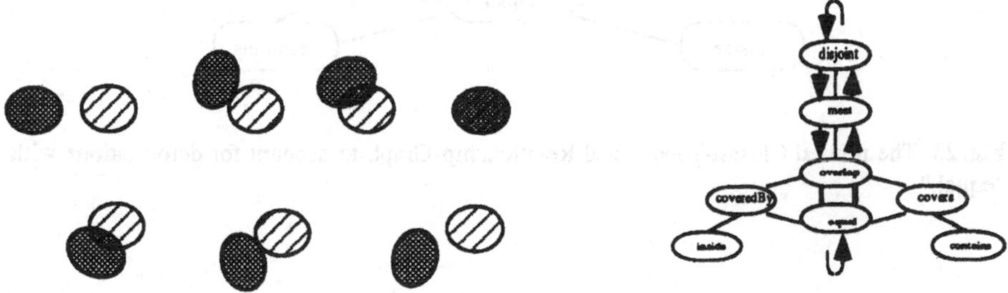

Fig. 22. Rotating *A*.

The sequence of their topological relationships for the first 360° rotation is disjoint, meet, overlap, equal, overlap, meet, and disjoint. This corresponds to a top-down-bottom-up traverse in the center of the graph.

5 Characteristic Patterns

Each of the deformations can be translated into a set of traverses of the Closest-Topological-Relationship-Graph. The corresponding graph coincides with the sequence of relationships for deformations in which the two regions cannot be equal; however, it demonstrated shortcomings if the topological relationship may take the value "equal" during the transformation. The graph of the closest topological relationships constructed from the shortest, non-zero topology distances lacks direct connections from equal to overlap, contains, and inside. Fig. 23 shows a revised graph, which contains the links with "equal" necessary to model accurately some of the scaling, translation, and rotation deformations. The introduction of these three direct links into the Closest-Topological-Relationship-Graph still guarantees that the sum of the length of any n edges between the relationships r_0 and r_1 is less than or equal to the sum the lengths of any $m > n$ edges linking r_0 and r_1.

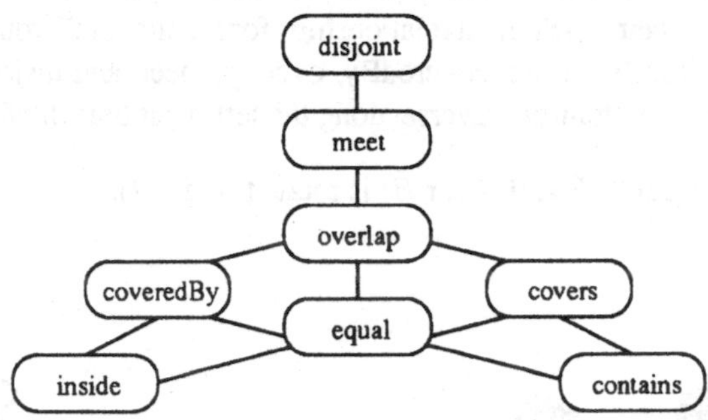

Fig. 23. The revised Closest-Topological-Relationship-Graph to account for deformations with "equal."

For each kind of deformation, the corresponding scenarios can be integrated into a single traverse. These integrated traverses allow for a comparison of the different deformations.

- Translation and rotation are primarily vertical traverses (Fig. 24). The only accountable difference is that the sequence for the rotation is a closed cycle at "disjoint," while the sequence for the translation ends at "disjoint."

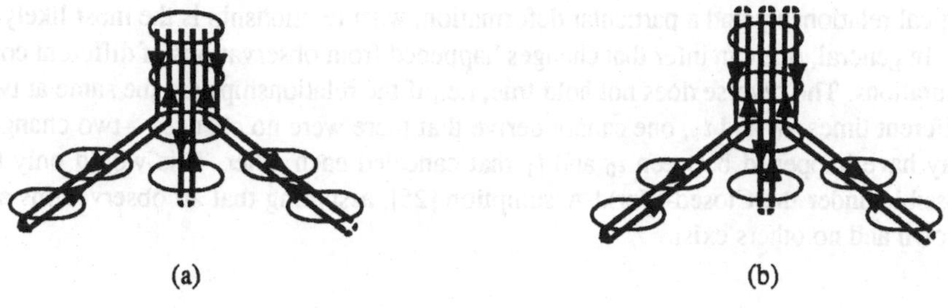

Fig. 24. The characteristic patterns for (a) translation and (b) rotation.

– The deformation of scaling shows four similar, but different patterns (Fig. 25). The patterns for expanding and reducing the same region are the same with reverse directions, indicating that expanding and shrinking are inverse operations. On the other hand, expanding one region or reducing the other region is generally not equivalent.

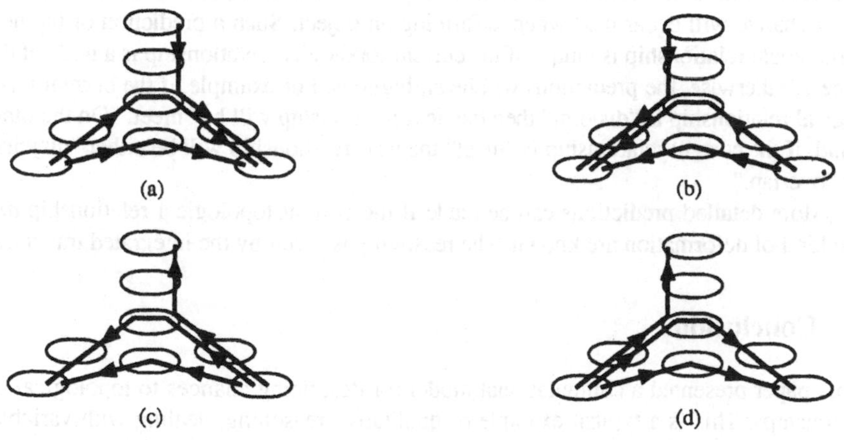

Fig. 25. The characteristic patterns for (a) expanding A, (b) expanding B, (c) reducing A, and (d) reducing B.

6 Reasoning about Deformations

These integrated traverses provides the necessary information to (1) infer from two or more observations what kind of deformation occurred and (2) predict for a given topological relationship and a particular deformation, what relationship is the most likely.

In general, one can infer that changes happened from observations of different configurations. The reverse does not hold true, i.e., if the relationships are the same at two different times, t_0 and t_1, one cannot derive that there were no changes—two changes may have happened between t_0 and t_1 that canceled each other. This would only be possible under the Closed-World-Assumption [25], assuming that all observations are known and no others exist.

6.1 Inferring the Kind of Deformation

Given two (or more) "topological snapshots," i.e., observations about topological relationships at different times, the deformation diagrams for the topological changes by shifting, expanding, reducing, and rotating can be used to infer what kind of deformation occurred. For example, the two observations t_0 = inside (A, B) and t_1 = covers (A, B), with $t_0 < t_1$, indicate that either A was expanded or B was reduced. The diagrams also indicate that such a deformation is impossible with just a rotation or translation.

6.2 Predicting the Next Change

The revised Closest-Topological-Relationship-Graph can be used as a means to predict what change will occur next when deforming an object. Such a prediction of the next topological relationship is unique if the current topological relationship is a node of degree 1; otherwise, the predictions will be ambiguous. For example, if the current topological relationship is "disjoint" then the next relationship will be "meet." On the other hand, if the current relationship is "meet" the next relationship will be either "disjoint" or "overlap."

More detailed predictions can be made if the current topological relationship *and* the kind of deformation are known. The reasoning is given by the integrated traverses.

7 Conclusions

This paper presented a computational model for describing changes to topological relationships. This is a typical example of qualitative reasoning, dealing with variables which can only take a small, predetermined number of values, here the eight topological relationships, and the inference rules use these values in lieu of numerical quantities approximating them [8].

Within a limited scope, it is possible to reason about deformation of topological relationships. We analyzed the three major kinds of deformations—gradual translation, rotation, and scalings. The second major result of this paper is a means to infer the kind of deformations from a series of $n > 1$ observations of topological relationships.

These investigations provided another significant result. While the 9-intersection is a means to determine the equality of two topological relationships, the Closest-Topological-Relationship-Graph provides a (partial) ordering over topological relationships and the topology distance is a measure to compare the differences between topological relationships. In terms of Stevens' taxonomy of measurements, the topology distance puts topological relationships onto a ratio scale of measurements [27] so that analyses typical for (quantitative) measurement data may be applied to (qualitative) topological observations.

References

1. P. Alexandroff, 1961. *Elementary Concepts of Topology*. Dover Publications, Inc., New York, NY.
2. K. Al-Taha and A. Frank, 1991. Temporal GIS Keeps Data Current. *1991-1992 International GIS Source Book*, 384–388.
3. J. Allen, 1983. Maintaining Knowledge about Temporal Intervals. *Communications of the ACM*, 26(11):832–843.
4. L. Buisson, 1989. Reasoning on Space with Object-Centered Knowledge Representations. In: A. Buchmann, O. Günther, T. Smith, and Y. Wang, editors, *Symposium on the Design and Implementation of Large Spatial Databases*, *Lecture Notes in Computer Science*, Vol. 409, pages 325–344, Springer-Verlag, New York, NY.
5. S.K. Chang, E. Jungert, and Y. Li, 1989. The Design of Pictorial Databases Based Upon the Theory of Symbolic Projections. In: A. Buchmann, O. Günther, T. Smith, and Y. Wang, editors, *Symposium on the Design and Implementation of Large Spatial Databases*, *Lecture Notes in Computer Science*, Vol. 409, pages 303–323, Springer-Verlag, New York, NY.
6. S.K. Chang, Q.Y. Shi, and C.W. Yan, 1987. Iconic Indexing by 2-D Strings. *IEEE Transactions on Pattern Analysis and Machine Intelligence*, PAMI-9(6):413–428.
7. W. Chase and M. Chi, 1981. Cognitive Skill: Implications for Spatial Skill in Large-Scale Environment. In: J. Harvey, editor, *Cognition, Social Behavior, and the Environment*, pages 111–136, Lawrence Erlbaum Associates, Hillsdale, NJ.
8. J. De Kleer and J. Brown, 1984. A Qualitative Physics Based on Confluences. *Artificial Intelligence*, 24:7–83.
9. S. Dutta, 1989. Qualitative Spatial Reasoning: A Semi-Quantitative Approach Using Fuzzy Logic. In: A. Buchmann, O. Günther, T. Smith, and Y. Wang, editors, *Symposium on the Design and Implementation of Large Spatial Databases*, *Lecture Notes in Computer Science*, Vol. 409, pages 345–364, Springer-Verlag, New York, NY.
10. S. Dutta, 1991. Topological Constraints: A Representational Framework for Approximate Spatial and Temporal Reasoning. In: O. Günther and H.-J. Schek, editors, *Advances in Spatial Databases—Second Symposium, SSD '91*, *Lecture Notes in Computer Science*, Vol. 525, pages 161–180, Springer-Verlag, New York, NY.
11. M. Egenhofer, 1991. Reasoning about Binary Topological Relations. In: O. Günther and H.-J. Schek, editors, *Advances in Spatial Databases—Second Symposium, SSD '91*, *Lecture Notes in Computer Science*, Vol. 525, pages 143–160, Springer-Verlag, New York, NY.
12. M. Egenhofer and R. Franzosa, 1991. Point-Set Topological Spatial Relations. *International Journal of Geographical Information Systems*, 5(2):161–174.
13. M. Egenhofer and J. Herring, 1990. A Mathematical Framework for the Definition of Topological Relationships. In: K. Brassel and H. Kishimoto, editors, *Fourth International Symposium on Spatial Data Handling*, pages 803–813, Zurich, Switzerland.
14. M. Egenhofer and J. Herring, 1992. Categorizing Binary Topological Relationships Between Regions, Lines, and Points in Geographic Databases. Technical Report, Department of Surveying Engineering, University of Maine, Orono, ME.
15. B. Faltings, 1990. Qualitative Kinematics in Mechanisms. *Artificial Intelligence*, 44:89–119.

16. K. Forbus, P. Nielsen, and B. Faltings, 1991. Qualitative Spatial Reasoning: The CLOCK Project. *Artificial Intelligence*, 51:417–471.
17. A. Frank, 1991. Qualitative Spatial Reasoning about Cardinal Directions. In: *Autocarto 10*, pages 148–167, Baltimore, MD.
18. C. Freksa, 1992. Temporal Reasoning Based on Semi-Intervals. *Artificial Intelligence*, 54(1-2):199–227.
19. P. Hayes, 1978. The Naive Physics Manifesto. In: D. Michie, editor, *Expert Systems in the Microelectronic Age*, pages 242–270, Edinburgh University Press, Edinburgh, Scotland.
20. D. Hernández, 1991. Relative Representation of Spatial Knowledge: The 2-D Case. In: D. Mark and A. Frank, editors, *Cognitive and Linguistic Aspects of Geographic Space*, Kluwer Academic Publishers, Dordrecht.
21. J. Herring, 1991. The Mathematical Modeling of Spatial and Non-Spatial Information in Geographic Information Systems. In: D. Mark and A. Frank, editors, *Cognitive and Linguistic Aspects of Geographic Space*, pages 313–350, Kluwer Academic Publishers, Dordrecht.
22. G. Hunter and I. Wiliamson, 1990. The Development of a Historical Digital Cadastral Database. *International Journal of Geographical Information Systems*, 4(2):169–179.
23. D.J. Peuquet and Z. Ci-Xiang, 1987. An Algorithm to Determine the Directional Relationship Between Arbitrarily-Shaped Polygons in the Plane. *Pattern Recognition*, 20(1):65–74.
24. S. Pigot, 1991. Topological Models for 3D Spatial Information Systems. In: *Autocarto 10*, pages 368–392, Baltimore, MD.
25. R. Reiter, 1984. Towards a Logical Reconstruction of Relational Database Theory. In: M. Brodie, J. Mylopoulos, and J. Schmidt, editors, *On Conceptual Modelling*, pages 191–233, Springer-Verlag, New York, NY.
26. E. Spanier, 1966. *Algebraic Topology*. McGraw-Hill Book Company, New York, NY.
27. S. Stevens, 1946. On the Theory of Scales of Measurement. *Science Magazine*, 103(2684):677–680.

The Meaning of "Neighbour"

Christopher M. Gold

Dept des Sciences Géodésiques,
Pavillon Casault, Université Laval,
Sainte-Foy, Québec, Canada G1K 7P4.
Telephone: (418) 656-3308
Email: CGOLD@VM1.ULAVAL.CA

Abstract. Traditional vector and raster spatial models as used in many computer systems are examined to determine what is meant by the term "neighbour". The limitations are examined and the Voronoi spatial model is proposed as a consistent alternative to both. It is then asked whether this new computer model of space bears any resemblance to human spatial reasoning and perception processes. Examination of the work of Blum, Ahuja, Tuceryan, Serra and others suggests that the Voronoi model may indeed relate to visual perception and the concept of "neighbour".

Introduction

Dutta [8] states that "spatial reasoning" refers to reasoning about entities occupying space. He mentions the differing approaches used by specialists in psychology, linguistics, robotics, vision, data bases, and artificial intelligence. In the GIS field various workers [10, 11,12 and others] have produced lists of words and/or concepts needed for "spatial reasoning". This paper makes no attempt to provide another such list: instead, it notes the presence of "neighbour" or "adjacent" concepts in most lists, and attempts to explore how this may be implemented and used in both human and computer situations. The philosophy used here is more closely allied with robotics in the use of skeletons and Voronoi diagrams, and with vision in the attempt to identify shapes. We start by reviewing the traditional raster and vector methods in order to find what *they* mean by "neighbour", and then suggesting that the Voronoi approach encompasses them both. This "integrated" Voronoi spatial model is largely based on concepts of neighbour and adjacency (the two words are here used interchangeably).

The paper then moves from the observable (computer methodology) to the largely unobservable (human or animal spatial processes or reasoning), with the question: does a more consistent computer method suggest anything about animal (brain) methods? While in no way covering the neurological issues, three previous collections of research activities are examined that suggest that the Voronoi method of handling perceived spatial objects may not be unreasonable. The first is the work of Blum who, in the 1960's and 1970's, attempted to define a type of shape description that would apply to the recognition of "biological" shapes. This included the discovery of the "skeleton" or medial-axis transform. The work suggested that if the skeleton of a shape was generated from the perceived edges by a growth or diffusion process then this skeleton would simplify the classification or recognition of that shape. He also suggested that even with an incomplete set of boundary segments a recognizable skeleton may be obtainable.

This idea was later developed in the work of Ahuja and Tuceryan, who examined the clustering of point patterns - the recognition of *groups* of objects - by examining the individual Voronoi regions of each point. The method conformed well with human visual decisions, and was later extended to develop methods for the recognition of texture.

In image analysis, these ideas were transferred to the regular square grid - although with the loss of true Euclidean distance. In "mathematical morphology", e.g. [22], operations of dilation and erosion involve the expansion of the raster "shape" by one pixel, or a similar contraction. Medial axis transforms can be generated, and some shape characteristics derived. Boundary smoothing and other operations are possible with the primitives of dilation and erosion.

These research directions, together with my own experience in communicating the underlying ideas of the Voronoi methods, suggest the plausibility of the Voronoi spatial model for resolving a large class of adjacency-based issues by using one basic underlying mechanism.

Section 1: Human Versus Computer Models of Space.

The management of space interior to the "system" is clearly based on different techniques for people and for computers, and it is evident that different categories of people reason about space differently, and also that different computer systems use differing "perceptions" of space. The biggest difference is obviously between people and computers - no human would consider reasonable a raster representation of the space in which he resides (although his initial visual perception may well be raster-like at the level of the retina). Similarly, the usual "vector" form of spatial representation in a GIS is equally unlikely as an internal human mechanism, as any neighbourhood relationships are only determined by line (or boundary) intersections. By comparison with this gulf, the cultural differences between humans appear small.

On this basis, it might be considered desirable to develop a computer method that approaches closer to the human. Even though the internal human mechanisms are not understood, we do know something about what they are not (see above). It appears reasonable that in the conversion from raw information to useable knowledge there must be a step involving the recognition of the spatial relationships among the objects perceived (either directly by imagery or retained in memory as a mental map). A spatial model in the computer that is at least not counter-intuitive may well be a step in the right direction.

It has been discussed elsewhere [16, 17] that the properties of a useable spatial modelling system must include as one of its steps the recognition of "adjacent" object relationships. (Other more elaborate relationships may then be described, but this one is the minimum.) For example, image analysis filtering procedures are dependent on the acceptance of at least the four pixels neighbouring the pixel being evaluated. Unfortunately current computer methods are - let us say fuzzy - about what is meant by "neighbour". The raster approach is attractive primarily because it has good implicit adjacency relationships - but these are between pieces of space, not perceived map objects.

The vector approach, on the other hand, is better at defining the map objects - but line segments have no intrinsic data structure ("topology") at all. They are merely pen movement commands, forming unconnected lines within the map space. Traditional vector systems then attempt to detect line intersections in order to construct a data structure that expresses any spatial relationships. Frequently the desired result is a polygonal data set, with polygons, arcs and nodes as separate map objects (see [13] for various alternatives). However, the spatial model is *not* a tiling, and hence the data structure must be formed by construction rather than spatial subdivision - a much more error prone operation, given the inevitable errors in the input data. A particularly serious problem is that the structure has little meaning until it is complete and error free: divide-and-conquer methods are usually used in an iterative cycle until the data errors have been eliminated.

As adjacency relations are definable entirely by detecting line intersections, this leads to a variety of oddities. My favourite is the necessity of counting the number of intersections between the boundary segments of a polygon and a line drawn from some query point and any point outside the map - merely to determine if that point lies within the polygon! I defy anyone to suggest that this is a plausible model of the internal spatial perception mechanism of the human brain (or even that of a pigeon). Clearly the line intersection model of space has been brought to the point of absurdity. In addition, the spatial relationships between sets of objects that have no common intersections are undefined - hence all of those problems with polygon islands, and the inability to use the same spatial model to process point data sets, line data sets (e.g. hydrology) and polygons. The line intersection model is fundamentally incomplete, even as a base set of relationships upon which can be built a more complex hierarchy. In addition, it is doubtful that the human brain needs differing spatial models for different types of data sets!

In the introduction we asked how differing computer models handled spatial adjacency. We may thus respond by saying that raster adjacency is based on adjacent regular tiles - usually squares of space. Vector adjacency depends on the detection of line intersections in order to form a polygonal graph, and it is this graph that forms conventional GIS "topology".

Of course, there are good things in both the raster and vector approaches, or else they would not have been used. What is needed is something that takes the good points of both, and leaves the absurdities. It would be nice, for example, to accept the simple spatial neighbour concept of the raster, but to reject space as a collection of sugar cubes - to have a spatial tiling, in effect, but with one tile representing one map object, however primitive. Given such a base spatial data structure, it would then be appropriate to examine it firstly to see if it is implementable in the computer (and hopefully to handle variation over time in a plausible fashion) and secondly to determine (if possible) if it is closer to the human spatial reasoning process than the current spatial models. It could hardly be worse!

Section 2: Towards a Consistent Computer Model of Space.

We will attempt here to form a consistent model of space, answering at least questions of the "neighbouring objects" type. This requires some definition of "neighbouring", "next to" or "adjacent" that can be built upon. About the only unambiguous definition of "adjacent" concerns polygons: two polygons are adjacent if they share a common boundary. This section, summarizing [13], starts with that.

Two polygons are adjacent if they have a common boundary. The existence of this adjacency relationship may be expressed as an edge of the dual graph. This edge connects two nodes, each node representing a polygon. For a planar polygonal graph the dual can be expressed as a triangulation (if a few easy modifications are permitted to account for more than three polygons meeting at a point, and for the case of islands). The adjacency relationships expressed by the dual triangulation may themselves contain information as to the form of adjacency (fuzzy boundary, flow between polygons, etc.) as illustrated in Figure 1.

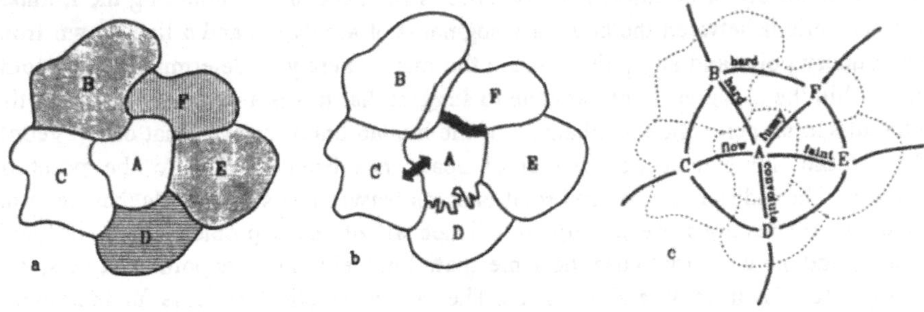

Figure 1: a) A Set of General Polygons b) Types of Boundaries c) The Dual Triangulation

If this holds true for any polygon set in two dimensional Euclidean space, then it is possible to draw a set of tiles, one around each map object, and consider objects with adjacent tiles to be themselves adjacent, or "neighbours". The map objects may be points, line segments, or more complex objects, such as roads or houses (Figure 2). One possible way of drawing tiles around map objects is to include within the tile all map locations that are closer to that object than to any other. The tile boundaries are thus equidistant between pairs of map objects, and are represented within the dual triangulation as a triangle edge. Each triangle thus represents three equidistant boundaries between three map objects. These three boundaries meet at a point that is equidistant from the three objects - the triangle circumcentre. The resulting tile set is the Voronoi diagram, and the dual graph is the Delaunay triangulation. While not the only possible tiling, this is intuitively simple and has many valuable properties.

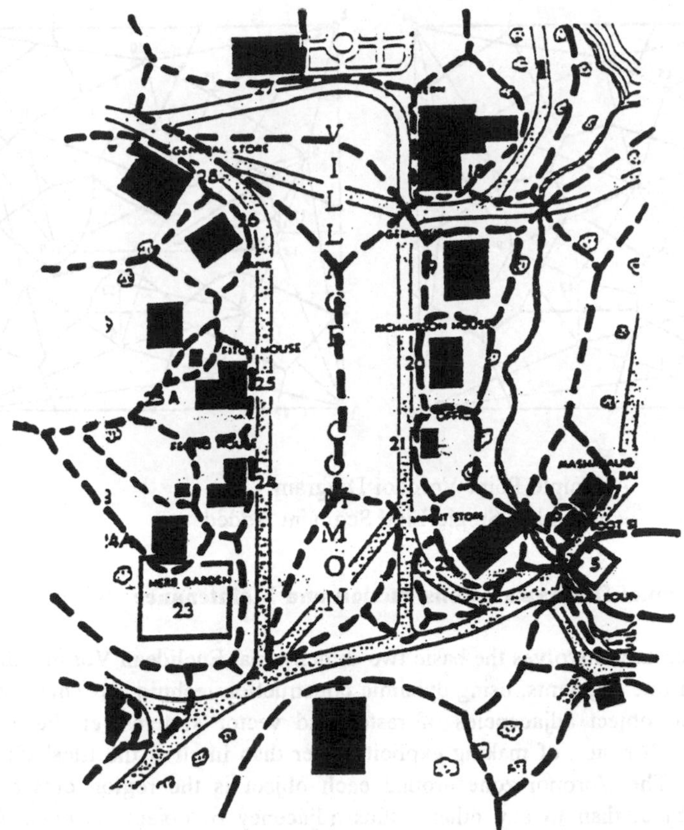

Figure 2: Sketch Map of a Village, with Voronoi Regions

The Voronoi diagram (also called Thiessen polygons, or the Dirichlet tessellation) subdivides the map space into a set of tiles, one for each map object, so as to assign any map location to the tile of the closest object - hence another equivalent term, a proximal mapping. A Voronoi region can, in principle, be constructed around *any* map object - a house, a river, a road (Figure 2). Implementation of the two dimensional Voronoi diagram (in Euclidean space) for points *and* line segments gives us the opportunity to construct more complex objects at a later date. Figure 3 shows the Voronoi diagram for a set of points, followed by the result of inserting a single line segment. While the second diagram appears complex, due to the parabolic boundary segments, the internal representation (the Delaunay triangulation) is the same. The line segment is formed by splitting point 18 from the original point 17, and then moving it to its final destination: the trailing line segment accumulates all the spatial relationships, or "history" of point 18 during its travels. This has various implications for the management of time-varying phenomena within the geometric data structure.

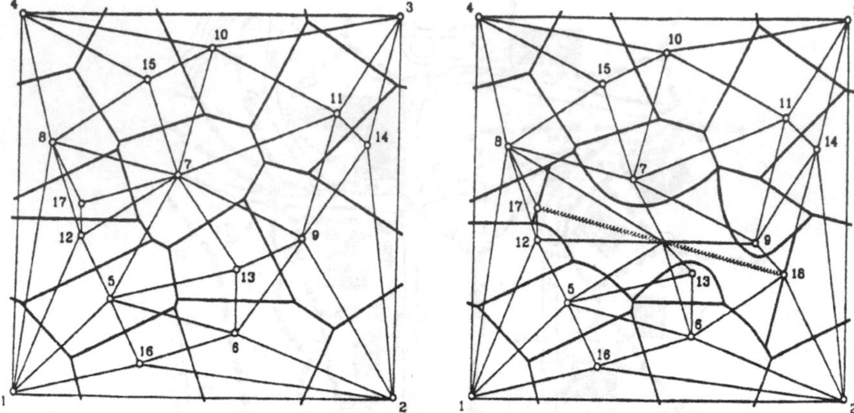

Figure 3: A Simple Point Voronoi Diagram; and with a Single Line Segment Added.

Dynamic Voronoi Diagrams - Construction and Maintenance

My current research involves the basic two-dimensional Euclidean Voronoi diagram of points and line segments, using dynamic construction techniques. This combines the tiling and object adjacencies of raster and vector systems, at the cost, by comparison with raster, of making explicit rather than implicit the tiles' adjacency relationships. The Voronoi zone around each object is the region closer to the generating object than to any other - thus adjacency of objects is equated with Voronoi zones having a common boundary. Points may be moved about within the map region, and the adaptive nature of the data structure provides a built-in collision warning system. In addition, the concept of an "interrogation point" moving about within the Voronoi map of data points, collecting stolen-area information as it goes, greatly facilitates the development of interpolation and simulation procedures, as well as robot navigation, etc. This point movement process is the *basis* of any dynamic maintenance [18]. The approach used to maintain the underlying triangulation during any data point movement is described in [15].

Apart from the ability to move a point, a few other simple operations are required. A point is *created* by splitting an existing point, which is then moved to its final destination. Points are *deleted* in the reverse process. *Lines* are drawn by letting the trail of a moving point accumulate all the spatial adjacency relationships held by the point in its travels, and deleted by having the moving point re-trace its path. This is closely related to turtle geometry, with the addition of the spatial adjacency relationships formed by the Voronoi zones or "bubbles" about each object. This gives a biological, cellular flavour to the process, the previous operations corresponding to the "birth, life, death and history" of a moving point in the data structure. Indeed, the similarity to turtle geometry is extremely close, as all commands consist of *selecting*

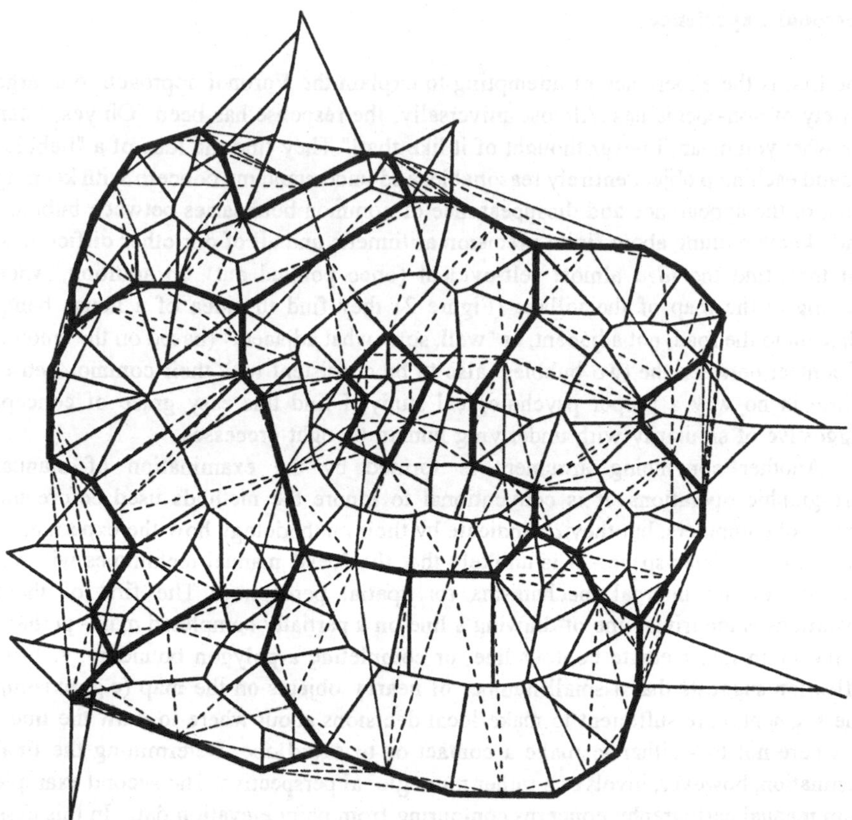

Figure 4: The Voronoi Diagram (solid lines) and Delaunay Triangulation (light lines) of a Polygon Set (heavy lines).

a turtle from one of the existing data points, and then ***passing it messages*** to perform the desired operation: both turtle and Voronoi geometry are ***object-oriented*** at the lowest level. Figure 4 shows the Voronoi regions of the line segments forming a polygon set, constructed using the Voronoi moving-point approach. The dashed lines show the equivalent dual triangulation - the only spatial data structure used in the method.

Section 3: The Human Model of Space.

We can conclude from this catalogue that it *is* possible to define a spatial data structure that contains the good points of traditional vector and raster systems. In addition, certain basic GIS operations "fall out of" the approach - in particular point-in-polygon, buffer zone and interpolation methods [16]. The question of interest here is whether a coherent computer approach says anything useful about human perception and reasoning. I believe that it does. There are several issues that convince me.

Personal Experience

The first is the experience of attempting to explain the Voronoi approach to a large variety of non-specialists. Almost universally, the response has been "Oh yes, I can see what you mean, I never thought of it like that!" They find the idea of a "bubble" around each map object entirely reasonable, and understand my concern with keeping track of the appearance and disappearance of common boundaries between bubbles. They know nothing about finite-precision arithmetic and all of our other difficulties, but they find the *idea* almost self-evident (once pointed out). In addition, when looking at the map of the village (Figure 2) they find the idea of a house being adjacent to the road, not adjacent, or "well, somewhat adjacent" (based on the amount of contact between the two bubbles) also to be consistent with their common sense. While in no way a proper psychological study, I find this easy grasp of concept suggestive of similarity with underlying human thought processes.

Another convincing argument is formed by the examination of manual cartographic operations. It is conventional to ignore the methods used before the arrival of computers, but they *do* indicate by their methodology how the experienced human manipulates space - it is unlikely that the "best" manual techniques will run contrary to the internal mechanisms for spatial perception. The first of these operations is the trivial one of drawing a line on a partially completed map - perhaps filling in an intermediate contour line, or completing a polygon boundary. A little reflection suggests that a small number of nearby objects on the map (e.g. existing line segments) are sufficient to make local decisions about where to draw the line - or where not to - either to make a contact or to avoid one. Determining the final destination, however, involves a rather more global perspective. The second example from manual cartography concerns contouring from point elevation data. In this case a selection of "close" pairs of points have lines drawn between them, and the positions of any intervening contour levels are placed, in an approximately linear fashion, along these lines. If the density of connected point pairs is sufficiently high, it is then possible to "connect the dots" to form the contour strings. Several years of teaching this method suggests that the most complete technique, especially for beginners, is to form a triangulation of the data points, and the "best" triangulation to use is the Delaunay one (which is known to include the minimum spanning tree of the "shortest" edges). Thus the visual estimation of the relative contribution of neighbouring data points is not based on metric decisions, but on the relative positions of the "neighbouring" data points (in a Voronoi sense).

Blum's Work

The second major issue follows from the work of Blum, where the original idea of a perceptual "skeleton" of a region was suggested as an appropriate intermediate step between the identification of the boundary of a region and its recognition as a particular type of object. His 1967 paper [4] is often cited as the origin of the medial axis transform, but his primary interest was in the field of shape classification of biological objects, and his direct interest was how shapes were identified and then classified by human or animal visual systems. His work was taken up in the raster domain by image analysts, and from this apparently developed much of the current activity in character recognition systems and mathematical morphology. Since current work on Voronoi methods is extending the original idea of the skeleton or medial axis transform in the computer domain, it should be of value to see how he felt his methods applied to human visual systems.

Blum states in the introduction to [4] that "I have approached the problem of shape by assuming that the current mathematical tools were somehow missing essential elements of the problem. For despite more than two millennia of geometry, no formulation which appears natural for the biological problem has emerged. ... I have chosen to enter the problem from the middle by hypothesizing simple shape processing mechanisms, and then exploring together the geometry and visual function that result. ... The output of the transformation merely gives a set of shape attributes on which the organism can perform selection, using criteria of usefulness and relevance similar to those used in other sensory processes."

Blum starts with the (now familiar) grass fire analogy, where wave fronts are generated from some initial set of points or boundaries, and examines what happens when wave fronts meet. Working originally with optical analogue equipment, these are imagined as diffusion, growth or blurring mechanisms that could easily be part of our visual processing system. He noted that cusps appear in the travelling wave front when a distance has been travelled equal to the local radius of curvature, and thereafter the wave front moves along the generated medial axis (making it a directed graph). (Figure 5.) This directed graph appears to be a great help in the "recognition" of particular shapes (e.g. Figure 6). The medial axis transform can generate graphs outside the shape ("polygon") as well as inside (giving the exoskeleton as well as the endoskeleton). A polygon set will produce one endoskeleton for each polygon (Figure 7). Even if the boundary of a shape is broken by some other feature, the skeleton of

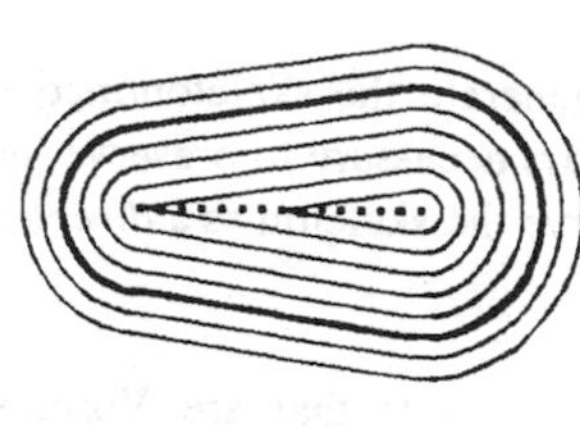

Figure 5: Wave Fronts and Skeleton of a Simple Shape. (After Blum, 1967)

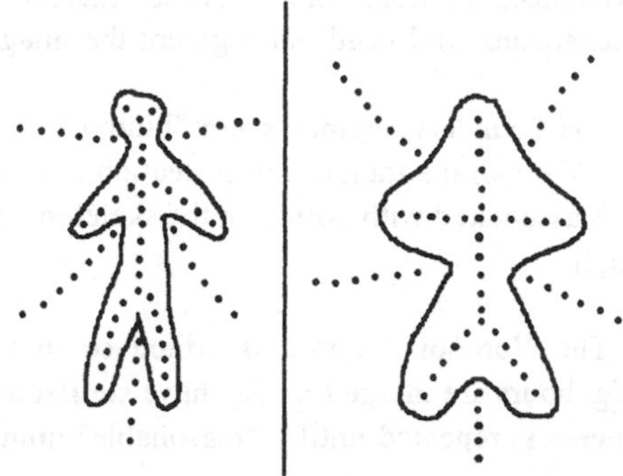

Figure 6: Skeletons of Two Figures. (After Blum, 1967)

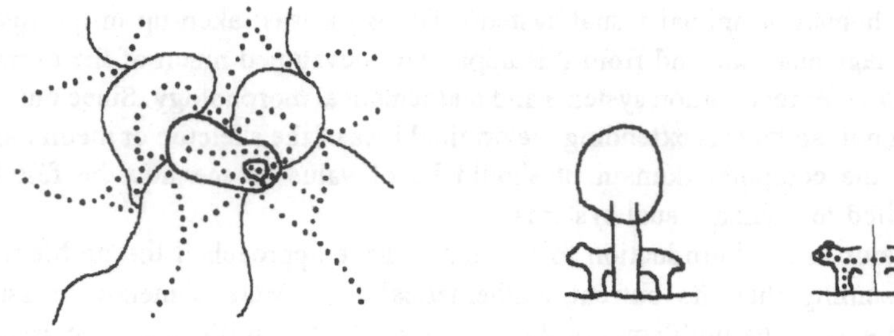

Figure 7: Skeletons of a Polygon Set (After Blum, 1967)

Figure 8: Completion of a Masked Object. (After Blum, 1967)

the identified components of the shape is frequently still recognizable (Figure 8). In his 1973 paper [5] he defines width and length measures that appear to be relatively stable with the flexing of the "biological" shapes he is primarily considering. In a later section of the paper he attempts to provide a possible classification scheme for objects depending on the number, in-valence and out-valence of the nodes of the medial axis and shows that this can be more stable than the original outline, suggesting a plausible mechanism of visual system function. This work is continued in [6].

Using Blum's approach one could envisage a visual system with the following processing stages:

1. An image is perceived (perhaps in a raster-like environment) and a variety of *boundary* segments are detected by various mechanisms (colour difference, intensity difference, motion, etc.). These merely provide elementary edge detection mechanisms, and need not segment the image fully.

2. The boundary segments are "blurred", in order to generate the skeleton/medial axis/Voronoi diagram of the collection of edges. It appears necessary to preserve the radii associated with points on the skeleton, and to preserve the skeleton as a *directed* graph.

3. The Voronoi diagram is edited so that boundary segments that are Voronoi neighbours are merged if they have similar attributes and are sufficiently close. This process is repeated until a "reasonable" number of shapes/polygons are formed.

4. Steps 1 to 3 may be repeated with different sensitivities if required. For example, on a dark night one must "stare" harder in order to receive a useful amount of information. With a very high contrast, bright and complex initial image one sometimes "de-focusses" in order to bring the information to manageable proportions.

5. The resulting "shapes" are examined for meaning. The skeleton of the shape is classified in some fashion (possibly using the node valences, among other properties -- which may include orientation, etc.). This is then *and only then* compared with the appropriate library of shape descriptors to attempt to define meaning in a particular context (forest, desert, urban, etc.) and decide if some appropriate action is necessary.

There is, of course, no direct evidence that this approach has any connection with the real internal visual mechanisms. Nevertheless, the development of a more plausible computer method for defining the neighbourhood relationships among discrete objects makes further work on the validation or invalidation of the approach intriguing. This would suggest a sequence of early (pre-meaning) visual operations that depend on only one basic mechanism - a form of blurring or diffusion.

Independently of Blum, Nordbeck and Rystedt [19] had developed, in a computer context, the "enlarged orientation theorem" for determining if a point is inside or outside a polygon. Although it uses a "sign of the determinant" type of calculation, it is based on the same "prairie fire" analogy used by Blum.

Ahuja and Tuceryan

Ahuja [1] was concerned with dot pattern recognition for use in image analysis. "Taking global features into account necessitates a top-down approach, and hence the availability of a model. Without a model, a bottom-up approach is required. Structural descriptions must be built up using the relative positions of neighbouring points. Therefore, a sound notion of neighbourhood is necessary. ... Our motivation for this correspondence came from the observation that humans find it easy to identify the neighbourhood and neighbours of a point in a wide variety of dot patterns, including those having a varying density. This would suggest the existence of a general parameter-free concept of neighbourhood." She reviews various neighbourhood clustering techniques,and concludes that the Voronoi region around a point is the best definition of its neighbourhood. "Since the perceived structure in a dot pattern results from the relative spatial arrangements of points, the geometric properties of Voronoi polygons may be useful for describing and detecting structure in dot patterns. In addition, such an approach lends a fully two-dimensional character to the problem in that the dot pattern is converted into a planar image or a mosaic. As a result, many common low-level computer vision techniques become relevant." She discusses applications to segmentation, pattern matching and perceptual boundary extraction based on properties of the Voronoi region of each point. For example, internal regions of a point cluster will have relatively compact shapes by comparison with the elongated regions of a boundary point.

Ahuja and Tuceryan [2] continued the work of extracting basic perceptual structure, or the lowest-level grouping in dot patterns. "It is not the intention here to model the grouping mechanisms used by the human visual system. Rather, the goal is only to achieve the same groupings as perceived by humans using steps which may or may not have analogues in human visual processing." They classify dots as "interior", "border", "curve" or "isolated", based on properties of the Voronoi regions such as compactness, area, elongation and eccentricity, (see Figure 9) and are able to improve on many traditional clustering techniques. Tuceryan and Jain [23] continue this work by examining the detection of texture, defining various order moments of area of the Voronoi regions that have geometric interpretations. From these moments they estimate the "break probabilities" of Delaunay edges, looking for those edges to be broken in separating regions of differing texture. It is clear that the use of the

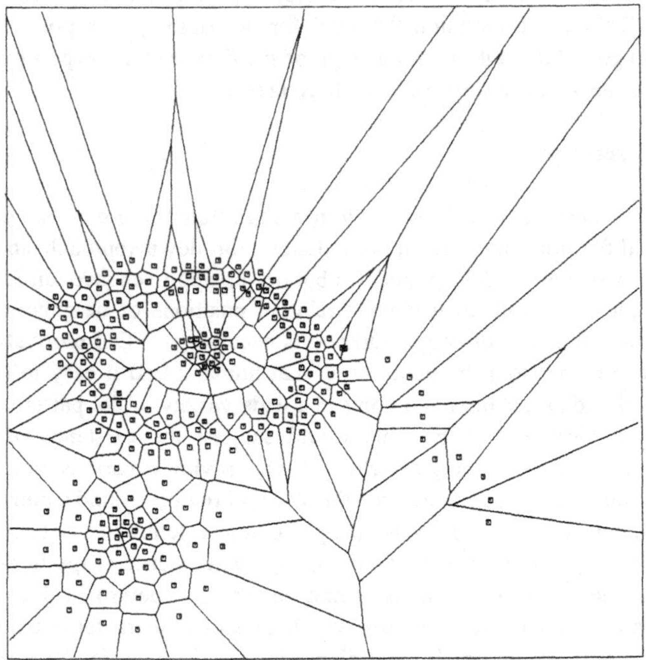

Figure 9: Boundary Detection of Point Patterns: Clusters and a Curve. (After Ahuja and Tuceryan, 1989)

Voronoi definition of neighbourhood and neighbour provides a valuable simulation of low-level pattern recognition processes - in this case for the *detection* of cluster boundaries. The encouraging feature is that the same underlying mechanism is used whether attempting to form "shapes" from clusters of significant points (Ahuja, and Tuceryan), or from perceived boundaries or fragments of boundaries (Blum).

Other Workers

Blum's skeleton approach also fits in with at least one of the mechanisms currently used for character recognition, e.g. [21] where the recognition of a simplified graph (so many loops, so many branches) greatly eases the classification of the symbol. The work of Ogniewicz and Ilg [20] on skeleton pruning has removed some of the limitations of this technique.

In image analysis similar techniques are used in shape analysis of raster images. Perhaps best known is the "mathematical morphology" of Serra [22]. His dilation and erosion mechanisms are local processes that can be combined into higher level functions for estimating the skeleton of a shape and hence providing a shape classification, a measure of elongatedness, etc. Smoothing techniques may be developed in the same way, by alternate dilation and erosion. In the Euclidean world this would be the original prairie-fire analogy used by Blum. Christensen [7] used this method to estimate the skeleton of polygons defined by vectors. Other applications and related approaches continue to be found. Aurenhammer's 1991 survey [3] of Voronoi algorithms and methods from a computational geometry viewpoint cites the opinion that "The Voronoi diagram is one of the most fundamental constructs defined by a discrete set of points".

Blum's concept of the "blurring" of object outlines in order to extract a skeleton may also relate to the way information is perceived hierarchically in an image. Edwards [9] noted a three level structure present in the way objects are perceived: the *image frame* (either the edge of the visual field, an imposed "frame" or a narrow "attention field"); the *scale* at which objects are perceived (for example, between a factor of one tenth to one half of the attention field); and a *fine scale texture* perceived inside such objects. The "blurring" mechanism for extracting the skeleton and shape information, as discussed by Blum, may also be used to select the intermediate object scale, given a framing attention field. Hence, objects that are "too small" or of "too low contrast" will be blurred beyond recognition, while objects of the "right size" will yield a skeleton. Objects which are "too large" also, with respect to the attention field (that is, their structure is not fully visible within the given frame), will not contain sufficient information for a skeleton to be obtained. Edwards noted that spatial reasoning about these intermediate scale objects depends on being able to name them by shape and/or other characteristics, and then to use relative directional and adjacency relations in a grammar to describe the relations between them. This grammar appears to be related to the formulation of a natural language description of the scene - i.e., human spatial reasoning.

Conclusions

The interrelation between the skeleton of a polygon and a buffer zone around its boundary [17] is related to the idea of blurring or defocussing an image. This is a basic technique of image and cartographic generalization - and appears to be part of our own perceptual toolkit. It is tempting to speculate that in our own image analysis system a variety of motion and edge detectors produce a set of perhaps disconnected boundary segments. A blurring or Voronoi process then links these together to form possibly useful regions, and the related skeletonization process attempts to produce a recognizable "object" from this information. Where the perceived image is a set of dots rather than a set of boundary segments, the same mechanism is capable of constructing a possible boundary - which is then fed into the previous shape construction and recognition process. Thus the idea of "neighbour" is the starting point for a set of elementary processes leading to a set of feature descriptors. These descriptors form the raw material from which reasoning about a composite object, or the relationships between discrete objects, may be initiated. Indeed, these spatial adjacency operators may also be involved in the spatial reasoning process itself.

The result of this work - in the computer implementation, as well as in perceptual speculation - is concerned with only a small part of spatio-temporal reasoning. This is the problem of providing a dynamic, scale and orientation independent description of the relationship of adjacent objects to each other. No attempt has been made to look further afield - into questions of orientation with respect to some agreed coordinate system, for example. While it is true that "general-purpose algorithms are always slower than special-purpose algorithms", many *more* applications can arise from a good general-purpose methodology. The mere development of a consistent, dynamic spatial structure that handles the adjacency of objects in a visual system, whether a pixel-based image or a drawn map, permits many applications to be explored in the fields of interpolation, adjacency and corridor analysis, and object detection in images. This is not yet "reasoning", which is perhaps not attainable, but it may well provide some of the pre-processing steps before reasoning can take place.

Acknowledgements

The funding for this research was made possible in part by an Energy, Mines and Resources Canada research agreement, and also by the foundation of an Industrial Research Chair in Geomatics at Laval University, jointly funded by the Natural Sciences and Engineering Research Council of Canada and the Association de l'Industrie Forestière du Québec. The author would also like gratefully to acknowledge the many fruitful discussions with Professors Jun Chen and Geoffrey Edwards, which were of great help in clarifying the ideas expressed here.

References

[1] N. Ahuja: Dot pattern processing using Voronoi neighbourhoods. IEEE Transactions on Pattern Analysis and Machine Intelligence PAMI-4, 336-343 (1982).

[2] N. Ahuja, M. Tuceryan: Extraction of early perceptual structure in dot patterns: integrating region, boundary and component Gestalt. Computer Vision, Graphics and Image Processing 48, 304-356 (1989).

[3] F. Aurenhammer: Voronoi diagrams - a survey of a fundamental geometric data structure. ACM Computing Surveys 23, 345-405 (1991).

[4] H. Blum: A transformation for extracting new descriptors of shape. In: W. Whaten-Dunn (ed.): Models for the Perception of Speech and Visual Form. Cambridge, Mass.: M.I.T. Press 1967, pp. 153-171.

[5] H. Blum: Biological shape and visual science (part I). Journal of Theoretical Biology 38, 205-287 (1973).

[6] H. Blum, R.N. Nagel: Shape description using weighted symmetric axis features. Pattern Recognition 10, 167-180 (1978).

[7] A.H.J. Christensen: Parallel pairs in automated cartography. Cartographica 23, 62-78 (1986).

[8] S. Dutta: Approximate spatial reasoning: integrating qualitative and quantitative constraints. International Journal of Approximate Reasoning 5, 307-331 (1991).

[9] G. Edwards: Spatial knowledge for image understanding. In: D. Mark, A. Frank (eds.): NATO Advanced Study Institute on Cognitive and Linguistic Aspects of Geographic Space. Kluwer Press 1992.

[10] M.J. Egenhofer, A. Frank: Object-oriented modelling in GIS: inheritance and propagation. Proceedings, Auto-Carto 9, Baltimore, 588-598 (1989).

[11] M. Feuchtwanger: Geographical logical database model requirements. Proceedings, Auto-Carto 9, Baltimore, 599-609 (1989).

[12] J. Freeman: The modelling of spatial relations. Computer Graphics and Image Processing 4, 156 (1975).

[13] C.M. Gold: Further research on Voronoi diagrams - a common basis for many applications. In: Y. Bedard (ed.): Trends and Concerns of Spatial Sciences: Proceedings, Third Annual International Seminar. Laval University, Québec City, Canada 1988.

[14] C.M. Gold: Surface interpolation, spatial adjacency and G.I.S. In: J. Raper (ed.): Three Dimensional Applications in Geographical Information Systems. London: Taylor and Francis Ltd. 1989, pp. 21-35.

[15] C.M. Gold: Spatial data structures -- the extension from one to two dimensions. In: L.F. Pau (ed.): NATO Advanced Research Workshop, Mapping and spatial modelling for navigation. NATO ASI Series, vol. F 65. Berlin: Springer 1990, pp. 11-39.

[16] C.M. Gold: Space revisited -- back to the basics. In: Proceedings, Fourth International Symposium on Spatial Data Handling, Zurich, pp. 175-189, (1990).

[17] C.M. Gold: Problems with handling spatial data - the Voronoi approach. CISM Journal 45, 65-80 (1991).

[18] C.M. Gold: Dynamic spatial data structures - the Voronoi approach. In: Proceedings, Fourth Canadian Conference on Geographic Information Systems, Ottawa, pp. 245-255, (1992).

[19] S. Nordbeck, B. Rystedt: Computer cartography point-in-polygon problems. B.I.T. 7, 39-64 (1967).

[20] R. Ogniewicz, M. Ilg: Skeletons with Euclidean metric and correct topology and their application in object recognition and document analysis. In: Proceedings, First European Conference on Geographic Information Systems, Amsterdam, pp. 15-24, (1990).

[21] T. Pavlidis: Algorithms for Graphics and Image Processing. Rockville, MD USA: Computer Science Press 1982, 416p.

[22] J. Serra: Image Analysis and Mathematical Morphology. London: Academic Press 1982.

[23] M. Tuceryan, A.K. Jain: Texture segmentation using Voronoi polygons. IEEE Transactions on Pattern Analysis and Machine Intelligence 12, 211-216 (1990).

A hierarchical triangle-based model for terrain description

Leila De Floriani
Dipartimento di Informatica e Scienze dell'Informazione
Università di Genova
Viale Benedetto XV, 3 - 16132 Genova - ITALY

Enrico Puppo
Istituto per la Matematica Applicata
Consiglio Nazionale delle Ricerche
Via L.B. Alberti, 4 - 16132 Genova - ITALY

Abstract

This article describes a new hierarchical model for representing a terrain. The model, called a Hierarchical Triangulated Irregular Network (HTIN), is a method for compression of spatial data and representation of a topographic surface at successively finer levels of detail. A HTIN is a hierarchy of triangle-based surface approximations, where each node, except for the root, is a triangulated irregular network refining a triangle face belonging to its parent in the hierarchy. In this paper we present an encoding structure for a HTIN and we describe an algorithm for its construction.

1 Introduction

In the last few years hierarchical surface models have been developed to describe terrains at different levels of resolution. Variable-resolution surface models provide a data compression mechanism which allows a reduction of the number of points needed to describe a surface: fewer points, for instance, should be used to represent large surface regions of almost constant slope. Such models are also used for robot navigation on a terrain, since a coarse map of the terrain is necessary to plan an initial path for the robot, while a more detailed description is required to plan local motions.

Hierachical models are used in a wide range of applications for representing point data, planar regions, surfaces, and 3D objects [Sam90]. Such models allow the manipulation of a geometric entity at different levels of resolution. Usually, they are classified into ***space-dependent*** representations (like the quadtree, the octree and their variants), which are based on a recursive decomposition of the space occupied by an object, and ***object-dependent*** representations (like different hierarchical triangulations or the Delaunay pyramid), which provide a description of the object in an object-centered coordinate frame.

A terrain can be described by a mathematical model, expressed as a pair $\mathcal{M} = (D, f)$, where $z = f(x, y)$ is a function (with suitable continuity properties) defined over a domain D in the x-y plane. In practice, a terrain is known through elevation values given at a discrete set of points in the x-y plane. Thus, we are interested in a discrete model of the terrain based on such data. A *Digital Elevation Model (DEM)* can be defined as a pair $\mathcal{F} = (\Sigma, F)$, where Σ is a partition of the domain D into regions $\{R_1, \ldots, R_n\}$ and F is a family of continuous functions $z = f_i(x, y)$, each defined on a region R_i of Σ, which provide a piecewise continuous approximation of the terrain.

Digital elevation models are usually classified into *Regular Grids (RGs)* and *Triangulated Irregular Networks (TINs)* depending on the characteristics of the domain subdivision Σ: The great advantage of TINs lies in their capability of adapting to the changes in the roughness of terrain. Also, surface specific points (peaks, pits, passes) and lines (ridges or valleys), which characterize the surface independently of the data sampling, can be included in a TIN as vertices and edges. Hence, in spite of the simplicity of regular grids, TINs provide a more appropriate and flexible means for describing a terrain. An arbitrary triangulation of the domain does not usually represent an acceptable basis for building a TIN, because of numerical interpolation problems. Thus, TINs are generally based on a Delaunay triangulation of the projections of the data points on the x-y plane. Delaunay triangulation has some important properties, like local definition, equiangularity (i.e., its triangles are as much equiangular as possible), minimal roughness (i.e., the surface described by a Delaunay-based TIN is as less rough as possible, independently of the elevation values) [Rip90]. In a Delaunay-based TIN, the domain subdivision depends only on the point distribution on the x-y plane. In [Dyn90] some domain triangulations that depend also on the elevation values are discussed, and corresponding TINs are compared with a Delaunay-based TIN.

In this paper, we present a new terrain model, which is based on an irregular domain triangulation and is hierarchical as well, thus providing a triangle-based representation at increasingly higher levels of resolution. The basic idea in such model, called a *hierarchical TIN*, is to combine the advantages of a TIN with the benefits of a hierachical description (for instance, local refinement in areas of interest). At a higher abstraction level, a hierarchical TIN consists of a Delaunay-based TIN, while each other node is a TIN refining a triangle belonging to its parent in the hierarchy. The refinement of a triangle is performed by inserting new points in its interior and/or on its edges and computing a Delaunay triangulation of such points. Thus, the underlying triangulation is locally a Delaunay one.

The remainder of the paper is organized as follows. Section 2 briefly reviews hierarchical models for terrain description both for regularly and irregularly spaced data. Section 3 introduces the hierarchical model we propose by giving the basic definitions and some examples. Section 4 describes a data structure for encoding a hierachical TIN, while Section 5 presents an algorithm for building such a model.

2 Hierarchical terrain models: an overview

We call *Hierarchical Digital Elevation Model (HDEM)* any DEM which provides a multiresolution description of a terrain. As standard DEMs, HDEMs can be classified depending on the shape of the underlying subdivision into: *quadtree-based models* and *hierarchical triangulated models.*

Quadtree-based models require regularly spaced data: they are based on a subdivision of the domain defined by the recursive partition of a rectangle enclosing the projections of the data points into a set of nested rectangles having vertices at such projections. Each rectangle is split into four subrectangles by joining each internal point to its projections on the four sides of the recatngle. Chen and Tobler evaluate different interpolation techniques for approximating a surface defined by a quadtree in terms of accuracy, computational speed and storage cost [Che86]. The problem with such interpolants is the difficulty in preserving the continuity of the surface approximation along the sides of the subdivision. Von Herzen and Barr propose a method for avoiding discontinuities [Von88]. Such method uses a modified version of the quadtree (that they call a *restricted quadtree*), and triangulates the leaves in the quadtree to achieve continuity at the borders of adjacent regions.

Hierachical triangulated models can be further classified into strictly hierarchical triangulations, which are described by a domain partition tree, and multiresolution triangulations, which are basically sequences of TINs. The first hierarchical triangulated models appeared in the literature are the *ternary* and the *quaternary* hierarchical triangulations [Gom79,Bar84,DeF84,Fek84,Pon87]. These models are based on the recursive subdivision of an initial triangle (with vertices at data points and containing all the other points inside) into a set of nested subtriangles with vertices at the data points. In a ternary triangulation, a subdivision of a triangle t consists of joining an internal point P to the three vertices of t, while, in a quaternary triangulation, each triangle is subdivided into four triangles formed by joining three points, each lying on a different triangle side. The major problem with a ternary triangulation lies in the elongated shape of its triangles, which leads to inaccuracies in numerical interpolation. On the other hand, a quaternary triangulation is only well suited when the data are regularly distributed and suffers of the same discontinuity problems at the boundaries of adjacent triangles as quadtree-based models. A quaternary triangulation, called *triarcon*, has been applied by Goodchild and Shiren as a hierarchical representation of the globe in a geographic information system [Goo92].

More recently, Scarlatos and Pavlidis have proposed a hierarchical triangulated model, which generalizes the ternary triangulation, by allowing splitting of the triangles along the edges as well [Sca90]. The idea of the method is to define alternative ways of refining a triangle either by adding internal points or by splitting its edges. The objective is to insert into the model significant terrain characteristics approximating critical lines and points at different levels of detail. The authors show experimentally that the number of edge and triangle splits necessary to achieve a certain degree of approximation is less than the number of refinements required in a ternary triangulation.

The Delaunay pyramid described in [DeF89] is a multiresolution hierarchical model consisting of an ordered sequence of Delaunay based TINs, each of which contains an increasing number of points and provides a more accurate surface description. Any two consecutive TINs are connected by a set of links which join the triangles modified between the two levels. The Delaunay pyramid has been extended to include also a set of segments as edges in the model at increasing resolution, thus producing a constrained Delaunay pyramid [Jon91]. This allows the explicit representation of surface-specific lines as well as their refinement when the resolution increases. A constrained Delaunay pyramid can be built by using the incremental method described in [DeF92].

A Delaunay pyramid cannot be described by a tree, since a triangle belonging to the triangulation at a given level i can intersect a portion of the domain covered by several triangles in the triangulation at level $i-1$. A Delaunay pyramid is encoded as a sequence of TINs plus a set of links which describe the connections among the triangles. One drawback of such model is thus its high storage cost. Moreover, it is difficult to reconstruct a surface approximation in which the approximation error is different in different regions of the domain.

3 Hierarchical Triangulated Irregular Network

In this section we introduce the definitions of *Hierarchical Triangulation (HT)* and of *Triangulated Irregular Network (TIN)*, and we combine such concepts to define our new hierarchical triangle-based surface model called the *Hierarchical Triangulated Irregular Network (HTIN)*.

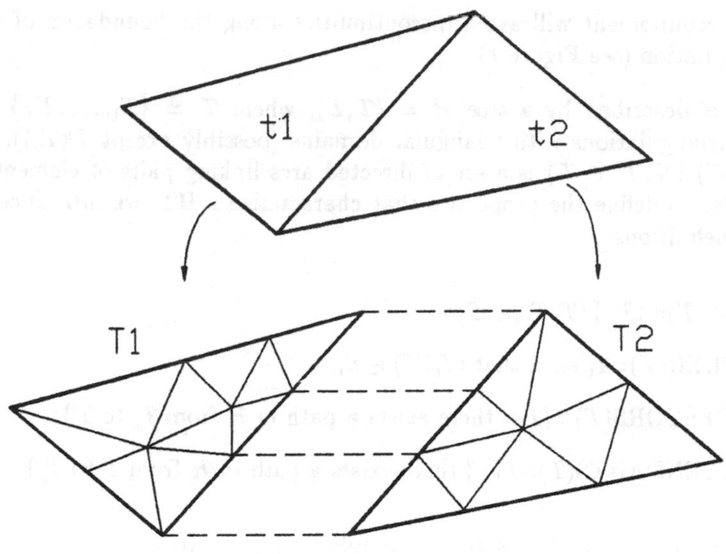

Figure 1: Two adjacent triangles and their refinement

All the structures we define are based on the *triangulation* of a finite set of points V in the Euclidean plane, defined as follows:

> a triangulation $T(V)$ of set V is a maximal Planar Straight Line Graph having V as set of vertices [Pre85].

$T(V)$ is a planar subdivision formed by triangular faces and covering the convex hull of V in $\mathbb{R}^2$; in the following, the domain of a triangulation T will be denoted $D(T)$. We also say that an edge e of a triangulation T is a *boundary edge* for T if it lies on the boundary of $D(T)$.

3.1 Hierarchical Triangulation

A *Hierarchical Triangulation (HT)* is obtained by applying the concept of recursive refinement to the triangulation model. Intuitively, given a triangulation, any of its triangles is seen as an individual entity. We can expand any such triangle at a higher level of detail into another triangulation, whose domain covers the triangle. Different triangles can be refined independently; nevertheless, the refinement of one triangle can produce splitting of its edges into chains of edges. As edges are entities shared by adjacent triangles, we enforce adjacent triangles to be expanded into triangulations that "match" along their common edge; this requirement will avoid discontinuities along the boundaries of each new triangulation (see Figure 1).

A HT is described by a tree $\mathcal{H} = (\mathcal{T}, \mathcal{E})$, where $\mathcal{T} = \{T_0, \ldots, T_N\}$ is a family of triangulations with triangular domains (possibly except $D(T_0)$), and $\mathcal{E} = \{(T,T') \mid T,T' \in \mathcal{T}\}$ is a set of directed arcs linking pairs of elements of $\mathcal{T}$. In order to define the properties that characterize a HT, we introduce the following definitions:

- SONS(T)=$\{T_j \mid (T,T_j) \in \mathcal{E}\}$;
- FATHER(T)=T_i such that $(T_i,T) \in \mathcal{E}$;
- ANCESTORS(T)=$\{T_j \mid$ there exists a path in $\mathcal{H}$ from T_j to $T\}$;
- DESCENDANTS(T)=$\{T_j \mid$ there exists a path in $\mathcal{H}$ from T to $T_j\}$;

A Hierarchical Triangulation satisfies the following properties:

- **hierarchy rule**: for every $T_j \in$ SONS(T) there exists exactly one triangle t_j in T such that $t_j = D(T_j)$; in other words, each triangulation, except for the root, is the refinement of some triangle of another (coarser) triangulation in the hierarchy; we say that T_j refines t_j and we denote:
  - t_j=ABSTRACTION(T_j)
  - T_j=REFINEMENT(t_j)
- **matching rule**: let T' and T'' be two triangulations of $\mathcal{T}$ and let V' and V'' be the sets of vertices of T' and T'' respectively; we say that T' and T'' are *adjacent* along a straight line l segment if their domains intersect only along l; we say that T' and T'' are *matching* along l if they are adjacent along l and $l \cap V' = l \cap V''$; then, if $T', T'' \in \mathcal{T}$ are adjacent along l, one of the following conditions must hold:
  (a) T' and T'' are matching along l;
  (b) $l \cap V' \subset l \cap V''$ and there exists $T^* \in$DESCENDANTS(T') that is matching with T'' along l;
  (c) $l \cap V' \supset l \cap V''$ and there exists $T^{**} \in$DESCENDANTS(T'') that is matching with T' along l.

In practice, the hierarchy rule guarantees the consistency of the hierarchical relations between triangulations in $\mathcal{H}$, while the matching rule ensures that any edge of any triangulation T of $\mathcal{T}$ is always refined consistently in the subtree rooted at T.

Figure 2: An approximation of terrain represented by a TIN

3.2 Triangulated Irregular Network

Let $z = f(x, y)$ be a function of two variables describing a terrain. A Triangulated Irregular Network (TIN) approximating such terrain is a continuous function interpolating f at a discrete set of points $V = \{v_1, \ldots, v_m\}$ in the plane, defined over a two-dimensional triangulation $T(V)$ of the points of V. A TIN is defined as a pair $\mathcal{F} = (T(V), F)$, where triangulation $T(V)$ is formed by triangles $\{t_1, \ldots, t_n\}$ and $F = \{f_1, \ldots, f_n\}$ is a family of functions, where each function f_i is defined over t_i and interpolates f at the vertices of t_i.

Here, we restrict to piecewise linear TINs, i.e., we impose that F is a set of linear functions. In practice, for every triangle t_i of T, a corresponding triangular planar patch $\overline{t_i}$ in $\mathbb{R}^3$ approximates $f(x, y)$, for all (x, y) lying inside t_i.

The precision of $\mathcal{F}$ in approximating function f is measured by some distance $E(f, \mathcal{F})$ between functions f and the linear interpolants over each triangle. Here, we define the precision of function $f_i \in F$ over triangle t_i as $E_i(f, f_i) = \max_{t_i} |f(x) - f_i(x)|$, and we define $E(f, \mathcal{F}) = \max_{i=1}^{n} E_i(f, f_i)$. We will call E the *error function*.

In Figure 2 a perspective view of a terrain represented by a TIN is shown.

3.3 Hierarchical Triangulated Irregular Network

In order to define a hierachical model of terrain surface, we combine the concept of TIN with the one of hierarchical triangulation. Given a function f defined as above, a ***Hierarchical Triangulated Irregular Network (HTIN)*** approximating f is a hierarchy of n TINs such that:

- for every $i = 1, \ldots, n$, TIN $\mathcal{F}_i = (T_i(V_i), F_i)$ approximates f in $D(T_i)$;
- triangulations $T_i(V_i)$, $i = 1, \ldots, n$, form a Hierarchical Triangulation $\mathcal{H}$.

In the following, we will refer interchangeably to a TIN $\mathcal{F}$ and to the triangulation T describing it, whenever no ambiguity arises. Similarly, we will refer to the precision of a triangulation or of a triangle by meaning the approximation error of the corresponding TIN or triangular patch, respectively. For simplicity, we will also denote with $E(T)$ the error of a TIN described by triangulation T, and with $E(t)$ the error of a triangular patch corresponding to triangle t.

A ***Hierarchical Delaunay TIN (HDT)*** is a HTIN with the further property that any triangulation in the hierarchy is a Delaunay triangulation.

The above definitions do not yield any particular criterion of refinement. For instance, one could build the HTIN by imposing that each triangle is refined into a triangulation containing no more than a maximum number n_{max} of triangles (such an approach could be useful, for instance, to speedup point location). In the next Section, we will show how a HTIN (a HDT) can be built based on a finite sequence of decreasing tolerance values, in such a way that each refinement causes an increase in the precision of the approximation of a portion of terrain.

4 A data structure for encoding a hierarchical TIN

In this Section, we describe a data structure for encoding a hierarchical TIN. The information stored in the data structure allow fast traversal of the model, as required by algorithms that build an "expanded" TIN at a specified level of accuracy, or more generally, which navigate the model at different degrees of resolution. Navigation algorithms are the basis, for instance, of algorithms for contour extraction or for visibility computation.

The internal encoding structure of a hierarchical TIN is a combination of individual data structures representing the various TINs composing the HTIN, and information describing the hierarchy as well as adjacency relations between triangulations sharing common boundaries.

Several data structures have been proposed in the literature for encoding a triangulation [Gui83,Pre85,Woo85]. Here, we use a variant of the symmetric structure developed by Woo [Woo85] for describing the triangulations forming the hierarchy. For each trianglulation $T \in \mathcal{T}$, we encode its three basic entities, namely vertices, edges and triangles, together with four incidence relations. Each edge e of T is described by its two extreme vertices (Edge-Vertex relation), and by the two triangles sharing it (Edge-Triangle relation). Each triangle t is related to its bounding edges (Triangle-Edge relation). Finally, we store with each vertex v one of the edges of T incident on v (partial Vertex-Edge relation). It can be shown that the data structure is optimal with respect to both storage cost and time complexity of the structure accessing algorithms operating on it.

The following information are stored to describe the hierarchical organizaition of a HTIN. For every node T in the HTIN, we store:

- a link to its parent triangulation in the hierarchy FATHER(T) together with an indirect link to triangle ABSTRACTION(T) in FATHER(T);
- for every triangle t in T that is refined in the hierarchy, a link to triangulation REFINEMENT(t);
- three sequences of boundary edges, corresponding to the refinements of the three edges of ABSTRACTION(T) respectively;
- for each boundary edge e of T, the sequence of boundary edges containing e and the position of e in such a sequence.

Information on boundary edges allow maintaining links towards the exterior of triangulation T in an implicit form. Such links allow navigation of the hierarchical structure at a given level of detail.

Let e be a boundary edge of T. We denote, for analogy, ABSTRACTION(e) the edge of ABSTRACTION(T) that is expanded in T into a sequence s containing e. Let us suppose for now that ABSTRACTION(e) is not a boundary edge of FATHER(T). Then, there must exist a triangle t' belonging to FATHER(T) and adjacent to ABSTRACTION(T) along ABSTRACTION(e); in the general case, t' is expanded in the hierarchy into a triangulation T' that matches with T along s. Then the position of e in s can be used to locate its corresponding edge in the corresponding boundary chain of T'. If also ABSTRACTION(e) is a boundary edge in FATHER(T), then the position of e is pushed onto a stack and upper levels in the hierarchy are searched following the same rule, until a non-boundary edge e^* is found. Then, the hierarchy is descended from e^* using the stack of positions, until the edge corresponding to e at the same level of detail is found (see Figure 3).

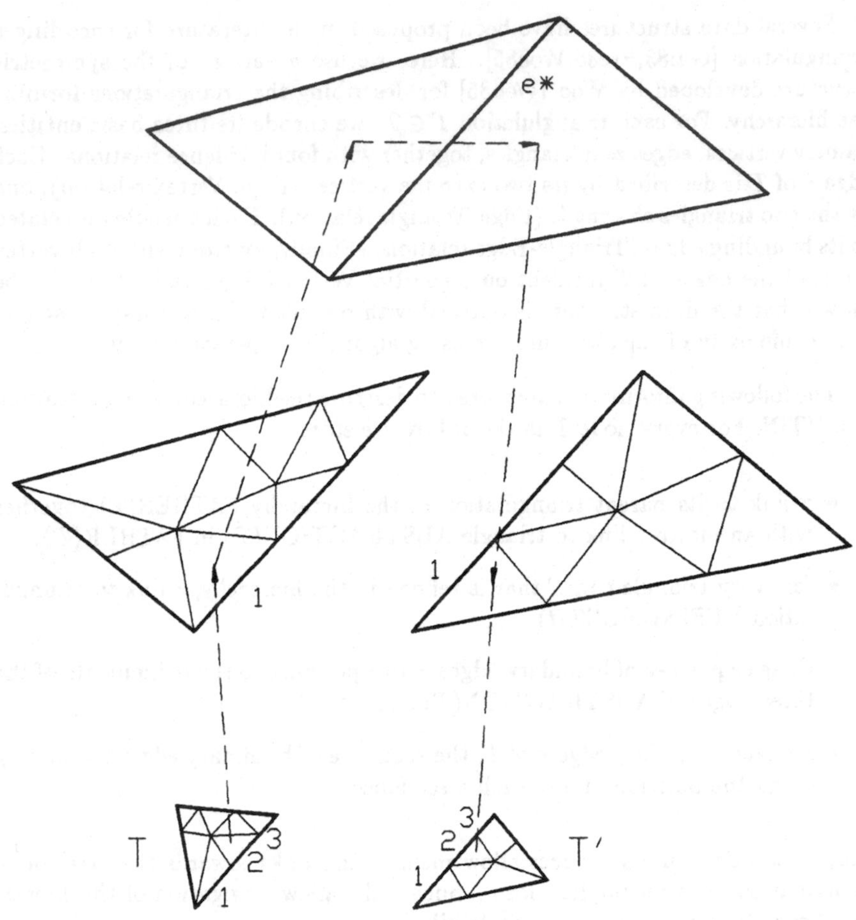

Figure 3: Navigation of a HTIN

5 Building a hierarchical TIN

We are interested in building a hierarchical terrain model at various levels of resolution. We assume to have an "exact" representation of a terrain (typically, an interpolation function based on a dense regular grid of sampled data), and to build our model by extracting points from it.

Techniques to obtain a TIN at a fixed level of resolution from a dense set of data have been described in [Fow79,DeF85,Sca90,Pup92]. In [DeF85] an algorithm was proposed that refines an existing Delaunay-based TIN by inserting one point at a time and updating the Delaunay triangulation until the required precision is met. The point inserted at each cycle is the one that causes the maximum error in the approximation; this criterion is named the ***Delaunay selector***. In [Pup92] a parallel algorithm based on the Delaunay selector is proposed, that performs refinement by inserting many points at a time (namely, one per existing triangle).

Let $\{\varepsilon_0, \ldots, \varepsilon_k\}$ be a given decreasing sequence of positive real values, called the ***tolerance values***. We build first the root of the HTIN T_0, which is a TIN at level of precision ε_0 (i.e., $E(T_0) \leq \varepsilon_0$). Then each triangle t_i of T_0 refined into a triangulation T_i such that $E(T_i) \leq \varepsilon_1$. This process is repeated on the new triangulations with decreasing tolerance values, until each portion of the initial domain has been refined at precision ε_k.

In order to build our HTIN, we produce first triangulation T_0 by applying a Delaunay selector algorithm with precision ε_0 to the initial data set. Then, an iterative refinement procedure is applied, that refines at each cycle all triangulations corresponding to the leaves of the current hierarchy tree whose error exceeds the current tolerance level.

The basic step of the refinement procedure consists in taking a triangulation $T = \{t_1, \ldots, t_n\}$ such that $\varepsilon_{i+1} < E(T) \leq \varepsilon_i$, and computing a set of triangulations $\{T_1, \ldots, T_n\}$, where $\forall j = 1, \ldots, n$, T_j approximates with precision ε_{i+1} the portion of terrain corresponding to triangle $t_j \in T$. In order to satisfy the matching rule, this task is performed in three steps (see Figure 4):

(i) **edge refinement**: each edge e of T is refined by inserting new data points on it; then, a chain of segments is obtained that approximates the terrain profile along e with precision ε_{i+1};

(ii) **first expansion**: for all j, a triangulation T_j is computed, that contains the vertices of t_j plus all vertices added to its edges;

(iii) **triangulation refinement**: for all j, a Delaunay selector algorithm with precision ε_{i+1} is applied to T_j.

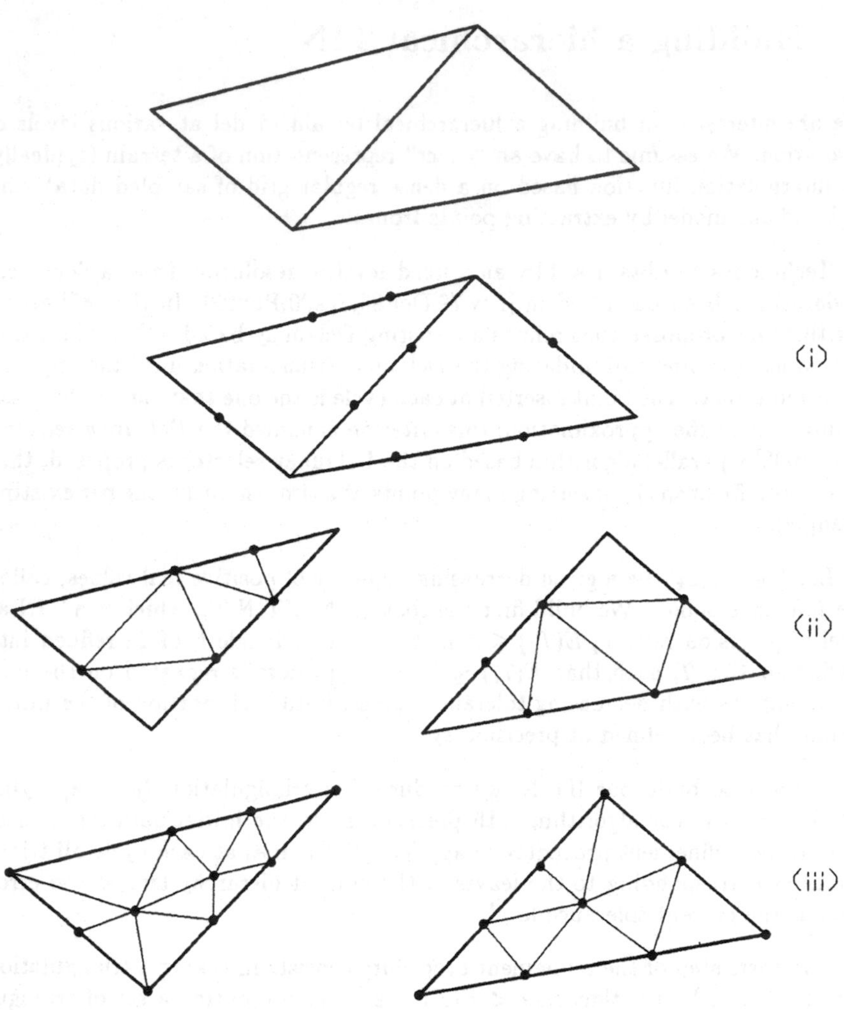

Figure 4: Steps of refinement algorithm.

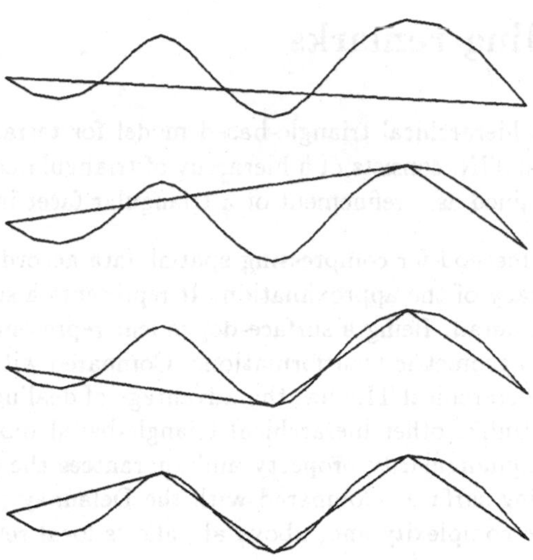

Figure 5: Refinement of an edge approximating a terrain profile

It is possible that some triangle t_j in T satisfies precision ε_{i+1}. In this case, t_j will be refined into a trivial triangulation formed by a single triangle. In order to reduce the storage complexity of the hierarchy, such a triangulation is eliminated at the next step (at precision ε_{i+2}) and replaced in the hierarchy by the refinement of the single triangle forming it. Trivial triangulations remaining as leaves of the final HTIN (at precision ε_k) are pruned. Thus, if we consider any triangle t belonging to any triangulation in the final hierarchy, either t satisfies precision ε_k and is not refined further, or there exists an index $i < k$ such that $\varepsilon_{i+1} < E(t) \leq \varepsilon_i$ and t is expanded into a triangulation satisfying at least precision ε_{i+1}.

Edge refinement can be produced independently for all triangulations and for all edges in each triangulation. Given an edge e, its approximation error that we denote $E(e)$, is the maximum difference between the terrain profile along e and its corresponding interpolated function (i.e., a straight-line segment). A refinement of e into a chain of edges to improve the approximation can be obtained through a well-known iterative algorithm that splits e by inserting at each cycle the point that causes the maximum error (see Figure 5) [Bal82].

After edge splitting has been performed, the first expansion can by computed for each triangle t independently, by applying any Delaunay triangulation algorithm to the set of vertices corresponding to the chains that refine the edges of t. The triangulation refinement can be performed on each new triangulation independently through a Delaunay selector algorithm (either sequential or parallel).

6 Concluding remarks

We have defined a hierarchical triangle-based model for terrains. This model, called a hierarchical TIN, consists of a hierarchy of triangulated surface approximations, each obtained as a refinement of a triangular facet in its parent.

The HTIN is a method for compressing spatial data according to a criterion based on the accuracy of the approximation. It represents a surface at increasingly finer levels of detail. Being a surface-dependent representation, the HTIN is invariant through geometric transformations. Compared with quadtree-based surface models, a hierarchical TIN has the advantage of dealing with arbitrarily distributed data. Unlike other hierarchical triangle-based models, a HTIN locally satisfies the equiangularity property and guarantees the global continuity of the approximating surface. Compared with the Delaunay pyramid, a HTIN has a lower storage complexity and, above all, allows local refinements in area of interests.

Further developments of this work will involve: experimenting the model with different underlying hierarchical triangulations, like those obtained by applying data dependent optimization criteria [Dyn90]; designing and implementing neighbor finding algorithms to navigate the model and to extract global surface approximations at different levels of precision; using HTIN as the basic data model for designing a hierarchical geographic database.

References

[Bal82] Ballard, D.H., Brown, C.M., *Computer Vision*, Prentice Hall, Englewood Cliffs, NJ, 1982.

[Bar84] Barrera, R., Vazquez, A.M., "A hierarchical method for representing relief", *Proceedings Pecora IX Symposium on Spatial Information Technologies for Remote Sensing Today end Tomorrow*, Sioux Falls, South Dakota, Oct. 1984, pp.87-92.

[Che86] Chen, Z.T., Tobler, W.R., "Quadtree representation of digital terrain", *Proceedings Autocarto*, London, 1986, pp. 475-484.

[DeF84] De Floriani, L., Falcidieno, B., Pienovi, C., Nagy, G., "A hierarchical data structure for surface approximation", *Computers and Graphics*, Vol.8, No.2, 1984, pp. 475-484.

[DeF85] De Floriani, L., Falcidieno, B., Pienovi, C., "Delaunay-based representation of surfaces defined over arbitrarily shaped domains", *Computer Vision, Graphics, and Image Processing*, 32, 1985, pp.127-140.

[DeF89] De Floriani, L., "A Pyramidal Data Structure For Triangle-based Surface Description", *IEEE Computer Graphics and Applications*, March 1989, pp.67-78.

[DeF92] De Floriani, L., Puppo, E., "An On-line Algorithm for Constrained Delaunay Triangulation", *CVGIP - Graphical Models and Image Processing*, Vol.54, No.3, May 1992.

[Dyn90] Dyn, N., Levin, D., Rippa, S., "Data dependent triangulations for piecewise linear interpolation", *IMA Journal of Numerical Analysis*, Vol.10, 1990, pp.137-154.

[Fek84] Fekete, G., Davis, L.S., "Property spheres: a new representation for 3-D object recognition", *Proceedings Workshop on Computer Vision: Representation and Control*, CS Press, Los Alamitos, CA, May 1984, pp.192-201.

[Fow79] Fowler, R.J., Little, J.J., "Automatic extraction of irregular network digital terrain models", *Computer Graphics* 13-3, Aug. 1979, pp.199-207.

[Gom79] Gomez, D., Guzman, A., "Digital model for three-dimensional surface representation", *Geo-Processing*, Vol.1, 1979, pp.53-70.

[Goo92] Goodchild, M.F., Shiren, Y., "A hierarchical spatial data structure for global geographic information systems", *CVGIP - Graphical Models and Image Processing*, Vol.54, No.1, January 1992.

[Gui83] Guibas, L.J., Stolfi, J., "Primitives for the manipulation of general subdivisions and the computation of Voronoi diagrams", *Proceedings 15th A.C.M. Conference on the Theory of Computing* , 1983, pp.221-234.

[Jon91] Jones, C.B., "Database architecture for multi scale GIS", *Proceedings Autocarto*, 1991, pp.1-14.

[Pon87] Ponce, J., Faugeras, O., "An object centered hierarchical representation for 3D objects: the prism tree", *Computer Vision, Graphics and ImageProcessing*, Vol.38, No.1, Apr. 1987, pp.1-28.

[Pre85] Preparata, F.P., Shamos, M.I., *Computational Geometry: An Introduction*, Springer-Veralg, Berlin, 1985.

[Pup92] Puppo, E., Davis, L., DeMenthon, D., Teng, Y.A., "Parallel terrain triangulation" in *Proceedings 5th International Symposium on Spatial Data Handling*, Charleston, SC, 3-7 August 1992 (in print).

[Rip90] Rippa, S., "Minimal roughness property of Delaunay triangulation", *Computer Aided Geometric Design*, 7, 1990, pp.489-497.

[Sam90] Samet, H., *The design and analysis of spatial data structures*, Addison Wesley, Reading, MA, 1990.

[Sca90] Scarlatos, L.L., Pavlidis, T., "Hierarchical triangulation using terrain features", *Proceedings IEEE Conference on Visualization*, San Francisco, CA, Oct. 1990, pp.168-175.

[Von88] Von Herzen, B., Barr, A.H., "Accurate triangulations of deformed, intersecting surfaces", *Computer Graphics*, 21, 4, July 1987, pp.103-110.

[Woo85] Woo, T.C., "A combinatorial analysis of boundary data structure schemata", *IEEE Computer Graphics and Applications*, 5, 3, pp. 19-27.

A Model for Expressing Topological Integrity Constraints in Geographic Databases

Thanasis Hadzilacos
and
Nectaria Tryfona
Computer Technology Institute
University of Patras, Greece
P.O. Box 1122, 26110, Patras, Greece
e-mail : thh@cti.gr, tryfona@cti.gr
tel, fax : +30 61 992061

Abstract. A major reccuring issue in spatial databases is that of handling topological relationships. Although topology can be determined from object positions it is often explicitly stored in geographic information systems for reasons of efficiency and integrity. No formal database models for expressing topological relationships at the conceptual and logical levels are available. This paper describes such a model by defining geographic objects, geometric types, and elementary spatial operations and relationships. The model can be used to express topological integrity constraints, to define geographic object classes and to express spatial queries. Examples are given on how to use the model for the whole cycle of design and development of a geographic application, including requirements analysis, conceptual and logical modeling and implementation.

1 Introduction

The topology of a set of objects refers to their relative positions in space, in abstraction of distances, shapes and sizes. The basic topological relationships are those of adjacency (or neighbourhood) and sharing (or overlapping) from which connectivity can be derived. Topological relationships can of course be determined from positions of objects (in terms of some fixed coordinate system); however, positioning of objects relative to one another can be known without information on the exact (absolute) object positions; topological information is useful and processable by itself; and when designing, it is sometimes necessary to manipulate objects topologically before distances, shapes and sizes have been determined. Furthermore the amount of processing required to extract topological relationships from absolute positions can be very large and the amount of information needed to describe topology can be much smaller than that needed to describe positions. This is why topological relationships play a prominent role in spatial information processing systems. In geographic information systems in particular, topological relationships are usually explicitly stored (see [6]) for reasons of efficiency and integrity.

A database represents part of the real world. A database state is a set of <entity, value> pairs. Some database states represent possible states of the real world; others do not. The former are called consistent. Static integrity constraints are conditions that express which database states are correct and which are not. Theoretically, static integrity constraints are sufficient to determine correct database states. In practice they are used to eliminate –some– incorrect states. Dynamic integrity constraints are conditions on the allowable transitions from one database state to another. Integrity constraints can refer to single <entity, value> pairs (e.g. no salary can be less than 10000 (static) or no salary can be decreased (dynamic)); or to a set of <entity, value> pairs (e.g. the sum of all assets equals the sum of all liabilities (static); or the sum of all forms of energy is constant (dynamic)). In spatial information processing systems an important consideration for determining whether a database state is correct or not is topology. Neighbouring countries, for example, must have a common border; seas and lakes do not overlap; and when a common wall is moved the sum of the areas of the two adjacent rooms remains constant. If we were to express topological integrity constraints in terms of absolute positions, they would be straightforward but cumbersome, and totally impractical. In the light of the discussion of the previous paragraph, however, it seems important to be able to formally express topological constraints directly. This is the purpose of the present paper.

Since static topological integrity constraints are conditions on the allowable values of spatial attributes of the database, a language to express them can be used not only to guard the integrity of the database, but also to define views or object classes and to express spatial queries. So the language we shall define should be able to express conditions such as "two land parcels cannot overlap", definitions such as "a candidate factory site is a land parcel that is road accessible and is not designated as residence area", and queries such as "find the private land parcels which abut upon Piazza Garibaldi", where "overlap", "road accessible" and "abut upon" are topological relationships among geographic objects.

The need to address this issue is very clear in the GIS literature where references to topological relationships abound, usually made with no particular explanation as they are considered to be "obvious". Several authors try to clearly set out the topological notions used and some even do so formally. Spooner in [12] states the need to store topological relationships in geographic databases and informally describes three such relationships (sharing, connectivity and adjacency) which he deems fundamental and from which all others are to be derived; examples are given from actual systems, but formal definitions are absent. Oxborrow and Kemp in [9] make a rather short reference to topological relationships of spatial objects, based on four types of objects (point, line, arc and region) for each of which operators such as distance, intersect, overlap are defined. Scholl and Voissard in [11] use the same types of objects along with an open set of functions and operators such as inside, border and Radjacent. Engenhofer and Herring in [2] present a theory which provides a complete coverage of binary topological relationships based on concepts of algebraic and set theory; we use this theory as the mathematical framework for our presentation. Pelagatti et al in [10] mention three operator types (geometric, arithmetic and set operators) and state that they can be used with propositional calculus to express topological integrity constraints. Oosterom and Vijlbrief in [8] distinguish geometric (such as length or perimeter), topological (such as right_polygon) and spatial comparison operators (such as inside). Finally, in [3] we see how a real GIS system handles topology, which is by distinguishing three types of topological connections (connectivity, area definition and contiguity) on the basis of which operators such as Union, Near, and Pointdistance are defined.

This proliferation of approaches in the modeling of topology in geographic systems clearly shows that what is needed is not yet another model of topological relationships with a slightly different set of basic operators, but a theory of such relationships which should be sound and complete on the one hand and able to accommodate the practical treatments of the subject (like the ones mentioned above) which stem from actual system needs.

Our approach is to use standard database models (object-oriented, semantic and relational) and extend them to incorporate topological relationships with the minimum of add-ons. In each model a different language must be used to express topological relationships; however they are just different syntactic versions of the same underlying concepts.

The contribution of this work is a unifying theory of topological relationships based on a lean set of concepts which makes it usable in a variety of environments at all levels of application development: semantic, logical, and physical design as well as implementation.

The rest of this paper is organized as follows: In Section 2 we define geographic objects and geometric operations, describe the model, and use it to develop a formal language for expressing topological integrity constraints. In Section 3 we give examples of using the model; we feel it is important to show how our formalism can be used for expressing topological integrity constraints in all levels of application development, so we give examples of utilization in a semantic data model, a logical data model and a working GIS environment (namely ARC/INFO). Section 4 concludes by reviewing the model in the context of a larger research effort, comparing it to the other models found in the literature and suggesting further research on the issue.

2 Definitions and the Model

2.1 Geographic Databases and Topological Integrity Constraints

A database is a set of *objects* which represent part of the real world; each object belongs to an *object class* (we ignore multiple inheritance, see [7], in order to make the presentation more clear, but our model does not depend on this); an object class is characterized by a set of properties, or ***attributes*** and a set of ***methods***; each attribute is associated with a ***domain***, which is an unrestricted set of *values*. Methods are the only means to access the attributes. So each object in a database instance is represented by a set of values each belonging to the domain of the corresponding attribute of the object class.

Domains are implemented by data types and methods by programs. Abstract data types constitute one way to encapsulate the implementation of both domains and methods. In order to serve the needs of spatial information handling applications, new data types, called cartographic, must be added to the classical database data types (real, integer, string, date etc). There are several such data types, of which we will use point, arc and region. **Points, Arcs** and **Regions** are the sets of data types point, arc and region respectively. The usage of the terms line and arc is often contradictory and confusing. We use "line segment" to mean a finite part of a straight line, "arc" to mean a set of consecutive line segments with only two end points (i.e. no branches allowed) and "line" to mean any finite set of connected linear segments.

In databases modeling geographic applications, objects have one special attribute, the *geometric type* which indicates the dimensionality of the object represented. Its domain is $\{point, arc, region, null\}$, or equivalently $\{0, 1, 2, \mathbf{null}\}$. Objects with non-null geometric type are called geographic objects, and have a special attribute, the ***spatial position*** or simply ***position***. In fact this is overloading of the term, see [7], as spatial position has different domains and methods depending on the geometric type.

The domain of the attribute position for objects of geometric type 0 is a finite set of points in $\mathbf{R}^2$. The domain of position for objects of geometric type 1 is a finite set of lines. The domain of position for objects of geometric type 2 is a finite set of regions.

Methods on geographic objects may involve spatial position; when they do they are called *geometric methods*.

A relationship is a condition on a tuple of values of attributes, possibly from different objects. Relationships which include position are called *topological*.

Some relationships must be stored in the database as they constitute primary information; others are derivable so they do not need to be stored. Sometimes derivable relationships are stored for practical reasons (mainly efficiency). This creates redundancy in the database and is a source of potential incorrectness. Integrity constraints, i.e. relationships that are true of any correct database state, delimit correctness. Topological integrity constraints are those which include position.

In order to study geometric methods and topological relationships we introduce *elementary geographic objects* or *pure geometric objects*. They are objects whose only attributes are geometric type and spatial position and which have simple domains for position and simple geometric methods as the only methods. There exist three types of elementary geographic objects: P, A and R.

- P is the set of elementary geographic objects with geometric type 0. The domain of their position has single points as values and **DISTANCE** as method. **DISTANCE** is a function from pairs of objects to $\mathbf{R}$.

- A is the set of elementary geographic objects with geometric type 1. The domain of position has simple lines as values and its method is **ENDPOINTS**, a function from objects to pairs of points.

- R is the set of elementary geographic objects with geometric type 2. The domain of position has simple polygons as values (a polygon is simple if both its interior and its boundary are connected) and the methods are **AREA**, (a function from objects to $\mathbf{R}$) and **NODES** (a function from objects to points).

We will refer to the topological notions of *interior* and *boundary* (see [2]) of the position of a geographic object as the interior and boundary of the object itself.

Objects in P have a boundary consisting of a single point and empty interior. Objects in A have two boundary points (the endpoints) and objects in R have a set of connected boundary points.

2.2 Elementary Geometric Methods

The methods of pure geometric objects are called elementary geometric methods. Geometric operations are operations on geographic objects among attributes which include spatial position. They are categorized according to the type of the value returned (real vs cartographic) and according to whether they are primary (i.e. defined along with the domain of the attribute) or derived.

a. Primary operations whose range is real:

1. **DISTANCE** takes two objects of type P and returns a real, their distance.

   DISTANCE: $P \times P \rightarrow \mathbf{R}$

2. **AREA** takes an object of type R and returns a real, its area.

   AREA: $R \rightarrow \mathbf{R}$

b. Primary operations whose range is a cartographic data type:

1. **UNION** takes a pair of similar elementary geographic objects and returns a set of points, arcs or regions which is the union of the areas of the positions of the objects.

   UNION: $P \times P \rightarrow$ **Points**, $A \times A \rightarrow$ **Arcs**, $R \times R \rightarrow$ **Regions**

2. **SETDIFFERENCE** takes a pair of similar elementary geographic objects and returns a set of points, arcs or regions which is the difference of the areas of the positions of the objects.

   SETDIFFERENCE: $P \times P \rightarrow$ **Points**, $A \times A \rightarrow$ **Arcs**, $R \times R \rightarrow$ **Regions**

3. **ENDPOINTS** takes an object of type A and returns a pair of points, its endpoints.

   ENDPOINTS: $A \rightarrow$ **Points x Points**

4. **NODES** takes an object of type R and returns a list of points, its nodes.

   NODES: $R \rightarrow$ **Points x...x Points**

5. **CONSLINE** takes a list of objects of type P and returns an arc.

   CONSLINE: $P \times ... \times P \rightarrow$ **Arcs**

6. Similarly **CONSREGION** is an operator to construct a region from its nodes; takes a list of objects of type P and returns a region.

   CONSREGION: $P \times ... \times P \rightarrow$ **Regions**

c. From the primary operations we can define **PERIMETER** and **LENGTH** as derived operations whose range is real.

d. Similarly we can define **INTERSECTION** as a derived operation whose range is a cartographic data type.

2.3 Elementary Topological Relationships

This section is based on the mathematical framework for binary topological relationships developed in [2]. In order to help the reader we summarize this framework here. In [2] the theory is applied to binary topological relationships between regions. We extend this to binary topological relationships between any two elementary geographic objects (region-region (R-R), region-arc (R-A), region-point (R-P), arc-arc (A-A), arc-point (A-P) and point-point (P-P)).

Let ∂ denote the boundary of an elementary object and ^{o} its interior. Given two elementary geographic objects, $\partial\partial$, ^{oo}, ∂^{o}, $^{o}\partial$ denote the intersection of their boundaries, that of their interiors, that of the boundary of the first with the interior of the second and last the intersection of the interior of the first with the boundary of the second. Each of these four intersections can be empty or non-empty, thus creating sixteen candidate binary topological relationships; for example if the intersection between the boundaries is non empty whereas all the other three intersections are empty then we say that the two objects *meet* (see Figure 1); this case can be designated as 1000 where each binary digit stands for one of the four intersections in turn, and 1 means non-empty while 0 means empty intersection. Of the sixteen candidate relationships, only 8 are possible for regions embedded in Euclidean 2-space. For example 0011 is not possible: if two regions have neither boundaries nor interiors in common, then it is not possible for the interior of the one to have common points with the boundary of the other or vice versa.

Table 1 summarizes the sixteen candidate binary topological relationships for each pair of elementary geographic objects showing which are possible and which are not. Since points have no interior some of the sixteen relationships are not applicable.

There is little point in trying to give names to the sixteen relationships, since any naming is bound to contradict some already existing usage or preferences.

More importantly it is not possible to give meaningfull names that would be consistent for all types of objects (observe, for example that r_3 for $R-R$ means "equal", for $A-A$ may mean "equal" whereas for $R-A$ is some sort of "internally connects"). What is important however is that with these sixteen relationships one can clearly define the meaning of one's prefered names.

Figure 1: Elementary topological relationship 1000

Figure 2: Elementary topological relationship 1111

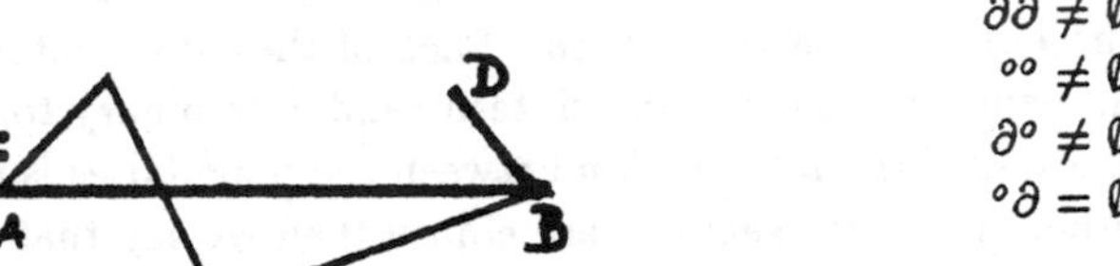

Figure 3: Elementary topological relationship 1110

	$\partial\partial$	$^{\circ\circ}$	∂°	$^{\circ}\partial$	R-R	R-A	R-P	A-A	A-P	P-P
r_0	0	0	0	0						
r_1	1	0	0	0						
r_2	0	1	0	0	n	n	-		-	-
r_3	1	1	0	0			-		-	-
r_4	0	0	1	0	n	n	-		-	-
r_5	1	0	1	0	n	n	-		-	-
r_6	0	1	1	0			-		-	-
r_7	1	1	1	0			-		-	-
r_8	0	0	0	1	n					-
r_9	1	0	0	1	n		n		n	-
r_{10}	0	1	0	1			-		-	-
r_{11}	1	1	0	1			-		-	-
r_{12}	0	0	1	1	n	n	-		-	-
r_{13}	1	0	1	1	n	n	-		-	-
r_{14}	0	1	1	1	n		-		-	-
r_{15}	1	1	1	1			-		-	-

n: Impossible in 2-d Euclidean space, -: non applicable since a point has no interior

Table 1: The sixteen cases for binary topological relationships

2.4 Expressing Complex Topological Relationships

In order to express complex topological relationships, integrity constraints, and queries, we shall use predicate calculus to construct topological expressions. A topological sentence is built out of atomic topological formulae with negation, conjunction, disjunction, and universal and existential quantification.

Definition 1. Let Θ be a geometric operation, r an elementary topological relationship, O an object class, O_1 and O_2 geographic objects of class O, x and y attributes of O, Δ a comparison operator ($<$, $\leq$, $>$, $\geq$, $=$, $\neq$) and c a constant. The following are atomic topological formulae:

1. $r[O_1,O_2]$
2. a. $\Theta[O_1]\ \Delta\ c$, b. $\Theta[O_1]\ \Delta\ \Theta[O_2]$
3. a. $O_1.x\ \Delta\ O_2.y$, b. $O_1.x\ \Delta\ c$
4. $O_1 \in O$

Definition 2. The following are topological sentences:

1. Every atomic topological formula is a topological sentence.
2. If P_1 is a topological sentence then so are $\neg\ P1$, (P_1).
3. If P_1, P_2 are topological sentences then so are $P_1 \vee P_2$, $P_1 \wedge P_2$.
4. If P_1, P_2 are topological sentences then so are $P_1 \Rightarrow P_2$, $P_1 \Leftrightarrow P_2$.
5. If $P_1(s)$ is a topological sentence and s a free variable then $\exists\ s\ P_1(s)$ and $\forall\ s\ P_1(s)$ are topological sentences.
6. In the absence of paretheses, operators are evaluated in the following order:

   $$\in, \exists, \forall, \neg, \wedge, \vee, \Rightarrow, \Leftrightarrow$$

7. Nothing else is a topological sentence.

3 Usage and Examples

The reason behind the theory and the model developed in the previous chapter is that it can be used to express topological integrity constraints, to define object classes and to query the database in a variety of settings. These include formal expression of user requirements, semantic and logical modeling as well as implementation. In this chapter we will give examples of all these, thus exibiting the power of the model.

Consider the following statement, in natural language, taken from a cadastral application:

"A Square is a landparcel which *abuts upon a street* and is not *contained in any building_block.*"

It is stated as a definition of an object class but could just as well be an integrity constraint ("Squares should abut upon some street and not be contained in any building_block") or a query ("Get landparcels which abut upon a street and are not included in any building_block").

During the normal application development cycle, such statements must be expressed in turn in a formal pseudo-language, in the language of the semantic data model, in the language of the logical data model and finally in the language of the application package. We shall present this statement in the formal language of Section 2.4, in G-IFO (a specialization of the semantic model IFO (see [1]) for the needs of spatial applications), in GDM (an extension of the relational model, see [5]) and in ARC/INFO.

For the first step we must clarify verbs in natural language expressing topological relationships such as "abut upon" and define them using the formal relationships r_0 through r_{15}. This is very useful in itself as it is often the case that users make such statements without sufficient precision.

1. *In the formal language proposed*

- ABUT_UPON(lp,st): r_9(lp,st) $\vee$ r_8(lp,st) $\vee$ r_1(lp,st) (between a region and a line)
- CONTAINED_IN(lp,bb): r_6(lp,bb) $\vee$ r_7(lp,bb) (between regions)
- SQUARE = { lp | lp $\in$ LANDPARCEL $\wedge$
  $\exists$ st $\in$ STREET (ABUT_UPON(lp,st)) $\wedge$
  $\neg$ $\exists$ bb $\in$ BUILDING_BLOCK (CONTAINED_IN(lp,bb)) }

2. *In the data manipulation language of G-IFO*

- CREATE OBJECT LANDPARCEL
  TYPE ABSTRACT

- CREATE OBJECT BUILDING_BLOCK
  TYPE ABSTRACT
  HIERARCHY SUBTYPE OF LANDPARCEL
- CREATE OBJECT STREET
  TYPE ABSTRACT
- CREATE OBJECT SQUARE
  TYPE FREE
  HIERARCHY SUBTYPE OF LANDPARCEL
  CONSTRAINT ABUT_UPON_A_STREET
  AND NOT CONTAINED_IN_BUILDING_BLOCK
- DEFINE CONSTRAINT ABUT_UPON_A_STREET
  AMONG (LANDPARCEL, STREET)
  AS r_9(LANDPARCEL, STREET) ∨
  r_1(LANDPARCEL, STREET) ∨ r_8(LANDPARCEL, STREET)
- DEFINE CONSTRAINT CONTAINED_IN_BUILDING_BLOCK
  AMONG (LANDPARCEL, BUILDING_BLOCK)
  AS r_6(LANDPARCEL, BUILDING_BLOCK) ∨
  r_7(LANDPARCEL, BUILDING_BLOCK)

3. *In the data manipulation language of GDM*

- DEFINE LAYER 1 LAND_OWNER ATTR LANDPARCEL
  TYPE REGION
  VALUES STRING
  RELATION LANDPARCEL
  POSITIONING STANDARD
  /* relation LANDPARCEL contains the descriptive attributes, like the name of each landparcel, its owner, etc. */
- DEFINE LAYER 2 BUILDING_BLOCK ATTR BUILDING_BLOCK
  TYPE REGION
  VALUES STRING
  RELATION BUILDING_BLOCK
  POSITIONING STANDARD

  DEFINE LAYER 3 ROAD_NETWORK ATTR STREET
  TYPE LINE
  VALUES STRING
  RELATION STREET
  POSITIONING STANDARD

- DEFINE OBJECT LANDPARCEL
  TYPE REGION
  ON LAYER [LAND_OWNER]

- DEFINE OBJECT BUILDING_BLOCK
  TYPE REGION
  ON LAYER [BUILDING_BLOCK]

- DEFINE OBJECT STREET
  TYPE LINE
  ON LAYER [ROAD_NETWORK]

- DEFINE OBJECT SQUARE
  TYPE LANDPARCEL
  ON LAYER [LANDPARCEL]
  CONSTRAINT ABUT_UPON_A_STREET
  AND NOT CONTAINED_IN_BUILDING_BLOCK

- DEFINE CONSTRAINT ABUT_UPON_A_STREET
  AMONG (LANDPARCEL, STREET)
  AS r_9(LANDPARCEL, STREET) $\vee$
  r_1(LANDPARCEL, STREET) $\vee$ r_8(LANDPARCEL, STREET)

- DEFINE CONSTRAINT CONTAINED_IN_BUILDING_BLOCK
  AMONG (LANDPARCEL, BUILDING_BLOCK)
  AS r_6(LANDPARCEL, BUILDING_BLOCK) $\vee$
  r_7(LANDPARCEL, BUILDING_BLOCK)

4. *In the data manipulation language of ARC/INFO*

- GENERATE LP
  /* arc command: creates layer (LP) for landparcel */

- INPUT LANDPARCEL.DATA
  /* generate command: the input file which contains the data for the creation of LP layer */

- LINES
  /* generate command: creates lines for the layer LP */

- CLEAN LP LPCN POLY
  /* arc command: creates topology (polygons and their relationships) for the layer LP */

  /* the following is an info command: defines a table which contains the descriptive attributes, like the name of each landparcel, its owner, etc. This table corresponds to the LANDPARCEL relation in GDM */

- **DEFINE LPCN.LUT** /* LUT: LookUpTable */

> **LPCN-ID**
/* item name */
> **4**
/* item width */
> **-return-**
/* item output width */
> **N**
/* item type */
> **0**
/* item decimal places */
> **LPCN-NAME**
/* item name */
> **8**
/* item width */
> **-return-**
/* item output width */
> **C**
/* item type */

- **JOINITEM LPCN.PAT LPCN.LUT LANDPARCEL.PAT**
  /* arc command. This table corresponds to the LANDPARCEL relation in GDM */

- **GENERATE BB**
- **GENERATE ST**
  /* layers and relations (tables) for building_block (BB) and street (ST) are created in the same way (also tables BBCN, STCN are created) */

- **RESELECT LPCN POLY OVERLAP BBCN PASSTHRU**
  /* arcplot command: selects a set of polygons of LPCN which fall (partially or not) in polygons of BBCN. PASSTHRU is an ARC/INFO topological relationship equivalent to $r_6 \vee r_7$ */

- **NSELECT LPCN POLY**
  /* arcplot command: selects the set of polygons of LPCN which do not fall (partially or not) in polygons of BBCN */

- **WRITESELECT LPCN.FILE**
  /* arcplot command: writes the currently selected set of layer features to a selection file */

- **RESELECT LPCN LPCN_NEW LPCN.FILE**

/* arc command: creates a new layer from LPCN.FILE */

- `RESELECT LPCN_NEW ARCS OVERLAP STCN 0`
  /* arcplot command: selects the set of arcs of LP_NEW which are connected to a street. Distance=0 is equivalent to $r_1 \vee r_8 \vee r_9$ */

- `WRITESELECT STCN.FILE`
  /* arcplot command: writes the currently selected set of layer features to a selection file */

- `RESELECT LPCN_NEW LPCN_ARC STCN.FILE`
  /* arc command: creates a new layer from STCN.FILE */

- `INTERSECT LPCN_ARC LPCN LP_SQUARE`
  /* arc command */

- `RESELECT LPCN SQUARE POLY LPCN# IN LP_SQUARE.AAT`
  /* arc command */

4 Conclusions and Further Research

This work is part of a larger research efford to develop a geographic application development methodology. Geographic applications lack a suitable design methodology, i.e. proper concepts and tools for data abstraction, data and process modeling and description of static and dynamic integrity constraints. Furthermore geographic systems lack proper database management support, i.e. facilities such as transaction handling, data sharing, crash recovery, logical and physical data independence, ease of design and administration, security and integrity.

Our research line is not to develop a whole new set of concepts and tools but to extend the available classic tools and provide interoperability among them specifically for geographic databases and applications. In this context a specialization of IFO has been defined in [14] and [13] (presented in [4]); GDM, a logical model for geographic data has been developed and applied to selected model applications.

We are currently developing rudimentaly geographic CASE tools to facilitate the automatic transition from each stage of application development to the next, especially going from semantic models to logical models and from there to specific GIS packages. Our goal is to develop maintainable and portable applications that will not be locked to any specific GIS.

In this paper we formalized topological relationships, since this is a major theme in spatial databases which has been dealt with so far in an adhoc manner. The examples in Section 3 show how the model can be used in different settings, which exibits its generality.

Next step from here is to develop software tools that will integrate this facility for expressing topological integrity constraints in actual working GIS environments.

Acknowledgements

The authors would like to thank the referees for suggesting reference [2] which led to a rewriting of Section 2.3.

References

1. Abiteboul, S. and Hull, R.: IFO: "A Formal Semantic Database Model", ACM Transactions on Database Systems, 12, 4 (March 1987).

2. Egenhofer, M. and Herring, J.: "A Mathematical Framework for the Definitions of Topological Relationships", in: Brazzel and Kishimoto, 4th International Symposium on Spatial Data Handling, pp 803–813, Zurich, Switzerland, July 1990.

3. ESRI: "Understanding GIS –The Arc/Info Method", Environmental System Research Institute, California (1990).

4. Hadzilacos, T. and Dedousi, I.: "Design of a Forest Fire Management System", Proceedings of the 3nd European Conference on Geographical Information Systems (EGIS'92), Munich, Germany, 23-26 March 1992.

5. Hadzilacos, T. and Tryfona N.: "A Conceptual Schema for Geographic Databases", Proceedings of the 2nd European Conference on Geographical Information Systems (EGIS'91), Brussels, Belgium. 2-5 April 1991.

6. Kasturi, Fernadez, Amlani and Feng: "Map Data Processing in Geographic Information Systems", IEEE Computer Magazine, (Dec 1989).

7. Nierstrasz, O.: "A survey of Object-Oriented Concepts", in Object-Oriented Concepts, Databases and Applications, W. Kim and F. Lochovsky (eds), ACM Press, 1989.

8. Oosterom, P. and Vijlbrief, T.: "Building a GIS on the top of the open DBMS POSTGRES", Proceedings of the 2nd European Conference on Geographical Information Systems (EGIS'91), Brussels, Belgium, 2-5 April 1991.

9. Oxborrow, E., Kemp, Z.: "An Object-Oriented Approach to the Management of Geographical Data", UK North West Regional Research Laboratory's Conference Managing Geographical Information Systems and Databases, U.K, (Sept 1989).

10. Pelagatti, G., Belussi, A., Negri, M., Rossi, M., Sbatella, L.: "Design and Implementation of a Geographic Information System: the Case of Regione Lombardia", Proceedings of the 2nd European Conference on Geographical Information Systems (EGIS'91), Brussels, Belgium, 2-5 April 1991.

11. Scholl, M. and Voissard, A.: "Object-Oriented Database Systems for Geographic Applications: an Experiment with O_2", in The Story of O_2 (1991).

12. Spooner, R.: "Advantages and Problems in the Creation and Use of a Topologically Structured Database", Seminar on Photogrammetry and Land Information Systems, Ecole Polytechnique de Lausanne, Switzerland, (March 1989).

13. Stefanopoulou, M.: "Database Design for Water Utility Management" (in greek), Department of Computer Engineering, University Patras, Greece (1991).

14. Tryfona, N.: "Geographic Database Design: Principles and a Cadastral Application" (in greek), Department of Computer Engineering, University Patras, Greece (1991).

Encoding Spatial Information: The Evidence for Hierarchical Processing

A. Stewart Fotheringham

and

Andrew Curtis

National Center for Geographic Information and Analysis
State University of New York at Buffalo
Wilkeson Quad
Buffalo, NY 14261
USA

Email: GEOASF@UBVMS

ABSTRACT: This paper describes how individuals process spatial information, how geographical location can affect the method of processing, how an understanding of spatial information processing is necessary to model spatial choices accurately, and how spatial variations in the way information is processed can be measured. Both non-hierarchical and hierarchical methods of processing information are discussed with the latter being the more likely means of processing spatial information. Results from an empirical example using migration flows within the U.S. suggest that individuals use a hierarchical method of spatial ordering and that there is a spatial pattern to the degree to which spatial information is processed hierarchically. This pattern is shown to be related to the amount of spatial information available to an individual.

1 INTRODUCTION

A continuing point of discussion across disciplines concerns the method by which individuals perceive space and the way in which they store and process the information that influences their perceptions. This is not a new issue; Gould (1974) suggests that geographic location influences the amount of information that an individual possesses about space, and that the different `information surfaces', formed through varying levels of contact, influence the way individuals respond to the environment. The basic premise is that the greater the population density of the region in which an individual lives, the more complex is that person's mental map. This leads to two interesting questions which form the focus of this paper: if individuals at different locations possess different levels of spatial information, to what extent does this variation influence the way they process information, and how can such variation be measured?

Before answering these questions it is useful to discuss briefly the two competing theories concerning spatial information processing that have evolved in the literature. One of these, a *hierarchical processing strategy*, postulates that spatial information is clustered into trees and information is retrieved by progressing through the branches of a tree. The other, a *non-hierarchical processing strategy*, postulates that spatial information is retrieved from a completely stored map in which locations have been `scanned'. Knowledge of the way in which individuals process spatial information has important implications for understanding behavior in space, and in particular, for modeling the outcomes of spatial choice processes such as migration, store choice and residential selection. In this paper, we will use migration flows to investigate spatial information processing because of their ready availability.

2 SPATIAL PROCESSING THEORIES

Individuals cluster space into subjective categories dependent on their own information surfaces, and the particular influences that they see as important. Shepard (1975, 1981, 1984) suggests that the physical constraints of our environment appear in the way we incorporate spatial structure in our language. But this environmental influence can extend beyond our language constructs to influence the very way we process spatial information. It is true that physical location will affect the amount of information available, and that this will lead to different ways of gathering' the information together. There are, however, other more subjective influences working on the way we cluster dependent on cultural and social backgrounds (Curtis 1992).

In cognition there are two main theories for the mental representation of spatial relations: non-hierarchical and hierarchical. *Non-hierarchical* theories presume that the spatial relationship between objects over space is mentally represented in either networks or image-like analog formats with continuously varying properties (Thorndyke 1981). In neither case does this theory allow that spatial information is stored at anything other than one level of representation. Byrne (1979), for example, suggests that the spatial representation of cities is nothing more than a series of interconnected links and nodes which preserve a topological connectedness but not a two-dimensional orientation. The suggested proof for this is in the way distances are perceived to be exaggerated when more `reference points' are encoded along a route (with increased familiarity), and in the way all angles are distorted towards 90 degrees (which suggest that angular information is not encoded in the spatial representation). One possible explanation for the over estimation of a familiar route (Briggs 1973), or one with many turns (Sadella & Magel 1980), or even with more intersections (Sadella & Staplin 1980) would be that more locations have been encoded and that by a simple heuristic the more locations remembered on a route, the longer the route must be. Sadella, Staplin & Burroughs (1980) found that distance judgements between reference points as compared with distance judgements between non-reference points of the same actual length were underestimated.

It has also been reported (Sadella, Staplin & Burroughs 1979) that distances between places with high frequency names tend to be overestimated compared to distances between places with low frequency names, which suggests some sort of cluster and boundary effect in the storage of spatial information. Although the presence of clusters does not necessarily eliminate the partitioning of space at any other than one level, it would be logical to assume that the clustering of any area would also contain a hierarchy of `priming' locations from which the cluster itself were derived.

Hierarchical theories suggest that knowledge is stored in a graph-theoretic tree with more detailed information appearing at the lower levels. The leaves for each branch of this tree, that is the cluster area, can either be drawn physically (an island), perceptually (a country border) or entirely subjectively (Hirtle & Jones 1985). Hierarchical theories can be sub-divided into two further groups: strongly hierarchical and partially hierarchical (Mcnamara 1986).

Strongly hierarchical theories suggest that the spatial representation between two entities is not encoded from two branches of the hierarchy but must be inferred from a higher order spatial knowledge. For example, the relative location of two settlements within different regions would not be stored in memory but would be inferred from the relative positions of the regions.

Alternatively, partially hierarchical theories' (Davis 1981, Stevens and Coupe 1978) allow cross-hierarchical spatial representation inferences. This means that it is also possible to judge distances between cities which lie on either side of a cluster boundary. The disadvantage of this type of encoding is that it becomes less efficient as greater amounts of information are stored in memory. The advantage is that it leads to more accurate judgements because encoded knowledge is more reliable than inferred knowledge (Mcnamara 1986).

Evidence for hierarchical spatial processing can be found in studies considering distortions in judged space, such as the schematic representation suggested by Stevens & Coupe (1978) who claim that spatial relations between cities in different regions are not explicitly represented. Examples of this are found in the way people make errors in the locational relations between cities, such as Seattle mistakenly perceived as being south of Montreal and Reno, Nevada mistakenly perceived as being east of Los Angeles, California. It is postulated that mistakes such as these arise because the two cities exist in different superordinates, and it is from these that people then judge subordinates. The common perception in the former is that Canada (one superordinate) is north of the U.S. (the other superordinate), from which it is inferred that subordinates existing in either superordinate will have the same relationship. In the latter case, California is "stored" as being west of Nevada (mostly correct), from which it is incorrectly inferred that this relationship holds for all pairs of subordinates (which is incorrect). Stevens and Coupe (1978) illustrate this process by creating a series of maps which were subdivided into fictitious counties and cities. Subjects were asked to learn these maps and then answer questions concerning the location of the cities to one another. Significant errors were found when one city was physically west of another city, but existing in a county that was generally east of the county hosting the other city. The reliance on `Higher order' information can lead to mistakes, and these mistakes would not be apparent on a `picture-map' which would be scanned and stored in its entirety.

Wilton (1979) found that the time needed to verify distances between locations found on either sides of a cluster boundary was greater than for pairs of locations being separated by the same distance but in this case situated within the same cluster. Stevens (1976) found a similar result with major cities acting as reference `primes' only for within cluster judgements, and that as soon as another judgement was needed from a prime city across such a boundary, mistakes were made, and the decision time extended. This is consistent with a movement up the hierarchical tree to the next node and then back down the other twig to the other cluster. This would explain the extended time taken. An example of this would be two cities, one being classed as a major or `prime' with both being situated on either side of a state line. In this case the cluster would be the state itself. The point though is that if the method of representation came from a scanned model, there should be no difference in the time taken to estimate these cross cluster distances.

These points can be summarized into three common findings that appear in the studies on clustering effects:

1: The superordinate relationship structures and biases judgements occurring across cluster boundaries;

2: Distances and response times are affected by the presence of boundaries, with across boundary judgements taking longer time and being more prone to errors, while within cluster judgements often being underestimated. Kosslyn, Pick & Fariello (1974) demonstrate this point by using cross boundary distance estimations extrapolated from rank order; and

3: Within cluster judgements are based upon reference point locations, such a `prime cities'.

The finding that there is a significant spatial boundary effect, and that these boundaries suggest a clustering of information into superordinates and subordinates, is consistent with the theory of hierarchical information processing. If we accept that spatial information is clustered, we must also consider the spatial implications of this, because as has been suggested, this would mean that there would be no such thing as a consistent hierarchy for all locations. Individuals located in more densely populated areas, with greater volumes of spatial information are likely to have more complex hierarchies and therefore process information hierarchically to a greater degree than an individual located in relatively sparsely populated areas. It has been suggested that as few as six pieces of information could be the limit of non-hierarchical processing and that increasing degrees of hierarchical processing will be required as information levels rise beyond this point. The spatial variation in the way in which spatial information is stored has important implications for the use of certain mathematical models of spatial choice. In turn, however, we demonstrate below how one type of spatial choice model can be used to demonstrate the existence of spatial variations in the degree to which spatial information is processed hierarchically.

3 SPATIAL CHOICE MODELS AND HIERARCHICAL INFORMATION PROCESSING

Consider an individual i making a destination choice from a set of spatial opportunities. Examples of such choices are commonplace and include store choice, residential choice and migration. The traditional method of modelling a set of spatial choices is with a multinomial logit model or share model which has the general form:

$$p_{ij} = \frac{\mathbf{X}_j\mathbf{B}}{\mathbf{X}_k\mathbf{B}} \tag{1}$$

where p_{ij} is the probability that an individual at i will select alternative j; $\mathbf{X}$ represents a vector of attributes describing alternative j; and $\mathbf{B}$ is a vector of parameters to be estimated and which describe the influence of each attribute on p_{ij}. The denominator of equation (1) is the numerator summed over all alternatives. Recently, Fotheringham (1986,1991a) and Fotheringham and O'Kelly (1989) have demonstrated that this model will invariably be a misspecification of reality for spatial choices because the theoretical derivation of the model is based on the assumption that an individual evaluates and compares every possible alternative. While this might be a tenable assumption in choice situations where the number of alternatives is small, such as in brand choice, for example, it is clearly untenable in most spatial choice situations where the number of alternatives is generally very large. Consider the typical range of alternatives in residential choice, for example, or in migration.

As a result of the inadequacy of equation (1) to model spatial choices, Fotheringham (1983,1988) has proposed an alternative choice model, termed a competing destinations model, which has the following general form:

$$p_{ij} = \frac{\mathbf{X}_j\mathbf{B} \;.\; p(j\varepsilon\mathbf{M})}{\sum \mathbf{X}_k\mathbf{B} \;.\; p(k\varepsilon\mathbf{M})} \tag{2}$$

where $p(j\varepsilon\mathbf{M})$ is the probability that alternative j is in the restricted choice set $\mathbf{M}$ which contains only those alternatives evaluated by the individual at i. This model is based on the assumption that individuals do not evaluate and compare all possible spatial alternatives but instead make decisions from a restricted choice set. It is therefore based on the assumption that spatial information is processed hierarchically and that individuals first select macro-sets of alternatives in which to focus their selection of an individual alternative. Consider residential search as an example: individuals cannot process all the information necessary to evaluate every possible alternative within a typical urban area and therefore initially make a decision about an area of the city in which to concentrate their search. Subsequently, more levels of the hierarchy may be formed depending on the size of the city, until eventually the choice set actually examined by the individual is reasonably small. In a migration context, the equivalent decision-making tree may be to select a broad region, then a sub-region, and then a city. In either case, the formulation in equation (2) explicitly recognizes the existence of this hierarchical choice process by allowing for variance in the likelihood that an individual alternative will be considered by an individual at i.

In order to operationalize the competing destinations model, it is necessary to define p(jεM). Clearly this will be related to attributes already in the model within the vector **X**, such as the distance a destination is from i, its size etc. However, Fotheringham (1987, 1991a) has shown that the probability of an alternative j being evaluated by an individual is also related to an attribute not contained in **X**, the level of spatial competition that alternative faces. The argument, stated succinctly, is as follows. The hierarchy in which an individual structures space is fuzzy and will vary across locations. However, a general psychophysical "law" is that individuals tend to underestimate the number of objects in a large cluster and this underestimation increases as the number of objects in the cluster increases. Therefore, individuals will tend to underestimate the number of opportunities in densely populated regions, making such regions less likely to be selected at the first level of the hierarchy than would be suggested by objective measurements. Hence, an alternative within such a region will have a lower probability of being selected, **ceteris paribus**, than would be suggested if hierarchical information processing and spatial competition were ignored. Fotheringham (1991b) therefore suggests operationalizing equation (2) as:

$$p_{ij} = \frac{\mathbf{X}_j \mathbf{B} \cdot c_{ij}{}^{\partial}}{\Sigma\, \mathbf{X}_k \mathbf{B} \cdot c_{ik}{}^{\partial}} \qquad (3)$$

where c_{ij} is a measure of the centrality of alternative j with respect to all other alternatives available to a person in i and is commonly measured in a spatial context by a potential measure which is simply an inverse weighted distance measure. Large values of c_{ij} indicate alternatives in densely populated regions and in close proximity to many other alternatives; small values indicate alternatives in relatively sparsely populated regions with few alternatives in close proximity. The parameter ∂ is thus an index of the degree to which choices are made hierarchically, and hence the degree to which spatial information is encoded hierarchically. If ∂ is not significantly different from 0, equation (2) is equivalent to equation (1) and the assumption that individuals evaluate all alternatives is valid. If individuals do process spatial information hierarchically and underestimate the numbers of opportunities in densely populated regions, ∂ will be negative (more central destinations are less likely to be selected, **ceteris paribus**.

When equation (2) is estimated separately for each origin in a system, a set of origin-specific parameter estimates is obtained. That is, $\mathbf{B}_i$ and ∂_i are estimated rather than $\mathbf{B}$ and ∂. Spatial variations in ∂_i indicate spatial variations in the degree of hierarchical processing. As discussed above, the hypothesis to be examined here is that individuals in more central origins have more spatial information and therefore must process that information hierarchically to a greater extent than individuals in less central origins. The hypothesis can be tested by examining the presence of a spatial trend in the estimates of ∂_i whereby more central origins have more negative estimates of ∂_i than do more peripheral origins. The presence of hierarchical spatial information processing and spatial variations therein is now examined with data on the spatial choices of US migrants.

4 EMPIRICAL EXAMINATION OF HIERARCHICAL INFORMATION PROCESSING

To examine if spatial information is processed hierarchically and whether the degree to which it is processed hierarchically varies by location, the competing destination formulation in equation (2) was calibrated on 1970 migration flow data between 74 of the largest State Economic Areas (SEAs) of the United States. All SEAs were at least 30 miles apart from each other to avoid measuring purely local moves. The specific aim of the calibration was to examine if the estimated parameter of the centrality variable is significantly less than zero for most origins and to examine if this parameter exhibits any systematic spatial variation related to the centrality of the origins. For comparison, we also calibrated the traditional choice model in equation (1) separately for each origin.

Both models contained the following destination attributes in the **X** vector:

1. The euclidean distance between the destination and the origin;

2. Population size for each of the SEAs.

3. Employment Status: the percentage of unemployed males aged 16 years and older (1970 Census: State Economic Areas (1972)). It was thought that a high unemployment value would deter migrants from travelling to an area due to the perceived poor state of its economy;

4. Mean Family Income (1970 Census: State Economic Areas, 1972)). It was thought that a high mean family income used as a proxy for a destination's economic standing would be attractive to in-migrants. Conversely a low mean family income should correlate with low migrant inflows;.

5. A climatic ranking system was used as designed by the "Places Rated Almanac". This system determined a score for climatic mildness including such considerations as: hot and cold months, variation in seasonal temperatures, heating- and cooling-degree days, freezing days, zero-degree days and ninety-degree days;

6.The final attribute calculated for inclusion in the model was the centrality or competing destinations variable measured as:

$$c_{ij} = \sum_{\substack{k=1 \\ k=j \\ k=i}}^{74} P_k / d_{jk} \qquad (4)$$

where P_k is the population of alternative k and d_{jk} is the distance between the two alternatives j and k. The higher the values of c_{ij}, the greater the centrality of destination $_j$; as expected, areas around the North East have higher values of this centrality index due to the clustered location of major cities in this area. The spatial distribution of the centrality measure is displayed in Figure 2a.

5 RESULTS

The results of calibrating the models in equations (1) and (2) are depicted in Figures 1 and 2. The focus of the discussion of these figures is on the significance and spatial pattern of the set of origin-specific estimates of ∂, the index of hierarchical information processing. However, we also demonstrate the misspecification that potentially can arise when spatial choice models that do not account for hierarchical information processing are calibrated.

Of the five variables described above, only the parameters estimates for population and distance were significant for every origin. The centrality parameter estimate, however, was significantly negative for 64 of the 74 SEAs (and insignificant for the other 10 origins) which strongly supports the hypothesis that destinations are selected hierarchically and that individuals discount the number of opportunities for migration in densely populated regions. The income parameter estimate was significant for only 36 of the SEAs and the climate parameter estimate was significant for only 5 of the origins and had conflicting signs.

To demonstrate that models of spatial choice which ignore hierarchical information processing are misspecifications of reality, the distance-decay parameter estimates from the logit and competing destinations models are displayed in Figures 1a and 1b, respectively and in Figures 2b and 2c, respectively. Figure 1a shows the relationship between the estimated distance-decay parameter from the logit model and the centrality of an origin and displays the common finding that the parameter estimates exhibit a strong spatial pattern whereby more central origins have less negative parameter estimates than peripheral ones (Fotheringham, 1981). Although the trend is clearly nonlinear, even a linear trend is significant when fitted through the scatter of points with an RSQ=.39 and the t-statistic for the slope parameter being -6.44.

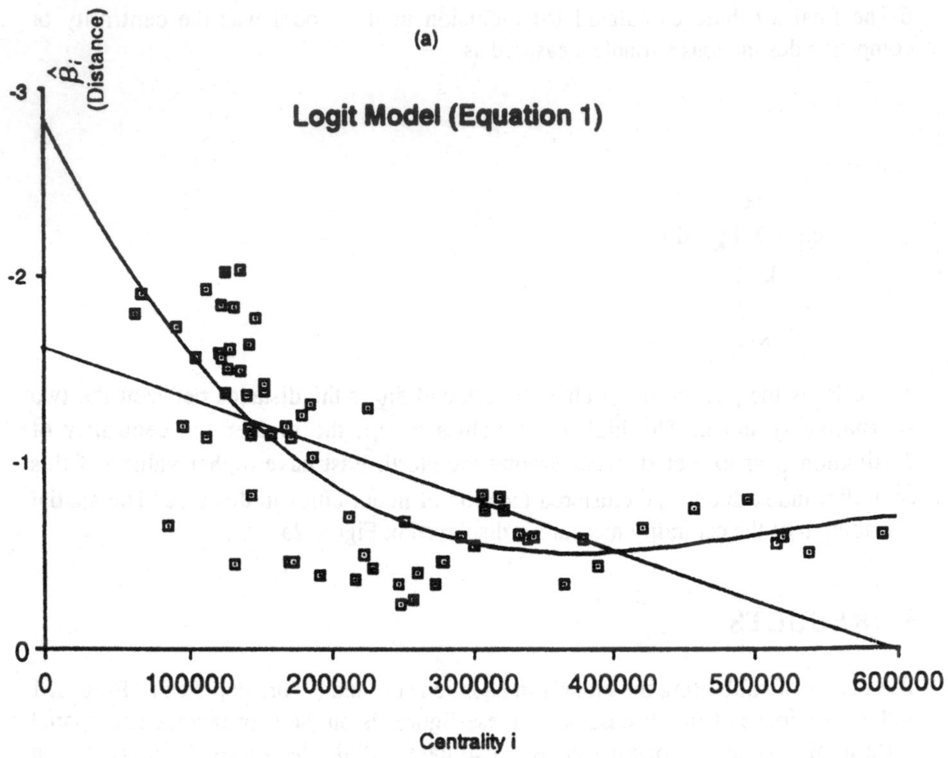
(a)
Logit Model (Equation 1)
$\hat{\beta}_i$ (Distance)
-3
-2
-1
0
0
100000
200000
300000
400000
500000
600000
Centrality i

Figure 1a

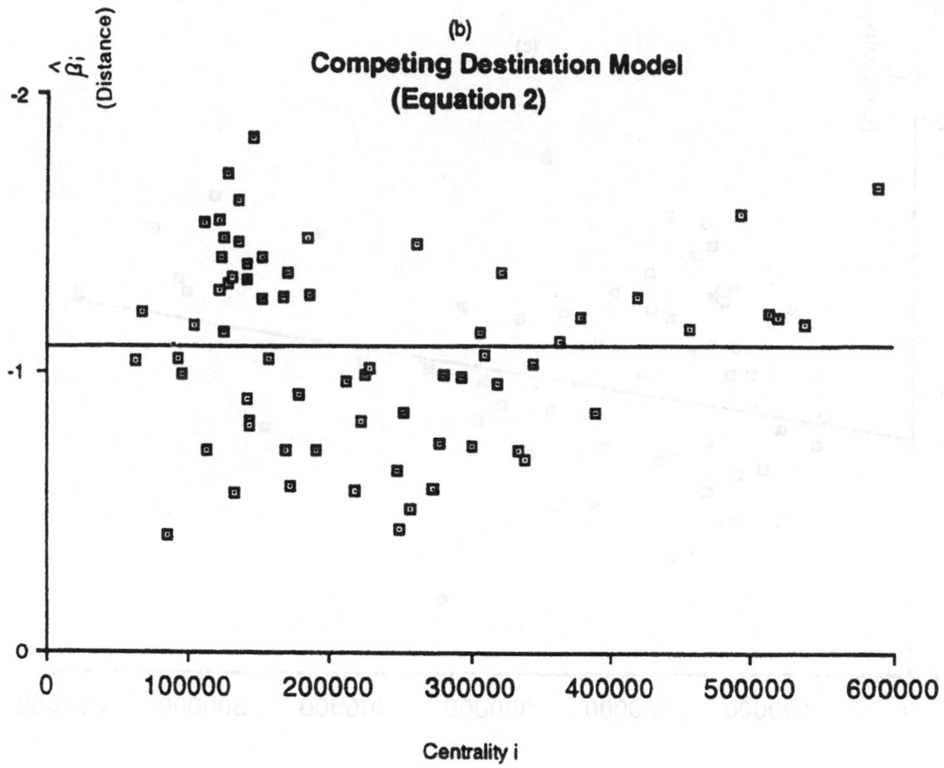
(b)
Competing Destination Model
(Equation 2)
$\hat{\beta}_i$
(Distance)
-2
-1
0
0
100000
200000
300000
400000
500000
600000
Centrality i

Figure 1b

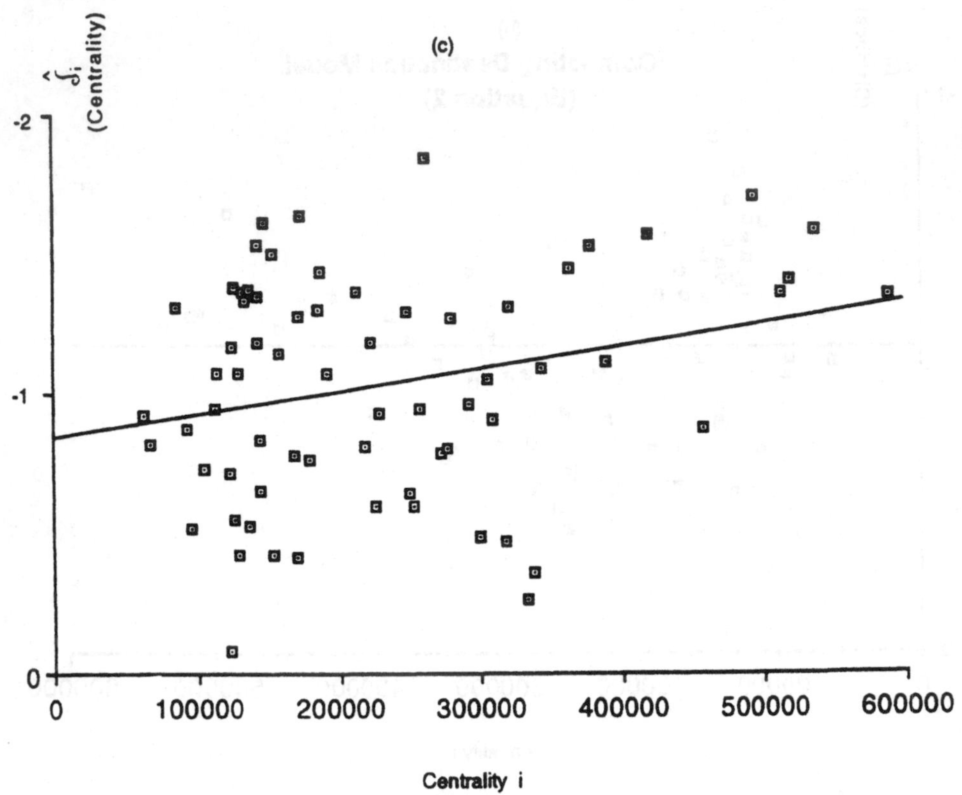
(c)
$\hat{\delta}_i$ (Centrality)
-2
-1
0
0
100000
200000
300000
400000
500000
600000
Centrality i

Figure 1c

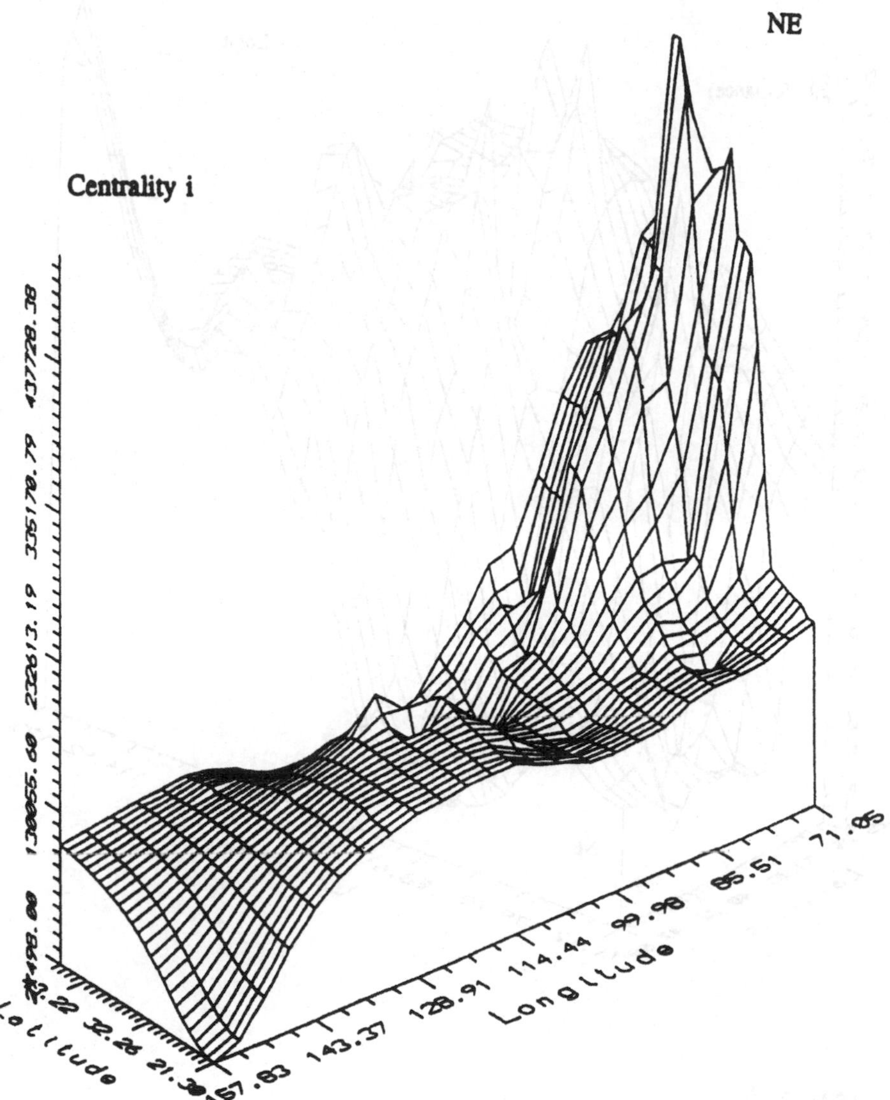
NE
Centrality i
437728.38
335170.79
232613.19
130055.60
Latitude
32.26
Longitude
143.37
128.91
114.44
99.98
85.51
71.05

Figure 2a

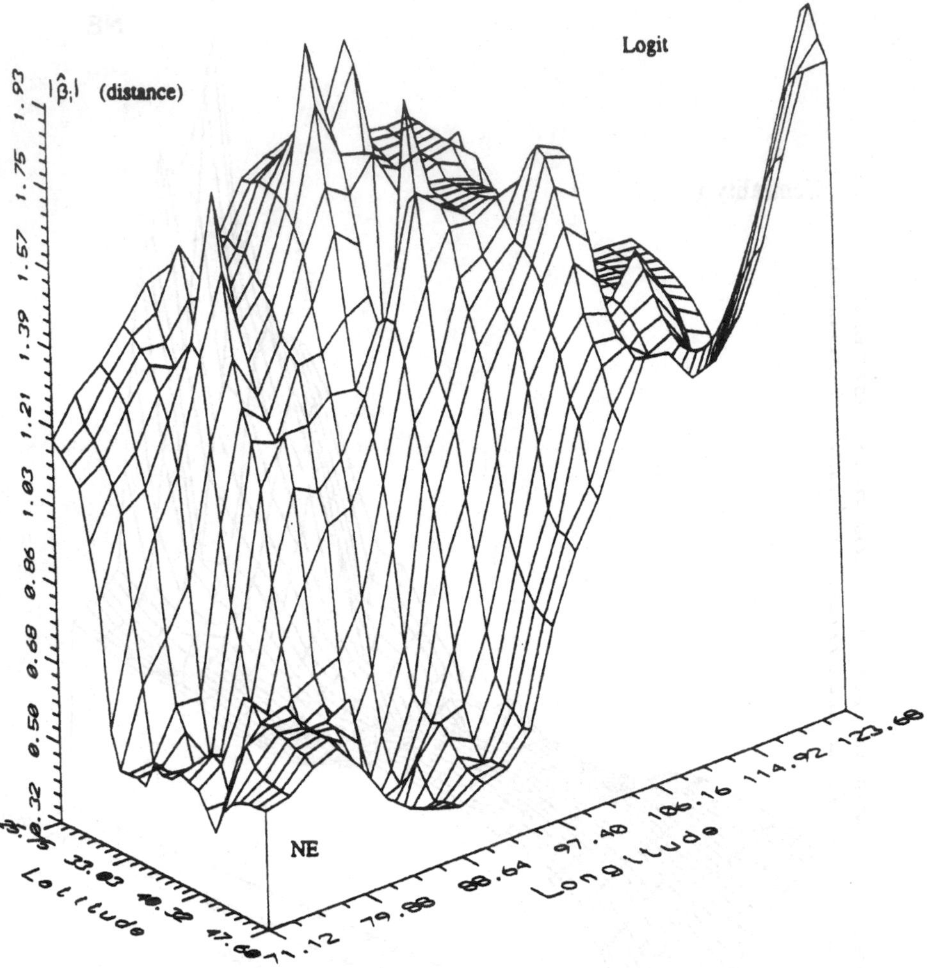
Logit
$|\hat{\beta}_i|$ (distance)
1.93
1.75
1.57
1.39
1.21
1.03
0.86
0.68
0.50
0.32
NE
Latitude
33.03
40.32
47.60
71.12
79.88
88.64
97.40
106.16
114.92
123.68
Longitude

Figure 2b

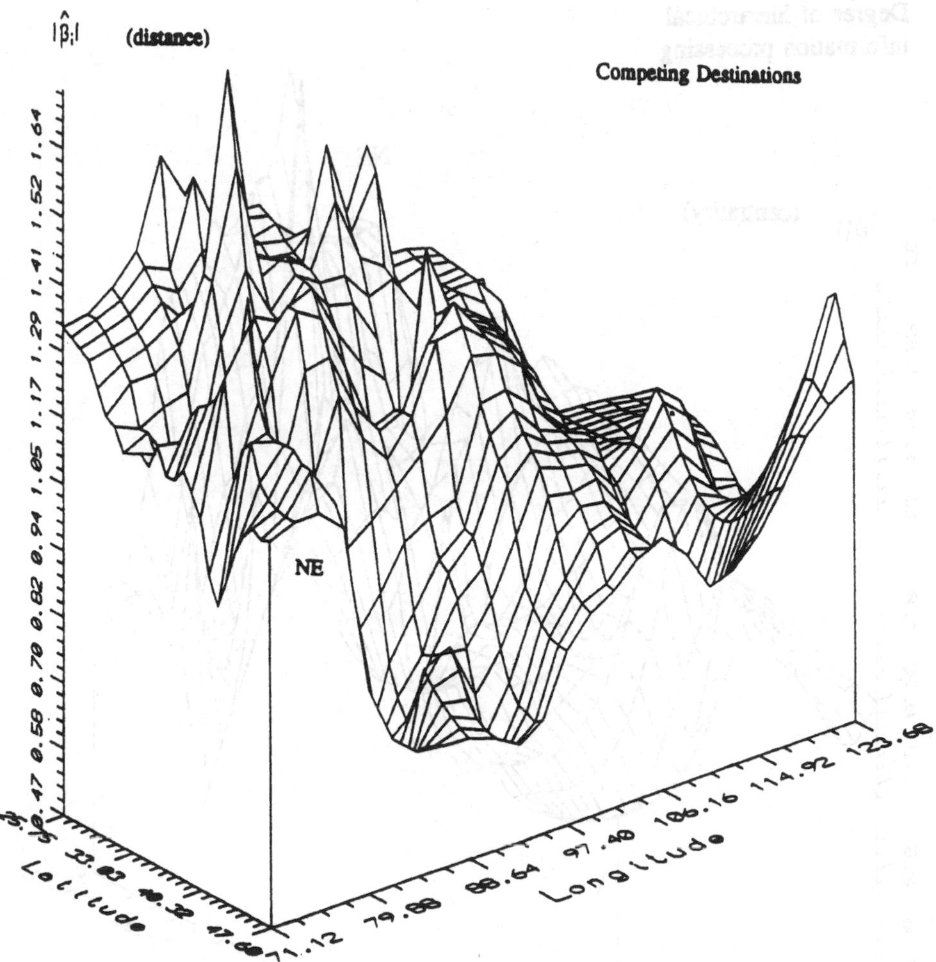

|β̂ᵢ| (distance)
Competing Destinations
0.47 0.58 0.70 0.82 0.94 1.05 1.17 1.29 1.41 1.52 1.64
NE
71.12 79.88 88.64 97.40 106.16 114.92 123.68
Longitude
33.83 40.72 47.60
Latitude

Figure 2c

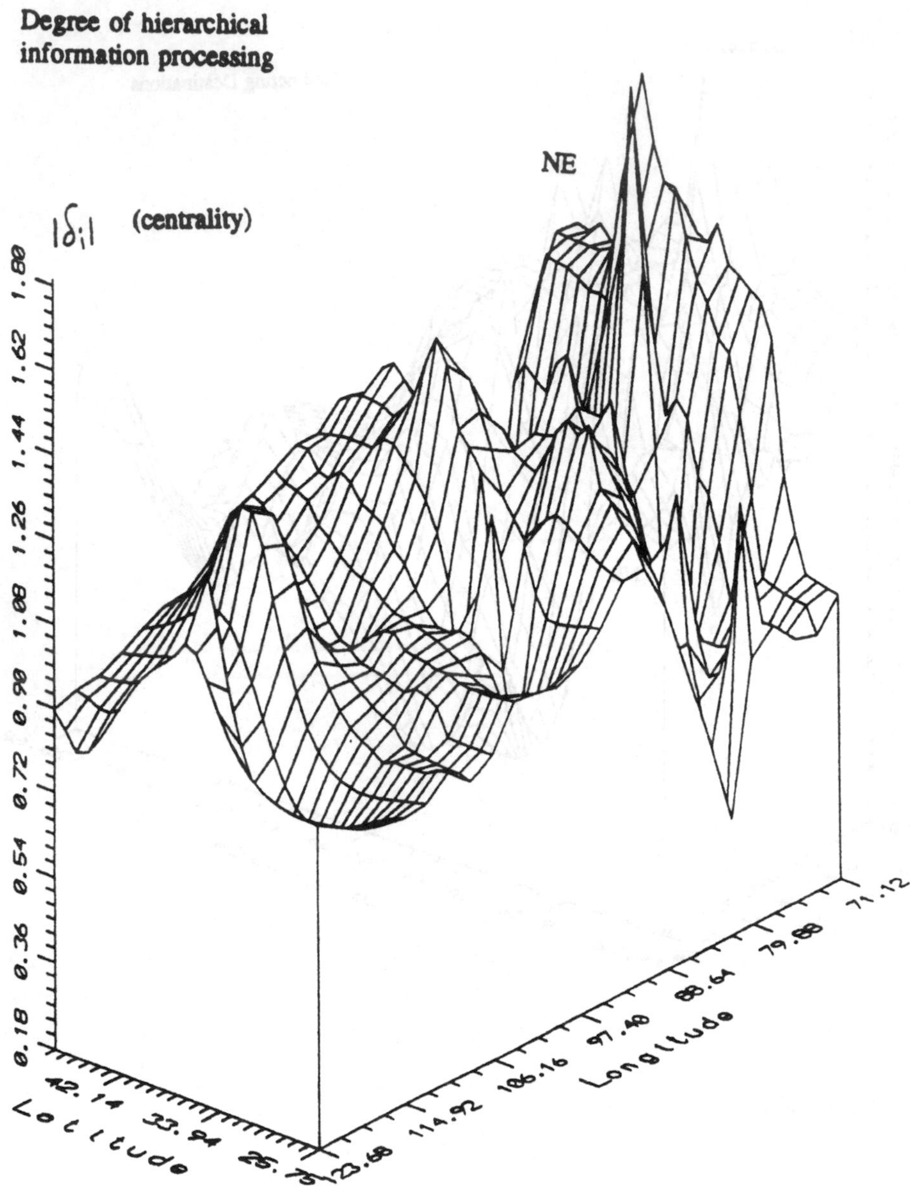
Degree of hierarchical information processing
NE
|δ;|
(centrality)
0.18
0.36
0.54
0.72
0.90
1.08
1.26
1.44
1.62
1.80
42.14
33.94
25.75
Latitude
23.68
114.92
106.16
97.40
88.64
79.88
71.12
Longitude

Figure 2d

Fotheringham (1984) has demonstrated the spurious nature of this counterintuitive trend in terms of a misspecification bias that has a direct spatial interpretation. Figures 1b and 2c also demonstrate the spurious nature of the data displayed in Figures 1a and 2b; when hierarchical information processing is accounted for, the relationship between the estimated distance-decay parameters and centrality disappears.

Finally, the results in Figure 1c and 2d depict the spatial pattern of the estimated values of ∂, the parameter indicating the degree of hierarchical information processing. There is a significant spatial trend (t=2.25) with more central origins having more negative estimates of ∂. This pattern is consistent with the hypothesis stated earlier that individuals in more central origins will have more spatial information to encode and will therefore process that information hierarchically to a greater extent that individuals in less central origins. if the estimate of ∂ were 0, no hierarchical information processing would be taking place and the competing destinations model would be equivalent to the logit model.

6 CONCLUSIONS

We have demonstrated how the degree to which information is processed hierarchically can be measured from the centrality parameter estimate in a competing destinations spatial choice model. Using this technique, the results from this study strongly support the hypothesis that spatial information is processed hierarchically, and that the degree to which spatial information is processed hierarchically depends on the amount of information needed to be processed, which in turn depends upon location in space. It appears that individuals in more central origins have more spatial information and hence process this information hierarchically to a greater degree than do individuals in less central origins. This is shown to have important implications for spatial choice modeling.

The results suggest several avenues for further research. It would be useful to examine choice data at several different levels of a hierarchy to examine the spatial scale at which branching begins in the encoding of spatial information. For example, do residents of the United States view space as a patchwork of states or are there broader definitional units to consider? Do perceptual hierarchies conform to political divisions or to some other spatial coverage?

It would be useful to combine this approach to measuring the degree to which spatial information is processed hierarchically with more controlled experiments. Obviously experiments undertaken in controlled environments give valuable insight into how people process spatial information although they lack the real world context of this study.

The establishment of a link between spatial movements and spatial information processing is particularly important because it provides a way of measuring the latter retroactively. That is, armed with the technique presented here, it is now possible to examine past migration patterns and make statements about the evolution of mental hierachies over time. In an historical study of US migration flows, for example, to what extent has the spatial distribution of the parameter ∂ changed and can any change be linked to presumed changes in information surfaces?

Finally, this study suggests a strong link between spatial choice and mental maps. It would be useful to link the literature on the latter with the findings from this type of study. For example, it would be useful to be able to produce representative mental maps for individuals in some of the origins covered in this study to reinforce the link between the complexity of one's perception of space and the degree to which one processes information hierarchically.

ACKNOWLEDGEMENTS

The National Center for Geographic Information and Analysis is supported in part by a grant from the National Science Foundation (SES88-10917); support by the NSF is gratefully acknowledged.

REFERENCES

Briggs, R., (1983) "Urban Cognitive Distance", Image and Environment, R.M. Davis & D.Stea (Eds.) Chicago:Aldine

Byrne, R.W., (1979) "Memory for Urban Geography", Quarterly Journal of Experimental Psychology, 31: 147-154.

Curtis, A. J., (1992) An Investigation Into The Hierarchical Processing Of Spatial Information Unpublished Master's thesis, New York State University at Buffalo.

Davis, E., (1981) Organizing Spatial Knowledge, Publication 193, Computer Science Department, Yale University, New Haven.

Fotheringham, A.S., (1981), "Spatial Structure and Distance-Decay Parameters", Annals of the Association of American Geographers, 71(3):425-436.

Fotheringham, A.S., (1983), "A New Set of Spatial Interaction Models: The Theory of Competing Destinations", Environment and Planning A, 15(1): 15-36.

Fotheringham, A.S., (1984), "Spatial Flows and Spatial Patterns", Environment and Planning A, 16(4): 529-543.

Fotheringham, A.S., (1986), "Modelling Hierarchical Destination Choice," Environment and Planning A, 18(3): 401-418.

Fotheringham, A.S., (1987), "Modelling Spatial Choice: A Geo-Psychological Approach", Papers in Planning Research, 110, Department of Town Planning,

University of Wales Institute of Science and Technology, Cardiff, Wales, 46 pp.

Fotheringham, A.S., (1988), "Consumer Store Choice and Choice Set Definition", Marketing Science, 7(3): 299-310.

Fotheringham, A.S., & Morton E. O'Kelly, (1989). Spatial Interaction Models: Formulations and Applications. xix and 224 pages, Kluwer Academic Publishers: Dordrecht/Boston/London, 1989. ISBN 0-7923-0021-1.

Fotheringham, A.S., (1991a), "Migration and Spatial Structure: The Development of the Competing Destinations Model", Chapter 4, pp.57-72 in Migration Models: Macro and Micro Approaches, J. Stillwell and P. Congdon (eds.), Bellhaven: London and New York, 1991.

Fotheringham, A.S., (1991b), "Statistical Modeling of Spatial Choice: An Overview", Chapter 5, pp. 95-118, in Spatial Analysis in Marketing: Theory, Methods, and Applications, A. Ghosh and C. Ingene (eds), JAI Press: Greenwich, CT and London, Research in Marketing Series.

Gould, P., (1975), "Acquiring Spatial Information," Economic Geography, 51:87-99.

Hirtle, S.C., Jonides, J. (1985), "Evidence of Hierarchies in cognitive maps", Memory & Cognition, 13(3):208:217.

Kosslyn,S., Pick,H.L.,& Fariello, G. (1974) "Cognitive Maps in Children and Men", Child Development, 45:90-94

McNamara, P., (1986), "Mental Representations of Spatial Relations," Cognitive Psychology, 18:87-121.

Muth, R.F., (1991) "Supply-Side Regional Economics" Journal of Urban Economics, 29, 63-69.

Sadella, E., & Magel, S., (1980) "The Perception of Traversed Distance", Environment and Behavior, 12: 167-182.

Sadella, E., & Staplin, L., (1980) "The Perception of Traversed Distance: Intersections." Environment and Behavior, 12:167-182.

Sadella,E., Staplin,L.J. & Burroughs,W.J., (1979), "Retrieval Processes in Distance Cognition", Memory and Cognition, 7:291:296.

Shepard, R.N. (1975) "Form Formation and Transformation of Internal Representation", In Information Processing and Cognition: The Loyola

Symposium, R. Solso (ed), Hillsdale, NY:Lawrence Erlbaum & Associates, pp. 87-122

Shepard, R.N., (1981) "Psychophysical Complementarity." In Perceptual Organization, M. Kubouy & J. Pomerantz (Eds.), Hillsdale, NJ: Erlbaum.

Shepard, R.N. (1984) "Ecological constraints on internal representation: Resonant kinematics of perceiving, imagining, thinking, and dreaming", Psychological Review, 91:417-447

Stevens, A., (1976), "The role of inference and internal structure in the representation of spatial information", Unpublished doctoral dissertation, University of California, San Diego, La Jolla, CA.

Stevens, A., Coupe, P. (1978), "Distortions in Judged Spatial Relations," Cognitive Psychology, 10: 422-437.

Thorndyke, P. W., (1981) "Distance Estimation from Cognitive Maps," Cognitive Psychology, 13: 526-550.

Wilton, R. (1979), "Knowledge of spatial relations: The specification of the information used in making inferences", Quarterly Journal of Experimental Psychology, 31:133-146.

IS THERE A RELATIONSHIP BETWEEN SPATIAL COGNITION AND ENVIRONMENTAL PATTERNS?

Scott M. Freundschuh

Department of Geography, Memorial University of Newfoundland
St. John's, Newfoundland, Canada A1B 3X9

Abstract. One aspect of a fundamental theory of spatial representations is human-cognitive representation. This research includes a review of cognitive models of spatial knowledge across disciplines, upon which a proposed comprehensive model is based. This model includes geographic facts, route, and configurational knowledge as kinds of (spatial) geographical knowledge. This research also investigates the acquisition of spatial knowledge. An experiment was designed to test the hypothesis that a regular environment (gridded road pattern) promotes the acquisition of metrical configurational knowledge from procedural knowledge and greater navigation experience, whereas an irregular environment (serpentine road pattern) does not. A irregular and regular environment were used in this study. Forty subjects performed orientation, distance, and location estimation tasks in each environment, and performance was compared. The results of the experiment were varied. There was, however, tentative support to suggest that the pattern of the environment does effect the accuracy of spatial knowledge.

1 Introduction

After what appears to have been a decline in the late 1970's and most of the 1980's in research concerning human understanding of space, there has been a renewed interest in this topic. Several factors are no doubt responsible for this rejuvenation, but one factor seems to be at the center of this revival, and that factor is the emergence of the discipline known as Cognitive Science. Gardner [17] defines cognitive science as the "empirically based effort to answer long-standing epistemological questions--particularly those concerned with the nature of knowledge, its components, its sources, its development, and its deployment (p. 6)". Cognitive science is having a profound impact on several disciplines, including geography. This impact on geography, though relatively recent, has focused much attention on research concerning navigation and wayfinding [1], and on spatial cognition in general [20, 22].

This paper reports the results of an experiment, of which only the research design and rationale were presented at a NATO Advanced Study Institute (ASI) in Las Navas, Spain in the summer of 1990, and subsequently published in the text that resulted from this ASI. To ensure the continuity of this paper, short summaries of the hypothesis and research design that have been previously published [12] will be provided here. The reader is referred to Freundschuh [11, 12] for further explanation and discussion.

2 Summary Of Spatial Knowledge Models

A review of spatial knowledge models [30, 6, 31, 29, 26, 24, 9, 13, 25, 16, 28, 10, 27, 32] reveals a variety of spatial knowledge types, and several means by which these knowledge types can be structured. As only a general summary of a spatial knowledge models will be provided here, one should refer to Hart and Moore [13], Heft and Wohlwill [14], or Freundschuh [11] for more extensive reviews. Putting aside differences in terminology between models, four distinct spatial knowledge types emerge.

2.1 The Body as a Reference Frame

The first, which has been called active space, action in space, topological, egocentric, and sensorimotor knowledge relies on the body as the reference frame. Acquisition of this knowledge comes from direct manipulation of objects, and therefore concerns geographic space that is in the immediate vicinity of the body (i.e., within arms length). The models that contain this knowledge type are developmental models that describe how a child learns his/her environment, beginning at birth.

2.2 Landmarks

The next knowledge type is that of landmarks. Landmarks (also referred to as declarative knowledge) have been defined as any salient environmental feature [25, 10, 27] though another meaning exists wherein landmarks are dominant landscape features that serve as organizing elements of a cognitive representation [18, 5]. Though these apparent differences in the definition of landmark exist, landmarks may be viewed generally as environmental cues for spatial cognition regardless of how 'cognitively prominent'.

2.3 Procedurally Based Knowledge

The third knowledge type, which has been referred to as strip-map, route map, projective, topological, and procedural knowledge is the first point at which general consensus between spatial knowledge models becomes apparent. This kind of spatial knowledge can be characterized as a procedurally based "linear" representation of space which relies in varying degrees on an egocentric reference frame.

2.4 Abstract Space

The last spatial knowledge type, which has been referred to as ego-centric, comprehensive map, survey, Euclidean, configurational, and metrical knowledge can be characterized as a two dimensional representation of space which includes metric measures such as angles and distances. It, in a general sense, entails full coordination of the environment upon which a Euclidean framework can be imposed. Though this appears to be the underlying similarity between these models at this level, there is actually a more poignant one. This is the belief that at this level, humans can deal with space at an abstract level and do so from a geocentric reference frame.

Two theories that were reviewed but not included in the summary of the four general spatial knowledge types are the theories of Yeap [32] and Gibson [9]. Though these two models are uniquely different from the other twelve, and offer interesting perspectives on spatial knowledge, at this time they are conceptions put forth by the authors that lack any compelling empirical support.

3 Integrating Spatial Knowledge

One aim of this research was to explore how kinds of spatial knowledge. are integrated. The following is a brief description of a model for spatial knowledge [12] that considers not only different spatial knowledge types, but proposes a framework within which spatial knowledge types are placed. This conceptual framework, synthesized from existing models, suggests how spatial knowledge types are related, and considers the component of time in acquiring these knowledge types.

3.1 Geographical Facts

The first kind of spatial knowledge in this model is *Geographical Facts*. Geographical facts are facts about places, and may include existence (*"X" exists*), factual descriptive characteristics (*"X" has characteristics*), and location (*"X" is located at*). Sources for geographical facts include direct real-world experiences, maps, television and movies, books and newspapers, and other people.

3.2 Route Knowledge

The second kind of geographical knowledge is *Route Knowledge*. This knowledge is the "linking together" of geographical facts, enabling travel between places. At a minimum, route knowledge consists of a set of choice points, the paths that link these points [roads, etc.], and the action executed at these points [go left/right, go straight]. Route knowledge is usually acquired through direct navigation experience, but it is possible that route knowledge can be gained from other sources such as map reading (via route planning), directions from other people, and from text.

3.3 Configurational Knowledge

The third kind of geographical knowledge is *Configurational Knowledge*. This type of knowledge is acquired most easily from maps and other sources of vertical perspective. Configurational knowledge of an environment may be a simple network of routes (i.e., topology), or it may be a network of routes where distance and direction is known, as well as the pattern the routes form (i.e., topology + metrics). In this sense, configurational knowledge is a continuum of spatial knowledge ranging from knowledge about the 'connectedness' of landmark (point) and route (linear) features in the environment, to knowledge of 'connectedness' as well as metrical information such as distance and angles between these features (areal and volumetric).

3.4 A Model of Spatial Knowledge

Thus far, models of spatial knowledge identify types of spatial knowledge and present them as individual entities seemingly separate from one another. The model presented here (see figure 1), instead of treating

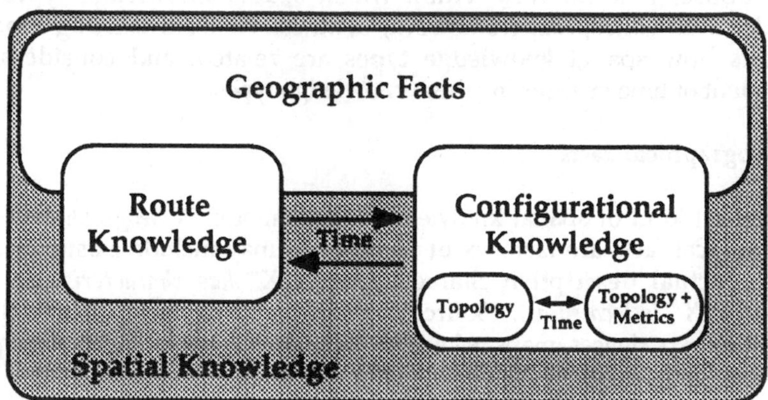

Fig. 1. Model of Spatial Knowledge. Spatial knowledge (i.e., spatial cognitive representation) considered not simply as a static representation of space, but instead as a dynamic representation that becomes refined through time (adapted from Freundschuh [12]).

kinds of spatial knowledge as separate components, integrates kinds of spatial knowledge. Here, spatial knowledge is considered not simply a static representation of space, but instead is a dynamic representation that becomes refined through time. Figure 1 shows that within the framework of spatial knowledge, there exists geographic facts, route knowledge, and configurational knowledge. Geographic facts are a necessary component of both route knowledge and configurational knowledge. In addition, geographic information that is lower in this hierarchy may be retrievable from higher levels. In other words, one could sometimes extract geographic facts from both route knowledge and configurational knowledge. It is also possible that some higher level geographic information is retrievable from lower levels. For instance, it is possible to integrate route knowledge to "build" a low level configurational knowledge.

4 Integrating Spatial Knowledge

In the literature, there is a question as to whether or not metrical configurational knowledge can be acquired from route knowledge with increased navigation in an environment [3, 4, 13, 2, 25, 15, 28, 17]. Specifically, research by Thorndyke and Hayes-Roth [28] suggests that metrical configurational knowledge can be acquired from route knowledge with increased navigation experience, whereas research by Lloyd [17] suggests that it can not. An important difference between these two experiments resides in the different environments used in each study. The test environment utilized by Thorndyke and Hayes-Roth was "regular", whereas the test environment used by Lloyd was "irregular".

4.1 Regular and Irregular Environments

Research by Lynch [18] and Moar *et al.*, [21] suggests that the arrangement or pattern of an environment does have an effect on the acquisition and recall of spatial knowledge of that environment. Arrangement of the environment involves the patterns formed by the paths or routes required to travel between places. One arrangement is a gridded pattern where paths are straight lines, and intersect at right angles (e.g., a gridded road pattern). Such gridded patterns are here considered regular environments. In contrast to a regular environment is an environment in which the paths are not necessarily straight, and the intersections between paths may or may not be right angles (e.g., a winding or serpentine road pattern). This pattern is here considered an irregular environment. Lynch [18] discovered that an irregular environment (i.e., Boston) was perceived to be "full of locational difficulties... crooked [and] confusing paths... [and] difficult to maintain [orientation] in" (pp. 14-17). In contrast, Lynch [18] found that a regular environment (i.e., Los Angles) was perceived to "[possess] a gridiron plan in its central area... [and easy] to maintain direction on the paths" (pp. 14-15, p. 38). Moar *et al.*, [21] discovered that an environment that appears to mimic a grid pattern is more likely to be remembered as a grid pattern. Given the results of Lynch and Moar, it would seem that both Thorndyke and Hayes-Roth's and Lloyd's results are reasonable, and one could certainly expect similar results under similar circumstances.

This raises the question: how does the arrangement of the environment affect the acquisition of spatial knowledge? Figure 2 is a conceptual model that shows a dynamic relationship between route and configurational

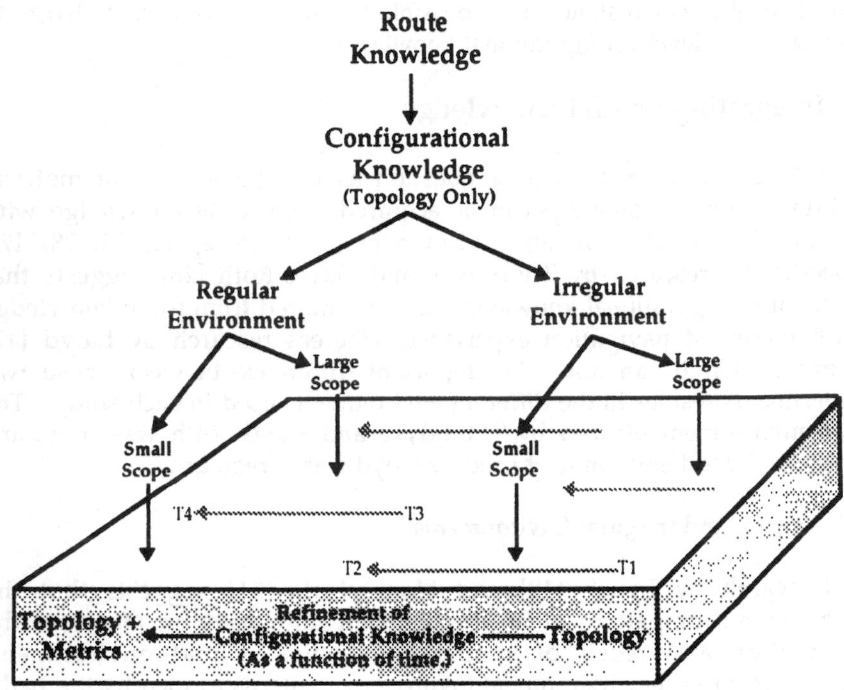

Fig. 2. Integrating Spatial Knowledge With Environment and Experience. This diagram demonstrates the relationship of route and configurational knowledge, as well as the arrangement and scope of an environment to the amount of navigation experience (length of time T) in an environment. (diagram reproduced from Freundschuh [12])

knowledge, arrangement and scope of the environment, and the dimension of time for learning an environment via navigation. Essentially, this model suggests that initially one acquires route knowledge of an environment, and with increased navigation experience within this environment, configurational (topology only) knowledge is acquired. After the topology is learned, the arrangement and scope of the environment begin to play a significant role in determining the "accuracy" and "extent" of one's knowledge about the metrical properties of this environment. In a regular environment of small scope, it is possible that both topology and metrical properties of an environment can be learned, whereas in an irregular environment of fairly large scope, due to the more complex nature of the geographical information, it is possible that only topology is learned.

4.3 Hypotheses

This study *investigates whether regularity of the environment promotes the acquisition of metrical configurational knowledge of an environment from route knowledge in subjects who learn an environment through navigation only.* Figure 3 represents the hypotheses that this experiment is designed to explore. The y axis in this diagram illustrates a progression of spatial learning from route knowledge to metrical configurational

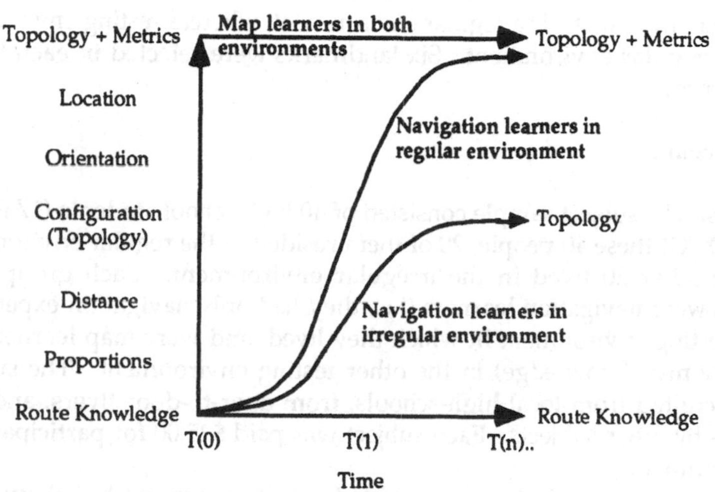

Fig. 3. This figure summarizes the hypotheses. It indicates that in both a regular and irregular environment, map learners acquire the topology of an environment, as well as distances and angles. Navigation learners, on the other hand, acquire only topology in an irregular environment, and acquire, through navigation experience, topology, distance and angles in a regular environment. (adapted from Freundschuh, 1991b).

knowledge. This progression begins with the learning of routes, followed by the acquisition of proportions, distances, topology, then angles and finally location. Figure 3 suggests that in both a regular and irregular environment, map-learners acquire metrical configurational knowledge, whereas a navigation learner acquires only topology in an irregular environment, and with increased navigation experience, topology, distance and angles in a regular environment. The length of time required to acquire this knowledge is a function of the scope (size) and complexity of the environment (number of features), and individual spatial cognitive ability.

5 Brief Review of Research Design

Only a brief review of the experimental design will be provided here. Parts of the experimental design as described below are taken from Freundschuh [12]; the reader is referred to Freundschuh [11, 12] for further explanation.

5.1 Testing Environments

Two testing environments were selected for this study. The testing environments are similar in size (1.1 square miles for environment 1 vs. 0.8 square miles for environment 2), and are both suburban "outside spaces". Testing environment 1 is a regular environment, whereas testing environment 2 is an irregular environment. Six landmarks were selected in each testing environment.

5.2 Procedure

Subjects. The subject sample consisted of 40 high school students (17 female, 23 male). Of these 40 people, 20 of them resided in the regular environment, and the other 20 lived in the irregular environment. Each group of 20 subjects were navigation learners (i.e., they had only navigation experience) in the testing environment in which they lived, and were map learners (i.e., had only map knowledge) in the other testing environment. The subjects were recruited from local high-schools, from door-to-door flyers, and from referrals by other subjects. Each subject was paid $25.00 for participating in the experiment.

Map learning subjects were divided into two groups based upon the amount of time they spent studying maps of the testing environments. The first group studied the map until they could label an unlabeled copy of the map (mean time of 18.5 minutes, range of 12 to 25 minutes). The second group studied the map until they reached the same criterion set for the first group, and then studied the map for an additional 15 minutes. Navigation learners were also divided into two groups, but in this case, group division was based on the amount of experience within the testing environment (i.e., length of residence). The resulting groups for testing environment 1 was from 1 to 14 years (10 subjects) and 15 to 17 years (10 subjects), and the resulting groups for testing environment 2 was from 1 to 6 years (10 subjects), and 7 to 16 years (again 10 subjects).

Orientation Task. Subjects were tested in groups of two, three, or four, (though performed the spatial tasks independently) and were taken by car to each landmark in turn. At each landmark, the other five landmarks were listed one at a time to each subject, after which the subject indicated, to the nearest degree, the direction to the center of the other five landmarks by pointing an arrow on a 2 ft^2 compass toward the other landmarks. The responses were recorded by the experimenter.

Distance Estimation Task. The six landmarks in each testing environment were paired such that no two landmarks were paired more than once, resulting in 15 landmark pairs for each environment. Each subject was given a form with these fifteen paired landmarks on it, and was asked to first estimate the distance in tenths of a mile on the shortest path (specified on the form) between paired landmarks, and then to estimate the straight line [Euclidean] distance in tenths of a mile between paired landmarks.

Location Task. Groups of three landmarks were determined for the six landmarks in each testing environment, resulting in 20 combinations for each environment. Each subject was given a booklet containing twenty 8.5 x 11 inch pages. On each page, two labeled dots designated the location of two of the landmarks in each combination. The subject was instructed to place a dot on the page indicating the location of the third landmark in the combination with respect to the two labeled landmarks on the page.

6 Results And Discussion

There were demonstrated differences in spatial knowledge based upon the pattern of the environment, and though some differences were significant, most were not. The results also indicated a large variation in individual spatial abilities. It should be noted that length of residence was not a significant factor between any groups. As this study was designed to specifically explore the nature of spatial knowledge based upon the pattern of the environment, a beginning point for discussion is to again look at the model proposed in figure 3.

6.1 Effect of Pattern of the Environment

The model illustrated in figure 3 made several predictions as to how subjects would perform. Based upon this model, it could be expected that there would not be a significant difference between map learners' and the most experienced navigation learners' spatial judgments in the regular environment, but that map learners' spatial judgments would be significantly more accurate than those of navigation learners in the irregular environment. Table 1 summarizes these results.

For distance estimates, both distance correlation's (r, Pearson's Product

Moment Correlation) and percent error were explored. Correlations were calculated between subjects' distance estimates and the actual distances, then a mean correlation was calculated for each group for comparison. Correlations provided a measure of the consistency in the accuracy of multiple judgments that was insensitive to absolute errors, therefore accounting for possible variation in scale in each subject's cognitive representation. Percentage error in distance estimates was calculated by converting the actual error for each estimate to a percent (estimate-actual/actual x 100). A mean percent error was then calculated for each subject from which a mean percent error was calculated for each group for comparison. For orientation estimates, the difference between the estimated orientation (angle in degrees from true North) and the true orientation from one landmark to another was computed for each subject (i.e., the angular error). A mean angular error was calculated for each landmark across subjects for each group, from which a total mean angular error was calculated for each group for comparison. For location estimates, error was calculated by first measuring the distance (in actual ground distance) between the estimated landmark location and its actual location, then dividing this distance by the baseline distance between the two reference landmarks. This resulted in a scale independent measure of locational error.

The results of subjects' distance, orientation, and location estimates were so varied that they failed to support the hypothesis (see table 1). For distance estimates, r was higher for map learners' Euclidean distance estimates than for navigation learners' in the regular environment but, as predicted, the difference was not significant. On the other hand, what was not predicted was that in the irregular environment, r was higher for navigation learners' Euclidean distance estimates than for map learners', though this difference too was not significant. Therefore, one result was predicted, the other was not. For route distance correlation's, as predicted r for navigation learners was higher in both the regular and irregular environment than for map learners, but again, the difference was not significant.

For percent error in distance estimates, in the regular environment map learners were unexpectedly more accurate than navigation learners in route distance estimates, though again the difference was not significant. In addition, map-learners were as predicted, not significantly more accurate than navigation learners in Euclidean distance estimates. In the irregular environment, navigation learners were unexpectedly more accurate than map learners in Euclidean distance estimates, and were as predicted more accurate than navigation learners in route distance estimates, but again, these differences were not significant.

For orientation estimates, though the differences were only mildly significant, navigation learners were more accurate than map learners in both the regular and irregular environment; a result that was only half expected. For location estimates, as predicted the map learners were more accurate than the navigation learners in the irregular environment, but the difference was not significant. In the regular environment, the map learners were significantly more accurate than the navigation learners, a result that was not expected. Therefore, it seems that the results do not support the hypotheses.

		Hypotheses Supported?		Significant Difference?	
		Regular Environment	Irregular Environment	Regular Environment	Irregular Environment
Distance Estimates	Correlations: Euclidean	y	n	n	n
	Route	y	y	n	n
	Error: Euclidean	y	n	n	n
	Route	n	y	n	n
Orientation Estimates		n *	n	only mildly	only mildly
Location Estimates (Proportional Error)		n	y	y	n

Table 1. Summary of map versus navigation learners within environments. Under the portion of the table labeled "Hypotheses Supported?", (y) indicates cases where the results seem to support the hypothesis, and (n) indicates cases where the hypotheses were not supported. Under the portion of the table labeled "Significant Difference?", the y's and n's indicate where differences between groups were statistically significant at $p < 0.05$, whereas "only mildly" indicates where differences were significant at $0.05 < p \leq .15$. The asterisk (*) indicates that the hypothesis was not supported because the navigation learners were not only as accurate as the map learners (which was the predicted result), but they performed more accurately.

6.2 Factors Influencing Subject Performance

There are several possible reasons that the hypotheses were not supported. One reason is the age of the subjects who participated in this study. Background statistics suggest that older subjects' spatial judgments were more accurate than those of younger subjects. In comparison to Thorndyke and Hayes-Roth's [28] and Lloyd's [17] studies, whose subjects were of college age and older, this study utilized subjects who were 18 years of age (two subjects) or younger.

In addition to age, it was shown that subjects who were drivers performed better than subjects who were not, and that more experienced drivers performed better than less experienced drivers. It would be reasonable to assume that the subjects in Thorndyke and Hayes-Roth's [28] and Lloyd's [17] experiment possessed a drivers license, and had varying levels of driving experience. It is difficult to say how driving experience affected the spatial judgments of the subjects in Thorndyke and Hayes-Roth's experiment, as this was not an out-of-doors environment. Though, it was shown in this experiment that subjects with driving experience performed better in an environment learned only from a map, which suggests that driving experience may foster the development of spatial problem solving skills. Whether this improved problem solving transcends all types of environments is unknown, but it is possible that it did have an effect.

Another factor related to age that may have affected the results concerns the maturity level of subjects. Subjects who did not approach the tasks seriously were the youngest subjects in both groups (9 subjects in the regular environment: 5 in 9th grade, 4 in 10th grade; and 10 subjects in the irregular environment: 6 in 9th grade, 3 in 10th grade, and one in 11th grade). These subjects generally did poorer than subjects who approached the tasks seriously. About two-thirds of the subjects who participated in the experiment did so with subjects who were their friends. The result was the creation of a jovial atmosphere, where subjects paid less attention to the specific tasks they were supposed to be attending to. In several cases, subjects had to be reminded that they were being paid for their time, and that it was important that they take the experiment seriously.

Another possible reason that these results do not support the hypotheses is due to variation in individual abilities, which was reflected in the wide range of subject performance. Subjects in each testing environment were ranked from most accurate to least accurate for all three spatial tasks in both environments. From this, subjects' rankings for each spatial task were divided into four classes: subjects who ranked as 1 through 5, 6 through 10, 11 through 15, 16 through 20 place. The median rank was calculated for each subject. Some subjects demonstrated a high spatial ability, and generally performed better than most other subjects. These subjects' median rank was above the 75th percentile (in the top five) within their residential group (see table 2). Other subjects demonstrated a lower spatial ability, and generally were ranked in the lower 25th percentile for all spatial tasks in their residential group. Then there were the subjects who filled the middle range, performing a bit better than average on some tasks, and less than average on other tasks. This group comprised the majority, and fell between the 25th and 75th percentile. Table 2 illustrates that subjects who performed well on one task, tended to perform well on all tasks, and vice-versa. The subjects in this experiment possessed a wide range of spatial abilities, and this variation masked differences between groups during comparisons. It is very possible that on an individual basis, subjects do progress through the lineage of spatial knowledge acquisition suggested in figure 3, but that each possesses a varying capability as to the kind and accuracy of the knowledge that he/she acquires. Further research is needed to explore individual differences, and to explore the progression of spatial knowledge acquisition for individual subjects.

Subject	Number of subjects with a median rank falling within one of the following percentiles.			
		25th	50th	75th
RRE	4	8	6	2
RIE	3	8	6	3

Table 2. Summary of subject ranking on task performance, within groups. This table shows the distribution of subjects' median ranking for all three spatial tasks. Median rank was based on rankings for twelve different situations for each subject: route and Euclidean distance correlation's for both environments [4], proportional error in route and Euclidean distance estimates for both environments [4], error in orientation estimates for both environments [2], and error in location estimates for both environments [2]. RRE represents residents of the regular environment, and RIE represents residents of the irregular environment.

A final possible reason as to why the results do not support the hypotheses is that the hypotheses may be incorrect. It may be the case that subjects do not really acquire spatial knowledge conforming to a Euclidean geometry, as suggested in figure 3. It may be that a model of spatial knowledge that assumes a Euclidean geometry is not appropriate for modeling human spatial cognition. Though some subjects, in comparison to other subjects, were able to make estimations that were termed "more accurate", in many cases even their estimates were in error of up to 50% (i.e., estimating an angle to be 60 degrees instead of 30 degrees). This relatively high level of error was common for distance and location estimations as well. There seems to be a certain amount of allowable error in a person's spatial cognitive representation which does not impede successful movement within an environment. There appears to be little need for subjects to acquire, and recall highly accurate knowledge of spatial relationships, an observation that is based upon the performance of the subjects in this study.

Of course, one could claim that people do not need *precise* spatial knowledge to get from point A to point B, or to any place else for that matter. Therefore, if the knowledge is not required, then there is no motivation to learn it [23].

6.3 Should the Spatial Knowledge Model be Revised?

The results of this study suggest that the spatial knowledge model proposed in this paper may not be the most appropriate for modeling human spatial cognition. It was demonstrated that subjects in this experiment possessed spatial knowledge that included geographical facts. All subjects knew of the six "landmarks" in their home environment, knew the type of geographic feature each landmark was, and "knew" the location of each landmark in relation to the road that the landmark was on (i.e., they knew how to get to each landmark). Of course, if the subjects knew how to get from one landmark to another, this is evidence that these subjects possessed route knowledge. So, it seems that there is evidence to suggest the existence of both geographical facts and route knowledge.

An extension of this spatial knowledge model, illustrated in figure 2, suggests a relationship between the acquisition of configurational knowledge (from topology only, to topology plus metrical information) and the pattern and scope of the environment, and the length of time within an environment. This diagram predicted that in a regular environment, the topology and metrical spatial relationships (distance and angles) would be learned sooner, and with a higher degree of accuracy, than would be learned in an irregular environment. The results of this study suggest that the pattern of the environment only tends to influence the accuracy of performance on some spatial tasks. This seemed especially true for distance and orientation estimates, but not for location estimates. Though pattern of the environment seemed to have an effect, based on the performance of the subjects in this study there was not a significant difference in the accuracy of spatial knowledge acquired from a regular versus irregular environment.

6.4 Integrating Individual Differences with the Spatial Knowledge Model

Individual differences in spatial abilities was a factor that influenced the results of this study, but was not part of the model illustrated in figure 2. This figure could be modified to include individual differences by simply labeling the Z axis of the conceptual plane as "individual spatial abilities". This suggests that subjects with a low spatial ability might only acquire topologic relationships of an environment, whereas subjects with a high spatial ability might acquire both topologic and metrical relationships. Results of this study suggest that individual differences should be considered, and that people's spatial abilities cannot be considered homogeneous [8].

7 Conclusions

The purpose of this research was to (1) review existing spatial knowledge models, (2) propose a model for spatial knowledge based upon prior research, the pattern of the environment, and the source of spatial knowledge, and (3) test whether this new model is a viable representation of human spatial cognition. All three objectives were completed, except the validation of the model. The results of the experiments were so varied that no definitive conclusions could be drawn as to whether the model is valid. Some results suggest that the pattern of the environment does have an effect, but then again, others did not support this. Clearly, further research is needed to explore the effects of the pattern of the environment on spatial learning, to compare spatial knowledge learned from maps versus navigation experience, and to clarify individual differences in spatial abilities.

The need for a comprehensive theory of spatial representation is recognized by geographers, as well as researchers in other disciplines. It is hoped that a theory of spatial representation is based on "those concepts used by human minds" [19, p. 539]. Fundamental to this theory is a need to know how people learn and understand the environment, and how they interact with the environment. From this, it is possible to gain a general understanding of human spatial cognition, thus resulting in useful and practical models of spatial cognition on which development of effective and useful navigation aids and their user interfaces can rely.

8 Acknowledgments

This paper represents part of Research Initiative #2, "Languages of Spatial Relations," of the National Center for Geographic Information and Analysis, supported by a grant from the National Science Foundation (SES-88-10917); support by NSF is gratefully acknowledged. David Mark, Hugh Calkins, Paul Densham and Michael Gould provided helpful comments throughout this work. Their comments are gratefully acknowledged.

9 References

1. Abler, Ronald F.: Awards, rewards, and excellence: Keeping geography alive and well. The Professional Geographer, 40(2), 135-140 (1988).
2. Acredolo, L., Pick, H., and Olsen, M.: Environmental differentiation and familiarity as determinants of children's memory for spatial location. Developmental Psychology, 11, 495-501 (1875).
3. Appleyard, D.: Styles and methods of structuring a city. Environment and Behavior, 2, 100-118 (1970).

4. Appleyard, D.: Why buildings are known. Environment and Behavior, 1, 131-156 (1969).
5. Blades, M., 1991. The development of wayfinding abilities. In Mark, D. M. and Frank, A. (eds.), *Cognitive and Linguistic Aspects of Geographic Space,* Kluwer Academic Press 1991.
6. Cassirer, E.: An Essay on Man: An Introduction to the Philosophy of Human Culture. Hew Haven: Yale University Press, 1944.
7. Gardner, H.: The Mind's New Science. Basic Books, Inc., New York: New York 1985, 423 pp.
8. Gentry, T. A. and Wakefield, J. A.: Methods for Measuring Spatial Cognition. In D. M. Mark and A. U. Frank (eds.), Cognitive and Linguistic Aspects of Geographic Space. Dordrecht: Kluwer 1991.
9. Gibson, J. J.: The Senses Considered as Perceptual Systems. Boston: Houghton Mifflin 1966.
10. Golledge, R.: Integrating spatial knowledge. Paper presented at the IGU Conference, Sydney, Australia, August 1988.
11. Freundschuh, S. M.: Spatial Knowledge Acquisition of Urban Environments from Maps and Navigation Experience. Unpublished Ph.D. Thesis, Department of Geography, State University of New York at Buffalo 1991a.
12. Freundschuh, S. M.: The Effect of the Pattern of the Environment on Spatial Knowledge Acquisition. In D. M. Mark. and A. U. Frank (eds.), *Cognitive and Linguistic Aspects of Geographic Space.* Dordrecht: Kluwer 1991b.
13. Hart, R. A. and Moore, G. T.: The development of spatial cognition: A review. In Downs, R. M. and Stea, D. (eds.), Image and Environment, Chicago: Aldine 1973.
14. Heft, H. and Wohlwill, J. F.: Environmental cognition in children. In Stokols, D. and Altman, I. (eds.), Handbook of Environmental Psychology. New York: John Wiley and Sons 1987.
15. Herman, J. F. and Siegel, A. W.: The development of spatial representations of large-scale environments. University of Pittsburgh: Learning Research and Development Center 1977.
16. Kuipers, B., 1978. Modeling spatial knowledge. Cognitive Science, 2, 129-153 (1978).
17. Lloyd, R.: Cognitive maps: Encoding and decoding information. Annals of the Association of American Geographers, 79(1), 101-124 (1989).
18. Lynch, K.: The Image of the City. Cambridge, MA: MIT Press 1960.
19. Mark. D. M., and Frank, A. U.: Concepts of space and spatial language. Proceedings of the Ninth International Symposium on Computer Assisted Cartography, Baltimore, Maryland, 538-556 (1989).
20. Mark, D. M., Frank, A. U., Egenhofer, M. J., Freundschuh, S. M., McGranaghan, M. and White, R. M.: Languages of Spatial Relations: Initiative II Specialist Meeting Report. Santa Barbara, CA: National Center for Geographic Information and Analysis, Report 89-2 (1989).

21. Moar, I., Hamer, N. J., and Woods, B. A.: The role of grid schemata in memory for large-scale environments. Proceedings of the Fifth Annual Conference of the Cognitive Science Society (1983).
22. National Center for Geographic Information and Analysis (NCGIA). The research plan of the National Center for Geographic Information and Analysis. International Journal of Geographical Information Systems, 3, 117-139 (1989).
23. Norman, D. A.: The Psychology of Everyday Things. New York: Basic Books, Inc 1988.
24. Piaget, J. and Inhelder, B.: The Child's Conception of Space. New York: Norton 1967.
25. Siegel, A. W., and White, S. H.: The development of spatial representations of large-scale environments. In H. W. Reese (ed.), Advances in Child Development and Behavior, (Vol. 10), New York: Academic 1975.
26. Shemyakin, F. N.: Orientation in space. In B. G. Ananyev *et al.* (eds.), Psychological Sciences of the USSR (Vol. 1, Report No. 62-11083). Washington, DC, Office of Technical Services 1962.
27. Stern, E., and Leiser, D.: Levels of spatial knowledge and urban travel modeling. Geographical Analysis, 20(2), 140-155 (1988).
28. Thorndyke, P. W. and Hayes-Roth, B.: Differences in spatial knowledge acquired from maps and navigation. Cognitive Psychology, 12, 137-175 (1982).
29. Tolman, E. C.: Cognitive maps in mice and men. Reprinted in Downs, R. M. and Stea, D. (eds.), Image and Environment, Chicago: Aldine 1973. (originally published in Psychological Review, 55, 189-208 (1948))
30. Trowbridge, C. C.: On fundamental methods of orientation and imaginary maps. Science, 38, 888-897 (1913).
31. Werner, H.: Comparative Psychology of Mental Development. New York: International Universities Press 1948.
32. Yeap, W. K.: Towards a computational theory of cognitive maps. Artificial Intelligence, 34, 297-360 (1988).

Counter-Intuitive Geographic 'Facts': Clues for Spatial Reasoning at Geographic Scales

David M. Mark
National Center for Geographic Information and Analysis
Department of Geography
State University of New York at Buffalo
Buffalo, New York 14261 U.S.A.

Telephone: (716) 636 3545
FAX: (716) 636 2329
Email: geodmm@ubvms.cc.buffalo.edu

Abstract. 'Counter-intuitive' geographic facts provide insight into spatial reasoning at geographic scales. Situations that are judged as counter-intuitive by many people probably result from 'correct' spatial reasoning based of distorted spatial knowledge that is common to populations. Systematic distortions of latitude and longitude are examined by asking subjects to judge whether certain cities were east or west (or, north or south) of a common city. When the proportion judging each city to be a certain direction is mapped, the isolines reveal systematic distortions of geographic configurations that are consistent with hierarchical knowledge representation and several prototype effects.

1 Introduction

It is reasonable to postulate that many people have a general idea of the relative locations of places and continental and global scales. Occasionally, however, geographic situations are encountered in which the actual situation surprises the majority. Some of these are sufficiently remarkable that they have become a part of popular culture as classic riddles or 'trivia' questions.

Whereas such ***counter-intuitive geographic facts*** are interesting in their own right, they raise a basic research question—if these facts are 'counter-intuitive', then there must be a standard, culturally-shared 'intuition' (common-sense reasoning process) that leads to a counterfactual. At least two possibilities arise: either reasoning procedures may be flawed (for an analysis of reasoning procedures regarding cardinal directions, see Frank, 1991), or the knowledge base to which those reasoning procedures are applied may have systematic errors.

This paper explores these issues by first reporting results of a survey to collect commonly-known counter-intuitive geographic facts. Next, two key papers on the topic are reviewed, and then an experiment to investigate cognitive maps is described and the results are discussed.

2 Counter-Intuitive Geographic 'Facts': A Survey

In April of 1990, I posted a request for "Counter-Intuitive Geographic 'Facts' to several Usenet electronic news groups and BITNET listservers: GEOGRAPH (a general geography discussion list); GIS-L (a GIS discussion list); comp.ai (artificial intelligence); sci.lang (linguistics); and rec.games.trivia (a news group for people interested in 'trivia' as a hobby). The request was worded as follows:

```
I am attempting to collect 'counter-intuitive' geographic
facts, of the sort that often crop up in riddles or
'trivia questions'.  In the United States, the classic
example seems to be:

"Which is farther west: San Diego, California, or Reno,
Nevada?"

The correct answer is "Reno", whereas many people would
think
that it should be "San Diego".

The idea is that this and other examples of 'counter-
intuitive' geographic facts may reveal the nature of some
of the intuitive 'rules' that people use by default in
spatial inference.

...

Please send me other examples, or post them.  I will post
a summary eventually.  I am especially interested in
examples from outside North America, and from non-English-
speaking areas.
```

I received almost 100 responses, some of which included more than one example—there were 106 examples in all, distributed as indicated in Table 1.

Table 1: Summary of responses to Electronic Media Survey of 'Counter-Intuitive Geographic Facts'

Cases	Situation
20	Atlantic end of Panama Canal is west of the Pacific end
18	Relative latitudes in Europe and North America
14	Extreme points of the United States of America
13	Detroit/Windsor situation
8	South America longitudes
4	Relative latitudes in Eastern and Western North America
1	Relative longitudes in the United States
28	Other Miscellaneous "Counter-Intuitive" Geographical Facts
106	Total

The most frequently-reported 'counter-intuitive' fact was that the Atlantic Ocean entrance to the Panama Canal is located west (by longitude) of the Pacific Ocean entrance. Evidently, since the Pacific is west of the Americas, and the Atlantic is east, people expect an Atlantic-to-Pacific trip through the Panama canal to run generally east to west. That the true geographic orientation of the canal is 'counter-intuitive' reveals that their intuition about the geography there would predict the contrary. Such a principle of whole-to-part inheritance of geographic relations seems to be one of the general properties of spatial reasoning at a geographical scale. The same principle would account for the fourth-most-common example from the survey, the 'counter-intuitive' fact that Windsor, Ontario, Canada is located The second most common set of counter-intuitive geographic facts reported in the informal survey were the 18 reports of facts regarding the relative latitudes of cities in Europe and in North America. In 6 examples, the European city given was Rome; in those examples, the U.S. city was New York (4 times), Boston, or Philadelphia, which are thought to be well north of Rome even though they are at about the same latitude. London England was paired with Boston (seems similar yet Boston is far south) and Winnipeg Canada (seems well north of London but actual latitude is about the same). The 'French Riviera' (Cote D'Azur) is intuitively believed to be well south of Boston or southern Ontario, when the latitude is about the same.

Ten of the people who gave Europe-America latitude examples volunteered possible explanations. Five added reasons that seem to be equivalent to Tversky's (1981) alignment hypothesis (see discussion below), but five others attribute the intuitive reasoning to comparative climate. In fact, one respondent from Italy (brescian@irst.it) suggested that "the 'wrong' rule used is:

IF (in north hemisphere) colder(climate(a),climate(b))
THEN probably north-of (a,b)

The author's intuition is that the effect is indeed mainly due to cognitive concepts of climate, rather than of alignment *per se*, but it is difficult to design an experiment that would objectively distinguish between these effects. Future work might, however, ask the subjects for introspective ideas on their reasons for making judgements that usually put Europe farther south relative to North America than it actually is.

Another block of counter-intuitive geographic facts (8 cases) involve the longitudinal position of South America compared with North America. It seems that at least North American residents think of the Americas being roughly aligned, such that the west coast of South America is approximately straight south from California. In fact, South America is relatively much farther east, and the Chilean Pacific seaport of Valparaiso is located at longitude about 72 degrees west, which is actually about 2 degrees ***east*** of New York City (about 74 degrees west), on the east coast of North America! Tversky's (1981) alignment hypothesis seems to be the obvious explanation here; this in turn lends credence to the idea the the latitude judgements comparing Europe and North America also are due simply due to assumed alignment.

3 Previous Research on Geographical-Scale Spatial Reasoning

In the literature of psychology and cognitive science, a paper by Stevens and Coupe (1978) in the journal *Cognitive Psychology* reports on a systematic study of spatial reasoning at geographic scales. As in the current study, their motivation was the nature of counter-intuitive geographic facts. They noted the Reno-San Diego and Panama Canal examples of east-west errors in judging geographic locations, and Madrid (Spain) vs. Washington D.C., and Seattle (Washington, U.S.A.) vs. Montréal (Quebec, Canada) examples for north-south distortions. They propose that these errors result from hierarchical mental representation of geographic information, and from whole-to-part inference about spatial relations, a sort of inheritance, with geographic regions serving as super-ordinate classes for the cities or other places within them.

Stevens and Coupe performed three experiments to examine the nature of such errors. The first involved judgements of relative orientations of five pairs of locations, which were included in a test instrument with 15 "filler pairs". Ten subjects were asked to draw lines from the center of a circle (representing the "from" city) to the edge of the circle in the direction of the "to" city; only the data for the five critical pairs were analyzed. The five pairs of locations tested are listed in Table 2. Responses were measured to the nearest 5 degrees, and circular histograms of orientation were plotted. All five averages, and all but 2 of the 50 judgements were "distorted in the direction of the superordinate units" (Stevens and Coupe, 1978, p. 424). They note (p. 425) that the results "do not seem to rely on unfamiliarity with the locations being judged", because although the experiment was done in San Diego, the San Diego-Reno results were at least as strongly biased as were each of the other four.

Table 2:
Location pairs tested by Stevens and Coupe

From	To
Portland, Oregon	Toronto
San Diego	Reno
Montreal	Seattle
Atlantic entrance of Panama Canal	Pacific entrance of Panama Canal
Portland, Oregon	Portland, Maine

The other experiments performed by Stevens and Coupe (1978) involved synthetic maps with either one or two regions, and three or four locations marked by letters. Each subject studied each map for 20 seconds, the map was then removed, and a question about the relative locations of two places was given. 'Errors' were about three times as common when the super-ordinate regions had a different relative orientation than did the two points; also, results were distorted toward the relative orientation of the superordinates. These results support the idea that systematic distortions in judgements of relative geographic locations arise from reasoning in which geographic information about point locations is inherited from relations between their enclosing regions.

Tversky (1981) continued this line of research by introducing another effect—alignment and rotation of regions to conform to right angles, etc. She claimed that people tend to remember oblique lines as being vertical or horizontal, curved lines are straighter than they are, and superordinate blocks as being more aligned than they actually are. These effects had been established in the literature on perception of diagrams, and Tversky extended these ideas to memory of maps.

Tversky tested the alignment hypothesis regarding memory for maps by having subjects draw lines pointing as would a line from one city to the other. The east-west city pairs, for which the north-south dimension of the subject's response was tabulated by the experimenter, were (southernmost city listed first): Philadelphia - Rome; Los Angeles - Algiers; Chicago - Monaco; Washington (D.C.) - Madrid; and Seattle - Paris. The north-south pairs, for which east-west relative location was of interest, were (westernmost city listed first): New York City - Santiago (Chile); Miami - Lima (Peru); and Boston - Rio de Janero. Tversky used much larger numbers of subjects, with a total of 895 judgements, ranging from 59 to 169 judgements per city pair, and all of her tests were performed at Stanford University, near San Francisco, California. 'Error' rates (that is, subjects reaching conclusions counter to the true relationships) were greater than 50% for all tests, because the city pairs were chosen so that they would violate intuitions based on the alignment of the continents being more nearly even than it actually is. The error rate was greatest for Miami-Lima; 86 percent of subjects judged Lima (Peru) to be west of Miami, when in fact it lies to the east by longitude. In the other part of the experiment, the greatest error was for Philadelphia-Rome, with 78% of subjects incorrectly placing Rome to the south of Philadelphia.

Tversky obtained results that seem to confirm the alignment hypothesis when she showed subjects pairs of maps in which the continents were moved to be more nearly aligned with each other. A majority of subjects (around 65% in each case) chose the more aligned map over the correct map. Tversky also tested some more local situations, and developed a series of experiments based on artificial maps which confirmed the general tendencies found for the judgements about real cities.

4 'Cognitive Latitudes, Cognitive Attitudes': An Empirical Study

In the present study, I used a somewhat different method to elicit information of judgements of relative latitude and longitude, and to analyze and present the results. One difference is that I simply elicited binary judgements of relative latitude, or relative longitude, allowing rapid collection of fairly large data sets in group testing situations. Another difference from the studies discussed above is that all test pairs included the testing location as one of the locations. In other words, subjects in Buffalo, New York were asked for each test city whether it is located north or south (or east or west) of Buffalo. There were 31 cities to compare with Buffalo in terms of latitude, 43 to compare by longitude, and 70 subjects in all. Taking into account the omits, the data set provides a total of 2140 binary judgments regarding east-west position compared with Buffalo, and 2849 north-south judgements. (Most of the omits were due to the fact that three subjects apparently did not notice that the test instrument was printed on both sides, and omitted the entire north-south city set.) The differences in analysis are described below.

4.1 Methods.

The test instrument consisted of a single, two-sided sheet of paper. One side was entitled "East or West of Buffalo?", and then gave the following instructions:

> Please complete this survey **without consulting any maps, atlases, reference books, or other people.** For each of the following cities, please indicate whether that city is **west** or **east** of Buffalo, New York, by longitude. (That is, if you drew a line north-south through Buffalo, would the city be west or east of that line?) If you are not sure of the correct answer, please make an "educated guess". Please indicate your choice by placing a check mark in front of the 'correct' answer

These instructions were then followed by the lists of test cities. On the other side, headed "North or South of Buffalo", had almost identical instructions, followed by a different set of cities. The cities for each test (North-South; East-West) were presented in two groups, first the test cities from the United States and Canada, and second the other cities. Within each group, the cities were arranged in alphabetical order. A Spearman's rank correlation test revealed that the order of presentation was not significantly correlated with latitude for the NS test (rs = -0.18 for the North American sub-sample, and rs = -0.19 for the other set of cities), nor with longitude for the EW test (rs = -0.02 for the North American cities, and rs = 0.25 for the Latin American cities). Lastly, some background information about the subject was elicited, but that information has not been analyzed.

The test instrument was administered to students in a first-year-level university course, "World Civilization Since 1500". Although the course was being taught by a geographer, the students were from almost all areas of the arts and sciences, and almost all were in their first year of university studies. Seventy students completed the questionnaire in the classroom. Results were then coded, and for each test city and question, the frequencies and proportions were tabulated.

4.2 East or West of Buffalo?: Cognitive Longitudes in North America

Ratings on the question "east or west of Buffalo?" were obtained for 1 Canadian and 16 U.S. cities, mostly distributed in a sector generally to the south of Buffalo. Chicago, Illinois, and Boston, Massachusetts, were included with the idea that they should be unambiguous. (In fact, all subjects did place Chicago west of Buffalo, although two subjects marked Boston as being *west* of Buffalo!) Figure 1 presents the locations of the test cities, and for each city the proportion of subjects who indicated that the city is "east of Buffalo". Isolines of equal proportion are also plotted on the map; these were drawn by eye, but on a blank sheet of tracing paper bearing only the locations and values.

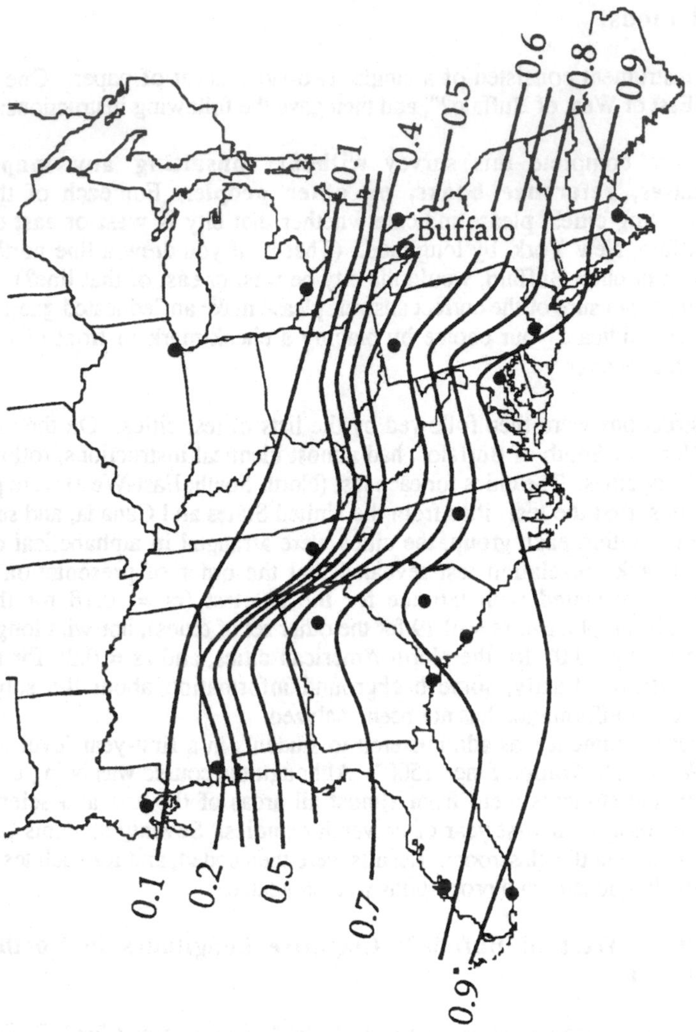

Figure 1: Isolines indicating the proportions of the subjects who felt that each test city (•) was 'east of Buffalo'

The location of the 0.50 isoline is of particular interest, because in a sense this equiprobability line represents a 'pseudo-longitude', or estimated cognitive longitude, of Buffalo. This line runs in a northeast-to-southwest direction, roughly paralleling the Atlantic Coast, as do the other equiprobability lines. This is strongly suggestive of a 'prototype' effect: since the Atlantic coast of the United States runs roughly north-south, it may be remembered as running much more directly north-south than it actually does; Michael Goodchild (personal communication, 1992) suggested that this effect may be reinforced by the fact that Americans typically see the U.S. on a conic projection such that the east coast is more nearly parallel to the right margin of the map than it would appear on a cylindrical projection.

Two of the cities reveal another common effect that distorts memories of geographic-scale-configurations: hierarchical inference. Knoxville, Tennessee ("K" in Figure 1) and Atlanta, Georgia ("A" in Figure 1) are only 352 km (219 miles) apart by road, and Atlanta is actually about 25 minutes of longitude ***west*** of Knoxville. Nevertheless, on most of these subjects' cognitive maps, Atlanta, in an east coast state, is clearly to the east of Buffalo (48 of 69 subjects rated it so), and Knoxville is thought to be west of Buffalo (59 of 68 subjects). This is consistent with hierarchical information processing, combined with a heuristic that the Atlantic coast runs north-south. Georgia, after all, runs from the Atlantic shore to the Appalachians, and Tennessee from the Appalachians west to the Mississippi River. People who cannot remember exact locations of towns within a state may recall them as closer to the state's centroid than they actually are; such effects would pull Knoxville westward and Atlanta east.

4.3 East or West of Buffalo?: Cognitive Longitudes in Latin America

Of the fourteen Latin American cities included in the study, only three were rated as being east of Buffalo by the majority of the subjects: Havana (Cuba), Rio de Janero (Brasil), and San Juan (Puerto Rico). In fact, one of those is wrong, since Havana is west of Buffalo. Its misplacement would seem to be due to the fact that Cuba may be 'anchored' to Florida, and pushed east with Florida by the effects discussed above that straighten the east coast of the U.S. in cognitive maps.

The other eleven cities were all placed to the west of Buffalo by the subjects. In fact, this is correct only for the three Mexican cities plus Guatemala City and (by a slight margin) Panama City. For the South American cities, these results confirm the fact that most people in the United States think that South America is more-or-less aligned with North America, and that places in western South America must be west of those in eastern North America. The variable ratings for the South American cities suggest that many of the subjects did not have much idea about the relative locations of countries within South America.

4.4 North or South of Buffalo?: Cognitive Latitudes in North America

Of the four analysis groups, the least interesting was the one involving judgements about latitudes in North America. The majority of subjects were incorrect for only two of the cities: Windsor, Ontario, and Boston, Massachusetts. The case of Windsor is another obvious example of hierarchical inference: since it is in Canada, which is generally north of the U.S., it is judged to be north of Buffalo when in fact it is not. This effect was weak in this study because Buffalo is south of almost all of Canada; a similar experiment run in Minneapolis or Seattle and with more cities from eastern Canada probably would confirm this effect. The case of Boston, somewhat south of Buffalo but rated as north by 39 subjects, and south by 28, is not as clear. It may be that subjects from New York City or Long Island are recalling that Boston is north of there, or to other effects not yet evident.

4.5 North or South of Buffalo?: Cognitive Latitudes in Europe

The proportions of subjects rating European cities to be south of Buffalo increases consistently with decreasing latitude (see Figure 2). By and large, the collective knowledge of the subjects would allow a reasonable reconstruction of relative latitudes. However, places well north of Buffalo are judged to be to the south, a result found in previous research (see Tversky, 1981). The results of the present study indicate that Europe is shifted southward by about 6 or 7 degrees of latitude relative to North America. That is, cities north of about 49 degrees north latitude are judged by a majority of subjects to be north of Buffalo (about 43 degrees north latitude), whereas cities south of 49 degrees N are judged by a majority to be south. Two hypotheses have been advanced for this effect. Tversky (1981) attributes it to the same alignment effect that seems to influence longitudinal judgements in the Americas: "... on the world map, it is compelling to group North America with Europe, and south America with Africa ... Here, alignment would lead to pulling Europe—Africa southward relative to the Americas" (Tversky, 1981, p. 411).

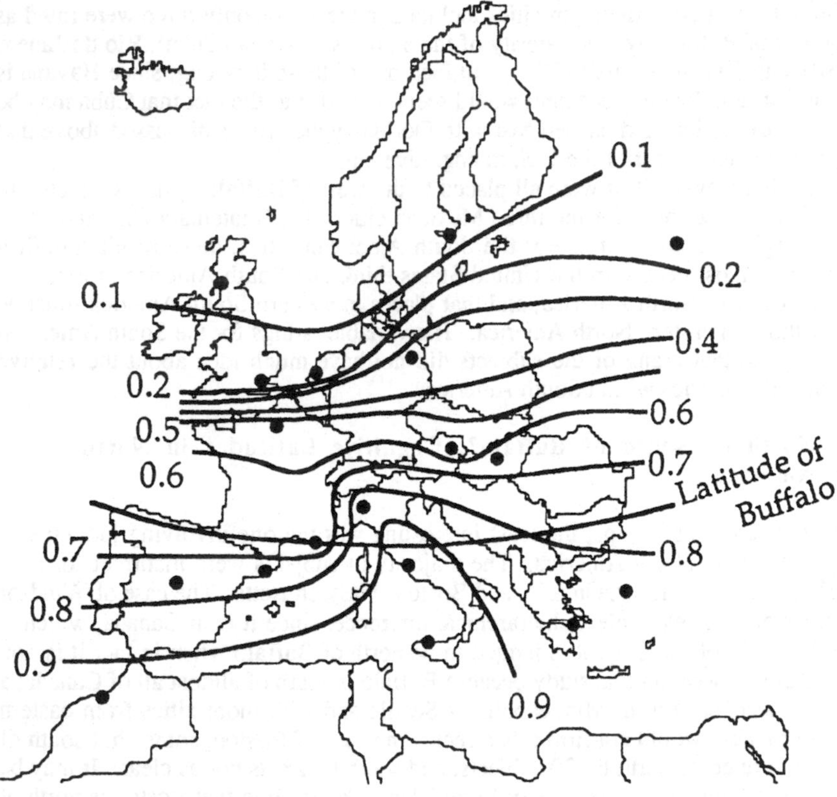

Figure 2: Isolines indicating the proportions of the subjects who felt that each test city (•) was south of Buffalo'; the actual latitude of Buffalo, 43 N, is indicated.

An alternative hypothesis, raised by several respondents to the survey of counter-intuitive facts, is that judgements of relative latitude across the Atlantic are at least in part inferred from perceived climate. Europe is much warmer in winter at equivalent latitudes because of the effects of the Gulf Stream, a fast warm-water ocean current that runs from the Gulf of Mexico northeastward to Europe. This hypothesis appeals to the author, but since its predictions are very similar to the expected effects of the alignment hypothesis, it is not obvious how to design an experiment to tease apart these effects. It is interesting to note that both the alignment hypothesis and the climate hypothesis would predict a much larger shift than is observed—the southern tip of Spain is about 11 degrees north of the southern tip of Florida, and to find January temperatures similar to, say, London (England) in eastern North America, one must go more than 15 degrees south of London. Perhaps the fact that London (England) is north of Buffalo and other parts of New York State has been systematically taught in the schools here, and that one fact anchors the cognitive map with a 6-7 degree shift.

Consistency of Latitude Rankings within Europe. Only six subjects rated the cities in a way that was completely consistent with the actual latitudes, except for the placement of Buffalo's latitude. Two subjects (33, 34) were almost perfectly correct—and since the responses were consecutive in the collected response sheets, they may have collaborated. Except for rating Marseille as south of Buffalo when in fact it is very slightly north, their ratings were correct for all European cities in the north-south study. Three identical responses rated Stockholm, Glasgow, Moscow, Berlin, Amsterdam, and London as north, and all the other cities as south—this represents the median placement of Buffalo's latitude within Europe, and is also consistent in rankings. Of course, this means that the north-south ratings of the other 61 subjects (91%) had one or more internal inconsistencies compared with actual latitude rankings, regardless of the relative alignment of Europe and North America. There were, however, nine subjects that gave identical responses, correctly placing Stockholm, Glasgow, Moscow, Amsterdam, and London to the north of Buffalo, but placing all other cities including Berlin in the 'south of Buffalo' category—this was by far the most frequent response pattern observed.

Collective Knowledge from Individual Ignorance: The Example of Ratings of Italian and French Cities. Considering the generally poor performance of Americans on tests of geographic knowledge, the results above are surprisingly consistent, except for the mis-alignment of North America and Europe. However, a more detailed analysis of two case studies indicates that the results do not provide evidence that the subjects had a high level of knowledge of relative latitudes in Europe.

Three Italian cities were included in the survey: Rome, Milan, and Palermo. In the summary statistics, these three cities have 'southness' ratings in the correct sequence. Even though 88.1 % of the subjects incorrectly judged Milan to be south of Buffalo, the proportion rose to 93.8 % for Rome and 95.4 % for Palermo (Sicily). The collective knowledge of the subjects allowed the three cities to properly ordered by latitude. However, a more detailed analysis reveals that the critical information is coming from just a few subjects. Fifty-six of the subjects (83.6 %) judged (incorrectly) that all three Italian cities in the survey were south of Buffalo—for these subjects, we have no idea whether they knew the relative positions of the cities within

Italy. The same is true for the one responded who judged all three Italian cities tested to be north of Buffalo. In both cases, the subjects probably were using hierarchically arranged knowledge, and judging Italy to be entirely south of Buffalo.

That leaves ten subjects who differentiated among three Italian cities tested. Five of these gave responses that were consistent with the correct internal geography of Italy. Three of the subjects gave the correct answer for the Italian cities, placing Milan to the north of Buffalo, but Rome and Palermo to the south. Two more placed Rome and Milan to the north of Buffalo, Palermo to the south. Only two subjects gave responses inconsistent with the true geography—1 subject had Rome and Palermo to the north of Buffalo, Milan south, and the other had Milan and Palermo to the north of Buffalo, Rome to the south. The remaining 3 subjects omitted the rating for one or two of the Italian cities. Two of these three gave "south of" ratings to Milan and one other of the cities and omitted the third, while the third rated Milan as "north of" Buffalo while not rating either Rome or Palermo. The information that allowed the cities to be correctly ranked by latitude thus came from 10 of 67 respondents, only 3 of whom actually placed all three of the Italian cities correctly with respect to Buffalo.

A similar result is found when the results for the two French cities included in the study, Paris and Marseille, are examined in detail. As was the case for the Italian cities, once again these cities were ordered correctly, with 64 percent of subjects reporting Marseille to be south of Buffalo, and 57 percent reporting Paris to be south. But again this information is coming from a small proportion of the subjects. Twenty of the subjects correctly placed both Paris and Marseille to the north; in fact, Paris is about 6 degrees of latitude farther north than Buffalo, and Marseille is almost at the same latitude, but about 1/2 degree north. But another 33 placed both cities to the south of Buffalo. The survey does not reveal whether any of these 53 people knew the ***relative*** latitudes of Paris and Marseille. Nine other respondents placed Paris to the north of Buffalo and Marseille to the south, implying the correct geographic relationship between the two French cities, but these only just 'out-voted' the four subjects who placed Marseille to the north of Buffalo and Paris to the south!

5 Discussion

How do the results above fit into a broader framework of spatial knowledge representation and spatial inference procedures? A detailed examination of the literature on this subject by Freundschuh (1991) revealed great variation in the details of descriptions of spatial knowledge, but common major themes. Previous work on spatial knowledge representation seems best accommodated by a general model that includes three distinct (yet inter-related) types of geographic knowledge:

1. **Geographic facts.** This type of geographic knowledge consists of isolated facts, such as "Paris is a large city" or "Cleveland is on Lake Erie". This type of geographic knowledge is acquired from a variety of sources, including direct real-world experience, books, television and movies, other people, maps, etc.
2. **Procedural knowledge.** This is knowledge of how to get from one place to another. An individual may or may not have the ability to express this knowledge verbally, or to draw a route map, yet they can

confidently find their way. Whereas geographic facts are embedded in procedural knowledge of routes, it may not be possible to access these facts outside of the context of the path-following in the world. This kind of knowledge is usually acquired through direct wayfinding experience in the real world, but can also be learned from others, from text sources, or by inference during map-reading.

3. **Configurational Knowledge.** This kind of geographic knowledge is "map-like", and if accurate would allow the person to draw an accurate map. This kind of knowledge may be imperfect, and and geometric properties (angles, distances) may be distorted while correct topology (connections) is preserved. This type of knowledge is most easily acquired from maps, or from views from high vantage points. In principle, configurational knowledge can be inferred from paths, but this may be greatly influenced by regularity of environment, etc. (see Freundschuh, 1991).

To this simple framework, we must add two additional factors. First is the fact that each of these types of knowledge can be stored hierarchically. Secondly, spatial reasoning (inference) procedures can transform or convert geographic knowledge from one of these forms to another, and/or up and down the organizational hierarchies within each type. Also, geographic knowledge can spontaneously "decay" to geographic facts by "forgetting" some properties: for example, someone might learn the capitals of European countries from maps, and later forget the locations within the countries, remembering only the enclosure relations.

The studies of judgements of relative location reported in this study, as well as in previous research by Stevens and Coupe (1978) and Tversky (1981) fall clearly into the configurational type of knowledge, best learned from maps. But the evidence from all of these studies strongly suggests that few if any of the subjects had access to accurate direct configurational knowledge of either relative or absolute locations of cities. Rather, the evidence suggests very strongly that most of the subjects in most of the tests inferred the requested spatial relations during testing.during testing.

For east-west judgements in eastern North America, results clearly suggest that inferences are based on an assumption that the east coast of the United States runs approximately north-south. Subjects probably can very quickly (and incorrectly!) judge that coastal cites are located to the east of inland cities, independently of latitude; it would be interesting to confirm this with reaction time studies. Buffalo is toward the western end of a reasonably large east-coast state; all test cities in other east-coast states were judged to be east of Buffalo by the majority of the subjects.

The east-west judgements for Latin America correctly rate Mexican and Central American cities as being west of Buffalo, perhaps by anchoring them more-or-less correctly to the western United States. Havana was incorrectly placed to the east of Buffalo, presumably by anchoring it to Florida, also inferred incorrectly to be east of Buffalo. The major discrepancy with fact is that all of the South American cities except Rio de Janero were judged to be west of Buffalo, when in fact they are east. This agrees with Tversky's (1981) data as well as the collection of counter-intuitive geographic facts reported earlier in this paper. Tversky's (1981) explanation that this misjudgement is a result of mistakenly assuming that South America is more-or-less aligned with North America seems compelling—certainly, I can suggest no alternative at this time. Tversky (1981) suggested a similar alignment hypothesis to account for

Europe being judged to be farther south (relative to eastern North America) that it is, a general cognitive 'error' that was further confirmed in this study. An alternative hypothesis that latitude is inferred from weather and climate seems plausible, but is difficult to separate from the alignment hypothesis.

6 Conclusions and Future Research

This study has confirmed several known systematic distortions in geographic knowledge of relative locations at continental and global scales, distortions that lead to incorrect judgements of relative locations and thus can produce 'counter-intuitive' facts. The new experimental design and data analysis procedures presented here have potential to facilitate further research on the topic. Similar experiments should be performed in other cities. Also, reaction time data for similar city-pair judgements of latitude and/or longitude may reveal useful data on the internal structure of mental representations of geographic information and on the spatial reasoning procedures used to make judgements about relative latitudes or longitudes of city pairs that may never have been explicitly considered previously in this regard by the subjects. Further research should involve repeating the procedures used in this study at other locations, and comparison of the resulting maps with those produced for the Buffalo subjects.

7 Acknowledgements

This paper is a part of Research Initiative #10, "Spatio-Temporal Reasoning and GIS", of the U. S. National Center for Geographic Information and Analysis (NCGIA), supported by a grant from the National Science Foundation (SES-88-10917); support by NSF is gratefully acknowledged. Thanks are also due to the many people from the electronic media who answered the original call for examples; to Michael Batty and Eric Williams for administering the questionnaire to their class; and to their students who completed the questionnaire.

8 References

Frank, A. U. (1991) Qualitative spatial reasoning about cardinal directions. **Proceedings, Auto Carto 10**, 148-167.

Freundschuh, S. M. (1991) Spatial Knowledge Acquisition of Urban Environments from Maps and Navigation Experience. Unpublished Ph.D. dissertation, Department of Geography, SUNY Buffalo.

Stevens, A. & Coupe, P. (1978). Distortions in judged spatial relations. **Cognitive Psychology**, 10, 422-437.

Tversky, B. (1981). Distortions in memory for maps. **Cognitive Psychology**, 13, 407-433.

Spatial-Linguistic Reasoning in LEI*

Shaun Futch, David N. Chin, Matthew McGranaghan, and Jinn-Guey Lay

University of Hawaii
Honolulu, HI 96822 USA

Abstract. In LEI, the Locality and Elevation Interpreter, lingusitic and geometric reasoning are joined to resolve natural language representations of locations as geodetic coordinates. The system uses the PAU (Parser and Understander) system to translate locality descriptions into semantic relations. The relations are then disambiguated by instantiation from USGS data bases. The project's goal is to replace operator intervention in locality interpretation.

1 Introduction

LEI, the Locality and Elevation Interpreter, is a software system for automated conversion of textual locality descriptions to systematic geodetic coordinates. It is being built to allow locational information, such as the locality descriptions associated with botanical collections, to be used in spatial analyses and to explore the human spatial reasoning reflected in those descriptions. It combines elements of both linguistic and spatial reasoning on the assumption that both are part of any communication about spatial arrangements.

Locations in geographic space are often described in terms of relations among objects (Lynch 1964, Downs and Stea 1977, Talmy 1983, 1987, 1989, Mark and Frank 1992). Some objects serve as landmarks, relating linguistic references to spatial positions. Other locations are specified by naming a landmark and then adding offsets and constraints to the description. Talmy (1983) found regularity in the types of objects which serve as the locative ground or landmarks.

Locality descriptions typically refer to political jurisdictions, place names, paths, and topography, but do not refer to geodetic coordinates. For example, one might find: *Oahu. Palolo Valley. Along the stream and up the northeast banks at elevations of 1100-1500 feet,* to indicate the site from which a botanical specimen was collected. In this description, two proper place names fix the place to a specific valley on a specific island, References to landscape elements, elevations, and the relations bewteen these and the site further constrain the location within the valley, and the intersection of these relations can be interpreted as the locus of the site.

The relations used to specify relative positions have been studied by a number of authors, several of whom have deduced minimal sets of terms purported to describe all possible spatial relations two objects might share. Mark and others (1988) discussed approaches to identifying a sufficient set of spatial relations. Freeman (1975) suggested that there are thirteen spatial relations for objects in an image: *left of, right of, beside, above, below, behind, before (in front of), near, far, touching, between, inside, outside.* Peuquet and Zhan (1987) suggested that the four cardinal directions (*north, south, east* and *west*) should be added for geographic relations. Herskovits (1986) indicates that relatively few schema, or prototypical relations, are used in locative descriptions. Each of these few prototypical relations is "stretched" for use in any particular instance, and reasoning based on the prototypical situation is tempered by context. She concentrated on the spatial prepositions *on, at* and *in.*

The recognition that linguistic representations of spatial realtions are often ambiguous and that natural languge allows communication inspite of this ambiguity is central to Herskovits' thesis, but the difficulty in using such representations to support spatial analysis is a well-known theme in several literatures. LEI reduces ambiguity through a combination of linguistic and spatial reasoning. Location descriptions are converted to representations which capture the central possible semantic interpretations. These representations are then resolved against cartographic databases to produce plausible coordinates for the place refered to by the description.

2 LEI

When people communicate about spatial locations, they use knowledge of both language and spatial relations to discern meaning. LEI attempts to use a similar strategy for understanding locality descriptions. The syntactic and semantic content of a description is considered and possible interpretations are verified against a database of geographic facts or beliefs. PAU, the Parser and Understander is the engine for parsing each description and buidling a schematic representation of its meaning. It scans locality descriptions for patterns indicating locative prepositional phrases, specified in PPI the Prepositional Phrase Interpreter, and returns sketches of their meanings. A Geographical Reasoner tests whether the relations in those sketches hold among objects represented in cartographic data sets.

The LEI project uses three US Geological Survey digital cartographic data bases as its geographic knowledge store. GNIS, the Geographic Names Information System provides links between the names of entities noted on USGS Topographic Quadrangles, their geodetic positions, and a categorization into one of 62 feature classes. GNIS exists as a single data file for the entire state. Digital Line Graph (DLG) data, provide planimetirc postions of hydrography, political and administrative boundaries, and roads, trails and transmission lines. These features are characterized into hierarchical categories. Elevations and topographic configurtations are derived from USGS Digital Elevation Models, DEMs. DLG and DEM data are organized as separate data layers, aligned to 7.5 minute quadrangles. These data sets are available for each of the major Hawaiian Islands and for nearly all of the US mainland.

2.1 Parser and Understander

PAU[1], the Parser and Understander (Chin 1992), performs linguistic processing to derive possible meanings of location descriptions. PAU is an all-paths, chart-based, unification parser. It scans it's input of English words from left to right and builds a chart (Kay, 1973) data structure to represent the course of the parse.

The first component of PAU analyzes the input words for morphology and performs spelling correction. The result is a series of syntactic instances corresponding to each word. For example, the word *in* is analyzed as an instance of the syntactic category `Prep` with the feature, `word = in`. Polysemy (multiple meanings for the same word) is allowed and results in more than one syntactic instance for an input word. Each syntactic instance is entered from left to right as a constituent in PAU's chart. Each time an instance is added to the chart, PAU looks for applicable grammar rules based on the syntactic category and semantics (meaning) of the instance.

The grammar rules for a domain guide PAU's interpretation of its input. A rule might, for instance, specify that a *preposition* followed by a *noun-phrase* is a *prepositional-phrase*. When PAU encounters a *preposition* in its input, it adds the rule as an active edge in the parse chart and continues with its input. If it next encounters a *noun-phrase*, then the rule is triggered and a *prepositional-phrase* is added to the chart as a new constituent. The new constituent may in turn activate new rules and/or extend or complete previous active edges (which represent other incomplete rules). In general, this recursive application of rules continues until no more new rules can be activated or old rule components matched. PPI, described below is a collection of such rules for locative prepositional phrases.

Matching of rule components to chart constituents is based on three factors: First, the syntactic category of the constituent must be the same as or more specific than the syntactic category of the rule component. Second, the features of the constituent must have the same or more specific values as the features of the component. Third, if there are any Unify relations emanating from the component, then the meaning of the component, which is specified at the opposite end of the Unify relation, must match the meaning of the constituent. That is, the category of the meaning of the constituent must be the same as or more specific than that of the component, the features of the constituent must have the same or more specific values as those of the component, and any relations that are common to both the constituent's meaning and the component's meaning must also match.

Because PAU combines syntactic parsing and semantic understanding in one integrated process, PAU can use semantics early in the parse to reject semantically anomalous parses. PAU is fully implemented in Common LISP and runs in real time (less than 1/2 second processing time for typical sentences) on a Sun sparcstation 2 running Franz Inc.'s Allegro CL.

2.2 Prepositional Phrase Interpreter

The Prepositional Phrase Interpreter (PPI) is a set of rules used by PAU to translate English prepositional phrases into relations that can be found and tested by the geographic reasoner. Locality descriptions consist almost entirely of actual or implied prepositional phrases. A typical location description contains several prepositional phrases and thus results in several relations. The goal of PPI is to unify each of these prepositional phrases with possible relations which can be asserted to the geometric reasoner. PPI currently handles the locative prepositions shown in Table 1 by mapping them onto a set of relations. The realtions that PPI unerstands are very much in flux as we attempt to find an appropriate balance an approach to interpreting prepositions. This set of locative relations covers essentially all of the locative prepositions in the 1340 locality descriptions with which we are currently working.

Table 1. Prepositions recognized by PPI.

Prepositions	Relations	Properties - Feature_Types
Above	At_elevation	greater elevation
Adjacent to	Adjacent_to	
Adjacent to	Near	
Along	Near	linear feature
Among	Within	between several objects
Around	Near	
At	Within	
At	Near	
At	At_elevation	specified elevation
(In) Back of	Beyond	oriented object/observer
Behind	Beyond	oriented object/observer
Below	At_elevation	lower elevation
Beside	Adjacent_to	oriented object/observer
Between	Within	two ground objects
Beyond	Beyond	oriented object/observer
By	Near	
Down	Down	lower elevation and path
East of	East_of	
From	From	oriented object/observer
(In) Front of	Front_of	oriented object/observer
In	Within	
Inside	Within	
Into	Within	
Left of	Left_of	
Near	Near	
Next to	Adjacent_to	
North of	North_of	
On	Within	
On	Adjacent_to	

On top of	Within	
Outside	Without	
Right of	Right_of	
South of	South_of	
To	Toward	oriented object/observer
Up	At_elevation	greater elevation and path
West of	West_of	

Our current thinking is that PPI should attempt to classify prepositional relations according to the type and/or form of ground object that should accompany the preposition, according to whether the spatial reference frame is relative to an object in the landscape, or the observer, and according to whether the relation implies (fictive) motion (along a path) or a fixed point in space. The most useful case is that in which the preposition indicates a relation to some object that can be uniquely identified and positioned. Somewhat less useful is that the form or type of a ground object is known, and a point in the area is also known.

The most common relationships involve containment or positional equivalence. These are topological in nature and include the relations: *At, Within, Adjacent_to, Along, Between* and *Among*. A very common situation is for a description to simply name an area or a physical feature, without explicitly indicating a relation. PPI currently treats this case as an *At* relation. *Within* indicates that the ground object should be conceptualized as an area, whereas *Adjacent_to* and *At* can have punctiform, linear, areal, or network features as the ground object. *Between* requires two ground objects and *Among* suggests several.

The relations *Above, Below, North_of, South_of, East_of,* and*West_of,* indicate that the figure position (the collection site) lies in the stated direction from the ground object. The direction of the offset is given relative to the Earth. PPI curently treats *Northeast of* as the conjuction of *North_of* and *East_of.* Other metric relations include *near* and *(distance) from.* These give relative distances of the figure object from the ground object. Several of these (almost) metric relations are open-ended in that they do not impose limits on the direction or distance between ground and figure. PPI need not deal with this but the geographic reasoner (see below) must.

Other descriptions describe location relationships from the viewpoint of an observer who may be either stationary or moving along a path, or from the viewpoint of a ground object which has a cannonical orientation.. *In_front_of, In_Back_of, Beyond, Left_of,* and *Right_of* depend on an orientation for the observer or a ground object . These types of relations arise when a locality description takes the form of a sequence of steps to make to reach a site. They relatively infrequently in our sample botanical locality descriptions.

Since a single English preposition may have several meanings depending on the context, there is not always a one-to-one correspondence between a preposition and the location relations previously described. This notion was discussed by

Herskovits (1987). To illustrate, *at* seems to have different meanings in the following two phrases:

at 750-900 ft.
at the head of the valley

In terms of the relations previously described, the first description would be mapped to the *At_elevation* relation. The second description would be mapped to the Within relation. But the phrase *head of* contains more information which should be used in deciding the location. Words and phrases which modify basic relations are treated as properties of the relation, one such property is `feature_type`.

`Feature_type` is a semantic property inherent to some prepositions. For example, the preposition *along* usually indicates a linear object such as a stream or a trail. This is coded by requiring the ground object to have a `feature_type linear`. *Above* and *below* have an `elevation` that indicates a height. PPI can use the `feature_type` to reduce ambiguity when examining GNIS for matching names.

Successful implementation of PPI involves creating various PAU grammar rules. With a predefined set of prepositions, prepositional relations, a mechanism to detect feature_types, and PAU grammatical patterns in place, the PPI is equipped to successfully process any prepositional phrase that indicates location.

The following illustrates the process of parsing the prepositional phrase *along rocky Aiea* according to a current PPI rule. When *along* is encountered, it is recognized as a preposition that unifies with the relation *Adjacent_to*. It also has the `feature_type Linear`. It triggers PAU to open the `PP-pat` pattern. The `Prepref` of this pattern is unified with the *Adjacent_to* relation. The next word encountered is *rocky*. This is identified by PAU as an adjective, and since one definition of a noun phrase (`NPhrase`) has components `Adjective` and `Noun`, a `NPhrase` pattern is opened. When the next word *Aiea* is encountered, it is recognized as a `noun`. The noun phrase pattern is fulfilled and closed, and its output is an object, Aiea, with certain features, including Rocky. Since Aiea is both a trail and a populated place according to the GNIS data base, two objects are passed back to the NPhrase entity in PP-pat, one with the `feature Linear` and the other with the `feature PopulatedPlace`. LEI then tries to unify both of these objects with Object2, the sink object of the Prepref. Since *along* maps to the relation *Adjacent_to* with `feature Linear`, only *Aiea Trail* will successfully unify. The final interpretation of the phrase is a relation of class *Adjacent_to* with a `sink object Aiea`, which in turn has the `feature_type Linear`. The source object is the unknown location at which the plant sample was collected.

Once a prepositional phrase has been successfully processed, LEI looks for more phrases. When the end of the line is encountered, all of the output relations are passed to the spatial reasoning portion of LEI.

2.3 Geographic Reasoner

The Geographic Reasoner (GR) component of LEI is currently under development. As initially conceived, GR relies heavily on overlay operations to resolve the spatial meaning of a locality description. Formalisms for the spatial aspect of these operations have been described by Egenhofer and Herring (undated ms). GR currently concentrates on relations among polygons as PAU considers all objects to be (possibly degenerate) polygons in specifying relations. GR first finds objects in the cartographic databases to satisfy the constraints on names, feature types, and rough proximity required by each relation found by PAU. The intersection of the coordinates for those features are returned as the spatial meaning of the locality description.

The GR attempts to instantiate relations between objects generated by PAU. Given a relation and the name of a ground object, GR searches the USGS databases for the named object and if it is found retrieves its coordinates, feature class and map sheet identifiers. Depending on the relation from PAU, the found coordinates maybe translated into a different spatial expression. For the*Within* relation the polygon itself is used. For the *Near* relation, a buffer is created around the object. For *Adjacent_to* a buffer-ring excluding the object is generated. If the site's elevation has been constrained, one or more polygons that include the relevant elevation ranges are created from the DEM data.

References to valleys and mountains as discrete terrain units are common in the locality descriptions but are not objects in the cartographic data sets. In the current implementation, we pre-compute the limits of these topographic features and store them as polygons in DLG format. The feature outline is then used as a constraint in the overlay process. This operation is currently done in a shell script using the GRASS GIS, but a better integrated approach is planned.

It is common also to refer to terrain features by their type but not specify a proper name (*along the stream* as opposed to *along Manoa Stream*). In this case, PAU will specify a ground object of a given type but with an unknown name. Given any named feature (most locality descriptions include the name of a nearby populated place) as a part of PAU's output, GR looks near the named object for ground objects of the correct type to use as the un-named objects.

For the metric relations involving distances and directions, GR will generate polygons based on metric offsets from ground objects, making assumptions about under-specified parameters. *Near* is handled as a buffer of limited width. Specific distances can be calculated either along geographic paths or as air distances. As a first approximation, unspecified distances are assumed to be no more than half the distance between the ground object and the nearest object of the same type. Techniques such as those of Peuquet and Zhan (1987) can be employed to convert directional relationships into polygonal areas. When no direction is specified a circular area is assumed. We are experimenting with different strategies for determining reasonable default assumptions for under-specified metric relations.

3 Discussion and Future Work

Understanding locality descriptions is a fairly constrained domain for a language understanding system. As a result we have met some limited success in our attempts and anticipate more. PAU's breadth-first approach to resolving multiple possible interpretations is proving superior to depth-first approaches for parsing in the face of the malleable way that place and relation names are used. PPI works for a number of prepositions in our sample and is at the stage that we can tinker with its rules to assess their robustness. PAU is generating the related constraints. The GR is still in very early development.

LEI uses USGS digital cartographic data as its source of name, feature_type and coordinate information for geographic entities. It was our initial hope that these data would be adequate in their raw form. However, considerable pre-processing is required to relate the information in the GNIS, DLG and DEM data. Entities in these data sets are not named directly, names are not attached to objects but rather to map coordinates that may or may not match those for related objects. The need to build associations of names in GNIS with spatial representations in DLG and DEM requires user intervention and has taken longer than anticipated.

Further, in USGS data, valleys and mountains do not exist as circumscribed polygons about which to reason. Several heuristics for delineating these features have been tried: region growing for topographic features in raster models; Theissen polygon modeling of named features of various classes; and ridge and valley line extraction in raster and TIN representations.

Of greater significance for linguistic processing is the lack of a common and consistent scheme for encoding the semantic properties of objects in the data sets. GNIS uses sixty-two feature class categories while the DLG data have more than two hundred combinations of major and minor attribute codes. There is no accepted direct mapping between these different categorizations.

Our group continues to debate the adequacy and constituents of the set of relationships recognized by PAU and PPI. This is made more complex by the ability to trade-off spatial reasoning against linguistic reasoning. Over the next fifteen months we will be working to establish the most useful balance between linguistic and spatial reasoning strategies for interpreting locality descriptions.

Notes

* Support from NSF Grant BSR-9019041 is gratefully acknowledged.

1 *Lei* and *Pau* are Hawaiian words for "flower garland" and "finished", respectively.

References

Adams, R. F., 1974, "Computer Graphics Plotting and Mapping of Data in Systematics", Taxon, 23, 53-70.

Allkin, R., and Bisby, F. A. (eds) 1984, Databases in Systematics, Academic Press, New York.

Brenan, J. P. M, Ross, R., and Williams, J.T. (eds), 1975 Computers in Botanical Collections, Plenum Press, New York.

Chin, David N., 1992, PAU: Parsing and Understanding with Iniform Syntactic, Semantic, and Idiomatic Representations, To appear in Computational Intelligence, vol. 8, no. 3, 1992.

Egenhofer, M. J., and Herring, J. R., (undated) Categorizing Binary Topological Relationships Between Regions, Lines, and Points in Geographic Databases, manuscript.

Frank, A., Palmer, B., and Robinson, V., 1986, "Formal Methods the for Accurate Definition of Some Fundamental Terms in Physical Geography", Proceedings: Second International Symposium on Spatial data Handling, July 5-10, Seattle, Washington, pp. 583-599.

Freeman, John, 1975, "The Modeling of Spatial Relations", Computer Graphics and Image Processing, vol. 4, pp. 156-171.

Herskovits, Annette, 1986, Language and Cognition, Cambridge University Press, New York.

Heywood, V.H., Moore, D.M. (eds), 1984, Current Concepts in Plant Taxonomy, Academic Press, New York.

Kay, M. 1973. The MIND System. In Natural Language Processing, Edited by R. Rustin. Algorithmics Press, New York, NY, pp. 155-188.

Lynch, Kevin, 1964, The Image of the City, M.I.T. Press, Cambridge, Mass.

Mark, David M. and Frank, Andrew, 1989, "Concepts of Space and Spatial Language", Proceedings of Auto-Carto 9, Baltimore, MD 2-7 April 1989, pp. 538-556.

Mark, D.M., 1988, (editor and compiler) "Cognitive and Linguistic Aspects of Geographic Space: Report on a Workshop", June 11-12, NCGIA, SUNY-Buffalo.

Mark , D. M. and Frank, A. U. (eds), 1992, Cognitive and Linguistic Representations of Geographic Space, Klewer Academic Press.

Mark, D.M., Frank, A.U., Egenhofer, M.J., Freundschuh, S.M., McGranaghan, M., and White, R.M., 1989, (compilers and editors), "Languages of Spatial Relations: Initiative Two Specialist Meeting Report", Technical Paper 89-2, NCGIA, University of California, Santa Barbara, CA.

McGranaghan, M, 1988, "Are Mental Manipulations of Surfaces Done in Language or Image Space", in D.M. Mark, ed. Cognitive and Linguistic Aspects of Geographic Space.

McGranaghan, M., and Wester, L., 1988, "Prototyping an Herbarium Collection Mapping System", Technical Papers: 1988 ACSM-ASPRS Annual Convention: GIS, v.5, pp. 232-238.

McGranaghan, M., 1989a, "Context-Free Recursive-Descent Parsing of Location Descriptive Text", Proceedings of Auto-Carto 9, Baltimore, MD, April 2-7, pp 580-587.

McGranaghan, M., 1989b, "Incorporating Bio-Localities in a GIS", Proceedings of GIS/LIS '89, 26-30 November 1989, Orlando, FL.

O'Callaghan, J., Mark, D., 1986, "The Extraction of Drainage Networks from Digital Elevation data", Computer Vision, Graphics and Image Processing, v. 28, pp. 323-344.

Peuquet, Donna J. and Zhan Ci-Xiang, 1987, "An Algorithm to Determine the Directional Relationship Between Arbitrarily-Shaped Polygons in the Plane", Pattern Recognition, vol. 20, pp. 65-74.

Sullivan, J., 1989, "Design Criteria for a Plant Geographic Information System", from "FLORA ONLINE" (ISSN 0892-9106) an electronic publication of TAXACOM, The Clinton Herbarium, Buffalo Museum of Science. Buffalo , NY 14211

Talmy, L., 1988, "Cognitive and Linguistic Aspects of Space", Presentation at a two day workshop, June 11-12, 1988, State University of New York at Buffalo.

Talmy, L. 1987, "The Relation of Grammar to Cognition" in B. Rudzka-Ostyn (ed) Topics in Cognitve Linguistics, John Benjamins Publishing, Philadelphia.

Talmy, L., 1983, "How Language Structures Space" in H. Pick and L. Acredolo (eds.) Spatial Orientation: Theory, Research, and Application, New York, Plenum Press.

US Geological Survey, 1987, "Geographic Names Information System", National Mapping Program Technical Instructions Data Users Guide 6, USGS, Reston, VA.

User models and information theory in the design of a query interface for GIS

Mikko Lindholm Tapani Sarjakoski

Finnish Geodetic Institute
Ilmalankatu 1 A
SF-00240 Helsinki
FINLAND

Abstract The design of user interfaces has lacked a firm theoretical foundation. A solid user interface theory would be particularily helpful in complex systems, such as GIS. Information theory and user modelling are presented here as a promising approach to building such a theory. Their applicability is considered in the context of querying a geographical database. Different theories of information are reviewed and some misunderstandings are corrected. Any communication can be examined on three different levels: syntactic, semantic and pragmatic. The syntactic information of a message is its relative frequency within language without any concern for the meaning of the message. The semantic information content of a message is defined as how many different states of the universe distinguishable in the language it excludes logically. The pragmatic information is the personal meaning of the message to the sender and the receiver. User modelling methodology is presented as a way to handle pragmatic information. Research into user models is reviewed and the potential of GIS applications and further study are investigated.

1 Introduction

Designing easily manageable and conceptually clear user interfaces to handle the complexity of the data and multiplicity of available operations in geographical information systems (GIS) has become an important topic of research in recent years. As the use of GIS technology spreads in society, it is becoming available to an increasingly large number of non-experts. Such people have considerable difficulty in understanding the inherent logic of the applications and memorizing all the operations needed. Especially applications designed for ordinary people, such as computer atlases and public information stands at offices, exhibitions and stations, must have a very clear and simple user interface without restricting the users unnecessarily.

In our research into hypermedia atlases for microcomputers (Lindholm, 1991), we have become acutely aware of the lack of any comprehensive theory for user interface design. Many design decisions have to be made on an insecure basis and learned through trial and error. We have set out to look for methods and formalisms which could give more rigour to user interface design.

The whole subject of user interface design for GIS applications is too wide to be covered completely in this presentation. Instead, we will concentrate on the query situation and ignore the user interface aspects of data input, maintenance and manipulation. On the most general level, the goal of querying a geographical database is to bring information from the database to the user's consciousness. It is from this very basic level that we think the development of user interfaces should start.

The aim of this presentation is to review the possibilities that different branches of information and communication theory together with techniques for user modelling offer as a basis for user interface research and design in GIS applications. At the same time, we want to correct some misinterpretations and misunderstandings concerning the applicability of information theory in a geographic/cartographic context.

2 Language and information

Niiniluoto (1990) has divided the concept of information into physical and linguistic information. Physical information refers to the organization level or complexity of material systems. When we say: "The more complex a DNA molecyle is, the more it contains information," we think of information in the physical sense. Linguistic information is related to communication. "The linguistic concept of information is based on the assumption that information has to have a *carrier*, i.e. a material object, event or process, which is able in certain circumstances to transmit and store *messages*. In general, information carriers can be called *signs* and systems of signs can be called *languages*" (Niiniluoto, 1990: 23).

2.1 Language

For our purposes, language is loosely defined as a set of signs – a vocabulary – and a set of rules – a grammar – governing the use of the signs. Thus a sentence may be defined as any collection of members of the vocabulary, which obeys the rules of the grammar. A sign has a form, which can be a word, a graphical or map symbol, etc., and a basic meaning, what the sign stands for. In a similar fashion, the grammar has a syntax which defines all the sentences allowed, while the semantics of the grammar define how each sign is to be interpreted in a given sentence or set of sentences.

A geographical information system may be seen as consisting of the languages of the user interface and the database. The vocabulary of a database language is the data items stored in it, and the grammar is the conceptual schema of the database coded as a data dictionary. The user interface consists of a language for input and a language for output. The input language is the means of transmitting user's commands to the database management system and the output language is the way of presenting of the database contents to the user.

The use of a GIS can be likened to the use of theory in science. According to Harvey (1969), a scientific theory consists of a set of primitive concepts and axioms from which all other concepts and statements are derived using some formal calculus or language, e.g. logic, probability theory or geometry. In addition to this, theory contains a text which maps the empirical observations to the concepts and statements of the theory and back again. In the abstract form of theory, the observations can be manipulated and new observations predicted. A GIS application is a theory of a certain part of the Earth's surface. The measurements from the object area are fed into the database, which acts as an abstract calculus for manipulating the data. Using this formal and internally consistent language new concepts and relationships may be derived. The user interface acts as the 'text' of this theory, forming a mapping between the real world experiences of the user and the abstract language. So the user interface has to work as an intermediate language between the fully formal abstract language of the database and the empirical unformal language of the user.

In this presentation, we will concentrate on the output language, i.e. the mapping of sentences from the abstract database language to a language comprehensible to the user. Now, what is this language or languages? In databases containing only alphanumeric data it is often some kind of forms-based display, where the data is presented in a tabular form. Statistical data is often better communicated visually using graphs, etc. GIS interfaces also use these when appropriate, but the most common way of presenting data in the geographical space is, of course, the map. It is important to remember, however, that the map is not the only way of presenting spatial data. Digitized photographs, sounds and video can also be used. Furthermore, the map does not have to be static. Animation is an efficient way of presenting change over time. It is important to note, that the output language and map are not synonyms. Maps are used in the sequel only as an example of the output language.

The issue, whether maps can be thought of as a form of language has been a subject of keen debate (Robinson & Petchenick, 1976; Board, 1981; Keates, 1982; Head, 1984; Andrews, 1990). To argue whether maps are or are not a language is useless, because it depends on our definition of language. If we define a language as above to be a set of signs and a set of rules governing their use and interpretation, then maps are, indeed, a language. In contrast to natural languages, in which sentences are formed and interpreted on the basis of sequence, the sentences of a map language are formed of the two-dimensional geometrical properties and spatial combinations of signs.

The form and basic meaning of a map symbol is defined in the legend. Thus each symbol in the legend can be compared to a word in a natural language. When put on the map, the map symbol changes into a sentence. A point symbol for a building says: "There is a building here." A 50 metre contour says: "The points on this line are 50 metres above sea level." Many contours together may be thought of as a compound statement, describing a hill, for instance. Andrews (1990) has taken this kind of analysis much further.

The idea of user interface as a language has been presented earlier for instance by Shneiderman (1987). In his theory, two levels in the user's knowledge of the application are distinguished, semantic and syntactic. Foley et al. (1990) developed a four-level model for the design of the output and input languages. The design begins on conceptual level, in which the central concepts and logic of operation of the application are defined. On the semantic level, the meaning of all the needed operations are defined. On the syntactic level, the form of each operation is described in detail. Lastly, on the lexical level, the actual implementation of each operation within the hardware and software is designed. Despite their similar names, these levels do not match precisely the levels of information presented in section 2.3, but they are parallel.

2.2 Communication system

Figure 1 represents the communication system first introduced in the information theory of Shannon (Shannon & Weaver, 1949). The sender[1] codes his message to a signal using some coding language. The signal is then sent to the communication channel. The receiver gets the signal, decodes it, and receives the message. In the channel, there may be noise which blurs the signal and is the cause of errors in communication.

In Shannon's model, information is treated syntactically (see below), i.e. with no reference to the semantic meaning of signals. The encoding and decoding processes are reversible mappings and the semantic information contents of the message do not change. If the signal comes through the channel unchanged, the message is transmitted correctly.

When talking about communication in the use of a GIS application, we assume the existence of a sender, be it the user himself or someone else, who has geographical data which he wants to communicate to others. He codes it into the form of a database. When the user – the receiver of the message – operates the application, the data, or signal, is decoded into the output language. The user receives the signal in the output and decodes this again to his internal mental representation.

[1] Shannon talks about 'source' and 'destination', but in the case of human communication 'sender' and 'receiver' might indicate their roles better.

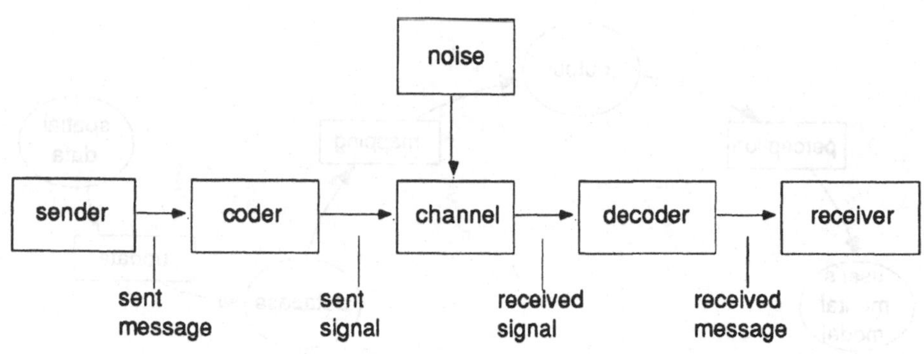

Figure 1. Communication system in the classical Shannon information theory.

A message is here understood as a sign, sentence or set of sentences. The channel is the computer system and the application software. Noise is anything which disturbs the message. Shannon theory concerns the removal of syntactic noise. In cartographic communication the main sources of disturbance in the message are the encoding and decoding processes. At least three sources of error in the cartographic communication system may be recognized. Firstly, the message may be encoded incorrectly; the cartographer uses map symbols erroneously. Secondly, the message may be decoded incorrectly; the reader does not understand map symbology. Thirdly, the cartographic language may not be suitable for expressing the phenomenon of interest. Carnap and Bar-Hillel (1952) have called such disturbances semantic noise.

A sketch of a communication system in a GIS query session is presented in Figure 2. The system is here seen as consisting of information sets coded in some language[2], and of the processes of translation between these languages. The two main parts are the user communicating with the database management system (DBMS). The human user can receive messages through the process of perception, mainly by seeing and hearing, and send messages through the process of physical action, e.g. by pressing the keys on the keyboard or moving the mouse. The DBMS can receive messages as queries and send messages via the process of mapping the result of the queries to the output language. 'Mapping' does not necessarily mean here producing geographical maps, but it is used in a more general, mathematical way, as a function from one set to another. The input and output languages act as common ground for the user and the DBMS, whose message sending and receiving methods are not otherwise compatible. Via the input the user can also affect the mapping process, i.e. how the data is to be displayed: as a map or a table, for instance. Because we are modelling the query situation, the creation and maintenance of the database are presented as happening outside the user's control.

[2] It can even be argued that no information can exist without coding.

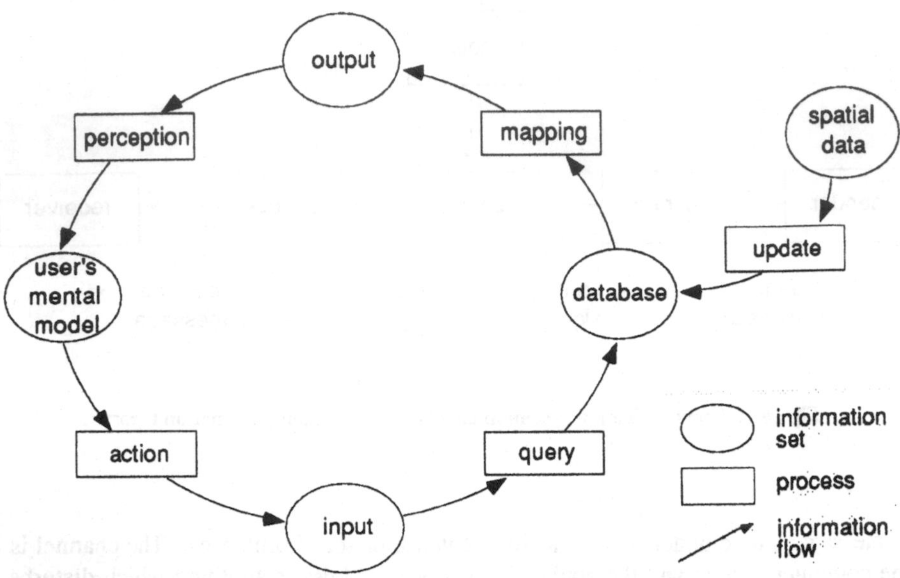

Figure 2. The communication system in a GIS query interface. The ovals represent information sets coded in some language, the rectangles represent processes of translation from one language to another, and the arrows indicate the flow of information or messages.

The study of processes of perception and action, which are the interfaces to the human user, is mostly the concern of ergonomics. The design of efficient query processes comes closest to the field of database theory. In this presentation, we are mainly dealing with the process of mapping information from the database to the output language. This has traditionally been the subject of cartography. The views presented here should nevertheless apply to the other three translations.

There are quite a few theories of cartographic communication, of which Board (1981) gives a good overview. However, most of these come roughly in the form: reality → cartographer → map → receiver. Communication is seen as unidirectional. The role of feedback from receiver to sender is unclear. In a GIS environment, on the other hand, it is very easy for the user to change the contents or the looks of the output, and the communication becomes circular, as in Figure 2.

MacEahren and Ganter have criticized the "cartography as a communication science" paradigm: "The most basic tenet of the cartographic communication model is that the goal of cartography is to effectively communicate a particular message. There is an assumption not only that the message is *known*, but that there is an *optimal* map for each message, and our objective as cartographers is to identify it" (MacEahren & Ganter, 1990: 65). Obviously they are talking about message in the pragmatic sense (see below). In this paper, the word 'message' is more neutral and less goal oriented in nature. In a query interface for GIS, we may ask whether there can be any specific intention on the part of the sender. The primus motor of all activity is the user, who gives commands to the DBMS. Entertainment aside, why would he use the system if he already possessed all the information stored in the database? Even in an educational application, if the user is given any choice in the manipulation and display of data, no precise purpose of the message can be identified, even though on a general level the aim is to supply knowledge about the phenomena of interest.

2.3 Types of information

Niiniluoto (1990) has written an excellent presentation on the different types of information. Unfortunately, it is in Finnish and thus unavailable to most readers of this paper. This section is based on his outline, with considerations of applicability in a GIS environment added. As we are here dealing with the linguistic concept of information, the information contained in a message can be divided into three common linguistic aspects or levels: syntactic, semantic and pragmatic.

Syntactic information. In Shannon's statistical communication theory (Shannon & Weaver, 1949) information is considered to consist only of messages to be transmitted without any interpretation. If $G=\{x_1,x_2,...x_n\}$ is a set of messages, and their probabilities of appearing in the communication system are $\{p_1,p_2,...p_n\}$, the one x_i which has the lowest probability p_i has the highest information content. The most unexpected message tells us most.

The Shannon entropy is a value that may be calculated for a random message variable X if the probabilities of the different message choices are known:

$$H(X) = H(p_1,p_2,...p_n) = -\sum_{i=1}^{n} p_i \log_2 p_i$$

H(X) tells us how much uncertainty the variable X has on average and, conversely, how much uncertainty is removed, when the value of X is known. H(X) is zero when the value of X is certain, or $p_i=1$ for some x_i. H(X) is at its maximum when all the messages have equal probability.

Entropy is thus a measure of the amount of information in a message. The higher the entropy of a language, the higher is its informativeness, because the more uncertain the receiver is about which message is to come next. When the message comes, its information amount is greater in a high entropy language than in lower entropy languages, because it relieves us from a greater uncertainty.

The joint entropy of two variables is defined as

$$H(X,Y) = -\sum_{i=1}^{n} \sum_{j=1}^{m} \pi_{ij} \log \pi_{ij},$$

where π_{ij} is the probability of x_i and y_j occurring together: $\pi_{ij} = P(X=x_i \ \& \ Y=y_j)$. Correspondingly, the entropy of Y on the condition X is

$$H(Y \mid X) = -\sum_{i=1}^{n} \sum_{j=1}^{m} \pi_{ij} \log q_{j/i}$$

which tells us the average uncertainty of Y when we know the value of X. If X and Y are probabilistically independent, the entropy of Y is not reduced. If X=Y, then $H(Y|X) = H(Y|Y) = 0$. The measure of transmitted information $I(Y|X)$ tells us how much information about Y is transmitted by X

$$I(Y \mid X) = H(Y) - H(Y \mid X) = -\sum_{i=1}^{n} \sum_{j=1}^{m} \pi_{ij} \log (q_j/q_{j/i}).$$

The relative entropy of a language is the ratio of the actual entropy to the maximum entropy possible with the same set of signs. One minus relative entropy is the redundancy of the language. Thus the redundancy is caused by the differences in the probabilities of signs. Shannon has estimated that the redundancy of ordinary English is about 50% (Shannon & Weaver, 1949). This means that 50% of the usage of the language is determined by the statistical structure of the language and 50% is chosen freely by the user. Redundancy is the part of the language which could be omitted without loss in the informativity of the language. On the other hand, redundancy clarifies the message. If the signal is blurred by noise, redundancy helps to reconstruct the original message. Colour-coding or patterning different areas on the display is redundant, because the areas may be represented with their borderlines. This form of symbolization does not yield any new information. Nevertheless, such redundancy is useful, because it reduces the possibility of confusing areas of different types.

Redundancy in the message may also be ergonomically wiser. If a GIS user would like to see, for instance, all farms which are no more than 10 metres higher than the mean level of a river, i.e. farms on the floodplain, the only information necessary is shown in Figure 3a. This kind of message transmitting is efficient, but the display is crude and unpleasant. It also omits the context, which may be of interest, even if not explicitly requested. Therefore, some amount of redundant information in the message is usually needed, as in Figure 3b. From a syntactic point of view, the redundant information in Figure 3b could be anything, even pure nonsense. It is only semantic or pragmatic interpretation which recognizes the redundant signs in Figure 3b as roads and contours.

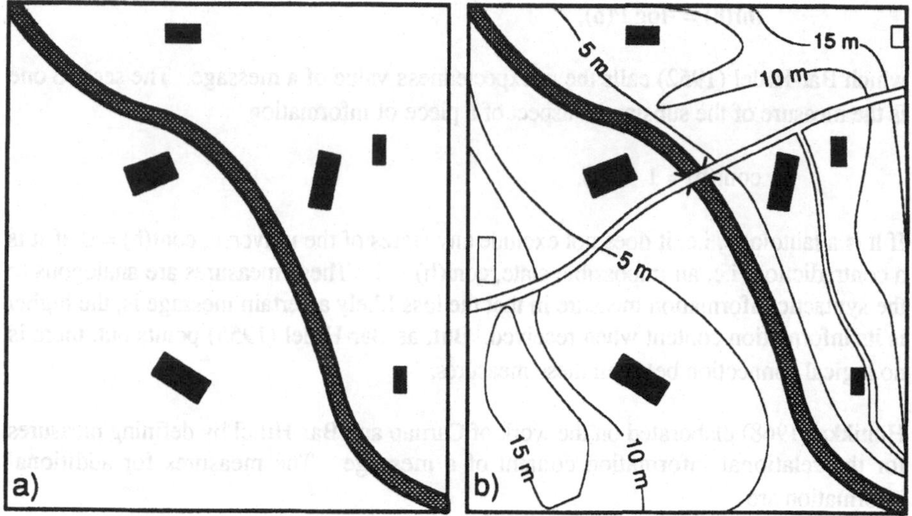

Figure 3. a) The result of a query when only those things which were explicitly requested are shown. b) The result of the same query when some redundant information is added to the display.

The Shannon information theory makes reference only to the relative frequency of signs. It has nothing to do with the form or meaning of the signs. Hence, this concept of information can be termed syntactic. One message in isolation does not have any information. Its information is defined only in relation to the frequency distribution of all possible messages.

Semantic information. Entropy, of course, cannot be the only measure of information of a message. Bar-Hillel (1955) gives as an example two sentences: "The enemy attacked at dawn." and "The enemy attacked in batallion strength at 5:30 AM." If the first message is more rare than the second one, then in a syntactic sense it conveys more information. But at the level of meaning, the second message is clearly more informative.

Carnap and Bar-Hillel (1952) developed a theory of semantic information. In this theory the semantic content of a sentence is defined as how many different states of the universe distinguishable in the language it excludes logically. We can think of h as a sentence in a language used to form state descriptions of the universe. The logical probability of h, P(h), is defined as a sum of probabilities of the states of the universe which are not excluded by h. The sum of all the probabilities of the states of the universe is 1. Now two measures of information are defined. The first one is a logarithm as in Shannon theory

$$\text{inf}(h) = -\log P(h),$$

which Bar-Hillel (1952) calls the unexpectedness value of a message. The second one is the measure of the substantial aspect of a piece of information

$$\text{cont}(h) = 1 - P(h).$$

If h is a tautology, i.e. it does not exclude any states of the universe, cont(h) = 0, if it is a contradiction, i.e. an impossible state, cont(h) = 1. These measures are analogous to the syntactic information measure in that the less likely a certain message is, the higher is its information content when received. But, as Bar-Hillel (1955) points out, there is no logical connection between these measures.

Hintikka (1968) elaborated on the work of Carnap and Bar-Hillel by defining measures for the relational information content of a message. The measures for additional information are

$$\text{inf}_{add}(h \mid e) = \text{inf}(h \,\&\, e) - \text{inf}(e)$$

$$\text{cont}_{add}(h \mid e) = \text{cont}(h \,\&\, e) - \text{cont}(e).$$

These measures tell us how much new information we get from h after knowing e. Measures for conditional information are defined as

$$\text{inf}_{cond}(h \mid e) = -\log P(h \mid e)$$

$$\text{cont}_{cond}(h \mid e) = 1 - P(h \mid e),$$

and they tell us what the information amount of h is if we know that e is true. The amount of transmitted information, i.e. how much information about the subject matter of h is conveyed by e, can be calculated in three different ways:

$$\text{inf}(h) - \text{inf}(h \mid e)$$

$$\text{cont}(h) - \text{cont}_{add}(h \mid e)$$

$$\text{cont}(h) - \text{cont}_{cond}(h \mid e).$$

These measures are parallels to Shannon's formula $I(Y|X)$. For instance inf(h) - inf(h|e) tells us how much the unexpectedness of h diminishes when we get to know e. Transmitted information is thus the measure of semantic information shared by e and h. See also Hilpinen (1970) on these measures.

In their theory, Carnap and Bar-Hillel assume an ideal receiver "...who 'knows' all of logic and mathematics, and together with any class of empirical sentences, all of their logical consequences" (Carnap & Bar-Hillel, 1952). Thus the logical content of a sentence contains the logical content of all the sentences which can be deducted from it. To make the theory of semantic information more realistic, Hintikka (1970) developed the concepts of surface information and depth information. The surface information of a message is its literal semantic meaning and the class of trivially equal statements in the language. The depth information corresponds to the information gained by the ideal receiver. By logically inferring non-trivial consequences from the message, its' surface information is deepened, thus approaching the depth information.

Pragmatic information. Even the theory of semantic information still has nothing to do with the actual communication situation. It does not tell us what information the sender was trying to transmit, or how the message was understood by the receiver. These questions belong to the field of pragmatics. As Carnap and Bar-Hillel (1952) point out, while the amount of semantic information in statement "17 × 19 = 323" is zero, its "psychological information" to some person might be quite high.

Agreement has not been reached on the definition of pragmatics and there is no clear theory of pragmatic information as there is for syntactic and semantic information. "To the pragmatic level we must relegate all questions of value or usefulness of messages, all questions of sign recognition and interpretation, and all other aspects which we would regard as psychological in character." (Cherry, 1957) Nauta (1972) defines pragmatic information as that which reduces uncertainty relevant to a given purposeful state of the receiver.

Distinguishing between pragmatic and semantic information is difficult. We can, for instance, use the above measures developed by Carnap and Bar-Hillel, if we can find out the probabilities the sender and the receiver believe the different states of the universe to have. Each individual is likely to assume a slightly different combination of probabilities for different states. The differences are presumably smaller between persons belonging to the same culture than between persons belonging to different cultures.

In addition to the expectations of the user, the interpretation of many signs is also culturally determined. Thus the content of a message depends on the place, time and situation in which it was received, even when the same signs are used. Semiotics is the study of culturally defined meanings for signs, and semiotic knowledge is needed in the coding of the message if the pragmatic information is to be transmitted correctly. Well-known semiotic studies in information graphics, including maps, are those of Bertin (1967) and Tufte (1983).

2.4 Applying information theory

The term "information theory" has often been wrongly understood as consisting merely of the statistical theory of communication by Shannon, and subsequent work based on it. The semantic and pragmatic considerations have received much less attention. Even worse, the Shannon entropy is repeatedly taken as a measure of meaning. Although Shannon explicitly stated that his theory does not in any way take into account the semantic aspects of information, considerable confusion has arisen in its later interpretations. The Shannon entropy measures just the amount of information of a message, not its logic, meaning, value or truthfulness. Bar-Hillel (1952; 1955) consistently emphasizes that no conclusions concerning the semantics of a message can be made on the grounds of Shannon theory and considers it better be named the theory of signal transmission.

Many of the writers who have examined information theory in the context of cartography have fallen into this same trap (e.g. Robinson & Petchenick, 1977 quoting Green & Courtis, 1966; Salichtchev, 1977). Guelke (1977) correctly points out that the problem of transmitting meaning is not solved by the statistical communication theory. Freitag (1980) has refined communication theory for cartography, and clearly distinguishes the syntactic and semantic aspects.

Within its limitations, the Shannon theory is still useful. Too much attention has been placed on the fact that the theory was developed for engineering purposes, e.g. for the transmission of signals in telephone or telegraph systems. Because of its generality, it is applicable to any communication system. Entropy can be calculated for any random variable whose frequency distribution is known. Thus redundancy can also be determined.

From the syntactic viewpoint, we can say that the rarest item, e.g. a map symbol on the display, has the highest information content. It tells us the most new things about the information source, in this case, the database. In a temporal sequence, be it a working session or a short animation, the most distinctive – i.e. the most unusual – display can be said to have the highest information content and is probably the best remembered.

Bjørke and Aasgaard (1990) have been developing a method of real-time cartographic zoom on the basis of the Shannon theory. It consists of selection and generalization of features. The entropy of a display is a measure of the amount of information of the display. The zoom can be realized by increasing or decreasing the entropy.

For the communication channel to be as efficient as possible, the most common message should have the smallest load on the channel (Shannon & Weaver, 1949). The channel in this situation is from the display to the consciousness of the user. This is in fact accomplished, for instance, in ordinary topographic maps, where contours are usually the most common symbol and are therefore coded in some neutral colour, such as brown or grey, so as not to distract the viewer. In the Finnish Basic Map Series, woodlands are left white because most of the land is covered with forest.

The central idea in the efficient transmission of a signal is that all the messages should have equal probability or, if that is not possible, then the load a message puts on the channel should be the lesser the more frequent the message is. This may be thought of as being the ideal basic form of communication, from which deviations are made for semantic and pragmatic reasons and to reduce the effect of noise.

The use of semantic information measures in a GIS context using spatial languages requires further study. If the information content of a sentence depends on how many other sentences it excludes logically, we might think that the areal coverage of some features could be used as a measure of the information content, at least in two-dimensional applications. If we were to study land use in some area, then each land use class excludes logically all the other uses[3].

As noted above, semantic and pragmatic information are difficult to separate. If the ideal receiver described above gets information only from that one given source, the measures inf and cont present the pragmatic information, too. For ordinary humans the pragmatic information is determined by the probabilities he has assigned to different states of the universe and by his ability to infer deeper information, new non-trivial consequences, from the given surface information. This brings us to the second subject of this paper. For a message to be correctly transmitted on semantic and pragmatic levels, which is of course the requirement for any useful communication, we have to have some knowledge of the receiver of the message. We have to have some kind of description – a model – of the user.

3 User models

3.1 A review

The method of user modelling began some twenty years ago in artificial intelligence and computer aided instruction research. Inherent in all applications there are some kind of assumptions about their users, but usually a user model refers to a systematic implementation of the important features describing the user. At its simplest, the user model may be thought of as consisting only of the possibility to change some default parameters in the system. The main interest in user model research, though, is in systems which can adapt themselves to different users at run time. The most important function of user models is to predict the user's actions and preferences and to change its functionality accordingly, for instance in database search. Rich (1983) has devised three dimensions for describing user models:

1) one model of a single canonical user versus a collection of models of individual users.

[3] In reality this is not true, but it is often desirable to classify land use on a nominal scale, in classes with no overlap.

2) models described explicitly by the system designer or by the users themselves versus models inferred by the system on the basis of users' behaviour.

3) models of fairly long-term user characteristics such as areas of interest or expertise versus models of relatively short-term user characteristics such as the problem the user is currently trying to solve.

Why should user models be employed? Each user is an individual and should treated as such if the computer is really to become a useful tool for everyone (Rich, 1983). Brajnik et al. (1990) list three advantages of employing user models: economy of interaction, user acceptability and the effectiveness and efficiency of the use of the target system. From our point of view, the effective transmission of information, the main benefit of user models is that they enable the control of pragmatic information.

Allen (1990) has listed some disadvantages of user models. Firstly, people may find it very unpleasant to be controlled by a computer. One solution might be to build the models so 'transparent' that users can control their function. Secondly, the model may be too mechanistic and discard much important information which the user has not explicitly requested. The model may become overspecialized and hinder the user instead of helping him. Thirdly, user models may present a risk to privacy. They contain much very personal information which could be end up in the wrong hands. The first two problems can be avoided by careful design, but the third may be more serious.

Rich (1983) has presented some techniques for building a user model. Broadly they fall into two categories: methods for inferring single facts at a time, and methods for inferring whole clusters of facts at once. Methods in the first class include monitoring the concepts and the form of the commands the user gives as input. From these, the application can infer facts such as the sophistication level of the user. Experienced users use more specialized commands and qualifiers than novices. A large collection of facts is inferred from some critical observations of the behaviour of the user via stereotypes. The idea of stereotypes is based on the fact that many human traits appear together. For instance, a wealthy person has supposedly travelled more widely than a poor one. A stereotype consists of attribute-value pairs, called facets, which describe the different characteristics of the stereotype, e.g. experience and age, etc. The facets may be given weights to describe how strongly they belong to a given stereotype. An individual user may also be modelled with facets, the weights of which tell the system how much it relies on the value of the facet. Some easily observable facets work like triggers that activate the stereotype. The triggers are also weighted to help in deciding whether to activate a given stereotype or not. The stereotypes can be organized into a hierarchy with the canonical user on top. The model of an individual user can be built by combining and modifying different stereotypes. Brajnik et al. (1990) describe in detail how to build a user modelling system based on stereotypes.

The application can derive information of the user either by asking directly or by quietly observing his actions. Rich (1983) suggests that the first method is not good, because it is time consuming and disturbs the user and because users are not always very good at evaluating themselves. A preferable way is to feed all user input into a kind of user processor, which infers from the input and its previous knowledge what the user might want to do and forwards this command to the appliction. If the user does not like the result, the model has to adapt itself.

User modelling has mostly been applied to text based applications such as editors (Zissos & Witten, 1985) and electronic news services (Allen, 1990). Holynski (1988) has determined a set of visual variables which can be used to express the users' preferences of display style: busyness, complexity, regularity, colour variety, shape variety, symmetry, grid size and balance. The variables are strongly interdependent, and thus lend themselves well to the construction of stereotypes in visual information systems, like GIS.

3.2 Scope of GIS

Figure 4 gives a diagram of the GIS communication system completed with a user model. The model receives new information of the user by examining the sentences of the input language the user gives. From these, certain traits are extracted which are thought to describe the user well, and the model of this individual user is updated.

The model may affect the translation of the user action into sentences of the input language, e.g. a long and tedious command sequence may be grouped into a single command. It may also formulate the actual query to the database, by modifying the user's input in the light of the knowledge and assumptions it has of the user's preferences and needs. Finally, the user model may affect how the data from the database is mapped to the output language. The same topographic data can be presented differently to a geologist and a landscape architect. The user model may be updated in the mapping process to indicate that the user's current level of knowledge of the study area has been raised.

Many attributes of a user, e.g. age, physical ability, education and cultural background, gender, taste and personal values, require study in many disciplines, such as psychology, sociology, anthropology, pedagogy and medicine. When modelling a user in practise, these characteristics are of course very important. What we are trying to do here, though, is to study some general principles of the transmission of information independently of these random factors.

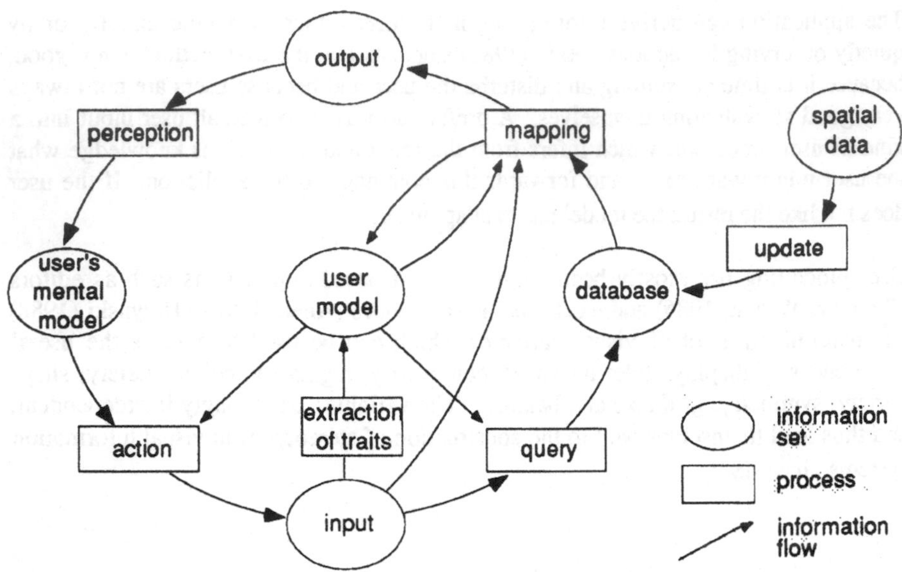

Figure 4. The position of a user model in the GIS communication system.

From the above discussion of information theory we have seen that the theory of syntactic information can be applied mainly to the coding of the message, e.g. the design of displays. From the discussion of semantic and pragmatic information we can conclude that in order to efficiently raise the user's level of knowledge, the system should present the user with messages which have as high a (semantic) information content as possible. In other words, the most unexpected news should be told first. For this we have to know the different probabilities the user assigns to different states of the universe, so we can pick the least probable. Three variables describing the user from the pragmatic viewpoint can now be extracted:

1) The information the user wants. This is needed for restricting the universe and all its different states to be finite, so it is possible to assign probabilities to all the different situations. In a GIS the restriction might be, for instance, on the basis of location, time or theme.

2) The information the user already has. This is needed for guessing the probabilities the user actually has assigned to the states of the universe. This knowledge of the user is accumulated during the period of working with the system.

3) The user's ability to infer deeper information from a given piece of surface information. This is used for determining the information that should be presented after the current message. It can be estimated by monitoring the queries the user makes.

Stereotypes can be used to make assumptions of all these variables. Zevenbergen (1990) presents a classification of GIS user interfaces which might serve as a basis for stereotype creation in GIS applications:

- the generic user interface
  - offers all functionality and access to all data of the GIS
  - for specialists maintaining the system and doing complex analyses
- the data-specific user interface
  - focused on a predefined dataset
  - offers all functionality
  - for specialists in an administrative sector or area, e.g. planners
- the task-specific user interface
  - a limited set of actions
  - the data set is not restricted
  - for people needing much different information but are not specialists in GIS, e.g. decision makers
- the restricted user interface
  - only some operations on some data
  - information stands for ordinary citizens

The idea of stereotypical receivers of geographic information is not new. As a matter of fact, in ordinary atlas books this has been common practice for about a century. The general maps are designed for a stereotypical atlas user. They contain information which is conventionally regarded as relevant to tell about a region. After the general map there is usually a collection of different thematic maps of the same region for people with more specialized information needs. Likewise in a computer atlas the first maps shown to the user might be of some generic type and, depending on the user's subsequent queries, more specialized presentations would be shown after that. The supposedly irrelevant information would be left out.

In recent years, the use of metaphors has become very popular in GIS user interface research and development (Gould & McGranaghan, 1990; Kuhn, 1990). One reason for this is that by using metaphors the applications can be made to look simpler without sacrificing their power. (Carroll et al., 1988). Interfaces based on metaphors, if well implemented, are also easier to learn, because the user can use his existing mental models of familiar things with little modification. However, it is difficult to find one metaphor to suit all the different tasks a GIS is needed to do. Gould and McGranaghan (1990) have suggested that a GIS should have several nested metaphors for different levels of the system operation. It is a small step from this to a system where different users could have different metaphors. Each metaphor presupposes a certain stereotypical user who is familiar with the concepts and operations of the real world phenomenon from which the metaphor is derived. On the other hand, within the context of a metaphor the pragmatic content of the user's actions is much easier to interpret and predict, because the concepts and operations are restricted and the logic of function of the real world counterpart is well understood.

Kuhn and Frank (1992) have shown, that the metaphors in human-computer interfaces can be treated formally using the methods of algebraic specification. The formalization of user interface metaphors would greatly improve the scope of formal handling of the context-dependent pragmatic information with stereotypical user models. A kind of ideal user interface could be realized. Each user would be able to communicate with the system in his "native language," i.e. with the concepts most familiar to him.

4 Conclusion

This presentation has been an attempt to put the study of user interfaces in a GIS environment on a more sound theoretical basis. Information theory combined with user modelling methods seems to be a promising way to approach the problem. We have reviewed some basic examples of their applicability. More studies dealing with the special problems of geographical information are needed for further conclusions. As seen above, information theory is rather well developed on the syntactic and semantic levels, but the theory is still inadequate to allow a decent analysis on the pragmatic level.

References

Allen, R. B. (1990). User models: theory method and practice. *International Journal of Man-Machine Studies*, 32(5): 511-543.

Andrews, J. H. (1990). Map as a language / a metaphor extended. *Cartographica*, 27(1): 1-19.

Bar-Hillel, Y. (1952). Semantic information and its measures. *Transactions of the Tenth Conference on Cybernetics*, Josiah Macy, Jr. Foundation, New York. pp. 33-48. Reprinted in Bar-Hillel (1964).

Bar-Hillel, Y. (1955). An examination of information theory. *Philosophy of Science*, 22: 86-105. Reprinted in Bar-Hillel (1964).

Bar-Hillel, Y. (1964). *Language and Information*. Addison Wesley and the Jerusalem Academic Press, Reading, Mass. & Jerusalem.

Bertin, J. (1967). *Semiologie Graphique*. Mouton & Gauthier-Villars, Paris.

Bjørke, J. T. & Aasgaard, R. (1990). Cartographic zoom. *Proceedings of the 4th International Symposium on Spatial Data Handling*, Zürich, Switzerland. pp. 345-353.

Board, C. (1981). Cartographic communication. *Cartographica*, 18(2): 42-78.

Brajnik, G., Guida, G. & Tasso, C. (1990). User modelling in expert man-machine interfaces: a case study in intelligent information retrieval. *IEEE Transactions on Systems, Man and Cybernetics*, 20(1): 166-185.

Carnap, R. & Bar-Hillel, Y. (1952). An outline of a theory of semantic information. *Technical Report No. 247* of the Research Laboratory of Electronics, Massachusetts Institute of Technology. Reprinted in Bar-Hillel (1964).

Carroll J. M., Mack, R. L., & Kellog, W. A. (1988). Interface metaphors and user interface design. In: M. Helander (1988), *Handbook of Human-Computer Interaction*, Elsevier Science Publishers, North-Holland.

Cherry, C. (1957). *On human communication*. MIT Press, Cambridge, Mass.

Foley, J. D., van Dam, A., Feiner, S. K. & Hughes, J. F. (1990). *Computer graphics: principles and practice*. Addison-Wesley, Reading, Mass.

Freitag, U. (1980). Can communication theory form the basis of a general theory of cartography? *Nachtrichten aus dem Karten- und Vermessungsvesen*, p.17-35, reihe II, heft nr. 38, Frankfurt A.M.

Gould, M. D. & McGranaghan, M. (1990). Metaphor in geographic information systems. *Proceedings of the 4th International Symposium on Spatial Data Handling*, Zürich, Switzerland. pp. 433-442.

Green, R. T. & Courtis, M. C. (1966). Information theory and figure perception: the metaphor that failed. *Acta Psychologica*, 25: 12-26.

Guelke, L. (1977). Cartographic communication and geographic understanding. *Cartographica* monograph no. 19. pp. 129-145.

Harvey, D. (1969). *Explanation in geography*. Edward Arnold, London.

Head, C. G. (1984). The map as natural language: a paradigm for understanding. *Cartographica*, 21(1): 1-32.

Hilpinen, R. (1970). On the information provided by observations. In: J. Hintikka & P. Suppes (eds.),*Information and inference*, D. Reidel, Dordrecht, Holland. pp. 97-122.

Hintikka, J. (1968). The varieties of information and scientific explanation. In: B. v Roostelaar & J. F. Staal (eds.),*Logic, Methodology, and Philosophy of Science III, Proceedings of the 1967 International Congress*, North-, Holland, Amsterdam. pp. 311-331.

Hintikka, J. (1970). Surface information and depth information. In: J. Hintikka & P. Suppes (eds.),*Information and inference*, D. Reidel, Dordrecht, Holland. pp. 263-297.

Holynski, M. (1988). User adaptive computer graphics. *International Journal of Man-Machine Studies*, 29(5): 539-548.

Keates, J. S. (1982). *Understanding maps*. Longman, London.

Kuhn, W. (1990). Are displays maps of views? *Proceedings, AutoCarto 10*, Baltimore, Maryland. Edited by D. M. Mark & D. White. pp. 261-274.

Kuhn, W. & Frank, A. (1992). A formalization of metaphors and image-schemas in user interfaces. In: D. Mark & A. Frank (eds.), *Cognitive and Linguistic Aspects of Geographic Space: Proceedings of the NATO Advanced Study*

Institute, 8.-20.7. 1990, Spain. Kluwer.

Lindholm, M. (1991). Tietokonekartasto hypermediaa soveltaen. (Applying hypermedia in a computer atlas, in Finnish) *Geodeettinen laitos, tiedote 4/kartografia.*

MacEahren, A. & Ganter, J. H. (1990). A pattern identification approach to cartographic visualization. *Cartographica*, 27(2): 64-81

Nauta, D. Jr. (1972). *The meaning of information.* Mouton, The Hague.

Niiniluoto, I. (1990). *Tieto, informaatio ja yhteiskunta – filosofinen käsiteanalyysi.* (Knowledge, information and society – a philosophical conceptual analysis, in Finnish) Valtion painatuskeskus, Helsinki.

Rich, E. (1983). Users are individuals: individualizing user models. *International Journal of Man-Machine Studies*, 18(3): 199-214.

Robinson, A. H. & Petchenick, B. B. (1976). *The nature of maps: essays toward understanding maps and mapping.* University of Chicago Press, Chicago.

Robinson, A. & Petchenick, B. (1977). The map as a communication system. *Cartographica* monograph no. 19. pp. 92-110.

Salichtchev, K. A. (1977). Some reflections on the subject and method of cartography after the sixth international cartographic conference. *Cartographica* monograph no. 19. pp. 111-116.

Shannon, C. & Weaver, W. (1949). *The mathematical theory of communication.* University of Illinois Press, Urbana, Illinois.

Shneiderman, B. (1987). *Designing the user interface.* Addison-Wesley, Reading, Mass.

Tufte, E. (1983). *The visual display of quantitative information.* Graphics Press, Chesire, Connecticut.

Zevenbergen (1990). Who's afraid of GIS – creating user interfaces for GIS users. *Proceedings of EGIS, First European Conference on Geographical Information Systems*, Amsterdam, the Netherlands. pp. 1210-1219.

Zissos & Witten, (1985). User modelling for a computer coach: a case study. *International Journal of Man-Machine Studies*, 23(6): 729-750.

A Conceptual Model of Wayfinding Using Multiple Levels of Abstraction*

Sabine Timpf, Gary S. Volta, David W. Pollock, and Max J. Egenhofer

National Center for Geographic Information and Analysis
and
Department of Surveying Engineering
Boardman Hall
University of Maine
Orono, ME 04469, U.S.A.
{SABINET, GARYV, DAVIDP, MAX}@mecan1.maine.edu

Abstract. Wayfinding is part of everyday life. This study concentrates on the development of a conceptual model of human navigation in the U.S. Interstate Highway Network. It proposes three different levels of conceptual understanding that constitute the cognitive map: the Planning Level, the Instructional Level, and the Driver Level. This paper formally defines these three levels and examines the conceptual objects that comprise them. The problem treated here is a simpler version of the open problem of planning and navigating a multi-mode trip. We expect the methods and preliminary results found here for the Interstate system to apply to other systems such as river transportation networks and railroad networks.

1 Introduction

Navigation is a fundamental human activity and an integral part of everyday life. People use their knowledge and their previous experiences with geographic space to find their way. Considerable research in the areas of cognitive science, psychology, and artificial intelligence has been carried out to examine the means by which humans navigate. Only recently, software design for Geographic Information Systems (GISs) has become interested in integrating these spatial concepts of navigation into their systems. This topic of research is related to the field of spatial reasoning, which is concerned with spatial task planning, navigation planning, representing large spatial databases, symbolic reasoning, the integration of reasoning with geometric constraints and accumulation of uncertain spatial evidence [1].

The cognitive basis for navigation is the concept of a mental map. *Cognitive maps* are mental maps which are built from experience or from expectations of the real world [16]. Many tasks, such as deciphering verbal route instructions, rendering scene descriptions and navigating, involve the creation of cognitive maps. Humans use their cognitive maps to carry out wayfinding tasks by retrieving information. Information is added or appropriate corrections are made when detecting differences between

* This work was partially funded by grants from Intergraph Corporation. Additional support from NSF for the NCGIA under grant number SES 88-10917 is gratefully acknowledged. Sabine Timpf acknowledges the support of the German Academic Exchange Service (DAAD).

cognitive maps and the real world. Humans may use several conceptual models representing different parts of geographic space to carry out a single navigation task. Different tasks require different models of space and this can be seen as using different levels of detail. Each task therefore is represented in a conceptual model and all models form a cognitive map for navigation. This paper adapts different conceptual models to wayfinding in geographic space within the U.S. Interstate Highway Network. The formal definition of the physical objects and actions of this network is the goal of this research. Therefore, only a part of the network (physical properties) has been defined for all levels of detail. The preliminary results of this work show that the levels are not independent from each other.

These different models of space need to be processed simultaneously or in succession to completely carry out a navigation task. Humans are very good at that type of reasoning and switch without great effort from one model of space to another. In the creation of these cognitive maps, humans are concerned with getting only the most important information. They use their commonsense to cope with partially unknown situations: they are using *default reasoning*. The theory of default reasoning involves a prerequisite, a justification and a consequent [5]. For example, airline passengers who must change flights in an unfamiliar airport assume that there will be a suitable method to do so and that they will find out the necessary details upon arrival. Other default reasoning deals with the hierarchy of space, like the Reno-San Diego problem [22]. Evidence of a hierarchy in cognitive maps has also been found in [11]. Default reasoning can be modelled as reasoning with multiple levels of detail, each lower level more precise than the higher one, each higher level representing a generalization of a lower one. We propose that default reasoning sufficiently supports the notion of multiple hierarchical levels of reasoning in the Interstate Highway Network.

Although cognitive maps are widely used in human navigation, they are seldom formally defined. The discovery and understanding of the underlying theory of real-world phenomena is critical to any scientific study. A formal description of such models of reality is crucial to provide a compact, consistent description of reality [2]. Formal models provide a framework for the analysis and comparison of various cognitive maps and formalization can facilitate the design and implementation of related software to a great extent. Many formal data models exist for spatial applications such as multi-sorted algebras or first-order predicate calculus. The method of formal investigation used here is known as algebraic specifications. The theory behind algebraic specifications has been developed and used in software design [15] and practical introductions can be found in [14] and [24].

We propose three levels of abstraction based on the different tasks that can be found in the process of navigating: planning, giving and receiving instructions, and driving. For example, one starts planning a trip by asserting that there is a way to drive by car from Boston to Baltimore, by estimating its approximate duration and by determining the Interstate highways to be used (Planning Level). Next, one determines entry and exit points for each leg of the trip (Instructional Level) and finally the driver makes decisions about which lanes to use (Driver Level). Humans do employ mental maps of these levels while planning and navigating. These maps are either graphical representations, lists of instructions, or a combination of both. Changes can be made to any of these mental maps. Some changes will affect all the maps similarly (e.g., destruction or construction of highways) and some will have no affect on the other maps (e.g., closing of one lane of traffic). The levels have been formalized with the help of algebraic specifications. A brief summary of the methodology of algebraic specifications and the complete set of algebraic specification for the three conceptual levels are given in the Appendix.

The remainder of this paper is organized as follows: section 2 gives a short introduction to the U.S. Interstate Highway Network and the tasks that are performed in it, section 3 defines and discusses the conceptual models of the Interstate Highway Network, section 4 compares the three models and presents some results, section 5 describes previous and related work, section 6 offers the conclusions and suggestions for future work, and in the appendix a brief overview on the method and a complete set of the algebraic specifications is given.

2 U.S. Interstate Highway Network

The U.S. Interstate Highway Network was conceived in the 1940's under the Department of Defense. Its purpose was to provide direct access to all parts of the country in case of emergency. The Interstate was also built to benefit the citizens of the United States. This latter use is exercised by a great number of Americans and visitors every day. One very important property responsible for the success of the system is national consistency. Highways in the Interstate Network follow a common naming convention, are of similar construction, and obey common rules [20]. These consistencies contribute to the formation of the conceptual models used in navigating the network. This section sets forth to describe the physical nature of the network. It discusses in greater detail some of the specific tasks that use these consistencies for carrying out the broader task of navigating in the Network.

2.1 Physical Nature of the Network

The physical properties of the network and the navigation of the network are conceptually different, although very interdependent. Only the physical properties of the network are addressed in this paper but we acknowledge that the navigation operations such as "proceed", "stop", and "turn" must be formalized to complete the model.

There are fundamentally two types of highways in the network which differ only in direction. One type of highway runs predominantly West to East and has even-numbered names ranging from 4 to 94. The other type of highway, that runs predominantly South to North, has odd-numbered names ranging from 5 to 95. In addition, "minor highways" exist within the interstate system. These highways typically run through or around cities and are named in connection with a "parent highway." For instance, I-495 is a minor highway associated with the major interstate highway I-95. These highways are typically contained within the same state and therefore occurrences of more than one I-495 may exist although never in the same state [25]. These facts are important to this study, because they define and describe the physical nature of the network and therefore influence the conceptual model of the network.

The mathematical model to describe networks is usually a graph. A graph consists of two basic objects: a vertex and an edge. These objects are combined to build a graph in the form of a list. We use the abstract objects of a vertex, an edge and a graph as basis for our objects in the three conceptual models.

2.2 Tasks in the Network

Several tasks are involved in planning and navigating a trip. There can be tasks that mean one set of actions in one level and another set of actions in another level. There are tasks that are very general (e.g., take exit) in one level but broken down to several tasks in another (e.g., change to appropriate lane for exiting, take offramp). There are tasks that require actions in one level but do not affect any other level (e.g., accelerating the vehicle).

A closer examination reveals that there must be even more tasks e.g., receive driving instructions, correct instructions, carry out instructions, drive a car, change plans because of some constraints. Time constraints can be expressed either as physical constraints (most effective route) or as a driving-constraint (drive as fast as possible with no breaks). In trying to group those different tasks, we found three distinctive groups. The "planning" group, the "instruction" group and the "driving" group. Looking in more detail into those groups we found that these groups operate in different domains. The planning group involves knowledge about the place where one is and about the place where one wants to go, as well as the time-frame and the places in between, if important. The instruction group involves knowledge about the decision points along the route given by the planning group. The driving group needs information about when to drive where, but also has a whole body of actions on its own that cannot be found in the other groups (change lane, accelerate).

Because there seems to be a hierarchy involved in these tasks, three levels of abstraction have been selected. The first and most general level is called the Planning Level (section 3.1). The information from the planning is also used to reason in the second level of detail, the Instructional Level (section 3.2). The most fundamental level is called the Driver Level (section 3.3) and describes the objects and actions necessary to drive a vehicle in the order of the instructions.

3 The Three Conceptual Levels

The following is an ontology of the cognitive model of Interstate navigation and its three conceptual levels. The objects in the three levels emerged from the formalization with the help of algebraic specifications. Selected parts of the algebraic specification are given for each level. A short introduction in the methodology of algebraic specifications and the complete set of algebraic specifications can be found in the Appendix.

3.1 Planning Level

The cognitive model in the *Planning Level* represents the U.S. Interstate Highway Network as a series of highways, places, and interchanges. The connectivity of edges expressed by the nodes is the critical information at this level. Dual directional travel is implied since it is a fundamental trait of the Interstate System. Also implied and therefore, not dealt with in this model is that points of entry and exit exist at sufficient intervals to allow more refined navigation to take place. This conceptual model is used for high-level wayfinding, involving the entire network, to judge the feasibility and scope of long distance travel. Its cognitive model is similar to the locator map found in the beginning of many road atlases (Figure 1). The objects in this conceptual level are the following:

Highway	a collection of edges between nodes.
Place	a location that a highway passes through.
Interchange	a place where more than one highway passes through.

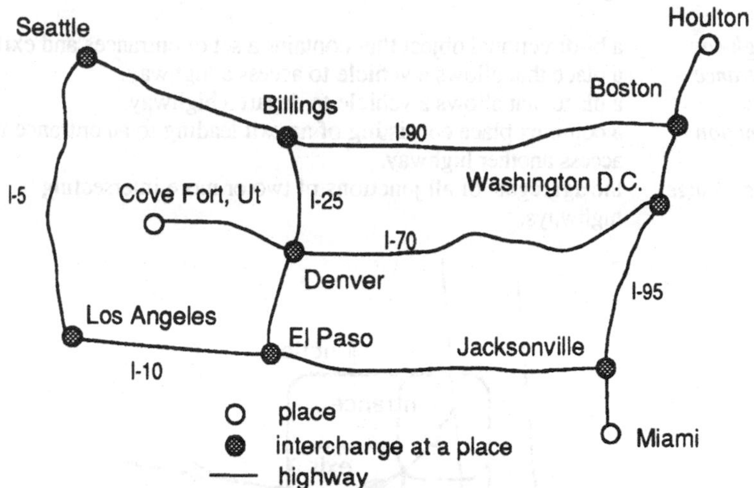

Fig. 1. Highways, interchanges, and places shown at the Planning Level.

A "place" at this level can be specified as demonstrated in Table 1. The object's underlying figure is a vertex (which is a node in the graph model) and the vertex is assumed to be already specified. The "place" is constructed by the operator "makePlace", that requires an identifier "id" and a position "pos". The observers "getPID" and "getPos" return the identifier "id" and the position "pos" respectively of a given place "pl".

```
sort  place is_a vertex
c     makePlace: id x pos-> pl
o     getPID: pl -> id
o     getPos: pl -> pos
axioms
      getPID(makePlace(id1, pos1))==id1
      getPos(makePlace(id1, pos1))==pos1
```

Table 1. An algebraic specification of the object "place."

3.2 Instructional Level

The *Instructional Level* involves the necessary conceptual information to provide sufficient driving instructions for navigating the system. This level deals with the interaction of more than one highway and the more specific elements of highways such as highways, junctions, entrances, and exits (Figure 2).

The objects and their properties are defined for one direction of travel. A driver usually is aware of travel in the opposite direction (lanes and vehicles going in the opposite direction can be seen). Unless a mistake is made (missing a desired exit), the driver would not be concerned with reversing direction. The objects in this conceptual level are the following:

Highway	a bi-directional object that contains a set of entrances and exits.
Entrance	a place that allows a vehicle to access a highway.
Exit	a place that allows a vehicle to depart a highway.
Junction	a complex place consisting of an exit leading to an entrance to access another highway.
Interchange	the aggregate of all junctions of two or more intersecting highways.

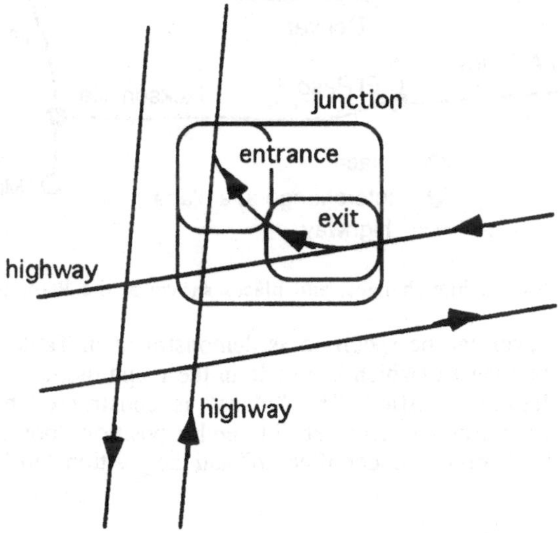

Fig. 2. Highways, junction, entrance, and exit for the Instructional Level.

Following are the algebraic specifications of a selected set of the objects of the Instructional level (Table 2). The objects "entrance" and "exit" correspond, when grouped, to the object "place" of the Planning Level. They are interrelated through the underlying structure of the vertex and, therefore, can be compared to each other.

sort entrance ***is_a vertex***
c makeVertex: id x dir -> ent
o getdir: ent -> dir
axioms
getdir (makeVertex(id1,dir1)) == dir1

sort exit ***is_a vertex***
c makeVertex: nb -> ex

```
o       getnb: ex -> nb
axioms
        getnb (makeVertex(nb1)) == nb1
```

Table 2. Algebraic specification of the objects "entrance" and "exit."

3.3 Driver Level

Navigation is carried out at a low level in large-scale space. This low level of conceptual abstraction contains the properties of the navigator's field of view (Figure 3). At this level, only one highway (specifically, a portion of a single highway) is involved in the model.

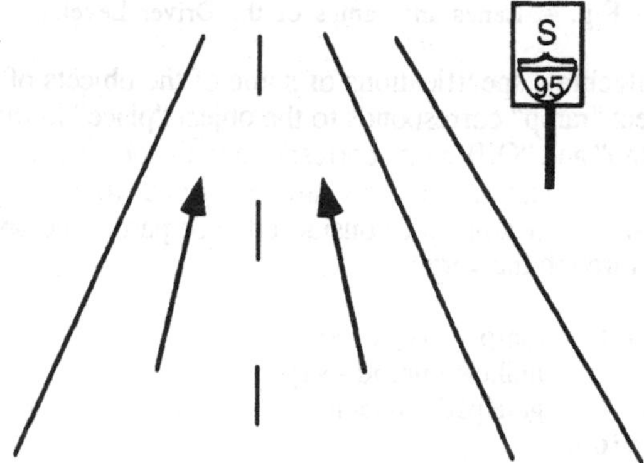

Fig. 3. A Model of the Interstate Highway at the Driver Level.

The salient information at this level consists of *lanes* (breakdown, travel, passing) and *ramps* (Figure 4). The driver is concerned with one direction of travel, and with maintaining the proper lane for travel, for passing, and for entry and exit. The objects in this conceptual model are the following:

Passing Lane	typically the left-most lane used for passing another vehicle.
Travel Lane	the lane(s) that contain(s) the steady traffic.
Breakdown Lane	an outer-most (right or left) lane that is used in case of vehicle malfunction or other emergency.
OnRamp	a ramp that brings the driver onto a highway.
OffRamp	a ramp that takes the driver off a highway.

A collection of objects of the Driver Level are shown in Figure 4 from an aerial perspective.

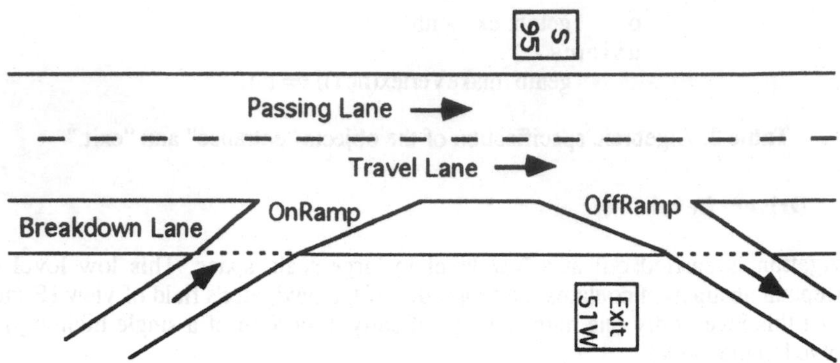

Fig. 4. Lanes and ramps of the Driver Level.

Following are the algebraic specifications of some of the objects of the Driver Level (Table 3). The object "ramp" corresponds to the object "place" in the Planning Level. The objects "OnRamp" and "OffRamp" correspond to the objects "entrance" and "exit" of the Instructional Level respectively. As can be derived from the specifications, the objects "onRamp" and "OffRamp" are considered to be part of the object "place" from the Planning Level through the vertex.

sort	ramp *is_a vertex*
c	makeRamp: id -> rp
o	getRpID: rp -> id
axiom	
	getRpID(makeRamp(i)) == i
sort	onRamp *is_a ramp*
c	makeRamp: id x direction -> onrp
o	getDirection: onrp -> direction
axioms	
	getDirection(makeOnRamp(i, d)) == d
sort	offRamp *is_a ramp*
c	makeRamp: id x number -> offrp
o	getNumber: offrp -> num
axioms	
	getNumber(makeOffRamp(rp, num)) == num

Table 3. Algebraic specifications of the objects "ramp", "onRamp", "OffRamp."

4 Comparison of the Conceptual Levels

Algebraic specifications were used to define the conceptual and physical objects of the Interstate Highway Network. This formal definition of the different levels of reasoning provides a basis for comparison of these levels. Our approach focused on definition of objects which are used as the theoretical basis for the specifications of the actual physical objects found in the U.S. Interstate Network. The formal definition of a generic graph (see Appendix) facilitates the comparison of the objects in the three levels of reasoning. Differences directly become apparent in the objects when defining generic objects and when using them as a basis for all three levels. The results of the comparison lead to a justification of the generalization processes that occurs in wayfinding on the U.S. Interstate Network.

The Interstate is an automobile transportation system, therefore, navigators of this system are expected to have a sufficient level of expertise in operating a vehicle. This would include accelerating, braking, turning and so on. These operations involve the maneuvering of the vehicle within our conceptual model of the Driver Level and do not enter into this discussion of assumptions made between levels. The following discussion shows the various levels we have proposed and their objects as they relate to each other, thereby, showing the foundation for default reasoning and generalization. We use the object *highway* and the composed object *interchange* as basis for our comparison, because they are the main objects in the most abstracted level and they best represent the differences in the three conceptual models.

Humans conceptualize space by navigating in it. Their experience in transportation systems leads to the creation of conceptual objects representing real-world objects found in large-scale space. These objects are then generalized to higher-level objects. Because the Driver Level of the conceptual model most closely resembles real-world objects, the generalizations are made based on this level. Figure 5 is an aerial view of a collection of ramps and lanes representing the interchange (Figure 5a) and the highway (Figure 5b) as perceived in the Driver Level.

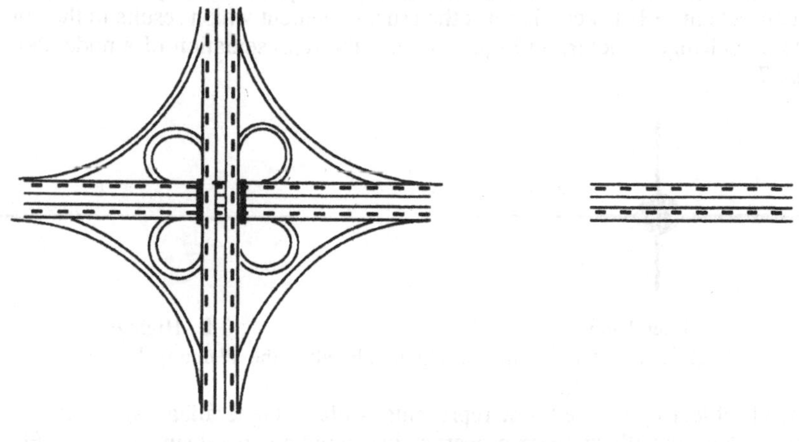

a. Interchange **b.** Highway

Fig. 5. A collection of ramps and lanes.

At the Instructional Level (Figure 6), the navigator is concerned with two or more highways and their objects. Lanes in the Driver Level are generalized to single lines in the Instructional Level. The existence of multiple lanes is assumed at this level, but is not needed for locating the correct exits and entrances. Also in the Instructional Level, entrances and exits are not seen as ramps in the physical sense, but rather as topological links to an intersecting highway or as gateways into, or out of the system. Figure 6a shows the Interchange shown in Figure 5a and Figure 6b shows the highway shown in Figure 5b as comprised by objects of the Instructional Level.

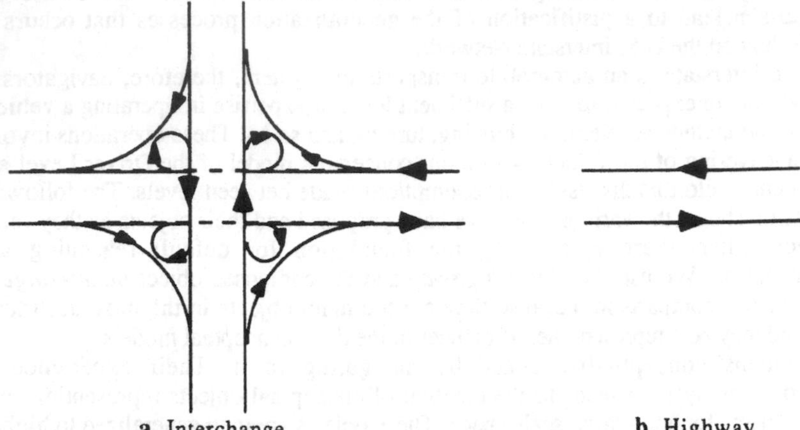

Fig. 6. Interstate components shown at the Instructional Level.

The Planning Level (Figure 7) is the highest level of the conceptual model and the navigator deals with the whole Interstate Highway Network. At this level, the bi-directional highway (Figure 6b) is generalized and implied in a single line (Figure 7b). The connectedness between places is the crucial element which results in the collapse of the interchange structure in Figure 6a into the representation of a node shown in Figure 7a.

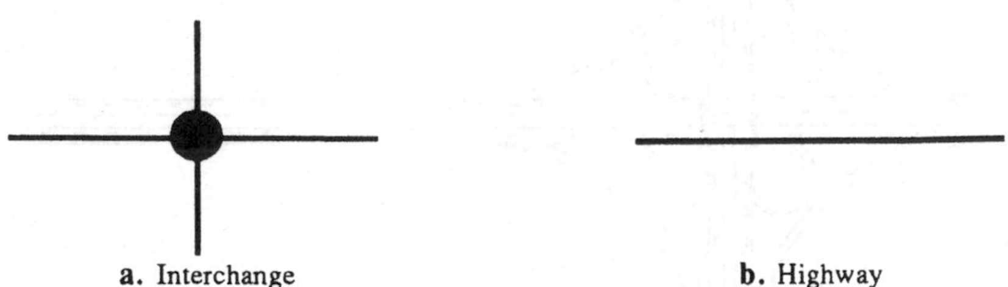

Fig. 7. Interstate components generalized at the Planning Level .

Each object of the network represents a class. Generalization groups several classes of objects with common properties into a more general superclass. In Figure 8 a graphical representation of the relationship between classes and their superclasses is given. Boxes describe classes, boxes in boxes describe the relationship of a superclass to a class. The classes entrance, exit, onramp, offramp, ramp, highway, lane, highwaysystem etc. belong to the superclasses vertex, edge and graph respectively.

In Figure 8, every object in one level has a corresponding object in the next higher level or next-lower level. Objects in the Driver Level are mostly the physical objects encountered while driving. Generalization changes them into different objects in the Instructional Level, which are already higher abstractions of reality. Generalizing even more, most details (even direction) vanish and as a result there are very coarse and very abstract objects in the Planning Level.

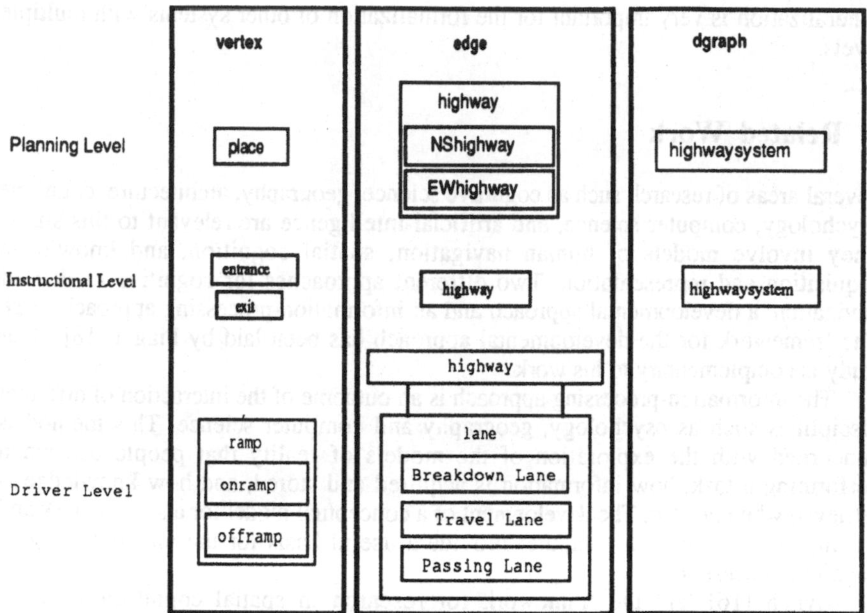

Fig. 8. Generalization

Classes inherit the properties of their superclasses. But they also can have properties on their own. In Figure 9 properties are represented on the bottom of the box with their names. For Instance, in the Driver Level, an edge is called a highway. It is composed of a specific set of lanes. In the Instructional Level the same abstract object also is called highway. Apparently there is no difference. Looking at Figure 9, however, reveals that the Diver Level highway has a *name* and is constructed as a *set of lanes*. The Instructional Level highway possesses an *identifier*, a *start-point*, an *end-point*, and a *length*. Similarly, the difference between the Instructional Level highway and the Planning Level highway is shown in the properties. The Planning Level highway has a *north-place* and a *south-place* but no length.

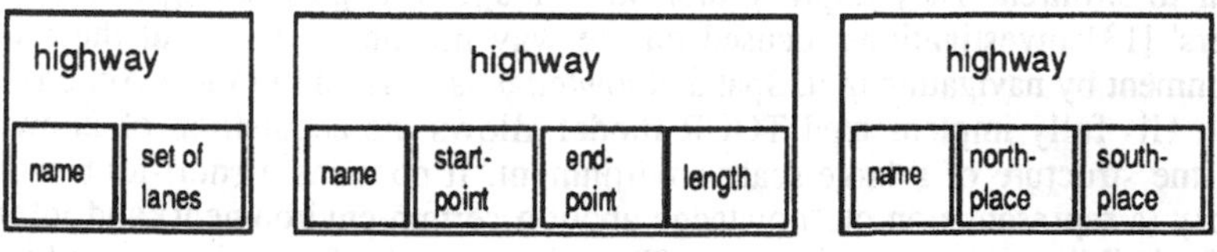

9a. Driver Level **9b.** Instructional Level **9c.** Planning Level

Fig. 9. Properties of *highway* at different levels.

As we have seen, there are different features in each level that correspond to the same object in a more abstracted point of view. Formalizing these objects helped uncovering the differences in the features. The discovery of the underlying process of generalization is very important for the formalization of other systems with multiple levels.

5 Related Work

Several areas of research such as cognitive science, geography, architecture, cognitive psychology, computer science, and artificial intelligence are relevant to this study. They involve models of human navigation, spatial cognition, and knowledge acquisition and representation. Two different approaches for cognitive models of navigation, a developmental approach and an information-processing approach exist. The framework for the developmental approach has been laid by Piaget [18]. Our study is complementary to his work.

The information-processing approach is an outcome of the interaction of different disciplines such as psychology, geography and computer science. This method is concerned with the exploration of the models of reality that people use when performing a task, how information is acquired and stored, and how knowledge is retrieved when needed. The development of a conceptual model for a specific task and its implementation on a computer provide a useful basis for the understanding of cognitive processes.

Lynch [16] laid the framework for research in spatial cognition with his investigation of sketch maps and path descriptions of people in different cities. He identified that people use five distinct elements to structure a city (to build a cognitive map or model of a city): landmarks, paths, nodes, edges and districts. *Landmarks* are outstanding features (buildings, places) in a city. They serve as reference points to the observer. *Paths* are streets or lanes. *Nodes* are located along paths and form important points (e.g., street intersection, bridges). *Edges* are boundaries to areas. They form a physical barrier (e.g., rivers). *Districts* are areas in a city that have one common property (e.g., shopping areas, residential areas). Lynch discovered that a individuals tend to use landmarks first in a new environment for the purpose of orientation. Gradually, the individuals add on to their knowledge until a cognitive map is constructed.

Several other models have been influenced by Piaget and Lynch's work: Siegel and White [21] dealt with the acquisition of spatial knowledge in adults. They propose, that adults acquire knowledge about a new environment in several stages, similar to children. They improve their knowledge through learning continuously. Kuipers' [13] investigations focused on the way humans learn about their spatial environment by navigating in it. Spatial knowledge is stored as a (View-Action)-View model. His fully implemented TOUR model allows the acquisition of knowledge about the structure of a large-scale environment. It contains a short-term working memory (a representation of knowledge about a certain environment) and inference rules for building a new cognitive map. The inference rules for navigating and finding position rely on the knowledge of hierarchy of regions, orientation frames, and boundaries. This is different from the present approach in which a hierarchy of routes is proposed. Gopal [9] describes a computational process model of spatial navigation in a large-scale environment. The model involves spatial learning about objects, representing, storing, and retrieving them when necessary. The reasoning process based on this accumulated knowledge will result in actions to carry out the task. The model helps to explain human performance and error while navigating. In this paper we are more concerned with the modelling of the human *concept* of navigation. McDermott and Davis [17] introduced multiple frames of reference that humans use when they plan routes through uncertain territory. Planning routes requires topological and metric information. A cognitive map is an assertional database for the topological information. Reference frames are stored with the metric information in multiple-frame maps called "fuzzy maps". Davis [5] bases commonsense inference mechanisms on Euclidian geometry and uses predicate calculus to define the inference mechanisms. In this paper we have dealt only with topological knowledge.

6 Summary

6.1 Conclusions

Humans use different levels of information when navigating the Interstate Highway Network. This paper described a conceptual model of the U.S. Interstate Network with three levels of reasoning. These levels were formalized using algebraic specifications such that they can be implemented and incorporated into a Human Navigation System. The simple everyday problem of navigating the Interstate Highway Network was exposed to contain a high degree of complexity. We applied diverse, previous research in such areas as spatial reasoning, default reasoning, formal methods, navigation and cognition to explore the problem. This opens new perspectives in the field of human navigation. Regardless of how the model has to be adapted to different tasks, it is always possible to formalize with the help of algebraic specifications.

Formal definitions provided a framework for comparison between the levels. There are differences that can be derived by generalizing the lowest level to the highest level (similar to zooming). The interaction between the levels of information was stressed to define a method of human wayfinding within the Interstate Highway Network. The conceptual models contain the physical structure of the network in this early stage of research. Navigation is an activity and formal definitions of actions in the Network are necessary to complete the model. The entire formal model can then serve as a foundation of a Human Navigation System for Interstate Highway travel. The larger goal of this research was to narrow the gap between the rigidity of computer processing and the flexibility of human reasoning.

6.2 Future Work

An implementation of the specifications is under way to reaffirm the interpretation of the conceptual model, to verify their completeness, and to confirm the method as a whole. The implementation consists of the direct translation of the graph specifications and the different level specifications into ThinkC source code. In addition, navigation actions such as proceed, locate, and exit must be formalized and integrated into the model presented here to form a comprehensive navigation system. Further investigations about the generalization process in the enlarged model will be necessary. A comparison to reasoning in other transportation networks, such as river and railroad networks would be beneficial.

Acknowledgement

The authors thank all the members of SVE 698-Spatial Reasoning for their valuable input to this paper.

References

1. AAAI Workshop on Spatial Reasoning and Multi-Sensor Fusion 1987
2. R.F. Abler: The National Science Foundation National Center for Geographic Information and Analysis. International Journal for Geographical Information Systems 1 (4), 303-326 (1979)
3. R.R. Baker: Human Navigation and the Sixth Sense. New York: Simon and Schuster 1981
4. H. Claussen, D.M. Mark: Vehicle Navigation Systems. In: J.C. Mueller (ed): Advances in Cartography. Elsevier Science Publishers Ltd. 1991, pp. 161-179
5. E. Davis: Representations of Commonsense Knowledge. San Mateo, California: Morgan Kaufmann Publishers, Inc. 1990
6. H.-D. Ehrich, M. Gogolla, U.W. Lipeck: Algebraische Spezifikationen abstrakter Datentypen. Stuttgart: Teubner Studienbuecher 1989
7. A.U. Frank, M.J. Egenhofer: Object oriented Software Engineering Considerations for Future GIS. Proceedings of the International Geographic Information System Symposium 1989 in Baltimore, Maryland
8. A. Gill: Applied Algebra for the Computer Sciences. Englewood Cliffs, NJ: Prentice-Hall 1976
9. S. Gopal: A Computational Model of Spatial Navigation. University of California, Santa Barbara: Unpublished Dissertation 1988
10. J.R. Herring, M.J. Egenhofer, A.U. Frank: Using Category Theory to Model GIS Applications. In: Proceedings of the 4th International Symposium on Spatial Data Handling 1990, Zurich, Switzerland, Vol. 2, pp. 820-829
11. S.C. Hirtle, J. Jonides: Evidence of Hierarchies in Cognitive Maps. Memory & Cognition, 13 (3), 208-217 (1985)
12. I.P. Howard, W.B. Templeton: Human Spatial Orientation: Geographical Orientation. John Wiley & Sons 1966, pp.256-271
13. B. Kuipers: Modeling Spatial Knowledge. Cognitive Science, 2, 129-153 (1978)
14. B. Liskov, J. Guttag: Abstraction and Specification in Program Development. MIT Press 1989
15. B. Liskov, S. Zilles: Specification Techniques for Data Abstraction. IEEE Transactions on Software Engineering, SE-1, 7-19 (1975)
16. K. Lynch: The Image of the City. Cambridge, MA: MIT Press 1960
17. D. McDermott, E. Davis: Planning Routes through Uncertain Territory. Artificial Intelligence, 22, 107-156 (1984)
18. J. Piaget, B. Inhelder: A child's Conception of Space. London: Routledge & Kegan Paul 1956
19. C.K. Riesbeck: "You can't miss it!" Judging the Clarity of Directions. Cognitive Science 4, 285-303 (1980)
20. M.H. Rose: Interstate, Express Highway politics, 1939-1989. Revised Edition, University of Tennessee Press 1990

21. A.W. Siegel, S.H. White, (1975). The development of Spatial Representations of Large-Scale Environments. In: H.W. Reese (ed.): Advances in Child Development and Behavior. New York: Academic Press 1975, vol 10, pp. 9-55
22. A. Stevens, P. Coupe: Distortions in Judged Spatial Relations. Cognitive Psychology, 10, 422-437 (1978)
23. C.W. Wixom: Pictorial History of Roadbuilding. American Road Builder's Association, 1975
24. J. Woodcock, M. Loomes: Software Engineering Mathematics. (The SEI Series in Software Engineering). Addison-Wesley Publishing Co. 1989
25. P.H. Wright, R.J. Paquette: Highway Engineering, 4th edition. John Wiley & Sons 1979

Appendix

A short introduction to the formalization with algebraic specifications is given before the actual specifications are listed. The formalization with the help of algebraic specifications is realized in three stages. First, the complete set of objects is collected (ontology). Second, the characteristics of the objects are determined. Third, the objects and their characteristics are translated into algebraic specifications.
Each object is an independent specification called sort "object." The object can be constructed and observed. The constructors and observers are two distinct characteristics of the object. Their interaction expresses the behavior of the object and is defined in the axioms. For example (see below) the vertex of the generic graph is constructed with an identifier and a position. So the constructor "makeVertex" acts on an identifier "id" and a position "pos" and then constructs a vertex "v."

makeVertex: id x pos -> v

The vertex can be observed regarding its identifier and its position. So the observer "getVId" acts on a vertex and returns an identifier "id" and the observer "getPos" acts on a vertex and returns the position "pos."

getVId: v -> id
getPos: v -> pos

The behavior of the vertex is defined through the axioms. The minimum amount of characteristics is determined by applying the observers on the constructors. In this case only the minimum amount is given, so there are no further constraints on the behavior.
Following are the specifications of the generic graph, that serves as basis for the specifications of the objects in the three levels, and the specifications of all the conceptual levels.

Directed Graph (adopted from Gill [8])

```
sort vertex
c       makeVertex:  id x pos -> v
o       getVID:  v -> id
o       getPos:  v -> pos
axioms
        getVID(makeVertex(id1, pos1)) = id1
        getPos(makeVertex(id1, pos1)) =pos1
```

```
sort edge
        import vertex
c       makeEdge: id x vs x ve-> e
c       addVertex: v x e -> e
o       getEID: e -> id
o       getVertex: e x vid -> v
o       getStart: e -> v
o       getEnd: e -> v
axioms
        getEID (makeEdge(id1,vs1,ve1)) == id1
        getEID (addVertex (v1,e1)) == getEID (e1)
        getVertex (makeEdge(id1,vs1,ve1),vid) == if getVID(vs1) = vid then vs1
        else if getVID(ve1) = vid then ve1
        else Error
        getVertex (addVertex (v1,e1),vid) == if getVID (v1) = vid then v1
        else getVertex (e1,vid)
        getStart (makeEdge(id1,vs1,ve1)) == vs1
        getStart (addVertex (v1,e1)) == getStart (e1)
        getEnd (makeEdge(id1,vs1,ve1)) == ve1
        getEnd (addVertex (v1,e1)) == getEnd (e1)

sort graph
        import edge
c       create: O -> dg
c       addEdge: e x vs x ve -> dg        {edges are added together with their vertices }
o       getEdge: eid x dg -> e
o       adjVerts: dg x v x v -> boolean
axioms
        getEdge (eid1,create) == ERROR
        getEdge (eid1,addEdge(e1,dg1)) == if getEid (e1) = eid1 then e1
                else getEdge (eid1,dg1)
        adjVerts ( create, v1,v2) == FALS E
        adjVerts ( addEdge (e1,vs1,ve1), v1,v2)=={trace to makeEdge or addVertex}
        adjVerts (dg1,v1,v2) == if there exists an edge that has those two vertices
        as start and end vertices.
```

Planning Level

```
sort    place       is_a  vertex
c       makePlace: id x pos-> pl
o       getPID: pl -> id
o       getPos: pl -> pos
axioms
        getPID(makePlace(id1, pos1))==id1
        getPos(makePlace(id1, pos1))==pos1

sort    highway  is_an edge
c       makeHighway: name x plf x pls-> hw
o       getHwName: hw -> name
o       getFirst: hw -> pl
o       getSecond: hw -> pl
axioms
        getHwName(makeHighway(nm1,plf1, pls1 ))-> nm1
```

```
        getFirst(makeHighway(nm1,plf1, pls1 )) -> plf1
        getSecond(makeHighway(nm1,plf1, pls1 )) -> pls1

sort    NSHighway    is_a highway
c       makeHighway: name x npl x spl-> vhw  {north-south hiway}
o       getHwName: vhw -> name
o       getNCity: vhw -> npl                  {get Northern termination}
o       getSCity: vhw -> spl                  {get Southern termination}

sort    EWHighway      is_a   highway
c       makeHighway: name x epl x wpl-> hhw   {west-east hiway}
o       getHwName: hhw -> name
o       getECity: hhw -> epl                  {get Eastern termination}
o       getWCity: hhw -> wpl                  {get Western termination}

sort    hiwaySystem
c       makeHSystem: Ø -> HS
c       addHighway: hw x HS -> HS
c       makeInterchange: hw x hw x pl x HS-> HS
o       isHighway: name x HS -> bool
o       canSwitch: name x name x HS x place -> bool
axioms
        isHighway(nm1, makeHSystem)== false
        isHighway(nm1, addHighway(hw1, HS1))==if getHWName(hw1)=nm1
                                               then true
                                               else isHighway(nm1, HS1)
        isHighway(nm1, makeInterchange(hw1, hw2, pl1, HS1))==
                                               isHighway(nm1, HS1)
        canSwitch(nm1, nm2, makeHighway, pl1)== false
        canSwitch(nm1, nm2, addHighway(hw1, HS1), pl1)==
                                   if getHwName(hw1)= nm1 or nm2 then false
                                   else canSwitch(nm1, nm2, HS1, pl1)
        canSwitch(nm1, nm2, makeInterchange(hw1, hw2, pl1, HS1), pl2)==
                           if getHwName(hw1) = nm1 or nm2 and
                              getHwName(hw2)=nm1 or nm2 and
                              pl1 =pl2
                           then true
                           else canSwitch(nm1, nm2, HS1, pl2)
```

Instructional Level

```
sort entrance is_a vertex
c       makeVertex: id x dir -> ent
o       getdir: ent -> dir
axioms
        getdir (makeVertex(id1,dir1)) == dir1

sort exit is_a vertex
c       makeVertex: nb -> ex
o       getnb: ex -> nb
axioms
        getnb (makeVertex(nb1)) == nb1

sort highway is_a edge
```

```
        import entrance, exit
c       makeEdge: id x start x end x length -> hi
o       getlength  : hi-> length
o       getdir: hi-> dir         { additional operators, serving facilitate the   }
o       getnb: hi-> nb           { access to vertices from the Interstatesystem  }
axioms
        getlength (makeEdge(id1,start1,end1,length1)) == length1
        getlength (addent (ent1,r1)) == getlength (r1)
        getlength (addex (ex1,r1)) == getlength (r1)
        getdir (makeEdge(id1,start1,end1,length1)) == getdir(start1)
        getdir (addent (ent1,r1)) == getdir ( getstart (r1))
        getdir (addex (ex1,r1)) == getdir ( getstart (r1))
                  { getdir is an observer in entrance }
        getnb (makeEdge(id1,start1,end1,length1)) == getnb(end1)
        getnb (addent (ent1,r1)) == getnb (getend (r1))
        getnb (addex (ex1,r1)) == getnb (getend (r1))
                  {getnb is an observer in exit }

sort  junction
        import highway
c       create  :  id x exhi x ex x enthi x ent  -> ju
o       getID: ju -> id
o       getexhiID: ju -> id
o       getnb: ju -> nb
o       getenthiID: ju -> id
o       getdir: ju -> dir
axioms
        getID (create (id1, h1, ex1, h2, ent1)) == id1
        getexhiID (create (id1, h1, ex1, h2, ent1)) == getID(h1)      { these are    }
        getnb (create (id1, h1, ex1, h2, ent1))  == getnb(ex1)        { observers    }
        getenthiID (create (id1, h1, ex1, h2, ent1)) == getID(h2)     { in highway }
        getdir (create (id1, h1, ex1, h2, ent1))  == getdir(ent1)

sort ISSystem is_a graph
        import highway, junction
c       addjun: ju x dg -> dg
o       getjun: id x dg -> jun
o       canswitch: ju x exhi x enthi -> boolean
axioms
        gethighway (id1,addjun (ju1,dg1)) == gethighway (id1)
        getent (id1,h1,addjun(ju1,dg1)) == getent (id1,h1,dg1)
        getex (nb1,h1,addjun(ju1,dg1)) == getex (nb1,h1,dg1)
        getjun (id1,addjun(ju1,dg1)) == if getID (ju1) = id1 then ju1
                                         else getjun (id1,dg1)
        canswitch (ju1, exhi1, enthi1) == if (getexhiID (ju1) = getID (exhi1)) and
                                             (getenthiID(ju1) = getID(enthi1))
                                           then TRUE else FALSE
```

Driver Level

```
sort    ramp        is_a vertex
c       makeRamp: id -> rp
o       getRpID: rp -> id
axiom
```

```
        getRpID(makeRamp(i)) == i

sort    onRamp  is_a  ramp
c       makeRamp: id x direction -> onrp
o       getDirection: onrp -> direction
axioms
        getDirection(makeOnRamp(i, d)) == d

sort    offRamp  is_a ramp
c       makeRamp: id x number -> offrp
o       getNumber: offrp -> num
axioms
        getNumber(makeOffRamp(rp, num)) == num

sort    lane
c       makeLane: id x leftNeighbor x rightNeighbor -> ln
o       getLnID: ln -> id
o       getLeftNeighbor: ln -> leftNeighbor
o       getRightNeighbor: ln -> rightNeighbor
axioms
        getLnID(makeLane(i)) == i
        getLeftNeighbor(makeLane(i, ltn, rtn)) == ltn
        getRightNeighbor(makeLane(i, ltn, rtn)) == rtn

sort    breakdownLane  is_a lane
{Note: Breakdown lanes can be on both sides of the highway}
c       makeLane: id x leftNeighbor x rightNeighbor -> bdLane
o       getLeftNeighbor: bdln -> leftNeighbor
o       getRightNeighbor: bdln -> rightNeighbor
axioms
        getLeftNeighbor(makeLane(i, ltn, rtn)) == ltn
        getRightNeighbor(makeLane(i, ltn, rtn)) == rtn

sort    travelLane  is_a  lane
c       makeLane: id x leftNeighbor x rightNeighbor -> tLane
o       getLeftNeighbor: tln -> leftNeighbor
o       getRightNeighbor: tln -> rightNeighbor
axioms
        getLeftNeighbor(makeLane(i, ltn, rtn)) == ltn
        getRightNeighbor(makeLane(i, ltn, rtn)) == rtn

sort    passingLane  is_a  lane
c       makeLane: id x leftNeighbor x rightNeighbor -> pLane
o       getLeftNeighbor: pln -> leftNeighbor
o       getRightNeighbor: pln -> rightNeighbor
axioms
        getLeftNeighbor(makeLane(i, ltn, rtn)) == ltn
        getRightNeighbor(makeLane(i, ltn, rtn)) == rtn

sort highway  is_an edge
c       makeHighway: name -> hw
c       addOnRamp: onrp x hw -> hw
c       addOffRamp: offrp x hw -> hw
c       addBreakdownLane: bdLane x hw -> hw
```

```
c       addTravelLane: tLane x hw -> hw
c       addPassingLane: pLane x hw -> hw
o       getOnRamp: onId x hw -> onrp
o       getOffRamp: offId x hw -> offrp
o       getLane:  lnId x hw -> ln
axioms
        getOnRamp(oni, makeHighway(n)) == error
        getOnRamp(oni, addOnRamp(onrp1, hw1)) == if oni = getRdID(onrp1)
                                    then onrp1 else getRamp(on1, hw1)
        getOnRamp(oni, addOffRamp(onffrp1, hw1)) == getOnRamp(oni, hw1)
        getOnRamp(oni, addBreakdownLane(bdln, hw1)) == getOnRamp(oni, hw1)
        getOnRamp(oni, addTravelLane(tln, hw1)) == getOnRamp(oni, hw1)
        getOnRamp(oni, addPassingLane(pln, hw1)) == getOnRamp(oni, hw1)
        getOffRamp(offi, makeHighway(n)) == error
        getOffRamp(offi, addOnRamp(onrp1, hw1)) == getOffRamp(offi, hw1)
        getOffRamp(offi, addOffRamp(onffrp1, hw1)) == if oni = getRpID(offrp1)
                                    then offrp1 else getOffRamp(off1, hw1)
        getOffRamp(offi, addBreakdownLane(bdln, hw1)) == getOffRamp(offi, hw1)
        getOffRamp(offi, addTravelLane(tln, hw1)) == getOffRamp(offi, hw1)
        getOffRamp(offi, addPassingLane(pln, hw1)) == getOffRamp(offi, hw1)
        getLane(lni, makeHighway(n)) == error
        getLane(lni, addOnRamp(onrp1, hw1)) == getLane(lni, hw1)
        getLane(lni, addOffRamp(onffrp1, hw1)) == getLane(lni, hw1)
        getLane(lni, addBreakdownLane(bdln, hw1)) == if lni = getLnID(bdln)
                                        then bdln
                                        else getLane(lni, hw1)
        getLane(lni, addTravelLane(tln, hw1)) == if lni = getLnID(tln)
                                    then tln
                                    else getLane(lni, hw1)
        getLane(lni, addPassingLane(pln, hw1)) == if lni = getLnID(pln)
                                    then pln
                                    else getLane(lni, hw1)
```

Towards Acquiring Spatio-Temporal Knowledge from Sensor Data

Kazuo Hiraki and Yuichiro Anzai

Department of Computer Science, Keio University,
3-14-1, Hiyoshi Kohoku-ku Yokohama 223 Japan
E-mail: {hiraki, anzai}@aa.cs.keio.ac.jp

Abstract. This paper presents an architecture for acquiring spatio-temporal knowledge. This architecture uses two different algorithms – *generalization to interval*(GTI) method and *feature construction* method – for learning from sensory/perceptual information. These methods generalize over positive/negative examples of target knowledge, and output a *constraint program* that can be used declaratively as a learned concept about spatio-temporal patterns, and procedurally as a method for reasoning about spatio-temporal relations. Thus our methods transform numeric spatio-temporal patterns to symbolic declarative/procedural representations. We have implemented these two algorithms with ACORN, a system that acquires spatio-temporal knowledge by observing examples. In this paper, we give two examples from different domains –layout problems and robot-commands learning – to demonstrate the ability of the system and the flexibility of constraint programs for knowledge representation.

1 Introduction

Acquiring spatio-temporal knowledge is the most important task for intelligent agents in order to behave in the world. For example, an intelligent robot has to have at least the following knowledge:

- *Relations between physical objects.*
- *How to move in the environment with avoiding obstacles.*
- *Physical attributes of objects, such as color, weight, shape and so on.*

Furthermore, this knowledge should be represented in a form that enables a human to understand. Since interaction with humans is the essential feature of an intelligent agent, there should be some symbolic representations for this knowledge.

In general, symbolic representation has the following properties:

1. *Vagueness* : If we use first-order logic for representing spatial relations, a predicate that represents a spatial relation and its actual instance do not correspond in a one-to-one fashion. For example, there are many interpretations of the predicate *left_of(block_a,block_b)*. On the other hand, we can use more than one predicate for representing a spatial relation between two blocks. There should be a mechanism to bridge the gap between symbolic expressions and varieties of actual instances.
2. *Context-dependency*: In general, symbolic representation depends on the situation/context. For example, suppose that you want a robot to make a big turn and say just "Big Turn". However, the robot cannot decide its behavior without information of the situation (e.g. the size of the room) where the robot behaves.

Classic reasoning systems such as STRIPS (Fikes 1971) or GPS(Newell 1963) use primitive predicates for representing spatio-temporal knowledge such as:

on(block1, table), right-of(block1,block2) and move(room1, room2).

In order to apply these systems to real-world domains, one would need a perceptual system to provide appropriate symbolic primitives. However, because of the above two properties of symbolic representation, the perceptual system has to deal with critical problems such as:

- How the system encodes spatio-temporal patterns into symbolic expressions.
- How many symbols should be prepared for reasoning.

These problems make it difficult to define symbolic representation *a priori*. Fig. 1 demonstrates one problem with using *a priori* primitives for concept learning. Suppose that a vision system has six primitives to represent the distance between two objects: very very near, very near, near, far, very far, very very far. Given two scenes of two objects A and B,their distances are supposed to be 11 and 19, as examples for the target concept. The vision system encodes these values to predicates: {very-near(A,B), near(A,B)} and { far(A,B) }. Some learning systems simply apply a kind of *dropping condition rule* to these predicates. Winston's ARCH system (Winston 1975) and Connell's system (Connell 1987) are designed in this fashion: a vision system translated images into a set of symbolic facts, which were then used by a concept learning system. This would mean that the system could not describe both examples with a single concept (all conditions would be dropped), even if this may be an appropriate decision.

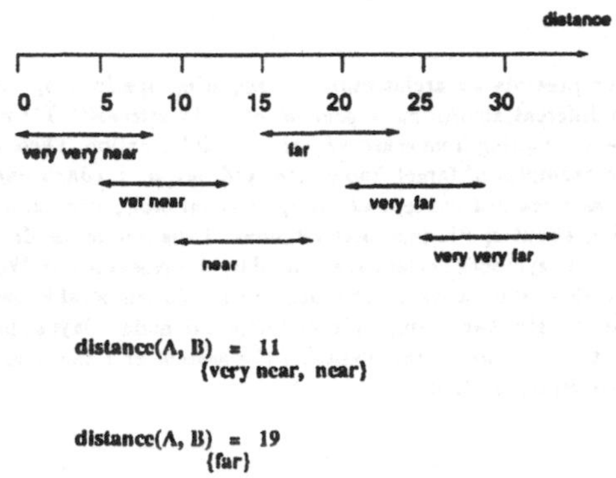

Fig. 1. Inappropriateness of using *a priori* primitives

To deal with these problems, we have proposed learning constraint expressions between symbol and sensory/perceptual information as intermediate representations. Based on this idea, a learning system called ACORN[1] was developed (Hiraki et al. 1991a ; Hiraki et al. 1991b). ACORN inductively learns symbolic constraints of spatial relations from positive and negative examples of simple visual images, and makes use of those constraints for a variety of performance tasks such as scene descriptions, layout tasks and so on. Recently, we have made the extension of ACORN's learning method to learning natural language commands for controlling a robot.

In the following, we describe ACORN and its learning architecture. Section 2 describes a general architecture for acquiring spatio-temporal knowledge. Section 3 describes in detail the learning method used in ACORN. Section 4 presents two examples to demonstrate ACORN system. One is learning spatial relations and the other is learning natural language commands for controlling robots. Section 5 gives concluding remarks.

2 A Learning Architecture for Spatio-Temporal Knowledge

In this section, we discuss an architecture for acquiring spatio-temporal knowledge. In relation to the two properties of symbolic representation (i.e. *vagueness* and *context-dependency*), a desired learning architecture must take account of the following points especially in real-world domains:

i. *Learning from numeric information*:
   Most perceptual/sensory information is expressed in continuous, numerical forms. The learning architecture has to transform continuous values into discrete ones.
ii. *Tractability of learned knowledge*:
   The learned knowledge should be useful for a variety of performance tasks. It should be possible to recognize examples, to generate examples of the concept, or to make inferences.

[1] ACquisition Of Relational ExpressioN

Fig.2 illustrates the architecture of ACORN that addresses these points. In this architecture, the *intelligent agent* has sensors and actuators, and the *human* gives some positive and negative instances with respect to the target concept(*symbolic knowledge*). Because all of the concepts are learned from information from sensors and/or actuators, we call the data from sensors and actuators *primary features* of the concepts.

There are three important characteristics in this architecture. First, both intelligent agents and human exist in the same environment (*Real-World*). To acquire situated symbolic knowledge, the human (i.e. teacher) and the intelligent agents must share the same situation. Second, this architecture uses two different learning algorithms – *generalization to Interval*(GTI) and *feature construction* – for learning from sensory/perceptual information (Section 3 describes these algorithms in detail). Finally, the learned knowledge is represented in *constraint programs*. Constraint programs represent relations between each sensor and/or actuator, and make it possible to perform various of tasks in terms of *constraint programming language*(Sussman 1980;Leler 1988). In our system, constraint programs are represented in EPOCH(Extended PrOlog with Constraint Handling), a new constraint logic programming system developed by ourselves(Nishizawa et al. 1991). The following section describes constraint programming in more detail.

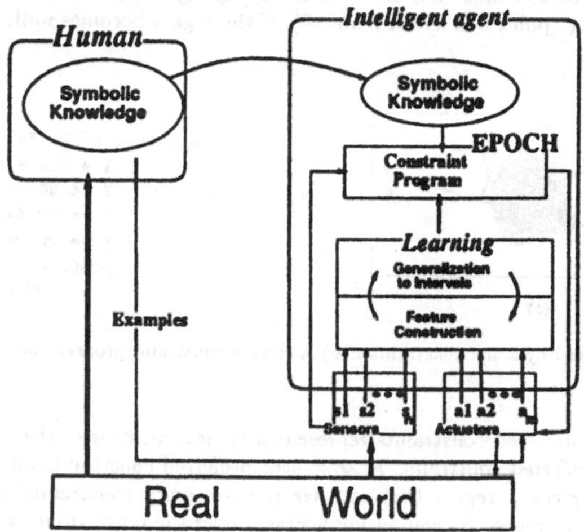

Fig. 2. An architecture for acquiring spatio-temporal knowledge

3 Constraint Programming

ACORN represents learned knowledge in a *constraint logic program* (Jaffar 1987). In general, a constraint logic program consists of a set of *extended Horn clauses*, each of which has the form:

$$Relation(\langle args \rangle) \leftarrow P_1 \wedge P_2 \wedge \ldots \wedge P_n \wedge C_1 \wedge C_2 \wedge \ldots \wedge C_m$$

where P_i is a *term* (as in Prolog) and C_j is an algebraic constraint expression such as an equation or inequality.

One of the most remarkable features of constraint-based languages is that the user does not have to write a procedure explicitly in order to solve constraints. The user has only to give *declarative* relations among variables. Therefore constraints can be used to make a variety of inferences. For example, the constraint

$$convert(C, F) \leftarrow (F = \frac{5C}{9} + 32)$$

can be used to make predictions either about F given C or C given F, without requiring separate rules. In general, constraint expressions make use of a powerful *constraint solver* that is used to make inferences or solve problems. This approach lets declarative knowledge be used procedurally, allowing ACORN to reason about its learned knowledge various tasks.

One of the advantages of using a constraint logic programming language is that semantics can be formulated more easily than other constraint-based languages(Sussman 1980;Leler 1988;Borning 1981), using logic programming semantics (see Jaffar(1991) for further discussion). Constraint logic programming has proved useful in a number of domains, such as option trading(Lassez 1987) and scheduling (Dincbas 1988).

ACORN uses EPOCH, a constraint logic programming system developed in our laboratory.[2] As noted earlier, EPOCH's constraint solver uses the simplex algorithm to solve linear programming problems. EPOCH is similar to CLP($\Re$) (Lassez 1987) in its ability as a constraint solver. However, EPOCH uses two types of constraints: *necessary constraints* that must be satisfied and *preferred constraints* that should be, but do not have to be satisfied. Preferred constraints are used to choose a preferred solution when there is more than one possible answer (see Nishizawa et al.(1991) for more details).

For example, the necessary constraints for "point a is left-of point b" are expressed by the fan-shaped region illustrated in Fig. 3a. Because EPOCH's constraint solver only works with linear problems, we approximate this region with linear inequalities; four linear inequalities in this case. EPOCH incorporates these inequalities in a constraint program that represents the fan-shaped region; Fig. 3b shows the program in Prolog form. The four inequalities (the necessary constraints) correspond to four lines delimiting the region used to define "left-of". The satisfying region shrinks as the number of constraints increases (e.g. by adding "point b is left-of point c"). If the region becomes null, the constraints cannot be satisfied.

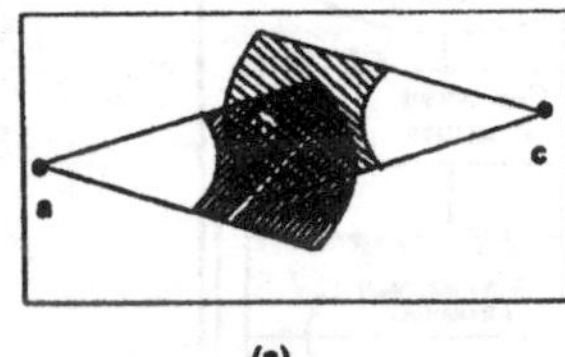

(a)

```
constraint( a([Xa,Ya]),b([Xb,Yb]) ) :-
        X = (Xb - Xa), Y = (Yb - Ya),
        Y =< 20.0*X - 100.0,
        Y >= -0.6*X, Y =< 0.4*X,
        Y >= 20.0*X - 200.0,
        pref:(X = 7.5), pref:(Y = 0.0).
```

(b)

Fig. 3. (a) A region defined by some constraints. (b) A simple constraint program for the region.

On the other hand, preferred constraints represent a typical member of the learned concept. In Fig. 3b, *pref:* indicates a preferred constraint. ACORN uses preferred constraints for finding an appropriate location of an object given a region that satisfies the necessary constraints of the learned relation. Preferred constraints are created by computing averages over the set of training instances.

4 Learning Method

ACORN uses two different algorithms – *generalization to interval*(GTI) method and *feature construction* method – for learning constraint programs. In this section, we first describe GTI method by using a simple example and then describe feature construction method.

4.1 Generalization to Interval Method

As described in the previous section, learned knowledge is represented in a constraint program of EPOCH. As the system observes positive and negative instances of the concept, it builds both necessary and preferred constraints.

In order to learn necessary constraints, ACORN uses GTI method that is essentially based on the simple learning rule:

> "For each attribute of the concept, given numeric values, x_1 and x_2, from two positive training instances, assume that all numeric values between x_1 and x_2 are also examples of positive instances".

This rule is an application to constraint expressions of Michalski's "closing interval generalization" heuristic (Michalski 1983).

[2] Both EPOCH and ACORN are implemented in Quintus Prolog.

This can be used directly with linear attributes such as distance, but for cyclic attributes, such as direction defined as an angle, two positive instances produce a pair of intervals. In this case ACORN adopts the heuristic of generalizing over the smaller interval.

Table 1 presents the incremental algorithm of GTI in more detail. Given a set of old constraint (region), R_n, and the new positive/negative instance, this algorithm returns a new set of constraints, where p_i is a parameter for dealing with noisy data, and q_i is for representing typicality of the concept.

Table 1. ACORN's learning algorithm GTI

```
For a set of Region R_n, parameter p_i and q_i w.r.t. r_i ∈ R_n and instance I
  If I is positive instance
      If exist r_i ∈ R_n that contains I
          then change p_i, q_i
      Else extend r_i(∈ R_n) so that it includes I
          and change parameters p_i, q_i
  If I is negative instance
      If exist r_i ∈ R_i that contains I
        and p > α
          then replace r_i with boundary points
      Else change q_i.
```

Fig. 4(1) - (5) illustrate how this algorithm makes constraints (regions) with incremental input of instances. Fig. 4 takes the instances of the spatial relation, "next-to", where a spatial object is assumed to be a point for simplicity. In this example, all of the instances are represented in two primary features - *distance* and *direction* between each pair of objects. ACORN already has a region illustrated in Fig. 4(1). Next, when a point **b1** is input to ACORN as a positive instance, the algorithm extends the region so that it includes b1 (See (2))[3]. Then, a negative example b2 is input to ACORN (see (3)) and the noise tolerance parameter p over a threshold α, the algorithm replaces the region with four boundary points (See (4)).

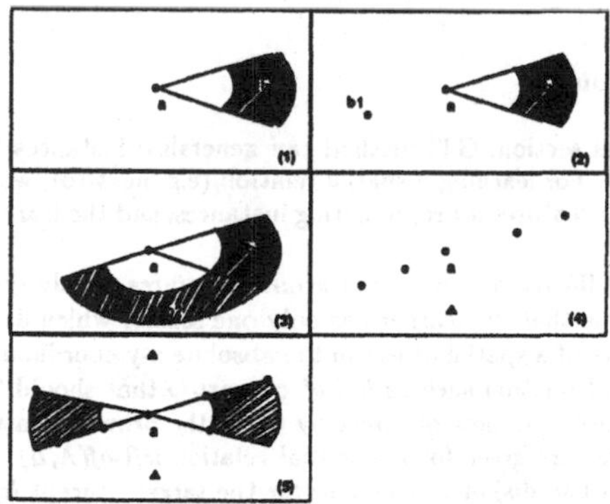

Fig. 4. Extending and replacing of regions for learning next-to (1) - (5)

[3] This region is selected in term of measuring the distance between the instance and the original region.

Constraint generator constructs EPOCH's constraint programs with respect to regions at each stage. The following programs correspond to the two regions in the Fig. 4(5). Note that there are two disjunctive clauses for two regions. As described before, "pref:(Exps)" means preferred constraint.

```
constraint(next_to,
   loc(A,[X1,Y1]), loc(B,[X2,Y2]) ):-
         X = X2 - X1, Y = Y2 - Y1,
         Y =< -0.345895*X,
         0.361615*X =< Y,
         pref:(X = 7.5), pref:(Y = 0.0).
constraint(next_to,
   loc(A,[X1,Y1]), loc(B,[X2,Y2]) ):-
         X = X2 - X1, Y = Y2 - Y1,
         -0.515502*X =< Y,
         Y =< 0.255538*X,
         pref:(X = -7.2), pref:(Y = 0.0).
```

In the above learning algorithm, two important parameters are used for dealing with real-world domains. First is the noise parameter p_i. In a real-world domain, perceptual data and/or sensor data might contain noisy data. Any system that tackles with this domain should care about this characteristic. The parameter p_i is defined as follows:

$$p_n = \frac{number\_of\_neg\_instance(R_n)}{number\_of\_instances(R_n)} \quad (0 \leq p_n \leq 1)$$

If $p_n > \alpha$ then replace R_n

Else $p_n := \frac{number\_of\_neg\_instance(R_n)+1}{number\_of\_instances(R_n)+1}$ (α is a positive value less than 1)

where *number_of_instances*(R_n) is a function which returns the number of all input instances. On the other hand, *number_of_neg_instance*(R_n) returns the number of all negative instances. Note that generalization to interval does not replace the region without the value beyond the threshold.

Second parameter, q_i, is the vector of feature values. This parameter represents typical values for a region and averages over the set of training instances. q_i is translated to EPOCH's preferred constraints. As described before, preferred constraints are used for finding an appropriate value of a region that is represented by the necessary constraints of the learned concept. By using this characteristic, ACORN can generate an instance from the learned concept (e.g. layout tasks described in the following section).

4.2 Feature Construction

As described in the previous section, GTI method can generalize instances to disjunctive regions that represent the target concept. For learning a spatial relation (e.g. next-to), we may assume that *distance* and *direction* are appropriate features for representing instances, and the learner has sensors for detecting these features.

In general, however, it is difficult to assume that *primary features* are always appropriate for the target concept. For example, assume that the learner has only one sensor, which detects the global location of spatial object(i.e. coordinates of a spatial object in the absolute x-y coordinate system). In this case, the learner cannot learn a spatial relation such as *left-of* or *next-to* that should be invariant under translation. Fig. 5 shows the inappropriateness of direct by using the primary features. In Fig. 5, three pairs of positive/negative instances are given for the spatial relation *left-of(A,B)*. If the learner directly uses GTI method, GTI generates two disjunctive regions for the target concept *left-of(A,B)*:

$$((X_A = 5) \wedge (Y_A = 5) \wedge (X_B = 10) \wedge (Y_B = 7)) \vee ((X_A = 15) \wedge (Y_A = 20) \wedge (X_B = 25) \wedge (Y_B = 17))$$

These constraints, however, have no meaning for the target concept. Direct using of primary features sometimes makes large numbers of disjunctions, which is inappropriate for representing the target concept.

For tackling this problem, ACORN uses *feature construction method*, which discovers new features appropriate for representing target concepts. The idea of feature construction method is based on *constructive induction*. Matheus (Matheus 1991) discusses some questions that a system must answer when constructing new features:

I. When should new features be constructed?
II. What constructive operators should be used and which of the existing features should they be applied to?
III. Which (if any) features should be discarded?

In ACORN, when disjuncts are over the given threshold, feature construction method is invoked and generates new features. After that, GTI reconstructs regions by using these new features. Table 2 illustrates the algorithm of feature construction method, and Table 3 describes relationship between feature

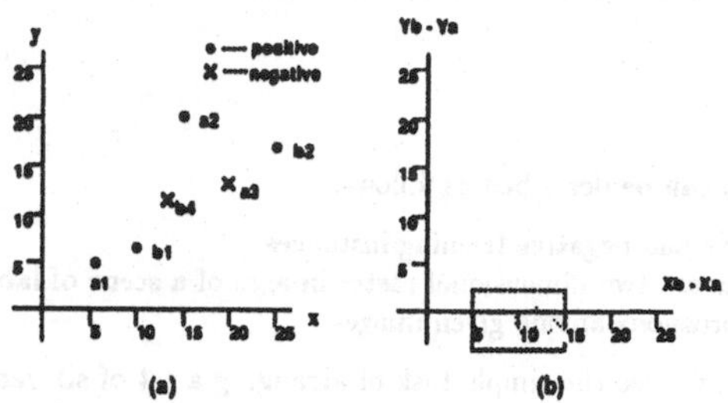

Fig. 5. An example of feature construction

construction and GTI method, where feature construction method selects two existing features and applies a operator from $\{-,+,*,/\}$ to these two features[4].

Table 2. Feature construction: algorithm for constructing new features

Let OP be a set of operators $OP = \{-,+,*,/\}$. For a set of existing features $F_{old} = \{f_1,\cdots,f_n\}$
    Select two features f_i, f_j from F_{old}
        $F_{old} := F_{old} - \{f_i, f_j\}$
    Select an operator op_k from OP
        f_{new} := New term which applies op_k to f_i, f_j
    $F_{new} := F_{old} + f_{new}$
    Return F_{new}

Table 3. Relation between GTI and feature construction

Let N be a number of regions constructed by GTI, F be a set of existing features $F = \{f_1,\ldots,f_n\}$ and γ be a positive integer
1. If $N > \gamma$
    Then F_{new} := feature_construction(F),
    M := a number of new regions constructed by GTI using F_{new}
2. If $M < \gamma$ then return M
3. Else goto 1.

For example, feature construction method can discover the new features:

$$X_B - X_A,\ Y_B - Y_A$$

for the example of Fig.5(a) and GTI method can generalize an appropriate region for the target concept *left-of(A,B)*. The shaded rectangle in Fig.5(b) shows the region generalized by using the new features.

[4] Feature construction method remembers the history of selected two features for avoiding redundancy

5 Examples

As we described earlier, the advantage of using constraint expressions is that the knowledge can be used in a variety of performance tasks without requiring special-purpose representations or rules. If knowledge about spatial relations is represented as a set of constraint expressions, the performance system should be able to recognize examples of a given relation, generate scenes that satisfy a set of relations, make inference from a set relations, or detect redundancy and inconsistencies in a set of relations. Also if a robot learns as constraint expressions relations between commands and actions, the robot becomes able to move according to learned commands and also to make moves in terms of combination of some commands. In order to show ACORN's abilities and generality, this section describes two examples from different domains – *acquiring spatial relations for a layout task* and *acquiring natural language commands for controlling a robot*.

5.1 The Layout Task

Learning for a layout task can be described as follows:

Given: A set of positive and negative training instances,
where instances are two-dimensional raster images of a scene of labeled objects.
Find: Constraint expressions among given images.

For the layout problem, we use the simple task of arranging a set of six rectangles into a 'face'. Fig. 6a shows the training instances given to ACORN. In order to learn relations, the system needs relation names, as well as labeled scenes. Thus, the rectangles in these figures are labeled *eye1*, *eye2*, *eyebrow1*, *eyebrow2*, *nose*, *mouth* , and there are two relations given: **above(X,Y)** and **right-of(X,Y)**. Fig. 6b gives a partial list of the relations that are associated with each scene. ACORN uses these as positive training instances for building the necessary constraints that define the spatial relation. In particular, it builds a *constraint program* for each relation as follows:[5]

$$\begin{array}{l} constraint(Relation\text{-}name, \\ \quad [Vertex^1_1, Vertex^1_2, Vertex^1_3, Vertex^1_4], \\ \quad [Vertex^2_1, Vertex^2_2, Vertex^2_3, Vertex^2_4]) \leftarrow \\ \quad necessary\_constr_1, \cdots, necessary\_constr_n, \\ \quad preferred\_constr_1, \cdots, preferred\_constr_m. \end{array}$$

Note that the two arguments in this relation are represented as lists of vertices.

After building constraint programs for the relations above and right-of, ACORN can construct arrangements of rectangles given a specification in terms of the two acquired relations. For example, given the specification:

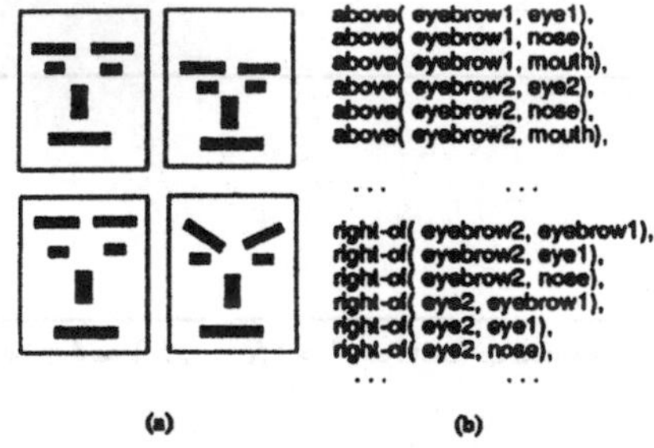

Fig. 6. Face domain input for ACORN: (a) Images (b) Partial list of training relations.

{**right-of(eye2,eye1)**,
above(eyebrow1,eye1), **above(eyebrow2,eye2)**,
above(eye1,nose), **above(nose,mouth)**} ,

ACORN generates the scene in Fig. 7a, while

{**right-of(eye2,eye1)**,
above(eyebrow1,eye1), **above(eyebrow2,eye2)**,
above(eye2,nose), **above(nose,mouth)**} ,

creates the scene in Fig. 7b. Note that the nose and mouth are 'off-center' in these scenes because the preferred constraint for above is straight above. If we add the constraints **right-of(eye1,nose)**, and **right-of(nose,eye2)** to the specification, we get the 'corrected' scene as in Fig. 7c.

[5] We use standard Prolog notation here.

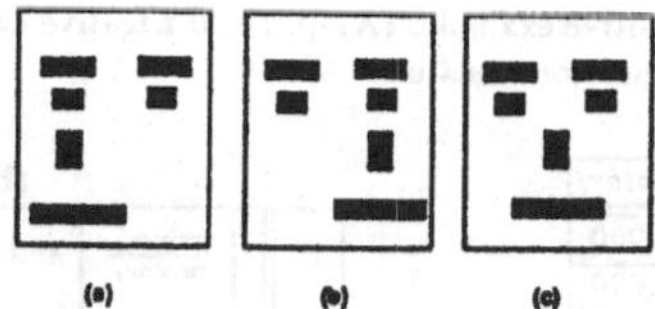

Fig. 7. Faces generated from specification.

This is a simple demonstration of the generality of ACORN's acquired knowledge, and the versatility of constraint expressions. Once the system has learned a few key spatial relations, it can use this knowledge in a variety of domains and performance tasks. In addition to this example, ACORN can use learned constraint programs to predict the location of missing objects. In this task, ACORN can predict the location of any number of missing components. As more and more components are missing, the necessary constraints become looser and looser. If all components are missing, then the system uses only the preferred constraints, and this becomes a form of the layout task.

5.2 Acquiring Natural Language Commands for Human-Robot Interaction

Recently, we have applied ACORN to learn natural language commands for controlling a robot. As described in the previous section, the meaning of symbolic knowledge depends on situation and/or context. In this section, we describe the example of learning the natural language command, "Big Turn".

Fig. 8 shows the positive instances((A) ~ (C)) and the negative instance(D) given to ACORN for learning the commands "Big Turn". Circles represent the locus of the robot and squares represent the room in which the robot is located. Note that Fig.8(D) is a negative instance even though its radius is larger than (A)'s because "Big Turn" depends on the size of the room. Table 4(a) shows the primary features and the time series values of these features[6]. In Table 4, $sensor_r$ and $sensor_l$ denote the data from the robot's right and left sonar sensor, and $motor_r$ and $motor_l$ denote the speed of right and left wheels respectively.

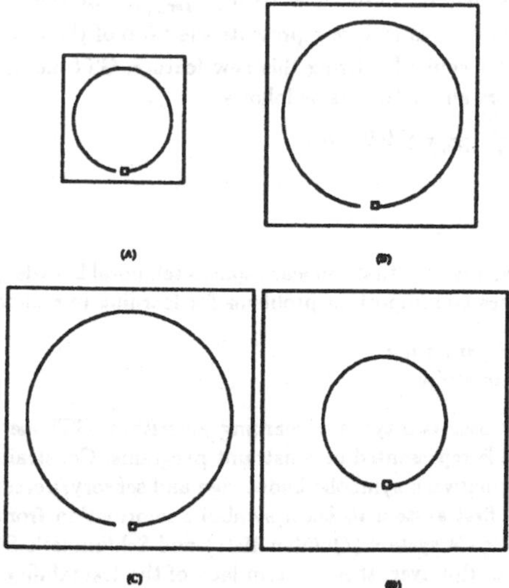

Fig. 8. Positive examples (A)-(C) and negative example (D) for command "Big Turn"

[6] It is not so simple to define the sampling interval and the correspondences between data. For simplicity, we assume that all instances can be represented with the same number of samples.

Table 4. (a) Primary features of positive examples (A)-(C) and negative example (D) for "Big Turn", and (b) the new features constructed by feature construction

(a)

		$sensor_r$	$sensor_l$	$motor_r$	$motor_l$
(A)	0	5.000	165.000	0.000	0.000
	1	17.293	176.762	5.965	4.080
	2	5.086	165.005	5.965	4.080
	3	21.668	181.068	5.965	4.080
(B)	0	15.000	305.000	0.000	0.000
	1	36.864	326.259	10.046	8.162
	2	15.150	304.999	10.046	8.162
	3	43.643	332.989	10.046	8.162
(C)	0	20.000	350.000	0.000	0.000
	1	44.589	373.973	11.302	9.418
	2	20.173	350.008	11.302	9.418
	3	52.809	382.133	11.302	9.418
(D)	0	85.000	285.000	0.000	0.000
	1	109.557	309.006	7.221	5.336
	2	85.139	285.040	7.221	5.336
	3	117.775	317.166	7.221	5.336

(b)

		$\frac{motor_l}{motor_r}$	$sensor_r + sensor_l$	$\frac{\frac{motor_l}{motor_r}}{sensor_r^0+sensor_l^0}$
(A)	1	0.684079	194.056	0.004024
	2	0.684079	170.092	0.004024
	3	0.684079	202.737	0.004024
(B)	1	0.812416	363.124	0.0025388
	2	0.812416	320.15	0.0025388
	3	0.812416	376.634	0.0025388
(C)	1	0.833258	418.564	0.00225205
	2	0.833258	370.182	0.00225205
	3	0.833258	434.943	0.00225205
(D)	1	0.739018	418.564	0.00199735
	2	0.739018	370.18	0.00199735
	3	0.739018	434.941	0.00199735

As described in the previous section, if we directly use primary features, GTI method generate a large number of disjunctions such as:
$\{(17.293 \le sensor_r^1 \le 44.589) \wedge (sensor_l^1 = 176.762) \wedge (motor_r^1 = 5.965) \wedge (motor_l^1 = 4.080)\}\ \vee$
$\{(17.293 \le sensor_r^1 \le 44.589) \wedge (326.259 \le sensor_l^1 \le 373,973) \wedge (motor_r^1 = 5.965) \wedge (motor_l^1 = 4.080)\}\ \vee$
$\{(17.293 \le sensor_r^1 \le 44.589) \wedge (sensor_l^1 = 176.762) \wedge (10.04 \le motor_r^1 \le 11.302) \wedge (motor_l^1 = 4.080)\}\ \vee$
$\{(17.293 \le sensor_r^1 \le 44.589) \wedge (326.259 \le sensor_l^1 \le 373,973) \wedge (10.04 \le motor_r^1 \le 11.302) \wedge (motor_l^1 = 4.080)\}\ \vee \cdots \vee$
$\{(17.293 \le sensor_r^1 \le 44.589) \wedge (326.259 \le sensor_l^1 \le 373,973) \wedge (10.04 \le motor_r^1 \le 11.302) \wedge (8.162 \le motor_l^1 \le 9.418)\}$
This is because the command "Big Turn" depends on the size of the room.

However, by using feature construction method, ACORN can discover the new feature that is appropriate for representing the target command. In Table 4(b), $\frac{\frac{motor_l}{motor_r}}{sensor_r^0+sensor_l^0}$ shows the new feature discovered by feature construction method. This feature represents the ratio of the radius of the circle ($\frac{motor_l}{motor_r}$) to the size of the room($sensor_r^0 + sensor_l^0$). Using this new feature, GTI method generates the constraint expression between the sensors and actuators as follows:

$$0.00225205 \le \frac{\frac{motor_l}{motor_r}}{sensor_r^0+sensor_l^0} \le 0.004024$$

6 Concluding Remarks

This paper described ACORN, a system that can learn spatio-temporal knowledge from sensory/perceptual information. ACORN addresses two important problems for learning in real-world:

1. *Learning from numeric information*
2. *Tractability of learned knowledge*

For these problems, ACORN uses two types of learning algorithm, GTI method and feature construction, and learned knowledge is represented in constraint programs. Constraint program can be seem as intermediate representations between symbolic knowledge and sensory/perceptual information.

Note that this is not the first system to learn symbolic information from numeric data. Aha's IBL system (Aha 1991), Quinlan's C4 system (Quinlan 1987) and Schlimmer's STAGER (?) are classifiers that work with numeric data. However, these system lack of the tractability of learned knowledge, and have only been used for classification task. On the other hand, ACORN's constraint program can be used to a variety of the performance tasks such as recognizing examples, generating examples that satisfy a set of constraints, making inference, and so on.

All of intelligent agents must acquire spatio-temporal knowledge from sensory/perceptual information and should make use of acquired knowledge for communicating with a human. ACORN is the our first step to overcome this problem.

Acknowledgment

This work is being carried out in the context of *PRIME* project. The authors would like to acknowledge the members associated with *PRIME*. The authors also wish to acknowledge Toyoshi Okada, Yoshinobu Yamamoto, John Gennari and Pat Langley for thier comments and discussion during the initial stages of this work.

References

Aha, D.W., Kibler, D. and Albert, M.K.: Instance-based learning algorithms, *Machine Learning*, 6, 37-66, 1991.

Borning,A.: The programming language aspects of ThingLab: A constraint-oriented simulation laboratory. *ACM Transactions on Programming Languages and Systems*, 3, 353-387, 1981.

Breiman, L., Friedman, J. H., Olshen, R. A. and Stone, C. J.:*Classification and Regression Trees*, Wadsworth International Group, 1984.

Connell,J. H. and Brady,M.: Generating and generalizing models of visual objects, *Artificial Intelligence*, 31, 159-183, 1987.

Dincbas, M., Van Hentenryck, P., Simmonis, H., Aggoum, A., Graf, T. and Berthier, F.: The constraint logic programming language CHIP, *In Proc. of the International Conference on Fifth Generation Computer Systems*, 693-702, 1988.

Fikes, R. E. and Nilson, N. J. : STRIPS: A new approach to the application of theorem proving to problem solving, *Artificial Intelligence*, 2, 1971.

Haar, R. L.: Sketching: Estimating object position from relational descriptions, *Computer Graphics and Image Processing*, 19, 227-247, 1982.

Hiraki, K., Gennari, J., Yamamoto, Y., and Anzai, Y. : Learning Spatial Relations from Images, *In Proc. of Eighth International Machine Learning Workshop ML'91*, 407–411, 1991.

Hiraki, K., Gennari, J., Yamamoto, Y., and Anzai, Y. : Encoding Images into Constraint Expressions, *In Proc. of Thirteenth Annual Conference of Cognitive Science Society*, 31–36, 1991.

Jaffar,J. and Lassez,J.: From unification to constraints, In Furukawa,K., Tanaka,H. and Fujisaki,T. (eds.), *Logic Programming '87, Lecture Notes in Computer Science*, Springer, 1987.

Lassez, C.: Constraint logic programming and option trading, *IBM Technical Report*, 1987.

Leler, W.: *Constraint Programming Languages: Their Specification and Generation*, Addison-Wesley, 1988.

Matheus, C.J.: *The Need for Constructive Induction*, In Proc. of Eighth International Machine Learning Workshop ML'91, 173–177, 1991.

Michalski, R.: A theory and methodology of inductive learning, In Michalski, R., Carbonell, J. and Mitchell, T. (eds.), *Machine Leaning: An Artificial Intelligence Approach*. Los Altos, CA: Morgan Kaufmann, 1983.

Newell, A. and Simon, H. A.: GPS, A program that simulates human thought, In Feigenbaum, E.A and Feldman, J. (eds.), *Computers and Thought*, McGraw-Hill, New York, 1963.

Nishizawa, T., Hiraki, K. and Anzai, Y.: EPOCH: A constraint logic programming language with goal constraint description, *Journal of Japanese Society for Artificial Intelligence*, 7, No. 3, 105–113, May, 1989.

Quinlan, J. R.: Simplifing decision trees, *Int. Journal Man-Machine Studies*, 27, 221-234, 1987.

Schilimmer, J.C.: Incremental adjustment of representations in learning, In *Proc. of the 4th International Workshop on Machine Learning*, 79–90,1987.

Sussman, G. J. and Steel, G. L.: CONSTRAINTS – A language for expressing almost-hierarchical descriptions, *Artificial Intelligence*, 14, 1-39, 1980.

Winston, P.H.: Learning structural descriptions from examples, In Winston, P.H. (ed.), *The Psychology of Computer Vision*, McGraw-Hill, 1975.

Yamada, A., Amitani, K., Hoshino, T., Nishida, T., Doshita, S.,: The analysis of the spatial description in natural language and the reconstruction of the scene, *Journal of Information Processing Society of Japan*, 31, No.5, 660-672, 1990.

Automatically Acquiring Knowledge by Digital Maps in Artificial Intelligence Planning Techniques (+)

A.Barbanente (*), D.Borri (**), F.Esposito, P.Leo (***), G.Maciocco (****), F.Selicato (**)

Abstract. Any ES research, in particular planner ES research, shows that knowledge acquisition is a bottleneck when building up the ES prototypes. From this viewpoint, the possibility of automatically acquiring knowledge for ES, at least with reference to special themes and problems, may be seen as constituting an interesting line of research.

Inductive and EBL methodologies, founded on quantitative and qualitative knowledge, are the main contributions that the ML (a branch of AI) makes to the above mentioned goal. Both approaches, even if very little investigated in the planning domain, seem to invite further research.

We refer in particular to the potentials of automatically learning by maps.

Relating to the research on planner ES prototypes for urban environmental control, this paper intends to set up a preliminary discussion on the perspectives offered by the automatic interpretation of key variables in order to make elementary inferences concerning urban typologies and situations.

1 Introduction

This contribution is based on the work that our research team has been carrying out for about two years, on building planner expert systems - like GREEN, for instance - aimed at performing environment-oriented town planning. GREEN, in particular, was built to suggest strategies for improving urban green and, more generally, open spaces as physical-social resources in a town [2, 3].

Working on GREEN we experienced great difficulty -not to cite other major problems- when collecting the domain expert knowledge and representing it

---

(+) The paper refers to the research coordinated by F. Clemente, University of Cagliari, "Integration of Environmental Control and Spatial Organization Methods", Ministry of Scientific Research, Research Program of National Interest and Relevant Interest for Science Development. The research unit of the University of Bari is directed by D. Borri.

The present paper is the result of a team work. The individual contributions are articulated as follows: paragraph 1 is by D. Borri, paragraph 2 is by A. Barbanente, paragraph 3 is by F. Selicato, paragraph 4 is by F. Esposito and P. Leo, paragraph 6 is by G. Maciocco.

(*) C.N.R. - I.R.I.S., Bari, Italy; (**) Department of Town Planning, Polytechnic of Bari, Italy; (***) Institute of Computer Sciences, University of Bari, Italy; (****) Institute of Town Planning, School of Engineering, Universty of Cagliari, Italy.

Working on GREEN we experienced great difficulty -not to cite other major problems- when collecting the domain expert knowledge and representing it through a profitable interaction between experts and knowledge engineers. In other words, we had to face in our small world, the "dark ages" of the exciting expert company, which by now is growing, as Wiggins jokingly says for the planning field [16]. Difficulties arose, we were to learn this later, because of the so-called representation mismatch, that is the difficulties of a knowledge representation process marked by the clash between the expert knowledge natural language on one hand, and the knowledge machine representation, on the other.
We came to share the idea, already accepted by other scholars, that the problem of a plural order in modelling the world (modelling the real world by the expert, modelling the expert models of the real world by the knowledge engineer) [5], will probably be overcome, in a not too distant future, in our perplexing planning domain too, through machine learning processes, that is through our intelligent systems' abilities to learn automatically.
The strategic expert knowledge which constituted the main target when building GREEN as a metaplanner and -at least till now- metarules processer, showed a marked sensitivity towards existing environmental structures, much less evident in our discipline's heritage.
In fact it is precisely the evaluation and the creative -more than stereotyped- classification of those environmental structures that some of the experts involved in the research assumed to be their major planning task. GREEN I, a problem solver for the shortage of green open spaces in an Italian town, firstly looked at the presence of emergencies and resources in the landscape around the town, aiming at their better use and preservation, abandoning the idea of building new artificial structures. A ravine on the borders of the town's historical centre first drew the attention of experts working at GREEN and triggered their strategies.
The potentials offered to a new kind of adaptive planning, by an automated classification of landscape key-elements as they relate to the solving task, and even a future creative discovering classification of those key-elements, with an emphasis on the connections in the environmental systems, led us to activate the research to which the present paper refers, suggesting in particular a hybrid learning system, where statistical induction by data is linked to symbolic concept operation.
In fact, the knowledge capital in the domain of environmental planning is not very substantial as yet, and by now machine learning processes can compete in the field with human learning, in less unfavourable terms than those dramatically presented by Lenat for current general learners [18, p. 255].
When we have robots that can walk into the ravine or along the cliff and stay there to subjectively perceive the characteristics that may candidate those natural elements as solutions to the specific planning problem (forms, colours, smells, vegetation etc.) the learning process will come closer to the human model. At present we look perspectively at a codification of environmental properties starting from "primitives" [18, p. 256], so as to correspond to the indirect perception of the environment by the expert when involved in analysing maps (hence, three levels of cognitive models interact in our solving task).

The character of the expert's mental models in an environmental analysis and representation aimed at changing the world by plans, the temporalization of the expert's virtual worlds, the markers of properties for objects in the world and the categorization functions which are founded on them [15], the transformation function through subsequent states of the world-system to be defined through cognitive forms and models involving time variables, are at the basis of the machine learning we are targeting, although we are fully aware of our limitations.
We think that an integration of the many learning methods along the hybrid line suggested -even if still in an embryonic stage- through the present approach, i.e. combining data, statistical induction, case-based and explanation-based induction, analogical induction [4, p. 251], and a deeper immersion into the world of these learners, will eventually result in a little step forward towards the complex reactive and strategical environment classification/ planning which we regard today as our main practical as well as ethical task.
The paper is divided into three sections.
Section one refers to the new interaction among different forms of knowledge within landscape/environmental planning, with an emphasis on the structural meaning and values of land morphology. It discusses dialectics between rules and anomalies, generalities and localisms, aiming at identifying the rules framing and modifying the environmental system within a specific local context.
The role played by mental models in this sort of analysis and the plural meanings of map models are also debated.
Section two illustrates the various steps taken when choosing some environmental key elements from a map in order to test the potentials of machine learners for recognition and classification procedures.
Finally, section three describes in detail the AI method we used to process numerical and non numerical information related to the above mentioned issues and perpectives.

2 Defining the Experimental Framework

Environmental issues have aroused a growing interest among Italian experts for regional planning and analysis in the last few years. This is in many ways coupled with the awareness that physical planning requires both a redefinition and an expansion of its forms and contents, and with a need to satisfy the ever- growing demand for environmental quality from large sections of the population.
This process has originated lines of research which had been explored to a lesser degree and from different viewpoints in the past. It has also led to a confrontation with other fields of knowledge and - thanks to this expansion of horizons - to the reconsideration of specific themes which had long been the prerogative of experts from other disciplines [20].
In this paper we shall focus in particular on the studies on regional morphology and on the closely related studies concerning the description and representation of a territory. What is meant by morphology here is not the mere recognition of formal characters but more properly an endeavor to find methods for the reading

and interpreting of forms starting from the very ways they were generated and transformed by man and nature in the course of time.

In spite of the diversity of methodological approaches, analytical contents and planning trends, a common field of research may be discerned which is geared to identifying the rules for framing and transforming the environmental system within specific local contexts. These rules are to be assumed as guidelines for defining the extent to which sites may be transformed, their compatible uses and the basic principles underlying any modification.

This does mean that the need to find extraordinary, specific and unique sites should be left unheeded. Quite the contrary: these are actually the main sites to be detected nowadays while well-established, tradition-based rules are disowned because modern man perceives them as dull and uniforming elements. But, to acknowledge rules as well as their exceptions is the result of our mental constructions: they do not exist in nature nor are they given us. Hence the problem we are confronted with is to make them both plausible by means of our analytical, descriptive and interpretative efforts [30].

It is plain that this interpretative effort will involve different levels of knowledge in environmental disciplines. But it is also clear that, while defining the rules governing the ways regional structures are transformed and shaped, the recognition of such rules and thus the description/representation of the formal characters of a region become particularly relevant [for different aspects of this problem, see 1, 11, 27]. The forms through which a region makes itself evident to our perception are a key element for investigating the network of relationships set up by the several community members using, modifying and "consuming" the region, in other words the relationships between the formal and the social features of regional transformations.

The research under way aims at giving an experimental contribution to the issues outlined above by resorting to artificial intelligence. The investigation was structured as follows: an expert or a team of experts made an accurate, exhaustive and complex description of the main elements of a region on technical maps in order to identify both the recurrent/regular and the abnormal/exceptional features of a region. Hence, morphological regional types were defined and classified within a system where each category was distinguished by specific attributes or correlations of attributes.

This preliminary part of the research is of a certain interest. First of all, the expert tends to avoid an aprioristic categorizing of the emergent morphological features which often confine the interpretation of regional resources within a pre-established framework and thus hamper any attempt to recognize the regular characters or morphological constants by which a physical space is organized. Such intrinsic values of environmental resources may be disclosed in certain social, economic and cultural contexts only through a "fresh" interpretation.

Moreover, the need to comprehensively describe regional structures in order to set up specifically characterized categories, the capacity to make complex, discursive descriptions based on numbers, together with the possibility of defining the systematic relations among the attributes of a certain typology all call for an in-depth investigation of regional structures. This will undoubtedly be a fruitful

source of issues to be compared with other items of the investigation at a later stage.
Finally, similar means of research may contribute to surmounting the traditional limitations of the analyses and classifications of regional resources, such as parallel and scarcely interrelated descriptions. In fact, this new approach would set up complex "environmental frames" based on the mere definition of some significant morphological characters of a region - albeit within the bounds of the present experimentation.

3 Some Environmental Key-Elements for Learning from Technical Maps

From the initial phases of the research, it was believed that, alongside and supporting the work of E.S. planners, automatic learning from maps could be directed towards finding out new potential areas useful for the planning, in this specific case, of green areas thus prospecting a choice of areas ready to be used and facilitating a solution for the E.S. planner.
The technical maps to be explored could support, on a generic scale of representation, any kind of information or thematic content. Traditional maps, drawn from aerophotogrammetric cartography were used even though, as the research develops, we envisage the use of numerical cartography. Cartography is the operating instrument which the experts are called to address together to build a structured set of meanings describing the contents, represented in order to classify them following the principles of coincidence, prevalence, rarity, singularity, vicinity, distance, etc., in typologies known as belonging to the different classes. The experts in these fields are required to supply typological descriptions, in a natural language, of objects that are prototypes of classes, that is significant examples of these classes, deduced from the graphic representation chosen. The inductive method of learning is still in the experimental phase and will have to set up the rules for the expert classes from the analysis of the symbolic descriptions so as to be able to identify all types of classes with the same characteristics.
However even within the limits imposed by the utilization of a normal graphic representation of territorial transformations in the natural environment, we included as one of our aims classification intended as a planning method essentially directed to some fundamental descriptive categories of the whole environment.
In a prevalently "pre-planning" phase, by using the informative contents of an aerophotogrammetric representation to a scale of 1:5000, in order to have a significant area offering the greatest number of different situations, we attemped to make a first classification of environment kind selecting, in particular, three classes characterized by well defined descriptive rules. In particular we analyzed a territory of about 15 kmq comprising the town of Mottola in the province of Taranto. The classes, marked C1, C2, and C3, describe respectively, a particular form of terrace slope called "cliff", a morphological configuration cutting along hill slopes called "ravine" and a particular model of rural space organization that

originated from the process of rural transformation defined "grid system of farms". They tipify the kind of environment often present in the Apulia region, which it is thought in the future could be submitted to automatic identification once the concordance of the descriptive rules has been verified. For each class a description is given in natural language (1) from which the experts were invited firstly to deduce the classification criteria following table 1. Lastly a modular grid was drawn to fit over the map corresponding to the classes C1, C2 with a square surface of one hectare and with a square surface of four hectares for the C3 class. This grid has the structural purpose of subdividing the territory into suitable units of form and dimension for recognizing their expert class once all the class rules are respected (figure 1). Specifically the básic module was dimensioned to make it possible both to identify all the essential elements defining the expert class and to make a generalization of the class itself (figure 1).

The automatic learning method permits the exploration of the grid covering the map, square by square recognizing the element E belonging to class C. To obtain this it is necessary to give the learning system characteristic examples of each class found in the modular dimensions of the chosen grid. The explanation of graphic symbols is given to understand the symbols on the map so avoiding doubts as to interpretation.

As the research stands today the direct experimentation of automatic learning has begun and it was beleived it should first regard classes C1 and C2, because the same grid can be used.

For both the chosen environmental categories, examples were given to the machine from which the automatic learning system drew the generalized description of the related expert classes. Thus for this generalization the system is able to recognize pieces of territory, belonging to the memorized environmental classes, only when all the conditions described as discriminant for the recognition itself are verified.

	CLIFF	RAVINE	SYSTEM OF FARMS IN REGULAR GRID
HEIGHTS			
	270-350 m.	190-270 m.	265-280 m. asl
GRADIENTS			
	20-35%	couples of parallel scarps, variably distant from 0 to 50 m., mark contour lines with cusp shapes	lower than 5%

	CLIFF	RAVINE	SYSTEM OF FARMS IN REGULAR GRID
PARTITION WALLS	absent	absent between scarps; the first wall external to the scarp is mostly parallel to the scarp itself	intersections between partition walls make angles of 80°-100°
BREAST WALLS	horizontal level measure: 5-10 m. main shape: parallel to contour lines	absent	absent
SETTLEMENTS	scattered, isolated if present, break-points or reduction of breast walls	absent	mainly 1, max 3 buildings with max surface of 200 sq. m., within a lot enclosed along the whole boundary (four sides, one of which coinciding with a road edge)
ROADS SYSTEM	only sheep tracks mainly intersecting breast walls, with variable angle of incidence	absent	mainly straight with different hierarchical level, with constant section within the single level
HIGH-TRUNK TREES	absent	absent	absent

Tab. 1. Classes and Classification Criteria

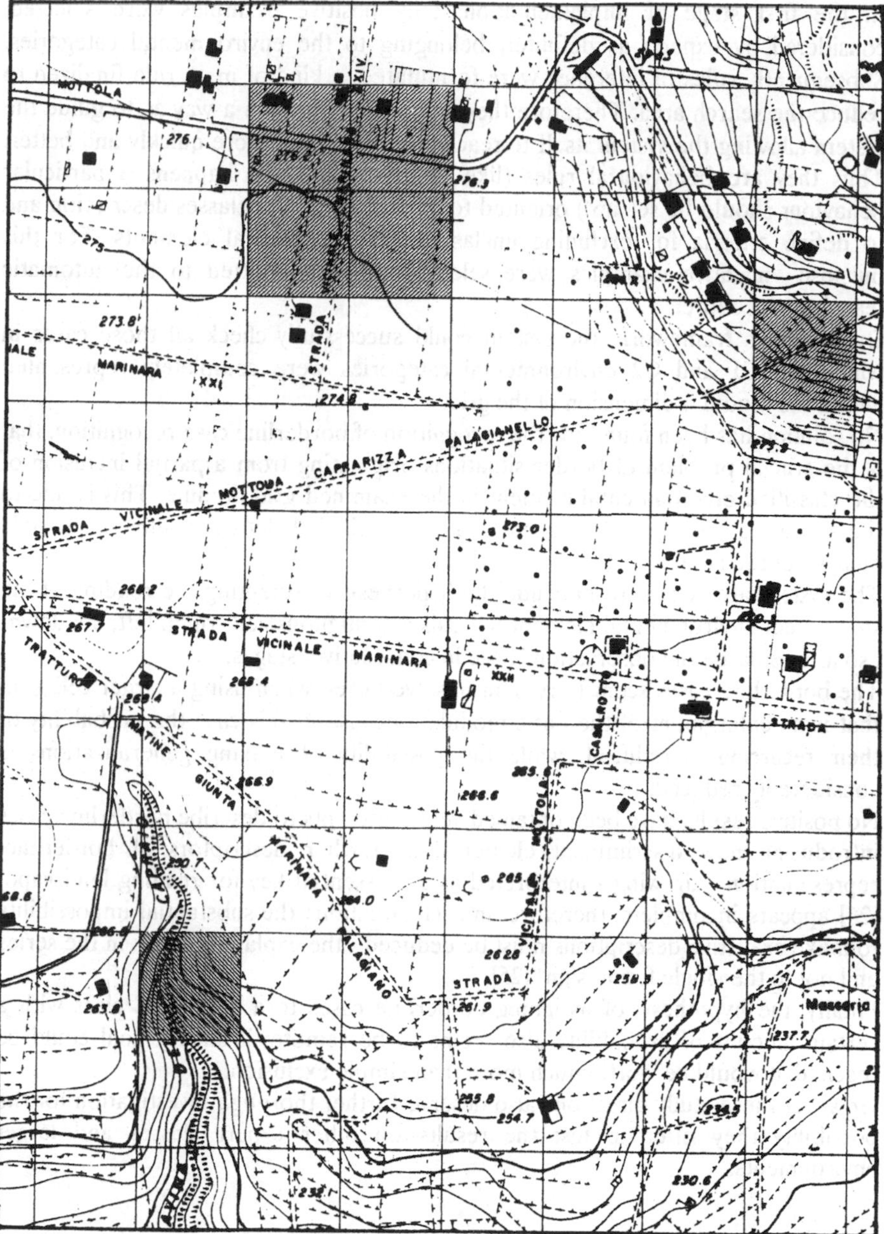

Fig. 1. Part of the 1:5000 map used for the description of C1, C2, and C3 classes, whose three characteristic examples are represented by their proper elementary dimension in the grid that covers the map.

In the first stage of implementation, only positive examples were selected, considered by experts as definitely belonging to the environmental categories. Subsequently rules of inference were formulated, a kind of meta-rule finalized to reduce the search area. Therefore they were set up in such a way as to guide the system allowing the system itself to reach the final result more quickly and better. Thus they are behavioural rules (like "if a certain thing happens a particular behaviour should be set up") oriented to enrich the expert classes description and to define criteria for excluding unclassified environmental elements. For this purpose negative examples were selected to be submitted to the automatic learning procedure.

By this rules framework, the system could successfully check all those cases in which the C1 and C2 environmental categories were completely represented within the modular dimension of the grid.

No solution has been found for the recognition of borderline case recognition, that is the crucial problem of border situations originating from a partial inclusion of the classified environmental element in the examined grid module. This is due to the specific automatic learning method approach that does not allow a possible analysis of the context.

The system also seems to preclude the hypothesis of orienting the reading of the subsequent environmental element towards a contiguous cell -right, left, up, down-, so as to enlarge the observation space in consecutive stages.

The borderline cases seem to remain unsolved even when using a larger cell grid, that is an enlargment of the basic module, because in this case the probability of their recurring is reduced; while the possibility of making generalizations is considerably reduced.

No positive results have been obtained yet in attempts to describe borderline cases introducing new discriminant elements, as further descriptors of borderline; representation - drawing - interpreted as an "essential key for reading landscape" [26] appears incomplete, therefore, in such situations the substantial impossibility to make exaustive descriptions must be deduced: "the explanation lies in the series and not to the single found sign" [25].

Finally, the hypothesis of assigning borderline cases to a specific C class with a certain amount of probability also seems to be remote: if such a goal could be reached, it would be worth much more than simple exclusion.

However these study directions also deserve further thorough investigation for the possibility they offer to test the results on other expert classes and larger environments.

4 An Inductive System Learning as a Knowledge Acquisition Tool in Developing Expert Systems

Techniques of inductive learning may be used to directly acquire knowledge in the form of production rules: from a series of facts describing some domain of application it is possible to induce general statements characterizing the domain [9, 22], by means of generalizations based on a defined number of pieces of evidence [23, 28]. More specifically, learning from examples (supervised learning) aims at classifying new objects, with a training set of preclassified objects available for which a description following a certain formalism is provided. Clustering (unsupervised learning) finds how a given set of not classified instances could be grouped into "natural" classes or clusters; it is a form of learning by observation and it is similar to the problem of categorization in psychology [31].

Symbolic languages are used in order to represent, in a close to natural language form, not only the observed events and the learned concepts, but also the a-priori knowledge, useful in a knowledge intensive approach to learning. The main advantage when using symbolic descriptions instead of classical feature vectors is in the possibility of treating structural descriptions, involving relations among the attributes.

In the following the possibility of using the inductive learning system RES [10] to automatically construct the knowledge base of a planning expert system will be investigated. The inductive method is intended for the acquisition, from preclassified examples, of the production rules of a system for the identification on a cartographic map of the spaces for the environmental control of green and parks.

RES is a supervised inductive learning system integrating statistical data analysis and probability-based techniques with symbolic concept learning methods. Such a hybrid approach is definable as empirical and supervised learning because it focuses on the classification of objects, with a training set of examples belonging to the given disjoint classes at disposal. The observations and the concepts are described in a symbolic language allowing relations between objects to be represented. RES combines a data analysis technique for linear classifying (Discriminant Analysis) with the conceptual algorithm INDUBI, inspired by INDUCE [21] algorithm. The system allows noisy and incomplete observations to set up a statistical guide in the generalization process (as a bias in selecting candidate concepts).

Formally, the problem of learning from examples can be formulated as follows:

given

1) an Example Description Language (EDL);
2) a Concept Description Language (CDL);
3) a set C of n concepts (intentional descriptions of classes) to learn:

$$C = \{C_i \mid i=1,2,...,n\}$$

4) a set F of examples for the concepts in C; the examples represent instances of such concepts and are supplied by the teacher and described by the EDL;
5) a background knowledge defining either problem constraints on the facts or domain specific knowledge;
6) a preference criterion, ranking plausible hypotheses according to expert's preferences;

determine:

a set H of hypotheses or concept descriptions, the most preferable among all sets of possible alternatives.

The examples are descriptions of objects preclassified by the trainer and can be viewed as a collection of decision rules of the form

$$F = \{E_{ik} ::> C_i\} \ i = 1,2,...,n$$

where n is the number of concepts, E_{ik} is an expression of the EDL and represents the event concerning the k-th object, example of the i-th concept C_i.

The result of learning are rules of the form

$$\text{Pattern} ::> C_i$$

where Pattern is an expression in a formal language describing the events characterizing the given class C_i. More precisely, the result of learning is the inductive assertion, i.e. the set of hypotheses H of the inductive paradigm expressed as a set of recognition rules of the kind

$$H = (G_i ::> C_i), \ i = 1,2,...n$$

where G_i are approximate descriptions of the i-th class or concept, expressed by the CDL.

4.1 The Representation Language

The choice of both the EDL and CDL is crucial in learning processes. Generally, the EDL is data-oriented as it should allow an adequate description of typical examples. The detail level of the descriptions can strongly influence the learning process complexity, since too detailed descriptions of objects increase the search space of possible hypotheses, while too simple descriptions may hide relevant characteristics. The CDL should be human oriented since the knowledge acquired should be comparable to that provided by an expert. As an extreme case, the input of an empirical learning system could be bitmap images, while the output hypotheses could be expressed in natural language. The gap existing between EDL and CDL is obviously filled by the learning system, thus the greater the difference the more difficult the inference process becomes.

Having a complex description language at disposal means drawing up multi-level class descriptions, involving attributes and measurable properties of objects, relations among them and higher level descriptors of concepts. The description language of RES is VL_{21}, a multi-valued version of the first order predicate calculus using typed function symbols [17]. The basic component of VL_{21} expressions is the "selector" or relational statement, written as

$$[\, L \# R \,]$$

where:

- L, called "referee", is a function symbol with its arguments;
- R, called "reference", is a set of values of the referee's domain;
- #, is a relational operator defining the relation between the referee and the reference.

Instead of predicates it is the selectors to assume a true or false value and these can be seen as tests in order to state if the predicate and the function values

belong to a defined domain or not. To each variable, predicate or function symbol a domain is associated: nominal, linear, tree structured.
Each VL_{21} expression may be obtained from a set of selectors by applying different operators, including decision operators (::>), logic implication (=>) and inference operators (==>).
VL_{21} may be used as EDL and CDL, its formulas being useful to specify the condition and the action part of a rule. It is possible to use different kinds of rules for different kinds of knowledge such as:

- decision rules to represent examples from a class (the action part defines the class to which the observation belongs);
- inference rules to represent the relationships among the different descriptors (background knowledge);
- generalization rules to define the transformations applicable to facts in the hypótheses generation (selective rules, constructive rules).

4.2 The Application of RES in the Classification of Areas from Cartographic Maps

A first step in order to verify the applicability of RES as an acquisition tool in our domain consists in defining the descriptors. In application, the examples are the symbolic descriptions of equidimensional square areas, elements of a grid, on a technical map. The classes are, initially, only two: the CLIFF-class and the RAVINE-class. In the future more classes will be considered.
Till now some descriptors have been pointed out:

contain_scarp(cell,scarp) — it denotes the scarps which are contained in the examined cell: it has a boolean domain, with cost 6.

contain_wall(cell,wall) — denoting the containment walls that are present in the examined cell: boolean, with cost 6.

contain_settl(cell,settl) — denoting the settlements which are evident within the observed cell: boolean, with cost 6.

contain_road(cell,road) — denoting the roads which are evident within the observed cell: boolean, cost 6.

contain_bottom_of_the_ravine(cell,bottom_of_the_ravine) — boolean descriptor representing the bottom of the ravine in the cell, with cost 6.

contain_contour_line(cell,contour_line) — denotes the contour line which are observable in the examined cell: boolean, with cost 6.

	nominal domain [vineyard, sownfield, treefield, uncultivated, with cost 8.
covered_area(cell)	defines the covered area which is present in the cell: interval domain [0,maxsup], cost 8.
form_contour_line(contour_line)	defines the form of contour line which is present in the cell: nominal domain [normal, cusp], with cost 8.
type_road(road)	defines the type of road present in the cell: structural domain 1 - road 1.1 primary 1.2 secondary 1.2.1 cattle_track with cost 8.
type_wall	defines the type of wall present in the cell: nominal domain: [partition_wall, containment_wall], cost 8.
num_contour_line(cell)	defines the number of contour lines which are present in the cell: interval domain [0..max_num_contour_line], cost 8.
scarp_pair(scarp1,scarp2)	defines the scarp pairs, i.e. scarps with a parallel configuration in the cell: boolean, with cost 10.
wall_pair(wall1,wall2)	denotes the existence in the cell of alligned containment walls: boolean, cost 10.
dis_scar_pair(scarp1,scarp2)	represents the distance between two scarps in the pair: it has an interval domain [0,..,maxdscar], with cost 10.
dis_wall_pair(wall1,wall2)	is the distance between two walls in a pair: the domain is [0,..,maxdwall], with cost 10.
*in_scarp_pair (scarp1, scarp2, *)*	denotes what is contained in a scarp pair: boolean. * can be a contour_line or a bottom_of_the_ravine. Cost 10.
intersection_road_wall(road,wall)	boolean descriptor defining the intersection between walls and roads, with cost 10.
class(cell)	defines the belonging class of the cell, if a CLIFF or a RAVINE.

The representation language VL_{21} is suitable to synthetically and completely describe the ground situations, as well as the relations among the elements that are useful to individuate particular soil configurations.
An example of the VL_{21} description of a cell is found in figure 2.

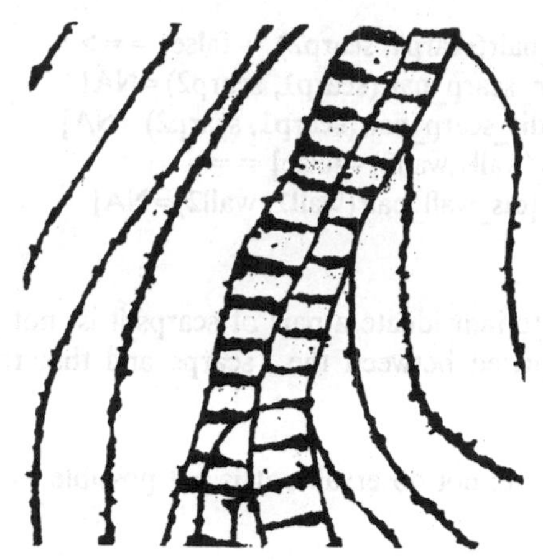

scarp1, scarp2, contour_line1, contour_line2, contour_line3, contour_line4, contour_line5

[contain_scarp(cell1,scarp1) = true]^
[contain_scarp(cell1,scarp2) = true]^
[contain_contour_line(cell1,contour_line1) = true]^
[contain_contour_line(cell1,contour_line2) = true]^
[contain_contour_line(cell1,contour_line3) = true]^
[contain_contour_line(cell1,contour_line4) = true]^
[contain_contour_line(cell1,contour_line5) = true]^
[quote(contour_line1 = 260]^
[quote(contour_line2 = 255]^
[quote(contour_line3 = 250]^
[quote(contour_line4 = 245]^
[quote(contour_line5 = 240]^
[scarp_pair(scarp1,scarp2) = true]^
[dis_scarp_pair(scarp1,scarp2) = 15]^
[in_scarp_pair(scarp1,scarp2) = partition_wall]::>
[class(cell1) = RAVINE]

Fig. 2. A cell example of the class ravine and its VL_{21} description

Some background knowledge is also definable, always as VL_{21} formulas. As inductive learning is a search in the area of inductive assertions, background knowledge is a form of bias and is very useful in order to restrict the search space, when producing the generalized descriptions of the classes.

For example it is possible to express two simple inference rules:

1) scarp1, scarp2 [scarp_pair(scarp1, scarp2) = false] = = >
[in_scarp_pair(scarp1, scarp2) = NA]^
^[dis_scarp_pair(scarp1, scarp2) = NA]
2) wall1, wall2 [wall_pair(wall1,wall2) = false] = = >
[dis_wall_pair(wall1, wall2) = NA]

meaning, respectively:
"when it is not possible to individuate a pair of scarps it is not possible to define that something is comprised between the scarps and that there is a distance between the two scarps"
and
"when two aligned walls are not observable it is not possible to define a distance between the walls".

The system is able to process a particular kind of functional relations between descriptors, related to the applicability of certain measurements to certain situations. Such a condition is expressed by the NA (Not Applicable) value whose semantics is defined. It has the effect of modifying both the generalization and the matching procedures at the level of "extension-against" and "extending references" trasformations.
Some authors [13] have already dealt with the condition of "non applicability" from a theoretical point of view: nevertheless not many examples of implementation are reported in machine learning literature.
The representation language VL_{21} is suitable for synthetically and completely describing the ground situations, as well as the relations among the elements that are useful for individuating particular soil configurations.
By a generalization process the system is able to produce consistent and complete descriptions of the class CLIFF and RAVINE, i.e. concepts. At present we are working to improve the training phase, that is, we are collecting consistent and significant examples of the chosen classes which will be the inputs to RES. Meanwhile the proposed descriptors will be evaluated aiming at verifying their relevance in describing the observed phenomena.

4.3 The Experimentation

The set of available examples were separated into two subsets for the training and testing phase. Specifically 28 and 22 examples were used for RAVINE and CLIFF classes respectively and 18 counter-examples for the two classes.

The used preference criteria concern the description complexity and the cost of generalization, specifically:

a) the most complex generalized descriptions have been preferred, i.e., those expressed by the max. number of selectors;
b) the minimization of the cost of a generalization has been perceived, that is, the min. value of the sum of the cost, associated with each descriptor in the description, has been searched.
The following rules were generalized:

```
[contain_bottom_of_the_ravine(cell1,bottom_of_the_ravine1)=true]^
                    [contain_scarp(cell1,scarp1)]^
                    [contain_scarp(cell1,scarp2)]^
[contain_contour_line(cell1,contour_line1)=true]^
[contain_contour_line(cell1,contour_line2)=true]^
                    [num_contour_line(cell1)=2..9]
                                    ::>
                                   [class(cell1)=ravine]
```

The meaning of generalization is:
If a part of the land contains at least two scarps and two contour lines and the slope is greater than 5%, then a ravine is recognizable in that area.

As to the CLIFF the following generalization was obtained:

```
                    [contain_wall(cell1,wall1)=true]^
                    [contain_wall(cell1,wall2)=true]^
                    [contain_wall(cell1,wall3)=true]^
                    [contain_wall(cell1,wall4)=true]^
                    [type_wall(wall1)=containment_wall]
                                         ::>
                                   [class(wall1)=cliff]
```

Whose meaning is:
If a part of the land contains at least four walls, one of which, at least, is a containment_wall, then in that area a cliff is recognizable.

The recognition rules which have been generalized basing them upon the training set were tested. In particular, we considered a complete map relative to an area of 140 hectars (fig. 3), that was divided into a grid of 140 examples. These elements were shown to a group of experts. They classified the examples into 3 classes: RAVINE (9 elements), CLIFF (10 elements) and REJECT (the rest of the world). This third class represents the grid elements not evidently belonging to the classes of interest. The examples recognized are reported in fig. 4.
It is necessary to observe that elements (13,5) and (14,5) represent limit cases for the class RAVINE: in fact, they do not exhibit all the elements characterizing the class and would constitute doubtful cases for human expert too.

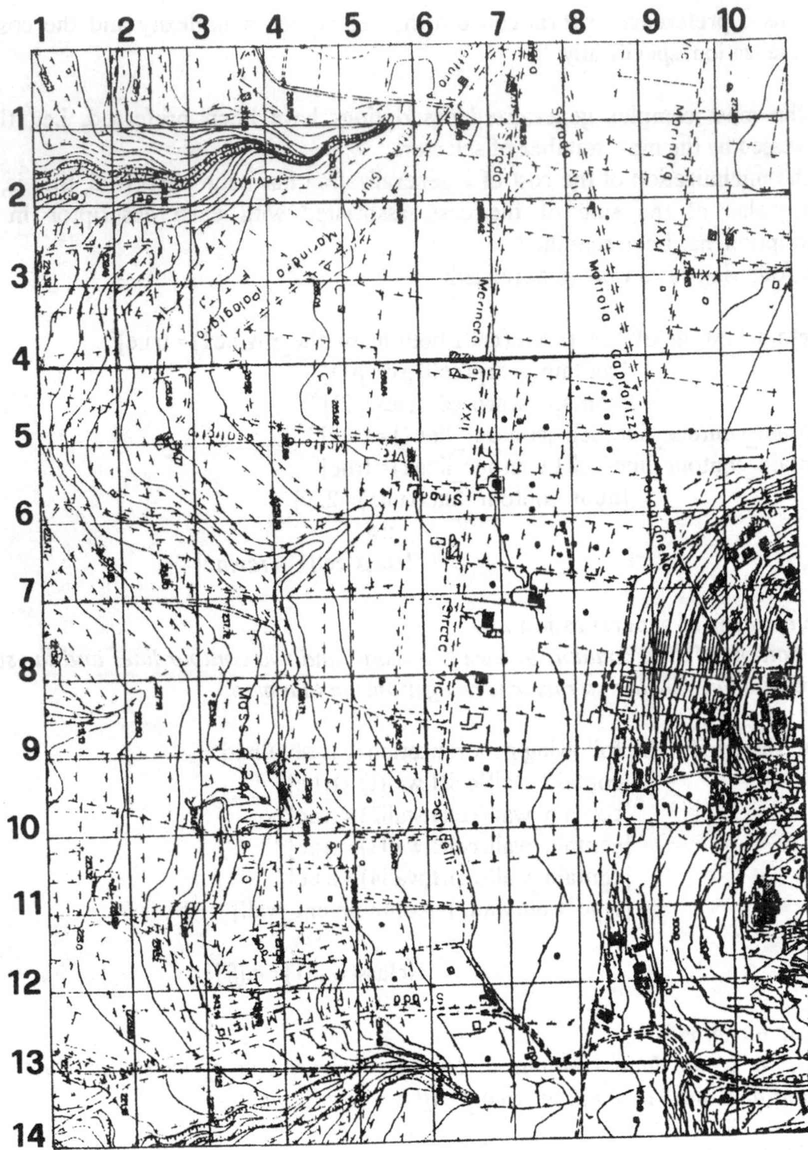

Fig. 3. Complete map of 140 Ha divided into a grid of 140 examples.

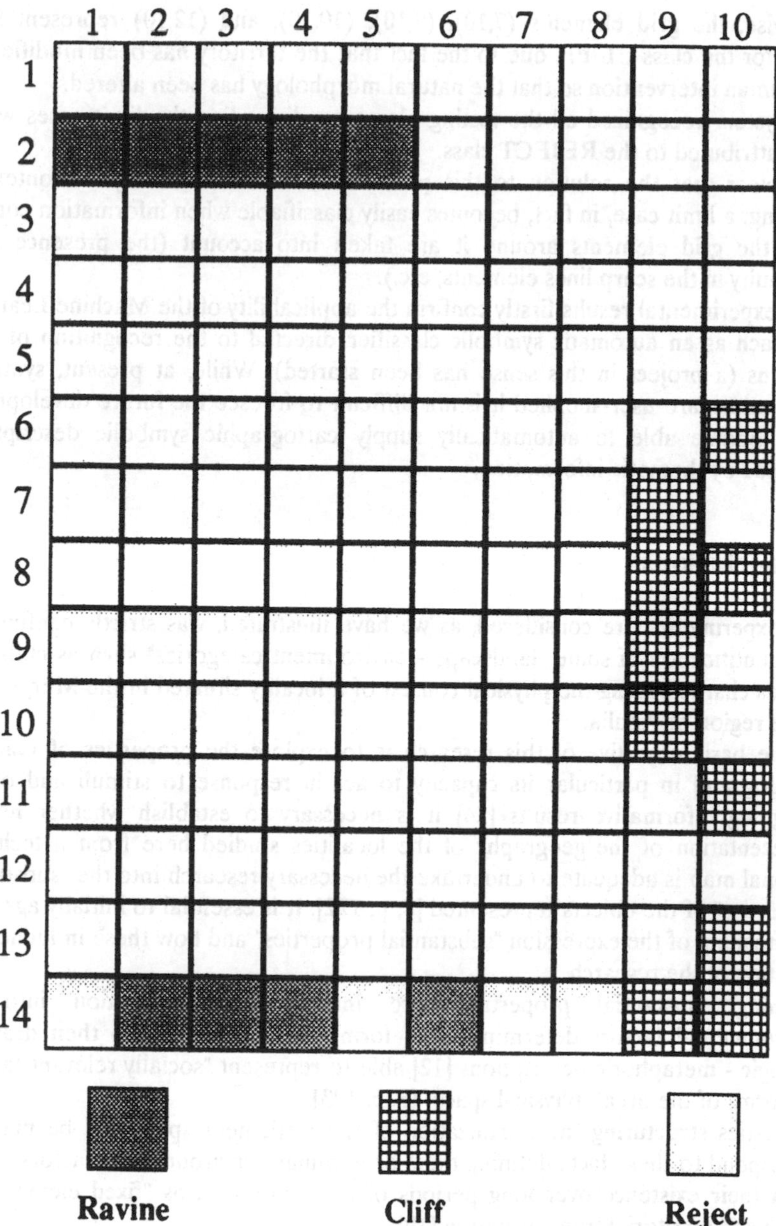

Fig. 4. Recognized examples.

Likewise, the grid elements (7,10), (9,10), (10,10), and (12,10) represent limit cases for the class CLIFF, due to the fact that the territory has been modified by the human intervention so that the natural morphology has been altered.
The system recognized all the testing elements, discarding the limit cases which were attributed to the REJECT class.
It is clear that the solution to this problem is in the possibility of contextual learning: a limit case, in fact, becomes easily classifiable when information coming from the grid elements around it are taken into account (the presence of a continuity in the scarp lines elements, etc.).
Such experimental results firstly confirm the applicability of the Machine Learning approach as an automatic symbolic classifier directed to the recognition of land patterns (a project in this sense has been started). While, at present, symbolic descriptions are user-supplied it is not difficult to foresee the future development of a module able to automatically supply cartographic symbolic descriptions enriched by thematic information.

6. Conclusions

The experiment here considered, as we have illustrated, was strictly confined to the identification of some "landscape - environment categories" such as cliffs and ravines characterizing the physical context of a locality situated in the Murgia hills in the region of Apulia.
As the basic objective of this research is to explore the properties of machine learning and in particular its capacity to act in response to stimuli and obtain intriguing informative results [24] it is necessary to establish whether normal representation of the geography of the localities studied here from a technical regional map is adequate to undertake the necessary research into the "substantial properties" of the objects represented [8, p. 122]. It is essential to initially agree on the meaning of the expression "substantial properties" and how these influence the direction of the research.
Defining substantial properties here implies an investigation into the environmental factors determining the forms of the territory to then draw up analogic - metaphoric descriptions [12] able to represent "socially relevant facts in the forms of the area's physical space" [8, p. 123].
Properties structuring the organization of the settlement space will be made to correspond to these facts defining them as dominant environmental factors which, given their existence over long periods of time, are seen as "fixed elements" of urban and territorial transformation [19].
A critical revision of the contents and usual planning methods accompanies this procedure. This is directed towards a "reflective" treatment [29] of the coherence between the urban and territorial intervention arising in the course of time and therefore not predictable, and fixed environmental features present before the organisation of the settlement space. Hence this research presents a stimulating prospect inasmuch as "machine learning" is expected to probe the hidden features influencing the settlement space. After this essential descriptive phase concerned

with "visible" environmental categories, a learning process is set up following an itinery passing through phases of discovery and exploration of values and leading to the comparision of different kinds of knowledge concerned with environmental oriented planning.

These brief considerations, aimed at explaining the inevitable restrictions of a preliminary machine learning experiment, therefore lead to the overcoming of a prevalently descriptive and taxonomic approach to vast environmental categories and the relative distributive nomenclature to set up a descriptive approach reproducing and developing an attitude to landscape centred around a "coherent relation of inseparable reciprocity with the environment" [7].

Such an approach tends to recover the original tension characterizing research into landscape - environment in some way devitalized, in particular in the building up of base knowledge when it is prevalently developed through taxonomies directed to the drawing up of generic thematic maps to be used for a number of possible combinations.

Representation should instead be based on the specifity of the areas and the problems to be solved, exposing the "signs" of the processes stratifying (in time and space) the relations between population, activities and areas. Problems of this nature naturally imply interdisciplinarity inasmuch as a moving away from accepted methods means a more committed approach involving the systematic comparison of the contributions of the different disciplines to the building up of basic knowledge [19, pp. 63-67].

If this work allows the identification of a "sign" through its describers - as in the experiment in question - some stimulating requisites of machine learning must be established namely:

- a catalogue of components based on the siting data of the sign should not necessarily be drawn up;
- the different readings of a sign as it is represented should be accepted, i.e. its ambiguity should be conserved [25];
- it is necessary, at the same time, to avoid falling into the trap of critical or projectual relativism but rather trigger a learning process of environmental relations underlying the visible manifestations of the sign, of which it is the outcome;
- different disciplines should be involved in the learning process and their critical aptitude for a possible deciphering of the environmental factors dominating the territory stimulated.

Notes

(1) With reference to classes C1, C2 and C3, we quote the original description in natural language as follows.

Cliff (Referring to class C1)

Strip of land parallel to the system of ravines, located between the system itself and the urban centre, 150-250 mt thick, sloping 20% to 35%, with a height of 275-350 mt a.s.l., increasing northwards.

The most peculiar element is a close series of terraces running sub-parallely, mainly at a distance of 5 to 10 mt from each other.
Both the peak and the lower versant of the cliff are flanked by some stretches of local roads following the morphological shape.
The few built-up areas, which are very small and isolated, can be observed where the terracing system is interrupted or becomes more gradual. As an exception, there is a big building towards the southern edge of the town, beyond the cliff-top road that separates the cliff itself from the town. Shape and dimensions of such building are quite atypical in comparison with others in the observed area. Its typology presents one open side, with its longer sides parallel to the road and contour lines.
Occasionally, and not only along the edges of roads, there are scarps parallel to terraces. There is absence of vegetation everywhere.
System of ravines (related to class C2, identifying the ravine).
Strip of land 200 to 250 mt high a.s.l., cut by contour lines with growing altimetry northwards, 200 to 400 mt large, sloping 12,5% to 25%, transversally cut by couples of scarps marking contour lines with cusp shapes.
On higher slopes there are more dry low walls functioning as breast walls. In places where the contour lines become closer, low walls are mostly parallel to them; where lines thin out, the walls are either parallel or perpendicular. Where they are perpendicular, their function is connected with the division of land into estates. On the whole, a marked absence of building settlements can be noted.
At the altitude of +175 mt a.s.l., following the axis cut by the ravine, the presence of farms can be noticed. From the same altitude on, the system of erosive furrows seems to reappear.
The road systems consist of sheep-tracks and local roads, branching from a quasi-straight road, at the constant altitude of about 270 mt a.s.l. -so beyond the highest point of the ravine system- perpendicularly to the ravines.
This historic environmental system is marked by recent changes, particularly due to the creation of important road axes, which have also determined the development of scattered settlements along the road system.
Regular grid system of farms (referring to class C3).
Plots of land substantially flat with maximum gradient lower than 5%, located between 265 and 280 mt a.s.l. on the west side of the compact town and between the ravine system and the cliff, south-west of the latter.
This is a particular model of rural space organization with lots set out on a grid, 9° E-SE rotated to E-W and N-S axes, comparable to geometric regular shapes such as squares and rectangles: in fact intersection angles between the sides limiting the surfaces are 80° to 100°.
Lots are located perpendicularly to a system of mainly straight roads, with different hierarchical levels and with constant sections at the same level. A particular element is the evident parallelism among some almost equi-distant roads -215 to 235 mt-, perpendicularly linked to each other by little lanes.
There is mainly one building inside the single lots; in some cases there can be at most 3, with the area for a single building up to 200 sq.mt.
On the map no kind of vegetation is indicated in the aforesaid lots.

References

1. B. Astori, R. Chiabrando: Tecnica cartografica. In: G. Abbate *et alii*. Enciclopedia di Urbanistica e Pianificazione Territoriale. Rappresentazioni. Milano: Angeli 1984, pp. 133-169

2. A. Barbanente, D. Borri. Artificial Intelligence, Expert Systems and Planning Knowledge. Paper Presented at the International Conference Planning Theory: Prospects for the 1990s. Oxford Polytechnic 2-5 april 1990

3. D. Borri *et alii*. GREEN: building an operational prototype of Expert System for planning control in urban environment. Paper Presented at the Regional Science Association European Conference. Istanbul 1990

4. B.G. Buchanan, D.K. Bartow, R.R. Bechtel, J.J. Bennet, W.J. Clancey, C. Kulikowski, T. Mitchell, D.A. Waterman. Constructing an Expert System. In: F. Hayes-Roth, D.A. Waterman, and D.B. Lenat (eds.): Building Expert Systems. Reading MA: Addison-Wesley 1983,

5. W.J. Clancey: The knowledge level reinterpreted: modeling how systems interact. Machine Learning 4, 285-291 (1989)

6. F. Clemente, G. Maciocco: I Luoghi della Città. Cagliari: Tema 1990

7. F. Clemente: Introduzione. In: G.Maciocco (ed.): La Pianificazione Ambientale del Paesaggio. Milano: Angeli 1991, pp. 7-9

8. G. Dematteis: Le Metafore della Terra. Milano: Feltrinelli 1986

9. T.G. Dietterich: Learning at the knowledge level. Machine Learning 1, (1982).

10. F. Esposito: Automated acquisition of production rules by empirical supervised learning. In: M. Schader (ed.): Knowledge, Data and Computer-Assisted Decisions. Berlin: Springer Verlag 1990,

11. F. Farinelli: La cartografia della campagna nel novecento. In: Storia d'Italia. Atlante. Vol.VI. Torino: Einaudi 1976, pp. 626-636

12. R.L. Flood, S.A. Robinson: Analogy and metaphor and systems and cybernetics methodology. Cybernetics and Systems: An International Journal 19, 501-520 (1988)

13. M. Gams, N. Lavrac: Review of five empirical learning systems within a proposed schemata. Proceeding of EWSL 87: 2nd European Working Session on Learning. Bled, Yugoslavia 1987, pp.46-65

14. F. Hayes-Roth, D.A. Waterman, D.B. Lenat (eds.): Building Expert Systems. Reading, MA: Addison-Wesley 1983

15. J.H. Holland, K.J. Holyoak, R.E. Nisbett, P.R. Thagard: Induction. Problems of Inference, Learning and Discovery. Cambridge, MA: The MIT Press 1989 (1st Edition 1986).

16. T.J.Kim, L.L.Wiggins and J.R. Wright (eds.): Expert Systems: Applications to Urban Planning. New York: Springer-Verlag 1990.

17. J. Larson: Inductive Inference in the Variable Valued Predicate Logic System. VL_{21}. Ph.D. Thesis. Urbana, Illinois: Dpt. of Computer Science 1977.

18. D.B. Lenat: When will machines learn. Machine Learning 4, 255-257 (1989)

19. G. Maciocco: La pianificazione ambientale del paesaggio. In: G. Maciocco (ed.): La Pianificazione Ambientale del Paesaggio. Milano: Angeli 1991, pp. 11-69

20. G. Maciocco: Le dimensioni ambientali della pianificazione urbana. In: G. Maciocco (ed.): Le Dimensioni Ambientali della Pianificazione Urbana Milano: Angeli 1991, pp. 15-71

21. R.S. Michalski: A theory and methodology of inductive learning. Artificial Intelligence 20, 111-161 (1983)

22. R.S. Michalski: Learning strategies and automated knowledge acquisition. In: L. Bolc (ed.) Computational Models of Learning. Heidelberg: Springer Verlag 1987

23. T.M. Mitchell: Generalisation as search. Artificial Intelligence 18, 203-226 (1982)

24. P. Nijkamp: Information Systems in an Uncertain Planning Environment - Some Methods. Working Papers. Luxenburg 1982

25. C. Olmo: Dalla tassonomia alla traccia. Casabella 575/576, 22-24 (1991)

26. F. Paulhan: L'Esthétique du paysage. Paris 1913

27. M. Quaini: L'Italia dei cartografi. In: Storia d'Italia. Atlante. Vol.VI. Torino: Einaudi 1976, pp. 5-24

28. L. Rendell: A general framework for induction and a study of selective induction. Machine Learning 1, (1986).

29. D. Schon: The Reflective Practitioner. New York: Basic Books 1983

30 B. Secchi: Un Progetto per l'Urbanistica. Torino: Einaudi 1989

31. R.E. Stepp and R.S. Michalski: Conceptual clustering of structured objects: a goal oriented approach. Artificial Intelligence 28, 43-69 (1986)

Machine Induction of Geospatial Knowledge

P A Whigham[1], R I McKay[2] (joint authors) & J R Davis[1]

[1]CSIRO Division of Water Resources, Canberra 2601, Australia
[2]Dept of Computer Science, ADFA, Canberra 2600, Australia

Abstract. Machine learning techniques such as tree induction have become accepted tools for developing generalisations of large data sets, typically for use with production rule systems in prediction and classification. The advent of computer based cartography and the field of geographic information systems (GIS) has seen a wealth of spatial data generated and used for decision making and modelling. We examine the implications of inductive techniques applied to geospatial data in a logical framework. It is argued that spatial induction systems will benefit from the ability to extend their initial representation language, through feature and relation construction. The enormous search spaces involved imply a need for strong biasing techniques to control the generation of possible representations of the data for all but the most trivial of cases. A heavily constrained geospatial domain, topographic representation, is described as one simplified example of induction across a vector description of space.

1 Introduction

The recognition that machine induction has become a useful tool for developing knowledge representations, especially when large amounts of data are involved, has led to the investigation of machine induction techniques for geospatial data. The need for spatial analyses that uncover cause/effect relationships has been noted for many years by geographers and mathematicians, as exemplified by techniques such as "spatial autocorrelation" and neighbourhood functions. The emphasis on spatial data handling (in particular geographic data) has led to the development of the field of geographic information systems. These geospatial systems offer limited modelling capabilities but do not use an integrated rule/spatial description for describing cause. One simple expert system that combines space with a rule based format, entitled ARX, is examined as a possible target language for geospatial induction.

Existing "spatial induction" systems have bypassed the problems inherent in generating spatial relations from raw data by pre-computing the relations that are believed to be relevant. This "de-spatialising", although useful with current induction systems, cannot uncover the spatial relations implicit in the data. This necessarily restricts the possible descriptions that may be generated, and is potentially a limitation when large amounts of geospatial data, containing diverse spatial relationships, are involved.

The spatial language of the ARX system may be viewed as a limited version of a logic-based language, and as such we examine the implications of generating a decision tree using a logic-based approach to induction. We describe the properties of formal logic applied to spatial descriptions, and find that many problems exist in the generation of spatial relations, indicating the need for strong biasing to limit the possible search space. The recognition that spatial relationships may involve complex quantification, multiple quantification and recursion demonstrate the difficulties that are faced in describing and generating spatial patterns. The use of feature and relation construction techniques are examined as possible elements of a geospatial induction system. We conclude with an example from a strongly biased geospatial domain, namely, induction over topographic descriptions.

2 Geospatial Induction: Why

The argument for "Why Induction" has been well developed by many authors [eg 15]. The argument for spatial methods to analyse cause has been noted for many years, and examined extensively by mathematicians [7]. For example, the recognition that observations over space are not random, and that typically many geographic elements are related by their spatial relationship with other geographic elements led to the development of spatial autocorrelation [22]. The diversity of problems with a strong spatial component, such as population patterns [23], plant dynamics [2], human geography [3], astronomy [18] and biology [22] indicate that spatial patterns are worthy of study. Recently, an additional focus has emerged in the development of models describing spatial variation [8].

The induction of geospatial knowledge would ideally represent deeper explanatory aspects than a description of purely local effects. For example, the location of a particular animal may be related to some particular vegetation type. The description that animal A exists where we find vegetation V is one form of knowledge. However, a deeper form of knowledge would represent why V exists at that location, which may involve other spatial elements such as surrounding landforms and soil types. These more primitive explanations may carry far more meaning in terms of prediction and explanation.

In general, spatial correlation is more complex than standard correlation between variables, because the exploration for relationships must cover geographic space as well as attribute space. This is emphasised by Maceachren and Ganter [12]: "..because of the difficulty of quantifying 'geographic meaningfulness', geographic correlation is a concept perhaps more suited to visualization and interactive exploration than to purely numerical analysis".

This suggests pattern classification methods alone are of limited use in situations which require either awareness of context or the use of pertinent heuristic knowledge. The scientist uses his knowledge of spatial causation when presented with a spatial analysis problem. It also suggests that strong biasing is used when developing spatial models, based on previous beliefs about the processes under consideration.

We now consider a limited form of spatial induction, namely induction over geographic descriptions. We commence this discussion by describing several ways of representing spatial information, given that any induction over space must have a suitable representation for that space.

3 Spatial Representation

The advent of the information era with computer technologies has led to a range of tools to represent and manipulate geospatial data. The concept of an information system was defined by Martin [13] as: "..a system in which the data stored will be used in spontaneous ways which are not fully predictable in advance for obtaining information."

The modern Geographic Information System (GIS) achieves this requirement of information processing by offering tools to create, store, manipulate and display spatial data.

3.1 The Geographic Information System

Typical GIS packages fall into two broad classes, based on their basic data forms: raster (or grid cell representation) and vector (point, line, polygon representation).

Raster Data Representation. In a raster GIS, spatial data is represented by a set of grid cells or tessellations. Each cell may have a number of associated attribute values, representing the value of selected conditions at that location. Data structures have been developed to minimise the storage requirements of the raster image and to offer efficient mechanisms to manipulate and display the spatial data. One common form of representation uses quadtrees [Abel, 1985] to allow data compaction, fast access and distributed organisation of large spatial databases. The size of the grid cell determines the precision of the spatial representation, and there is typically a tradeoff between storage requirements and required resolution.

Vector Data Representation. The vector data model is based on the concept that geographic data can be represented as a set of geographic elements (or items), each of which has associated locational and thematic data. The GIS represents spatial elements as a collection of points, lines and polygons. The locational data for these elements are explicitly stored as a set of (x,y) values in cartesian coordinates or some equivalent representation (eg latitude/longitude). Attribute values may be associated with any element, thereby creating a spatial database. Most vector GIS allow spatial indexing mechanisms to explicitly represent spatial relationships that are to be used extensively for analyses and spatial selection. Other techniques to speed the search strategies include using bounding rectangles for elements, and storing the data in a form that reflects some spatial property.

3.2 Geospatial Modelling

Most GIS perform some form of modelling based on the spatial and attribute data. The most common operation involves overlaying several maps to produce a new map which represents the combination of selected attributes. This is commonly done with raster data, as each grid cell from one map has an associated partner on another map layer. The selection process may be represented by a set of rules or mathematical expressions that transform the set of attributes to some new values. Although the overlay technique may also be applied in a vector system, the process is slow and tedious due to the creation of new spatial boundaries, and the propensity to create unwanted spatial elements (slivers). A second form of modelling involves buffering map items to select elements that fall within or are excluded from a specified distance around the element. This spatial selection procedure allows the modelling of spatial relationships between map elements; however it is normally a complex operation requiring a detailed understanding of the GIS and its spatial mechanisms.

Recently there has been an interest in building GIS tools using Artificial Intelligence (AI) techniques to increase the usability and functionality of the GIS [21]. These methods have focussed on search techniques, storage issues and execution times, rather than integrating the representational techniques of AI with GIS.

The building of a geospatial inference system requires a formal target language defined as part of the system. The forms of spatial data that are to be used, and the possible operations that may be applied between them, must be defined. One such system, entitled ARX [25], will be described after we examine the basic concepts involved in learning from geographic data.

4 What is Machine Learning?

Machine learning may be defined as the acquisition by a computer based system of knowledge that was neither originally explicitly present in the system, nor explicitly input into the system. Such a wide definition allows of many possibilities, only some of which are of interest in our domain of geospatial reasoning. In particular, machine learning systems can be classified according to:

.the type of knowledge that the system can learn
.the types of input that the system requires in order to learn
.the types of existing knowledge the system can use to build new knowledge

The Type of Knowledge that the System Can Learn. At the highest level, knowledge may be subdivided into two main categories: procedural knowledge and declarative knowledge. Procedural knowledge is knowledge of how to accomplish something, whereas declarative knowledge is knowledge of what is correct. The distinction is perhaps best illustrated by an example: in tennis, the skill and knowledge required to hit the ball into the opposing court, rather than into the net or out of bounds, is procedural knowledge; the knowledge, that it is one of the goals of the game to do so, is declarative knowledge.

Here we will be exclusively concerned with declarative knowledge, since the goal is to construct knowledge that could be used in a declarative reasoning system. In particular, we rule out consideration of neural nets and other connectionist learning systems, since in their present form, these systems can learn only procedural knowledge - how to make particular distinctions - not declarative knowledge - what those distinctions mean.

Artificial Intelligence research has investigated a wide range of formalisms for representing declarative knowledge: semantic nets, frames, and the predicate calculus with its sublanguages (notably Horn Clause logic/production rules). The majority of machine learning systems (particularly those which fit into the further categories we define below) learn knowledge expressed in some subset of the predicate calculus (or an equivalent formalism). We will follow this direction, purely from the pragmatic viewpoint that it is currently the best understood form of machine learning. To delimit the area of interest even further, we will limit our discussion to systems which learn rules (if A and B and C then D) or closely related formalisms, such as decision trees.

The Types of Input the System Requires. Not all machine learning systems require input. For example, Lenat's AM system [11] learns mathematical concepts purely by introspection. However, input-free learning can only acquire tautological concepts, which, while interesting to mathematicians, are not the stuff of an observational science such as geography.

There is an important distinction between systems that learn from unselected data, and systems which assume that the data has been selected by a benevolent teacher. Such guided learning systems mimic much of human learning, which is often directed by a teacher, author etc. From a utilitarian viewpoint, though, a benevolent teacher allows the system to assume that every irregularity in the data is important, whereas systems using unselected data must await the accumulation of sufficient evidence to determine whether an irregularity is relevant. Thus guided learning systems can be more parsimonious in their data requirements. In most geospatial problems, however, there is abundant data and a shortage of teachers, so unguided learning is the more appropriate technique.

Related to input data are the questions of noise and completeness: as in most observational sciences, geospatial data is rarely 100% clean or complete, so any learning approach used must be able to deal with noisy and/or incomplete data.

The Use of Preexisting Knowledge. The primary form of preexisting knowledge is knowledge of what concept the system is intended to learn. Thus we may usefully distinguish between systems which have this knowledge, and those that do not, or following Michalski [15], between concept acquisition (the learning of a sufficient definition of some predetermined concept) and descriptive generalisation (the learning of new concepts which are interesting or useful according to some heuristic). We shall be interested in concept acquisition as the primary goal; however, descriptive generalisation will be required as a means of generating subdescriptions for use during concept acquisition.

Detailed and accurate knowledge of the structure of a domain - for example a preexisting theory - is an important asset to a human learner, and presumably to a machine learning system. Even an inaccurate but suggestive theory can be of assistance in learning. Explanation based learning [5, 16] is the main stream of interest here. Unfortunately, the relevance of this work to geospatial systems is limited, as there are major difficulties in handling large bodies of noisy and inconsistent data, although there have been attempts to alleviate the difficulties [10].

Recent work on incremental version space learning [9] has suggested an alternative approach, but it is too early to evaluate its computational feasibility in geospatial learning. For the moment, it seems appropriate to assume the absence of any preexisting theory.

4.1 Existing Spatial Induction Systems

The term "spatial induction" has been used previously to describe the application of standard induction methods such as ID3 [19], CART [1, 24] and INDUCE [6] to spatial attributes. These methods rely on 'de-spatialising' the data before the induction commences. Spatial operations are performed to select attributes across space that are considered to be "related" (by the modeller), and the system then treats these selected terms as if they were non-spatial entities. If, for example, the distance from the nearest stream is thought to be important, then the distance from the nearest stream is computed for each point in the region, and appended to the data provided to the learning system. The constraint of pre-generated spatial relationships obviously limits the possibilities for exploration.

Another form of limited spatial induction has been previously studied by Michalski [15]. Symbolic descriptions are used to represent spatial relations between attributes of interest. The induction relies on all spatial predicates being defined before the induction, and the search for generalisations of the data becomes a manipulation of symbols with no explicit spatial understanding. The properties of space must be defined as logical predicates that represent the totality of what can be expressed spatially. This approach ensures no new spatial relationships between entities can be uncovered.

5 Formal Logic & Geospatial Properties

In this section, we consider how various geospatial concepts relate to the conceptual categories of formal logic.

5.1 The Propositional Case

The simplest situation arises where the properties involved are all attributes of one particular item in question: 'if the site has rich soil and the site has high moisture levels and the site is not on a hilltop then mammals are abundant at the site' which might be expressed formally as:

if rich_soil(site)
and high_moisture(site)
and not on_hilltop(site)
then abundant_mammals(site)

Since only the one variable 'site' occurs in the formulae, it is usually left implicit, effectively reducing the problem to one of learning propositional rules:

if p and q and r then s

5.2 Simple Relations

Propositional representation languages are not sufficient to handle geospatial reasoning, however. Geography is quintessentially about spatial relationships involving at least two locations, hence must be represented formally as at least binary relations. The next simplest case, then, involves rules relating two sites, such as:

if Y is_within_10_kilometres_of X
and Y is_a_nesting_site_for_Ernests_Eagle
then X is_within_a_feeding_range_of_Ernests_Eagle

While the distance relation can be represented as a ternary relation, within_distance(X,Y,10), the distance parameter (ie 10) has a different role from the other parameters, and is best viewed as an index over an infinite set of relational predicates: within_distance(10)(X,Y).

5.3 Quantification

The conditions of the previous case involved an implicit existential quantification over Y: if any Y at all satisfies the conditions, then the conclusion is justified. Geospatial relations, however, often involve other quantifiers: either the logician's traditional universal quantifier, 'for all', or more typically quantifiers such as 'for most' or 'for 10% of'. At a formal level, these indefinite quantifiers can be translated into the traditional quantifiers, but at the cost of introducing complex mathematical relationships into the formulae which hinder, rather than help, machine learning. It is better to represent these heterodox quantifiers directly, as in Michalski's [1983] annotated predicate calculus.

5.4 Bulk Properties; Multiple Quantification

Bulk properties - 'mountainous', 'patchwork' - refer not just to the pairwise relationships between individual locations in the area under consideration, but to the interrelationships between the locations as a whole. Despite their importance in some geographic domains, they are difficult to formalise cleanly. In some cases, at least, it is possible to approximate them with formulae involving a complex interplay of nested quantifiers. Thus 'the region around X is a patchwork' might be approximately defined as:

'for most Y within some reasonably large distance of X
and for most Z1 & Z2 within some reasonably small distance of Y
Z1 and Z2 have the same value of the relevant attribute
{ie the region is homogeneous in the attribute on a small scale}
but it is not the case that for most Z3 & Z4 within some intermediate distance of Y
Z3 and Z4 have the same value of the relevant attribute
{ie the region is inhomogeneous on an intermediate scale}'

The complexity of this (still inadequate) definition is indicative of the difficulties involved in formally defining such bulk properties.

5.5 Recursion

The concepts defined above are non-recursive: ie they are not defined self-referentially. But recursively defined concepts can be important in geospatial domains: thus 'permissible path' may be defined in terms of 'permissible step':

if permissible_step(X,Y)
then permissible_path(X,Y)
if permissible_step(X,Y)
and permissible_path(Y,Z)
then permissible_path(X,Z)

or 'upstream' might be defined similarly in terms of 'immediately upstream'.

It is not clear to us whether these simple 'transitive closure' recursions cover all important geospatial concepts, or whether some geospatial concepts require more complex recursion schemes.

6 ARX - A Vector-Based Spatial Expert System

We will briefly describe an existing logic based spatial modelling system (ARX) to illustrate the type of representation under discussion.

ARX developed from a series of expert system shells developed at CSIRO since 1985 [4], based on a need for natural resource modelling across spatial boundaries. The rule base is defined as a set of IF/THEN rules where each component of the premise or conclusion is a quadruplet:

<Quadruplet>: <parameter> <relation> <expression><spatial-expression>

The <spatial-expression> component selects elements of space to apply the <parameter> <relation> <expression> triplet. Spatial element selection is based on the combination of spatial relationships between selected elements, and allows the spatial operators "Within", "Further", "Enclosed", "Adjacent", and compass direction. A complete formal description of this language may be found in [25].

The inference engine "knows" about space in the sense that it is always operating at some locational element on some map layer. This location may be referred to implicitly in the spatial- expression by "the current location". Hence we may express generalised spatial rules that can be applied to different elements across a spatial layer. A simple example from a knowledge base used to predict the "Wetness Index" for a landscape unit illustrates this point:

if landunit is one of terrace or gentle slopes
(in the current location)
and landunit is not "lower footslopes"
for all allocations Adjacent to the current location
then wetness index is seasonally waterlogged
(in the current location).

Note that in ARX's syntax, the quantification over space may use "For All", "For Any" "For <number>" and "For <ratio>", as found in annotated predicate calculus statements such as Michalski [15]. The parameters of the expert system (such as "landunit" and "wetness index") are unstructured. Many expert systems offer structured objects such as frame based, slot based and hierarchical definitions. The ARX spatial language has no way of defining multiple quantification over an element of space. These limitations do not appear overly restrictive for our current investigations.

7 Categorising Geospatial Learning

7.1 Feature-based spatial learning

In existing geospatial learning systems, the user identifies the spatial relationships of interest. Our goal is a system which can learn in domains where human experts are not clear which spatial properties are important.

We may distinguish here between learning of concepts whose derivation may involve relations, but which are not relational concepts themselves, and direct learning of relational concepts. It is usually the case that the top level goal of a geospatial system is the prediction of unobserved properties of particular spatial locations, or the explanation of observed properties in terms of other more primitive properties. In either case, the top level goal is a unary property, rather than a relational one.

This is important for geospatial learning, since it implies that well understood learning mechanisms such as decision tree induction can be used at the top level. It suggests a model in which tree induction, say, is used on the concepts supplied by the initial language, but where it reaches an impasse (where a leaf node is insufficiently pure in the goal concept for the learning to be considered successful, but no remaining concept produces a worthwhile gain) other techniques are used to extend the initial language before a further round of tree induction.

Essentially, then, we are concerned with the concept learning of unary properties, but involving the construction of such unary properties not only from other unary properties, but also from higher arity relations.

7.2 Feature and Relation Construction

Even in purely feature-based learning, there is a need to construct new features not present in the initial representation. For instance, where one of the data properties has a continuous range of values (eg a temperature T), it is necessary to synthesise properties such as 'T > 0', 'T < 100'. Alternatively, some physical properties do not affect a value directly, but only in interaction with other properties. Thus the force between two bar magnets depends on the relationship between the orientations of the two magnets and the angular displacement between them. Any one of these three properties taken in isolation gives absolutely no information about the force between the two magnets; it is only when all three are determined together that any effect can be detected.

Thus learning systems which consider properties serially will find such a relationship only if they conduct computationally expensive lookahead; but if the base language can be extended by the addition of conjunctive concepts, lookahead can be avoided. In other words, we need to construct features that are either generalisations of one attribute, or syntheses of multiple attributes. For a fuller justification of such feature construction, see Matheus [14].

As the previous discussion has shown, geospatial learning requires the extension of the initial language with features defined not only in terms of the unary properties of the initial language, but also in terms of the relations of that language, perhaps involving complex quantification and recursion.

7.3 Matheus' Framework for Feature Based Learning

Matheus [14] has given a useful framework for the classification of feature based learning systems. While the framework was initially proposed in the context of the construction of new features (ie unary properties) from old, it also provides a useful clarification of the difficulties in building a fully generalised geospatial learning system. Matheus distinguishes four components of a learning system involving feature construction:

Determining the Need for Feature Construction. A concept learning system may provide a means of detecting the need for feature construction. Since feature construction can be computationally expensive, there are advantages in only attempting to construct new features when it becomes clear that the learning system cannot otherwise progress. Matheus argues that an efficient feature construction system requires hypothesis based need detection (ie the detection occurs in the process of learning that particular hypothesis). Yet as we shall see, the search spaces involved in constructing general geospatial predicates are far larger than those required for non-relational feature construction; thus efficient need detection, performing feature construction only when necessary, is critical. Matheus' arguments for the requirement for hypothesis based detection apply a fortiori.

Selection of Constructors. In the feature construction case considered by Matheus, the only available constructors are the pre- existing features as operands, and boolean functions as operators. Matheus argues that initial selection of only the basic boolean connectives (using repeated application of the construction method to obtain higher order boolean functions), combined with hypothesis based and knowledge based biasing of runtime selection, can sufficiently constrain the search space.

In our case, the search space is larger, since the operators include also universal quantifiers. In addition, the operands themselves are complex, allowing all permutations of variables to be parameters to the various relations. Moreover the distance and/or orientation component of any spatial relations involved add a further complexity.

Recursion adds yet further complexity. Each form of recursion permitted will require the addition of a corresponding recursion schema to the initial selection of constructor operators. The implications of these additions have yet to be determined. It may well be that simple 'transitive closure' - recursion of the form

'P(<variables>) if <other predicates> and P(<other variables>)'

- will suffice for geospatial domains. But any geospatial concept requiring deeper recursion will greatly extend the search.

Learning of relations - even recursive relations - has recently received considerable attention [17, 20]. This work will undoubtedly be of importance in geospatial learning, in determining and constructing the relevant relational concepts.

Constructor Generalisation. In Matheus' work, only relatively simple generalisation operators are available: in a tic-tac-toe example, translation of board configurations. In geospatial learning, many of the spatial operations are best treated as generalisation operations. Thus specific distance and orientation values (in a polar coordinate domain) generalise to ranges of distance or orientation, and universal quantifiers generalise to existential or more indefinite quantifiers. Matheus argues that, even for feature construction, only biases based on domain knowledge can provide the selectivity required for efficient learning; this conclusion is all the more appropriate with the wide range of generalisations available in geospatial learning.

Feature Evaluation. Matheus argues that the autonomy provided by automatic evaluation of the utility of new features outweighs the greater accuracy provided by user evaluation. Given the dramatically larger search spaces involved in geospatial learning, automatic evaluation is unlikely to be sufficiently selective; on the other hand, user evaluation, for the same reasons, could well become unacceptably onerous. Thus user evaluation must allow the user to specify not only whether the proposed feature is acceptable (as in CIGOL [17]), but also to indicate why a feature is unacceptable, so that this may be used to guide further search and so reduce the need for further interaction with the user.

8 Bias in Learning Geospatial Predicates

8.1 How Space Helps

Because of the enormous search spaces required for geospatial learning, good heuristics to guide search are crucial. Fortunately, the structure of space provides a convenient basis for constructional biases.

.The total ordering of the distance relation imposes an obvious and appropriate bias, particularly as many geospatially interesting processes are polynomial functions of distance: 'prefer relations involving small distances to those involving large distances'.

Moreover, in most geospatial systems, space is quantised, either regularly, as in raster based systems, or irregularly, as in point-line-polygon systems. Thus an even stronger bias can be used: 'investigate nearest neighbours first, then next-nearest-neighbours, etc'

.Orientation relations are unfortunately not ordered; nevertheless, they readily lend themselves to biases such as 'select angular quadrants first, then octants, etc.'

Again, the quantisation of the underlying GIS helps to reduce the overall search space.

Similarly, with the generalisation stage, assumptions about the homogeneity of space lead naturally to a bias towards distance or orientation relations involving continuous intervals rather than discrete values; ie we would prefer a concept that involved 'points between 10 and 20 km distant' to one that involved 'points at 3, 17 or 23 km distance'.

8.2 Non-Spatial Biases

The general spatial biases discussed above, arising from our overall beliefs about the operation of natural processes in space, are useful; but they will be insufficient to permit efficient learning of general geospatial concepts. They will inevitably require supplementation with further biases specific to the particular domain of application. Bias in a learning system can arise in a number of ways:

The Choice of the Basic Terms of the Representation Language. We have argued that there are advantages in a geospatial learning system constructing new terms when required, rather than relying on human detection and despatialising of the important relational concepts. Nevertheless, where it is known - or even suspected - that a particular concept is important for a given problem, the simplest way to impart that knowledge to the system is to add it directly as a basic term of the representation language (not necessarily by adding it to the data - it will generally be simplest to provide the learning system with the means to construct the value of the property when required).

The Preferred Structure of the Overall Knowledge Organisation. Thus a tree induction system with a goodness measure which prefers concepts that split the data into approximately equal sized subsets will preferentially construct relatively balanced trees; other preference relations will lead to a preference for differently shaped trees. It is not clear whether biases of this sort will be useful in geospatial learning.

The Priority Ordering of the Term Construction and Generalisation Operations. There are some obvious general heuristics. Thus feature construction is preferable to relational construction, if only because of the smaller search spaces involved, so should be applied first. In general, though, the number of possible preference relations is very large - is it preferable to quantify before/after attempting recursion? Should evaluation beyond nearest neighbours precede consideration of orientation? - and domain specific, so can only be specified by a user with a knowledge of the structure of the domain. The investigation of appropriate means for user specification of such bias appears to be an interesting line of future research.

The Priority of the Different Spatial Aspects. (ie. in a polar coordinate system, should the system evaluate out to ten kilometres before or after subdividing below 10 degrees). Again, user specification of bias appears relevant here.

Nevertheless, even with this degree of biasing, the general problem of induction over space still appears very difficult for all but the simplest of geospatial domains.

9 A Heavily Biased Domain : Topographic Induction

From the relatively formal viewpoint given above, this subproblem consists of a language in which the following biases are applied:
i) quantification is omitted (ie implicitly, all variables are existentially quantified),
ii) the only distance relation allowed is 'nearest neighbour',
iii) there is a mechanism bias, ie. particular elements of space are initially selected for examination based on the assumption that gross properties of material movement are easily identified (ie. select property X over property Y)
iv) there is a transitive relational bias, ie. if the most recently constructed relation r(X,Y) was useful, then there is a bias towards constructing the same relation with Y as its first parameter: r(Y,Z)

9.1 Assumptions

The following assumptions define our method for extracting spatial causality from a topographic description of space (assuming a vector spatial framework) :

Certain Map Items Perform the Role of "Information" Transport. Certain elements in the natural world appear to transport elements across spatial boundaries. Wind will carry particles through the air, water will transport nutrients down a stream to the ocean, the slope of a landform will influence the pattern of soil movement, etc. These elements are recognised for their special influence in causality, and are intended to be part of the biasing mechanism when we perform topographic induction.

There may be a Flow of "Information" across Item Boundaries. All spatial items are represented as points, lines or polygons. All spatial items that share a boundary (ie. share the side of a polygon, line which crosses a polygon boundary, point enclosed by a polygon, etc.) may have an influence upon each other. The term "information" is intended to represent the abstract mechanism that causes influence between items. The form of this mechanism is not considered. We merely want to detect that some particular locational properties are influencing other properties.

The limitation that we examine immediate neighbours for possible influences does not limit the possibility of a spatial item n neighbours away from some item being detected, as we apply the search procedure recursively to each selected neighbourhood item when detecting spatial similarity.

If we assume that the set of spatial items X that share a boundary with some item Y have neighbours that are not part of the boundary set X, we effectively allow the possibility of influence from one spatial item to any other spatial item. This assumption appears valid for topographic information.

9.2 Bias for Topographic Induction.

The following description sketches a heavily-biased approach to the problem of detecting spatial similarity for a topographic description of space. The ordering of preferences represents the bias towards gross mechanisms as the most likely influence between spatial items.

The Ordering of Preferences is
Macro Transport. Gross movements of "information" (eg. downstream along a river).

Single Attribute Micro Transport. Movements of "information" across shared boundaries of spatial items based on attribute values of only one of the items involved (eg slope: an item at the bottom of a hill is likely to be influenced by elements transported down the hill slope, such as surface water).

Shared Classification Micro Transport. Movement of "information" across shared boundaries affected by the boundary attribute (ie the attribute which classifies the spatial units into separate entities). Eg in a map layer whose classification attribute is land use, two items classified as 'forest' are more likely to support bird migration than two differently classified items.

Other Shared Attribute Micro Transport. Movement of "information" across shared boundaries based on any other common attributes (ie adjacent items that have other attributes in common with the current items being inspected). Eg in the previous birds example, shared vegetation type may be important: birds preferring conifers are more likely to migrate between two patches of coniferous forest than between adjacent broad leaved and coniferous forests.

The Basic Approach. These preferences are used to direct the selection of the next set of spatial items to compare for similarity. The transport relations would be defined by a set of spatial rules in the target spatial language.

This exploratory approach to finding common spatial causes for topographic data will create rules that generate a chain of adjacent spatial selections. Our logic-based approach has been biased to generate only adjacent relations, and is further directed by the (user) definition of macro and micro transport relations amongst spatial items.

This example places the emphasis on eliminating spatial relations and using the effect of boundary conditions as the only exploratory mechanism. This limitation does not prevent detection of distance relations, however it will not recognise an effect due to the relative orientation of spatial items.

10 Conclusion

Machine learning techniques, such as tree induction, have become accepted tools for developing generalisations of large data sets, typically for use with production rule systems in prediction and classification. The proliferation of spatial data used by organisations over the last decade indicates a need for tools that explore the spatial relations inherent in these data forms. In particular, the discovery of relations between elements of space that are not easily recognised by the human expert would greatly benefit the development of predictive and explanatory models. We have argued that spatial induction systems would benefit from the ability to extend their initial representation language, through feature and relation construction. The enormous search spaces involved imply a need for strong biasing techniques to control the generation of possible representations of the data for all but the most trivial of cases. This paper highlights the main aspects of geospatial induction in a logical framework, and indicates some basic areas of research for further investigation.

Acknowledgements

The ideas in this paper have been partly incubated in discussions with David Stockwell of the Australian National University. Robert Pearson and Brian Studman of University College, Australian Defence Force Academy have made a number of useful suggestions. Dr. Peter Laut, CSIRO Division of Water Resources, offered useful discussions from the geographic viewpoint.

References

1. L. Breiman, J.H. Friedman, R. Olshen & C. Stone: Classification and Regression Trees. Monterey: Wadsworth & Brooks 1983
2. I. Broner, P. King, and A. Nevo: Structured Induction for Agricultural Expert Systems Knowledge Acquisition. Computers & Electronics in Agriculture 5, 87-99 (1990)
3. A.D. Cliff and J.K. Ord: Model Building and the Analysis of Spatial Patterns in Human Geography'. Journal of the Royal Statistical Society, Series B 37, 297-348 (1975)
4. J.R. Davis, J.R.L. Hoare and P.M. Nanninga: Developing a Fire Management Expert System for Kakadu National Park, Australia. Journal of Environmental Management 22, 215-227 (1986)
5. G.F. De Jong and R. Mooney: Explanation-based Learning: An Alternative View. Machine Learning 1 (2), 145-176 (1986)
6. T.G. Dietterich and R.S. Michalski: Learning and Generalization of Characteristic Descriptions: Evaluation Criteria and Comparative Review of Selected Methods. Proc 6th IJCAI, Tokyo, 1979
7 P.J. Diggle: Statistical Analysis of Spatial Point Patterns. London: Academic Press 1983
8. R. Haining: Spatial Models and regional science: A comment on Anselin's paper and research directions. Journal of Regional Science 26(4) (1986)
9. H. Hirsh: Incremental Version-Space Merging: A General Framework for Concept Learning. Mass: Kluwer 1990
10. M. Lebowitz: Complex Learning Environments: Hierarchies and the Use of Explanation. in T.M. Mitchell, J.G. Carbonell and R.S. Michalski (eds): Machine Learning: A Guide to Current Research. Mass: Kluwer 1986
11. D.B. Lenat: AM: An Artificial Intelligence Approach to Discovery in Mathematics as Heuristic Search. PhD Thesis, Stanford University, 1976

12. A. Maceachren and J.H. Ganter: A Pattern Identification approach to cartographic visualization. Cartographica 27(2), 64-81 (1990)
13. J. Martin: Principles of Database Management. Englewood Cliffs: Prentice Hall 1976, p332
14. C.J. Matheus: Feature Construction: An Analytic Framework and an Application to Decision Trees. PhD Thesis, University of Illinois at Urbana-Champaign, 1990
15. R.S. Michalski: A Theory and Methodology of Inductive Learning. in R.S. Michalski, J.G. Carbonell and T.M. Mitchell (eds): Machine Learning, an Artificial Intelligence Approach. Berlin: Springer, 1983
16. T.M. Mitchell, R.M. Keller and S.T. Kedar-Cabelli: Explanation Based Generalization: A Unifying View. Machine Learning 1(1), 47-80 (1986)
17. S. Muggleton and W. Buntine: Machine Invention of First Order Predicates by Inverting Resolution. Proc. 5th Int. Conf. on Machine Learning, Morgan Kaufmann, 1988, pp339-352
18. P.J.E. Peebles: The nature of the distribution of galaxies. Astronomy and Astrophysics 32, 197--202 (1974)
19. J.R. Quinlan: Learning Efficient Classification Procedures and their Application to Chess End Games. in R.S. Michalski, J.G. Carbonell and T.M. Mitchell (eds): Machine Learning, an Artificial Intelligence Approach. Berlin: Springer, 1983
20. J.R. Quinlan: Determinate Literals in Inductive Logic Programming. Proc. 12th IJCAI, Sydney, 1991
21. T. Smith, D. Peuquet, S. Menon and P. Agarwal: A Knowledge-Based Geographic Information System. Int. J. Geographic Information Systems 1(2), 149-172 (1987)
22. R.R. Sokal and N.L. Oden: Spatial Autocorrelation in biology. Biological Journal of the Linnean Society 10, 199-22 (1978)
23. D.R.B. Stockwell, S.M. Davey, J.R. Davis and I.R. Noble: Using Induction of Decision Trees to Predict Greater Glider Density. AI Applications in Natural Resource Management 4(4), 33-44 (1990)
24. P.A. Walker and K.D. Cocks: Habitat: a Procedure for Modelling a Disjoint Environmental Envelope for a Plant or Animal Species. Global Ecology and Biogeography Letters 1, 108-118 (1991)
25. P.A. Whigham, J.R. Davis and S. Cuddy: Modelling with a Spatial Expert System. Proc. Australian Artificial Intelligence Conf., Perth, 1990 pp 448-461.

Treatment of Qualitative Geographic Information in Monitoring Environmental Pollution

Ombretta Paladino

ISTIC - Facoltà di Ingegneria -Università di Genova
Via Opera Pia 15, 16145 GENOVA (I)

Abstract. The inverse problem of material sources identification, with particular reference to air polluting sources and their detection from experimental data, is a difficult task to solve and it is classified as a typical ill-posed problem. The traditional approach to these problems uses the additional information available on the system in order to limit the number of solutions consistent with the data by means of regularization techniques. In this paper we propose a method that allows to find reliable solutions by treating qualitative spatial and geographic information. It is shown how to code in a general fuzzy optimization algorithm the experimental knowledge, quantitative models and the a-priori knowledge about territory configuration such as urban areas, lakes, parks and high-traffic motorways. The architecture of an automatic system that allows to handle the coupled qualitative and quantitative knowledge about the system is presented.

1 Introduction

The general problem of real time detection of polluting sources provides the establishment of air and ground monitoring networks, data acquisition and subsequent data treatment. The difficulties arising in material sources identification are not only related to the adoption of a systematic and suitable measuring procedure, but also to a correct management of the available information.

In the last few years environmental monitoring passed from a local scale (typically a regional scale) to a larger scale due to the extension of the polluting sources, the increasing of dangerous compounds and the interdependence of polluting phenomena. Hence the necessity, in addition to the traditional predictive models that allows to compute the environmental impact of known polluting sources, of developing new techniques for detecting sources and evaluate their intensity. Monitoring can provide an important aid in the choice of polluting control strategies and in the choice of new industrial sites. Furthermore it assumes a fundamental role in prevenction of industrial accidents and in planning emergency policy.

However, from the theoretical point of view, this problem presents many difficulties. It is in fact a typical ill-posed problem, i.e. it is characterized by highly different solutions from small changes in the data. Physically this means that different source configurations giving the same polluting ground distribution could exist.

Ill-posed problems in the sense of Hadamard [1] are frequent in all fields of data analysis and imply lack of continuity of the solution with respect to the experimental data. Typical ill-posed problems are Fredholm integral equations of the first kind [2] which occur in deconvolution problems and the inverse problem of the heat or mass equation. The traditional approach to tackle this class of problems uses the additional information available to restrict the domain of the possible solutions consistent with the data. Regularization methods are often based on constraining the solution to fall in a compact set using algorithms based on some extremum property such as the search of the smallest or the smoothest solution.

2 The Monitoring Problem

In order to understand the ill conditioning of a similar problem let us express the ground concentration at each point (x,y) and time t as a function of the density of the polluting source. Then we have:

$$c(x,y,t)=q(x_0,y_0,\tau)*K(x-x_0,y-y_0,t-\tau|\theta)*dx_0\,dy_0\,d\tau \tag{1}$$

where c indicates the concentration, q the source density, K an appropriate convolution kernel and θ a certain number of known parameters such as atmospheric coefficients, orografic information and so on. The direct problem consists in the prediction of c when q and K are known; it is a well posed problem, which means that the operator F:(q,K) → C (where C indicates the vector space of the solutions in R^3) is continuous. The converse of this statement is not true, which means that the operator F^{-1}:(c,K) → q is not continuous. To demonstrate this statement let us consider two different polluting distributions q (the exact one) and q' given by:

$$q'(x_0,y_0,\tau)=q(x_0,y_0,\tau)+\int N*\cos[\omega(x_0,y_0,u\tau)]\,d\omega \tag{2}$$

where u is a speed parameter (typically the mean wind speed). Ground concentration takes the form of:

$$c'(x,y,t)=c(x,y,t)+\int N*\cos[\omega(x_0,y_0,u\tau)]*K(x-x_0,y-y_0,t-\tau|\theta)*dx_0\,dy_0\,d\tau \tag{3}$$

By supposing K is limited, i.e.

$$\left|\int k(x,y,\tau)*dx\,dy\,d\tau\right|<\delta<\infty \tag{4}$$

we have:

$$c'(x,y,t) = c(x,y,t) + \alpha \tag{5}$$

where α is given by $N\beta/\omega$. Now for all values of N and ß, α can be made arbitrarily small by choosing a high frequency ω . The result is that while the distance $| q-q' |_\alpha$ measured in an opportune metric ß can be very large, the corresponding distance |c-c'| can be small. The choice of the cosine function is by no means arbitrary if we realize that every function can be expanded in terms of a Fourier integral.

The general expression (2) now becomes:

$$q'(x_0,y_0,\tau)=q(x_0,y_0,\tau)+\int N(\omega)*\cos[\omega(x_0,y_0,u\tau)]d\omega \tag{6}$$

This example refers to the simple case of computing the polluting flow q from a single component concentration measures. Furthermore the stochastic nature of mesurements is not considered. The real monitoring problems are more complex and ill-posedness, individuated in this simple example, can only increase due to the relevant number of parameters which in real cases are present.

The real monitoring problems can be grouped in the following cases:

a) Compute K being known c and q. It can be shown that the problem does not admit a single solution. Tracing techniques have to be used in order to reduce the solution domain [3].

b) Compute q being known c and K. It is the problem discussed in the previous example.

c) Compute q and K being known c. Acting on the experimental data correlation matrix, a transformation of the matrix eigenvalues allows to express the solutions as linear relations of polluting concentration measures. This correspond to the well known source receptor relations [4] [5].
The problem is always ill-posed.

3 Traditional Regularization Techniques

While ill-posed problems were considered void of physical meaning until some years ago, it is nowadays generally recognized that the experimental information cannot be obtained by well posed physical experimentation and therefore that opportune techniques are to be made use of to better utilize this amount of information. Hence the regularization techniques, which can be divided into two different procedures: the inverse operator F^{-1} can be modified so that it becomes continuous, or the solution domain can be restricted to a compact set. This give rise to a certain degree of arbitrariness that reflects the experimentalist's confidence in a certain number of subjective assumptions.
Referring to a simple least squares parameter estimation scheme we have to solve:

$$\|Ag-\Psi\|^2=\min$$

Whithout regularization the solution is given by:

$$g=\left(A^{*}A\right)^{-1}A^{*}\Psi$$

Ill-posedness derives from the poor conditioning of the matrix ($A^{*}A$).
The most common frequently used procedures are briefly rewieved:

1) Non-negativity [6]
The original problem changes to:

$$\|Ag-\Psi\|^{2}=\min \qquad ; \ g\geq 0$$

which is a well known quadratic programming problem.

2) Smallness (damped least squares) [7]
This method derives from the attempt to limit the norm of g. The original problem becomes:

$$\|Ag-\Psi\|^{2}=\min \qquad ; \ \|g\|^{2}=\varepsilon$$

or equivalently

$$\|Ag-\Psi\|^{2}+\lambda\|g\|^{2}=\min$$

where λ is connected with the value of ε. The analytical solution of the problem is:

$$g=\left[\left(A^{*}A\right)+\lambda I\right]^{-1}A^{*}\Psi$$

Ill-conditioning can be removed by keeping opportune λ values.

3) Smoothness [8]
Similarly to the previous method, in this case we attempt to limit the derivatives of g. Tha analytical solution of the problem is:

$$g=\left[\left(A^{*}A\right)+\lambda T\right]^{-1}A^{*}\Psi$$

where T depends on the constraints used. Also in this case the value of λ depends on the a-priori knowledge about the problem.

4) Pseudoinverse [6]
Regularization can be performed by using the pseudoinverse matrix A^{+}. The

pseudoinverse coincides with $(A^*A)^{-1}A^*$ if $(A^*A)^{-1}$ exists and to a suitable approximation (based on singular value decomposition) if it does not exist.

5) Filtering techniques [9]
These methods (and also Wiener filters) are based on the approximation of the Fourier transform of the deconvolution problem. Regularization is a trade-off between consistency and stability.

6) Maximum entropy [10]
The method consists in the determination of the least-biased solution consistent with the experimentally computed moments of the data. The regularization is given by the finite number of moments that are considered.

The use of all these regularization methods is due to the necessity of employing deterministic and possibly simple procedures. Anyway these techniques, based on parsimony criteria, are often used even when the available information does not agree with the extremum property implied by them [11]. In fact the solution which is being looked for may not be small, smooth or whatever condition is being imposed. Furthermore, even if we expect some degree of regularity, we do not necessarily expect an extremum. Finally the available information can often be fuzzy. The monitoring problem obey these conditions: we can hardly think of a smallness or smoothness condition applied to a polluting source and we generally only possess a certain degree of confidence in the solution having certain properties. Hence the necessity of developing a procedure that does not limit the solution and that use fuzzy and subjective knowledge.

4 Regularization Techniques Based on Fuzzy Optimization

In this section is briefly described a general fuzzy optimization theory that embeds traditional regularization as particular cases. More details on the implementation of numerical algorithms are reported in [12].

Let us consider again the problem

$$\|Ag-\Psi\|^2=\min$$

If some additional a-priori knowledge on the solution domain is available, it can be cast into the form:

$$f_i=f_i[B_i(g)] \;\;;\;\; f_i:\Re\rightarrow L \;\;;\;\; B_i:G\rightarrow\Re$$

where L is the set

$$\{x|x\in\Re\,;\,0\leq x\leq 1\}$$

In this notation f_i is the membership function of the property B_i of the expected solution g. This formulation implies a translation of the available information from qualitative to quantitative:

i) Definition of B_i

ii) Definition of a membership function of the kind:

$$\chi_i[B_i(g)]:\Re \rightarrow \Lambda$$

where Λ is a qualitative set of properties.

iii) Definition of a new membership function of the kind:

$$f_{\chi_i}(g):\Lambda \rightarrow L$$

The estimation problem assumes the form of a fuzzy minimization problem, i.e. a system of fuzzy constraints together with a crisp objective function [13]. The solution vector g is fuzzy due to the presence of constraints. Formally the solution can be expressed as the membership function ξ of the fuzzy set F_g defined as:

$$\xi(g)=\sup\{\alpha\neq 0 | g\in M_\alpha\} \; if \; g\in\bigcup M_\alpha$$
$$\xi(g)=0 \; otherwise$$
$$with \; \xi:G\rightarrow[0,1]$$

where

$$M_\alpha=\{g\in L_\alpha(d);\, P(g)=\inf_{g\in L_\alpha} P(g)\}$$
$$L_\alpha(d)=\{g\in G;\, D(g)\geq\alpha\}$$
$$D(g)=\inf(f_1,\ldots,f_m)$$

This means that among all solutions $g \in F_g$ which satisfy the constraints at a confidence level of at least α [$D(g) \geq \alpha$] we pick the ones which provide the minimum value of the objective function P. The solution vectors thus determined are assigned a membership value equal to α
Also in the fuzzy case we can perform a-posteriori data analysis:
Thus for instance if

$$M_\alpha = \{0\}$$
$$\alpha \le \overline{\alpha}$$
$$f_i > \alpha \ ; \quad i \ne k$$
$$f_k = \alpha$$

This means that f_k should be changed a-posteriori in such a way so as to set to zero all the membership values which have been supposed to lie between 0 and $\overline{\alpha}$ In this way we can check if information supplied by the user is consistent with the experimental data.

The main difficulties in solving the problem are linked to the construction of a membership function for each fuzzy constraint. We have chosen a simple piecewise constant expression that depends on four parameters (y_1, y_2, y_3, y_4). It has been supposed that for every constraint B_i there is an interval y_2_y_3 whose values can be fully accepted. Values lower than y_1 or greater than y_4 are not allowed and values inside the intervals y_1_y_2 and y_3_y_4 are accepted with a confidence of 0.5. This choice seems to be good enough to handle the qualitative a-priori knowledge about the problem.

The procedure for the computation of the solutions is:

1. Find the solutions g_0 of the problem:

$$\|Ag - \Psi\|^2 = \min$$
$$y_{2i} \le B_i(g) \le y_{3i} \quad i = 1, \ldots, m$$

2. Set up all the combinations:

$$f_k = \tfrac{1}{2} \quad k = 1, \ldots, m$$
$$f_{j \ne k} = (\tfrac{1}{2}, 1)$$

Let there be N of them.

3. Set n=1

4. Solve the problem:

$$\|Ag - \Psi\|^2 = \min$$

subject to:

a) $y_{1i} \leq B_i(g) \leq y_{2i}$
$y_{3i} \leq B_i(g) \leq y_{4i}$
if in the n combination $f_i=0.5$

b) $y_{2i} \leq B_i(g) \leq y_{3i}$
if in the n combination $f_i=1$

Let be g_n the vector of solutions.

5. Set n=n+1. If n<N return to step 4.

6. The solution is given by:

$F_g = \bigcup_{i=1}^{N} g_i$

where g_0 has full membership and $g_i \neq 0$ has membership degree equal to 0.5.

Generally it is not necessary to solve all the combinations connected with the f values of the contraints. In fact if two constraints apply to elements that do not interfere (a lake and an urban area and so on) in the determination of the solution, the principle of superposition [12] can be used.

More details about the whole procedure for solving a simulated simplified air quality monitoring problem, are given elsewhere [14].

5 Geographic A-Priori Knowledge Representation

As shown previously, instead of a-priori deciding in which compact set the solution has to be looked for and then carrying out the numerical procedure, we use an optimization technique that provides various solutions in different compact sets and union of them. The user can supply additional information that derives from geographic knowledge on the codomain or from subjective hypotheses on the possible location of the polluting sources. This information allows to bound some domain areas and to set up the constraints. Examples of available information are listed below.

a - bounds of an high density urban area;
b - location of a single polluting source (industrial site);
c - presence of an high traffic motorway;
d - location of gates in the motorway;
e - location of natural bounds such as coasts and mountains;
f - presence of lakes and parks.

Knowledge about this zones can be qualitatively expressed as follows:

1 - A sharp decrease of emission rate is expected at the boundary of the urban area;
2 - A minimum value of emission rate is expected inside the boundary of the urban area;
3 - Emission inside the urban area is approximately constant;
4 - Emission along the motorway is approximately constant;
5 - Emission along the motorway in the stretch close to the urban area could be higher than in other parts of the motorway due to local traffic;
6 - Absence of sources inside lakes and parks;
7 - negative sources (for certain compounds) inside parks.

As we easily can see, knowledge about a certain area can be expressed in different ways. The existence of an urban area could give rise to at least three (1, 2, 3) possible qualitative statements. The difference among the three can be well understood if we refer to three typical italian urban areas: statement 1 well describes the geographic situation of a city with real natural bounds. Pollutant flowrate effectively decreases (at limit until the zero value) on the boundary constituted by the coast or the mountains in a city like Genoa, Italy. On the other hand, if we have to describe an urban area placed on a large plain, statement 2 seems more true. A defined city contour does not exist and a gradual density decrease appears. Statement 2 could be used only to limit the central urban area: the constraint on the threshold value does not prevent the algorithm from finding high polluting flowrates also in the suburbs. Finally, statement 3 is suggested to describe only residential areas where no industrial sites exist.

A possible translation of the above reported qualitative statements into fuzzy constraints is:

1) $B_m(g)=g_k-g_h$

where the sets {k} and {h} refer to elements close to the boundary from the inside and the outside respectively. The index m refers to all combinations {k}*{h}. Suitable parameters for the membership function are: y1=0, y2=δ , y3=y4=+∞

2) $B_n(g)=g_n$

where the set {n} contains all the elements inside the boundary. A suitable membership function can be defined with y1=0, y2=β , y3=y4=+∞

3) $B_l(g)=g_{ni}-g_{nj}$

where the set {n} contains all the elements inside the boundary and the index l refers to all the combinations i*j of the n elements. Parameters y are: y1=-Ka, y2=-a, y3=a, y4=Ka

4) $B_i(g)=g_{i+1}-g_i \quad ,i=1,p \quad ; \quad B_p(g)=g_1-g_p$

where p is the number of discrete elements into which the linear source (motorway) is divided. We have y1=y2=-b, y3=y4=b.

5) $B_m(g)=g_k-g_h$

where the set {k} contains elements close to the surface source (urban area) and the set {h} contains the elements immediately close to the previous ones. In this case some of the membership functions (i.e. those connected with elements close to the surface source) should be changed with the following parameters: y1=y2=-b, y3=b, y4=c.

6) $B_q(g)=g_q$

where the set {q} contains all the elements inside the boundary. A suitable membership function can be defined with y1=y2= -ε , y3= y4 = +ε

7) $B_q(g)=g_q$

where the set {q} contains all the elements inside the boundary. A suitable membership function can be defined with y1=y2= -∞ , y3= ξ , y4=0.

Once all the constraints have been defined, the optimization procedure can be stated by computing all the combinations connected with the values (1/2,1) assigned to the constraints and reducing the number of them by using the principle of superposition.

The a-posteriori solution analysis can finally be performed on the basis of traditional regression theory applied to the fuzzy case and on some reasonable knowledge on the problem such as:

- Negative values (pollutant absorption) very close to peaks (apodizing effect);
- Absence of merging of known sources (converse of apodizing effect);
- Feeble dependance on the number of measurements (i.e. persistence of the pollutant distribution if some measurements are dropped);
- Permanent distribution if steady state conditions of the emitting sources are known;
- Coincidence of sinks and sources of secondary pollutants resulting from chemical reactions;
- Coincidence of sources of different pollutants produced by the same polluting structure;
- Persistence of pollutant distribution when the atmospheric parameters present in the model vary;

- Agreement of the time behaviour with the expected daily or seasonal (day/night or winter/summer) behaviour;
- Sensitivity to sudden changes (accidents with sudden releases) and absence of negative sources close to a sudden change.

Since the whole optimization procedure depends on the values assigned to the membership functions, and changing one of them means the change of all the optimization steps, an expert system has to be designed to set up the constraints and to create the source code without the user intervention.

6 Expert Monitoring Problem Solver

In this section we analyse the features of a man machine interface that allows to automatize the fuzzy optimization procedure. The system helps the user in defining and discussing the starting monitoring problem in terms of qualitative variables, than it transforms the information in order to solve the problem in terms of quantitative variables only. The main role of the expert solver is the translation of all the a-priori knowledge.

6.1 Main Working Steps

1) Input: problem setup

a) knowledge about the monitoring experimental runs:
- definition of the investigated geographic zone;
- measured variables, type and units (for example soil concentration of compound x);
- experimental data;
- variance-covariance matrix of the experimental data, if known;

b) Physical and spatial knowledge about the monitoring problem:
- choice of the model;
- spatial description of the solution domain.

c) Quantitative and qualitative variables:
- model crisp parameters (wind speed, stability class, etc.) if exactly known;
- model fuzzy parameters, if known with a certain degree. Definition of the membership function for these parameters.

2) Input: qualitative additional information setup

a) global knowledge on the solution domain:
- qualitative relation;
- translation method (from qualitative fuzzy into quantitative fuzzy);
- membership function construction (input y_i).

b) local knowledge on the solution domain by means of:
- zone contour defining;
- qualitative relation;
- translation method (from qualitative fuzzy into quantitative fuzzy);
- membership function construction (input y_i).

If a user proposed relation is not coded into the system, the system provides:

- situation defining (zone and possible qualitative relation to describe it);
- translation method defining;
- membership function construction (input y_i).

The first two inputs are coded into the system knowledge base.

3) Translation:

a) the system transforms the chosen qualitative information into a fuzzy constraint.

b) fuzzy optimization procedure explication by:
- computing the different combinations with _=1,1/2 and the corresponding runs. For each run the expert solver generates source code routines (in FORTRAN or C language) containing:
- the model
- the constraints

4) Procedure Execution

- compiling
- linking
- run

5) Output:

a) results:
- graphics or numerical data;
- certainty degree of the solution.

b) a-posteriori data analysis:
- statistical analysis;
- consistency of results (using rules).

6.2 Modules Description

Language Processor. It performs the translation of the qualitative knowledge supplied by the user into fuzzy constraints. It is not a real language processor since it proposes the qualitative relationships (according to the user input) by means of some rules but uses a deterministic translator that transforms rules expressed in natural language into the possible quantitative fuzzy constraints. The language processor consists in a graphic shell that presents to the user the geographical relations contained in the knowledge base and in an algorithm selecting the constraints.

Knowledge Base. The expert solver knowledge base is coded in three different data bases and is composed of qualitative geographic facts and relations, quantitative fuzzy constraints and their membership functions, rules for choosing facts and relations on the basis of the user supplied information and rules for choosing the optimal solution during the a-posteriori solution analysis.

1) Qualitative knowledge: it contains global and local information on the objects such as "industrial zone", "city" or "park" and "highway".

2) Quantitative knowledge: it contains the previous information formally coded into fuzzy disequations. As explained in the previous paragraph a correspondence 1-n between the two could exist, since the same qualitative fact can be expressed in different ways.

3) Rules: These inference rules can be used as both a-priori or a-posteriori information treatment. During the input step they allow to help the user in furnishing the available information and to classify the user input into the previously defined qualitative global and local knowledge. Once the optimization algorithm has found the set of solutions, the expert solver uses these rules to perform the solution validation in order to propose the most reliable solution. The inference mechanism is forward-chaining.

Conclusions

An approach for using geographic information in solving monitoring environmental problems has been proposed. It is shown how to use fuzzy optimization to perform the experimental data analysis. All the available information about the interested monitored zone can be coded into a quantitative algorithm that uses fuzzy logic to find the solutions. Since knowledge handling results very complex an expert system that helps the user during the whole process steps has been designed.

References

1. A. Tikhonov and V. Arsenine: Methodes de Résolution de Problèmes Mal Posés. Moskow: Mir Editors 1974.

2. K. Miller: Least squares methods for ill-posed problems with a prescribed bound. SIAM J. Mathl. Analysis, **1**, 52-74 (1970).

3. K. Keiding and J. Pedersen: A Comparison of two procedures for modelling of absolute source contributions in urban air. Atmosph.

Environ., 22, 4, 763-767 (1988).

4. K. E. Thrane: Application of air pollution models - a comparison of different techniques for estimating ambient air pollution levels and source contributions. Atmosph. Environ., 22, 3, 587-594 (1988).

5. D. Kronborg: Determination of sources of atmospheric aerosol in Copenhagen based on receptor models. Atmosph. Environ., 21, 9, 1877-1889 (1987).

6. C. L. Lawson and R. J. Hanson: Solving Least Squares Problems. New Jersey: Prentice-Hall, Englewood Cliffs 1974.

7. A. E. Hoerl and R. W. Kennard: Ridge regression: biased estimation for nonorthogonal problems. Technometrics, 12, 55-68 (1970).

8. R. Twomey: On the numerical solution of certain integral equations of the first kind. J. Assoc. Comput. Mach., 9, 84-97 (1962).

9. E. L. O'Neill: Introduction to Statistical Optics. Addison-Wesley 1963.

10. B. R. Frieden: Picture processing and digital filtering. Topics in Applied Physics. Vol.6, Berlin: Springer 1975.

11. O. Paladino, B. Canepa and G. Randi: Expert systems and chemical engineering problems: knowledge representation. Proc. of CHEMASIA '89, Singapore, 7, 4 (1989).

12. V. G. Dovì and O. Paladino: Use of fuzzy optimization algorithms for the solution of a class of ill-posed problems in data analysis. Comput. Chem. Engng., 14, 9, 957-966 (1990).

13. A. Kandel: Fuzzy Mathematical Techniques with Application. Addison-Wesley 1986.

14. O. Paladino, Realizzazione di una procedura di calcolo fondata sulla teoria dell'ottimizzazione fuzzy per l'individuazione di sorgenti inquinanti, Ph.D thesis (1989).

Lecture Notes in Computer Science

For information about Vols. 1–549
please contact your bookseller or Springer-Verlag

Vol. 550: A. van Lamsweerde, A. Fugetta (Eds.), ESEC '91. Proceedings, 1991. XII, 515 pages. 1991.

Vol. 551:S. Prehn, W. J. Toetenel (Eds.), VDM '91. Formal Software Development Methods. Volume 1. Proceedings, 1991. XIII, 699 pages. 1991.

Vol. 552: S. Prehn, W. J. Toetenel (Eds.), VDM '91. Formal Software Development Methods. Volume 2. Proceedings, 1991. XIV, 430 pages. 1991.

Vol. 553: H. Bieri, H. Noltemeier (Eds.), Computational Geometry - Methods, Algorithms and Applications '91. Proceedings, 1991. VIII, 320 pages. 1991.

Vol. 554: G. Grahne, The Problem of Incomplete Information in Relational Databases. VIII, 156 pages. 1991.

Vol. 555: H. Maurer (Ed.), New Results and New Trends in Computer Science. Proceedings, 1991. VIII, 403 pages. 1991.

Vol. 556: J.-M. Jacquet, Conclog: A Methodological Approach to Concurrent Logic Programming. XII, 781 pages. 1991.

Vol. 557: W. L. Hsu, R. C. T. Lee (Eds.), ISA '91 Algorithms. Proceedings, 1991. X, 396 pages. 1991.

Vol. 558: J. Hooman, Specification and Compositional Verification of Real-Time Systems. VIII, 235 pages. 1991.

Vol. 559: G. Butler, Fundamental Algorithms for Permutation Groups. XII, 238 pages. 1991.

Vol. 560: S. Biswas, K. V. Nori (Eds.), Foundations of Software Technology and Theoretical Computer Science. Proceedings, 1991. X, 420 pages. 1991.

Vol. 561: C. Ding, G. Xiao, W. Shan, The Stability Theory of Stream Ciphers. IX, 187 pages. 1991.

Vol. 562: R. Breu, Algebraic Specification Techniques in Object Oriented Programming Environments. XI, 228 pages. 1991.

Vol. 563: A. Karshmer, J. Nehmer (Eds.), Operating Systems of the 90s and Beyond. Proceedings, 1991. X, 285 pages. 1991.

Vol. 564: I. Herman, The Use of Projective Geometry in Computer Graphics. VIII, 146 pages. 1992.

Vol. 565: J. D. Becker, I. Eisele, F. W. Mündemann (Eds.), Parallelism, Learning, Evolution. Proceedings, 1989. VIII, 525 pages. 1991. (Subseries LNAI).

Vol. 566: C. Delobel, M. Kifer, Y. Masunaga (Eds.), Deductive and Object-Oriented Databases. Proceedings, 1991. XV, 581 pages. 1991.

Vol. 567: H. Boley, M. M. Richter (Eds.), Processing Declarative Kowledge. Proceedings, 1991. XII, 427 pages. 1991. (Subseries LNAI).

Vol. 568: H.-J. Bürckert, A Resolution Principle for a Logic with Restricted Quantifiers. X, 116 pages. 1991. (Subseries LNAI).

Vol. 569: A. Beaumont, G. Gupta (Eds.), Parallel Execution of Logic Programs. Proceedings, 1991. VII, 195 pages. 1991.

Vol. 570: R. Berghammer, G. Schmidt (Eds.), Graph-Theoretic Concepts in Computer Science. Proceedings, 1991. VIII, 253 pages. 1992.

Vol. 571: J. Vytopil (Ed.), Formal Techniques in Real-Time and Fault-Tolerant Systems. Proceedings, 1992. IX, 620 pages. 1991.

Vol. 572: K. U. Schulz (Ed.), Word Equations and Related Topics. Proceedings, 1990. VII, 256 pages. 1992.

Vol. 573: G. Cohen, S. N. Litsyn, A. Lobstein, G. Zémor (Eds.), Algebraic Coding. Proceedings, 1991. X, 158 pages. 1992.

Vol. 574: J. P. Banâtre, D. Le Métayer (Eds.), Research Directions in High-Level Parallel Programming Languages. Proceedings, 1991. VIII, 387 pages. 1992.

Vol. 575: K. G. Larsen, A. Skou (Eds.), Computer Aided Verification. Proceedings, 1991. X, 487 pages. 1992.

Vol. 576: J. Feigenbaum (Ed.), Advances in Cryptology - CRYPTO '91. Proceedings. X, 485 pages. 1992.

Vol. 577: A. Finkel, M. Jantzen (Eds.), STACS 92. Proceedings, 1992. XIV, 621 pages. 1992.

Vol. 578: Th. Beth, M. Frisch, G. J. Simmons (Eds.), Public-Key Cryptography: State of the Art and Future Directions. XI, 97 pages. 1992.

Vol. 579: S. Toueg, P. G. Spirakis, L. Kirousis (Eds.), Distributed Algorithms. Proceedings, 1991. X, 319 pages. 1992.

Vol. 580: A. Pirotte, C. Delobel, G. Gottlob (Eds.), Advances in Database Technology – EDBT '92. Proceedings. XII, 551 pages. 1992.

Vol. 581: J.-C. Raoult (Ed.), CAAP '92. Proceedings. VIII, 361 pages. 1992.

Vol. 582: B. Krieg-Brückner (Ed.), ESOP '92. Proceedings. VIII, 491 pages. 1992.

Vol. 583: I. Simon (Ed.), LATIN '92. Proceedings. IX, 545 pages. 1992.

Vol. 584: R. E. Zippel (Ed.), Computer Algebra and Parallelism. Proceedings, 1990. IX, 114 pages. 1992.

Vol. 585: F. Pichler, R. Moreno Díaz (Eds.), Computer Aided System Theory – EUROCAST '91. Proceedings. X, 761 pages. 1992.

Vol. 586: A. Cheese, Parallel Execution of Parlog. IX, 184 pages. 1992.

Vol. 587: R. Dale, E. Hovy, D. Rösner, O. Stock (Eds.), Aspects of Automated Natural Language Generation. Proceedings, 1992. VIII, 311 pages. 1992. (Subseries LNAI).

Vol. 588: G. Sandini (Ed.), Computer Vision – ECCV '92. Proceedings. XV, 909 pages. 1992.

Vol. 589: U. Banerjee, D. Gelernter, A. Nicolau, D. Padua (Eds.), Languages and Compilers for Parallel Computing. Proceedings, 1991. IX, 419 pages. 1992.

Vol. 590: B. Fronhöfer, G. Wrightson (Eds.), Parallelization in Inference Systems. Proceedings, 1990. VIII, 372 pages. 1992. (Subseries LNAI).

Vol. 591: H. P. Zima (Ed.), Parallel Computation. Proceedings, 1991. IX, 451 pages. 1992.

Vol. 592: A. Voronkov (Ed.), Logic Programming. Proceedings, 1991. IX, 514 pages. 1992. (Subseries LNAI).

Vol. 593: P. Loucopoulos (Ed.), Advanced Information Systems Engineering. Proceedings. XI, 650 pages. 1992.

Vol. 594: B. Monien, Th. Ottmann (Eds.), Data Structures and Efficient Algorithms. VIII, 389 pages. 1992.

Vol. 595: M. Levene, The Nested Universal Relation Database Model. X, 177 pages. 1992.

Vol. 596: L.-H. Eriksson, L. Hallnäs, P. Schroeder-Heister (Eds.), Extensions of Logic Programming. Proceedings, 1991. VII, 369 pages. 1992. (Subseries LNAI).

Vol. 597: H. W. Guesgen, J. Hertzberg, A Perspective of Constraint-Based Reasoning. VIII, 123 pages. 1992. (Subseries LNAI).

Vol. 598: S. Brookes, M. Main, A. Melton, M. Mislove, D. Schmidt (Eds.), Mathematical Foundations of Programming Semantics. Proceedings, 1991. VIII, 506 pages. 1992.

Vol. 599: Th. Wetter, K.-D. Althoff, J. Boose, B. R. Gaines, M. Linster, F. Schmalhofer (Eds.), Current Developments in Knowledge Acquisition - EKAW '92. Proceedings. XIII, 444 pages. 1992. (Subseries LNAI).

Vol. 600: J. W. de Bakker, C. Huizing, W. P. de Roever, G. Rozenberg (Eds.), Real-Time: Theory in Practice. Proceedings, 1991. VIII, 723 pages. 1992.

Vol. 601: D. Dolev, Z. Galil, M. Rodeh (Eds.), Theory of Computing and Systems. Proceedings, 1992. VIII, 220 pages. 1992.

Vol. 602: I. Tomek (Ed.), Computer Assisted Learning. Proceedings, 1992. X, 615 pages. 1992.

Vol. 603: J. van Katwijk (Ed.), Ada: Moving Towards 2000. Proceedings, 1992. VIII, 324 pages. 1992.

Vol. 604: F. Belli, F.-J. Radermacher (Eds.), Industrial and Engineering Applications of Artificial Intelligence and Expert Systems. Proceedings, 1992. XV, 702 pages. 1992. (Subseries LNAI).

Vol. 605: D. Etiemble, J.-C. Syre (Eds.), PARLE '92. Parallel Architectures and Languages Europe. Proceedings, 1992. XVII, 984 pages. 1992.

Vol. 606: D. E. Knuth, Axioms and Hulls. IX, 109 pages. 1992.

Vol. 607: D. Kapur (Ed.), Automated Deduction – CADE-11. Proceedings, 1992. XV, 793 pages. 1992. (Subseries LNAI).

Vol. 608: C. Frasson, G. Gauthier, G. I. McCalla (Eds.), Intelligent Tutoring Systems. Proceedings, 1992. XIV, 686 pages. 1992.

Vol. 609: G. Rozenberg (Ed.), Advances in Petri Nets 1992. VIII, 472 pages. 1992.

Vol. 610: F. von Martial, Coordinating Plans of Autonomous Agents. XII, 246 pages. 1992. (Subseries LNAI).

Vol. 611: M. P. Papazoglou, J. Zeleznikow (Eds.), The Next Generation of Information Systems: From Data to Knowledge. VIII, 310 pages. 1992. (Subseries LNAI).

Vol. 612: M. Tokoro, O. Nierstrasz, P. Wegner (Eds.), Object-Based Concurrent Computing. Proceedings, 1991. X, 265 pages. 1992.

Vol. 613: J. P. Myers, Jr., M. J. O'Donnell (Eds.), Constructivity in Computer Science. Proceedings, 1991. X, 247 pages. 1992.

Vol. 614: R. G. Herrtwich (Ed.), Network and Operating System Support for Digital Audio and Video. Proceedings, 1991. XII, 403 pages. 1992.

Vol. 615: O. Lehrmann Madsen (Ed.), ECOOP '92. European Conference on Object Oriented Programming. Proceedings. X, 426 pages. 1992.

Vol. 616: K. Jensen (Ed.), Application and Theory of Petri Nets 1992. Proceedings, 1992. VIII, 398 pages. 1992.

Vol. 617: V. Mařík, O. Štěpánková, R. Trappl (Eds.), Advanced Topics in Artificial Intelligence. Proceedings, 1992. IX, 484 pages. 1992. (Subseries LNAI).

Vol. 618: P. M. D. Gray, R. J. Lucas (Eds.), Advanced Database Systems. Proceedings, 1992. X, 260 pages. 1992.

Vol. 619: D. Pearce, H. Wansing (Eds.), Nonclassical Logics and Information Proceedings. Proceedings, 1990. VII, 171 pages. 1992. (Subseries LNAI).

Vol. 620: A. Nerode, M. Taitslin (Eds.), Logical Foundations of Computer Science – Tver '92. Proceedings. IX, 514 pages. 1992.

Vol. 621: O. Nurmi, E. Ukkonen (Eds.), Algorithm Theory – SWAT '92. Proceedings. VIII, 434 pages. 1992.

Vol. 622: F. Schmalhofer, G. Strube, Th. Wetter (Eds.), Contemporary Knowledge Engineering and Cognition. Proceedings, 1991. XII, 258 pages. 1992. (Subseries LNAI).

Vol. 623: W. Kuich (Ed.), Automata, Languages and Programming. Proceedings, 1992. XII, 721 pages. 1992.

Vol. 624: A. Voronkov (Ed.), Logic Programming and Automated Reasoning. Proceedings, 1992. XIV, 509 pages. 1992. (Subseries LNAI).

Vol. 625: W. Vogler, Modular Construction and Partial Order Semantics of Petri Nets. IX, 252 pages. 1992.

Vol. 626: E. Börger, G. Jäger, H. Kleine Büning, M. M. Richter (Eds.), Computer Science Logic. Proceedings, 1991. VIII, 428 pages. 1992.

Vol. 628: G. Vosselman, Relational Matching. IX, 190 pages. 1992.

Vol. 629: I. M. Havel, V. Koubek (Eds.), Mathematical Foundations of Computer Science 1992. Proceedings. IX, 521 pages. 1992.

Vol. 630: W. R. Cleaveland (Ed.), CONCUR '92. Proceedings. X, 580 pages. 1992.

Vol. 631: M. Bruynooghe, M. Wirsing (Eds.), Programming Language Implementation and Logic Programming. Proceedings, 1992. XI, 492 pages. 1992.

Vol. 632: H. Kirchner, G. Levi (Eds.), Algebraic and Logic Programming. Proceedings, 1992. IX, 457 pages. 1992.

Vol. 633: D. Pearce, G. Wagner (Eds.), Logics in AI. Proceedings. VIII, 410 pages. 1992. (Subseries LNAI).

Vol. 634: L. Bougé, M. Cosnard, Y. Robert, D. Trystram (Eds.), Parallel Processing: CONPAR 92 – VAPP V. Proceedings. XVII, 853 pages. 1992.

Vol. 635: J. C. Derniame (Ed.), Software Process Technology. Proceedings, 1992. VIII, 253 pages. 1992.

Vol. 636: G. Comyn, N. E. Fuchs, M. J. Ratcliffe (Eds.), Logic Programming in Action. Proceedings, 1992. X, 324 pages. 1992. (Subseries LNAI).

Vol. 637: Y. Bekkers, J. Cohen (Eds.), Memory Management. Proceedings, 1992. XI, 525 pages. 1992.

Vol. 639: A. U. Frank, I. Campari, U. Formentini (Eds.), Theories and Methods of Spatio-Temporal Reasoning in Geographic Space. Proceedings, 1992. XI, 431 pages. 1992.